RSF: The Russell Sage Foundation Journal of the Social Sciences

Criminal Justice Contact and Inequality

VOLUME 5, NUMBER 1, FEBRUARY 2019

RSF: The Russell Sage Foundation Journal of the Social Sciences — ISSN 2377-8261

The Russell Sage Foundation

The Russell Sage Foundation, one of the oldest of America's general purpose foundations, was established in 1907 by Mrs. Margaret Olivia Sage for "the improvement of social and living conditions in the United States." The foundation seeks to fulfill this mandate by fostering the development and dissemination of knowledge about the country's political, social, and economic problems. While the foundation endeavors to assure the accuracy and objectivity of each book it publishes, the conclusions and interpretations in Russell Sage Foundation publications are those of the authors and not of the foundation, its trustees, or its staff. Publication by Russell Sage, therefore, does not imply foundation endorsement.

Board of Trustees

Claude M. Steele, *Chair*
Larry M. Bartels
Cathy J. Cohen
Karen S. Cook
Sheldon H. Danziger
Kathryn Edin
Jason Furman
Michael Jones-Correa
Lawrence F. Katz
David Laibson
Nicholas Lemann
Sara S. McLanahan
Martha Minow
Peter R. Orszag
Mario Luis Small
Hirokazu Yoshikawa

Mission Statement

RSF: The Russell Sage Foundation Journal of the Social Sciences is a peer-reviewed, open-access journal of original empirical research articles by both established and emerging scholars. It is designed to promote cross-disciplinary collaborations on timely issues of interest to academics, policymakers, and the public at large. Each issue is thematic in nature and focuses on a specific research question or area of interest. The introduction to each issue will include an accessible, broad, and synthetic overview of the research question under consideration and the current thinking from the various social sciences.

RSF Journal Editorial Board

Elizabeth O. Ananat, Duke University
Sheldon H. Danziger, Russell Sage Foundation
Mesmin Destin, Northwestern University
Shigeo Hirano, Columbia University
Maria Krysan, University of Illinois, Chicago
Michal Kurlaender, University of California, Davis
Helen Levy, University of Michigan
Martha Minow, Harvard University
Mary E. Pattillo, Northwestern University
Becky Pettit, University of Texas at Austin
Miguel S. Urquiola, Columbia University

Copyright © 2019 by Russell Sage Foundation. All rights reserved. Printed in the United States of America. No part of this publication may be reproduced, stored in a retrieval system, or transmitted in any form or by any means, electronic, mechanical, photocopying, recording, or otherwise, without the prior written permission of the publisher. Reproduction by the United States Government in whole or in part is permitted for any purpose.

Opinions expressed in this journal are not necessarily those of the editors, editorial board, trustees, or the Russell Sage Foundation.

We invite scholars to submit proposals for potential issues through the *RSF* application portal: https://rsfjournal.onlineapplicationportal.com/. Submissions should be addressed to Suzanne Nichols, Director of Publications.

To view the complete text and additional features online please go to **www.rsfjournal.org**.

Open Access Policy

RSF: The Russell Sage Foundation Journal of the Social Sciences is an open access journal. It is published under a Creative Commons Attribution-NonCommercial-No Derivs 3.0 Unported License.

Russell Sage Foundation
112 East 64th Street
New York, NY 10065

ISSN (print): 2377-8253
ISSN (electronic): 2377-8261
ISBN: 978-0-87154-746-0

RSF: The Russell Sage Foundation
Journal of the Social Sciences

VOLUME 5, NUMBER 1,
FEBRUARY 2019

Criminal Justice Contact and Inequality

ISSUE EDITORS
Kristin Turney, University of California, Irvine
Sara Wakefield, Rutgers University–Newark

CONTENTS

Criminal Justice Contact and Inequality 1
Kristin Turney and Sara Wakefield

Part I. Surveillance

Police Contact and the Legal Socialization of Urban Teens 26
Amanda Geller and Jeffrey Fagan

Family Surveillance: Police and the Reporting of Child Abuse and Neglect 50
Frank Edwards

Digital Vulnerability: The Unequal Risk of E-Contact with the Criminal Justice System 71
Robert Vargas, Kayla Preito-Hodge, and Jeremy Christofferson

The Great Decoupling: The Disconnection Between Criminal Offending and Experience of Arrest Across Two Cohorts 89
Vesla M. Weaver, Andrew Papachristos, and Michael Zanger-Tishler

Part II. Unexplored Forms of Punishment

Bail and Pretrial Detention: Contours and Causes of Temporal and County Variation 126
Katherine Hood and Daniel Schneider

A Debt of Care: Commercial Bail and the Gendered Logic of Criminal Justice Predation 150
Joshua Page, Victoria Piehowski, and Joe Soss

Statutory Inequality: The Logics of Monetary Sanctions in State Law 173
Brittany Friedman and Mary Pattillo

Part III. Consequences of Criminal Justice Contact

Level of Criminal Justice Contact and Early Adult Wage Inequality 198
Robert Apel and Kathleen Powell

Racial Inequality in the Transition to Adulthood After Prison 223
Heather M. Harris and David J. Harding

Where the Other 1 Percent Live: An Examination of Changes in the Spatial Concentration of the Formerly Incarcerated 255
David S. Kirk

Criminal Justice Contact and Inequality

KRISTIN TURNEY AND SARA WAKEFIELD

The American incarceration rate, though recently stabilized, increased rapidly over the past half century. Today, compared with the 1970s, more than five times as many people spend time in prison annually (National Research Council 2014; Wakefield and Uggen 2010). The historically unprecedented incarceration rates have wide-ranging consequences for the well-being of individuals, families, and communities. The confinement associated with incarceration disrupts employment and, on release, formerly incarcerated individuals face challenges to finding stable employment (Pager 2003; Western 2006). Incarceration also impairs relationships with parents and romantic partners (Comfort 2007), increases physical and mental health problems (Massoglia and Pridemore 2015), and reduces civic participation (Manza and Uggen 2006). Furthermore, perhaps unsurprisingly given the severe and often compounding difficulties encountered by individuals and their families during and after confinement, incarceration has intergenerational consequences. Children of incarcerated parents experience impairments in their educational, behavioral, and health outcomes (Foster and Hagan 2015; Murray, Farrington, and Sekol 2012).

Although incarceration is consequential for millions of individuals and families in the United States, and accordingly has been the focus of much social science investigation, incarceration is only one component of a much larger criminal justice system. Even in an era of mass incarceration, with historically and comparatively novel incarceration rates, incarceration is a relatively rare experience. Many more individuals engage with an increasingly repressive criminal justice system—through arrests, misdemeanor convictions, or the accumulation of fines and fees, for example—without spending time behind bars in jails or prisons. Relatedly, incarceration is usually a late stop along a much longer path of criminal justice contact. Moreover, the focus on incarceration obscures a broader landscape of carceral contact, institutional spillover, and vicarious experiences with the criminal justice

Kristin Turney is associate professor at the Department of Sociology at the University of California, Irvine. **Sara Wakefield** is associate professor at the School of Criminal Justice at Rutgers University–Newark.

© 2019 Russell Sage Foundation. Turney, Kristin, and Sara Wakefield. 2019. "Criminal Justice Contact and Inequality." *RSF: The Russell Sage Foundation Journal of the Social Sciences* 5(1): 1–23. DOI: 10.7758/RSF.2019.5.1.01. The authors thank participants at the Russell Sage Foundation conference "Criminal Justice Contact and Inequality" and three reviewers for feedback on this article. Direct correspondence to: Kristin Turney at kristin.turney@uci.edu, Department of Sociology, University of California, Irvine, 3151 Social Science Plaza, Irvine, CA 92697; and Sara Wakefield at sara.wakefield@rutgers.edu, School of Criminal Justice, Rutgers University, 123 Washington St., Newark, NJ 07102.

Open Access Policy: *RSF: The Russell Sage Foundation Journal of the Social Sciences* is an open access journal. This article is published under a Creative Commons Attribution-NonCommercial-NoDerivs 3.0 Unported License.

system. For example, many individuals are affected by the criminal justice system vicariously via surveillance in their communities, the criminal justice contacts of kith and kin, or the importation of criminal justice logic and practice to noncarceral organizations and bureaucracies (such as schools). The wide-ranging scope of the criminal justice system, with its concentration among people of color and the poor and its insidious consequences across the life course, has implications for creating, maintaining, and exacerbating inequalities in the United States.

This volume focuses on how criminal justice contact, broadly defined, structures inequality in the United States. In the pages that follow, we introduce a series of new studies that examine a range of criminal justice stages and associated institutions and all reflect on the meaning of their results for social inequality. The essays included in this volume use a mix of methods to explore, describe, and explain inequality that flows from criminal justice contact. They leverage old and new data sources, always to innovative ends, and cover topics including predatory bail systems, pretrial detention, child welfare, and system legitimacy. All of them break new ground—some by returning to basic and critical questions and others by shifting our gaze to new inquiries—and provide an expanded foundation for thinking broadly about criminal justice contact and inequality.

CRIME, PUNISHMENT, AND THE CARCERAL STATE

Research on the criminal justice system, much like the criminal justice system itself, has grown substantially in recent years, encompassing a diverse set of disciplines and an ever-growing set of outcomes of interest. In just our home disciplines, sociology and criminology, a new student of the criminal justice system will find an astonishing number of pieces in the annual reviews devoted to summarizing research and developing a research agenda on the criminal justice system (see, for example, Beckett 2018; Comfort 2007; Foster and Hagan 2015; Kirk and Wakefield 2018; Kreager and Kruttschnitt 2018; Martin et al. 2018; Massoglia and Pridemore 2015; Morenoff and Harding 2014; Phelps 2016; Wakefield and Uggen 2010; Wildeman and Muller 2012; Wildeman, Fitzpatrick, and Goldman 2018). The criminal justice system is also a core interest for developmental psychologists, economists, public health scholars, socio-legal scholars, and policy analysts, among others, who bring a diverse set of interests and expertise to the questions raised in this volume (see, for example, Agan and Starr 2016; Arditti 2012; Doleac and Hansen 2016; Gottschalk 2014; Lynch 2016; Raphael and Stoll 2009; Simon 2007).

Although we cannot do justice to the diversity of arguments detailed in the works just cited, we first wish to orient readers to three insights generated from the research focused on the prison boom in the United States. Parts of these insights are well known but not well accounted for in current research. Others represent new ways of conceiving of the criminal justice system and its role in structuring inequality in the United States. First, the relationship between crime and changes in punishment and criminal justice practice is neither simple nor direct. Such relationships present a substantial challenge for researchers, but a focus on one or the other often obscures the ways crime and punishment work in concert to produce durable inequalities. Second, diversity in criminal justice experiences and stage-by-outcome interactions represent a new and important area of research for inequality outcomes. A wealth of research links differential criminal justice processing outcomes to later recidivism (Green and Winik 2010; Listwan et al. 2013; Manski and Nagin 1998; Mears, Cochran, and Cullen 2015). Research on other outcomes is disproportionately focused on adult incarceration in state prisons, but many fewer studies focus on earlier stage contacts (but see Augustyn and Loughran 2017; Grogger 1995; Lerman and Weaver 2014). Third, the focus on core criminal justice agencies (police, courts, or corrections) and inequality has more recently given way to much broader investigations of the institutional and administrative linkages between the criminal justice system and other systems, agencies, and institutions. All of these insights, on which we elaborate, form the foundation for the pieces brought together by this volume.

Crime and the Criminal Justice System

The relationship between the criminal justice system and crime provides the backdrop to much research in this volume. Yet changes in the scope and contours of crime in the United States are less directly responsible for the growth in the criminal justice system than a host of other political, legal, demographic, and social factors (Alexander 2010; Beckett 1997; Forman 2017; Lynch 2016; National Research Council 2014; Pfaff 2017; Simon 2007; Wakefield and Uggen 2010). Crime levels today are not the primary explanation for continuing high rates of criminal punishment in the United States; and the payoff to high incarceration rates for crime, beyond a certain threshold, is not large (Durlauf and Nagin 2011; Johnson and Raphael 2012).

That said, the size of the population involved in the criminal justice system ought to be, at least theoretically, related to the number of people involved in crime (Weaver, Papachristos, and Zanger-Tishler 2019). However, the National Academy of Sciences report on high incarceration rates in the United States presents an extensive review of the relationship between crime and incarceration, concluding that "the link between crime and the growth of the penal population is neither immediate nor direct" (National Research Council 2014, 45). An accompanying decomposition analysis attributes the growth in the incarcerated population specifically not to crime per se, but to shifts in the likelihood of prison admission on conviction and to the increases in time served once incarcerated.[1] In the aggregate, the volume of crime is lower today than at any point since the 1990s and yet rates of criminal punishment remain very high. The United States experienced large growth in the volume of crime from the 1960s through the 1980s, peaking in the early 1990s and then dropping precipitously thereafter. The peak differs slightly for violent crime relative to property crime but the two follow roughly the same trend. Drug arrests followed a rather different trend, peaking later, and are especially unconnected to rates of drug use in the population (Baumer, Velez, and Rosenfeld 2018; Lauritsen and Rezey 2018).

Although high rates of criminal punishment are not a direct or natural response to crime and victimization, the politicized race- and class-structured fear of crime and victimization certainly contributes to high rates of punishment. Such processes are important for understanding both inequality and criminal justice contact. Much as national-level incarceration rates mask significant variation between states and localities, aggregate crime rates mask large variation in exposure to crime and to the agents of the criminal justice system deployed to control it. Crime rates across cities became more heterogeneous in the 2000s (Baumer, Velez, and Rosenfeld 2018). Also, much as a particularly heinous crime can have an outsized influence on sentencing policy or public opinion related to punishment, temporary crime spikes in a small number of cities can change perceptions of the rate of crime in all places (on heinous crime, Enns 2016; Zimring, Hawkins, and Kamin 2003; on crime spikes, Gramlich 2016). Thus even in a period of historically low crime rates, some communities will be subject to high rates of surveillance, exposure to violence, and criminal justice contact, and a few places or events can potentially drive punitive criminal justice policies over the entire population (Geller and Fagan 2019; Kirk 2019; Sharkey 2018).

Exposure to crime and criminal involvement patterns present a number of challenges for analyzing the relationship between criminal justice contact and inequality. At the individual level, it is simply not plausible to ignore criminal involvement in the estimation of the effects of criminal justice contact. We wholeheartedly support work that pays more attention to the processes that produce criminal justice populations. The volume includes sev-

---

1. It is beyond the scope of this essay to engage all of the arguments for the growth in the incarcerated population, but we note that the explanations are complex and hotly contested (Alexander 2010; Beckett 2018; Pfaff 2017). It is sufficient for our purpose here to simply note that few scholars of mass incarceration view crime levels as the main, direct, or exclusive driver of current high and racially disparate rates of criminal punishment in the United States.

eral articles reporting on innovative and rigorous attempts to isolate unexplored forms and consequences of criminal justice contact, for example. We suggest also that treating criminal involvement as simply a selection problem to be overcome may introduce other problems for inequality scholars. Such a view ignores that exposure to violence, state-sponsored surveillance, and criminal punishment are core features of concentrated disadvantage in American life. Simply "netting out criminal involvement" makes somewhat less sense when violence, punishment, and surveillance are viewed holistically with respect to inequality and disadvantage. The articles in this volume tackle the selection problems associated with crime in innovative ways but many fold crime, surveillance, and exposure to violence in more concrete ways, using crime and punishment together to produce new ideas about the growth, scope, and contours of inequality in the United States.

Punishment

Similar complexities arise when trying to distinguish the effects of different types of criminal justice contact for attainment and inequality. As we demonstrate in more detail shortly, many people are stopped by police and never arrested, arrested but not charged, charged but not convicted, and convicted but not sentenced to prison (University at Albany 2018). The criminal justice system, often conceptualized as a (leaky) funnel, processes large numbers of people, and a host of factors—including crime seriousness, quality of evidence, bureaucratic priorities, criminal history, and demographic characteristics—determine who proceeds from one stage of the system to the next. Such a process presents a substantial selection problem for researchers, and includes multiple decision points that account for the end-stage observation that a single individual becomes incarcerated, for example.

As a basic matter, many types of criminal justice contact are simply not well measured in available surveys, and administrative criminal history information is notoriously difficult to link to other sources (Kirk and Wakefield 2018). Information on long-term incarceration, a discrete and easily recalled event, is easier to measure relative to numerous transitory contacts with police officers or frequent short stints in jails. Partially as a result of data availability, criminal justice contact in the form of incarceration thus represents the most commonly studied exposure, but as the essays in this volume amply demonstrate, incarceration represents a very late stage of contact. Such a focus on incarceration misses substantial contacts within the core of the criminal justice system that do not involve easily measured forms of incarceration.

By making this point, we do not suggest that incarceration is unimportant. Prison incarceration rates in the United States are nearly five times as high today as they were in 1970, growing from a stable 105 per 100,000 from 1925 to 1976 to a peak of 506 per 100,000 in 2007 (Kirk and Wakefield 2018). Incarceration is arguably the most intrusive and repressive form of criminal justice system exposure. Beyond incarceration in state and federal prisons, almost eleven million people passed through a local jail in 2015 alone (Minton and Zeng 2016). Relatedly, pretrial detention, largely a result of the inability to make bail at the state level and immigration-related detentions at the federal level, has increased alongside the more commonly recognized rise in sentenced incarceration (Cohen 2013; Dobbie, Goldin, and Yang 2018). Less commonly known is that most people in local jails have been convicted of no crime; of the roughly 646,000 people in local jails on any given day in 2016, about 451,000 (70 percent) had not been convicted of anything (Wagner and Rabuy 2016; see also Minton and Zeng 2015).

It is also well known that exposure to incarceration is not equally distributed across demographic and socioeconomic groups in the population. Instead, incarceration is concentrated among men, people of color, and those with low educational attainment (Pettit and Western 2004). Demographic estimates show that 20 percent of black men, versus 3 percent of white men, can expect to experience imprisonment by their mid-thirties. Among black men who did not complete high school, nearly 65 percent can expect to be imprisoned by their mid-thirties (Pettit and Western 2004). Similarly, pretrial detention, largely because of an inability to pay bail, is quite clearly related to poverty status.

Although the rise and unequal distribution of incarceration is well known and critically important for understanding inequality, the prevalence and correlates of other types of criminal justice contact are less well understood. Such contacts may be short in duration but long-lasting in their consequences. Consider first a (potential) precursor to incarceration such as being stopped by the police. In 2011, about one-quarter of the U.S. population had contact with the police; of these, half were involuntary or otherwise police-initiated interactions (Langton and Durose 2016). Like incarceration, such stops are concentrated primarily on those in a very small number of places, typically populated by poor residents and residents of color. Small surveys of residents in heavily patrolled, high-crime neighborhoods in New York City routinely yield reports of youth who are stopped multiple times over the course of very short periods (Fratello, Rengifo, and Trone 2013; Geller and Fagan 2019; Lambson 2014).

Consider another (potential) precursor to incarceration such as arrest. More than twelve million individuals are arrested annually (Federal Bureau of Investigation 2013). Recent research from the 1997 National Longitudinal Study of Youth (NLSY), a nationally representative panel data set of individuals who have been followed annually since 1997, finds that between 30 percent and 41 percent of individuals have been arrested by age twenty-three (Brame et al. 2011). Like incarceration, the prevalence of arrest varies by gender and race-ethnicity. For example, 38 percent of non-Hispanic white males, versus 20 percent of non-Hispanic white females, are arrested by age twenty-three. Further, racial-ethnic disparities in arrest exist among males, but not among females, with 44 percent of Hispanic males and 49 percent of non-Hispanic black males being arrested by age twenty-three (Brame et al. 2014).

Finally, community supervision—most commonly in the form of probation (supervision with a threat of incarceration if conditions are not met) or parole (supervision following a term of incarceration, with a threat of reincarceration if conditions are not met)—is an understudied form of criminal justice contact with respect to inequality. In 2016, almost seven million people (about one in thirty-seven) were under some form of correctional supervision. The population subject to correctional supervision via probation and parole is more than double the number incarcerated, although probationers and parolees face the constant threat of incarceration and reincarceration (Kaeble 2018). Community supervision may be independently consequential for health and well-being and, ultimately, contribute to inequalities in these outcomes (Phelps 2017). For example, the constant monitoring that comes along with such supervision may be a chronic stressor that increases feelings of depression and anxiety (Pearlin 1989). It may also alter family relationships, by making family members responsible for providing those on supervision a place to stay or by putting family members into contact with law enforcement officials such as probation officers (Goffman 2009).

A primary goal for this volume was to encourage the submission of essays that examine the importance of incarceration for inequality in new, rigorous, and innovative ways but also to include works that move beyond (or before) it. Several articles examine other forms of criminal justice contact beyond incarceration in state or federal prisons (such as policing or incarceration via pretrial detention) or present innovative examinations of incarceration's effect on social inequality. These essays are a mere sampling of the many recent studies along these lines (Dobbie, Goldin, and Yang 2018; Patler and Branic 2017; Sugie and Turney 2017; Uggen et al. 2014). As such, they contribute to a broader conversation about all forms of criminal justice contact and their implications for social inequality.

The Carceral State and the Nature of Spillover

The rapid and unequal rise in criminal justice contact is a source of considerable research attention. As noted, much early research focused on incarceration experiences. Yet other forms of criminal justice exposure and the spillover of carceral logics and practices highlight a number of missed opportunities for researchers to understand the full implications of the criminal justice system for inequality. For example, exposure to regular interactions with police has the power to shape social life and culture, even when it does not result in further criminal justice processing in the form of citation, tickets, or arrest. Forrest Stuart describes the adaptations of Skid Row residents who navigate heavily policed areas using "cop-wisdom" to predict and ideally reduce unwanted attention from police (2016). Related work examines adaptations among Chicago youth hoping to avoid interactions with police while on the street (Stuart and Benezra 2017). Police contact is also increasingly common in American public schools, which has core implications for inequality in educational settings (Haskins 2014; Shedd 2015). Adolescents, especially those in large urban areas, are routinely exposed to security personnel and law enforcement while in school; more than half of all public middle and high school students attend schools with law enforcement, and this percentage rises inversely with the proportion of students who are nonwhite (Gray and Lewis 2015). As Amanda Geller and Jeffrey Fagan explain later in this volume, such experiences contribute to legal cynicism and "risks weakening teens' deference to law and legal authorities" (2019).

Much of the early work on mass incarceration or collateral consequences narrowly focused on incarceration or attainment outcomes, such as employment or educational attainment. Such work is important, laying a foundation for later research that expanded to other forms of criminal justice contact and made transparent the often unexamined linkages between the criminal justice system and other forms of state intervention (such as schooling or child welfare). What has become clear from this body of research as it has broadened, however, is that clearly demarcating where the criminal justice system starts and ends is increasingly difficult.

A parallel line of research and theory takes as given that the boundaries of the criminal justice system expand well beyond the core agencies typically associated with it. As one salient example, Katherine Beckett and Naomi Murakawa eschew the narrow confines of core agencies within the criminal justice system, noting that criminal justice agencies "represent only the most visible tentacles of penal power," in favor of a "shadow carceral state" (2012, 222). The carceral state, as opposed to the criminal justice system, more adequately captures the "legally hybrid and institutionally variegated" nature of criminal punishment in the United States and not only allows examination of conventional forms of carceral spillover but also expands the lens to a much larger swath of entanglements and institutional links (Beckett and Murakawa 2012, 222; Gottschalk 2014; L. Haney 2018; Lara-Millan and Gonzalez Van Cleve 2016; Miller 2014; Miller and Stuart 2017; Reiter and Coutin 2017; Zedner 2016).

The works in this volume recognize that significant engagement with the criminal justice system may occur in the absence of confinement in a jail or prison. Such contact may come in the form of lengthy surveillance in the community, as in mass probation (Phelps 2013). It may describe the spillover of criminal justice contact to the families of the incarcerated (Comfort 2007). It may describe the importation of criminal justice logics and culture (Stuart and Miller 2016) to the creation of prison-like settings, as many describe secondary schools today (Hirschfield 2018). It may also describe surveillance in adjoining systems, such as child welfare (Edwards 2016; L. Haney 2018) or the bail industry (Page, Piehowski, and Soss 2019). These additional and vicarious engagements represent still other settings that form a larger carceral state that builds from and grows beyond the criminal justice agency core (Beckett and Murakawa 2012; Beckett 2018; Gottschalk 2014; L. Haney 2018; Hernandez, Muhammad, and Thompson 2015; Lageson and Maruna 2017).

Research along these lines contributes to a welcome move in the literature to expand the scope of inquiry. It highlights the unwieldy nature of the criminal justice system, especially in the current era. It outlines the many challenges ahead for researchers as well as champions of criminal justice reform (see, for example, Beckett 2018). It remains to be seen whether, how, and to what extent hidden tentacle-like forms of carceral state engagements contribute to social inequality in the aggregate, but such a project focuses on experiences that are too often defined (or missed) as something other than criminal justice contact.

OPPORTUNITIES FOR RESEARCH ON CRIMINAL JUSTICE CONTACT AND INEQUALITY

We view criminal justice contact as fitting into one of three (sometimes overlapping) categories: transitory (sometimes sporadic but oftentimes recurring) contacts with criminal justice agents (which include police stops, arrests, and tickets and fines); sustained contacts with criminal justice agents (which include felony conviction, pretrial detention, and correctional supervision); and spillover consequences of the criminal justice system (such as in schools or child welfare agencies). We suggest that these three types of contact can both create and exacerbate inequality. Importantly, many of the contacts we describe (and are explored further in the essays in this volume) do not include (or end with) incarceration yet have important implications for social inequality arising from the criminal justice system.

In departing somewhat from the usual demarcation between carceral and noncarceral criminal justice experiences, we suggest that the duration of direct contact with the criminal justice system is less tightly linked to harm than might be expected. When long terms of incarceration are the reference point, everything else has a tendency to seem trivial or like a one-shot experience. Yet even within carceral environments, duration is often not the most important predictor of harms imposed. As an extreme example, very short terms of solitary confinement may be much more detrimental to mental health and well-being relative to lengthier terms of confinement under better conditions (C. Haney 2018). One of the recent innovations of the literature is to focus more squarely on other forms of criminal justice contact beyond, before, or in place of incarceration. Some of these forms mirror the sustained engagement with criminal justice agencies that characterizes imprisonment; others are wholly different, characterized by short (and often repeated) contact with criminal justice system actors. Such events are as consequential—and for some outcomes, more so—as a term served in a correctional facility.

Consequences of Transitory Forms of Criminal Justice Contact

Social scientists tend to conceive of criminal justice contact as a path, as we have done here thus far, beginning with arrest and ending with incarceration. This makes good sense for distinguishing initial contacts from experiences in the deep end of the system but obscures several forms of contact that result in consequential life changes and are central to understanding the creation and maintenance of inequality. For example, consider the tragic case of Philando Castile. Mr. Castile was shot and killed by a police officer within moments of being pulled over in St. Anthony, Minnesota. Mr. Castile had no serious criminal record, no felony convictions or incarceration experience, but had been pulled over by police almost fifty times, mostly for minor traffic violations, and amassed significant legal debt related to tickets and fines (LaFraniere and Smith 2016; see also Harris 2016). One uneventful police stop or citation on its own might be considered inconsequential. Some might also be tempted to consider even many police stops less consequential if they never lead to deeper contact within the system. But how many is too many and what are the consequences for inequality? Such transitory contacts accumulate over time, structuring the lives of those who, like Philando Castile, interacted with police officers every few months. Engagement like this, occurring more and more often with agents of today's criminal justice system, shares much with any more general conception of cumulative disadvantage (DiPrete and Eirich 2006) as well as with a burgeoning literature on the health consequences of a lifetime of experiences with racial discrimination (Phelan and Link 2015; Williams, Neighbors, and Jackson 2003).

Recall that more than 25 percent of the population reports police contact in a single year, but that some groups within the population are regularly subject to police interaction, questioning, and surveillance. Evidence is accumulating that this form of criminal justice contact has implications for physical and mental health. For example, a telephone survey of New

York City men ages eighteen to twenty-six, in which 46 percent reported being stopped by the police in the past year, finds that police stops are positively associated with trauma and anxiety. This study also finds that perceptions of intrusiveness are positively associated with trauma and anxiety (Geller et al. 2014). Other research based in New York City—combining data from the New York City Community Health Survey (NYC-CHS) and the 2009–2012 NYC Stop, Question, and Frisk (NYC-SQF) dataset—finds that living in a neighborhood with higher levels of invasive police stops is associated with poor health outcomes including fair or poor health, diabetes, asthma, and being overweight or obese (Sewell and Jefferson 2016). Other research using these data finds that neighborhood-level frisk and use of force proportions, but not neighborhood-level stop rates, are associated with higher psychological distress among men (Sewell, Jefferson, and Lee 2016).

Consider also how many police stops can lead to substantial legal debt through the accumulations that may arise from several small tickets or fines. Police stops, tickets, and arrests for minor crimes can all occur independent of incarceration (or prior to incarceration), and there is some research suggesting that these types of criminal justice contact can have deleterious consequences for individuals. For example, one ethnographic study documents both the prevalence and consequences of misdemeanor arrests. It shows that misdemeanor arrests are much more common than the more commonly studied felony arrests. It also shows that, despite the fact that these arrests are commonly dismissed, they have wide-ranging consequences for individual lives. These arrests are a system of marking, which creates a formal sanction on a person's record, denigrates a person's social status, and facilitates bureaucratic and procedural hassles (Kohler-Hausmann 2013).

The important point here is that the accumulation of low-level or very brief criminal justice contact can be consequential for an individual's daily life as well as aggregate-level inequality. Criminal justice contact prior to—or independent of—incarceration can be consequential for a variety of outcomes. Here we offer examples for two domains of outcomes where research is especially strong: health and employment. With respect to health, recent research using data from the NLSY97 finds that changes in arrests, independent of other types of criminal justice contact such as conviction or incarceration, are independently associated with changes in mental health (Sugie and Turney 2017). Such research suggests that, for some, minor contacts with the criminal justice system are neither transitory nor inconsequential.

With respect to employment, there is evidence that both arrests and convictions can be consequential for outcomes. For example, Devah Pager's experiment shows that individuals with a felony conviction, relative to their matched counterparts without a felony conviction, are less likely to receive a callback for a job (2003). She finds that race intersects with felony conviction; blacks without a felony conviction are less likely to receive a callback than whites with a felony conviction (Pager 2003; but see Agan and Starr 2016). The effects of criminal justice contact on employment outcomes are not limited to those stemming from felony conviction, however. A recent experiment documents that individuals reporting a disorderly conduct arrest on a job application receive fewer callbacks compared to those not reporting an arrest, suggesting that employers perceive arrests as stigmatized credentials (Uggen et al. 2014; also see Grogger 1995; Wiesner, Capaldi, and Kim 2010).

Consequences of Sustained Forms of Criminal Justice Contact

Despite a large and growing literature linking incarceration and inequality, with few exceptions, little is known about how variation in the experience of incarceration structures resulting outcomes or inequalities. For example, how is a long prison sentence differentially associated with outcomes compared to a series of short jail stints? What are the long-term consequences of incarceration if that experience occurs in a prison unit with high rates of violence?

Research has begun to explore how a long imprisonment term may differ from a series of short jail terms, for example, or how confinement experiences differ according to security levels, such as federal, state, local, public, or private facilities (Andersen 2016; Bushway 1998; Gaes and Camp 2009; Kling 2006; Loughran et al. 2009; Mueller-Smith 2015; Wildeman, Turney, and Yi 2016; Yi, Turney, and Wildeman 2017). Facilities and even units within facilities may differ with respect to the availability of programs (Phelps 2011). They may also differ in regard to the level of disorder, violence, and misconduct (Listwan et al. 2013; Skarbeck 2014). Individuals within the same prison, or within the same unit, may also have vastly different experiences based on their level of connection to outside friends and family (Cochran and Mears 2013), their exposure to solitary confinement (C. Haney 2018; Reiter 2016; Smith 2006), their connections to other inmates (Haynie et al. 2018), and the prevailing inmate culture (Crewe 2009; Kreager and Kruttschnitt 2018; Skarbeck 2014; Sykes 2007). Most important for this volume is that despite a relatively large literature examining such incarceration experiences for later recidivism, almost none of this research explores the broader set of outcomes that are often the focus of the collateral consequences and inequality literature.

Incarceration may also occur in the absence of or prior to conviction in the form of pretrial detention. In addition to the employment consequences of arrest and conviction, there is evidence that pretrial detention is negatively associated with formal sector employment, employment benefits, and tax-related government benefits (Dobbie, Goldin, and Yang 2018). This research, which draws on quasi-experimental data of randomly assigned judges, also shows that pretrial detention is positively associated with conviction, which may be one mechanism through which pretrial detention is linked to employment outcomes. Similarly, Naomi Sugie and Kristin Turney disaggregate two types of incarceration—pretrial incarceration and incarceration with conviction (2017). They find that the association between incarceration and mental health is concentrated among those awaiting trial, suggesting that it is especially important to consider the consequences of jail incarceration in addition to the more commonly considered prison incarceration.

Beyond incarceration, sustained community surveillance in the form of probation and parole is more common than detention in prisons or jails. In 2016, about 4.5 million people were supervised in the community via probation or parole, relative to 2.1 million people incarcerated (Kaeble 2018). The population on probation and parole has grown at a rate greater than the incarcerated population and represents another form of criminal justice reach that is likely to have consequences for life outcomes and inequality (Petersilia 2003). Yet, as is true of incarceration, few studies link varying forms of probation and parole to inequality outcomes, and probation populations often simply stand in as a convenient referent group for the incarcerated population. Those on probation or parole are vulnerable to experiencing parole sanctions or to punishment resulting from a violation of the terms of their parole, such as failing to report to a parole officer or being suspected of using alcohol or drugs. These parole sanctions, like the criminal justice system more broadly, have the potential to further marginalize poor and minority populations (Alexander 2010).

Research shows that surveillance may be consequential for the individuals being surveilled. For example, recent research using a sample of individuals released from prison in Michigan finds that nearly two-thirds experienced a jail custodial sanction and nearly half experienced a custodial sanction other than jail while on parole in the six years following release from prison. This research also finds that these parole sanctions are associated with a 37 percent decrease in income in the quarter following their sanction, suggesting that this form of back-end net widening has implications for labor marker inequality (Harding, Siegel, and Morenoff 2017). Other research shows that surveillance may be consequential for those connected to the surveilled. Alice Goffman's ethnographic account documents how police officers interact with family members—particularly mothers and romantic partners—of men "on the run," for example, by threatening a child welfare investigation if they do not cooperate (2009).

Finally, as is true in regard to the accumulation of fines and fees associated with transitory contacts with police, opportunities are ample for research on legal debt that accompanies incarceration and community supervision. The majority of individuals who experience conviction or incarceration experience monetary sanctions in the form of fines, fees, and other legal debt (Harris, Evans, and Beckett 2010). As is true of fines and fees that flow from transitory criminal justice contact, debt associated with incarceration can have wide-ranging and long-term implications for individuals; these financial consequences may impair one's ability to accumulate assets or wealth; they may facilitate future criminal involvement, perpetuating a cycle of inequality; and they may impair fathers' abilities to pay child support (Harris, Evans, and Beckett 2010; Holzer, Raphael, and Stoll 2004; Piquero and Jennings 2017). Given that child support arrears are associated with decreased father involvement with children, these debts may also have important implications for children's relationships with their parents and their well-being (L. Haney 2018; Turner and Waller 2017).

Spillover Consequences of Criminal Justice Contact

Finally, particularly in an era of increasing surveillance, the influence of the criminal justice system is not limited to those who have direct contact with it nor is it confined to spheres clearly related to criminal justice. Other institutions—such as schools and child welfare agencies—intersect with the criminal justice system in identifiable ways that are consequential for outcomes over the life course. In other cases, criminal justice experiences spill over into institutional and social engagements in ways that often seem surprising or complex.

The intersection between the criminal justice system and other systems may be easily identified or largely unexplored. The reach of criminal justice culture is clearly evident in the public school system, as police officers are increasingly likely to be found in schools across the country (Hirschfield 2008; Kupchik 2010). Existing literature evaluating the presence of police officers (or school resource officers) is complicated by large issues of selection and endogeneity, but the evidence does not suggest that more prison-like conditions in schools are a boon for adolescent well-being. A host of studies find that, unsurprisingly, the introduction of police officers in schools has the effect of criminalizing adolescence (Hirschfield 2018; Na and Gottfredson 2013). It also has clear implications for racial inequalities in school discipline (Kupchik 2010; Payne and Welch 2010; Rocque and Paternoster 2011; Shedd 2015; Welch and Payne 2010).

The criminal justice system also intersects with the child welfare system in readily measurable ways. For example, children placed in foster care are more likely than their counterparts to have experienced parental incarceration (Andersen and Wildeman 2016; Turney and Wildeman 2017). Child welfare investigations, which precede foster care placement, are often initiated by police (Edwards 2019). Understanding these interrelations and their implications for inequality are an important yet understudied phenomenon (Yi and Wildeman 2018). Children placed in foster care experience educational and health inequalities throughout the life course, especially when they transition to adulthood (Brown, Courtney, and McMillen 2015). These individuals also have a high probability of getting ensnared in the criminal justice system themselves (Lee, Courtney, and Tajima 2014).

Those with criminal records tend to avoid formal institutional engagements of all sorts (Brayne 2014; Goffman 2009) but the full range of the consequences of system avoidance remains unclear. More informally, criminal records reduce participation in social life in less obvious ways, including avoidance of mundane parenting activities (Lageson 2016) and influencing treatment received in emergency rooms (Lara-Millan 2014).

VOLUME OVERVIEW

As detailed, existing research documents the expansive scope of criminal justice contact, the intersections between various types of criminal justice contact, and the consequences of criminal justice contact for inequality across domains such as employment, health, and family life. The articles in this volume, building on this research, all highlight the myriad ways that criminal justice contact can structure inequality in the United States. The articles fit into three broad categories: surveillance, unexplored forms of punishment, and consequences of criminal justice contact. We review these articles, highlighting their contributions and synergies and detailing how they move forward scholarship on criminal justice contact and inequality.

Surveillance
Four articles in the volume focus on surveillance, an aspect of the criminal justice system that has received less attention than many other types of criminal justice contact. These articles, all of which employ original data collection or creatively use existing data sources, independently contribute to our knowledge of how criminal justice surveillance can shape outcomes across the life course and how such surveillance can structure inequality. Together, they provide a solid foundation for future investigations of causes, consequences, and processes associated with surveillance.

Amanda Geller and Jeffrey Fagan use newly available data from the Fragile Families and Child Wellbeing Study, a cohort of children born in urban areas around the turn of the century and followed for fifteen years, to examine the relationship between adolescents' contact with the police and legal socialization (for example, "I have a great deal of respect for the police"). Understanding legal socialization in adolescence, in particular, is important because it is during this life-course stage when first interactions with the criminal justice system are common and when individuals are developing perceptions of the police and the law.

Geller and Fagan contribute to our understanding of police surveillance in three ways. First, the authors provide recent and broadly representative evidence about the frequency of police contact. They find that, on average, more than one-quarter (27 percent) of adolescents report at least one police stop and more than three-quarters (78 percent) report vicarious contact (such as witnessing a police stop or personally knowing someone who has experienced a police stop). Second, the authors find that both personal and vicarious police contact, particularly more intrusive police contact, engenders greater levels of legal cynicism. That is, the consequences of surveillance go beyond those who directly experience surveillance themselves and further proliferate to those who experience vicarious contact. This suggests that the consequences of police surveillance may be more widespread than previously considered, therefore suggesting that vicarious contact is an important form of spillover rarely examined in social science research. Third, the authors find that the deleterious consequences of police stops are consistent across race-ethnicity; that is, white, black, and Hispanic adolescents are similarly affected by both personal and vicarious police stops. Given that adolescents of color are more likely to be exposed to both personal and vicarious police stops, these findings suggest that police contact has implications for race-ethnic inequalities in legal cynicism.

Second, Frank Edwards uses data from the National Child Abuse and Neglect Data System, combined with administrative data from police departments (including information about the resources available to the departments and the number of arrests), to examine the consequences of police surveillance for family life. This article highlights how two powerful institutions, the criminal justice system and the child welfare system, are intertwined to shape family life. The police regularly interact with families, as Edwards notes, though little existing research considers the correlates and consequences of this form of criminal justice contact. The contributions of this research are twofold. First, by documenting a positive association between county-level arrest rates and county-level police reports of child abuse and neglect, these findings provide evidence that these two institutions are linked and, more generally, that the consequences of surveillance are both spatially patterned and extend to family life. Second, by showing that county-level arrest rates explain some variation in police reports of child abuse and neglect among American Indian–Alaska Native families, these findings document another way through which the criminal justice system facilitates racial-ethnic inequality in family life. That is, some families experience unnecessary police interventions while other families lack police interventions that may be necessary.

Third, Robert Vargas, Kayla Preito-Hodge,

and Jeremy Christofferson examine an aspect of surveillance that occurs daily in communities across the United States but is almost entirely unexplored in social science research: police-dispatcher radio communication. Using sixty hours of police-dispatcher radio communication across three racially disparate police zones—a predominantly white (and affluent) area, a predominantly black area, and a predominantly Latinx area—they examine inequality in exposure to data breaches (that is, when police dispatchers reveal identifying information about individuals reporting criminal activity). They find that these data breaches are not uncommon, with the disclosure of a caller's name or address occurring in about 10 percent of police calls. Furthermore, they find that these data breaches are spatially patterned, with disclosure occurring in 12 percent of police calls in the black area, 8 percent in the Latinx area, and 0 percent in the white area. They suggest that dispatchers in neighborhoods with a high concentration of people of color, compared with dispatchers in predominantly white areas, might be more overworked, both in terms of the number of hours they are working and the number of calls they must handle during each shift. They further suggest that this overwork might make dispatchers more vulnerable to disclosure of personal information. Taken together, the findings suggest that radio dispatchers are an important form of criminal justice contact, a form of criminal justice contact that is unequally distributed across community context and can create a form of digital vulnerability (also see Lageson 2016).

Finally, Vesla Weaver, Andrew Papachristos, and Michael Zanger-Tishler take a different approach to examining surveillance, by providing an accounting of the changing relationship between criminal offending and criminal justice contact. They examine these changes by using data from two nationally representative cohorts, the NLSY79 (a cohort of individuals who turned eighteen in 1980) and the NLSY97 (a cohort of individuals who turned eighteen in the late 1990s). A key premise of their article is that criminal offending and criminal justice contact should be tightly linked, as detailed earlier; that is, individuals who report engaging in criminal activity should be the same individuals who report having criminal justice contact and, conversely, individuals who do not report engaging in criminal activity should not report having criminal justice contact.

This article advances our understanding of the link between criminal offending and criminal justice contact with three key findings. First, individuals in the earlier cohort, compared to those in the later cohort, engaged in more criminal activity (which is consistent with national declines in crime over time). Second, despite lower rates of criminal activity in the later cohort, those in the later cohort were more likely than those in the earlier cohort to experience an arrest (10 percent versus 25 percent). Relatedly, the association between criminal offending and arrest is weaker in the later cohort than in the earlier cohort. Third, racial inequalities exist in the disconnect between criminal offending and arrest, with black men being more likely than white men to report an arrest with no criminal offending, and these racial inequalities increased dramatically over the two cohorts. These findings point to a remarkable shift in the decoupling of criminal offending and criminal justice contact. Given the deleterious consequences of criminal justice contact for outcomes across the life course (for reviews, see Kirk and Wakefield 2018; Wakefield and Uggen 2010), these findings may also have profound implications for racial-ethnic inequality in domains such as employment, family life, and health.

Unexplored Forms of Punishment

Three articles examine two aspects of the criminal justice system that have both changed substantially during the prison boom and have been relatively unexplored in social science observation: bail and monetary sanctions. As these articles demonstrate, these two unexplored forms of punishment are common, are consequential, and have implications for inequality.

Two of the articles examine the correlates and consequences of bail, the temporary release of an individual awaiting trial (often in the form of a financial payment). Bail is an important element of the criminal justice system because it structures who spends time in jail awaiting trial and for how long. Indeed, about two-thirds of individuals in jail are being held in pretrial detention (Minton and Zeng 2015), all of whom have not been convicted of the crime with which they have been charged and most of whom are being confined because they cannot afford monetary bail. Katherine Hood and Daniel Schneider further our understanding of bail processes by using unique data from the State Court Processing Statistics series to examine county-level variation in severity of bail practices, measured by nonfinancial release and amount of bail (conditional on having a financial bail set). This extends existing research, which mostly examines single locations, by documenting substantial between-county variation in the severity of the bail practices. The authors also extend existing research by documenting that the severity of bail practices is structured by a number of political (such as the political affiliation of the district attorney), socioeconomic (such as county-level unemployment rate), and demographic characteristics (such as percentage of black individuals in the county). For example, the state-level Gini coefficient, a way of measuring income inequality, is negatively associated with nonfinancial release. These analyses provide an important foundational description of the trends and correlates of the use of bail. Given both the inequalities in who experiences pretrial detention, as well as the consequences of pretrial detention for a number of life-course outcomes including employment and recidivism, understanding bail processes—which is at the center of pretrial experiences—is particularly important (on consequences, Dobbie, Goldin, and Yang 2018).

This analysis of the contextual determinants of bail severity is complemented by another article on the bail industry, which has increased in scope alongside the increase in pretrial incarceration. Joshua Page, Victoria Piehowski, and Joe Soss rely on eighteen months of ethnographic fieldwork as a bail bond agent to examine how the bail industry produces opportunities for predation. In particular, their analysis highlights the role of gender, suggesting that women—mostly women of color—connected to incarcerated individuals are primary targets of predation in the bail bond industry. They describe how bail bonds agents engage in a form of emotional labor to target female relatives (particularly mothers, grandmothers, and long-term romantic partners) to secure bail for incarcerated men. This ethnographic examination suggests an important yet to date understudied way through which the criminal justice system has spillover consequences for relatives, particularly female relatives, of the incarcerated. Also, because securing bail can be quite costly, especially if the accused does not show up for trial, this examination suggests another way through which the criminal justice system can affect economic inequality among women.

A third article examines an aspect of the criminal justice system that has been relatively understudied by social scientists: monetary sanctions. Brittany Friedman and Mary Pattillo offer a broad picture of monetary sanctions—defined by the fines, fees, restitution, and other legal costs that individuals accumulate from criminal justice contact—and, therefore, the costs of criminal justice contact. To do so, they conduct a content analysis of statutes related to monetary sanctions in Illinois. Their findings highlight how these statutes impose many economic penalties for a conviction. Their findings also highlight that they collectively define the poor and indigent as irresponsible, rarely providing an opportunity for the predominantly poor individuals affected by the statutes to be relieved of their debt. Because the economic penalties for not paying these monetary sanctions are severe, as outlined in the statutes, this suggests that monetary sanctions can increase inequality among an already severely poor and economically marginalized population.

Consequences of Criminal Justice Contact

The third and final set of articles examines the consequences of criminal justice contact, specifically considering how forms of criminal justice contact—such as arrest, conviction, and incarceration—maintain and exacerbate inequality throughout the life course. These articles highlight the cumulative nature of disadvantages imposed by the criminal justice system and how these disadvantages persist across diverse outcomes such as socioeconomic outcomes, the transition to adulthood, and neighborhood attainment. The articles remind us to examine all stages of criminal justice contact, including contact that precedes incarceration such as arrest and contact that follows incarceration such as parole, to fully understand the role that the criminal justice system plays in the American stratification system.

Robert Apel and Kathleen Powell use data from the NLSY97, examining the consequences of two types of criminal justice contact—arrest and incarceration—for hourly wages. This research, which uses a series of modeling strategies to account for selectivity into criminal justice contact, contributes to existing literature on the consequences of criminal justice contact for inequality in two ways. First, the authors extend prior research by simultaneously considering arrest (a form of noncarceral contact with the criminal justice system) and incarceration (a form of carceral contact with the criminal justice system), finding that the consequences of criminal justice contact for these outcomes are limited to the consequences of incarceration. They find that arrests are only consequential for hourly wages when they accumulate. Second, the authors extend prior research on the consequences of criminal justice contact for inequality by considering two types of heterogeneity: race-ethnic heterogeneity and distributional heterogeneity. They find the negative consequences of incarceration for hourly wages are concentrated among blacks (but not among whites or Latinx). Therefore, as both exposure and (in some cases) consequences of criminal justice contact are unequally distributed, these findings highlight one pathway through which incarceration can entrench existing socioeconomic inequalities.

Using novel administrative data from Michigan, Heather Harris and David Harding use group-based trajectory models to examine whether black-white disparities in precriminal justice contact outcomes can explain racial-ethnic disparities in postcriminal justice contact outcomes. This research contributes to existing literature on the consequences of criminal justice contact by focusing on inequalities within a sample of parolees (as opposed to comparing individuals with criminal justice contact to individuals without criminal justice contact, as is common in most research) and by focusing on adulthood transitions (measured by completing education, finding employment, establishing independent households, and desisting from criminal justice contact). They characterize parolees, who were young adults (ages eighteen to twenty-five) when released from prison, into the following five groups: transitioning, continuing education, persisting, unsettled, and disconnected. They find racial inequalities in group membership; whites make up 71 percent of those in the transitioning group (characterized by the highest rates of employment, independence, and desistance) and blacks make up 63 percent of those in the persisters group (characterized by high unemployment, nonresidential independence, and steady involvement in the criminal justice system). They also find that neither characteristics prior to prison (including human capital and prior criminal justice contact) nor characteristics after prison (including social contexts) can explain these black-white differences in transition to adulthood outcomes. These findings suggest that racial inequalities in the transition to adulthood are entrenched among those receiving community supervision in the form of probation.

Finally, David Kirk draws on sixteen years of prisoner release data in Illinois, focusing on the neighborhood contexts where formerly incarcerated individuals live. He finds that the spatial dynamics of prisoner reentry have changed over time, in respect both to where prisoners return after incarceration and to the clustering of these released prisoners in neighborhoods. Over time, fewer former prisoners return to the city of Chicago; instead, former prisoners are more likely to return to suburban areas. Additionally, former prisoners have become more spatially concentrated and, compared to in the past, there is a larger correlation between these returning residences and household poverty levels. Taken together, these findings suggest linkages between the consequences of incarceration and the spatial geography of poverty and, further, document another way that the criminal justice system has spillover consequences.

CONCLUSIONS

The criminal justice system, expansive in its scope and deleterious in its consequences, is an institution of social stratification in the United States. Although the correlates and consequences of incarceration have been the focus of much social science inquiry, the wide-ranging and consequential nature of the criminal justice system necessitates inquiry into forms of criminal justice contact beyond incarceration. These include both transitory (sometimes sporadic but oftentimes recurring) contacts with criminal justice agents (including police stops, arrests, and tickets and fines) and sustained contacts (including felony conviction, pretrial detention, and correctional supervision). Further, the reach of the criminal justice system can extend into other institutions, such as the educational system or child welfare agencies.

The articles in this volume document the implications of the criminal justice system for social stratification in the United States in three primary ways. First, the articles show that many forms of criminal justice contact, often beyond but certainly related to incarceration, contribute to inequality across stages of the life course including adolescence (Geller and Fagan), the transition to adulthood (Harris and Harding), and adulthood (Kirk). These disadvantages likely compound across the life course, with earlier disadvantages creating later disadvantages and further entrenching race-ethnic and social class inequalities. Second, the articles demonstrate that the consequences persist across an array of outcomes. These outcomes include but are not limited to wages (Apel and Powell), legal socialization (Geller and Fagan), and family life (Edwards). Third, the articles document that the consequences of criminal justice contact proliferate in expansive and complicated ways. The consequences of criminal justice contact spill over across individuals, as evidenced by Geller and Fagan's research documenting how vicarious police stops are consequential for teenagers' legal socialization. The consequences of criminal justice contact also spill over into communities, as evidenced by Kirk's research showing that prisoners return to predominantly disadvantaged neighborhoods. They also spill over across institutions, as shown by Edwards's research on the role that police officers play in the child welfare system.

Individually and collectively, the articles forward our understanding that the criminal justice system—broadly defined to include both noncarceral and carceral contact—has implications for creating, maintaining, and exacerbating inequality in the United States. Also, as many of the articles document, many aspects of the criminal justice system remain unexplored and many opportunities for research on criminal justice contact and inequality have yet to be undertaken. Moving forward, investigations into criminal justice contact and inequality could benefit from a comprehensive theoretical understanding about how the various independent and sometimes overlapping components of the criminal justice system are consequential for individuals, families, and communities. Specifically, advancing theoretical discussions about how stages of the criminal justice system (police stops, arrests) may be differentially associated with diverse outcomes (employment, recidivism), across distinct stages of the life course (adolescence, adulthood), and across heterogeneous subgroups of the population (race-ethnicity, gender) is both necessary and important. Indeed, it is unlikely that all aspects of the criminal justice system similarly affect all outcomes, across all stages of the life course, and across all subgroups of the population. It is equally important to understand when and how the criminal justice system may be consequential and when and how it is not. Further, understanding the various contingencies and sources of heterogeneity has policy implications.

Consider the potentially differential consequences of two sometimes overlapping and sometimes not overlapping forms of criminal justice contact—arrest and incarceration. Theoretically, it is important to understand why arrest might be differently associated with outcomes than incarceration. It is also important to understand why both arrest and incarceration might be consequential for some outcomes but not for others. Two recent studies are instructive for thinking through the theoretical distinctions between these two forms of criminal justice contact. Both studies use the

NLSY97—and modeling strategies that adjust for unobserved heterogeneity—to examine the consequences of arrest and incarceration, one study examining mental health outcomes (Sugie and Turney 2017) and one examining socioeconomic outcomes, specifically, hourly wages (Apel and Powell 2019). The former study finds that both arrest and incarceration have deleterious consequences for mental health. The latter finds that incarceration, but not arrest, is significantly associated with decreases in hourly wages. Why might that be? Why might arrest lead to impairments in mental health but not hourly wages? One possible explanation for the relationship between arrest and mental health is that the anticipatory stress associated with an arrest—and, specifically, the uncertainty about the future (if they will be convicted, if they will experience prison incarceration, if they will be able to communicate with family members)—is a key mechanism (Sugie and Turney 2017). Such anticipatory stress likely matters little for socioeconomic outcomes such as hourly wages (as arrests are not necessarily immediately apparent to an employer). Researchers should embrace these complexities.

Similarly, consider the consequences of immigrant detention. Relatively little is known about the consequences of immigrant detention for the well-being of individuals, families, and communities (for exceptions, see Golash-Boza 2015; Menjívar and Abrego 2012). How might immigrant detention, versus pretrial jail incarceration or prison incarceration, be similarly or differently associated with outcomes? Immigrant detention is certainly consequential for deportations; more than two hundred thousand immigrants were deported in 2012, the most recent peak for deportations as a result of a criminal offense. The number is now slightly less than 150,000 annually but remains large. Most notably, deportations of this nature often involve very low-level offenses (for more detail, see Kirk and Wakefield 2018). It is likely that those detained have many experiences and consequences similar to those of individuals incarcerated in other capacities. For example, being detained is likely consequential for employment, those detained losing their jobs and likely having difficulty finding employment if they are released. Additionally, much like other forms of jail and prison incarceration, being detained is likely a stressful event for families and children. But immigrant detention may have unique consequences. For example, undocumented immigrants who are detained may experience particular uncertainties about their future; in addition to being unsure when they will be released, it is likely they are also unsure whether they will be released at all or whether they will be deported to their country of origin. Indeed, research suggests there is great variation in bond decisions (Ryo 2016; Wadhia 2015). Undocumented immigrants who are detained may also receive fewer visits than others who are incarcerated, given that family members and friends who are also undocumented may be unlikely to visit in fear of criminal justice repercussions related to their own legal status (Patler and Branic 2017). Researchers need to develop theories to distinguish how immigrant detention might affect outcomes relative to incarceration.

Relatedly, it is important for researchers to consider, theoretically, how criminal justice contact might affect individuals over the life course or subgroups of the population. The intergenerational consequences of incarceration is one area of research where such theoretical development could be instructive. For example, paternal incarceration is not associated with test scores among young children but is associated with educational attainment. The reasons for these different associations across life-course stages remain relatively unexplored, however (Foster and Hagan 2009; Geller et al. 2012). Similarly, consensus is growing that the consequences of paternal incarceration for children's behavioral outcomes is stronger among boys than among girls, at least in early childhood. The reasons for these contingent effects remain relatively unexplored (Geller et al. 2012; Wildeman 2010). Researchers need to develop theories to guide understandings of such contingencies.

In addition, research on criminal justice contact and inequality faces additional challenges. One involves data limitations. Many of the criminal justice processes researchers are interested in—such as pretrial detention, conditions of confinement, and plea bargaining, to name a few—are generally unexplored by social science researchers. Other processes, such as arrest or incarceration, are often asked about in large and representative data sources (such as NLSY97 or Add Health) but the information ascertained is limited. For example, the NLSY97 collects detailed information on arrests but does not provide information about the processes underlying the arrest (such as the degree of intrusiveness), which may be particularly important for outcomes. Indeed, Geller and Fagan find in their article in this volume that heterogeneity in police stops structures legal socialization, and that it is possible that heterogeneity is also consequential for linking arrests to outcomes throughout the life course. Relatedly, existing data sources rarely allow researchers to link the various stages of the criminal justice system. An overfocus on incarceration, to the exclusion of building knowledge on the inequalities that result from other forms of criminal justice contact, prevents a full accounting of the numerous and massive changes in criminal justice processing over the last five decades.

Another challenge to research on criminal justice contact and inequality, as evidenced by some articles in this volume, is the tremendous variation across place. This variation exists across all stages of criminal justice contact (including in official policies and in the enactment of these policies). For example, Vargas, Preito-Hodge, and Christofferson show in this volume that individuals across different neighborhoods are differentially vulnerable to digital exposure. In their article in this volume, Hood and Schneider show that bail regimes are quite different across counties. In his, Kirk documents the causes and consequences of the changing spatial distribution of returning prisoners. Further, other research outside of this volume shows that conditions of confinement vary dramatically across facilities (Kreager and Kruttschnitt 2018; Wildeman, Fitzpatrick, and Goldman 2018), that policing practices vary across neighborhoods (Rios 2011), and that sentencing decisions vary across counties (Ulmer and Kramer 1996). This variation across neighborhoods, counties, and states is one reason it is challenging to provide a comprehensive accounting of the link between criminal justice contact and inequality. It also suggests that scholars be attuned to these types of variation in their own research.

Variation in criminal justice practices across time and place also highlights the need for greater sensitivity to the enormous range of outcomes and processes still to be understood. That mass incarceration and surveillance is inefficient, racist, repressive, destructive, and irrational in a host of ways has been amply demonstrated. The next steps are much more difficult, however, and a full accounting of the problem as well as the most effective ways to reduce it remain elusive. Moving forward, we note that more research is needed to link different stages of the criminal justice system and to move beyond incarceration to interrogate the main sources of inequality that derive from criminal justice contact. Similarly, we suspect that scholars focused on entry points in the criminal justice system (policing, arrest, school discipline) and those focused further along in the system (probation, incarceration, and parole) would have much to learn from another.

REFERENCES

Agan, Amanda Y., and Sonja B. Starr. 2016. "Ban the Box, Criminal Records, and Statistical Discrimination: A Field Experiment." *Law & Economics* research paper no. 16-012. Ann Arbor: University of Michigan.

Alexander, Michelle. 2010. *The New Jim Crow: Mass Incarceration in the Age of Color Blindness*. New York: The New Press.

Andersen, Lars H. 2016. "How Children's Educational Outcomes and Crimininality Vary by Duration and Frequency of Paternal Incarceration." *Annals of the American Academy of Political and Social Science* 665(1): 149-70.

Andersen, Signe Hald, and Christopher Wildeman. 2014. "The Effect of Paternal Incarceration on Children's Risk of Foster Care Placement." *Social Forces* 93(1): 269-98.

Apel, Robert, and Kathleen Powell. 2019. "Level of Criminal Justice Contact and Early Adult Wage Inequality." *RSF: The Russell Sage Foundation Journal of the Social Sciences* 5(1): 198-222. DOI: 10.7758/RSF.2019.5.1.09.

Arditti, Joyce. 2012. *Parental Incarceration and the Family: Psychological and Social Effects of Im-*

prisonment on Children, Parents, and Caregivers. New York: New York University Press.

Augustyn, Megan Bears, and Thomas A. Loughran. 2017. "Juvenile Waiver as a Mechanism of Social Stratification: A Focus on Human Capital." *Criminology* 55(2): 405–37.

Baumer, Eric P., Maria B. Velez, and Richard Rosenfeld. 2018. "Bringing Crime Trends Back into Criminology: A Critical Assessment of the Literature and a Blueprint for Future Inquiry." *Annual Review of Criminology* 1: 39–61.

Beckett, Katherine. 1997. *Making Crime Pay: Law and Order in Contemporary American Politics*. New York: Oxford University Press.

———. 2018. "The Politics, Prospects, and Peril of Criminal Justice Reform in an Era of Mass Incarceration." *Annual Review of Criminology* 1: 235–59.

Beckett, Katherine, and Naomi Murakawa. 2012. "Mapping the Shadow Carceral State: Toward an Institutionally Capacious Approach to Punishment." *Theoretical Criminology* 16(2): 221–44.

Brame, Robert, Shawn Bushway, Raymond Paternoster, and Michael G. Turner. 2014. "Demographic Patterns of Cumulative Arrest Prevalence by Ages 18 and 23." *Crime and Delinquency* 60(3): 471–86.

Brame, Robert, Michael G. Turner, Raymond Paternoster, and Shawn D. Bushway. 2011. "Cumulative Prevalence of Arrest from Ages 8 to 23 in a National Sample." *Pediatrics* 129(1): 21–27.

Brayne, Sarah. 2014. "Surveillance and System Avoidance: Criminal Justice Contact and Institutional Attachment." *American Sociological Review* 79(3): 367–91.

Brown, Adam, Mark E. Courtney, and J. Curtis McMillen. 2015. "Behavior Health Needs and Service Use Among Those Who've Aged-Out of Foster Care." *Children and Youth Services Review* 58: 163–69.

Bushway, Shawn D. 1998. "The Impact of an Arrest on the Job Stability of Young White American Men." *Journal of Research in Crime and Delinquency* 35(4): 454–79.

Cochran, Joshua C., and Daniel P. Mears. 2013. "Social Isolation and Inmate Behavior: A Conceptual Framework for Theorizing Prison Visitation and Guiding and Assessing Research." *Journal of Criminal Justice* 41(4): 252–61.

Cohen, Thomas H. 2013. "Pretrial Detention and Misconduct in Federal District Courts, 1995–2010." Washington: Bureau of Justice Statistics.

Comfort, Megan. 2007. "Punishment Beyond the Legal Offender." *Annual Review of Law and Social Science* 3: 271–84.

Crewe, Ben. 2009. *The Prisoner Society: Power, Adaptation and Social Life in an English Prison*. Oxford: Oxford University Press.

DiPrete, Thomas A., and Gregory M. Eirich. 2006. "Cumulative Advantage as a Mechanism for Inequality: A Review of Theoretical and Empirical Developments." *Annual Review of Sociology* 32: 271–97.

Dobbie, Will, Jacob Goldin, and Crystal Yang. 2018. "The Effects of Pre-Trial Detention on Conviction, Future Crime, and Employment: Evidence from Randomly Assigned Judges." *American Economic Review* 108(2): 201–40.

Doleac, Jennifer L. and Benjamin Hansen. 2016. "Does 'Ban the Box' Help or Hurt Low-Skilled Workers? Statistical Discrimination and Employment Outcomes When Criminal Histories Are Hidden." Cambridge, Mass.: National Bureau of Ecnomic Research

Durlauf, Steven N., and Daniel S. Nagin. 2011. "Imprisonment and Crime: Can Both Be Reduced?" *Criminology and Public Policy* 10(1): 13–54.

Edwards, Frank. 2016. "Saving Children, Controlling Families: Punishment, Redistribution, and Child Protection." *American Sociological Review* 81: 575–95.

———. 2019. "Family Surveillance: Police and the Reporting of Child Abuse and Neglect." *RSF: The Russell Sage Foundation Journal of the Social Sciences* 5(1): 50–70. DOI: 10.7758/RSF.2019.5.1.03.

Enns, Peter K. 2016. *Incarceration Nation: How the United States Became the Most Punitive Democracy in the World*. New York: Cambridge University Press.

Federal Bureau of Investigation. 2013. *Uniform Crime Report: Crime in the United States, 2012*. Washington: U.S. Department of Justice.

Forman, James, Jr. 2017. *Locking Up Our Own: Crime and Punishment in Black America*. New York: Farrar, Straus, and Giroux.

Foster, Holly, and John Hagan. 2009. "The Mass Incarceration of Parents in America: Issues of Race/Ethnicity, Collateral Damage to Children, and Prisoner Reentry." *Annals of the American Academy of Political and Social Science* 623(1): 179–94.

———. 2015. "Punishment Regimes and the Multi-level Effects of Parental Incarceration: Intergenerational, Intersectional, and Interinstitutional Models of Social Inequality and Systemic Exclusion." *Annual Review of Sociology* 41: 135–58.

Fratello, Jennifer, Andres F. Rengifo, and Jennifer Trone. 2013. "Coming of Age During Stop, Question, and Frisk." New York: Vera Institute of Justice.

Friedman, Brittany, and Mary Pattillo. 2019. "Statutory Inequality: The Logics of Monetary Sanctions in State Law." *RSF: The Russell Sage Foundation Journal of the Social Sciences* 5(1): 173–96. DOI: 10.7758/RSF.2019.5.1.08.

Gaes, Gerald G., and Scott D. Camp. 2009. "Unintended Consequences: Experimental Evidence for the Criminogenic Effect of Prison Security Level Placement on Post-Release." *Journal of Experimental Criminology* 5(2): 139–62.

Geller, Amanda, Carey E. Cooper, Irwin Garfinkel, Ofira Schwartz-Soicher, and Ronald B. Mincy. 2012. "Beyond Absenteeism: Father Incarceration and Child Development." *Demography* 49(1): 49–76.

Geller, Amanda, and Jeffrey Fagan. 2019. "Police Contact and the Legal Socialization of Urban Teens." *RSF: The Russell Sage Foundation Journal of the Social Sciences* 5(1): 26–49. DOI: 10.7758/RSF.2019.5.1.02.

Geller, Amanda, Jeffrey Fagan, Tom Tyler, and Bruce G. Link. 2014. "Aggressive Policing and the Mental Health of Young Urban Men." *American Journal of Public Health* 104(12): 2321–27.

Goffman, Alice. 2009. "On the Run: Wanted Men in a Philadelphia Ghetto." *American Sociological Review* 74(3): 339–57.

Golash-Boza, Tanya Maria. 2015. *Immigration Nation: Raids, Detentions, and Deportations in Post-9/11 America*. New York: Routledge.

Gottschalk, Marie. 2014. *Caught: The Prison State and the Lockdown of American Politics*. Princeton, N.J.: Princeton University Press.

Gramlich, John. 2016. "Voters' Perceptions of Crime Continue to Conflict with Reality." Washington, D.C.: Pew Research Center.

Gray, Lucinda, and Laurie Lewis. 2015. "Public School Safety and Discipline: 2013–14." Washington: National Center for Education Statistics.

Green, Donald P., and Daniel Winik. 2010. "Using Random Judge Assignments to Estimate the Effects of Incarceration and Probation on Recidivism among Drug Offenders." *Criminology* 48(2): 357–87.

Grogger, Jeffrey T. 1995. "The Effect of Arrests on the Employment and Earnings of Young Men." *Quarterly Journal of Economics* 110(1): 51–72.

Haney, Craig. 2018. "Restricting the Use of Solitary Confinement." *Annual Review of Criminology* 1: 285–310.

Haney, Lynne. 2018. "Incarcerated Fatherhood: The Entanglements of Child Support Debt and Mass Imprisonment." *American Journal of Sociology* 124(1): 1–48.

Harding, David J., Jonah A. Siegel, and Jeffrey D. Morenoff. 2017. "Custodial Parole Sanctions and Earnings After Release from Prison." *Social Forces* 96(2): 909–34.

Harris, Alexes. 2016. *A Pound of Flesh: Monetary Sanctions as Punishment for the Poor*. New York: Russell Sage Foundation.

Harris, Alexes, Heather Evans, and Katherine Beckett. 2010. "Drawing Blood from Stones: Legal Debt and Social Inequality in the Contemporary United States." *American Journal of Sociology* 115(6): 1753–99.

Harris, Heather M., and David J. Harding. 2019. "Racial Inequality in the Transition to Adulthood After Prison." *RSF: The Russell Sage Foundation Journal of the Social Sciences* 5(1): 223–54. DOI: 10.7758/RSF.2019.5.1.10.

Haskins, Anna R. 2014. "Unintended Consequences: Effects of Paternal Incarceration on Child School Readiness and Later Special Education Placement." *Sociological Science* 1(11): 141–58.

Haynie, Dana L., Corey Whichard, Derek A. Kreager, David R. Schaefer, and Sara Wakefield. 2018. "Social Networks and Health in a Prison Unit." *Journal of Health and Social Behavior* 59(3): 318–34.

Hernandez, K. L., Khalil Gibran Muhammad, and Heather Ann Thompson. 2015. "Introduction: Constructing the Carceral State." *Journal of American History* 102(1): 18–24.

Hirschfield, Paul J. 2008. "Preparing for Prison? The Criminalization of School Discipline in the USA." *Theoretical Criminology* 12(1): 79–101.

———. 2018. "Schools and Crime." *Annual Review of Criminology* 1: 149–69.

Holzer, Harry J., Steven Raphael, and Michael A. Stoll. 2004. "How Willing Are Employers to Hire Ex-Offenders?" *Focus* 23(1): 40–43.

Hood, Katherine, and Daniel Schneider. 2019. "Bail and Pretrial Detention: Contours and Causes of Temporal and County Variation." *RSF: The Russell Sage Foundation Journal of the Social Sciences* 5(1): 126–49. DOI: 10.7758/RSF.2019.5.1.06.

Johnson, Rucker, and Steven Raphael. 2012. "How Much Crime Reduction Does the Marginal Prisoner Buy?" *Journal of Law and Economics* 55(2): 275–310.

Kaeble, Danielle. 2018. "Probation and Parole in the United States, 2016." NCJ 251148. Washington: U.S. Department of Justice. Accessed September 8, 2018. https://www.bjs.gov/content/pub/pdf/ppus16.pdf.

Kirk, David S. 2019. "Where the Other 1 Percent Live: An Examination of Changes in the Spatial Concentration of the Formerly Incarcerated." *RSF: The Russell Sage Foundation Journal of the Social Sciences* 5(1): 255–74. DOI: 10.7758/RSF.2019.5.1.11.

Kirk, David S., and Sara Wakefield. 2018. "The Collateral Consequences of Punishment: A Critical Review and Path Forward." *Annual Review of Criminology* 1: 171–94.

Kling, Jeffrey R. 2006. "Incarceration Length, Employment, and Earnings." *American Economic Review* 96(3): 863–76.

Kohler-Hausmann, Issa. 2013. "Misdemeanor Justice: Control Without Conviction." *American Journal of Sociology* 119(2): 351–93.

Kreager, Derek, and Candace Kruttschnitt. 2018. "Inmate Society in an Era of Mass Incarceration." *Annual Review of Criminology* 1: 261–83.

Kupchik, Aaron. 2010. *Homeroom Security: School Discipline in an Age of Fear*. New York: New York University Press.

LaFraniere, Sharon, and Mitch Smith. 2016. "Philando Castile was Pulled Over 49 Times in 13 Years, Often for Minor Infractions." *New York Times*, July 16.

Lageson, Sarah E. 2016. "Found Out and Opting Out: The Consequences of Online Criminal Records for Families." *Annals of the American Academy of Political and Social Science* 665(1): 127–41.

Lageson, Sarah E., and Shadd Maruna. 2017. "Digital Degradation: Stigma Management in the Internet Age." *Punishment and Society* 20(1): 113–33.

Lambson, Suvi Hynynen. 2014. "Community Perceptions of Brownsville: A Survey of Neighborhood Quality of Life, Safety, and Services." Brooklyn, N.Y.: Center for Court Innovation.

Langton, Lynn, and Matthew Durose. 2016. "Police Behavior During Traffic and Street Stops, 2011." NCJ 242937. Washington: Bureau of Justice Statistics.

Lara-Millan, Armando. 2014. "Public Emergency Room Overcrowding in the Era of Mass Imprisonment." *American Sociological Review* 79(5): 866–87.

Lara-Millan, Armando and Nicole Gonzalez Van Cleve. 2016. "Interorganizational Utility of Welfare Stigma in the Criminal Justice System." *Criminology* 55(1): 59–84.

Lauritsen, Janet L., and Maribeth L. Rezey. 2018. "Victimization Trends and Correlates: Macro- and Microinfluences and New Directions for Research." *Annual Review of Criminology* 1: 103–21.

Lee, JoAnn S., Mark E. Courtney, and Emiko Tajima. 2014. "Extended Foster Care Support During the Transition to Adulthood: Effect on the Risk of Arrest." *Children and Youth Services Review* 42(1): 34–42.

Lerman, Amy E., and Vesla M. Weaver. 2014. *Arresting Citizenship: The Democratic Consequences of American Crime Control*. Chicago: University of Chicago Press.

Listwan, Shelley Johnson, Christopher J. Sullivan, Robert Agnew, Francis T. Cullen, and Mark Colvin. 2013. "The Pains of Imprisonment Revisited: The Impact of Strain on Inmate Recidivism." *Justice Quarterly* 30(1): 144–68.

Loughran, Thomas A., Edward P. Mulvey, Carol A. Schubert, Jeffrey Fagan, Alex R. Piquero, and Sandra H. Losoya. 2009. "Estimating a Dose-Response Relationship Between Length of Stay and Future Recidivism in Serious Juvenile Offenders." *Criminology* 47(3): 699–740.

Lynch, Mona. 2016. *Hard Bargains: The Coercive Power of Drug Laws in Federal Court*. New York: Russell Sage Foundation.

Manski, Charles F., and Daniel S. Nagin. 1998. "Bounding Disagreements About Treatment Effects: A Case Study of Sentencing and Recidivism." *Sociological Methodology* 28(1): 99–137.

Manza, Jeff, and Christopher Uggen. 2006. *Locked Out: Felon Disenfranchisement and American Democracy*. New York: Oxford University Press.

Martin, Karin D., Bryan L. Sykes, Sarah Shannon, Frank Edwards, and Alexes Harris. 2018. "Monetary Sanctions: Legal Financial Obligations in US Systems of Justice." *Annual Review of Criminology* 1: 471–95.

Massoglia, Michael, and William Alex Pridemore. 2015. "Incarceration and Health." *Annual Review of Sociology* 41: 291–310.

Mears, Daniel P., Joshua C. Cochran, and Francis T. Cullen. 2015. "Incarceration Heterogeneity and Its Implications for Assessing the Effectiveness of Imprisonment on Recidivism." *Criminal Justice Policy Review* 26(7): 691–712.

Menjívar, Cecilia, and Leisy Abrego. 2012. "Legal Violence: Immigration Law and the Lives of Central American Immigrants." *American Journal of Sociology* 117(5): 1380–421.

Miller, Reuben Jonathan. 2014. "Devolving the Carceral State: Race, Prisoner Reentry, and the Micro-Politics of Urban Poverty Management." *Punishment and Society* 16(3): 305–35.

Miller, Reuben Jonathan, and Forrest Stuart. 2017. "Carceral Citizenship: Race, Rights, and Responsibility in the Age of Mass Supervision." *Theoretical Criminology* 21(4): 532–48.

Minton, Todd D., and Zhen Zeng. 2015. "Jail Inmates at Midyear 2014." NCJ 248629. Washington: Bureau of Justice Statistics.

———. 2016. "Jail Inmates in 2015." NCJ 250394. Washington: Bureau of Justice Statistics.

Morenoff, Jeffrey D., and David J. Harding. 2014. "Incarceration, Prisoner Reentry, and Communities." *Annual Review of Sociology* 40: 411–29.

Mueller-Smith, Michael. 2015. "The Criminal and Labor Market Impacts of Incarceration." Working paper. Ann Arbor: University of Michigan. Accessed September 8, 2018. https://sites.lsa.umich.edu/mgms/wp-content/uploads/sites/283/2015/09/incar.pdf.

Murray, Joseph, David P. Farrington, and Ivana Sekol. 2012. "Children's Antisocial Behavior, Mental Health, Drug Use, and Educational Performance After Parental Incarceration: A Systematic Review and Meta-Analysis." *Psychological Bulletin* 138(2): 175–210.

Na, Chongmin, and Denise C. Gottfredson. 2013. "Police Officers in Schools: Effects on School Crime and the Processing of Offending Behaviors." *Justice Quarterly* 30(4): 619–50.

National Research Council. 2014. *The Growth of Incarceration in the United States: Exploring Causes and Consequences*, edited by J. Travis, B. Western and S. Redburn. Washington, D.C.: National Academies Press.

Page, Joshua, Victoria Piehowski, and Joe Soss. 2019. "A Debt of Care: Commercial Bail and the Gendered Logic of Criminal Justice Predation." *RSF: The Russell Sage Foundation Journal of the Social Sciences* 5(1): 150–72. DOI: 10.7758/RSF.2019.5.1.07.

Pager, Devah. 2003. "The Mark of a Criminal Record." *American Journal of Sociology* 108(5): 937–75.

Patler, Caitlin, and Nicholas Branic. 2017. "Patterns of Family Visitation During Immigration Detention." *RSF: The Russell Sage Foundation Journal of the Social Sciences* 3(4): 18–36. DOI: 10.7758/RSF.2017.3.4.02.

Payne, Allison Ann, and Kelly Welch. 2010. "Modeling the Effects of Racial Threat on Punitive and Restorative School Discipline Practices." *Criminology* 48(4): 1019–62.

Pearlin, Leonard I. 1989. "The Sociological Study of Stress." *Jounral of Health and Social Behavior* 30(3): 241–56.

Petersilia, Joan. 2003. *When Prisoners Come Home: Parole and Prisoner Reentry*. New York: Oxford University Press.

Pettit, Becky, and Bruce Western. 2004. "Mass Imprisonment and the Life Course: Race and Class Inequality in US Incarceration." *American Sociological Review* 69(2): 151–69.

Pfaff, John. 2017. *Locked In: The True Causes of Mass Incarceration—and How to Acheive Real Reform*. New York: Basic Books.

Phelan, Jo C., and Bruce G. Link. 2015. "Is Racism a Fundamental Cause of Inequalities in Health?" *Annual Review of Sociology* 41: 311–30.

Phelps, Michelle S. 2011. "Rehabilitation in the Punitive Era: The Gap Between Rhetoric and Reality in US Prison Programs." *Law & Society Review* 45(1): 33–68.

———. 2013. "The Paradox of Probation: Community Supervision in the Age of Mass Incarceration." *Law & Policy* 35(1): 51–80.

———. 2016. "Possibilities and Contestation in 21st-Century US Criminal Justice Downsizing." *Annual Review of Law and Social Science* 12: 153–70.

———. 2017. "Mass Probation: Toward a More Robust Theory of State Variation in Punishment." *Punishment and Society* 19(1): 53–73.

Piquero, Alex R., and Wesley G. Jennings. 2017. "Research Note: Justice System-Imposed Financial Penalties Increase the Likelihood of Recidivism in a Sample of Adolescent Offenders." *Youth Violence and Juvenile Justice* 15(3): 325–40.

Raphael, Steven, and Michael A. Stoll, eds. 2009. *Do Prisons Make Us Safer? The Benefits and Costs of the Prison Boom*. New York: Russell Sage Foundation.

Reiter, Keramet. 2016. *23/7: Pelican Bay Prison and the Rise of Long Term Solitary Confinement*. New Haven, Conn.: Yale University Press.

Reiter, Keramet, and Susan Bibler Coutin. 2017. "Crossing Borders and Criminalizing Identity: The Disintegrated Subjects of Administrative Sanctions." *Law & Society Review* 51(3): 567–601.

Rios, Victor M. 2011. *Punished: Policing the Lives of Black and Latino Boys*. New York: New York University Press.

Rocque, Michael, and Raymond Paternoster. 2011. "Understanding the Antecedents of the 'School-to-Jail' Link: The Relationship Between Race and School Discipline." *Journal of Criminal Law and Criminology* 101(2): 633–65.

Ryo, Emily. 2016. "Detained: A Study of Immigration Bond Hearings." *Law & Society Review* 50(1): 117–53.

Sewell, Abigail A., and Kevin A. Jefferson. 2016. "Collateral Damage: The Health Effects of Invasive Police Encounters in New York City." *Journal of Urban Health* 93 (Suppl. 1): 42–67.

Sewell, Abigail A., Kevin A. Jefferson, and Hedwig Lee. 2016. "Living Under Surveillance: Gender, Psychological Distress, and Stop-Question-and-Frisk Policing in New York City." *Social Science & Medicine* 159(6): 1–13.

Sharkey, Patrick. 2018. "The Long Reach of Violence: A Broader Perspective on Data, Theory, and Evidence on the Prevalence and Consequences of Exposure to Violence." *Annual Review of Criminology* 1: 85–102.

Shedd, Carla. 2015. *Unequal City: Race, Schools, and Perceptions of Injustice*. New York: Russell Sage Foundation.

Simon, Jonathan. 2007. *Governing Through Crime: How the War on Crime Transformed American Democracy and Created a Culture of Fear*. New York: Oxford University Press.

Skarbeck, David. 2014. *The Social Order of the Underworld: How Prison Gangs Govern the American Penal System*. New York: Oxford University Press.

Smith, Peter Scharff. 2006. "The Effects of Solitary Confinement on Prison Inmates: A Brief History and Review of the Literature." *Crime & Justice* 34(1): 441–528.

Stuart, Forrest. 2016. "Becoming 'Copwise': Policing, Culture, and the Collateral Consequences of Street-Level Criminalization." *Law & Society Review* 50(2): 279–313.

Stuart, Forrest, and Ava Benezra. 2017. "Criminalized Masculinities: How Policing Shapes the Construction of Gender and Sexuality in Poor Black Communities." *Social Problems* 65(2): 174–90.

Stuart, Forrest, and Reuben Jonathan Miller. 2016. "The Prisonized Old Head: Intergenerational Socialization and the Fusion of Ghetto and Prison Culture." *Journal of Contemporary Ethnography* 46(6): 673–98.

Sugie, Naomi F., and Kristin Turney. 2017. "Beyond Incarceration: Criminal Justice Contact and Mental Health." *American Sociological Review* 82(4): 719–43.

Sykes, Gresham. 2007. *The Society of Captives: A Study of Maximum Security Prisons*, 2nd ed. Princeton, N.J.: Princeton University Press.

Turner, Kimberly J., and Maureen R. Waller. 2017. "Indebted Relationships: Child Support Arrears and Nonresident Fathers' Involvement with Children." *Journal of Marriage and Family* 79(1): 24–43.

Turney, Kristin, and Christopher Wildeman. 2017. "Adverse Childhood Experiences Among Children Placed In and Adopted from Foster Care: Evidence from a Nationally Representative Survey." *Child Abuse & Neglect* 64 (February): 117–29.

Uggen, Christopher, Mike Vuolo, Sarah Lageson, Ebony Ruhland, and Hilary K. Whitham. 2014. "The Edge of Stigma: An Experimental Audit of the Effects of Low-Level Criminal Records on Employment." *Criminology* 52(4): 627–54.

Ulmer, Jeffery T., and John H. Kramer. 1996. "Court Communities Under Sentencing Guidelines: Dilemmas of Formal Rationality and Sentencing Disparity." *Criminology* 34(3): 383–408.

University at Albany. 2018. *Sourcebook of Criminal Justice Statistics*. Albany, N.Y.: Hindelang Criminal Justice Research Center.

Vargas, Robert, Kayla Preito-Hodge, and Jeremy Christofferson. 2019. "Digital Vulnerability: The Unequal Risk of E-Contact with the Criminal Justice System." *RSF: The Russell Sage Foundation Journal of the Social Sciences* 5(1): 71–88. DOI: 10.7758/RSF.2019.5.1.04.

Wadhia, Shoba Sivaprasad. 2015. *Beyond Deporta-*

tion: The Role of Prosecutorial Discretion in Immigration Cases*. New York: New York University Press.

Wagner, Peter, and Bernadette Rabuy. 2016. "Mass Incarceration: The Whole Pie 2016." Northampton, Mass.: Prison Policy Initiative.

Wakefield, Sara, and Christopher Uggen. 2010. "Incarceration and Stratification." *Annual Review of Sociology* 36(1): 387–406. DOI: 10.1146/annurev.soc.012809.102551.

Weaver, Vesla M., Andrew Papachristos, and Michael Zanger-Tishler. 2019. "The Great Decoupling: The Disconnection Between Criminal Offending and Experience of Arrest Across Two Cohorts." *RSF: The Russell Sage Foundation Journal of the Social Sciences* 5(1): 89–123. DOI: 10.7758/RSF.2019.5.1.05.

Welch, Kelly, and Allison Ann Payne. 2010. "Racial Threat and Punitive School Discipline." *Social Problems* 57(1): 25–48.

Western, Bruce. 2006. *Punishment and Inequality in America*. New York: Russell Sage Foundation.

Wiesner, Margit, Deborah M. Capaldi, and Hyoun K. Kim. 2010. "Arrests, Recent Life Circumstances, and Recurrent Job Loss for At-Risk Young Men: An Event-History Analysis." *Journal of Vocational Behavior* 76(2): 344–54.

Wildeman, Christopher. 2010. "Paternal Incarceration and Children's Physically Aggressive Behaviors: Evidence from the Fragile Families and Child Wellbeing Study." *Social Forces* 89(1): 285–309.

Wildeman, Christopher, Maria D. Fitzpatrick, and Alyssa W. Goldman. 2018. "Conditions of Confinement in American Prisons and Jails." *Annual Review of Law and Social Science* 14. Published online July 11, 2018. DOI: 10.1146/annurev-lawsocsci-101317-031025.

Wildeman, Christopher, and Christopher Muller. 2012. "Mass Imprisonment and Inequality in Health and Family Life." *Annual Review of Law and Social Science* 8:11–30.

Wildeman, Christopher, Kristin Turney, and Youngmin Yi. 2016. "Paternal Incarceration and Family Functioning: Variation across Federal, State, and Local Facilities." *Annals of the American Academy of Political and Social Science* 665(1): 80–97.

Williams, David R., Harold W. Neighbors, and James S. Jackson. 2003. "Racial/Ethnic Discrimination and Health: Findings from Community Studies." *American Journal of Public Health* 93(Suppl. 1): 200–208.

Yi, Youngmin, and Christopher Wildeman. 2018. "Can Foster Care Interventions Diminish Justice System Inequality?" *Future of Children* 28(1): 37–58.

Yi, Youngmin, Kristin Turney, and Christopher Wildeman. 2017. "Mental Health Among Jail and Prison Inmates." *American Journal of Men's Health* 11(4): 900–909.

Zedner, Lucia. 2016. "Penal Subversions: When Is a Punishment Not Punishment, Who Decides, and on What Grounds?" *Theoretical Criminology* 20(1): 3–20.

Zimring, Franklin E., Gordon Hawkins, and Sam Kamin. 2003. *Punishment and Democracy: Three Strikes and You're Out in California*. New York: Oxford University Press.

PART I
Surveillance

Police Contact and the Legal Socialization of Urban Teens

AMANDA GELLER AND JEFFREY FAGAN

Contemporary American policing has routinized involuntary police contacts with young people through frequent, sometimes intrusive investigative stops. Personal experience with the police has the potential to corrode adolescents' relationships with law and skew law-related behaviors. We use the Fragile Families and Child Wellbeing Study to estimate how adolescents' experiences with the police shape their legal socialization. We find that both personal and vicarious police contact are associated with increased legal cynicism. Associations are present across racial groups and are not explained by teens' behaviors, school settings, or family backgrounds. Legal cynicism is amplified in teens reporting intrusive contact but diminished among teens reporting experiences characterized by procedural justice. Our findings suggest that aggressive policing risks weakening teens' deference to law and legal authorities.

Keywords: policing, legal socialization, legal cynicism, adolescents

Recent high-profile incidents of police violence toward citizens have underscored the everyday presence of police in the lives of young people. Contemporary policing, including "proactive policing" models, has routinized police contacts between citizens and police (Kubrin et al. 2010; Tyler, Fagan, and Geller 2014). These regimes expose teens to police in their everyday routines, translating into regular and involuntary police-citizen interactions through frequent and sometimes intrusive investigative stops and frisks, often on threadbare suspicion of criminal behavior (Fagan et al. 2010; Fagan and Geller 2015; White and Fradella 2016). In both large and small cities, these contacts can lead to official sanctions in the form of noncriminal summons for violations of municipal codes or arrests for minor misdemeanors (Fagan and Ash 2017). Studies show that the burden of these police contacts and arrests condi-

Amanda Geller is clinical associate professor of sociology at New York University. **Jeffrey Fagan** is Isidor and Seville Sulzbacher Professor of Law and professor of epidemiology at Columbia University.

© 2019 Russell Sage Foundation. Geller, Amanda, and Jeffrey Fagan. 2019. "Police Contact and the Legal Socialization of Urban Teens." *RSF: The Russell Sage Foundation Journal of the Social Sciences* 5(1): 26–49. DOI: 10.7758/RSF.2019.5.1.02. The Fragile Families and Child Wellbeing Study was funded by the Eunice Kennedy Shriver National Institute of Child Health and Human Development (NICHD) of the National Institutes of Health under award number R01HD36916, R01HD39135, and R01HD40421, as well as a consortium of private foundations. The content is solely the responsibility of the authors and does not necessarily represent the official views of the National Institutes of Health. The authors are grateful for feedback from participants at the Russell Sage Foundation authors' conference and from anonymous reviewers. Direct correspondence to: Amanda Geller at amanda.geller@nyu.edu, Department of Sociology, New York University, 295 Lafayette St., New York, NY 10012.

Open Access Policy: *RSF: The Russell Sage Foundation Journal of the Social Sciences* is an open access journal. This article is published under a Creative Commons Attribution-NonCommercial-NoDerivs 3.0 Unported License.

tional on police encounters fall on young minority males (on burden, U.S. Department of Justice 2015, 2016, 2017; on arrests, Kochel, Wilson, and Mastrofski 2011).

Police are also regularly present in urban and suburban schools, and often have the authority to make arrests and engage in other enforcement activity, often for minor incidents that could be handled informally by school officials (Kupchik 2010). As is true of aggressive street policing, the burden of police contact in schools falls predominantly on black and Latino youth (on policing, Fagan et al. 2010; Weitzer, Tuch, and Skogan 2008; on schools, Nance 2016; Rocque and Paternoster 2011; on youth, White 2015).

Personal experience with the police and other forms of interpersonal racial discrimination are critical factors in the legal socialization of adolescents (Berg et al. 2016; Brunson 2007; Burt, Lei, and Simons 2017; Fagan and Tyler 2005; Fagan and Piquero 2007). By legal socialization, we refer to the interaction of natural maturation with a broad set of situational experiences. Interactions with legal authorities are a key feature of those experiences, because for most adolescents, police stand alongside school authorities as the face of the state (Shedd 2015). Through those interactions, children and adolescents develop values and attitudes about law and the legal actors that enforce it; these legal interactions frame their cognitive schema of the socio-legal landscape around them (Burt, Lei, and Simons 2017).

The frequency of police-youth contacts in poor neighborhoods skews the locus of adolescent socialization in those places toward their interactions with police. Carla Shedd finds that Chicago youths stopped by the police show high rates of distress and perceptions of injustice (2015). Rod Brunson and Ronald Weitzer identify feelings of "hopelessness" and being "dehumanized" (2009). Benjamin Justice and Tracey Meares contend that people gain information about their position in society from interactions with the legal system throughout adolescence (2014). This forms the basis of their relationship with legal authorities and their sense of democratic belonging and obligation to the law (Epp, Maynard-Moody, and Haider-Markel 2014; Bell 2016; Soss and Weaver 2017).

Others show that legal cynicism runs deeper among youths and adults in neighborhoods that are more heavily policed (Kirk and Matsuda 2011; Desmond, Papachristos, and Kirk 2016). Particularly if the "dosage" of police contact is strong, citizens who feel they have been treated harshly or unfairly by the police, experienced procedural injustice (Bell 2016), or were stopped due to racial discrimination are at risk of diminished perceptions of police legitimacy (Tyler, Fagan, and Geller 2014) and the development of legal cynicism (Brunson 2007; Fagan and Tyler 2005; Kirk and Matsuda 2011). Because policing is woven into the social fabric of urban neighborhoods, teens' legal socialization might also be influenced by police activity that they witness in their neighborhoods, even if they are not personally involved (Stuart 2016). Both Dennis Rosenbaum and his colleagues and Brunson and Weitzer identify a "vicarious" experience of policing, in which perceptions of the police are influenced not only by one's own experiences, but also by the experiences of others (Rosenbaum et al. 2005; Brunson and Weitzer 2009; compare Fagan and Piquero 2007). Each additional direct or vicarious interaction provides new information and experiences that can add to their evaluations of legal authorities (Fagan, Tyler, and Meares 2016). These interactions and socialization experiences influence crime over time, especially in the distinct contexts of adolescent development for African American youths (Burt, Lei, and Simons 2017).

In this article, we examine the intersection of aggressive policing and legal socialization of teenagers and young adults, with a focus on one dimension of legal socialization: legal cynicism (Sampson and Bartusch 1998; Bell 2016). Following Robert Sampson and Dawn Bartusch, we define legal cynicism as "anomie about law" (1998, 778). "Anomie" was a state of disconnection of individuals from both community and the social and legal norms of the state. More recent expressions of legal cynicism emphasize the rejection of the law and its agents as "illegitimate" and "unresponsive" to concerns about safety and justice (Kirk and Papachristos 2011, 1191). These perspectives view legal cynicism as disrupting willing deference to legal actors and as unraveling social cohesion and the social bonds that connect people to each other and the state (on legal actors, Tyler and Huo 2002; Carr, Napalitano, and Keating 2007; on bonds, Sampson and Bartusch 1998). Monica Bell expands the concept of legal cynicism to include an animating process resulting from experiences of procedural injustice in a situational context of social exclusion and marginalization (2016). Exposure to young adults to these policing tactics is woven into the developmental landscape of children and adolescence, potentially skewing their socialization to law, legal actors, and underlying social norms.

From this framework, we assess how police-youth interactions shape the legal socialization of adolescents under social conditions of intense police surveillance and contact. We focus on adolescents with high exposure to the criminal justice system and estimate the extent to which their personal and vicarious contacts with the police are associated with a reduction in their respect for the police and an increase in legal cynicism. Using regression and matching models, we find that adolescents who have been stopped by the police, witnessed police stops, or know people who were stopped report greater levels of legal cynicism than their counterparts without police contact. Moreover, the conduct of these police encounters matters: legal cynicism is amplified in teens reporting more intrusive contact but diminished among teens who report that the police behaved with consideration for procedural justice. These associations are present for black, white, and Hispanic teens, robust across multiple model specifications, and not explained by the teens' behavior, school settings, or family backgrounds.

PROACTIVE POLICING

Policing in the United States has changed substantially over the past four decades (Skogan and Frydl 2004; Braga and Weisburd 2010; Weisburd and Majmundar 2018). Many urban police departments have shifted from a reactive posture to aggressive tactics such as "proactive policing" (Kubrin et al. 2010), "order maintenance policing" (Livingston 1997), and "broken windows" policing (Kelling and Coles 1996; Kelling and Wilson 1982). These models emphasize the active engagement of citizens at low levels of suspicion and aggressive enforcement of minor crimes and civil violations. Debra Livingston and Philip Heymann each describe this as the "new policing," featuring the integration of advanced statistical metrics, new forms of organizational accountability, and aggressive enforcement of minor crimes (Livingston 1997; Heymann 2000). Police also apply this model to use field interrogations or investigative stops as prophylactics to scrub from local areas the social conditions thought to contribute to crime (Skogan 1990; Harcourt 1998; Taylor 2001). The model has been adopted in large and small cities, and institutionalized in everyday police-citizen interactions, especially among residents of poorer, minority, and higher crime areas (Fagan et al. 2016; Livingston 1997; Skogan and Frydl 2004; Kohler-Hausmann 2014; Soss and Weaver 2017; Weisburd and Majmundar 2018).

Applying these tactics, police have saturated many communities with surveillance and proactive contacts. In 2011, more than 62.9 million U.S. residents, 26 percent of the population age sixteen or older, reported contact with the police over the previous twelve months (Langton and Durose 2013). About half of those experienced police-initiated, or involuntary, contact, such as an investigative stop while driving or as a pedestrian (Langton and Durose 2013). The rich data on police stops in New York City provide a basis for estimating the prevalence of police stops (White and Fradella 2016). Between 2004 and 2012, the New York City Police Department recorded more than two hundred thousand police-initiated stops of youth between the ages of thirteen and fifteen (NYPD 2016). Jeffrey Fagan and colleagues estimated that up to 80 percent of African American males between sixteen and twenty-four may have been stopped once or more by the NYPD in 2008, versus 38 percent of Latino males and 10 percent of white males (2010). Precision in these estimates is difficult given variations in police reporting, the presence of nonresidents in the population of those stopped, and the possibility that individuals are stopped multiple times. Tom Tyler, Jeffrey Fagan, and Amanda Geller estimate, based on a 2012 stratified random sample of eighteen to twenty-six year old males living in New York City, that 43.2 percent of respondents were stopped by police in the year leading up to the survey (2014).

A survey of Chicago public school students found that approximately half had been stopped, questioned, and "told off or told to move on" by ninth or tenth grade (Shedd 2015). Police officer presence has also become prevalent in schools, and police often have the authority to make arrests and engage in other enforcement activity (*B.H. v. City of New York.* Amended Complaint 10 CV 0210 (RRM)(ALC) (2010); Fowler et al. 2010; Kupchik 2010; Na and Gottfredson 2011; Owens 2017). Driven in part by this police contact, evidence from the National Longitudinal Survey of Youth shows that by age eighteen, cumulative arrest prevalence rates range from 30.2 to 41.4 percent (Brame et al. 2012).

Police exposure and resulting sanctions are racially skewed. The cumulative arrest rate by age twenty-three is 49 percent for black males and 38 percent for their white counterparts (Brame et al. 2012). With greater exposure to police who are applying these aggressive patrol tactics comes a greater risk of police contact and violence during those contacts (Fagan 2017; Eckhouse 2018). Even in a period of declining police stops in New York, racial and neighborhood disparities in intrusive policing persist, with the distribution by race no different in 2015 than in the peak year of police stop activity in 2011 (Zimroth 2017).

Police Contact and Legal Socialization

Legal socialization is a developmental process of forming a relationship to the law and legal authority (Trinkner, Jackson, and Tyler, in press). It begins in early adolescence and continues into young adulthood (Fagan and Tyler 2005; Piquero et al. 2005; Fagan and Piquero 2007; Stewart et al. 2009; Berg et al. 2016). During this period, from their everyday exposure to policing, young people develop views about the social and moral norms that legal actors enforce and about the norms and rules that those authorities represent. These views develop from adolescents' interactions in social institutions and social settings where authority can exert control and has the capacity to punish and to confer status about a person's social value and societal role (Justice and Meares 2014). Adolescents also expand the empirical basis for their judgments by observing the interactions of family, peers, and neighbors with legal authorities to broaden their views of the moral authority and fairness of law.

Three features of legal socialization or experience with law inform this project. First, police matter more than other authorities. In an era when school discipline overlaps with policing, and when policing is integrated into the school environment and embedded in many neighborhoods, police figure prominently in how adolescents view legal authority and legal rules (Weitzer and Tuch 2006). The totality of adolescents' contacts with police in schools and on the street in the new policing models places the locus of legal socialization in their contacts with police, particularly during early to mid-adolescence.

Second, legal socialization is inherently a learning process. Through interactions with legal actors, adolescents and young adults experience "teachable moments" that signal the underlying rules and norms of legal regimes and actors (Stewart et al. 2009; Tyler, Fagan, and Geller 2014; Justice and Meares 2014; Berg et al. 2016). Experiences move from teachable moments to socialization processes through not just the content, but also the emotional and cognitive weight of the sum of their experiences. Positive experiences with legal actors can reinforce law; negative experiences can teach the opposite lesson through anger and fear reactions to the unfair or abusive exercise of legal power. These competing and reinforcing processes create a tension between viewing legal authorities as fair and respectful or as abusive and illegitimate (Fagan and Piquero 2007). The elements of procedural justice can be thought of as powerful emotional engines that can bind or distance adolescents from the police or other legal actors (Kirk and Papachristos 2011).[1] When interactions with police are harsh or intrusive, the psychological fallout—stress, stigma, anger—can skew the meaning

---

1. They also can shape the evaluations of law and its rewards and punishments, which has implications for the salience of deterrence processes (Fagan and Piquero 2007; Fagan and Meares 2008).

of legal actors and the laws they stand for (Geller et al. 2014). Moreover, the effects of these experiences are cumulative, so the emotional weight of one experience can shape the cognitive frame through which subsequent experiences are evaluated and internalized.

Third, legal reasoning and decision-making are influenced by these experiences. Both Monica Bell and Mark Berg and his colleagues, using quite different methods, show how perceived injustices can produce legal cynicism and alienation from—or even opposition to—the law or its agents (Bell 2016; Berg et al. 2016). Legal socialization can influence deference to the law by conferring or withholding the law's legitimacy, and the emotional aftermath of accumulated negative experiences can produce cynicism that changes legal reasoning (Tyler and Fagan 2008). Both at the individual and neighborhood levels, high rates of legal cynicism can lead to higher offending rates (individual, Tyler and Fagan 2008; Fagan and Piquero 2007; neighborhood, Kirk and Papachristos 2011; Tyler, Fagan, and Geller 2014). Legal cynicism also can reduce incentives to cooperate with police in solving crimes, leading to a spiral of crime, intensive policing, and legal cynicism in the most heavily policed communities (see Kirk and Matsuda 2011; Tyler, Fagan, and Geller 2014; Gau and Brunson 2010; Desmond, Papachristos, and Kirk 2016).

Race Differences in the Effects of Police Contact

There are reasons to think that the effects of police contact on legal socialization may vary by race; however, the nature of race moderation is theoretically ambiguous. If police officers use racial invective, or subjects believe they were targeted because of their race, the stress and stigma of an encounter may be compounded and have consequences for legal socialization (Anderson 2013; Hatzenbuehler et al. 2010; Krieger 1999; Phelan and Link 2015; Sawyer et al. 2012). The effects of police contact on legal cynicism may also be amplified for minority youth if they perceive racial targeting and that their encounter was therefore unjust (Stewart et al. 2009; Gau and Brunson 2010; Berg et al. 2016). On the other hand, the increased exposure of minority youth to the police has the potential to foster resilience, depending on the neighborhood, family, and other social contexts of interactions with police, and may attenuate any adverse effects of a given encounter on their legal socialization (Burt, Lei, and Simons 2017; Geller, Fagan, and Tyler 2017).

METHODS

The current project extends our understanding of these implications of adolescents' contacts with the police for legal socialization, using new data from a large multiwave population-based sample of urban teens across multiple cities and social contexts.

Data

Data are drawn from the Fragile Families and Child Wellbeing Study (FFCWS), a birth cohort survey of children born in large cities that has become a leading source of data on urban families and the social environment. The study follows a cohort of nearly five thousand couples with children born between 1998 and 2000 in twenty large U.S. cities (Reichman et al. 2001). The study systematically oversamples unmarried parents, providing a sample that contains mostly racial and ethnic minorities and faces significant social disadvantage, but when weighted or regression-adjusted is nationally representative of urban births. Parents are surveyed at the time of their child's birth, and follow-up surveys are conducted when the children are one, three, five, nine, and fifteen years old (Y1, Y3, Y5, Y9, and Y15 follow-up waves). The study's "focal children" were interviewed at the Y9 and Y15 follow-ups; at Y15 more than three thousand were asked about their experiences with the police, police contact among their peers and others they know, and their perceptions of the law and police-community relations. These data build on five previous waves of interviews with parents and other caregivers, assessments of child development and behavior, and various measurements of the children's social environments.

Key Measures

Key measures in this study include legal cynicism and legal socialization; adolescent-police contact; and demographic, socioeconomic, and behavioral characteristics.

Legal Cynicism and Legal Socialization

Legal cynicism is measured using a series of six questions related to the focal teens' perceptions of the police and the law (Sampson and Bartusch 1998; Kirk and Papachristos 2011; Berg et al. 2016; Geller et al. 2014). Subjects report their level of agreement (on a 5-point Likert scale) with the following six statements: "I have a great deal of respect for the police." "It's okay to do anything you want." "There are no right or wrong ways to make money." "Laws were made to be broken." "If I fight with somebody it's nobody else's business." "The police create more problems than they solve." Responses are combined in an additive scale ($\alpha = 0.66$), each coded so that higher values indicate a greater legal cynicism.

Adolescent-Police Contact

Adolescent experiences with the police are measured using self-reports of personal contact (in which the teen reports having been stopped by the police), and vicarious contact (in which the teen reports having witnessed a police stop of someone else, or personally knowing someone who has been stopped by the police). Although teens have opportunities to report both personal and vicarious contact, and many (approximately 25 percent) report having experienced both, our analyses examine differences between mutually exclusive groups: teens reporting personal contact, teens reporting vicarious but not personal contact, and teens reporting no contact.

Teens reporting personal or vicarious police contact report on several domains of the contact that they have experienced, witnessed, or heard about. (Adolescents with personal and vicarious experience are asked specifically about their encounters rather than encounters they witnessed or heard about). Asked about "the incident that stands out most in [their] mind" (their *critical stop* or *most memorable stop*), teens report whether the stop involved the officer frisking them (or, for vicarious contact, the person stopped), searching their bags or pockets, using harsh language, using racial slurs, threatening physical force, and using physical force. Binary indicators of these force domains are totaled to form an index of police intrusion in the critical stop ($\alpha = 0.75$). Teens with stop experience (personal or vicarious) also complete a three-item omnibus measure of procedural justice that measures, in the incidents the youth experienced, witnessed, or heard about, whether the police "explained why they stopped [the person stopped] in a way that was clear to them," "treat[ed them] with dignity and courtesy," and "respected [their] rights" (on procedural justice, see Tyler 2003). Questions were answered "often," "sometimes," or "never," and were totaled with higher values on the scale ($\alpha = 0.71$) indicating greater procedural justice.

Demographic, Socioeconomic, and Behavioral Characteristics

Adolescent experiences with the police, and their potential consequences for legal socialization, were evaluated in the context of teens' demographic, socioeconomic, and behavioral characteristics. Respondent race is self-reported, and supplemented by parents' self-reported race when teens' responses cannot be coded. Analyses also consider adolescent age, their mothers' educational attainment, and their parents' relationship status at the time of their birth. Finally, we consider adolescents' likely exposure to the police and criminal justice system, measured individually (based on self-reported measures of their early externalizing and delinquent behavior, both reported at Y9), and as an aspect of their family background (such as whether either of their parents is known to have ever been incarcerated) and school environment (specifically, whether a police officer is regularly stationed at their school).

Analysis

Our analysis sample includes the 3,001 teens interviewed who provided information on their experiences with the police (whether they had ever been stopped or experienced vicarious police contact), and their attitudes about the law. Table A1 presents a model, based on the 4,897 families interviewed at baseline, predicting inclusion in our analysis sample, and suggests that our sample differs from the broader FFCWS sample in several ways. Teens in the analysis sample are significantly ($p < .05$) less likely to be born to Hispanic or "other race" mothers, reflecting greater attrition over fifteen years in these minority families, but marginally

(p < .10) more likely to be born to black mothers than white mothers. Children born to mothers in deep poverty (below 50 percent of the federal poverty line) are also significantly less likely to be included in our analysis sample (p < .01). Controlling for mothers' race and poverty status, teens in our analysis sample do not differ from their counterparts in terms of their parents' baseline relationship status. Missing covariate values are imputed in fifty datasets. Most covariates are missing 1 percent of observations or fewer; exceptions include whether the teens report a police officer stationed at their school (3 percent), peer delinquency (6 percent), teens' self-reported delinquency (7 percent) and Y9 externalizing behavior (7 percent), and their fathers' incarceration histories (13 percent).

Table 1 provides descriptive statistics for the analysis sample. Teens reporting either personal or vicarious police contact also report significantly more cynicism than their counterparts who have no experience with the police. However, those reporting police contact also report more delinquency, externalizing behavior, and aspects of socioeconomic disadvantage that may contribute to their elevated levels of both police contact and legal cynicism. We estimate the association between legal cynicism and stop experience net of these additional factors.

Our analysis proceeds in three stages. In the first, we use regression and propensity score analyses to assess differences in legal cynicism between teens with and without police contact. We next assess outcome differences by the nature of contact that teens report: whether the teens report that they were personally stopped or that they witnessed involuntary police contact or knew someone stopped, as well as their reports of officer behavior during these encounters. Finally, we assess the moderating effects of respondent race and ethnicity on our estimates of the relationship between police contact and legal socialization.

Socialization Differences by Police Contact
Our first models examine how legal cynicism differs between teens with and without contact with the police, whether personal or vicarious. Model 1 is an ordinary least squares regression estimating differences with controls for race, age, sex, and a series of behavioral and socioeconomic characteristics likely to be associated with adolescents' police exposure and their subsequent legal cynicism: mothers' baseline educational attainment, parents' relationship status at baseline, their own externalizing behavior, and their exposure to the police through self-reported delinquency (measured at Y9), fathers' criminal justice history, and their school environment.

Model 2 uses propensity score matching to estimate the effects of police contact experience, controlling for the distributions of the covariates of police contact. Within each of the fifty imputed datasets, we use a probit specification to generate a propensity score for each individual, and use nearest-neighbor matching with replacement to identify outcome differences in each dataset and combine estimates across imputations (Dehejia and Wahba 2002). We next estimate two parallel models (models 3 and 4) focusing on differences in legal cynicism between teens who report personal experience with the police and those who have not. In these models, teens reporting only vicarious experience are modeled as having been "untreated," whereas in models 1 and 2 they were considered to be part of the treatment group.

Socialization Differences by the Nature of Contact
In the second stage, we move from examining binary indicators of police contact to indicators that provide additional detail on the nature of police contact that teens report. Model 5 parallels models 1 and 3 to examine associations between police contact and legal cynicism, with controls for the complete set of covariates laid out in table 1 but identifies differences in legal socialization between teens with personal, vicarious, and no experience with the police. Model 6 controls not only for whether respondents had personal or vicarious experience with the police, but also for the level of intrusion they reported in their critical stop. This model includes an interaction term to distinguish whether the respondents' critical stop was personally or vicariously experienced. In these models, teens with no stop experience (personal or vicarious) are coded as having ex-

Table 1. Sample Description: Means, Standard Errors, and Percentages

	Total (N = 3,001)	Personally Stopped (N = 799)	Vicarious Contact (N = 1,580)	No Contact (N = 622)
Legal cynicism (min = 6, max = 30)	10.5	12.3***	10.2***	9.2
	(0.06)	(0.13)	(0.08)	(0.1)
Police experience				
Ever stopped	27%	100%	0%	0%
With vicarious contact	78%	94%	100%	0%
Intrusion of critical stop	1.1	1.25***	1.51***	0
	(0.03)	(0.06)	(0.04)	
Procedural justice in stop experience	6.8	7.0	6.7	N/A
(N = 2,379 with personal or vicarious contact)	(0.4)	(0.06)	(0.04)	
Background				
Male	51%	69%***	44%	45%
White	18%	14%***	19%	21%
Black	50%	58%***	48%+	44%
Hispanic	24%	20%**	25%	27%
Other race	2%	1%	2%	2%
Two or more races	6%	7%	6%	6%
Age	15.5	15.5***	15.5*	15.4
	(0.01)	(0.02)	(0.01)	(0.02)
Mother has less than high school education	31%	34%**	32%*	27%
Mother finished high school or GED	31%	35%*	31%	28%
Mother has some college	26%	23%*	26%	29%
Mother finished college	11%	8%***	11%*	15%
Parents married at birth	24%	17%***	26%*	30%
Parents cohabiting at birth	35%	39%	33%	35%
Parents nonresident at birth	41%	44%***	41%**	35%
PCG past-year drug use (Y15)	5%	7%***	5%*	3%
PCG public assistance (between Y9 and Y15)	68%	76%***	67%***	60%
Neighborhood collective efficacy	19.8	19.8	19.7	20.2
	(0.11)	(0.23)	(0.16)	(0.24)
Father ever incarcerated (by Y15)	52%	61%***	50%**	44%
Police officer at school	81%	82%+	81%	78%
Delinquency (Y9)	1.2	1.7***	1.1***	0.87
	(0.3)	(0.07)	(0.04)	(0.06)
Externalizing behavior (Y9)	0.91	1.12***	0.87**	0.77
	(0.01)	(0.03)	(0.02)	(0.03)

Source: Authors' calculations based on the Fragile Families and Child Wellbeing Study.
Note: Standard errors in parentheses. Percentages may not total 100 percent due to rounding. Statistical significance indicates differences between teens with personal and vicarious police contact, respectively, and no contact. Less than 1 percent of primary caregivers have unknown status on each of drug use and public assistance.
+*p* ≤ .10; **p* ≤ .05; ***p* ≤ .01; ****p* ≤ .001

Table 2. Intrusion Reported by Teen Respondents in Most Memorable Police Contact

	Personally Stopped (N = 799)	Vicarious Contact (N = 1,580)
Officer frisked them	34	49
Officer searched their bags or pockets	38	57
Officer used harsh language	21	15
Officer used racial slurs	8	6
Officer threatened physical force	14	15
Officer used physical force	12	19

Source: Authors' calculations based on the Fragile Families and Child Wellbeing Study.
Note: Numbers in percentages. Between one and four respondents reporting personal contact report that they "don't know" whether each type of intrusion took place. Of teens reporting vicarious contact, between 9 and 11 percent of respondents do not know whether the specified contact took place in the stop they witnessed or heard about. Percentages are based on the stops in which respondents report that each type of force did or did not happen.

perienced zero police intrusion. Finally, model 7 controls not only for the intrusion in respondents' critical stops, but also for respondents' perceptions of procedural justice in their experiences with the police. We again use an interaction term to distinguish between procedural justice in personal and vicarious stops. Teens reporting no police contact are assumed to perceive the maximum level of procedural justice.

Racial Differences in the Legal Socialization Relationship
The final stage of our analysis re-estimates models 5 through 7 separately, in turn, for respondents who are white, black, and Hispanic. The FFCWS has too few respondents of other race or multiple races for race-specific models to be meaningful.

RESULTS

Our analyses indicate that the criminal justice system is deeply embedded in the lives of urban adolescents. As shown in table 1, more than 25 percent report having personally been stopped by police once or more, and nearly 80 percent report vicarious police contact.

Exposure to Criminal Justice
Table 2 provides details of these contacts and criminal justice exposure generally. Rates of police contact are racially skewed: black and Hispanic teens are significantly more likely than others to have personal police contact. Adolescent exposure to the criminal justice system extends beyond police stops: more than half of teens in the analysis sample have fathers who have been incarcerated, and more than 80 percent report a police officer regularly stationed at their school.

Respondents report considerable intrusion in their critical police encounters. More than one-third of teens with personal experience and approximately half of those reporting vicarious contact report that they (or the person stopped in the vicarious contact) were frisked or searched during their most memorable stops. More than 20 percent of teens personally stopped and approximately 15 percent of those reporting vicarious contact report that the officers used harsh language (a smaller proportion noted that the officer used racial slurs), and more than 10 percent reported that the officer threatened or used physical force.

Police Contact and Legal Cynicism
Table 3 presents the estimated associations between the binary indicators of police contact and respondent legal cynicism. Respondents with police contact (personal or vicarious) report significantly more legal cynicism than those with no contact, a difference that is

Table 3. Associations Between Adolescent Stop Experience and Legal Cynicism

	Models 1 and 2: Any (Personal or Vicarious) Contact		Models 3 and 4: Personal Contact Only	
	Model 1: Demographic, SES, and Behavioral Controls	Model 2: Propensity Score Matching	Model 3: Demographic, SES, and Behavioral Controls	Model 4: Propensity Score Matching
Any stop	1.344***	1.494***	1.494***	
	(0.143)	(0.183)	(0.183)	
Personal contact			1.838***	1.761***
			(0.133)	(0.198)
Respondent race (reference = white)				
Black	1.323***		1.231***	
	(0.179)		(0.176)	
Hispanic	1.076***		1.042***	
	(0.194)		(0.190)	
Other	0.464		0.497	
	(0.455)		(0.448)	
Multiple races	1.934***		1.828***	
	(0.274)		(0.269)	
Respondent male	0.549***		0.279*	
	(0.117)		(0.117)	
Respondent age	0.347***		0.319**	
	(0.103)		(0.102)	
Police at school	−0.207		−0.209	
	(0.146)		(0.144)	
Father ever incarcerated (Y15)	0.270*		0.224+	
	(0.127)		(0.125)	
N	3,001	3,001	3,001	3,001

Source: Authors' calculations based on the Fragile Families and Child Wellbeing Study.
Note: Standard errors in parentheses. Models also control for mothers' educational attainment, parents' baseline relationship status, PCG past-year drug use (Y15) and public assistance between Y9 and Y15, and teens' delinquency and externalizing behavior at age nine.
+$p \leq .10$; *$p \leq .05$; **$p \leq .01$; ***$p \leq .001$

slightly amplified when focusing on personal contact. Notably, estimates obtained through propensity score matching are of comparable magnitude to those obtained through regression analysis with our full set of controls, increasing our confidence that regression analysis is a suitable approach for our subsequent analyses, which focus on the nature of the stops that teens report.

In addition to being linked to personal experience with the police, legal cynicism is also significantly associated with other indicators of social disadvantage. Minority (specifically, black, Hispanic, and multiracial) teens report significantly more legal cynicism than their white counterparts, net of racial differences in their reported personal and vicarious police experience. Boys report greater cynicism than girls, and reported legal cynicism increases with respondent age. Finally, legal cynicism is greater among teens whose fathers have incarceration histories, though the difference is only marginally significant in the model focusing on personal contact.

The Nature of Police Stops

Table 4 shows results from analyses examining the nature of police stops and their implications for adolescent legal cynicism. Model 5, which separately examines personal and vicarious contact, indicates that although personal and vicarious police contact are associated with increases in legal cynicism, teens with personal contact report significantly greater legal cynicism than those reporting only vicarious contact. Notably, legal cynicism is significantly associated not only with whether teens report (personal or vicarious) contact with the police, but also with the adolescents' reports of what happened during the stop. Model 6 finds that controlling for the indicators of police contact, teens reporting more intrusive encounters with the police also report significantly greater levels of subsequent legal cynicism. The significant negative interaction between stop intrusion and vicarious stops indicates that intrusion in a stop the teen witnessed or heard about is a weaker predictor of legal cynicism than intrusion in a stop they experienced. However, a significance test of the sum of the main effect and interaction term indicate that stop intrusion is associated with increases in legal cynicism for teens reporting vicarious as well as personal police contact.

Model 7 shows that teens perceiving greater procedural justice in their police encounters report less legal cynicism than teens reporting lower levels of procedural justice. As in model 6, the interaction between perceived procedural justice and having only vicarious, rather than personal, contact with the police is in the opposite direction than the estimated main effect, suggesting that effects of procedural justice are stronger for teens with personal, rather than vicarious contact. However, the interaction is not statistically significant, and the combined procedural justice estimate indicates significantly less legal cynicism for teens reporting greater levels of procedural justice in the encounters they have witnessed or heard about.

Our binary indicator of personal experience with the police is independently associated with teens' legal cynicism, as is stop intrusion for teens with both personal and vicarious contact. However, model 7 shows that controlling for stop intrusion and perceived procedural justice in the encounters they witnessed or heard about, adolescents reporting only vicarious contact report less legal cynicism than those reporting no contact. Accordingly, the association between vicarious police contact and adolescent legal cynicism is inextricably linked to the interaction quality in the stops that teens see and hear about. Teens with vicarious exposure to stops with minimal intrusion, and stops with high levels of procedural justice, report little cynicism; those with intrusive stops, and stops with low levels of procedural justice, report significantly more.

Race Differences in Police Contact and Legal Cynicism

Notable in tables 3 and 4 are the increased levels of legal cynicism reported by black, Hispanic, and multiracial teens relative to their white counterparts, controlling for their personal and vicarious contact with the police and multiple alternate sources of criminal justice exposure (such as their fathers' incarceration histories and the presence of police officers at their schools). Selected coefficients from a race-specific estimation of models 5 through 7 are presented in table 5. Although estimated associations between legal cynicism and personal experience with the police are slightly greater in magnitude for racial and ethnic minority teens than for white teens, the most notable finding in table 5 is the relative consistency of the estimated relationships between personal experience with the police and legal cynicism. Regardless of race, teens stopped by the police report significantly more legal cynicism than their counterparts with no contact, and this relationship increases significantly with critical stop intrusion and declines significantly with their perceptions of procedural justice.

For all three racial groups, the relationship between police contact and legal cynicism is less pronounced for teens experiencing vicarious contact only, particularly in model 6 and model 7, which consider stop intrusion and perceptions of procedural justice. For white teens, model 7 indicates that vicarious contact is not consistently associated with increased

Table 4. Associations Between Aspects of Adolescent Stop Experience and Legal Cynicism

	Model 5: Distinguishing Personal and Vicarious Contact	Model 6: Considering Stop Intrusion	Model 7: Considering Intrusion and Procedural Justice
Personal contact	2.480***	1.718***	1.080***
	(0.170)	(0.184)	(0.200)
Vicarious contact	0.873***	0.373*	−1.657*
	(0.145)	(0.162)	(0.721)
Stop intrusion		0.697***	0.424***
		(0.069)	(0.077)
Stop intrusion x vicarious		−0.342***	−0.188*
		(0.086)	(0.095)
Reported procedural justice			−0.507***
			(0.067)
Reported procedural justice x vicarious			0.156+
			(0.084)
Respondent race (reference = white)			
Black	1.246***	1.061***	0.874***
	(0.175)	(0.172)	(0.170)
Hispanic	1.065***	0.947***	0.843***
	(0.189)	(0.185)	(0.183)
Other	0.502	0.453	0.405
	(0.445)	(0.435)	(0.428)
Multiple races	1.837***	1.632***	1.466***
	(0.268)	(0.262)	(0.259)
Respondent male	0.285*	0.197+	0.268*
	(0.117)	(0.114)	(0.113)
Respondent age	0.302**	0.260**	0.261**
	(0.101)	(0.099)	(0.097)
Police officer at school	−0.224	−0.282*	−0.253+
	(0.143)	(0.140)	(0.138)
Father ever incarcerated (Y15)	0.215+	0.182	0.142
	(0.124)	(0.121)	(0.119)
N	3,001	3,001	3,001

Source: Authors' calculations based on the Fragile Families and Child Wellbeing Study.
Note: Standard errors in parentheses. Testing the sum of the intrusion and interaction terms in model 6 indicates that intrusion in vicarious stops is associated with greater reports of legal cynicism ($p < .001$). Model 7 indicates that intrusion in a vicarious stop is associated with elevated reports of legal cynicism ($p < .001$), while procedural justice in vicarious stop experience is associated with a reduction in legal cynicism ($p < .001$). Models also control for mothers' educational attainment, parents' baseline relationship status, PCG past-year drug use (Y15) and public assistance between Y9 and Y15, and teens' delinquency and externalizing behavior at age nine.
+$p ≤ .10$; *$p ≤ .05$; **$p ≤ .01$; ***$p ≤ .001$

Table 5. Race-Specific Estimations of Models Predicting Legal Cynicism

	Model 5	Model 6	Model 7
White respondents (N = 540)			
Personal contact	1.852***	1.336***	0.796*
	(0.343)	(0.354)	(0.368)
Vicarious contact	0.764**	0.519+	−4.778*
	(0.269)	(0.297)	(1.986)
Stop intrusion		1.118***	0.549*
		(0.243)	(0.271)
Stop intrusion x vicarious		−0.858**	−0.384
		(0.279)	(0.305)
Reported procedural justice			−0.858***
			(0.200)
Reported procedural justice x vicarious			0.544*
			(0.224)
Black respondents (N = 1,494)			
Personal contact	2.696***	1.902***	1.212***
	(0.231)	(0.277)	(0.303)
Vicarious contact	0.927***	0.353	−1.921+
	(0.231)	(0.261)	(1.002)
Stop intrusion		0.607***	0.342***
		(0.090)	(0.102)
Stop intrusion x vicarious		−0.263*	−0.093
		(0.118)	(0.129)
Reported procedural justice			−0.485***
			(0.092)
Reported procedural justice x vicarious			0.181
			(0.117)
Hispanic respondents (N = 731)			
Personal contact	2.603***	1.790***	1.133**
	(0.341)	(0.381)	(0.422)
Vicarious contact	1.000***	0.445	0.002
	(0.274)	(0.305)	(1.500)
Stop intrusion		0.738***	0.552***
		(0.158)	(0.167)
Stop intrusion x vicarious		−0.337+	−0.315
		(0.190)	(0.201)
Reported procedural justice			−0.433***
			(0.135)
Reported procedural justice x vicarious			−0.037
			(0.175)

Source: Authors' calculations based on the Fragile Families and Child Wellbeing Study.
Note: Standard errors in parentheses. All models control for respondent age, sex, Y9 delinquency and externalizing, fathers' incarceration history, mothers' BL education, parents' BL relationship, police presence at school.
+$p \le .10$; *$p \le .05$; **$p \le .01$; ***$p \le .001$

legal cynicism in these models, nor is stop intrusion. For minority teens, the opposite is true: stop intrusion and legal cynicism are significantly associated for black and Hispanic teens with vicarious contact.

Sensitivity Analyses
Because our analyses are based on data from fifty datasets created by multiple imputation, we test the robustness of our findings to an alternate mode of dealing with missing data. Table A2 presents estimates of models 5 through 7 based on the 2,155 teens with complete data on all included measures. Our estimated relationships of primary interest are almost identical in magnitude and direction to those in table 4, differing by magnitudes of tenths or hundredths of scale score points. Statistical significance declines somewhat in our complete case sample, presumably partly because our complete case sample is 28 percent smaller than the imputation datasets. However, most relationships that are statistically significant in our full sample are also significant in our complete case sample. It is thus highly likely that our estimated associations are the result of a substantive relationship between police contact and legal socialization, rather than a statistical artifact of the process used to account for missing data.

We also examined the sensitivity of findings to our choice of outcome measure. As noted, our measure of legal cynicism is an additive scale consisting of six items, each coded as four-point Likert measures with higher values indicating greater legal cynicism. We re-estimated models 1, 3, and 5 using ordered logit models to predict each item individually, as a function of, respectively, any police contact, personal experience with the police, and separately, personal and vicarious experience with the police. Results, presented in table A3, indicate that the estimated relationship between police contact and legal cynicism is largely robust to our choice of outcome. Five of the six survey items are significantly and positively associated with all measures of police contact in all three models examined; the sixth ("It's okay to do anything you want") is significantly and positively associated with both any contact and personal contact, but its association with vicarious contact is not statistically significant. We also re-estimate models 5, 6, and 7 predicting a two-item outcome combining only the items specifically measuring attitudes toward the police ("I have a great deal of respect for the police" and "The police create more problems than they solve") and including the other items as control variables. Results from these models are largely substantively consistent with those in table 4. Taken together, these results suggest that the associations in tables 3 through 5 are not the result of a particularly influential survey item, but are instead robust to our measure of legal cynicism.

Finally, we examined the sensitivity of our findings to a measure of whether, in addition to contact with the police, the adolescent respondents report having been arrested. Our results, presented in table A4, indicate that arrests are indeed significantly associated with legal cynicism: teens who have been arrested score more than a unit higher on their legal cynicism scales. However, the estimated associations between stop experience (personal and vicarious), stop intrusion, reported procedural justice and legal cynicism remain strong and statistically significant when controlling for arrest experience. This finding suggests that the association between stop experience and legal cynicism is not simply the result of an adverse outcome (such as arrest), but is associated with the stops themselves.

DISCUSSION
We identify a significant and robust relationship between adolescent exposure to the police and legal cynicism. In nearly all models, teens reporting personal or vicarious police contact report more legal cynicism than their counterparts with no contact, and teens with personal contact report significantly more cynicism than teens with vicarious contact. Our main findings are consistent across racial and ethnic groups; however, we identify significant moderation in these relationships by the nature of teens' reported contact with the police. Teens reporting intrusive stops report significantly more cynicism, while teens reporting encounters with greater procedural justice report less. Notably, model 7 indicates that intrusion and procedural justice are both significant predictors of

legal cynicism, and one relationship is not wholly accounted for by the other. The simultaneous significance of both relationships underscores that intrusion and procedural justice are, at least in part, independent descriptors of teens' police contact.

Our method relies on reports of stop intrusion that reflect specific actions by police, which teens recall from a particular stop that stands out in their mind. Although these reports are open to interpretation (one teen may report an officer's language as harsh but another may not) and are at some risk of misinterpretation (the teen may not understand the difference between a frisk and a search), they are likely to be relatively well measured and consistently interpreted. The procedural justice scale measures—in part—the emotional salience of experience with the police. Rather than recalling a single, specific stop, respondents are asked to draw on all encounters they experienced or witnessed or heard about. Some teens draw on a single incident, others a diverse array of personal or vicarious experiences. The procedural justice measure is also based on more subjective aspects of the stop—whether the police officer explained the reason for the stop "in a way that was clear" to the person stopped, whether they treated the person stopped "with dignity and courtesy," and whether they "respected [their] rights"—and more open-ended measures of quantity, such as whether the officer conduct occurred often, sometimes, or never. This linkage of emotion to a rejection of institutional authority and social norms provides a processual picture of the development of legal cynicism (see Bell 2016; Sampson and Bartusch 1998; Kirk and Papachristos 2011; Berg et al. 2016).

Policing, Legal Cynicism, and Social Inequality

The importance of legal cynicism for law-related behavior, and the increased levels of legal cynicism reported by teens with police contact, is of particular concern given the well-documented racial disparities in police-public interactions (Fagan et al. 2010; Nance 2016; Rocque and Paternoster 2011; Weitzer, Tuch, and Skogan 2008; White 2015). Strong and significant associations between personal police contact and legal socialization are observed among black, white, and Hispanic adolescents. The concentration of police contact among minority teens, particularly when coupled with concentrated racial residential segregation, suggests that legal cynicism may also be ecologically concentrated in minority communities (on segregation, Massey and Denton 1989; on minority communities, Kirk and Papachristos 2011; Kirk and Matsuda 2011; Sampson and Bartusch 1998). To the extent that legal cynicism is associated with subsequent offending behavior, police activity may undermine public safety in these communities (Fagan and Piquero 2007; Kirk and Papachristos 2011; Tyler and Fagan 2008).

When police routinely intervene in the everyday lives of teens, they impose psychological and social interaction costs that inevitably deter young people from moving freely (Fagan and Ash 2017). And when these police actions have legal and economic consequences for those already in disadvantaged social positions, those consequences effectively lock such individuals in by constraining choices of neighborhood selection. Because police deployments and actions are racialized and focused in poor, segregated places, police in effect reproduce inequality, racial stratification, and segregation through their criminal legal enforcement actions and in turn constrain social and economic mobility. More policing in poor neighborhoods leads to more arrests in those places, deepening the ecological concentrations of criminal stigma and social exclusion in places sometimes characterized as *poverty traps* (Sampson and Morenoff 2006; Fagan and Ash 2017).

Racial segregation and intrusive contact with the police seem to be inextricably linked (Desmond, Papachristos, and Kirk 2016; see also Brunson and Weitzer 2009). The aggressive policing of minority communities and neighborhoods place black and Hispanic youth at increased risk of arrest and subsequent criminal justice involvement (Kochel, Wilson, and Mastrofski 2011). The adjudication process, even for low-level arrests, involves considerable burdens, including financial impositions, exacerbating economic inequality, and impeding the ability of minority residents to move out of high-crime and heavily policed neighborhoods (Feeley 1979; Geller 2016; Kohler-Hausmann 2014; Harris 2016). The conflation of racial segregation and economic mobility means that, typically, a black adolescent or young adult male in a U.S. city lives in very different economic and social circumstances than his white counterpart: different types of schools, different social networks, different levels of access to social capital leading to crime, and different exposure to the police and to violence (Sharkey 2013). The burdens of police contact combined with the blocking effects of segregation mean that these teens are far less likely to better their economic circumstances in adulthood.

These disadvantages extend to health and mental health. The adverse health outcomes associated with police contact also threaten to exacerbate racial disparities in health (on contact, Geller et al. 2017, 2014; Sewell 2017; Sewell and Jefferson 2016; Sewell, Jefferson, and Lee 2016; on health, Harris et al. 2006; Hill 2016). To the extent that the link between policing and legal cynicism undermines public safety in minority neighborhoods, and in turn, increases the perceived need for police surveillance, these disparities may be exacerbated further still.

Limitations and Future Research

Although our analyses identify robust relationships between adolescent reports of police contact and their self-reported legal cynicism, we caution against causal inferences. Our analyses are limited by a dataset that, though it provides a rich description of family circumstances over the teens' first fifteen years, includes only periodic interviews with family members and has interviewed the study's teen respondents only twice, about the time of their ninth and their fifteenth birthdays. We have a single measure of legal cynicism and are therefore unable to measure whether the teens' (personal or vicarious) experience with the police caused a change in their attitudes toward the law, or whether their reports at age fifteen reflect long-standing attitudes unaffected by police contact.

It is also possible that long-standing attitudes about the law (or other personal characteristics) might cause teens to engage in illegal or other risky activities that increase their exposure to the police, escalate the level of intrusion in an encounter they are exposed to, or influence their perception of procedural justice in their reported encounters. To guard against this risk, we control for the teens' self-reports of early (Y9) delinquency and externalizing behavior, which precede nearly all reported police contact and would likely be affected by longstanding legal cynicism. However, without a pretreatment measure of legal cynicism, our observed associations may still reflect aspects of a *reverse causal* relationship, as well as any direct effects of police encounters and their conduct on subsequent attitudes.

Our conclusions are also limited by the risk of shared method variance—that our treatment of police contact and our legal socialization outcome are measured by the same teen reporters (on shared method variance, see Bank et al. 1990). Specifically, unmeasured characteristics of the teen respondents may be drivers of behavior that increases their exposure to the police, their perceptions of any police contact they experience or hear about, and their attitudes toward the law. For example, teens who are pessimistic by nature may both perceive a reported encounter as more intrusive or involving more procedural injustice than their peers would and report greater legal cynicism. Such unobserved characteristics of our adolescent respondents may drive a spurious relationship between reports of their personal and vicarious experiences and their legal socialization that are conflated with any causal effects of police contact. A contextual analysis incorporating measures of police activity, including arrests and use of force, can begin to address this limitation, at least in part. Our analyses are also limited by sample attrition. Our analysis sample represents approximately 60 percent of the initial Fragile Families sample, and as noted is less disadvantaged and has a racial composition that differs from the sample as a whole. The extent to which our sample can generalize to a broader population is therefore limited. Nonetheless, the robust associations between police experiences and adolescent attitudes observed, particularly given the high prevalence of contact reported by teens in the sample, suggest that exposure to the police—both positive and negative experiences—have the potential to shape legal cynicism at a turning point of their social development. Future research would advance the field by unpacking the emotional content of legal cynicism and legal socialization more broadly.

One final potential implication remains unstudied for now: city differences in the aggregate behaviors of adolescents exposed to city-specific differences in policing. Policing regimes matter in this framework because they determine the extent and nature of police contact for adolescents. Integrating city indicators of crime and policing is another critical next step.

Table A1. Odds Ratios from Model Predicting Analysis Sample Retention from Baseline Family Characteristics

	OR/SE
Parents' baseline relationship status (reference = married)	
Cohabiting	0.947
	(0.078)
Nonresident	1.091
	(0.094)
Mother's race (reference = white)	
Non-Hispanic black	1.152+
	(0.097)
Hispanic	0.72***
	(0.064)
Non-Hispanic other	0.674*
	(0.107)
Race unknown	1.108
	(0.701)
Mother's poverty status (reference = no poverty)	
Deep poverty (<50 percent of federal poverty line)	0.781**
	(0.070)
In poverty (50 to 99 percent of federal poverty line)	0.873
	(0.080)
Near poverty (100 to 199 percent of federal poverty line)	0.976
	(0.078)
Constant	1.76***
	(0.134)
N	4897

Source: Authors' calculations based on the Fragile Families and Child Wellbeing Study.
Note: Standard errors in parentheses.
+$p \leq .10$; *$p \leq .05$; **$p \leq .01$; ***$p \leq .001$

Table A2. Complete Case Estimation of Legal Cynicism Models, Selected OLS Coefficients

	Model 5	Model 6	Model 7
Personal contact	2.419***	1.716***	0.993***
	(0.193)	(0.208)	(0.226)
Vicarious contact	0.869***	0.337+	−2.509**
	(0.169)	(0.192)	(0.823)
Stop intrusion		0.658***	0.350***
		(0.078)	(0.087)
Stop intrusion x vicarious		−0.297**	−0.091
		(0.099)	(0.108)
Reported procedural justice			−0.574***
			(0.076)
Reported procedural justice x vicarious			0.251**
			(0.096)
Respondent race (reference = white)			
Black	1.220***	1.036***	0.833***
	(0.213)	(0.210)	(0.207)
Hispanic	1.036***	0.933***	0.816***
	(0.230)	(0.225)	(0.221)
Other	0.201	0.180	0.135
	(0.538)	(0.526)	(0.516)
Multiple races	1.394***	1.175***	1.024***
	(0.326)	(0.319)	(0.314)
Respondent male	0.216	0.119	0.200
	(0.138)	(0.136)	(0.133)
Respondent age	0.193	0.159	0.152
	(0.120)	(0.118)	(0.116)
Police officer at school	−0.249	−0.271+	−0.224
	(0.168)	(0.164)	(0.161)
Father ever incarcerated (Y15)	0.135	0.108	0.076
	(0.146)	(0.143)	(0.140)
N	2,155	2,155	2,155

Source: Authors' calculations based on the Fragile Families and Child Wellbeing Study.
Note: Testing the sum of the intrusion and interaction terms in model 6 indicates that intrusion in vicarious stops is associated with greater reports of legal cynicism ($p < .001$). Model 7 indicates that intrusion in a vicarious stop is associated with elevated reports of legal cynicism ($p < .001$), and procedural justice in vicarious stop experience is associated with a reduction in legal cynicism ($p < .001$). Models also control for mothers' educational attainment, parents' baseline relationship status, PCG past-year drug use (Y15) and public assistance between Y9 and Y15, and teens' delinquency and externalizing behavior at age nine.
+$p \le .10$; *$p \le .05$; **$p \le .01$; ***$p \le .001$

Table A3. Selected Regression Coefficients from OLR models

	Indicator 1 "I have a great deal of respect for the police."	Indicator 2 "It's okay to do anything you want."	Indicator 3 "There are no right or wrong ways to make money."	Indicator 4 "Laws were made to be broken."	Indicator 5 "If I get into a fight with somebody it's nobody else's business."	Indicator 6 "The police create more problems than they solve."
Model 1 coefficient (any contact)	0.694*** (0.100)	0.212* (0.096)	0.340*** (0.096)	0.595*** (0.131)	0.607*** (0.085)	0.815*** (0.089)
Model 3 coefficient (personal contact)	1.049*** (0.086)	0.254** (0.087)	0.400*** (0.085)	0.536*** (0.099)	0.761*** (0.080)	0.918*** (0.081)
Model 5 coefficient (personal)	1.352*** (0.118)	0.363* (0.115)	0.574*** (0.114)	0.880*** (0.146)	1.075*** (0.104)	1.367*** (0.107)
Model 5 coefficient (vicarious)	0.401*** (0.105)	0.146 (0.100)	0.234* (0.101)	0.447*** (0.136)	0.421*** (0.088)	0.595*** (0.092)

Source: Authors' calculations based on the Fragile Families and Child Wellbeing Study.

Note: All survey items are 4-point Likert scales, coded so that higher values indicate greater legal cynicism.

†p ≤ .10; *p ≤ .05; **p ≤ .01; ***p ≤ .001

Table A4. Sensitivity Analysis Examining Arrest as a Predictor of Legal Cynicism, Selected OLS Coefficients

	Model 5	Model 6	Model 7
Personal contact	2.230***	1.678***	1.074***
	(0.173)	(0.184)	(0.199)
Vicarious contact	0.917***	0.393*	−1.432*
	(0.144)	(0.162)	(0.721)
Stop intrusion		0.595***	0.348***
		(0.072)	(0.079)
Stop intrusion x vicarious		−0.238**	−0.110
		(0.089)	(0.097)
Reported procedural justice			−0.486***
			(0.067)
Reported procedural justice x vicarious			0.133
			(0.084)
Reported arrest	2.052***	1.277***	1.114***
	(0.287)	(0.299)	(0.295)
Respondent race (reference = white)			
Black	1.235***	1.067***	0.881***
	(0.174)	(0.171)	(0.170)
Hispanic	1.036***	0.936***	0.836***
	(0.188)	(0.185)	(0.182)
Other	0.507	0.466	0.418
	(0.441)	(0.434)	(0.427)
Multiple races	1.837***	1.643***	1.478***
	(0.265)	(0.262)	(0.258)
Respondent male	0.279	0.205	0.276
	(0.116)	(0.114)	(0.113)
Respondent age	0.270	0.244	0.250**
	(0.100)	(0.099)	(0.097)
Police officer at school	−0.232	−0.283*	−0.253+
	(0.142)	(0.139)	(0.137)
Father ever incarcerated (Y15)	0.162	0.151	0.115
	(0.123)	(0.121)	(0.119)
N	3,001	3,001	3,001

Source: Authors' calculations based on the Fragile Families and Child Wellbeing Study.
Note: Models also control for mothers' educational attainment, parents' baseline relationship status, PCG past-year drug use (Y15) and public assistance between Y9 and Y15, and teens' delinquency and externalizing behavior at age nine.
+$p \leq .10$; *$p \leq .05$; **$p \leq .01$; ***$p \leq .001$

REFERENCES

Anderson, Katherine Freeman. 2013. "Diagnosing Discrimination: Stress from Perceived Racism and the Mental and Physical Health Effects." *Sociological Inquiry* 83(1): 55–81.

Bank, Lewis I., Thomas J. Dishion, Martie Skinner, and Gerald R. Patterson. 1990. "Method Variance in Structural Equation Modeling: Living with GLOP." In *Depression and Aggression in Family Interaction*, edited by Gerald R. Patterson. Hillsdale, N.J.: Lawrence Erlbaum.

Bell, Monica C. 2016. "Police Reform and the Dismantling of Legal Cynicism." *Yale Law Journal* 50(2): 314–47.

Berg, Mark T., Eric A. Stewart, Jonathan Intravia, Patricia Y. Warren, and Ronald L. Simons. 2016. "Cynical Streets: Neighborhood Social Processes and Perceptions of Criminal Injustice." *Criminology* 54(3): 520–47.

Braga, Anthony A., and David Weisburd. 2010. *Policing Problem Places: Crime Hot Spots and Effective Prevention*. New York: Oxford University Press.

Brame, Robert W., Michael G. Turner, Raymond Paternoster, and Shawn D. Bushway. 2012. "Cumulative Prevalence of Arrest from Ages 8 to 23 in a National Sample." *Pediatrics* 129(1): 21–27.

Brunson, Rod K. 2007. "'Police Don't Like Black People': African-American Young Men's Accumulated Police Experiences." *Criminology and Public Policy* 6(1): 71–102.

Brunson, Rod K., and Ronald Weitzer. 2009. "Police Relations with Black and White Youths in Different Urban Neighborhoods." *Urban Affairs Review* 44(6): 858–85.

Burt, Callie H., Man Kit Lei, and Ronald L. Simons. 2017. "Racial Discrimination, Racial Socialization, and Crime over Time: A Social Schematic Theory Model." *Criminology* 55(4): 938–79.

Carr, Patrick J., Laura Napolitano, and Jessica Keating. 2007. "We Never Call the Cops and Here Is Why: A Qualitative Examination of Legal Cynicism in Three Philadelphia Neighborhoods. *Criminology* 45(2): 445–80.

Dehejia, Rajeev H., and Sadek Wahba. 2002. "Propensity Score-Matching Methods for Nonexperimental Causal Studies." *Review of Economics and Statistics* 84(1): 151–61.

Desmond, Matthew, Andrew W. Papachristos, and David S. Kirk. 2016. "Police Violence and Citizen Crime Reporting in the Black Community." *American Sociological Review* 81(5): 857–76.

Eckhouse, Laurel. 2018. "Everyday Risk: Disparate Exposure and Racial Inequality in Police Violence." Unpublished manuscript, University of Denver.

Epp, Charles R., Steven Maynard-Moody, and Donald P. Haider-Markel. 2014. *Pulled Over: Howe Police Stops Define Race and Citizenship*. Chicago: University of Chicago Press.

Fagan, Jeffrey. 2017. "Point/Counterpoint: Recent Evidence and Controversies in 'The New Policing.'" *Journal of Policy Analysis and Management* 36(3): 690–700.

Fagan, Jeffrey, and Elliott T. Ash. 2017. "New Policing, New Segregation: From Ferguson to New York." *Georgetown Law Journal* 106. Accessed September 17, 2018. https://georgetownlawjournal.org/articles/246/new-policing-new-segregation/pdf.

Fagan, Jeffrey, Anthony A. Braga, Rod K. Brunson, and April Pattavina. 2016. "Stops and Stares: Street Stops, Surveillance, and Race in the New Policing." *Fordham Urban Law Journal* 43(3): 539–614.

Fagan, Jeffrey, and Amanda Geller. 2015. "Following the Script: Narratives of Street Stops in Terry Stops in Street Policing." *University of Chicago Law Review* 82: 51–88.

Fagan, Jeffrey, Amanda Geller, Garth Davies, and Valerie West. 2010. "Street Stops and Broken Windows Revisited: The Demography and Logic of Proactive Policing in a Safe and Changing City." In *Race, Ethnicity, and Policing: New and Essential Readings*, edited by Stephen K. Rice and Michael D. White. New York: New York University Press.

Fagan, Jeffrey, and Tracey L. Meares. 2008. "Punishment, Deterrence, and Social Control: The Paradox of Punishment in Minority Communities." *Ohio State Journal of Criminal Law* 6(1): 231–75.

Fagan, Jeffrey, and Alex R. Piquero. 2007. "Rational Choice and Developmental Influences on Recidivism Among Adolescent Felony Offenders." *Journal of Empirical Legal Studies* 4(4): 715–48.

Fagan, Jeffrey, and Tom R. Tyler. 2005. "Legal Socialization of Children and Adolescents." *Social Justice Research* 18(3): 217–42.

Fagan, Jeffrey, Tom R. Tyler, and Tracey L. Meares. 2016. "Street Stops and Police Legitimacy in New York." In *Comparing the Democratic Governance of Police Intelligence: New Models of Participation and Expertise in the United States and Europe,* edited by Thierry Delpeuch and Jacqueline E. Ross. Cheltenham, UK: Edward Elgar.

Feeley, Malcolm M. 1979. *The Process Is the Punishment: Handling Cases in a Lower Criminal Court.* New York: Russell Sage Foundation.

Fowler, Deborah, Rebecca Lightsey, Janis Monger, and Elyshia Aseltine. 2010. *Texas' School to Prison Pipeline: Ticketing, Arrest and Use of Force in Schools.* Austin: Texas Appleseed. Accessed September 17, 2018. http://www.njjn.org/uploads/digital-library/Texas-School-Prison-Pipeline_Ticketing_Booklet_Texas-Appleseed_Dec2010.pdf.

Gau, Jacinta M., and Rod K. Brunson. 2010. "Procedural Justice and Order Maintenance Policing: A Study of Inner-City Young Men's Perceptions of Police Legitimacy." *Justice Quarterly* 27(2): 255–79.

Geller, Amanda. 2016. "The Process Is Still the Punishment: Low-Level Arrests in the Broken Windows Era." *Cardozo Law Review* 37(3): 1025–58.

Geller, Amanda, Jeffrey Fagan, and Tom R. Tyler. 2017. "Police Contact and Mental Health." *Columbia Public Law Research Paper* no. 14-571. New York: Columbia Law School.

Geller, Amanda, Jeffrey Fagan, Tome R. Tyler, and Bruce G. Link. 2014. "Aggressive Policing and the Mental Health of Young Urban Men." *American Journal of Public Health* 104(12): 2321–27.

Harcourt, Bernard E. 1998. "Reflecting on the Subject: A Critique of the Social Influence Conception of Deterrence, the Broken Windows Theory, and Order-Maintenance Policing New York Style." *Michigan Law Review* 97(2): 291–389.

Harris, Alexes. 2016. *A Pound of Flesh: Monetary Sanctions as Punishment for the Poor.* New York: Russell Sage Foundation.

Harris, Kathleen M., Penny Gordon-Larsen, Kim Chantala, and J. Richard Udry. 2006. "Longitudinal Trends in Race/Ethnic Disparities in Leading Health Indicators From Adolescence to Young Adulthood." *Archives of Pediatric and Adolescent Medicine* 160(1): 74–81.

Hatzenbuehler, Mark L., Katie A. McLaughlin, Katherine M. Keyes, and Deborah S. Hasin. 2010. "The Impact of Institutional Discrimination on Psychiatric Disorders in Lesbian, Gay, and Bisexual Populations: A Prospective Study." *American Journal of Public Health* 100(3): 452–59.

Heymann, Philip B. 2000. "The New Policing." *Fordham Urban Law Journal* 28(2): 407–56.

Hill, Shirley A. 2016. *Inequality and African American Health: How Racial Disparities Create Sickness.* Bristol, UK: Policy Press.

Justice, Benjamin, and Tracey L. Meares. 2014. "How the Criminal Justice System Educates Citizens." *Annals of the American Academy of Political and Social Science* 651(1): 159–77.

Kelling, George L., and Catherine M. Coles. 1996. *Fixing Broken Windows: Restoring Order and Reducing Crime in Our Communities.* New York: Free Press.

Kelling, George L., and James Q. Wilson. 1982. "Broken Windows." *Atlantic Monthly* 249(3): 29–36, 38.

Kirk, David S., and Mauri Matsuda. 2011. "Legal Cynicism, Collective Efficacy, and the Ecology of Arrest." *Criminology* 49(2): 2011.

Kirk, David S., and Andrew V. Papachristos. 2011. "Cultural Mechanisms and the Persistence of Neighborhood Violence." *American Journal of Sociology* 116(4): 1190–233.

Kochel, Tammy R., David B. Wilson, and Stephen D. Mastrofski. 2011. "Effect of Suspect Race on Officers' Arrest Decisions." *Criminology* 49(2): 473–512.

Kohler-Hausmann, Issa. 2014. "Managerial Justice and Mass Misdemeanors." *Stanford Law Review* 66(3): 611–94.

Krieger, Nancy. 1999. "Embodying Inequality: A Review of Concepts, Measures, and Methods for Studying Health Consequences of Discrimination." *International Journal of Health Services* 29(2): 295–352.

Kubrin, Charis E., Steven F. Messner, Glenn Deanne, Kelly McGeever, and Thomas D. Stucky. 2010. "Proactive Policing and Robbery Rates Across U.S. Cities." *Criminology* 48(1): 57–97.

Kupchik, Aaron. 2010. *Homeroom Security: School Discipline in an Age of Fear.* New York: New York University Press.

Langton, Lynn, and Matthew R. Durose. 2013. "Police Behavior During Traffic and Street Stops, 2011." NCJ 242937. Washington: Bureau of Justice Statistics. Accessed August 9, 2018. http://www.bjs.gov/content/pub/pdf/pbtss11.pdf.

Livingston, Debra. 1997. "Police Discretion and the Quality of Life in Public Places: Courts, Communities, and the New Policing." *Columbia Law Review* 97(3): 551–672.

Massey, Douglas S., and Nancy A. Denton. 1989. "Hypersegregation in U.S. Metropolitan Areas: Black and Hispanic Segregation Along Five Dimensions." *Demography* 26(3): 373–91.

Na, Chongmin, and Denise C. Gottfredson. 2011. "Police Officers in Schools: Effects on School Crime and the Processing of Offending Behaviors." *Justice Quarterly* 30(4): 619–50.

Nance, Jason P. 2016. "Over-Disciplining Students, Racial Bias, and the School-to-Prison Pipeline." *University of Richmond Law Review* 50: 1063–74.

New York City Police Department (NYPD). 2016. "Stop, Question, and Frisk Data." City of New York. Accessed September 17, 2018. https://www1.nyc.gov/site/nypd/stats/reports-analysis/stopfrisk.page.

Owens, Emily G. 2017. "Testing the School-to-Prison Pipeline." *Journal of Policy Analysis and Management* 36(1): 11–37.

Phelan, Jo C., and Bruce G. Link. 2015. "Is Racism a Fundamental Cause of Inequalities in Health?" *Annual Review of Sociology* 41: 311–30. DOI: 10.1146/annurev-soc-073014-112305.

Piquero, Alex R., Jeffrey Fagan, Edward P. Mulvey, Laurence Steinberg, and Candice Odgers. 2005. "Developmental Trajectories of Legal Socialization among Serious Adolescent Offenders." *Journal of Criminal Law and Criminology* 96(1): 267–98.

Reichman, Nancy, Julien Teitler, Irwin Garfinkel, and Sara McLanahan. 2001. "Fragile Families: Sample and Design." *Children and Youth Services Review* 23(4/5): 303–26.

Rocque, Michael, and Raymond Paternoster. 2011. "Understanding the Antecedents of the 'School-to-Jail' Link: The Relationship Between Race and School Discipline." *Journal of Criminal Law and Criminology* 101(2): 633–65.

Rosenbaum, Dennis P., Amie M. Schuck, Sandra K. Costello, Darnell F. Hawkins, and Marianne K. Ring. 2005. "Attitudes Toward the Police: The Effects of Direct and Vicarious Experience." *Police Quarterly* 8(3): 343–65.

Sampson, Robert J., and Dawn J. Bartusch. 1998. "Legal Cynicism and (Subcultural?) Tolerance of Deviance: The Neighborhood Context of Racial Differences." *Law and Society Review* 32(4): 777–804.

Sampson, Robert J., and Jeffrey D. Morenoff. 2006. "Durable Inequality: Spatial Dynamics, Social Processes, and the Persistence of Poverty in Chicago Neighborhoods." In *Poverty Traps*, edited by Samuel Bowles, Steve N. Durlauf, and Karla R. Hoff. New York: Russell Sage Foundation.

Sawyer, Pamela J., Brenda Major, Bettina J. Casad, Sarah S.M. Townsend, and Wendy Berry Mendes. 2012. "Discrimination and the Stress Response: Psychological and Physiological Consequences of Anticipating Prejudice in Interethnic Interactions." *American Journal of Public Health* 102(5): 1020–26. DOI:10.2105/AJPH.2011.300620

Sewell, Abigail A. 2017. "The Illness Associations of Police Violence: Differential Relationships by Ethnoracial Composition." *Sociological Forum* 32(51): 975–97. DOI:10.1111/socf.12361.

Sewell, Abigail A., and Kevin A. Jefferson. 2016. "Collateral Damage: The Health Effects of Invasive Police Encounters in New York City." *Journal of Urban Health: Bulletin of the New York Academy of Medicine* 93(1, Supplement): 42–67.

Sewell, Abigail A., Kevin A. Jefferson, and Hedwig Lee. 2016. "Living Under Surveillance: Gender, Psychological Distress, and Stop-Question-and-Frisk Policing in New York City." *Social Science and Medicine* 159(3): 1–13. DOI:10.1016/j.socscimed.2016.04.024.

Sharkey, Patrick. 2013. *Stuck in Place: Urban Neighborhoods and the End of Progress Toward Racial Equality*. Chicago: University of Chicago Press.

Shedd, Carla. 2015. *Unequal City: Race, Schools, and Perceptions of Injustice*. New York: Russell Sage Foundation.

Skogan, Wesley G., and Kathleen Frydl, eds. 2004. *Fairness and Effectiveness in Policing: The Evidence*. Washington, D.C.: National Academies Press.

Soss, Joe, and Vesla Weaver. 2017. "Police Are Our Government: Politics, Political Science, and the Policing of Race–Class Subjugated Communities." *Annual Review of Political Science* 20: 565–91.

Stewart, Eric A., Eric P. Baumer, Rod K. Brunson, and Ronald L. Simons. 2009. "Neighborhood Racial Context and Perceptions of Police-Based Racial discrimination Among Black Youth." *Criminology* 47(3): 847–87.

Stuart, Forrest. 2016. "Becoming 'Copwise': Policing,

Culture, and the Collateral Consequences of Street-Level Criminalization." *Law and Society Review* 50(2): 279–313.

Taylor, Ralph. 2001. *Breaking Away from Broken Windows: Baltimore Neighborhoods and the Nationwide Fight Against Crime, Grime, Fear, and Decline.* Boulder, Colo.: Westview Press.

Trinkner, Rick, Jonathan Jackson, and Tom R. Tyler. In press. "Bounded Authority: Expanding 'Appropriate' Police Behavior Beyond Procedural Justice." *Law and Human Behavior.*

Tyler, Tom R. 2003. "Procedural Justice, Legitimacy, and the Effective Rule of Law." *Crime and Justice: A Review of Research* 30: 431–505.

Tyler, Tom R., and Jeffrey Fagan. 2008. "Legitimacy and Cooperation: Why Do People Help the Police Fight Crime in Their Communities?" *Ohio State Journal of Criminal Law* 6(1): 173–229.

Tyler, Tom R., and Yuen J. Huo. 2002. *Trust in the Law: Encouraging Public Cooperation with the Police and Courts.* New York: Russell Sage Foundation.

Tyler, Tom R., Jeffrey Fagan, and Amanda Geller. 2014. "Street Stops and Police Legitimacy: Teachable Moments in Young Urban Men's Legal Socialization." *Journal of Empirical Legal Studies* 11(4): 751–85.

U.S. Department of Justice. 2015. *Investigation of the Ferguson Police Department.* Washington: Government Printing Office. Accessed August 11. 2018. https://www.justice.gov/sites/default/files/opa/press-releases/attachments/2015/03/04/ferguson_police_department_report.pdf.

———. 2016. *Investigation of the Baltimore City Police Department.* Washington: Government Printing Office. Accessed August 11. 2018. https://www.justice.gov/crt/file/883296/download.

———. 2017. *Investigation of the Chicago Police Department.* Washington: Government Printing Office. Accessed August 11, 2018. https://www.justice.gov/opa/file/925846/download.

Weisburd, David L., and Malay K. Majmundar. 2018. *Proactive Policing: Effects on Crime and Communities.* Washington, D.C.: National Academies Press.

Weitzer, Ronald, and Steven A. Tuch. 2006. *Race and Policing in America: Conflict and Reform.* Cambridge: Cambridge University Press.

Weitzer, Ronald, Steven A. Tuch, and Wesley G. Skogan. 2008. "Police-Community Relations in a Majority-Black City." *Journal of Research in Crime and Delinquency* 45(4): 398–428.

White, Karletta M. 2015. "The Salience of Skin Tone: Effects on the Exercise of Police Enforcement Authority." *Ethnic and Racial Studies* 38(6): 993–1010.

White, Michael D., and Henry Fradella. 2016. *Stop and Frisk: The Use and Abuse of a Controversial Policing Tactic.* New York: New York University Press.

Zimroth, Peter L. 2017. "Fifth Report of the Independent Monitor of NYPD Stops Reported, 2013–2015." New York: Arnold and Porter Kaye Scholer. Accessed August 11, 2018. http://nypdmonitor.org/wp-content/uploads/2017/06/2017-05-30-MonitorsFifthReport-AnalysisofNYPDStopsReported2013-2015-Asfiled.pdf.

Family Surveillance: Police and the Reporting of Child Abuse and Neglect

FRANK EDWARDS

Police are responsible for producing about one-fifth of all reports of child abuse and neglect investigated by local child welfare agencies, and low-level interactions with police often result in the initiation of a child welfare investigation. Because police contact is not randomly or equitably distributed across populations, policing has likely spillover consequences on racial inequities in child welfare outcomes. This study shows that police file more reports of child abuse and neglect in counties with high arrest rates, and that policing helps explain high rates of maltreatment investigations of American Indian–Alaska Native children and families. The spatial and social distribution of policing affects which children and families experience unnecessary child protection interventions and which children who are victims of maltreatment go unnoticed.

Keywords: child protection, surveillance, policing, family, child abuse, neglect

Police routinely interact with families and children and have exceptionally intimate access to the interactions of parents and children. Unlike doctors, educators, or social service providers, police can gain access to observe the daily lives of children and families at home with or without the consent of a subject family. Whereas other street-level bureaucrats use passive surveillance of children and families, police can engage in an active and coercive manner to monitor and regulate family life (Lipsky 1980). State and federal policymakers have long recognized the capacity of the police to engage in intensive family surveillance. In all U.S. states, police are required to report suspected child abuse and neglect to local child protection agencies. They do so quite frequently. In 2015, police originated about four hundred thousand reports to child welfare agencies alleging abuse or neglect, nearly one-fifth of the national total (Children's Bureau 2017).

This study describes the interactions between police and child welfare agencies and explores whether exposure to policing helps explain how and why certain children enter the child welfare system. After describing the kinds of cases police report to child welfare agencies and the distribution of police reporting of child abuse and neglect across U.S. counties, it constructs a series of regression models to evaluate

---

Frank Edwards is a postdoctoral associate at the Bronfenbrenner Center for Translational Research at Cornell University and incoming assistant professor of criminal justice at Rutgers University–Newark.

© 2019 Russell Sage Foundation. Edwards, Frank. 2019. "Family Surveillance: Police and the Reporting of Child Abuse and Neglect." *RSF: The Russell Sage Foundation Journal of the Social Sciences* 5(1): 50–70. DOI: 10.7758/RSF.2019.5.1.03. Direct correspondence to: Frank Edwards at fedwards@cornell.edu, Martha Van Rensselaer Hall, Room 1302D, Cornell University, Ithaca, NY 14850.

Open Access Policy: *RSF: The Russell Sage Foundation Journal of the Social Sciences* is an open access journal. This article is published under a Creative Commons Attribution-NonCommercial-NoDerivs 3.0 Unported License.

whether variation in police activities is predictive of the intensity of maltreatment reporting. It then evaluates whether racial inequalities in exposure to policing contribute to racial inequalities in contact with the child welfare system (Roberts 2002; Wulczyn et al. 2013). These analyses use restricted data from the National Child Abuse and Neglect Data System (NCANDS), and provide the first systematic analysis of police involvement in the child welfare system across nearly all U.S. counties.[1]

Contact with the criminal justice system has a host of consequences for families (Comfort 2008; Braman 2007; Wildeman and Muller 2012; Roberts 2012; Wildeman and Wang 2017). The incarceration of a family member strains the emotional and material resources of children's caregivers in ways that can have complex and disruptive effects on families (Wakefield and Wildeman 2014; Wildeman 2014; Turney 2014; Foster and Hagan 2015). The arrest or incarceration of a parent or caregiver may present both an immediate and a long-term crisis for the care of children, demanding that either kin, fictive kin, or the state step in to provide care for children (Andersen and Wildeman 2014; Berger et al. 2016; Comfort 2008, 2016; Roberts 2012). We know that parental incarceration has detrimental impacts on children and families. What this study illustrates is that even low-level contact with the criminal justice system exposes children and families to the risk of serious disruption through the deep interconnection of policing and child protection.

Policing likely provides a partial explanation for racial inequalities in child welfare system outcomes (Roberts 2002; Kim et al. 2016; Wildeman et al. 2014). As a key component of American family surveillance systems, local police agencies play a role in shaping the composition of the population of children and families singled out for maltreatment investigations. Agency and officer decisions about where to patrol, what to enforce, who is suspicious, and whether to make an arrest all play a role in determining which families are subject to surveillance and which are not.

THE INTERSECTIONS OF CRIMINAL JUSTICE AND CHILD PROTECTION

Contact with the child welfare system is incredibly common. About 37 percent of children in the United States will experience a child welfare maltreatment investigation during their childhood (Kim et al. 2016). About 12 percent will experience a confirmed case of child maltreatment before they turn eighteen (Wildeman et al. 2014). The likelihood of interacting with child welfare systems is dramatically higher for children of color. About half of all African American children will experience a child welfare investigation before their eighteenth birthday (Kim et al. 2016). In 2015, about four million children were reported to local child welfare agencies, of whom more than three million were screened in and received some form of agency response. About 5 percent of the U.S. child population was the subject of a report to child welfare agencies at some point in 2015 (Children's Bureau 2017). The prevalence of arrest follows a strikingly similar distribution: about 30 percent of Americans but 49 percent of young black men will experience an arrest by age twenty-three (Brame et al. 2012, 2014). The FBI Uniform Crime Reports show a national arrest rate in 2015 of about forty-five arrests per thousand adults, an incidence rate quite similar to the per capita rate of child abuse and neglect reporting (author's calculation).

Criminal justice and child welfare systems are likely to be most active in similar communities and neighborhoods, and overlapping contact with criminal justice and child welfare systems within families is common (Berger et al. 2016; Roberts 2012). Using administrative data in Wisconsin, Lawrence Berger and his colleagues find that 28 percent of children in-

---

1. The data used in this article were made available by the National Data Archive on Child Abuse and Neglect at Cornell University in Ithaca, New York. The data from the Substantiation of Child Abuse and Neglect Reports Project were originally collected by John Doris and John Eckenrode. Funding support for preparing the data for public distribution was provided by a contract (90-CA-1370) between the National Center on Child Abuse and Neglect and Cornell University. Neither the collector of the original data, funding agency, nor the National Data Archive on Child Abuse and Neglect bears any responsibility for the analyses or interpretations presented here.

volved in the child welfare system between 2004 and 2012 in Milwaukee County had a parent in jail or prison within a year of their contact with the child welfare system (2016). They further find that 18 percent of incarcerated eighteen- to twenty-one-year-olds in Wisconsin were involved with child welfare agencies as adolescents. Ethnographic work suggests that the communities in which child protection and police departments are most aggressive and most active often overlap (Fernandez-Kelly 2015; Roberts 2008).

Police agencies have deep institutional ties to child protection agencies. Child welfare agencies routinely conduct joint investigations with police, many police departments have created special units directed at child abuse and neglect, and police themselves handle noncriminal maltreatment investigations in some jurisdictions (Cross et al. 2015; Cross, Finkelhor, and Ormrod 2005). Regardless of jurisdiction, however, police play a fundamental role in child protection: they conduct front-line surveillance of children for signs of abuse and neglect; they produce information about the fitness of an adult to parent through the application of criminal stigma; and they create both short- and long-term crises of care when they incapacitate caregivers.

Police suspicion is likely to affect bureaucratic appraisals of the incidence of abuse or neglect within a family through the application of criminal stigma. Criminal records and arrests convey a powerful social signal to street-level bureaucrats and other community members. Places with more aggressive police forces mark larger proportions of their population with racialized and gendered criminal stigmas connoting irresponsibility and dangerousness (on racialized stigmas, Asad and Clair 2017; Harris, Evans, and Beckett 2011; on gendered stigmas, Rios 2011; Haney 2010). These stigmas likely affect child welfare system decision-making about the fitness of parents (Vesneski 2012).

Police are not dispassionate or objective instruments of social measurement. The social (and spatial) organization of policing is informed by and reproduces entrenched racialized and gendered inequalities (Beckett, Nyrop, and Pfingst 2006; Haney 2010; Gilmore 2007; Epp, Maynard-Moody, and Haider-Markel 2014; Lerman and Weaver 2014; Soss and Weaver 2017; Roberts 2012). The distribution of policing is not socially uniform (Carmichael and Kent 2014; Capers 2009; Perry 2009b). Further, criminal-legal decision-making is systematically related to race, class, and gender (Harris 2016; Murakawa and Beckett 2010; Haney 2000; Steen, Engen, and Gainey 2005; Rios 2011). These persistent and widespread inequalities in exposure to policing may be responsible for exacerbating racial inequalities in family exposure to the child welfare system.

CHILD PROTECTION SYSTEMS, FAMILY SURVEILLANCE, AND FAMILY REGULATION

Child protection systems are responsible for the investigation of alleged child abuse and neglect and are empowered to separate children from their families. Like the police, they are charged with the identification and regulation of unlawful and deviant behavior. However, unlike the police, child welfare agencies are tasked with an explicitly therapeutic and rehabilitative mission. Agencies often help children and families access housing, medical, counseling, and other benefits and services, and children in state custody become automatically eligible for a wide range of state and federal benefits. However, participation in these services is often unwanted and involuntary, because agencies may require compliance with case plans as a condition to allow children to remain or return. American child protection agencies operate in a distinctly coercive and paternalistic manner (Edwards 2016; Gilbert 2012). They require families to pursue what the state determines to be the best interests of children. Child welfare systems ensure that parents comply with agency and court mandates through the implicit or explicit threat of family separation.

However, child welfare agencies lack the direct surveillance capacities required to detect child abuse and neglect in communities. They depend on schools, police, medical professionals, social service agencies, and the community at large to act as their eyes and ears (Wells et al. 2014; Aleissa et al. 2009). This diffuse surveillance system is formalized by mandated reporting laws. In all states, professionals who routinely interact with families and children are required by law to report suspected child abuse or neglect, and a growing number of states have passed universal mandated reporting laws, which extend this obligation to a state's entire adult population (Krase and DeLong-Hamilton 2015; Drake and Jonson-Reid 2015; Raz 2017). This dependency on external agencies to originate reports of abuse and neglect is a likely source of variation in the flow of cases into the child welfare system. This institutional feature—a multi-organizational system of maltreatment surveillance—also creates conditions under which inequalities generated from one set of state actors can cause inequalities in proximate policy areas.

Surveillance is a process that requires a series of interactions and decisions. Prior to the generation of an agency investigation, a child or family must have contact with some professional or community member capable of monitoring the family. That observer must then use cultural scripts and institutional routines to classify a family interaction as normal or deviant. Following this classification, the observer may choose to submit a formal report to the relevant agency, and that agency must decide whether to respond to the allegation. Under this model, exposure to potential reporters, classification and reporting routines, local law, and agency rules for responding to cases all play a role in determining which children and families come under investigation. In this analysis, I direct attention to the first stage of this process by evaluating whether the rate of contact between police and community members is systematically related to the rate at which police report suspected child abuse and neglect.

DATA AND MEASURES

Outcomes for this study are constructed from the National Child Abuse and Neglect Data System, the federal data system responsible for tracking child maltreatment investigations and responses. NCANDS records case-level information on all investigated reports of child maltreatment annually with data reported from state and local child welfare agencies to the federal government. It is the most comprehensive source for national information on suspected child abuse and neglect, and contains several million records annually.

Child Maltreatment Surveillance

I construct counts of investigated maltreatment reports initiated by police at the county-year level. NCANDS does not capture reports of child abuse and neglect that are screened out as not requiring an investigation by child welfare agencies. Processes for classifying reports of alleged child abuse and neglect as worthy of investigation or response vary by jurisdiction, but are not quantifiable with current federal data. Because NCANDS does not record reports that are screened out and receive no agency response, the rates of police reporting of maltreatment presented here are conservative estimates.

Although comprehensive, the quality of NCANDS data varies by jurisdiction. Some counties have high levels of missing data on focal variables for this study likely related to agency data collection practices. All county-years in which more than 10 percent of reports are missing data on the original source of the investigated maltreatment report are treated as missing, as are those in which more than 10 percent of reports are missing data on the race of the investigated child. This procedure results in treating about 8 percent of county-year counts of police-initiated maltreatment reports as missing. Multiple imputation models address this and other sources of missing data and measurement error.[2] Because they are subject to unstable rate measures, all observations for county-years in which the population of children in the county by race is less than ten are excluded from the regression models.

Restricted versions of the NCANDS data allow for much higher coverage of U.S. counties and the U.S. child population than was possible with alternative versions of the data. Data are included on maltreatment reporting in 3,064 of the 3,142 U.S. counties or county-equivalent

---

2. These procedures do not affect the substantive conclusions presented. Parameter estimates are generally of the same direction, significance, and magnitude in models with imputed data and models that exclude these missing cases.

units. By contrast, previous work using these data has been able to include geographic information on about only six hundred counties. In 2015, this sample includes data from counties representing 99 percent of the U.S. Asian–Pacific Islander child population, 96 percent of the American Indian–Alaska Native child population, and more than 99 percent of the African American, Latino, white, and total U.S child population. Descriptive statistics on police-initiated maltreatment reports with Latino/a child subjects are presented, but the role of Latino/a ethnicity is not evaluated in regression models that include criminal justice data because federal criminal justice data systems systematically underreport Latino/a arrests (Nellis 2016).

CRIME, POLICING, AND ARRESTS

Focal predictors are constructed from the Uniform Crime Reports (UCR) arrests by age, sex, and race annual data for 2009 through 2015 (Federal Bureau of Investigation 2014a). The UCR, collected by the FBI and maintained by the National Archive of Criminal Justice Data, provides the only national time series data on law enforcement activity available at the jurisdiction level and covering the period of interest for this study. This series provides data on arrests by race at the police agency level aggregated to the county level. I also include information on the number of officers employed by police agencies at the county-year level from the UCR Police Employee Data (Federal Bureau of Investigation 2014b).

Using four offense categories, I create county-year sums for all arrests, and for arrests by race. Violent offenses include murder, manslaughter, rape, robbery, and aggravated assault, following the FBI's classification of violent offenses in the UCR index crime classification system. I also rely on the UCR's classification of drug offenses, a set that includes either possession or sale of opiates, marijuana, synthetic narcotics, and other dangerous non-narcotic drugs.

Quality-of-life policing captures a more diffuse set of offenses that are generally low level and subject to high officer and agency discretion in enforcement. These include vandalism, liquor laws, drunkenness, disorderly conduct, vagrancy, general suspicion, curfew and loitering, and various gambling offenses.

Reporting to the UCR is voluntary. Some police agencies faithfully report data annually, some do so intermittently, some never do, and some submit reports subject to clear error (these limitations are described in more detail in the discussion). For agencies with intermittent reporting, I replace all unreported years with linear interpolations constructed from the 2002 through 2015 data.[3] I treat counties as missing that include agencies with known or likely reporting error, including all counties with more than one thousand adults that report no arrests.[4] I construct imputation models to address both these explicit and identified implicit missing cases (Honaker, King, and Blackwell 2011; Honaker and King 2010).

DEMOGRAPHIC DATA AND MEASURES

Of course, rates of reported child abuse and neglect are sensitive to actual rates of child abuse and neglect. No direct measures of the incidence of child abuse and neglect are available, and few measures of child well-being, child injury, and family stability are available for all U.S. counties by race in reliable time series. Child poverty is widely regarded by child maltreatment researchers as among the best predictors of abuse and neglect (Sedlak et al. 2010). Although the measure has many known flaws, it provides a crude indicator of child and family well-being available for all U.S. counties annually by race (Brady 2009). I include measures of child poverty per capita by race between 2009 and 2015 using the American Community Survey (ACS) five-year data (Ruggles et al. 2010). Because many U.S. counties have very small populations, ACS five-year estimates are far more reliable than three-year or single-year

---

3. I classify arrest reports as missing if an agency reported more than fifty arrests in any included reporting year (by race) and reported zero arrests in an included reporting year. I use all observed years to produce a linear interpolation for these missing values.

4. The New York Police Department's submissions to the UCR are known to be unreliable, and I identify several other agency-years that are extreme outliers and are likely errors in reporting.

estimates. Five-year estimates are available only beginning in 2009, however, so I limit the regression models to the years 2009 through 2015.

I also include urban-rural classifications from the National Center for Health Statistics to control for potential differences in policing and child welfare system operations across metropolitan types. The Centers for Disease Control and Prevention produce annual population estimates for counties by race, sex, and age through the Surveillance, Epidemiology, and End Results Program, providing a reliable time series of adult and child populations by race for all counties and years available in the NCANDS data.

ANALYTIC STRATEGY

I first describe the kinds of cases police report to child protection agencies, the kinds of children and families police report, and the outcomes of police-reported maltreatment cases. I also evaluate national temporal trends in police-reported child maltreatment. I compare patterns of police-originated maltreatment reports to all maltreatment reports to explore whether police are more likely than other kinds of reporters to capture particular kinds of maltreatment, to report children of color, or to generate substantiated cases of child abuse and neglect.[5]

Next, I evaluate whether the activities of local police agencies are systematically related to police-originated child maltreatment reporting. I construct a series of multilevel regression models that evaluate the relationships between rates of arrest by offense and race and the volume of police-originated maltreatment reports by race at the county-year level. These models include child poverty rates, measures of county racial composition, urban-rural classification codes, police staffing levels, county-level random intercepts, and a national linear trend. Arrest, poverty, and composition measures interact with race, allowing for varying linear relationships between police reporting of maltreatment and regression predictors for all children, African American children, Asian–Pacific Islander children, American Indian–Alaska Native children, and white children. The outcomes for all regression models are counts of investigated reports of child abuse or neglect initially filed by police offset by the size of the focal child population.

Different kinds of enforcement may be more likely to result in police interaction with families and are subject to varying degrees of agency discretion. Police responses to violent and property offenses are largely reactive, in response to public calls or complaints. By contrast, police departments have more flexibility in deciding whether, where, and how to enforce drug laws (Beckett, Nyrop, and Pfingst 2006). They also have considerable flexibility in deciding whether to aggressively police low-level violations, in strategies frequently described as broken windows or quality-of-life policing (Fagan and Davies 2000; Gelman, Fagan, and Kiss 2007). We are more likely to capture discretion in law enforcement by comparing rates of drug and quality-of-life arrests across jurisdictions. I therefore separately model the relationships between police-initiated child protection reports and all arrests, for arrests for violent offense arrests, for drug offenses, and for quality-of-life offenses.

Because both policing and child protection are deeply racialized and gendered legal and administrative practices, heterogeneity may be substantial in the relationships between policing and family surveillance for families of color relative to white families (Roberts 2012; Rios 2011; Soss and Weaver 2017). Ideas about parental fitness are deeply intertwined with race, class, and family structure in ways that may affect the likelihood of a maltreatment report (Roberts 1997, 2012; Masters, Lindhorst, and Meyers 2014). Police may assess families of color as more dangerous to children's well-being than similar white families and may be more likely to have routine contact with families of color than with white families. Racial heterogeneity in risk of maltreatment surveillance and reporting would produce varying relationships between policing and reporting even after accounting for racial inequalities in rates of police contact. To account for these

---

5. Regression models that restrict the analysis to only cases in which a child is substantiated as a victim of abuse or neglect (not presented) yield substantively similar conclusions to models including all investigated cases.

varying relationships, I model race-specific relationships for arrests, child poverty, and racial composition.

Fixed-effects approaches to multilevel data have the advantage of purging unmeasured heterogeneity in individual units from models, enabling close evaluation of longitudinal within-unit trends, but they also inhibit cross-unit comparisons and provide little insight into time-stable features or slow-moving processes. I pursue a random-effects approach that estimates parameters for both average values of county-level covariates and for annual mean-difference values for county-year level covariates (Bell and Jones 2015). Evidence for short-term within-county relationships may provide stronger evidence of a potentially causal relationship; cross-county relationships identify whether variation in policing regimes across places helps explain the high geographic variation in maltreatment reporting.

For county i, year j, race k, child population m, and predictors X, I estimate multilevel Poisson models for counts of investigated maltreatment reports Y. These models estimate county-level intercepts, observation-level intercepts to model overdispersion, and race-specific intercepts and slopes for focal variables. Additionally, they estimate parameters for relationships between police maltreatment reporting and both county-average values (cross-sectional variation) and annual changes (longitudinal variation) for focal measures. I separately estimate models for each offense category. These models take the following general form:

$$Y \sim \text{Poisson}$$

$$\log \frac{\lambda_{ijk}}{m_{ijk}} = \gamma_{ijk} + \beta_2 \bar{x}_{ik_1} + \beta_3 (x_{ijk_1} - \bar{x}_{ik_1}) \cdots \beta_{n-1} \bar{x}_{ik_n} + \beta_n (x_{ijk_n} - \bar{x}_{ik_n})$$

$$\gamma_{ijk} = \beta_{0k} + \beta_{1k} \cdot j + \zeta_i + \varepsilon_{ijk}$$

$$\zeta_i \sim N(0, \sigma_\zeta^2)$$

$$\varepsilon_{ijk} \sim N(0, \sigma_\varepsilon^2).$$

FINDINGS

Police are less likely than others are to file maltreatment reports involving physical abuse (see table 1). In 2015, about 17 percent of all investigated maltreatment reports filed by police involved physical abuse, versus 22 percent of reports from all sources. Given the central role of police in responding to family violence, this is surprising. Police were more likely than other reporters to file reports involving allegations of psychological maltreatment or sexual abuse of children. As with other reporters, neglect is the primary form of suspected maltreatment in most police-filed reports. More than 70 percent of police maltreatment reports involving American Indian–Alaska Native children in 2015 centered on allegations of neglect.

Children are far more likely to be classified as victims of child abuse and neglect following a child welfare agency assessment when they are reported by police than when reports originate from another source. Although 22 percent of all investigations result in a conclusion that a child was a victim of abuse or neglect, 39 percent do when police file the initial report. Substantiation rates for children of all racial and ethnic groups are similar, concentrated at around 40 percent for police-filed reports and 22 percent for reports from all sources (see table 2).

Rates of Police Reporting

Police filed at least 394,482 reports of child abuse and neglect in 2015, about 19 percent of the more than 2.2 million investigated reports that year (see table 3).[6] Among professionally mandated reporters of child abuse and neglect, teachers and police have nearly identical rates and most frequently report maltreatment to local child welfare agencies (Children's Bureau 2017). About 30.9 reports of child maltreatment per thousand children in 2015 were investigated and about 5.8 were initiated by police.

Racial and ethnic inequalities in the rates at which child abuse and neglect are reported and investigated are substantial (see table 3). In

---

6. All counts of police reports used for these analyses are conservative. NCANDS records only those cases that receive an agency response, and many reports in NCANDS have an unidentified report source. The counts reported here are lower bounds to the numbers of maltreatment reports originated from police. Descriptive counts and rates presented in text are the original values in the NCANDS data.

Table 1. Reports by Type of Alleged Maltreatment in 2015

Type	Total	African American	American Indian–Alaska Native	Asian–Pacific Islander	Latino/a	White
All reports						
Neglect	0.56	0.52	0.67	0.43	0.52	0.55
Physical abuse	0.22	0.25	0.16	0.28	0.22	0.23
Psychological maltreatment	0.04	0.03	0.06	0.09	0.08	0.03
Sexual abuse	0.06	0.06	0.04	0.05	0.07	0.08
Police reports						
Neglect	0.57	0.50	0.71	0.52	0.54	0.54
Physical abuse	0.17	0.19	0.12	0.16	0.14	0.19
Psychological maltreatment	0.05	0.05	0.09	0.12	0.11	0.04
Sexual abuse	0.08	0.06	0.04	0.07	0.09	0.10

Source: Author's calculations based on NCANDS data (Children's Bureau 2016).

Table 2. Substantiation Rates for All Cases and for Police-Initiated Maltreatment Reports

	All Cases	Police-Reported Cases
Total	0.22	0.39
African American	0.23	0.38
American Indian–Alaska Native	0.24	0.42
Asian–Pacific Islander	0.20	0.37
Latino/a	0.22	0.39
White	0.22	0.39

Source: Author's calculations based on NCANDS data (Children's Bureau 2016).

Table 3. Investigated Child Abuse and Neglect Reports in 2015

	All Reports	Police Reports	Report Rate	Police Report Rate	Proportion of Reports from Police
Total	22,11,869	394,482	30.85	5.79	0.19
African American	462,913	85,096	49.24	9.73	0.20
American Indian–Alaska Native	21,068	4,521	18.49	4.28	0.23
Asian–Pacific Islander	20,979	3,877	6.48	1.23	0.19
Latino/a	331,018	63,912	23.65	4.68	0.20
White	813,124	144,305	27.10	5.10	0.19

Source: Author's calculations based on NCANDS data (Children's Bureau 2016).
Note: Counts and rates per thousand children.

2015, about 9.7 police reports of child maltreatment were investigated per thousand African American children, about 4.3 per thousand American Indian–Alaska Native children, about 1.2 per thousand Asian–Pacific Islander children, about 4.7 per thousand Latino/a children, and about 5.1 per thousand white children. Black children were subject to 1.9 times more police-initiated maltreatment investigations than white children; American Indian–Alaska Native, Latino/a, and Asian–Pacific Islander children were all subject to a lower rate of police reporting of maltreatment than their white counterparts. Although the share of maltreatment reports filed by police appears relatively constant by race in 2015, the increase in both the share of maltreatment reports filed by police and the volume of police reporting of maltreatment between 2002 and 2015 for most children has been notable (see figure 1).

The rate of police reporting of maltreatment increased for three groups—African American, Latino/a, and white children—between 2002 and 2015. Black families saw a 60 percent increase, Latino/a families a 23 percent increase, and white families a 39 percent increase. Rates of police reporting on Asian–Pacific Islander and American Indian–Alaska Native families remained relatively stable between 2002 and 2015. The proportion of all investigated maltreatment reports filed by police increased for all groups except Asian–Pacific Islanders between 2002 and 2015. This increase was most pronounced for American Indian–Alaska Native families. Although the rate of police reporting of maltreatment remained relatively stable over the period, police have been responsible for initiating a growing proportion of cases involving native families.

Spatial and Temporal Heterogeneity
Policing varies dramatically across U.S. counties. Table 4 presents the coefficients of variation by race for between and within-county rates of police reporting of maltreatment and rates of arrest.[7] Police reporting varies more between counties than it does within counties for all groups. The rates at which American Indian–Alaska Native and Asian–Pacific Islander families are reported show exceptionally high between-county variation.

Variation between counties in rates of arrest is also extreme. For all arrests, the standard deviation of county-average arrest rates is twice as large as the national average. Variation in arrest rates within counties is much lower than variation between counties. However, within-county variation in arrests is on the same order of magnitude as within-county variation in police reporting of maltreatment.

As shown in figure 1, national trends in police reporting of maltreatment over time are clear. Asian–Pacific Islander families experience particularly high degrees of fluctuation in reporting rates within counties over time. Although most of the variation in police reporting of maltreatment is between counties, within-county variation is substantial.

Regression Results
The results of multilevel regression models of police reporting of maltreatment show that policing is closely tied to the intensity of family surveillance at the county level. I present results for focal regression variables in table 5, a full table of regression parameter estimates in tables A1 and A2, and expected values for marginal changes in focal variables in figure 2. Both between-county average levels of arrest and annual within-county differences in arrests are significantly related to the number of police reports of child abuse and neglect for all categories of offenses and for nearly all racial groups. The expected change in police reporting of maltreatment for a marginal increase in within-county arrests is small, but the expected rate of police abuse and neglect reporting for a county with high county-average arrest rates is substantially greater than the expected rate for a county with national mean arrest levels.

County-average arrest rates are positively and significantly associated with rates of police reporting of maltreatment for all offense categories. The magnitude of this positive relationship is greatest for models including all arrests and smallest for models of quality-of-life arrests. In the model of total arrests, a county with average arrest rates at one standard de-

---

7. The coefficient of variation is calculated as the ratio of the standard deviation to the mean.

Figure 1. Police-Initiated Reporting Rate and Proportion of All Police-Initiated Investigated Reports

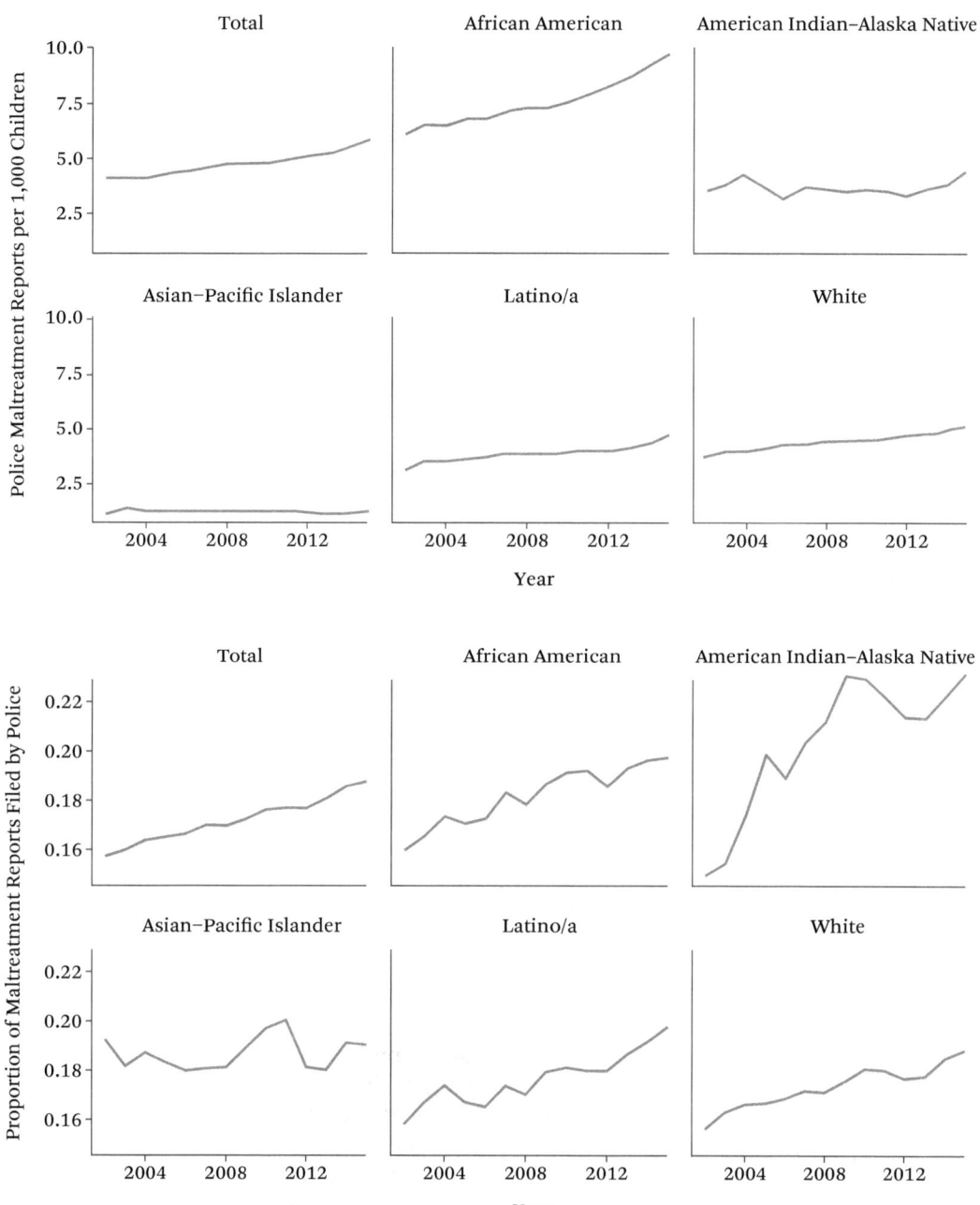

Source: Author's calculations based on NCANDS data, 2003–2015 (Children's Bureau 2016).

viation above the national mean is expected to have 8 percent more police reports of suspected child abuse or neglect. Within-county changes in arrest rates are significantly and positively associated with police reporting of maltreatment for all offenses, drug offenses, and quality-of-life offenses, but not for violent offenses. These associations have a relatively small magnitude; a one standard deviation increase in year-to-year total arrest rates is expected to correlate with an increase in police reporting of maltreatment rates of about 2 percent.

Table 4. Coefficients of Variation for Police-Initiated Reporting Rates and Arrest Rates

	Within-County Reports	Between-County Reports	Within-County Arrests	Between-County Arrests
Total	0.40	0.69	0.29	2.02
African American	0.52	1.08	0.32	0.73
American Indian–Alaska Native	0.73	1.94	0.60	1.95
Asian–Pacific Islander	1.09	1.46	0.55	1.97
Latino/a	0.72	0.91		
White	0.42	0.71	0.30	1.53

Source: Author's calculations based on NCANDS data, 2009–2015 (Children's Bureau 2016), and UCR data, 2009–2015 (Federal Bureau of Investigation 2014a).

Table 5. Parameter Estimates and Significance of Focal Regression Predictors

	Parameter	All Arrests	Violent Arrests	Drug Arrests	Quality-of-Life Arrests
Total	Between counties	0.09*	0.06*	0.07*	0.04*
	Within county	0.02*	0.01*	0.01*	0.01*
African American	Between counties	0.24*	0.18*	0.22*	0.21*
	Within county	0.02*	0.01*	0.02*	0.02*
Asian–Pacific Islander	Between counties	0.31*	0.25*	0.25*	0.24*
	Within county	0.03*	0.02*	0.00	0.02*
American Indian–Alaska Native	Between counties	0.54*	0.56*	0.60*	0.38*
	Within county	0.04*	0.03*	0.02*	0.03*
White	Between counties	0.28*	0.29*	0.25*	0.15*
	Within county	0.03*	0.01*	0.02*	0.02*

Source: Author's calculations based on NCANDS data, 2009–2015 (Children's Bureau 2016), and UCR data, 2009–2015 (Federal Bureau of Investigation 2014a).
Note: Mean-centered and scaled into standard deviation units.
*$p < .05$

I next model rates of police reporting of maltreatment by race of the child reported as a function of rates of arrest by race and category of offense. These models specify interactions of race, arrest, child poverty, and population composition. County-average arrest rates are positively and significantly associated with police reporting of maltreatment for all groups and for all offense categories. Within-county annual changes in arrest rates are positively and significantly associated with police reporting of maltreatment for all offenses and groups save Asian–Pacific Islander drug arrests, though again, the magnitude of this positive association is relatively small. I illustrate the expected rate of police reporting of maltreatment for marginal increases in both the county-average arrest rate and for marginal increases in the year-to-year within-county arrest rate by category of offense and race in figure 2. I also plot expected values for marginal increases in child poverty for comparison.

I expect police in a county with a cross-period average arrest rate of Asian–Pacific Islanders at one standard deviation above the national mean observed value to generate 36 percent more investigated reports of child abuse and neglect involving Asian–Pacific Islander children than a county with arrest rates at the national average. For African American

Figure 2. Expected Changes in Police-Initiated Maltreatment Reporting for Marginal Changes in Focal Variables

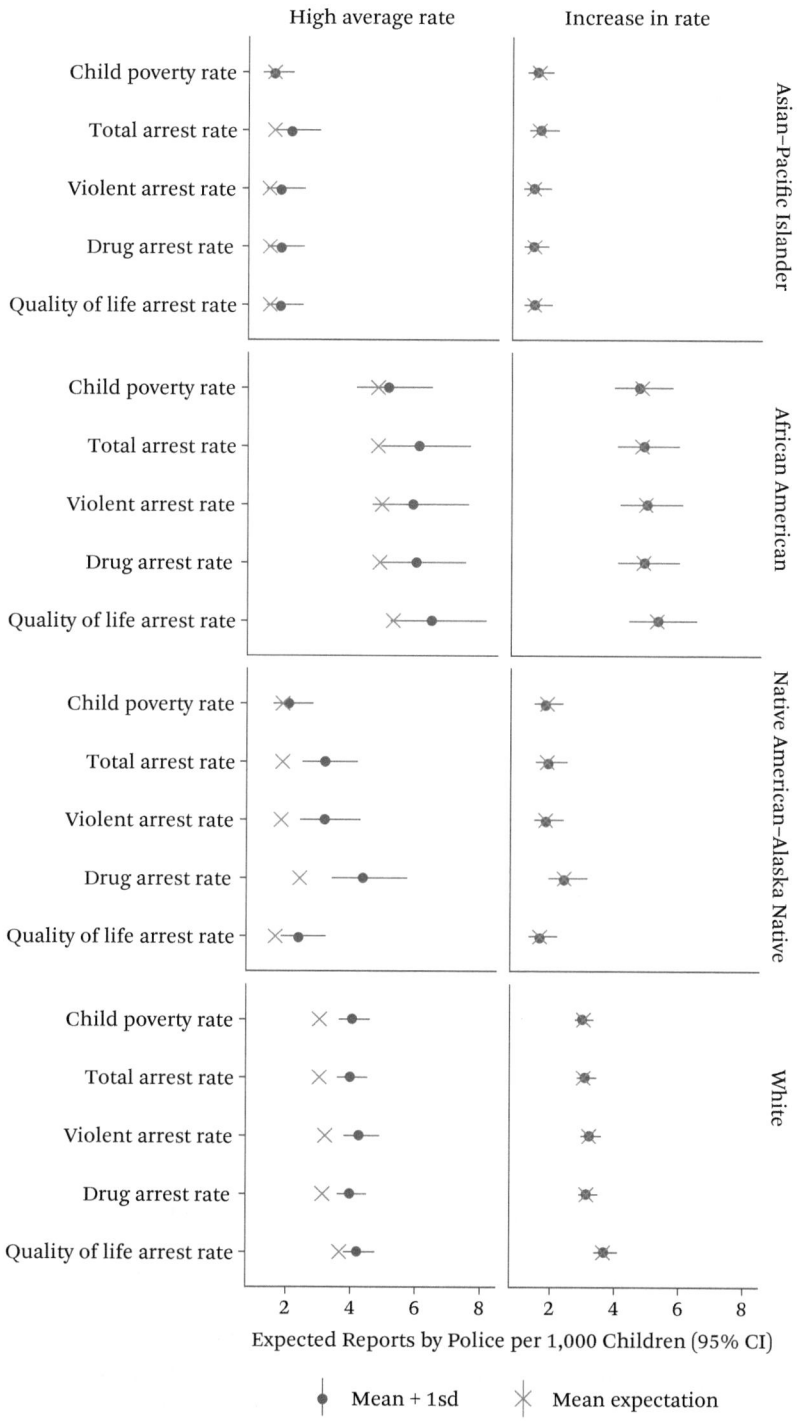

Source: Author's calculations based on NCANDS data, 2009–2015 (Children's Bureau 2016), and UCR data, 2009–2015 (Federal Bureau of Investigation 2014a).

children and families, police in a county with high average arrest rates are expected to produce 27 percent more reports of child abuse and neglect. For American Indian–Alaska Native children, counties with high average rates of native arrest are predicted to have 72 percent more police-investigated police reports of child maltreatment. For white children and families, counties with high average arrests are expected to have 32 percent more police maltreatment reports than those with average white arrest rates. Although within-county changes in arrest are significantly associated with police reporting of maltreatment rates, the magnitude of the relationship is relatively small. A within-county increase in arrests is predicted to increase reporting rates on average by about 3 percent for white children, 6 percent for Asian–Pacific Islander children, 4 percent for American Indian–Alaska Native children, and 2 percent for African American children.

Average arrest levels are incredibly strong predictors of the volume of police maltreatment reports involving American Indian–Alaska Native children and families. Although the magnitude of the relationship between average arrests and police reporting of maltreatment is relatively stable across offense types, for American Indian–Alaska Native children and families, drug arrests have an especially powerful association with police reporting. Counties with high average rates of American Indian–Alaska Native drug arrests are expected to have 82 percent more police reports of child maltreatment involving native children than counties at the national mean.

For white children, the magnitude of the estimated relationship between child poverty and police reporting is nearly identical to the magnitude of the estimated relationship between arrest rates and police maltreatment. A county with high white child poverty is expected to have about 35 percent more reports of child abuse and neglect filed by police than a county with average levels of white child poverty. However, for children and families of color, arrests are a far stronger predictor of the volume of maltreatment reports filed by police than child poverty is. For American Indian children, the expected rate of police reporting for a place with higher than average native child poverty is 13 percent higher than a county with average child poverty. For Asian–Pacific Islander children and families, high child poverty is not significantly associated with police reporting of maltreatment. For black children and families, counties with high black child poverty are only expected to have 8 percent more police maltreatment reports than counties with average rates. The relationships between child poverty and family surveillance appear to be highly sensitive to race.

Although not illustrated in figure 2, racial composition also has a powerful relationship to police reporting of maltreatment (see table A2). Counties with larger than average white populations are expected to have 50 percent more police maltreatment reports involving white children than counties with average proportional white populations. By contrast, population composition is negatively associated with police reporting of maltreatment for children and families of color. Counties with a greater than average share of Asian–Pacific Islanders are expected to have 18 percent fewer maltreatment reports than an average county. For American Indian children, high population composition predicts a 16 percent lower rate of police reporting of maltreatment, and for African American children and families, 42 percent fewer reports than would be expected in an average county.

DISCUSSION
Police are central components of local regimes for family surveillance. Contact with police is a key vector through which children and families come under the scrutiny of child welfare systems. These results show that average levels of arrest are tightly associated with the rates at which police report child abuse and neglect across counties. The results further show that within-county changes in arrest rates are associated with small changes in rates of child abuse and neglect reporting by police. But further research—ideally with micro-level data—is needed to investigate a possible causal relationship between police contact with families and the reporting of child abuse and neglect. These results suggest that involvement with the child

welfare system is a spillover consequence of arrest, particularly for American Indian–Alaska Native children. Contact with police is a common precondition to a child welfare investigation, and opens the possibility of a child's separation from their family through entry into the foster care system.

Race plays a powerful role in explaining the geography of family surveillance (Roberts 2008). For children and families of color, population composition and policing powerfully explain the intensity of family surveillance, whereas child poverty—typically considered a key correlate of child abuse and neglect (Sedlak et al. 2010)—is only weakly associated with the rate of police reporting of maltreatment for children of color. Although reporting rates are certainly associated with the actual incidence of child abuse and neglect, reports and investigations are organizational artifacts. Reporting is contingent on the observation of a family by a street-level bureaucrat, the cognitive classification of a child as a potential victim or a parent as unfit, the decision to file a report, and a child welfare agency formally classifying a report as credible and deserving of a response. Race, gender, and entrenched ideas about the family have central roles in structuring both the infrastructure of family surveillance and the micro-level interactions that lead to the decision to file a report.

The racial politics of policing and crime, driven by complex dynamics of threat, control, and predation (Soss and Weaver 2017; Smith and Holmes 2014; Carmichael and Kent 2014; Capers 2009), result in a distinctively punitive style of policing in many communities of color: a simultaneous overpolicing of perceived black and brown criminality and underpolicing in response to victims of color (Rios 2011; Perry 2009a; Beckett, Nyrop, and Pfingst 2006). Tight symbolic and legal associations among race, gender, ethnicity, criminality, and parental fitness inform both cognitive and institutional classification routines that lead officers, caseworkers, and agencies to view poor women of color as unfit parents who may pose a danger to their children (Roberts 2014; Haney 1996). These processes lead to a racialized spatial distribution of both the quantity of police and the qualitative character of their interactions with community members.

Surveillance infrastructure is likely related to both the production of excess child welfare cases and the underdetection of child maltreatment. Because surveillance is not equitably distributed, we should expect some communities to experience a high volume of false or needless reports, and others a high volume of false negatives (nonreports). The decoupling of offending and arrest has likely expanded contact between families and police over time (Weaver, Papachristos, and Zanger-Tishler 2019). It may also be a source of racial inequity in exposure to family surveillance, the generation of excess maltreatment reporting in communities of color, and underreporting in communities where police are less active or aggressive. Disparities originating in criminal justice may drift across organizational boundaries to reinforce the deep racial inequalities that are a defining feature of American child protection (Roberts 2002; Jacobs 2014).

Although it is reasonable to assume that the distribution of surveillance has a significant effect in generating the over- and underreporting of child abuse and neglect, no reliable data on actual maltreatment incidence across places currently exists. Using data on childhood injuries may provide some insight, but the overwhelming volume of maltreatment cases involve neglect, which is subject to tremendous discretion in identification and classification. Because many types of maltreatment are not cleanly demarcated, it is unlikely that the development of an objective surveillance procedure is possible. Street-level bureaucrats enforce maltreatment statutes by leveraging formal information (including stigmas such as criminal or arrest records) and informal biases in an always subjective process that classifies parents as abusive or neglectful and classifies children as victims or nonvictims.

The geography of policing has likely spillover consequences on child protection beyond the direct reporting of child abuse and neglect by police. Legal cynicism resulting from direct and vicarious experiences of negative interactions with police may lead to a generalized cynicism that extends to other coercive state institutions, such as the child welfare system (on police, Geller and Fagan 2019; on other institutions, Lerman and Weaver 2014; Fernandez-Kelly 2015). Legal cynicism may lead to a reduction in reporting of suspected child abuse and neglect by community members, suspicion of the motives of child welfare agencies and family courts, and avoidance of institutions that interface with either law enforcement or the child welfare system (Fong 2017).

Strengths and Limitations of NCANDS and UCR Data

Like the UCR, the NCANDS data offer the promise of comprehensive national data on a critically important social policy sector. The UCR is the sole longitudinal data on arrests across police agencies, but its limitations are substantial. Because reporting to the UCR is voluntary, the availability and quality of the data varies tremendously across places and within places over time. Many jurisdictions fail to report data, and others report data that are subject to various kinds of measurement error. Some researchers have challenged the validity of the UCR for subnational inferences of the sort presented in this analysis (Maltz and Targonski 2002), though others have suggested that nonreporting may have little impact on substantive conclusions (Lott and Whitley 2003), or have offered imputation and interpolation procedures to address nonreporting (Lynch and Jarvis 2008). Multiple imputation procedures that adjust for the longitudinal structure of the UCR offer an opportunity to quantify the extent to which missing data may affect inferences by introducing reasonable levels of missing data–induced measurement error into regression models (Honaker and King 2010).

The NCANDS data offer valuable insights into the activities of state and local child welfare organizations and afford the opportunity for the systematic comparison of child welfare systems across counties and states. However, as with all administrative data, the NCANDS has several distinct limitations that are a function of the organizational processes that generate the data. Most important, the data do not record cases that child welfare agencies screen out as not warranting an agency response. These screening processes are a function of varying statutes, policies, and routines that agencies use to determine when to respond to a case. Heterogeneity in screening affects the composition of cases that receive agency responses and hence are recorded in NCANDS. The implications of variation in case screening are difficult to estimate with current data but are likely small. Variance in the screening-in of police-initiated maltreatment reports across places is likely low because police tend to be seen as credible maltreatment reporters by child welfare agency staff. Future work could consider whether automatic screening policies, in effect in some jurisdictions later in the period, reveal shifts in the estimated relationships between policing and maltreatment reporting.

Because NCANDS submissions from state agencies to the federal government are all constructed from internal data systems, the quality of NCANDS variables can differ across jurisdictions. Some measures, such as report source, case substantiation, and child race, are recorded well across the data. Others, including service provision and child and parent risk factors, have a much lower quality across jurisdictions. These data quality issues can make individual-level analyses that take advantage of the multilevel structure of child welfare service provision challenging. However, those high-quality variables do offer researchers a unique opportunity to construct comparable indicators of child welfare agency activity across jurisdictions.

CONCLUSION

American child protection systems are deeply multi-institutional. Lacking their own capacity to monitor children and families for signs of abuse and neglect, they depend on police, medical personnel, teachers, and other professionals and community members to leverage their routine interactions with children and families into a broad and diffuse network for maltreatment surveillance. This dependence turns practices and biases from external organizations into key features of the processes through which maltreatment reports are generated. Neither the geographic distribution of police officers nor the qualitative character of police-public interactions are uniform. The social and spatial organization of policing plays a central role in selecting children and families for scrutiny by child protection agencies. Exposure to policing plays an important role in determining which children do, and which children do not, come to the attention of child protection agencies.

Table A1. Investigated Police Child Maltreatment Reports, Parameter Estimates and Standard Errors for Multilevel Poisson Regression

	All Arrests	Violent Arrests	Drug Arrests	Quality-of-Life Arrests
Intercept	−5.34***	−5.34***	−5.34***	−5.33***
	(0.02)	(0.02)	(0.02)	(0.02)
Mean arrest	0.09***	0.06***	0.07***	0.04***
	(0.01)	(0.01)	(0.01)	(0.01)
Change in arrest	0.02***	0.01**	0.01**	0.01***
	(0.00)	(0.00)	(0.00)	(0.00)
Mean child poverty	0.07***	0.06***	0.07***	0.08***
	(0.01)	(0.01)	(0.01)	(0.01)
Change in child poverty	0.00	0.00	0.00	0.00
	(0.00)	(0.00)	(0.00)	(0.00)
Year	0.10***	0.10***	0.09***	0.10***
	(0.00)	(0.00)	(0.00)	(0.00)
Number of police departments	0.04**	0.04*	0.04**	0.04*
	(0.01)	(0.02)	(0.01)	(0.02)
Large fringe metropolitan area	0.20***	0.20***	0.20***	0.17**
	(0.05)	(0.04)	(0.05)	(0.05)
Medium metropolitan area	−0.08	−0.10*	−0.09*	−0.10*
	(0.04)	(0.05)	(0.04)	(0.05)
Small metropolitan area	0.01	−0.02	−0.03	−0.02
	(0.04)	(0.04)	(0.04)	(0.04)
Micropolitan	−0.03	−0.04	−0.03	−0.04
	(0.03)	(0.03)	(0.03)	(0.03)
Noncore	−0.01	0.01	−0.01	−0.01
	(0.03)	(0.03)	(0.03)	(0.03)
Officers per capita	−0.03**	−0.02*	−0.03**	−0.02
	(0.01)	(0.01)	(0.01)	(0.01)
Residual variance	0.16	0.16	0.16	0.16
County intercept variance	0.30	0.31	0.31	0.31

Source: Author's calculations based on NCANDS data, 2009–2015 (Children's Bureau 2016), and UCR data, 2009–2015 (Federal Bureau of Investigation 2014a).
Note: Results combined across imputations.
*$p < .05$; **$p < .01$; ***$p < .001$

Table A2. Investigated Police Child Maltreatment Reports for Multilevel Poisson Regression

	All Arrests	Violent Arrests	Drug Arrests	Quality-of-Life Arrests
Intercept	-5.80***	-5.74***	-5.77***	-5.61***
	(0.04)	(0.04)	(0.04)	(0.04)
Asian American–Pacific Islander	-0.66***	-0.83***	-0.79***	-0.94***
	(0.06)	(0.07)	(0.06)	(0.07)
American Indian	-0.48***	-0.56***	-0.26***	-0.79***
	(0.05)	(0.06)	(0.05)	(0.06)
African American	0.45***	0.42***	0.43***	0.36***
	(0.04)	(0.04)	(0.04)	(0.04)
Mean arrest	0.28***	0.29***	0.25***	0.15***
	(0.02)	(0.02)	(0.02)	(0.01)
Change in arrest	0.03***	0.01***	0.02***	0.02***
	(0.01)	(0.01)	(0.01)	(0.01)
Mean child poverty	0.30***	0.30***	0.31***	0.34***
	(0.02)	(0.02)	(0.02)	(0.02)
Change in child poverty	0.00	0.00	0.00	0.00
	(0.01)	(0.01)	(0.01)	(0.01)
Year	0.09***	0.08***	0.08***	0.09***
	(0.00)	(0.00)	(0.01)	(0.00)
Number of police departments	0.05***	0.04***	0.04***	0.04***
	(0.01)	(0.01)	(0.01)	(0.01)
Large fringe metropolitan area	0.07	0.11	0.09	0.07
	(0.04)	(0.04)	(0.05)	(0.04)
Medium metropolitan area	-0.04	-0.09	-0.07	-0.09
	(0.04)	(0.04)	(0.04)	(0.04)
Small metropolitan area	0.01	0.01	-0.01	0.02
	(0.03)	(0.03)	(0.03)	(0.03)
Micropolitan	-0.03	-0.07	-0.03	-0.06
	(0.03)	(0.03)	(0.03)	(0.03)
Noncore	0.02	0.03	0.03	0.03
	(0.02)	(0.03)	(0.03)	(0.03)
Officers per capita	-0.03*	-0.02*	-0.02*	-0.01*
	(0.01)	(0.01)	(0.01)	(0.01)
Percentage of the population	0.40***	0.34***	0.35***	0.20***
	(0.04)	(0.04)	(0.04)	(0.04)
Asian American–Pacific Islander x mean arrest	0.03	-0.04	-0.00	0.09
	(0.04)	(0.03)	(0.04)	(0.03)
American Indian x mean arrest	0.26***	0.27***	0.35***	0.23***
	(0.02)	(0.02)	(0.02)	(0.02)
African American x mean arrest	-0.04*	-0.11*	-0.03*	0.06*
	(0.02)	(0.02)	(0.02)	(0.02)
Asian American–Pacific Islander x change in arrest	0.03	0.02	0.00	0.02
	(0.02)	(0.03)	(0.02)	(0.02)
American Indian x change in arrest	0.01	0.02	0.00	0.01
	(0.02)	(0.02)	(0.02)	(0.01)
African American x change in arrest	-0.01	0.00	-0.00	-0.00
	(0.01)	(0.01)	(0.01)	(0.01)

Table A2. (continued)

	All Arrests	Violent Arrests	Drug Arrests	Quality-of-Life Arrests
Asian American–Pacific Islander x mean child poverty	−0.27***	−0.26***	−0.28***	−0.30***
	(0.03)	(0.03)	(0.03)	(0.02)
American Indian x mean child poverty	−0.18***	−0.13***	−0.16***	−0.15***
	(0.03)	(0.03)	(0.03)	(0.03)
African American x mean child poverty	−0.22***	−0.22***	−0.23***	−0.26***
	(0.02)	(0.02)	(0.02)	(0.02)
Asian American–Pacific Islander x change in child poverty	−0.01	−0.01	−0.01	−0.01
	(0.02)	(0.02)	(0.02)	(0.02)
American Indian x change in child poverty	−0.01	0.00	−0.01	−0.00
	(0.02)	(0.02)	(0.02)	(0.02)
African American x change in child poverty	−0.01	−0.01	−0.01	−0.01
	(0.01)	(0.01)	(0.01)	(0.01)
Asian American–Pacific Islander x percent population	−0.60***	−0.56***	−0.56***	−0.36***
	(0.07)	(0.07)	(0.07)	(0.07)
American Indian x percent population	−0.57***	−0.51***	−0.38***	−0.37***
	(0.05)	(0.05)	(0.05)	(0.05)
African American x percent population	−0.95***	−0.93***	−0.89***	−0.72***
	(0.05)	(0.05)	(0.05)	(0.05)
Residual variance	0.36	0.36	0.36	0.36
County intercept variance	0.19	0.19	0.20	0.20

Source: Author's calculations based on NCANDS data, 2009–2015 (Children's Bureau 2016), and UCR data, 2009–2015 (Federal Bureau of Investigation 2014a).
Note: Results combined across imputations.
*p < .05; **p < .01; ***p < .001

REFERENCES

Aleissa, Majid A., John D. Fluke, Bernard Gerbaka, Lutz Goldbeck, Jenny Gray, Nicole Hunter, Bernadette Madrid, Bert Van Puyenbroeck, Ian Richards, and Lil Tonmyr. 2009. "A Commentary on National Child Maltreatment Surveillance Systems: Examples of Progress." *Child Abuse & Neglect* 33(11): 809–14.

Andersen, Signe Hald, and Christopher Wildeman. 2014. "The Effect of Paternal Incarceration on Children's Risk of Foster Care Placement." *Social Forces* 93(1): 269–98.

Asad, Asad L., and Matthew Clair. 2017. "Racialized Legal Status as a Social Determinant of Health." *Social Science & Medicine*. Online pre-print: doi.org/10.1016/j.socscimed.2017.03.010.

Beckett, Katherine, Kris Nyrop, and Lori Pfingst. 2006. "Race, Drugs, and Policing: Understanding Disparities in Drug Delivery Arrests." *Criminology* 44(1): 105–37.

Bell, Andrew, and Kelvyn Jones. 2015. "Explaining Fixed Effects: Random Effects Modeling of Time-Series Cross-Sectional and Panel Data." *Political Science Research and Methods* 3(1): 133–53.

Berger, Lawrence M., Maria Cancian, Laura Cuesta, and Jennifer L. Noyes. 2016. "Families at the Intersection of the Criminal Justice and Child Protective Services Systems." *Annals of the Ameri-*

can Academy of Political and Social Science 665(1): 171–94.

Brady, David. 2009. *Rich Democracies, Poor People: How Politics Explain Poverty*. New York: Oxford University Press.

Braman, Donald. 2007. *Doing Time on the Outside: Incarceration and Family Life in Urban America*. Ann Arbor: University of Michigan Press.

Brame, Robert W., Shawn D. Bushway, Ray Paternoster, and Michael G. Turner. 2014. "Demographic Patterns of Cumulative Arrest Prevalence by Ages 18 and 23." *Crime & Delinquency* 60(3): 471–86.

Brame, Robert W., Michael G. Turner, Raymond Paternoster, and Shawn D. Bushway. 2012. "Cumulative Prevalence of Arrest From Ages 8 to 23 in a National Sample." *Pediatrics* 129(1): 21–27.

Capers, I. Bennett. 2009. "Policing, Race, and Place." *Harvard Civil Rights-Civil Liberties Law Review* 44(1): 43–78.

Carmichael, Jason T., and Stephanie L. Kent. 2014. "The Persistent Significance of Racial and Economic Inequality on the Size of Municipal Police Forces in the United States, 1980–2010." *Social Problems* 61(2): 259–82.

Children's Bureau. 2016. National Child Abuse and Neglect Data System (NCANDS) Child File, FFY 2015 [Dataset]. Washington: U.S. Department of Health and Human Services, Administration for Children and Families.

———. 2017. *Child Maltreatment 2015*. Washington: U.S. Department of Health and Human Services, Administration for Children and Families. Accessed July 26, 2018. https://www.acf.hhs.gov/sites/default/files/cb/cm2015.pdf.

Comfort, Megan. 2008. *Doing Time Together: Love and Family in the Shadow of the Prison*. Chicago: University of Chicago Press.

———. 2016. "'A Twenty Hour a Day Job': The Impact of Frequent Low-Level Criminal Justice Involvement on Family Life." *Annals of the American Academy of Political and Social Science* 665(1): 63–79.

Cross, Theodore P., Emmeline Chuang, Jesse J. Helton, and Emily A. Lux. 2015. "Criminal Investigations in Child Protective Services Cases: An Empirical Analysis." *Child Maltreatment* 20(2): 104–14.

Cross, Theodore P., David Finkelhor, and Richard Ormrod. 2005. "Police Involvement in Child Protective Services Investigations: Literature Review and Secondary Data Analysis." *Child Maltreatment* 10(3): 224–44.

Drake, Brett, and Melissa Jonson-Reid. 2015. "Competing Values and Evidence: How Do We Evaluate Mandated Reporting and CPS Response?" In *Mandatory Reporting Laws and the Identification of Severe Child Abuse and Neglect*, edited by Ben Mathews and Donald C. Bross. New York: Springer.

Edwards, Frank. 2016. "Saving Children, Controlling Families: Punishment, Redistribution, and Child Protection." *American Sociological Review* 81(3): 575–95.

Epp, Charles R., Steven Maynard-Moody, and Donald P. Haider-Markel. 2014. *Pulled Over: How Police Stops Define Race and Citizenship*. The Chicago Series in Law and Society. Chicago: University of Chicago Press.

Fagan, Jeffrey, and Garth Davies. 2000. "Street Stops and Broken Windows: Terry, Race, and Disorder in New York City." *Fordham Urban Law Journal* 28(2): 457–504.

Federal Bureau of Investigation. 2014a. "Uniform Crime Reporting Program Data: Arrests by Age, Sex, and Race, 2012." Ann Arbor, Mich.: ICPSR—Interuniversity Consortium for Political and Social Research.

———. 2014b. "Uniform Crime Reporting Program Data: Police Employee (LEOKA) Data, 2012." Ann Arbor, Mich.: ICPSR—Interuniversity Consortium for Political and Social Research.

Fernandez-Kelly, María Patricia. 2015. *The Hero's Fight: African Americans in West Baltimore and the Shadow of the State*. Princeton, N.J.: Princeton University Press.

Fong, Kelley. 2017. "Child Welfare Involvement and Contexts of Poverty: The Role of Parental Adversities, Social Networks, and Social Services." *Children and Youth Services Review* 72 (January): 5–13. DOI: 10.1016/j.childyouth.2016.10.011.

Foster, Holly, and John Hagan. 2015. "Punishment Regimes and the Multilevel Effects of Parental Incarceration: Intergenerational, Intersectional, and Interinstitutional Models of Social Inequality and Exclusion." *Annual Review of Sociology* 41: 135–58.

Geller, Amanda, and Jeffrey Fagan. 2019. "Police Contact and the Legal Socialization of Urban Teens." *RSF: The Russell Sage Foundation Journal* of the Social Sciences 5(1): 26–49. DOI: 10.7758/RSF.2019.5.1.02.

Gelman, Andrew, Jeffrey Fagan, and Alex Kiss. 2007. "An Analysis of the New York City Police Department's 'Stop-and-Frisk' Policy in the Context of Claims of Racial Bias." *Journal of the American Statistical Association* 102(479): 813–23.

Gilbert, Neil. 2012. "A Comparative Study of Child Welfare Systems: Abstract Orientations and Concrete Results." *Children and Youth Services Review* 34(3): 532–36.

Gilmore, Ruth. 2007. *Golden Gulag: Prisons, Surplus, Crisis, and Opposition in Globalizing California*. Berkeley: University of California Press.

Haney, Lynne A. 1996. "Homeboys, Babies, Men in Suits: The State and the Reproduction of Male Dominance." *American Sociological Review* 61(5): 759–78.

———. 2000. "Feminist State Theory: Applications to Jurisprudence, Criminology, and the Welfare State." *Annual Review of Sociology* 26: 641–66.

———. 2010. *Offending Women: Power, Punishment, and the Regulation of Desire*. Berkeley: University of California Press.

Harris, Alexes. 2016. *A Pound of Flesh: Monetary Sanctions as Punishment for the Poor*. American Sociological Association's Rose Series in Sociology. New York: Russell Sage Foundation.

Harris, Alexes, Heather Evans, and Katherine Beckett. 2011. "Courtesy Stigma and Monetary Sanctions: Toward a Socio-Cultural Theory of Punishment." *American Sociological Review* 76(2): 234–64.

Honaker, James, and Gary King. 2010. "What to Do About Missing Values in Time Series Cross-Section Data." *American Journal of Political Science* 54(3): 561–81.

Honaker, James, Gary King, and Matthew Blackwell. 2011. "Amelia II: A Program for Missing Data." *Journal of Statistical Software* 45(7): 1–47.

Jacobs, Margaret D. 2014. *A Generation Removed: The Fostering and Adoption of Indigenous Children in the Postwar World*. Lincoln: University of Nebraska Press.

Kim, Hyunil, Christopher Wildeman, Melissa Jonson-Reid, and Brett Drake. 2016. "Lifetime Prevalence of Investigating Child Maltreatment Among US Children." *American Journal of Public Health* 107(2): 274–80.

Krase, Kathryn S., and Tobi A. DeLong-Hamilton. 2015. "Comparing Reports of Suspected Child Maltreatment in States with and Without Universal Mandated Reporting." *Children and Youth Services Review* 50 (March): 96–100.

Lerman, Amy E., and Vesla M. Weaver. 2014. *Arresting Citizenship: The Democratic Consequences of American Crime Control*. Chicago Studies in American Politics. Chicago: University of Chicago Press.

Lipsky, Michael. 1980. *Street-Level Bureaucracy: Dilemmas of the Individual in Public Services*. New York: Russell Sage Foundation.

Lott, John R., and John Whitley. 2003. "Measurement Error in County-Level UCR Data." *Journal of Quantitative Criminology* 19(2):185–98.

Lynch, James P., and John P. Jarvis. 2008. "Missing Data and Imputation in the Uniform Crime Reports and the Effects on National Estimates." *Journal of Contemporary Criminal Justice* 24(1): 69–85.

Maltz, Michael D., and Joseph Targonski. 2002. "A Note on the Use of County-Level UCR Data." *Journal of Quantitative Criminology* 18(3): 297–318.

Masters, N. Tatiana, Taryn P. Lindhorst, and Marcia K. Meyers. 2014. "Jezebel at the Welfare Office: How Racialized Stereotypes of Poor Women's Reproductive Decisions and Relationships Shape Policy Implementation." *Journal of Poverty* 18(2): 109–29.

Murakawa, Naomi, and Katherine Beckett. 2010. "The Penology of Racial Innocence: The Erasure of Racism in the Study and Practice of Punishment." *Law & Society Review* 44(3–4): 695–730.

Nellis, Ashley. 2016. "The Color of Justice: Racial and Ethnic Disparity in State Prisons." Washington, D.C.: Sentencing Project. Accessed September 1, 2018. https://www.sentencingproject.org/publications/color-of-justice-racial-and-ethnic-disparity-in-state-prisons.

Perry, Barbara. 2009a. *Policing Race and Place in Indian Country: Over-and Underenforcement*. Lanham, Md.: Lexington Books.

———. 2009b. "Impacts of Disparate Policing in Indian Country." *Policing and Society* 19(3): 263–81.

Raz, Mical. 2017. "Unintended Consequences of Expanded Mandatory Reporting Laws." *Pediatrics* 139(4) (April): e20163511.

Rios, Victor M. 2011. *Punished: Policing the Lives of*

Black and Latino Boys. New York: New York University Press.

Roberts, Dorothy. 1997. *Killing the Black Body: Race, Reproduction, and the Meaning of Liberty*. New York: Pantheon Books.

———. 2002. *Shattered Bonds: The Color of Child Welfare*. New York: Basic Civitas Books.

———. 2008. "The Racial Geography of Child Welfare: Toward a New Research Paradigm." *Child Welfare* 87(2): 125–50.

———. 2012. "Prison, Foster Care, and the Systemic Punishment of Black Mothers." *UCLA Law Review* 59(6): 1474–500.

———. 2014. "Complicating the Triangle of Race, Class and State: The Insights of Black Feminists." *Ethnic and Racial Studies* 37(10): 1776–82.

Ruggles, Steven J., J. Trent Alexander, Katie Genadek, Ronald Goeken, Matthew B. Schroeder, and Matthew Sobek. 2010. Integrated Public Use Microdata Series: Version 5.0 [Machine-Readable Database]. Minneapolis: University of Minnesota.

Sedlak, Andrea, Jane Mettenburg, Monica Basena, Ian Peta, Karla McPherson, Angela Greene, and Spencer Li. 2010. "Fourth National Incidence Study of Child Abuse and Neglect (NIS-4)." Washington: U.S. Department of Health and Human Services.

Smith, Brad W., and Malcolm D. Holmes. 2014. "Police Use of Excessive Force in Minority Communities: A Test of the Minority Threat, Place, and Community Accountability Hypotheses." *Social Problems* 61(1): 83–104.

Soss, Joe, and Vesla Weaver. 2017. "Learning from Ferguson: Policing, Race, and Class in American Politics." *Annual Review of Political Science* 20: 565–91.

Steen, Sara, Rodney L. Engen, and Randy R. Gainey. 2005. "Images of Danger and Culpability: Racial Stereotyping, Case Processing, and Criminal Sentencing." *Criminology* 43(2): 435–68.

Turney, Kristin. 2014. "The Consequences of Paternal Incarceration for Maternal Neglect and Harsh Parenting." *Social Forces* 92(4): 1607–36.

Vesneski, William M. 2012. "Judicial Criteria for Terminating Parental Rights: A Content Analysis of 2010 North Carolina Appellate Court Opinions." Ph.D. diss., University of Washington.

Wakefield, Sara, and Christopher Wildeman. 2014. *Children of the Prison Boom: Mass Incarceration and the Future of American Inequality*. New York: Oxford University Press.

Weaver, Vesla M., Andrew Papachristos, and Michael Zanger-Tishler. 2019. "The Great Decoupling: The Disconnection Between Criminal Offending and Experience of Arrest Across Two Cohorts." *RSF: The Russell Sage Foundation Journal of the Social Sciences* 5(1): 89–123. DOI: 10.7758/RSF.2019.5.1.05.

Wells, Rebecca, Monica Perez Jolles, Emmeline Chuang, Bowen McBeath, and Crystal Collins-Camargo. 2014. "Trends in Local Public Child Welfare Agencies 1999–2009." *Children and Youth Services Review* 38 (March): 93–100.

Wildeman, Christopher. 2014. "Parental Incarceration, Child Homelessness, and the Invisible Consequences of Mass Imprisonment." *Annals of the American Academy of Political and Social Science* 651(1): 74–96.

Wildeman, Christopher, Natalia Emanuel, John M. Leventhal, Emily Putnam-Hornstein, Jane Waldfogel, and Hedwig Lee. 2014. "The Prevalence of Confirmed Maltreatment Among U.S. Children, 2004 to 2011." *JAMA Pediatrics* 168(8): 706–13.

Wildeman, Christopher, and Christopher Muller. 2012. "Mass Imprisonment and Inequality in Health and Family Life." *Annual Review of Law and Social Science* 8: 11–30.

Wildeman, Christopher, and Emily A. Wang. 2017. "Mass Incarceration, Public Health, and Widening Inequality in the USA." *The Lancet* 389 (10077): 1464–74.

Wulczyn, Fred, Robert Gibbons, Lonnie Snowden, and Bridgette Lery. 2013. "Poverty, Social Disadvantage, and the Black/White Placement Gap." *Children and Youth Services Review* 35(1): 65–74.

Digital Vulnerability: The Unequal Risk of E-Contact with the Criminal Justice System

ROBERT VARGAS, KAYLA PREITO-HODGE, AND
JEREMY CHRISTOFFERSON

Increased citizen interaction with the criminal justice system on digital platforms renders citizens more vulnerable to breaches of information to third parties. We introduce the concept of digital vulnerability to measure the extent to which technology produces unequal exposure to risk of data breaches. Using police-dispatcher radio communication, we examine the extent to which dispatchers reveal identifiable information about callers reporting crime. Data come from sixty audio-recorded hours of police-dispatcher radio communication across three racially distinct police radio zones in Chicago. Findings revealed that one of every ten calls made to police in zones serving racial minorities disclosed caller names or home addresses. We discuss implications for research on racial inequality in criminal justice contact, police-community relations, and policies concerning police-dispatcher radio communication.

Keywords: criminal justice contact, 911 emergency service, policing, technology, race

Of the 240 million calls made to 911 every year, a significant portion are for police assistance (NENA 2017). In Chicago alone, from 2000 to 2010, 911 dispatchers made an annual average of five million calls for police service on citizens' behalf. This form of electronic contact, or e-contact, with the criminal justice system occurs more frequently than physical forms of criminal justice contact, such as the twelve million individuals arrested or the eleven million individuals jailed each year in the United States (Federal Bureau of Investigation 2013). Equally important is that details about these calls for assistance can be heard by anyone over public radio frequencies. Most city police departments and 911 dispatchers still rely on open access radio frequencies to communicate, meaning that anyone with a radio, cell phone,

Robert Vargas is Neubauer Family Assistant Professor of Sociology and director of the Violence, Law, and Politics Lab at the University of Chicago. **Kayla Preito-Hodge** is a graduate student in the sociology department at the University of Massachusetts-Amherst and a recipient of the National Science Foundation's Graduate Research Fellowship. **Jeremy Christofferson** is a graduate student in the sociology department at the University of Notre Dame.

© 2019 Russell Sage Foundation. Vargas, Robert, Kayla Preito-Hodge, and Jeremy Christofferson. 2019. "Digital Vulnerability: The Unequal Risk of E-Contact with the Criminal Justice System." *RSF: The Russell Sage Foundation Journal of the Social Sciences* 5(1): 71–88. DOI: 10.7758/RSF.2019.5.1.04. We thank Ariel Azar and Anil Sindhwani for research assistance on this project, as well as Dan Gillion, Jothie Rajah, the American Bar Foundation, the Russell Sage Foundation, and the anonymous reviewers for comments and critiques on earlier components of this article. Direct correspondence to: Robert Vargas at robvargas@uchicago.edu, 1126 E. 59th St., Chicago, IL 60637.

Open Access Policy: *RSF: The Russell Sage Foundation Journal of the Social Sciences* is an open access journal. This article is published under a Creative Commons Attribution-NonCommercial-NoDerivs 3.0 Unported License.

or computer can eavesdrop on police-dispatcher communication.[1] On the one hand, this enables journalists or citizen groups to monitor and scrutinize police behavior; on the other, it provides criminals, gangs, or predatory businesses with the ability to collect personal information about citizens for malicious or exploitive purposes (Jacobs 2015; Lageson 2016; Vargas 2016).

The ease by which police-dispatcher communication can be compromised is one of many recent examples of how technological advances in the administration of criminal justice policies is having detrimental and often unintended consequences for citizens. The challenge of protecting callers' or witnesses' identities is becoming even more challenging as police departments incorporate "big data" in their everyday activities (Jacobs and Wright 2006; Brayne 2017). Similarly, the advent of criminal record databases is placing citizens at greater risk of having their personal information hacked or exploited by third parties (Jacobs 2015; Lageson 2016; Vuolo, Lageson, and Uggen 2017). The adoption of new technologies is increasing citizens' e-contact with the criminal justice system and, in doing so, producing new forms of digital racial inequalities.

This article introduces the concept of *digital vulnerability* to help scholars begin to unpack the extent to which e-contact with the criminal justice system is placing citizens at unequal risk of harm. Digital vulnerability refers to citizens' risk of having incriminating information publicly disclosed and exploited by third parties. Although the article focuses on 911 calls, digital vulnerability is a concept that can be applied more broadly to other criminal justice technologies.

We introduce digital vulnerability through a comparative case study of interaction between police officers and 911 dispatchers over public radio frequencies in Chicago. Using sixty hours of audio recordings across three radio zones, defined as bounded geographical areas in which officers and dispatchers communicate, we examine the extent to which officers or dispatchers disclose identifiable information about callers: the caller's first name, last name, or home address. Each radio zone in the study served a demographically distinct community—the first predominantly African American, the second predominantly white, and the third predominantly Latino.

Findings revealed startling racial inequality in digital vulnerability. Black and Latino communities had far greater digital vulnerability than white communities. Approximately one of every ten calls made to police in zones serving racial minorities disclosed identifiable information about the caller—12 percent for blacks (44 of 371 calls), 8 percent for Latinos (11 of 148). In contrast, not a single call of 121 in the white police zone disclosed identifiable information. When we exclude citizen calls for direct police assistance, where the caller is in immediate danger and needs help at their home address, the inequality is even greater. Forty percent of third-party calls (47 of 116) in the black radio zone and 25 percent in the Latino (30 of 120) revealed identifiable information, whereas none of the forty-three in the white radio zone revealed identifiable information. In Chicago, where gangs have been shown to retaliate against residents who call police as well as use police radio scanners to identify callers in order to retaliate, these data disclosures put racial minorities at greater risk of harm than whites (Hagedorn 2015; Venkatesh 2006; on scanners, Vargas 2016).

Our findings have several implications. First, we show that digital vulnerability can be a useful concept for identifying inequalities rooted in technology and citizen e-contact with the criminal justice system. For example, our study reveals that the lack of citizen cooperation with police may stem not only from instances of overt police brutality or cultural dispositions, but also from local government's inability to digitally protect callers' identities (Desmond, Papachristos, and Kirk 2016; Kirk and Papachristos 2011). Second, our findings

---

1. One of the arguments police use for continuing use of open radio frequencies is the ease of communication it allows across city agencies in the event of a major emergency. Encrypting a communication channel (whether radio or digital) would require agencies to bypass security interfaces, which may delay or inhibit interagency coordination.

show the importance of studying intermediaries such as 911 dispatchers, who are trusted to provide private information about citizens to agents of the criminal justice system. Such intermediaries, though well intentioned, may unknowingly be doing more harm than good to citizens. Finally, as one of the first to systematically examine police-dispatcher communication, this study has policy implications for training emergency dispatchers as well as for debates over regulating public access to police radio frequencies.

TECHNOLOGY AND CRIMINAL JUSTICE CONTACT

Technological advances in media and communication are pivotal symbols of economic progress in society, but these advances have also accelerated growth in surveillance practices, hacking, and data breaches. With respect to law enforcement, technological advances are making citizen e-contact with the criminal justice system more prevalent. For example, local governments are increasingly using big data to learn more about wanted or "potential" criminals through algorithms estimating citizens' likelihood of committing crime (Asher and Arthur 2017). Police are also collecting data on citizens by sifting through databases produced by other governmental agencies such as immigration, social security, and departments of children and family services (Brayne 2017; Stuart 2016). Scholars describe such integration as parallel state structures, whose left and right hands govern disadvantaged populations through welfare and criminal justice policy (Soss, Fording, and Schram 2011).

Despite the growth of citizen e-contact with the criminal justice system, much of the literature to date has focused on physical contact between law enforcement agents and citizens through arrests or police stops. Researchers have used cross-sectional or longitudinal data on individuals to show how experiencing incarceration, arrest, or conviction can negatively affect health (Massoglia and Pridemore 2015; Turney 2014), political participation (Manza and Uggen 2008; Sugie 2015), and economic life chances (Wakefield and Wildeman 2013). Contact with the criminal justice system is thought to affect individuals physically, organizationally, or legally. For example, experiencing arrest or incarceration can be a stressor that, compounded with others, has deleterious effects on mental or physical health (Sewell and Jefferson 2016; Sugie and Turney 2017). Similarly, the trauma of incarceration or police brutality can operate organizationally, formerly incarcerated individuals being less likely to participate, apply for, or seek help from public agencies (Brayne 2014; Desmond, Papachristos, and Kirk 2016). Contact also has legal effects, in that laws that disenfranchise ex-convicts from employment or social services create poverty traps for the formerly incarcerated (Pager 2003).

Digital or electronic forms of contact have been less explored, but a handful of scholars are charting important new ground in this area by studying online criminal record databases (Lageson 2016; Jacobs 2015; Vuolo, Lageson, and Uggen 2017). Companies that run these databases acquire criminal information from the federal government for mass distribution on the internet (Jacobs 2015). These websites include mug shots and police reports of the accused and have the reputation of presenting false and misleading information. Sarah Lageson argues that such sites constitute a new form of punishment and discrimination for individuals impacted by the criminal justice system, many of whom are unaware these records even exist (2016).

By typing the names of job applicants into a search engine, employers are provided a baseless platform on which they can judge applicants' moral character. Proponents of online criminal record databases argue that their services fulfill the "public's right to know." Scholars, however, maintain that these databases are far from genuine in intent and are financially exploitative and socially damaging (Jacobs 2015; Lageson 2016; Vuolo, Lageson, and Uggen 2017). For instance, on Mugshots.com, web publishers disclaim the accuracy of the records on the database, but refuse to remove the information in the event an individual is found not guilty or the case is dismissed—ultimately leaving permanent marks of criminality. Third-party companies, such as Internetreputation.com, advertise their removal services for hundreds of dollars a month to individuals damaged by online criminal record databases. James Jacobs argues that these companies are highly predatory and that "On the surface, the mug shot sites and the reputation firms are mortal enemies. But behind the scenes, they have a symbiotic relationship that wrings cash out of the people exposed" (2015, 84). Laws governing the dissemination of private criminal information online remain largely absent; however, some states have begun taking preventative approaches by regulating how criminal justice agencies disseminate citizens' personal information (Jacobs 2015).

Law enforcement and private companies are not the only actors seeking private electronic information about citizens. Criminal groups do as well. In the age of the internet, hackers have targeted government databases to steal citizen identities. For example, in 2015, a group of hackers broke into databases of the Office of Personnel Management and stole 20.5 million social security numbers (Davis 2015). Similar data breaches have occurred among local governments in Minnesota, Georgia, and California. Hackers have even compromised some of the most secretive government agencies, such as the National Security Administration and Internal Revenue Service (Shane, Perloth, and Sanger 2017).

Stealing sensitive information about citizens from government data sources does not require significant technological expertise. With respect to policing, technological advances have made it easy for anyone with a smart phone, tablet, or computer, to listen and monitor police radio communication at any time and from any location on the planet. Prior to the internet, listening to police chatter over radio frequencies required purchasing a handheld scanner and doing research to learn the frequencies and geographies in which police communicated. Journalists were the most likely to be adept at these skills, given their goal to be the first to break a news story.

Today, monitoring police scanners is becoming more common among criminal groups. Some use scanners while committing a crime to learn precisely when police are on their way to the scene (Liebowitz 2012). Most troubling are criminal groups that monitor police radio communication to conduct countersurveillance on citizens reporting crimes to police (Vargas 2016). Scholars of organized crime have long argued that Omerta, or code of silence, is essential to the survival of organized criminal groups (Gambetta 1996; Sanchez-Jankowski 1991). Omerta is an informal expectation that criminal groups enforce through the threat of violence that no citizen is to report the organization's activities to police or cooperate with any police investigations (Gambetta 1996). In the United States, Omerta is often referred to as an inner-city code of silence, which scholars have found among Mexican and African American organized criminal groups (Vargas 2016; Venkatesh 2006).

The practices and policies of police-dispatch communication provide another way to explore inequalities generated through e-contact with the criminal justice system. While providing police with as much information as possible can expedite calls for service, dispatchers may be unaware of the consequences resulting from divulging identifiable information about callers over public radio frequencies.

DIGITAL VULNERABILITY

The notion of vulnerability is familiar in the criminal justice contact literature and sociology more broadly. It is the idea that social structures render groups more likely to experience pain, suffering, or marginalization than others (Fineman 2008). The idea of a digital vulnerability extends prior research by emphasizing that citizen vulnerability occurs not only physically during police stops on the streets or trials in county courts, but also digitally across cyberspace and radio waves. It concerns governments' ability to safeguard citizen's private information from groups with malicious intentions. Therefore, we define digital vulnerability as citizens' risk of having incriminating information publicly disclosed and exploited by third parties. By defining digital vulnerability this way, we aim to advance research identifying inequalities generated by the criminal justice system's use of technology.

We use radio communication between 911 dispatchers and police officers to assess the degree of digital vulnerability across three racially distinct geographical areas in Chicago. The goal is to assess how much identifiable information is revealed about callers that criminal groups could use to retaliate which, in turn, would have deleterious consequences on police-community relations. The concept of digital vulnerability, however, is not meant to be unique to citizens' 911 phone calls. Other forms of e-contact with the criminal justice system may render citizens digitally vulnerable to a wider variety of consequences than retaliation from criminal groups. For example, in Chicago, police collect data on Latino youth in disadvantaged neighborhoods and erroneously label many as "gang affiliated" (Serrato 2017). Other government agencies looking to employ or provide services to Latino youth can access these data when running background checks, which can lead to unwarranted denials of jobs or benefits. Thus, living in a disadvantaged neighborhood with high degrees of e-contact with the criminal justice system can render certain populations more digitally vulnerable to a host of negative consequences.

THE RISKS OF DIGITAL VULNERABILITY OVER POLICE RADIO FREQUENCIES IN CHICAGO

This study of digital vulnerability over police radio frequencies was motivated by a systematic qualitative study on citizen police reporting in Chicago, conducted by the lead author, that discovered the risks of dispatchers disclosing identifiable information about callers. After canvassing sixty randomly selected blocks of Chicago's Little Village neighborhood, Robert Vargas identified a cluster of eight blocks where the majority of residents refused to report crimes to police because allegedly corrupt officers disclosed caller identities directly to gang members (2016). To assess the validity of residents' allegations against police, Vargas conducted additional fieldwork with gang members and police officers on residential blocks and discovered that gang members were identifying callers by monitoring police radio communication, retaliating by firebombing callers' houses, and spreading misinformation by claiming the police had intentionally "ratted out" residents.

"You got to understand," said Freddy, a former gang member, "some of the gang members have police scanners. Not just any scanner, but the actual police scanner. So when cops make the call, they hear caller's names and addresses."

Vargas confirmed these findings by directly observing gang members with police scanners in their possession and learning addresses of residents with whom the gang had retaliated. Gang members acquired police-issued scanners by breaking into police squad cars, and regularly used them to, as one gang leader described, "listen in on what the cops were up to" as well as "tell [residents] it was the cops who ratted them out to scare the shit out of them" (2016, 131).

Through interviews with gang members, Vargas learned the addresses of seven residents against whom the gang had retaliated as a result of information disclosed over police radio frequencies. In each of the retaliated households, residents had called 911 to report witnessing gang members carrying weapons or acting suspiciously, only to have their homes set on fire within the next twenty-four hours. In the aftermath of these fire bombings, gang members engaged in additional work of deceiving residents by claiming that corrupt police officers intentionally disclosed caller identities to the gang. In total, Vargas identified seven instances of gang members identifying and retaliating against residents through monitoring police radio communication between 2009 and 2011, which influenced residents on these four blocks to refrain from reporting crime to police (2016). Aside from the Chicago context, researchers have similarly found gangs or criminals listening to police radio communication to either retaliate against residents or evade police capture in Maryland (Liebowitz 2012), Washington, D.C. (Paquette 2015), and St. Louis (Patrick 2014).

Ideally, one would survey gangs of Chicago to assess the extent to which they monitor police radio communication and retaliate against callers, but such an approach is not feasible given the low likelihood that these groups would readily divulge such information. Thus, in this study, we aim to advance this line of inquiry by examining the extent to which residents are vulnerable to retaliation by having identifiable information disclosed over open

Table 1. Radio Zone Characteristics

	White Zone 4	Black Zone 8	Latino Zone 13
Frequency	460.15	460.2	460.45
Police districts	1, 18	4, 6	9
Neighborhoods	Gold Coast, Lincoln Park	Auburn-Gresham, Chatham	Bridgeport, Brighton Park, New City
Total population	156,424	77,201	156,424
Number of gangs	2	7	15
Homicide rate	2	40	28
Citizen complaints	1.04	4.77	0.87

Source: Authors' calculations based on American Community Survey five-year Estimates, 2010–2015 (U.S. Census Bureau 2016); Invisible Institute 2016; City of Chicago Data Portal 2016; Chicago Crime Commission 2012.
Note: Rates are per 100,000.

airwaves. To do so, we systematically examined police radio communication across three geographical areas of Chicago.

METHODS AND COMPARATIVE CASE STUDY DESIGN

The Chicago Police Department is structured into twenty-five geographical administrative units known locally as districts. In these districts, 911 dispatchers relay calls for service to patrol officers across fourteen radio zones, each having a unique frequency. Data for this study come from sixty hours of audio recordings across three police radio zones, twenty hours per zone. In each zone, we recorded one-hour increments from 7 to 8 p.m. and from midnight to 1 a.m., Monday through Friday, for two weeks. Audio recordings were conducted in July of 2016 for zones 8 and 13, and July through August of 2017 for zone 4. We recorded audio from police radio zones using www.broadcastify.com, a free website that plays a live feed of all police radio zones on the internet. We played the radio zones on loud speakers and used a handheld recording device to record audio.[2]

To assess racial differences, we sampled three police radio zones that served racially homogenous neighborhoods. Zone 8 included patrol officers from districts 4 and 6, which served the predominantly black neighborhoods of Auburn-Gresham and Chatham. Zone 13 included district 9, which served the predominantly Latino neighborhoods of Brighton Park, Bridgeport, and New City. Zone 4 included districts 1 and 18, which served the predominantly white and affluent downtown central business district, the Gold Coast, and Lincoln Park.

Table 1 provides an overview of each radio zone's characteristics derived from census data averaged across the police districts or neighborhoods in each zone. The figures in table 1 should be interpreted with some caution as the neighborhood and police radio zone boundaries do not perfectly match (see figure 1).

The black and Latino radio zones had high homicide rates, rates of citizen complaints against police officers, and greater presence of street gangs.[3] Zone 8 serves neighborhoods home to infamous black gangs like the Black P. Stones, Gangster Disciples, and the Black Disciples. Zone 13 is home to violent Latino gangs such as the Maniac Latin Disciples, Satan Disciples, and Insane Spanish Cobras. Disclosing identifiable information about callers in

---

2. For this study, we do not have access to interactions between callers and 911 dispatchers. Audio of citizen calls to 911 dispatchers in Illinois are only accessible to researchers making Freedom of Information Act (FOIA) requests within thirty days that the call was made. This severely hampers any effort to systematically assess audio of 911 calls over time.

3. Data on citizen complaints against officers from the Invisible Institute's citizen police data project, which aggregates the number of complaints filed against police officers at the district level. Our calculation is based on the sum of complaints across districts in each zone from 2010 to 2015.

Figure 1. Locations of Police Zones in Chicago Community Areas

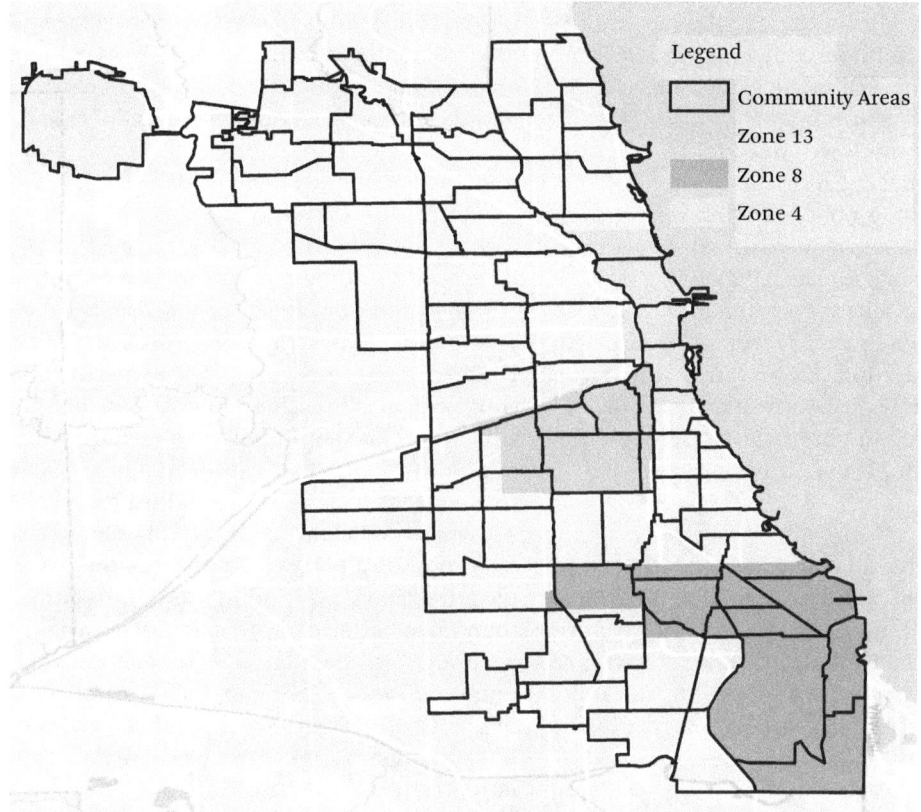

Source: City of Chicago Radio Communications 2016.

these gang-infested areas heightens the risk of citizens' digital vulnerability in these radio zones.

To analyze the data, we conducted multiple rounds of coding using the audio coding tool in NVivo. We spliced the calls in the audio files into segments and assigned each a unique ID. These audio segments were instances of dispatchers introducing calls for service to a police officer. Segments ranged between ten and forty-five seconds depending on how much information the dispatcher provided. Consider the following example of how we coded a segment, using pseudonyms, when a dispatcher introduced a new call for service to a police officer:

Call 71
DISPATCHER: 723, check for a suspicious person at 73rd and Vincent. A woman named Jennifer says there are two vehicles following her. She lost sight of them, but is scared to go home. One was a tan Toyota Camry, the other was a gray Astro van.

Sometimes chatter between officers and dispatchers for a case such as call 71 would continue for a few minutes while other calls would come in, thereby increasing the difficulty in following the thread of a conversation over time. Thus, to have as clean a sample as possible, we only coded the first interaction between the dispatcher and officer, such as in call 71, to avoid miscoding prolonged radio chatter to wrong calls. A total of 650 calls like call 71 formed the sample of our study.

The next round of coding consisted of entering call characteristics into an Excel spreadsheet. Specifically, we coded as zero (no) or 1 (yes) the following characteristics of each call: address provided for crime scene, first name of caller disclosed, last name of caller disclosed, home address of caller disclosed, and whether the caller was described as anonymous. In addition, we coded the type of crime for each call, as well as the date, time, and district where it occurred.

Most important, we coded for whether the caller was requesting direct assistance from police or requesting police assistance as a third-party or bystander. This distinction is crucial for our analysis because callers requesting direct assistance, like the woman in call 71, need to give identifiable information to receive help as soon as possible. As our study focuses on digital vulnerability, third-party calls are of most relevance to our analysis. Consider the following example of a third-party call:

> Case 86
> DISPATCHER: Suspicious person. 6000 S. Main Street. John Smith is calling. Male black, bald, and a mustache. White shirt, black shorts. Walking northbound trying to hold up people for money. John's family members trying to get more information by going door-to-door.

From the audio, we can deduce that a man named John Smith called police to investigate a suspicious person attempting to rob people on the street. In this example, we code the call with a 1 indicating that the call reported the address of the crime scene. Although the dispatcher did not disclose the caller's home address, he did disclose the caller's first and last name and shared that the caller's family was seeking more information from neighbors, which suggests that the caller lived on that block or nearby. Such a call, we argue, exemplifies dispatchers rendering citizens digitally vulnerable to retaliation from gangs. Third-party calls, rather than calls for direct assistance from people needing immediate police assistance, are the focus of our analysis across police radio zones.

To protect the privacy of callers, police officers, and dispatchers in this study, we used pseudonyms throughout the analysis and presentation of results. The audio files contain identifiable information, and we stored these data in a password-protected computer with no internet access. According to Illinois law and the Federal Communications Commission (FCC), police radio communication is considered public record, and can thus be recorded, analyzed, and scrutinized (FCC 2008). However, in the spirit of protecting the privacy of callers, police officers, and dispatchers, we use pseudonyms for all individuals in this study.

The process of coding and cleaning the data took six months. Afterward, we created graphs describing findings across the three police zones. In addition, we use two measures to calculate digital vulnerability across each radio zone. The first measure is the share of total calls with disclosed identifiable information, which uses the sum of direct-assistance calls and third-party calls as the denominator. The second measure is the share of third-party calls with disclosed identifiable information, which only uses third-party calls as the denominator. Last, we report our findings as counts rather than rates because of the inability to produce accurate total population estimates for each police radio zone. As figure 1 shows, police radio zone boundaries are smaller than neighborhood boundaries, which means that any population estimate derived from neighborhoods would overestimate the population within each radio zone.

FINDINGS

The disclosure of identifiable information about callers over the radio occurred when dispatchers or officers stated a caller's first name, last name, or home address. Consider the following example:

> Case 278 in the Black Radio Zone
> DISPATCHER: Suspicious car with occupants. 2116 West State. Dana says that a red and silver car, 4-door, several occupants, male and female, parked outside of her house, and they have been there for a while.

In this call, the dispatcher disclosed the caller's first name. Although it is unclear whether 2116 West State is Dana's address, the dispatcher provides the caller's approximate home address when saying the suspicious car's occupants are parked outside Dana's house. Outside parties interested in identifying and re-

Figure 2. Total Calls and Third-Party Calls that Disclose Identifiable Information

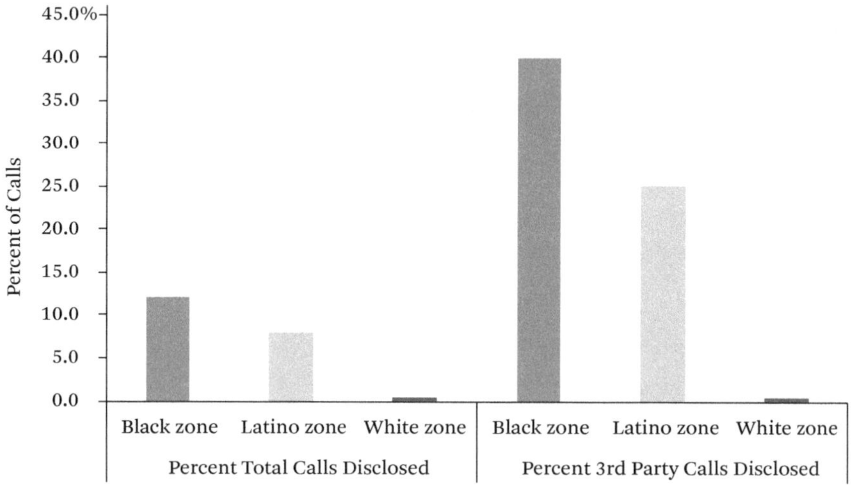

Source: Authors' calculations.

taliating would only have to find a woman named Dana near the address of 2116 West State. At other times, dispatchers were more explicit when disclosing a caller's address.

Case 115, Latino Radio Zone
DISPATCHER: Person wanted at 4700 S. Chester. Diana Rodriguez is calling from 4872 Washington Street. She says a male is wanted, and that he was at that address.

In case 115, the dispatcher provides the full name and home address of a caller informing the police of the location of a man wanted by police. This disclosure renders the caller especially vulnerable to retaliation, as the consequences of her call may result in jail time for the wanted criminal. Moreover, if the caller's tip is not true, any criminal or friend of a criminal listening would know that Diana Rodriguez provides information to police on wanted suspects.

Case 298 in the Latino Radio Zone
DISPATCHER: There is a criminal damage to property in progress at 2543 S. May, where James was calling. Says that there is a male trying to remove a boot from an unknown vehicle. He has no other information. Although we are trying to reach him on the radio.

Case 298 is another example of dispatchers disclosing identifiable information about a citizen making a third-party call. In contrast to other calls that reference a block such as 2500 S. May, the dispatcher gives an exact address (2543 S. May). These select cases exemplify the types of third-party calls that we quantify and analyze in the following section. Findings reveal stark patterns about each police radio zone as well as the kind of crimes reported to police that are likely to result in caller identities being disclosed.

Quantitative Results
Figure 2 illustrates descriptive statistics from the two measures of digital vulnerability in each police radio zone. If we use the total number of calls as the denominator, 12 percent disclosed identifiable information in the black zone (forty-four of 371) relative to 8 percent in the Latino zone (eleven of 148) and 0 percent in the white zone (total of 131). This means that, in the black and Latino zones, approximately one of every ten calls reveals an identifiable piece of information about the caller. Even further, this means that 2.2 caller identities are disclosed per hour in the black zone and 0.55 per hour in the Latino zone.

Focusing on third-party calls illuminates more troubling findings. Forty percent in the black zone (forty-four of 111) and 25 percent in the Latino zone (eleven of forty-four) revealed identifiable information about callers. These figures signified that black and Latino citizens had greater digital vulnerability than whites and were at greater risk of retaliation.

Examining variation in digital vulnerability by type of crime across each zone reveals more detailed findings. Figure 3 provides a breakdown of the crime type reported by the caller. It also breaks down calls by zone and whether they were third-party calls or direct-assistance calls. Figure 3 illuminates the importance of distinguishing between calls for direct assistance and third-party calls given that, understandably, to receive assistance as soon as possible, victims of domestic abuse or batteries in progress should have their names and home addresses disclosed to police.

Looking exclusively at third-party calls, however, reveals a different pattern. In the black zone, dispatchers disclosed identifiable information especially of citizens reporting batteries, gang disturbances, noise complaints, and shots fired. Relative to Latinos and whites, citizens reporting crimes on people carrying guns or knives had their identities disclosed at by far the highest rate (27 percent). This might reflect the higher number of people carrying weapons in these areas, or a higher chance that dispatchers reveal more information about callers when discussing weapons-related crimes on radio frequencies. Because a call about weapons is an especially dangerous one for the police officers investigating it, dispatchers may want to give as much information to the police as possible out of concern for officers' safety.

In the Latino zone, dispatchers disclosed identifiable information for citizens reporting noise complaints and suspicious persons. It makes sense for these crime types to be common among third-party calls, given that they are crimes a citizen is likely to observe by being in a public space or looking out on the street from a window. In addition, 911 dispatchers are required to ask for the name and address of the caller for police to follow up if necessary (Preusse and Gibson 2016). Interestingly, in both black and Latino zones, dispatchers do not reveal identifiable information about crimes typically associated with organized criminal groups or the informal economy. Fewer than 5 percent of calls reporting prostitution, drug dealing, or gang disturbances revealed identifiable information about the caller. This might reflect dispatchers being careful with caller's information, or the fact that few citizens even report these crimes in the first place.

Figure 4 displays data exclusively from third-party calls but groups them by the kind of identifiable information revealed and radio zone. The figure reveals that first and last names account for a larger proportion of identifiable information disclosed by dispatchers than home addresses. This suggests that, in most cases, criminals eavesdropping to identify "snitches" deduce caller identities by names and crime locations. Identifying a caller based on this limited information, according to gang ethnographers, would not be difficult because gangs tend to be adeptly aware of the community members within their territories (Sanchez-Jankowski 1991; Vargas 2016; Venkatesh 2006). Gangs inquire through family members, friends, or surrogates at community policing meetings to learn the names of neighbors who call police. On identifying callers, gangs may coerce residents into refraining from calling police again using strategies ranging from bribery to violent retaliation.

Figure 4 also illuminates some interesting racial differences. The black radio zone not only had the highest percentage of calls disclosing first and last names, it was also the only zone where dispatchers gave away callers' home addresses. Not a single caller home address was disclosed in the white or Latino zone. This finding illuminates a wide disparity in digital vulnerability across communities: African Americans were far more vulnerable to data breaches over police radio zones than any other group. It is also important that in both figure 3 and figure 4, not a single call in the white zone disclosed any piece of identifiable information about the caller.

To gain further insight on factors driving differences across districts, we ran four logistic regression models displayed on table 2. Models 1, 2, and 3 predict the probability of the police reporting the first name, last name, and home address of the caller. Model 4 predicts the probability of reporting at least one of these three pieces of identifiable informa-

Figure 3. Disclosed Calls by Call Type and Crime Type

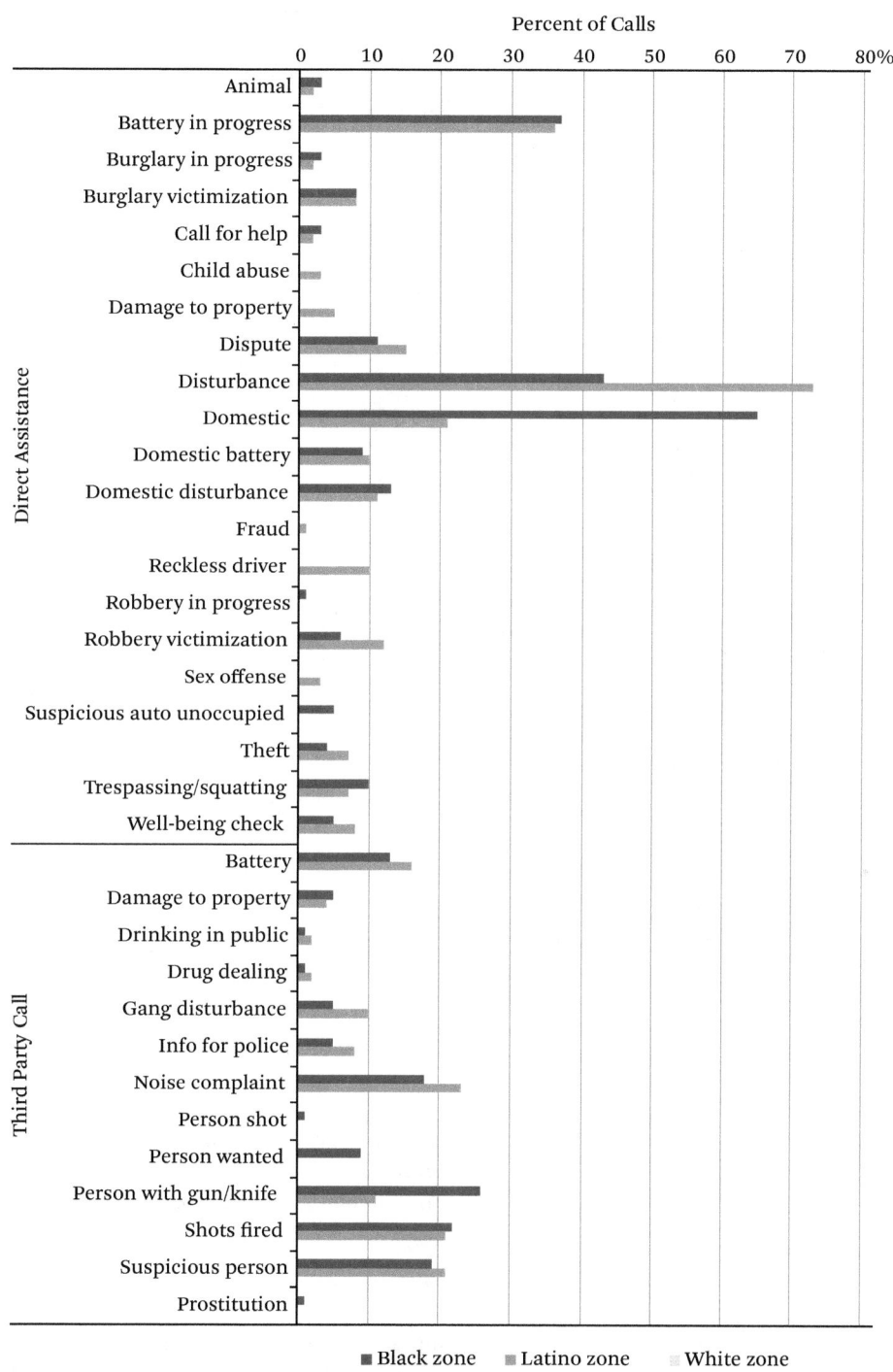

Source: Authors' calculations.

Figure 4. Disclosed Calls by Identifiable Information

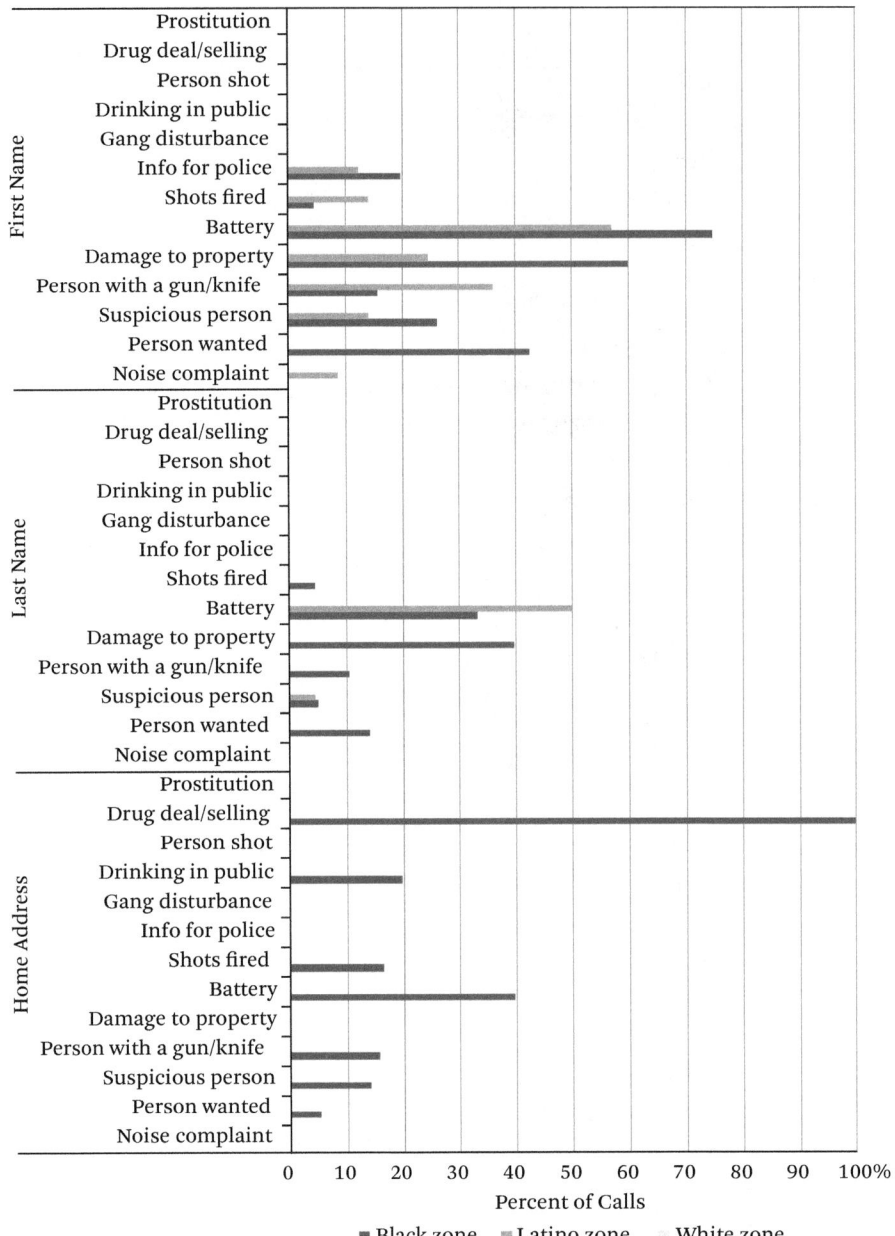

Source: Authors' calculations.

tion. Each of the models contains the same independent variables for radio zone, the white radio zone being the reference category, and type of call, and public disorder calls the reference category. Public disorder calls involved less serious crimes such as noise complaints, public disturbances, suspicious persons, suspicious automobiles, reckless drivers, and public drinking.

With respect to police radio zones, the models show no significant differences between zones on the probability of reporting callers' last names. The Latino and black zones, however, disclose callers' first name and home ad-

Table 2. Logistic Regression Models: Probability of Reporting Different Kind of Information

	Model 1 First Name		Model 2 Last Name		Model 3 Home Address		Model 4 At Least One Piece of Information	
	Coef.	AME	Coef.	AME	Coef.	AME	Coef.	AME
District (ref = district 18)								
District 3	1.077*	0.154**	0.329	0.022	0.278	0.026	1.093**	0.164***
	(0.554)	(0.062)	(0.765)	(0.045)	(0.652)	(0.058)	(0.515)	(0.064)
District 6	1.148**	0.166***	0.842	0.068	1.214*	0.144**	1.554***	0.253***
	(0.555)	(0.063)	(0.757)	(0.046)	(0.642)	(0.060)	(0.514)	(0.065)
Type of call (ref = disorder)								
Intelligence	0.360	0.058	0.784	0.040	1.232***	0.148**	0.750**	0.147*
	(0.412)	(0.071)	(0.684)	(0.043)	(0.448)	(0.068)	(0.368)	(0.080)
Violent	0.465**	0.077**	1.265***	0.081***	0.575**	0.054**	0.696***	0.135***
	(0.215)	(0.036)	(0.379)	(0.023)	(0.292)	(0.027)	(0.200)	(0.039)
Property	0.931***	0.173***	1.619***	0.122***	1.394***	0.176***	1.312***	0.280***
	(0.307)	(0.063)	(0.473)	(0.047)	(0.371)	(0.057)	(0.294)	(0.066)
Domestic	2.312***	0.501***	2.180***	0.210***	3.013***	0.536***	2.988***	0.619***
	(0.259)	(0.050)	(0.390)	(0.042)	(0.302)	(0.050)	(0.303)	(0.044)
Constant	−2.630***		−3.874***		−3.215***		−2.609***	
	(0.556)		(0.792)		(0.657)		(0.517)	
Observations	650		650		650		650	

Source: Authors' calculations.
Note: Coef. = Coefficients. AME = Average Marginal Effect.
*$p < .1$; **$p < .05$; ***$p < .01$

dresses at a significantly higher rate than the white zone. A call made in the Latino police radio zone has a 16.4 percent higher probability of disclosing identifiable information, and one made in the black zone has a 25.3 percent higher probability, both relative to the white zone.

Across all four models, calls reporting domestic violence had the highest probability of disclosing first names (50.1 percent), last names (21 percent), home addresses (53.6 percent), or at least one piece of identifiable information (61.9 percent) relative to public disorder calls. Calls reporting property crimes such as trespassing, squatting, damage to property, burglary, and property theft had the second highest level of probability of disclosing identifiable information across all four models. Intelligence calls involving instances where callers had intelligence for police on wanted persons and violent calls involving persons shot, kidnappings, robberies, batteries, and people carrying guns, also had significantly higher probabilities of disclosing all types of information, but with smaller probabilities than domestic and property calls.

Model results confirm that dispatchers most frequently disclose identifiable information during direct-assistance calls for domestic violence and third-party calls involving property crime. Third-party calls on violent crimes or intelligence were less common but still significantly more likely to reveal identifiable information than public disorder calls. Overall, findings show that police radio chatter reveals identifiable information about callers at a troubling rate. Moreover, findings show substantial racial inequality as dispatchers disclosed information about callers in black and Latino neighborhoods but no information about callers in white neighborhoods.

MAKING SENSE OF UNEQUAL DIGITAL VULNERABILITY

All dispatchers serving Chicago work from a central hub station in the West Loop neighborhood that field calls for police, fire, and medical emergency services from throughout the city. Each dispatcher is assigned a zone or an area in which they take calls. Informal interviews with dispatchers suggest four factors that could help explain our findings. The first is a lack of resources to adequately staff Chicago's 911 dispatch system. In 2016, a report by Chicago's Office of Emergency Management found that 49 percent of the city's 911 emergency call takers are absent on any given day, which leaves the rest of the operators overrun with work. All 911 dispatchers qualify for the Family and Medical Leave Act, which permits employees up to twelve weeks of unpaid time off work. Advocates of 911 dispatchers argue that such time off is essential to the mental health of dispatchers, who have higher rates of depression, anxiety, and post-traumatic stress disorder (Pierce and Lilly 2012). Even worse, to address staff shortages, supervisors force dispatchers to work overtime, sometimes up to sixty hours a week. In fact, one Chicago dispatcher earned $91,000 worth of overtime pay in 2016; his base salary was $77,784 (Sargent 2013). The city government's underfunding of dispatchers, coupled with the trauma of the job, has created an environment where dispatchers are extremely overworked. In such work conditions, it is reasonable to expect mistakes to be made.

The second possible factor contributing to our results are the lax rules governing dispatcher conduct. According to the Office of Emergency Management & Communications in Chicago, rules protecting the release of callers' names and addresses over public radio frequencies are limited. Protocol instructs dispatchers to ask callers if they would like to request anonymity, but it is not a requirement. Protocol also does not discipline dispatchers for revealing identifiable information about callers. In fact, the Chicago Police Department website instructs citizens to "inform the call taker if you do not want your name given to responding police units." Thus, the burden of choosing whether to remain anonymous is on citizens, not dispatchers.

A third factor is dispatchers' well-intentioned desire to help. Conversations with three dispatchers in Chicago with whom we shared our findings revealed that during most calls dispatchers are simply trying to provide as much information to the police as possible. One dispatcher explained that revealing a caller's address happens because "you want to get that call out to as many people as possible." The dispatchers we spoke to were hesitant to provide more detail on their firsthand experiences.

In 2016, however, a journalist interviewed a Chicago dispatcher in-depth and found that the intense trauma dispatchers hear makes them want to help callers as much as possible, and that this can often translate into providing caller information. Yana Kunichoff writes that "the dispatchers say their jobs are often misunderstood, and the criticisms levied against them are misguided at best. Their work is performed in a constantly tense environment, using a complicated and demanding technological system, under the looming threat of budget cuts" (2016, n.p.). Our inquiry into the workings of 911 dispatch in Chicago suggest that an underfunded and inadequately staffed emergency management office bears much of the responsibility for the findings in our study.

Fourth, neighborhood conditions also matter. Police officers in black and Latino neighborhoods have a significantly higher number of calls for service related to violent crimes, which may overburden dispatchers or police officers and make them prone to mistakes (Klinger 1997; Vargas 2016). Similarly, the low rates of violent crime in Chicago's white neighborhoods, which tend to be more affluent, such as the white zone in this study, make it less likely for 911 dispatchers to disclose identifiable information about white callers. Perhaps if we included a low-income white neighborhood in the study, the racial differences in our findings would have been less dramatic. Such a comparison, however, would be impossible because Chicago lacks a low-income white community comparable to black or Latino low-income communities.

It is likely that a combination of these four factors contributes to the inequality in digital vulnerability across the three radio zones. An overworked and severely mentally stressed workforce coupled with high volumes of calls from high-crime neighborhoods produces the conditions generating racially stratified digital vulnerability in Chicago.

CONCLUSIONS

In this article, we examine police-dispatcher radio communication, an older, simple, and frequently used technology, to introduce the concept of digital vulnerability for measuring inequality in citizens' risk of personal data disclosures by government agencies. Our findings suggest digital vulnerability, with respect to 911 calls for police assistance, is a real concern, especially in low-income, high-crime, minority neighborhoods. Although many residents of such communities come into contact with the criminal justice system through police stops or arrests, millions more have indirect e-contact through emergency 911 calls for police assistance, and the information conveyed in these interactions is being dangerously disclosed over public radio frequencies. This finding has several scholarly and policy implications.

First, studying digital vulnerability can illuminate inequalities generated by technologies that remain largely hidden because of the dearth of research on citizen e-contact with the criminal justice system. In the case of police-dispatcher communication, growth in low-cost smartphones and wireless internet access has made it easier for criminals to monitor police radio communication. Broadcastify.com, the website that broadcasts the Chicago Police Department's radio frequencies, averages nearly thirty thousand listeners per day. Although it is impossible to determine exactly how many individuals are listening to police scanner chatter for malicious purposes, it only takes a small portion of the thirty thousand to inflict sizable damage to police-community relations by retaliating against a caller. For example, Matthew Desmond, Andrew Papachristos, and David Kirk show that a single event such as the police beating of Frank Jude can contribute to a net loss of twenty-two thousand calls for 911 emergency service (2016). More research, however, is needed to understand the degree to which disclosing identifiable information about callers over police radio frequencies leads to violent retaliation. Nevertheless, our findings establish that the disclosure of caller information over police radio frequencies should be a concern to scholars and policymakers concerned with improving relationships between police and minority communities. Individuals' refusal to report crimes or cooperate with police investigations may stem not only from reluctance to inform on a friend or family member but also from police and dispatchers' inability to protect caller identities.

Second, our findings show the importance of studying third parties who broker contact between citizens and agents of the criminal justice system. Our case study focused on 911 dispatchers, but lawyers (Van Cleve 2016), social workers (Stuart 2016), tax preparers (Sykes et al. 2015), and health-care staff (Lara-Millán 2014) are also occupations that share information about citizens to government bodies via digital platforms. How do these third parties safeguard private information about citizens? More research is needed on the complicated bureaucratic layers of interaction between citizens and the state, and the degree to which sensitive information may be vulnerable to exploitation.

Scholars also need to consider the digital platforms in which citizen contact with the criminal justice system occurs. Much scholarly attention has been paid to physical police stops or, in our case study, 911 calls over radio frequencies. Other forms of contact, however, occur on Facebook, Twitter, or film footage from surveillance cameras or police body cameras. To better understand the consequences of e-contact with the criminal justice system, the field sites and social contexts in which scholars observe need to evolve and incorporate cell phone usage, email usage, and data security systems. The notion of digital vulnerability, introduced in this article, can help scholars identify and measure inequalities produced from digital forms of criminal justice contact.

Finally, the article offers several policy implications for the 911 dispatch system in Chicago and possibly other cities. First, findings suggest the need to fund and adequately staff the 911 emergency system in Chicago. Given the austere financial situation of U.S. cities, funding these agencies is probably easier said than done. Nevertheless, our findings at minimum suggest that dispatchers need to be far more careful with sharing caller information. Although it makes sense for dispatchers to provide police identifiable caller information when direct assistance is needed, dispatchers need to recognize that third-party callers do not need to be identified, especially when criminal groups listen to identify and retaliate against callers. Training dispatchers to recognize the difference between direct-assistance calls and third-party calls may decrease digital vulnerability in black and Latino communities.

Some may argue that our findings suggest the need for police departments to scramble their radio frequencies, which would prevent any third party from listening. We would caution any reader from drawing this conclusion. Cities such as Washington, D.C., and Santa Monica have already taken their police radio frequencies offline (Hudson 2011), but no evidence suggests that this has improved police-community relations, officer safety, or citizen calls for service. The debate between government transparency on the one hand and the need for security on the other is real and important. However, research remains scant on this issue and policymakers should not rush to conclusions. At the moment, we contend that simply training 911 dispatchers to be more discreet when sharing identifiable information about third-party callers should help reduce digital vulnerability. Hastily scrambling police radio frequencies may result in an unnecessary trade-off between the Democratic value of government transparency and citizen security.

REFERENCES

Asher, Jeff, and Rob Arthur. 2017. "Inside the Algorithm That Tries to Predict Gun Violence in Chicago." *New York Times*, June 13. Accessed September 8, 2018. https://www.nytimes.com/2017/06/13/upshot/what-an-algorithm-reveals-about-life-on-chicagos-high-risk-list.html.

Brayne, Sarah. 2014. "Surveillance and System Avoidance: Criminal Justice Contact and Institutional Attachment." *American Sociological Review* 79(3): 367–91.

———. 2017. "Big Data Surveillance: The Case of Policing." *American Sociological Review* 82(5): 977–1008.

Chicago Crime Commission. 2012. *The Gang Book*. Chicago: Cook County Crime Commission.

City of Chicago Data Portal. 2016. "Crimes 2001–Present." Accessed July 1, 2016. https://data.cityofchicago.org/Public-Safety/Crimes-2001-to-present/ijzp-q8t2.

City of Chicago Radio Communications. 2016. "General Order G03-01-01." Chicago Police Department. July 13. Accessed September 17, 2018.

http://directives.chicagopolice.org/directives/data/a7a57be2-128ff3f0-ae912-8ff7-442a6e5fde43e2df.html.

Davis, Julie. 2015. "Hacking of Government Computers Exposed 21.5 Million People." *New York Times*, July 9. Accessed September 8, 2018. https://www.nytimes.com/2015/07/10/us/office-of-personnel-management-hackers-got-data-of-millions.html.

Desmond, Matthew, Andrew V. Papachristos, and David S. Kirk. 2016. "Police Violence and Citizen Crime Reporting in the Black Community." *American Sociological Review* 81(5): 857–76.

Federal Bureau of Investigation. 2013. "Crime in the United States: Uniform Crime Reports for the United States 2012." Washington: U.S. Department of Justice.

Federal Communications Commission. 2008. "The Public and Broadcasting." Washington: The Media Bureau. Accessed September 17, 2018. https://www.fcc.gov/sites/default/files/public-and-broadcasting.pdf.

Fineman, Martha Albertson. 2008. "The Vulnerable Subject: Anchoring Equality in the Human Condition." *Yale Journal of Law & Feminism* 20(1): Article 2. Accessed September 8, 2018. https://digitalcommons.law.yale.edu/yjlf/vol20/iss1/2.

Gambetta, Diego. 1996. *The Sicilian Mafia: The Business of Private Protection*. Cambridge, Mass.: Harvard University Press.

Hagedorn, John. 2015. *The Insane Chicago Way: The Daring Plan by Chicago Gangs to Create a Spanish Mafia*. Chicago: University of Chicago Press.

Hudson, Travis. 2011. "Police Departments Encrypting Radio Traffic as Scanner Technology Proliferates." *Dallas News*, November 21.

Invisible Institute. 2016. "Citizens Police Data Project." Accessed July 1, 2016. https://cpdp.co/.

Jacobs, James B. 2015. *The Eternal Criminal Record*. Cambridge, Mass.: Harvard University Press.

Jacobs, Bruce A., and Richard Wright. 2006. *Street Justice: Retaliation in the Criminal Underworld*. Cambridge: Cambridge University Press.

Kirk, David S., and Andrew V. Papachristos. 2011. "Cultural Mechanisms and the Persistence of Neighborhood Violence." *American Journal of Sociology* 116(4): 1190–233.

Klinger, David A. 1997. "Negotiating Order in Patrol Work: An Ecological Theory of Police Response to Deviance." *Criminology* 35(2): 277–306.

Kunichoff, Yana. 2016. "Why Are Half of Chicago's 911 Operators Absent from Work?" *Chicago Magazine*, October 21. Accessed September 8, 2018. http://www.chicagomag.com/city-life/October-2016/911-call-takers.

Lageson, Sarah. 2016. "Found Out and Opting Out: The Consequences of Online Criminal Records for Families." *Annals of the American Academy of Political and Social Science*. 665(1): 127–41.

Lara-Millán, Armando. 2014. "Public Emergency Room Overcrowding in the Era of Mass Imprisonment." *American Sociological Review* 79(5): 866–87.

Manza, Jeff, and Christopher Uggen. 2008. *Locked Out: Felon Disenfranchisement and American Democracy*. Oxford: Oxford University Press.

Massoglia, Michael, and William Alex Pridemore. 2015. "Incarceration and Health." *Annual Review of Sociology* 41: 291–310.

NENA. 2017. "911 Statistics." Accessed September 8, 2018. https://www.nena.org/?page=911Statistics.

Pager, Devah. 2003. "The Mark of a Criminal Record." *American Journal of Sociology* 108(5): 937–75.

Paquette, Danielle. 2015. "Why Some Police Departments Let Anyone Listen to Their Scanner Conversations—Even Criminals." *Washington Post*, December 4.

Patrick, Robert. 2014. "St. Louis Police Encrypting Radio to Foil Listeners." *St Louis Post-Dispatch*, October 10.

Pierce, Heather, and Michelle M. Lilly. 2012. "Duty-Related Trauma Exposure in 911 Telecommunicators: Considering the Risk for Postraumatic Stress." *Journal of Traumatic Stress* 25(2): 211–15.

Preusse, Kimberly C., and Christina Gipson. 2016. "Dispatching Information in 911 Teams: A Case Study." In *Proceedings of the Human Factors and Ergonomics Society Annual Meeting*, vol. 60. Los Angeles: SAGE Publications.

Sanchez-Jankowski, Martin. 1991. *Islands in the Street: Gangs and American Urban Society*. Berkeley: University of California Press.

Sargent, Jordan. 2013. "The Chicago City Employee That Made $91,000 in Overtime in 2012 Has Things Figured Out." *Gawker*, January 22. Accessed September 8, 2018. http://gawker.com/5978182/the-chicago-city-employee-employee-that-made-91000-in-overtime-in-2012-has-things-figured-out.

Serrato, Jacqueline. 2017. "Ice Raids Could Crack Down on Mexican-American Gangs in Chicago." *Chicago Tribune*, July 24.

Sewell, Abigail A., and Kevin A. Jefferson. 2016. "Collateral Damage: The Health Effects of Invasive Police Encounters in New Yok City." *Journal of Urban Health* 93(1): 42–67.

Shane, Scott, Nicole Perloth, and David E. Sanger. 2017. "Security Breach and Spilled Secrets Have Shaken the N.S.A. to Its Core." *New York Times*, November 12.

Soss, Joe, Richard C. Fording, and Sanford Schram. 2011. *Disciplining the Poor: Neoliberal Paternalism and the Persistent Power of Race*. Chicago: University of Chicago Press.

Stuart, Forrest. 2016. *Down, Out, and Under Arrest: Policing and Everyday Life in Skid Row*. Chicago: University of Chicago Press.

Sugie, Naomi F. 2015. "Chilling Effects: Diminished Political Participation Among Partners of Formerly Incarcerated Men." *Social Problems* 62(4): 550–71.

Sugie, Naomi F., and Kristin Turney. 2017. "Beyond Incarceration: Criminal Justice Contact and Mental Health." *American Sociological Review* 82(4): 719–43.

Sykes, Jennifer, Katrin Kris, Kathryn Edin, and Sarah Halpern-Meekin. 2015. "Dignity and Dreams: What the Earned Income Tax Credit Means to Low-Income Families." *American Sociological Review* 80(2): 243–67.

Turney, Kristin. 2014. "Stress Proliferation Across Generations? Examining the Relationship Between Parental Incarceration and Childhood Health." *Journal of Health and Social Behavior* 55(3): 302–19.

U.S. Census Bureau. 2016. "Summary File." 2010–2015 American Community Survey. Washington: U.S. Census Bureau.

Van Cleve, Nicole Gonzalez. 2016. *Crook County: Racism and Injustice in America's Largest Criminal Court*. Stanford, Calif.: Stanford University Press.

Vargas, Robert. 2016. *Wounded City: Violent Turf Wars in a Chicago Barrio*. New York: Oxford University Press.

Venkatesh, Sudhir Alladi. 2006. *Off the Books*. Cambridge, Mass: Harvard University Press.

Vuolo, Mike, Sarah Lageson, and Chris Uggen. 2017. "Criminal Record Questions in the Era of 'Ban the Box.'" *Criminology and Public Policy* 16(1): 139–65.

Wakefield, Sara, and Christopher Wildeman. 2013. *Children of the Prison Boom: Mass Incarceration and the Future of American Inequality*. Oxford: Oxford University Press.

The Great Decoupling: The Disconnection Between Criminal Offending and Experience of Arrest Across Two Cohorts

VESLA M. WEAVER, ANDREW PAPACHRISTOS, AND MICHAEL ZANGER-TISHLER

Our study explores the arrest experiences of two generational cohorts—those entering adulthood on either side of a large shift in American policing. Using the National Longitudinal Survey of Youth (1979 and 1997), we find a stark increase in arrest odds among the later generation at every level of offending, suggesting a decoupling between contact with the justice system and criminal conduct. Furthermore, this decoupling became racially inflected. Blacks had a much higher probability of arrest at the start of the twenty-first century than both blacks of the generation prior and whites of the same generation. The criminal justice system, we argue, slipped from one in which arrest was low and strongly linked to offending to one where a substantial share of Americans experienced arrest without committing a crime.

Keywords: criminal justice contact, carceral state, criminal offending, generational change

"Black teens who commit a few crimes go to jail as often as white teens who commit dozens." So read a recent *Washington Post* headline (Ehrenfreund 2015). This finding emerged alongside other news that nearly three of every four young black men had been stopped and frisked by police in New York City but were much less likely than whites who were stopped to have contraband or be engaged in unlawful activity (Fagan et al. 2009). Although scholars have penned volumes on the rise of the carceral state, expansion of surveillance, several "wars on" policy developments, and their racially disparate consequences, the possibility that contact with criminal justice was increasingly disconnected from criminal offending (and that this disconnect was racially inflected) was barely taken up.[1]

Vesla M. Weaver is Bloomberg Distinguished Associate Professor of Political Science and Sociology at Johns Hopkins University. **Andrew Papachristos** is professor of sociology and a faculty fellow at the Institute for Policy Research, Northwestern University. **Michael Zanger-Tishler** is a recent graduate of Yale University.

© 2019 Russell Sage Foundation. Weaver, Vesla M., Andrew Papachristos, and Michael Zanger-Tishler. 2019. "The Great Decoupling: The Disconnection Between Criminal Offending and Experience of Arrest Across Two Cohorts." *RSF: The Russell Sage Foundation Journal of the Social Sciences* 5(1): 89–123. DOI: 10.7758/RSF.2019.5.1.05. Direct correspondence to: Vesla M. Weaver at vesla@jhu.edu, Departments of Political Science and Sociology, 338 Mergenthaler Hall, 3400 N. Charles St., Baltimore, MD 22181; Andrew Papachristos at avp@northwestern.edu, Institute for Policy Research, Northwestern University; and Michael Zanger-Tishler at michael.zanger-tishler@yale.edu.

Open Access Policy: *RSF: The Russell Sage Foundation Journal of the Social Sciences* is an open access journal. This article is published under a Creative Commons Attribution-NonCommercial-NoDerivs 3.0 Unported License.

1. There are of course several exceptions, particularly work by legal scholar Jeffrey Fagan. In general, however, scholars interested in crime rarely engage scholars motivated to understand punishment.

Figure 1. Basic Depiction of the Relationship Between Contact and Conduct

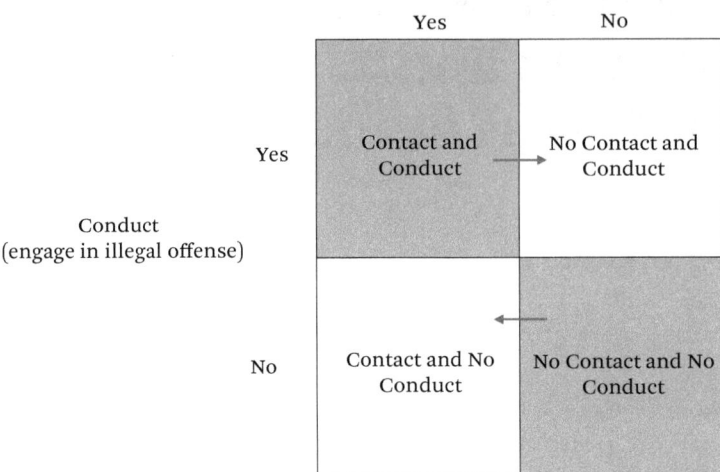

Source: Authors' compilation.

We argue that existing bodies of knowledge mischaracterize one of the most fundamental relationships in the modern era between Americans and the carceral state—namely, that between criminal offending and criminal justice contact. A sizable body of research tacitly assumes the relationship to be unidirectional, with more offending leading to more contact and, subsequently, more incarceration. Yet research on mass incarceration documents that shifts in policies are a primary mechanism to increasing contacts with the justice system (and subsequent punishment) net of individual criminality (Tonry and Melewski 2008). One crude measure of this change is the shift in confinements per crime: in 1970, the ratio was twenty inmates per thousand crimes; by 2000, it had increased to 112 for every thousand. Given this dynamic, how might exposure to criminal justice connote something other than offending patterns? How might criminality and justice involvement be intertwined in ways that get lost in academic debates? In addition, how might larger policy changes—such as the war on drugs and broken windows policing—which increased contact, affect the risk of justice involvement for different generations of individuals and different generations of racial groups?

This study would be the first (to our knowledge) to examine how the relationship between reported criminality and justice involvement has changed across two generations, slipping from a system under which involvement was a good proxy for having run afoul of the law to one defined by increasingly separate constituencies of criminal offender and custodial citizen (Lerman and Weaver 2014).

We start from a fairly uncontroversial assumption that contact should follow, not lead, criminal offending. The idea is so simple and straightforward as to be obvious: that criminal justice exposure should exhibit a strong relationship to being engaged in crime. Otherwise said, individual criminal justice contact should be strongly predicted by criminal behavior and offending patterns. Imagine a two-by-two table with four quadrants (figure 1). We take it as uncontroversial that under a criminal justice system that promotes public safety while confining abuses of power, most Americans should fall in the shaded diagonal and a very small share should fall in the opposite diagonal—those people who did not engage in crime but were arrested or jailed or, conversely, those individuals who were not law abiding but were also not arrested (or, therefore, convicted). In other words, for a non-arbitrary system of justice, contact should closely follow conduct. The share of Americans having involuntary encounters with criminal justice institutions (police, courts, probation or parole agencies, jails, and prisons) should be tightly coupled and have considerable overlap with those who engage in unlawful behavior. There will be mistakes in interpreting law abiding and assessing guilt, of course, but the exceptions should not mock the rule.

This article descriptively examines the distributions within these quadrants for two distinct generational cohorts, those coming of age as the prison boom was beginning in earnest and those moving through early adulthood two decades later when incarceration would soon reach its peak, based on a representative and over-time data source, the National Longitudinal Survey of Youth (NLSY 2014). This survey is particularly suited to our aims because it queries respondents about their criminal behavior as well as about being arrested by police (which we use as a proxy for criminal justice contact).

Our preliminary findings are striking and carry troubling implications. First, the members of the late-1990s cohort were much more likely to have contact with legal authorities than the 1979 cohort, even though the earlier cohort reported engaging in substantially more offending. Given that the latter cohort reached adulthood under the policy and practices of broken windows policing, zero tolerance in schools, the drug war, and mandatory minimums, the greater odds of being arrested makes sense. Concretely, in the 1979 cohort of eighteen- to twenty-three-year-olds, only 10 percent had been arrested by police, versus 25 percent of their counterparts in the 1997 cohort.

Second, we find that the predictive value of criminal offending for estimating justice involvement waned for Generation X. Self-reported criminal conduct, thus, is a less good predictor among the more recent generation of having contact with criminal justice. In the 1979 cohort, if one did not report unlawful behaviors, one was somewhat unlikely to report experiencing arrest (18 percent of those who reported being arrested reported no offending). By the 1997 cohort, it was the opposite: fully 70 percent of the people who reported that they had been arrested did not report engaging in a property or violent crime. So distinct are these trends in contact that we find that reported criminal involvement in the earlier cohort triggers arrest by police at the same rate as no reported offending in the later cohort. By the later generation, the underlying relationship between crime and contact with criminal justice had transformed.

Third, and more troubling still, we find the growth of a cavernous disparity by racial membership across the generations. In the 1979 cohort, quadrant membership does not differ significantly by racial group. In the 1997 cohort, it does—and dramatically so. By 1997, the share who reported no criminal offending but being arrested grows and differs by racial group. Crime self-report distributions by race do not shift by more than a few percentage points across the two cohorts; contact with the law does. In the 1997 cohort, black men were more likely than white men to be arrested and report no illegal activity. In addition, the group that is the least visible in scholarly or popular discourse, namely, those who report engaging in property damage, theft, or violence but are not arrested or convicted, is also racially inflected; white men were more likely than black men to indicate engaging in criminal offenses but not being arrested.

Our conclusion is stark: security from state discipline and oversight is increasingly decoupled from law-abidingness, conditioned less on patterns of behavior than in prior generations. This decoupling is what characterizes criminal justice in the twenty-first century, which has dire consequences for the lives of those who are at high risk of oversight despite not having engaged in crime.

THE CRIME-CONTACT CONUNDRUM
The idea that criminality is tightly linked to contact with the criminal justice system is so foundational to most criminological theory, political rhetoric, and public policy that we take it for granted. Quite simply, we by and large assume that many if not most of those involved in the criminal justice system are engaged in some criminal activity or other wrongdoing (or that if they were not at the time of arrest, they were at some point doing something unlawful). Innocence (or mistaken criminality) is assumed to counter the modal experience and as something that should be sorted out by the system itself—such as false charges dropped, mis-

taken identities clarified, or innocent citizens freed. From this perspective, the severe inequities by race and place observed in arrest and incarceration rates are driven by how, where, and when the criminal justice system directs its gaze on particular parts of the population and not, so much, the underlying criminality of that population. The unequal effects of the war on drugs, for example, were driven by policies that applied more severe enforcement and sentences on those drug-related offenses found in minority communities (Alexander 2012). But scholarly analyses suggested that it was the enforcement, adjudication, and sentencing that was racially disparate and excessive (Tonry 1995), not necessarily that a significant share of those who were arrested were innocent of criminal activity or drug-related behaviors.

Alarming recent evidence from the fields of law, political science, sociology, and criminology suggest a decoupling of criminality from criminal justice contact, leading one of us to argue for the importance of distinguishing the criminal offender, who is characterized by his or her behavior and the "custodial citizen," who "is defined by his or her relationship to the state," a relationship predicated more on who one is than what one has done (Lerman and Weaver 2014, 32). Examples abound. Many studies began to document that racial disparities in arrest outcomes were poorly explained by individual-level differences in delinquency, and that black arrest odds remained substantially higher and racial arrest disparities appeared to strengthen even after taking into account differential crime involvement and criminal history (Unnever, Cullen, and Barnes 2017; Huizinga et al. 2007; Tapia 2012; Andersen 2015; Kirk 2008; Gase et al. 2016; Mitchell and Caudy 2017; but see Beaver et al. 2013).

One set of studies found stark disparities between actual drug possession and drug distribution arrests—namely, that higher drug arrest rates is not explained solely by greater involvement in drug distribution. To be sure, although a link between drug possession and being arrested for drug possession does exist, other factors such as where and under what condition the drug was purchased, what type of drug was purchased, and citizen complaints about crime all play a prominent role in who is arrested for drug possession (Beckett et al. 2005; Ramchand, Pacula, and Iguchi 2006; Engel, Smith, and Cohen 2012). Those who purchased crack cocaine or who purchased drugs in public places from strangers were more likely to be arrested (Beckett et al. 2005; Ramchand, Pacula, and Iguchi 2006). These inequities are related to the fact that "open air" drug markets in disadvantaged urban neighborhoods are more likely to attract the attention of police than indoor drug operations often found in white suburbs (Hagedorn 1994). In a Seattle study, for instance, Katherine Beckett and her colleagues find that police practices targeting crack offenders and outdoor markets were directly related to the significant overrepresentation of blacks in drug arrest rates (2006, 105, 129). In a national sample, blacks and Latinos were much less likely to be engaged in drug offending but more likely to report experiencing a drug distribution arrest (Mitchell and Caudy 2017). Thus, enforcement decisions can create a situation in which blacks are just under 15 percent of all drug users but become 33 percent of all drug-related arrests, 46 percent of drug convictions, and 45 percent of those serving time in state prison for drug offenses (Bobo and Thompson 2010).

The pattern observed by Beckett and her colleagues for drug arrests also applies more generally to low-level misdemeanor arrests. The movement toward "broken windows" and "order maintenance" policing, first by New York and quickly followed by jurisdictions across the United States, provides a case in which exposure to the justice system becomes increasingly associated not with crime in the sense of malum en se criminality but, instead, for minor transgressions or perceived transgressions such as loitering, attempting to clean car windows at a stoplight, and so on (Sampson and Raudenbush 2004; Harcourt 2009; Fagan and Davies 2000). Often conducted without probable cause, misdemeanor arrests are often deployed against people who are legally innocent. Selection for arrest, not evidence of guilt, often drives outcomes in this low-level domain: "the petty offense process is permitted to distribute criminal liability based on race and social vulnerability rather than individual fault" (Natapoff 2012, 119–22). The result, as Issa Kohler-Hausmann describes it, is a system of "misdemeanor justice" that places a massive burden upon tens-of-thousands of New York residents each year that leads to no findings of guilt, fine, or legal assessment that a crime was committed (2013). As the law professor and former prosecutor Paul Butler recounts of his own experience, "When I got arrested, I thought it would matter that I was innocent. It turns out, however, for misdemeanor arrests, whether you are innocent or guilty is not the most important thing" (2017, 64).

New York's Stop, Frisk, and Question (SFQ) exemplifies perhaps the most dramatic decoupling of criminality from contact. Emerging from the "broken windows" approach to policing, New York's SFQ's explicit purpose was to maximize contacts with citizens purely for the purpose of questioning them in non-arrest situations "in the hope that some yield fruit" (Epp, Maynard-Moody, and Haider-Markel 2014, 8). In effect, this not only increased the number of contacts with the justice system but also introduced a new mechanism by which the system contacted Americans outside of the context of criminal offending. The result, in short, was the large-scale surveillance of minority communities. Through careful empirical studies, SFQ was shown to target blacks and Latinos far more frequently than whites, even when controlling for crime participation, and to target residents in minority neighborhoods regardless of their levels of neighborhood disorder and crime (Gelman, Fagan, and Kiss 2007, 821; Grunwald and Fagan, forthcoming). Not only did blacks and Latinos represent 51 and 33 percent of the stops, while only comprising 26 and 24 percent of the total population, respectively, these stops were characterized by a significant disconnection from actual criminality: they were much less likely to lead to arrests than stops of whites, a pattern that strongly suggests blacks were being stopped despite little evidence of criminal wrongdoing (Gelman, Fagan, and Kiss 2007, 816, 822). Although various legal and investigatory justifications were often given in support of SFQ, the racial disparities in police stops have often been linked to little more than race, where the only "crime" in play at the time of the stop was "racial incongruity" with the location in which one was stopped (being black in a majority white area or vice versa) or racial belonging (Capers 2009; Meehan and Ponder 2002). Two-thirds of all police stops failed to meet the "reasonable suspicion" standard, particularly when blacks were stopped. "Racial composition," Jeffrey Fagan and his colleagues argue, was "as important as local crime conditions in predicting police stop activity" (Fagan et al. 2009, 330). Indeed, if one looks at the reasons police gave for making the stops, the connection to crime was dubious; many were stopped for making "furtive movements" or being in a high-crime area, a designation that itself was "virtually uncorrelated with actual crime rates," for instance (Lerman and Weaver 2014; Grunwald and Fagan, forthcoming).

Strikingly similar patterns were found in police stops of motorists, though with a notable twist. In *Pulled Over*, Charles Epp and his colleagues document the emergence, acceptance, and eventual institutionalization of a new kind of stop tactic in police departments—the investigatory stop—that which is not intended to stop crime but to use any pretext to "merely check people out." As police training manuals described, stopping a surplus of people was an explicit goal: "you have to stop a lot of vehicles to get the law of averages working in your favor" (quoted in Epp, Maynard-Moody, and Haider-Markel 2014, 39). Using this kind of stop to observe as many people as possible became accepted, even celebrated. Unlike traffic safety stops, which show some parity, the racial disparities in these investigatory stops were large, leading the authors to conclude that drivers were stopped less by "how they drive" than by "who you are" (25).

Studies in a variety of locations and contexts find that minority drivers are stopped at a disproportionate amount relative to their total composition of the driving population (Browning et al. 1994; Lamberth 1996; Smith and Pertocelli 2001; Baumgartner, Epp, and Shoub 2018). Although the levels of such disparities vary by study—as does who is doing the stopping (local versus state or traffic police)—the consensus is that the disparities in stops by race are so persistent to warrant the act of "driving while black" itself to be viewed as something that is considered criminal, in that it leads to unequal contact with police. Similarly, Amada Armenta finds that Latino residents in Nashville, Tennessee, are often fearful of driving as it might lead to (now legal) immigration checks (2017). In both instances, enforcement strategies and policies have blurred the distinction between criminality and other ordinary acts such as commuting to work or driving down the expressway.

A final example merits attention. A recent study of adolescent boys calls into question the strength of the connection—and even the directionality of the relationship—between arrests and offending in recent years. It demonstrates not only that police contact was likely to trigger subsequent offending in a sample of adolescent boys, but that self-reported delinquency bore no relationship to subsequent police contact and prior law-abidingness did not "protect" them from police stops: "at each wave of the survey, boys who reported little or no involvement in delinquency at the prior wave were just as likely to have been stopped by police six months later as boys who had reported higher levels of delinquent behavior at the previous wave" (Del Toro et al., n.d.).

A second dimension to our decoupling argument often evades academic discussion: the lack of contact with criminal justice among some who report criminality. In contrast to the experiences of black and Latino youth who are treated as suspicious for "offenses" as mundane as walking down the street or driving in a car, the relationship between criminal offending and criminal justice contact is problematic in the opposite direction in more affluent and whiter suburbs and college campuses, the so-called antitargets of the war on drugs (Richards, Berk, and Forster 1979; Singer 2014; Jacques and Wright 2015; Wooden and Blazak 1995; Mohamed and Fritsvold 2010). A study of Amherst, New York, a wealthy, largely white suburb outside of Buffalo, finds that police practice a "maximum tolerance" rather "zero tolerance" approach to youth offending (Singer 2014, 239). Generally, Amherst police had a high level of tolerance for low-level offending often treated along the lines of the old adage "boys will be boys." Simon Singer concludes that though as many as 64 percent of the youth in the study could have been arrested based on their delinquent behavior, few were (238). Although 22 percent had been picked up by police, only 10 percent of them had been adjudicated in some way for their behavior (238). Additionally, young people living in affluent white suburbs such as Amherst are unlikely to be arrested for possession of small amounts of pot (Singer 2014, 21; Hagedorn 1994). Such maximum tolerance approaches in suburbs thus is also implicated in a decoupled relationship between offending and contact in these communities but in the direction of a false negative, or underenforcement and diminished probability of contact among offenders.

The central objective of our study is to determine whether and how the basic relationship between criminality and criminal justice contact has shifted across the past several decades. To this end, we use nationally representative data from two cohorts, young adults in the 1970s and young adults in the 1990s, to compare their reported experiences with both criminal offending and criminal justice contact. The timing of these two cohorts provides a unique lens into the experiences of those living under very different criminal justice regimes. The 1970s cohort was surveyed prior to the war on drugs and just as the institutional changes of the late 1960s war on crime were being reflected on the ground. The 1990s cohort entered young adulthood in a policy era characterized by broken windows policing, increased prosecutorial activism (Pfaff 2017), and a sweeping set of legislative changes that together bent the criminal justice system toward a focus on low-level or non-offenders (National Research Council 2014).

Figure 1 provides a conceptualization of our theoretical and analytic approach by depicting a binary distinction between a respondent's self-reported criminal activity (whether they engaged in an illegal offense) against a respondent's experience of criminal justice contact. The top left yes–yes quadrant of figure 1 is the area assumed by most: the vast majority of those involved with the criminal justice system have been so engaged because of their involvement in criminal behavior. The no–no quadrant provides the logical opposite: lack of criminal justice contact is generally associated with lack of criminal involvement. The yes offending–no contact quadrant is, essentially, a system failure—the inability of the criminal justice system to contact those actually committing the crimes. The no offending–yes contact quadrant is a different type of system failure, and the one of interest in this study: individuals who are contacted by the criminal justice system without engaging in an illegal activity. The arrows depict movement from a criminal justice system tightly connected to offending. Our argument is that, over time and particularly among the generation coming of age before and after one of the largest transformations in criminal justice to date, the share of Americans shifted between these quadrants in ways that are troubling for a system predicated on few "errors" (few yes–no combinations)—and that this maladaptation is heavily skewed by race.

DATA AND METHODS

To explore our argument, we rely on the National Longitudinal Survey of Youth. The NLSY asks a nationally representative survey sample of more than eight thousand young adults questions about their criminal offending and direct experiences with the criminal justice system in two generational cohorts, one that turned eighteen around 1980 and one that did so in the late 1990s.[2] The NLSY includes a detailed battery of self-reported offenses as well as several measures of reported contact with police, courts, and correctional institutions. Despite some differences in question wording between the two years of the survey and its reliance on offense and arrest self-report, which we discuss in detail in the following section, and a slightly smaller sample in the later cohort, the NLSY is an ideal data source for making comparisons across cohorts, given that it kept its sampling procedures identical across the cohorts, includes large oversamples of nonwhites, and has high response rates in the 82 percent to 93 percent range (Stevens and Morash 2014).[3] Using a self-weighting representation of households with youth between ages twelve and sixteen in 1996 and between fourteen and twenty-two in 1978 yields cohort samples that are representative of the American young adult population.

Following existing approaches to ensuring the cohort samples are as similar as possible, we remove the military and low-SES oversamples from the 1979 cohort and exclude respondents under eighteen in both cohorts. After that adjustment, 5,837 respondents remain in the 1979 cohort analysis and 8,683 in the 1997 analysis. We examine the 1980 wave, the only year of the 1979 NLSY that includes queries about criminal justice contact; we use the 2002 wave of the 1997 NLSY, the year that most closely approximates the age distribution of the 1979 cohort analysis (once those under eighteen are removed). About 1,008 of the original 1997 cohort were not available for re-interview in 2002, and 395 of the original 1979 cohort were not in 1980. We assume that these cases are missing at random, an assumption consistent with past research using NLSY (Brame et al. 2014).[4]

Our primary outcome of interest is arrest, a critical entry point into the criminal justice system and experience with police and, as others have argued, a key mechanism for further involvement and embeddedness with the crim-

---

2. The NLSY was not originally designed for research on crime and delinquency, but its nationally representative sample—especially with significant numbers of racial and ethnic minorities—has produced a string of important criminological investigations into a variety of theoretical and methodological topics, including several of those discussed here.

3. As Tia Stevens and Merry Morash explain, "Both have a similar questionnaire design, a sample based on birth year using similar sampling methods, and oversampling of Black and Hispanic youth to allow for reliable statistical analysis for these subgroups" (2014, 80).

4. Robert Brame and his colleagues conducted sensitivity analysis using various estimators (lower and upper bounds) to ensure that those respondents missing from the analysis either because they weren't interviewed in that round or because they did not answer the arrest question did not bias the prevalence estimates by subgroup (2014). They find that even if the missing cases were not missing at random, "only an extreme difference in the missing data patterns" of blacks and whites and of men and women "could overcome the difference we see in the observed data" (480).

inal justice system (Sampson and Laub 2003). Arrest, even absent formal conviction or adjudication, has been linked to several disconcerting outcomes including less earnings, unemployment, lowered educational attainment, and greater risk of dropping out of school (Grogger 1995; Bushway 1998; Uggen 2000; Bernburg and Krohn 2003; Blumstein and Nakamura 2009). As one recent study bluntly put it, "the collateral social and personal damage created by an arrest mortgages the futures of young people as they make the transition to adulthood" (Brame et al. 2012). Unfortunately, only the NLSY 1980 data include measures of being stopped by police (without arrest), so we cannot track changes over time in this lower-level contact that may show even less connection to criminality given the rationales of broken windows policing. We use arrest as a proxy for contact, given that it is asked in both cohorts and a large enough share of each cohort and by racial group experienced arrest to make analysis of subgroups possible. We focus on the "front end" of experiences with criminal justice, and future research should consider other points of contact. To compile the arrest measure, we use the initial question in 1980 and 1997 about whether the respondent has "ever been" arrested, booked, or charged. For the 1997 cohort, we also rely on the follow-up questions in each later round (up to and including 2002) of whether the respondent has been arrested "since the date of last interview."[5] Although some respondents are missing from subsequent rounds of the 1997 NLSY, we use the NLSY's event history arrest measure.

Our main explanatory variable is self-reported criminal offending in the previous year measured in both cohorts. Respondents are asked whether they committed one of several offenses since the date of last interview (that is, over the past year) as well as the number of times the act was committed. Offending in one year has a strong correlation with offending in other years and in the absence of explicit longitudinal measures, can be assumed to reflect prior offending (Stevens and Morash 2014; Jolliffe et al. 2003; Herrenkohl et al. 2000). Because the 1980 NLSY does not query respondents about prior criminal offending in 1980 or include measures of offending in the initial 1979 wave of that cohort survey, we use a one-year measure in both. The criminal offending profiles of the two cohorts show substantial divergence. On balance, a much larger share of the 1979 cohort reported doing at least one unlawful act. Among the 1979 cohort, 52 percent reported one offense in the last year (not including drug use; including drug use, the share is 56 percent); in comparison, only 15 percent of the 1997 cohort reported engaging in at least one illegal offense (if drug use is included, that share rises to 31 percent).

Our first measure of self-reported offending is a dichotomous measure that equals 1 if the respondent reported any of the offenses excluding drug use and a 0 if they reported no illegal acts excluding drug use.[6] We further divide the crime measure into reported property and violent offenses, again as dichotomous measures. For a subset of analyses, we use a continuous measure of self-reported offending based on an index of crime severity and frequency.

Beyond offending profiles, few differences between the respondent samples in each cohort in terms of gender, age, region, and urbanicity are notable; in both the 1979 and 1997 cohort, about half of the sample are non-Hispanic whites, and roughly similar proportions are Latino and black. College enrollment and the share in poverty were both higher in the later cohort and a larger share lived in the central city in the later cohort. Respondent

---

5. Although our main analysis relies on a cumulative measure of arrest among young adults in the NLSY, in the appendix, we replicate the results using a more limited arrest measure, namely, arrest in the last year alone. Doing so attempts to deal with the concern that our measure is biased towards finding greater arrest prevalence in the later cohort given multiple opportunities to report in 2002 relative to 1980 and addresses the mismatch between measuring cumulative arrest and noncumulative offending.

6. Our measure excludes items that were not asked in both cohorts—gambling, fighting, threatening to hit someone, and membership in a gang.

demographics by cohort are presented in table A2. For most of the analyses to follow, our focus remains on a comparison between black and non-Hispanic white respondents. The reason for this is simple: the Latino population in 1979 is not comparable to that in the late 1990s for many reasons, the most important being that the 1982 and 1993 immigration acts changed migration patterns, bringing many more low-skilled immigrants and many more of Mexican descent.

Scope of Study and Limitations

Although the NLSY was not explicitly designed for the study of crime, its inclusion of questions on self-reported delinquency and arrest has made it an important source of data to examine a range of criminological phenomena such as self-control theory (Hay and Forrest 2008), the relationship between gang membership and drug use (Bjerregaard 2010), and the effects of dropping out of school on delinquency (Apel et al. 2008). Our study builds on and advances prior work using the NLSY to study crime and delinquency in two important ways. First, we focus on shifts occurring between cohorts rather than on cohort-specific behaviors. Several recent studies have used the 1979 and 1997 NLSY to compare outcomes and expectations across cohorts. These include behaviors such as the changing skills of youth and labor market outcomes (Altonji, Bharadwaj, and Lange 2012, 783); the role of education in determining wages (Castex and Dechter 2014, 689); inequality in postsecondary education (Bailey and Dynarski 2011, 1, 19); the changing effect of family income and ability in education achievement (Belley and Lochner 2007); changing college expectations (Reynolds and Pemberton 2001); high school dropout rates in urban and rural areas; and the association between dropout rates and paid employment during high school (Jordan, Kostandini, and Mykerezi 2012; Warren and Cataldi 2006). Although some note difficulties in comparing specific variables across surveys and the change from pencil and paper to computer-assisted instruments, these studies provide evidence of the reliability of making cohort comparisons using the NLSY once attrition is accounted for through survey weights. Despite recent attention to the cumulative prevalence of arrest among today's youth, our study is one of the first to take a similar cross-cohort perspective on arrest and criminality.[7]

Second, instead of exploring criminal offending or contact with legal authorities in isolation, we examine the relationship between self-reported offending and arrests. Only two studies to our knowledge have used the NLSY cohort comparisons to examine patterns in justice system involvement (conditional on delinquency) among adolescent youth, finding that minority youth were more likely to be convicted and confined after accounting for offending and that this disparity grew over time (Stevens and Morash 2014, 77; Stevens, Morash, and Chesney-Lind 2010).

Our study is not without limitations, though we took steps to minimize their impact on our analyses and inference. First, relying on a population survey not designed for the specific task of measuring and tracking offending and contact with legal authorities raises some concerns. Such a survey likely underrepresents offenders as well as those currently incarcerated (though the NLSY makes efforts to re-interview in correctional facilities), so our estimates of criminal justice contact and offending are likely to be more conservative than what actually exists in the United States. In addition, our examination of self-reported offending and arrest rely on measures that are not as expansive as we would ideally like; delinquency measures exclude more serious offenses like rape and vehicular

---

7. A set of studies by Brame and colleagues analyze the cumulative prevalence of arrest in the NLSY 1997, finding that a commanding share of American youth were arrested at least once by young adulthood (2012, 2014). Roughly 30 percent of the cohort had experienced arrest by the time they reached twenty-three years old. Arrest risk was extremely high for black young men, just shy of half (48 percent) by age twenty-three and 30 percent by age eighteen, versus 38 percent and 21.5 percent for white young men. Our study differs from Brame's by focusing on arrest by a given year rather than cumulative arrests by a certain age.

homicide and do not represent all index and non-index offense possibilities.[8]

Second, our analysis proceeds from the assumption that our measures of offending and arrest are reliable and valid; that they are equally so for both blacks and whites; and that they do not become more or less valid depending on the cohort or period. The analysis of self-reported delinquency and arrest measures is a mainstay in criminological research, and despite its unique advantages, it is also not without limitations. Because our key explanatory and dependent variables rely on subjective recollections of arrest and offending that are not validated in official records, they may contain measurement error that could bias results and our conclusions. This error is of two sorts. On the delinquency measure, respondents may misreport actual offenses as not being a crime (or vice versa), have difficulty recalling the frequency or severity of offenses, or face social desirability incentives to underreport their offending behavior. On the arrest measure, respondents may misremember the age, timing, or frequency of arrest, confuse a police stop for an arrest and thus overreport arrests, or face similar social desirability concerns to conceal their contact with legal authorities, resulting in biased reports. These possibilities have been the subject of extensive scholarly debate in criminology. We discuss each in turn.

A central debate surrounds the relationship between self-reported arrest as compared to official arrest records.[9] In general, in reviews of the many studies in this domain, there is "moderate" to "moderate-to-strong" agreement in the reliability and validity of self-reported measures of arrest vis-à-vis official records (Thornberry and Krohn 2003; Piquero, Schubert, and Brame 2014), and congruence between self-reported and official arrests is stable over time (Piquero, Schubert, and Brame 2014). Validations have occurred across both general and serious offending samples and in a host of datasets: The Pathways to Desistance, the Project on Human Development in Chicago Neighborhoods, The National Longitudinal Study of Adolescent to Adult Health, the Seattle Social Development Project, the Pittsburgh Youth Study, The Dunedin Longitudinal Study, the Cambridge Study in Delinquent Development, and the National Youth Survey Family Study (Bersani and Piquero 2017; Hindelang, Hirshi, and Weis 1981; Krohn et al. 2013; Maxfield, Weiler, and Widom 2000; Farrington et al. 1996; Thornberry and Krohn 2000; Pollock et al. 2015; Piquero, Schubert, and Brame 2014). The findings from these studies suggest that self-reports are a "fairly good representation of official reports" of petition-arrest, capturing approximately 80 percent of arrests in arrest records and exhibiting a high level of agreement in both the prev-

---

8. The lack of some index crimes makes it difficult to compare these self-report arrests with official UCR data, which is generally tracked based on index crimes.

9. For a review of this and related debates, see Terrence Thornberry and Marvin Krohn (2003), Delbert Elliot (1995), and Alex Piquero and his colleagues (2014). "The overall validity of self-report data is in the moderate-to-strong range, especially for self-reports of being arrested" (Thornberry and Krohn 2003, 61). As Elliot describes:

> Self-reported data have their own sources of error and should not be accepted uncritically.... But conceptually and operationally they are more appropriate measures for studying the causes of criminal behavior and describing the distribution and dynamics of criminal behavior in a general population. Subject to some variation, the validity of self-reported offending based on "known" arrests is about 80 percent. Validity of arrests based on known self-reports is as high as 25 to 50 percent for serious offenses and as low as 1 percent for minor offenses. Given that arrest and self-report data produce different distributions of offenders and offenses in the general population and specific subpopulations, self-reports are likely to produce the better estimates. (1995, 3)

More recently, Alex Piquero and his colleagues conclude that "the high level and stability of the agreement is striking and adds to the emerging story about the validity of these two methods for measuring arrest" (2014, 547, and, for a comprehensive summary of the studies that have assessed concordance between official records and self-reports, see table 1).

alence and frequency of arrest (Piquero, Schubert, and Brame 2014; Pollock et al. 2015). Michael Maxfield, Barbara Weiler, and Cathy Widom, for example, found that 47.5 percent of those in their sample of 1,196 young adults from a Midwestern metropolitan area had an arrest officially recorded by authorities, close to the 45.6 percent who self-reported an arrest (2000, 98).

More recent studies have gone beyond simple correspondence to explicitly match self-reported arrests to official arrests (Farrington et al. 2010; Hirschfield et al. 2006). For example, Nancy Morris and Lee Ann Slocum systematically investigated self-reported arrest errors in a sample of 350 women in a jail and found an extremely high degree of congruence between whether an arrest was reported and whether it was officially documented: 88 percent of women who reported that they were arrested over a period of three years could be matched to official arrest (2010). Recall of the frequency of arrest also exhibited high levels of matches to official data, and to a lesser extent, the timing of arrest: between 35.1 and 39.9 percent of reported arrests were recalled accurately to within just a month of the official arrest date.

In general, where measurement error was evident, it was most likely to be in the direction of overreporting of arrest by those who did not have official arrest documented (most of those with an arrest accurately report being arrested), misidentification of the date or age of the arrest (accuracy erodes for arrests further in the past), and errors in arrest frequency for those who reported more frequent arrests; accuracy was lowest among those with more trivial offenses or adjudication outcomes and accuracy highest among serious offenders and adult relative to juvenile offenders (Pollock et al. 2015; Krohn et al. 2013; Morris and Slocum 2010; Huizinga and Elliot 1986; Elliot 1995). Thus, the preponderance of studies, we and others find, point to self-report of arrest as a valid and reliable indicator.[10]

The validation of self-reported offending is much more difficult because no objective measure of offending exists.[11] Although many studies find a positive correlation between self-reports of offending and arrest, for obvious reasons (selection for arrest is not the same as delinquency) it is less strong than findings between self-report arrests and official arrests. Criminologists have rightly questioned, and some have abandoned, the practice of using arrest to understand the dynamics and distribution of offending or to generalize to criminals in the population, one calling it "indefensible" (Elliot 1995, 9). Instead, they tap official responses to offending and the discretion of agencies. Official arrests neither do an adequate job at describing the incidence and distribution of offending in the population, which is far more extensive in self-reports, victimization surveys, and crimes known to police, nor adequately capture the individuals who self-report offending. Most offenders are never arrested and most crime is never reported, and the probability of "arrest per self-reported serious violent offense" is shockingly low (2 percent). Specifically, the correlations between arrests for index crimes and self-reported index offending rates are small, hovering around 0.38, and arrest rates explained just 9 to 14 percent of the variation in offending based on self-reports (Elliot 1995). Arrest rates are not necessarily accurate predictors of offending patterns nor do they accurately distinguish offenders from non-offenders. Even the "worst offenders" based on official arrests bear almost no relationship to the worst offenders based on self-reports, with more than 75 percent of one group missing from the other (Elliot 1995). Offense patterns and estimates of the prevalence of offending by demographic group based on both sources of data look remarkably different

---

10. One notable exception is a study of Chicago youth by David Kirk, which finds that 45.5 percent of youth who had an official arrest did not report an arrest and 23.4 percent who were not arrested reported that they were (2006). Nonetheless, Kirk concludes that self-report measures can serve as a reliable indicator of actual arrests particularly when trying to explain between person differences or when comparing group differences and not "within-individual change" (126).

11. For a trenchant and seminal critique of the field's tendency to put faith in official arrest as an unbiased indicator of actual offending, see Elliot 1995.

(Pollock et al. 2015). Knowing arrest history, in short, does not allow one to say much of anything about offending in the population, nor do arrest samples come close to being representative of the population of offenders. On these grounds, we follow a growing group of experts who have argued for relying on offending self-reports as a more suitable method.[12] Readers should note, however, that our measure of offending is subject to errors in recall, flawed understanding of whether something is a criminal offense, and social desirability pressures.

Another concern with implications for our study is differential validity, or the extent to which the correspondence between self-report and actual incidence of arrest or court referral might vary for different groups. Because one of our central theoretical arguments surrounds growing black-white differences in the relationship between offending and contact across cohorts, and our modeling strategy assumes that self-reports of offending and arrest are equally valid, caution is warranted given the spectrum of different findings about the validity of self-reported offending and criminal history by black Americans. Disagreement across studies exists about whether and how extensive a problem differential validity is. Some studies find evidence of substantial differences in validity, and thus challenge our assumption (Hindelang et al. 1981; Huizinga and Elliot 1986; Maxfield, Weiler, and Widom 2000; Kirk 2006). Other studies contradict them, finding little significant variation by race and a strong agreement between self-reported and official records obtained regardless of race or ethnic group (Farrington et al. 1996; Bersani and Piquero 2017; Jolliffe et al. 2003; Piquero, Schubert, and Brame 2014; Thornberry and Krohn 2003; Piquero and Brame 2008).[13]

The studies finding systematic underreporting of offending by blacks were based on a concordance strategy using an unrepresentative sample of local arrest records that assumed no differential validity by race in official arrest records (Huizinga and Elliot 1986; Hindelang et al. 1981). As Elliot contends, this "assumption [was] seriously challenged by Geerken (1994) who concluded that there were serious racial biases in local arrest records which overstate the arrests of blacks relative to whites" (1995, 7). Many other studies using different methods to assess validity of self-reports from polygraph tests to peer reports of offending and others, Elliot goes on to observe, "have all failed to show significant race differences" (1995, 7).

Second, and more important, is that in all of the studies that support differential validity, the direction of bias was in underreporting, not overreporting; in other words, blacks with a criminal record were more likely than whites to underreport offenses (Hindelang et al. 1981; Huizinga and Elliot 1986) and arrests (Kirk 2006; Maxfield, Weiler, and Widom 2000; Krohn et al. 2013). Positive bias—reporting an arrest when there was no official arrest—when it occurred was more likely among whites (Maxfield, Weiler, and Widom 2000; Krohn et al. 2013). Thus, if differential validity of arrest self-reports by race is a problem in our study, it will lead to bias our results in a conservative direction. If differential validity of offending (given greater underreporting of offenses among blacks) is a problem, there is little reason to believe that offense underreporting would not affect both the earlier and later cohorts *and* that it would be accompanied by the simultaneous underreporting of arrests. In both scenarios, the conclusions we reach about a changed relationship between offending and contact are unlikely to be exaggerated.

12. "Although the two measures are positively related, as we would expect, the two cannot reasonably be regarded as measures of the same phenomenon, and it is self-reports, not arrests, that provide the more complete picture of illegal behavior" (Pollock et al. 2015, 70; see also Elliot 1995). And, given the limits of official administrative data and differences in reporting across jurisdictions, "the best option currently available is to rely on self-reported survey data" (Brame et al. 2014, 482).

13. One study not only failed to replicate findings of underreporting by blacks, but also found that "black males generally had the *highest validity* in these analyses" (Jolliffe et al. 2003, 194, emphasis added). Similarly, Alex Piquero, Carol Schubert, and Robert Brame find that the "correspondence between the prevalence estimates for the two arrest measures appears to be consistently higher for Blacks" than for whites and Hispanics (2014, 541).

A final issue related to the reliance on self-reports for testing claims of cross-cohort shifts is that self-reports may themselves exhibit a cohort effect, that the manifestation of under- or overreporting depends on the era or period in question. Studies have found that under- or overreporting of arrests remains remarkably consistent over the adolescent through young adult life course (Emmert et al. 2017; Piquero, Schubert, and Brame 2014). Research addressing whether self-reporting behavior remains unchanged across cohorts, a crucial assumption on which our analysis rests, is conspicuously lacking, however. One possibility is that perceptions of arrest differ across the periods; given proactive policing tactics that made stops more common in the later period, perceptions about what constitutes an arrest may have been subject to more confusion (Piquero, Schubert, and Brame 2014; Pollock et al. 2015).

It is also possible that the self-reporting of offending may have been more prone to social desirability bias in the later NLSY cohort, given the politicization of crime and drugs in the 1980s and 1990s and their accompanying stigmas in political discourse. If true, then we would expect the crime measures to be biased in the direction of less reported offending among more recent cohorts, a trend that was an artifact of social desirability concerns and not representative of actual offending in the young adult population. However, on this logic, such bias should also have affected reporting of arrests by the later survey cohort. Thus, if social desirability bias was driving cohort-specific underreporting of offending and contact with legal authority, we should see more pronounced underreporting of both arrest and offending in the later NLSY cohort. It is highly unlikely that we would see both overreporting of arrest concurrent with underreporting of offending among the later cohort. More likely would be underreporting of both. Social desirability bias, therefore, may lead to artificially lower levels of both arrest and offending in the later period, but would not pose significant problems to our decoupling argument or finding of a changed relationship between offending and arrest.

With these limitations acknowledged generally and with attention to how our analysis specifically might suffer from bias introduced by the deficits of the self-report method, we proceed cautiously. Fortunately, the design of the NLSY is helpful in this regard; arrests are collected using a life event calendar method, which has been shown to reduce recall error; in addition, each arrest event is followed through to adjudication outcomes, which increases the likelihood that the data provide accurate estimates (Morris and Slocum 2010). Our decisions in the construction of our NLSY merged cohorts dataset were designed to specifically minimize these potential limitations and biases. To minimize the danger of false positives of arrest in the self-reports, our measures of arrest exclude those who cannot recall the year of their arrest, thus producing a conservative estimate of arrest by excluding those who offer hazy arrest details.[14] To address the possibility of greater self-reporting of arrest in the 1997 cohort, we conduct additional analysis among only those who reported an arrest and an official charge.[15] We also confine our analysis to respondents in their early adult years. The logic is that adolescents are more likely to mistakenly recall arrest given greater ambiguity in police practices (Pollock et al.

---

14. According to the NLSY, "if respondents cannot provide the arrest date (both month and year) or the year of the arrest, the arrest is not populated in the arrest event history array."

15. If they reported that they had been arrested, respondents were asked several additional questions about whether the police had formally charged them with a specific offense. In 2002, 387 respondents (4.3 percent) reported being charged with an offense in the last year. Using a cumulative measure based on this item in prior waves, 1,558 respondents (17.4 percent) reported being charged with an offense. Using this more restrictive measure, a smaller share of respondents in 2002 reported ever having a charge or having a charge in 2002 (relative to the original arrest measure, which included 25 percent of respondents who "ever" had an arrest and 6 percent who reported being arrested in the last year). Using this measure is likely an underestimate of arrest relative to the 1979 cohort.

2015).[16] When validity in self-reporting behavior differs by race, it "disappears in the early adult years" (Elliot 1995; Pollock et al. 2015; Thornberry and Krohn 2003). Finally, our analysis does not depend on the details of the arrest—when it occurred, how frequently, for what offense, or even what took place as a result—just whether it took place; thus, we are less concerned about self-report errors that arise from the inability of respondents to locate their arrests in time or recall frequency.

Question Wording and Sample Design Differences

Our analysis is also based on the viability of comparing the 1979 and 1997 NLSY cohorts. Some minor changes in the survey instruments and design occurred between the 1979 and 1997 cohorts, raising potential concerns about comparisons. Of note, in the 1997 survey, respondents were asked a binary yes or no question for each offense, and then asked the number of times they committed particular acts, whereas in the 1979 survey respondents were only asked the number of times they committed a particular delinquent act on a scale of 0 (never) to 6 (more than fifty times). For our analysis, we recode the 1997 data into a frequency item so that it lines up with the 1979 data. It may be that the framing of the response choices elicited more self-reported delinquency in 1979 than 1997. Additionally, a few other questions were only asked of respondents who said they had stolen something valued at more than $50 in the 1997 survey (such as a question about joy riding), whereas in the 1979 cohort this question was asked of all respondents and may have elicited more responses.

Another difference is that more crime questions were asked in 1979 than in the 1997 cohort, which year tends to collapse the same information into fewer queries. In 1979, respondents are explicitly asked whether they broke into a building to steal something as well as about auto theft and shoplifting. In 1997, only those who reported stealing something were subsequently asked whether they stole by breaking and entering or whether they stole a car. In addition, whereas 1979 respondents are asked about using force to obtain things, only those who reported stealing are asked whether they used a weapon in 1997. Finally, 1979 respondents are simply asked about conning someone and about knowingly holding or selling stolen goods, but 1997 respondents are asked whether they engaged in other property crimes.

Although the wording of the items related to offending does differ in important ways between the 1979 NLSY and the 1997 NLSY, we do not think that offending-pattern differences are merely an artifact of question wording or respondents being asked more items in regards to offending behavior. For example, studies based on the Monitoring the Future survey of youth document similar trends in delinquency that support higher criminal offending among the 1979 cohort (Keyes et al. 2017). If we compare the self-reported criminal offense measures item by item, and focus on items that have very similar question wording, a larger share of the 1979 cohort consistently reports unlawful behavior than the 1997 cohort (for the raw share of each cohort that self-reported each of several offenses, see table A2).

Queries on contact with legal authorities also show some differences in wording between the two cohorts. In 1980, respondents are asked, "Not counting minor traffic offenses, have you ever been booked or charged for breaking a law, either by the police or by someone connected with the courts?" In 2002, they are asked, "Have you ever been arrested by the police or taken into custody for an illegal or delinquent offense (do not include arrests for minor traffic violations)?" Because of the different question wordings used to compile our arrest measure, we examine whether the results are sensitive to different measures. Because the question in 2002 is not as specific as it is in 1980, it is possible that the slight wording difference in 2002 was more prone to overreporting of arrests. To address this possibility, we examine how the results hold up if we use the

---

16. For example, police in one study indicated that they would sometimes decide "to file the case as arrest after dropping the individual off so the adolescent might not know whether he or she was arrested" (Pollock et al. 2015, 78–79).

Figure 2. Odds of Arrest by Self-Reported Offending and Cohort

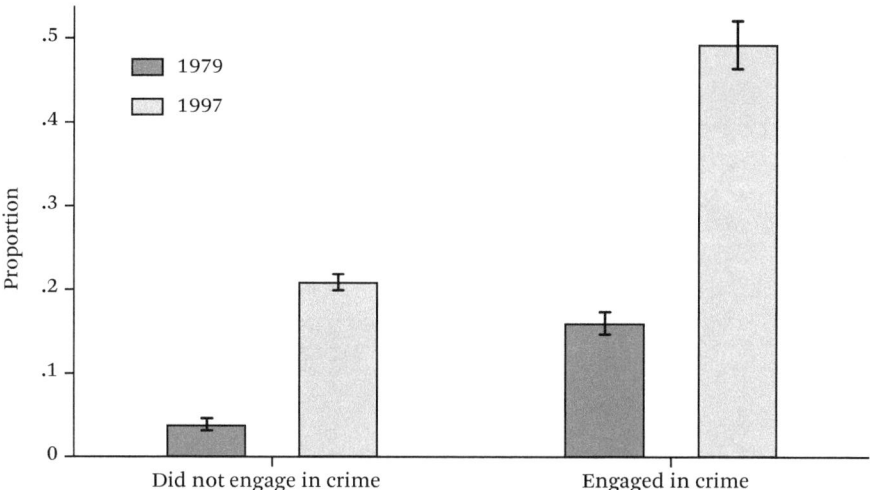

Source: Authors' compilation based on the NLSY (Bureau of Labor Statistics 2014, 2015).
Note: Self-reported crime does not include drug use. Analysis limited to those respondents at least eighteen years of age. The 1979 cohort analysis excludes military and low-SES white oversamples. Analysis is unweighted; analysis with weights is not different.

more conservative measure: "Did the police charge you with an offense?"

It is also possible that respondents in the 1997 cohort misreported being stopped by police as an arrest (Pollock et al. 2015), especially since NLSY 1997 did not separately query respondents specifically about police stops (as distinct from formal arrests or charges) as it had for the NLSY 1979 cohort. Unfortunately, we know of no studies that examine the link between police stops and arrest perceptions, though some do suggest that confusion is likely (Elliot 1995). However, as discussed, we use a more conservative measure of arrest (being charged) and replicate our findings.

Other changes, such as a switch from PAPI (paper and pencil interviewing) in the 1979 cohort, to CAPI (computer-assisted personal interviewing) in the 1997 cohort, may have increased the level of delinquency reported among the 1997 respondents. Despite the potential that these changes altered the overall self-reported delinquency between the cohorts, we have no reason to suspect that these changes would have differentially affected white and black respondents. In other words, we have no reason to suspect that these changes would impact our findings regarding the differences in predicted probability of arrests for blacks and whites between the two cohorts.

RESULTS

We begin with basic plots of bivariate relationships of arrest outcomes for those who reported being engaged in crime and those who did not by cohort and race. Next, we turn to a multivariate investigation of the cohort data. Instead of distributions, we explore the importance of self-reported offending as a predictor of arrest in each cohort and by racial group. We examine whether the influence of offending differs by cohort and by racial group within and across cohorts. Finally, we return to the quadrants from figure 1 using a multinomial logit to examine the odds of landing in each quadrant.

Bivariate Results

The bivariate relationship between arrest and offending among the two NLSY cohorts offers a first descriptive consideration of our argument (see figure 1). Figure 2 plots the basic odds of arrest separately by self-reported criminal offending for both cohorts. As it clearly

Figure 3. Odds of Incarceration by Self-Reported Offending and Cohort

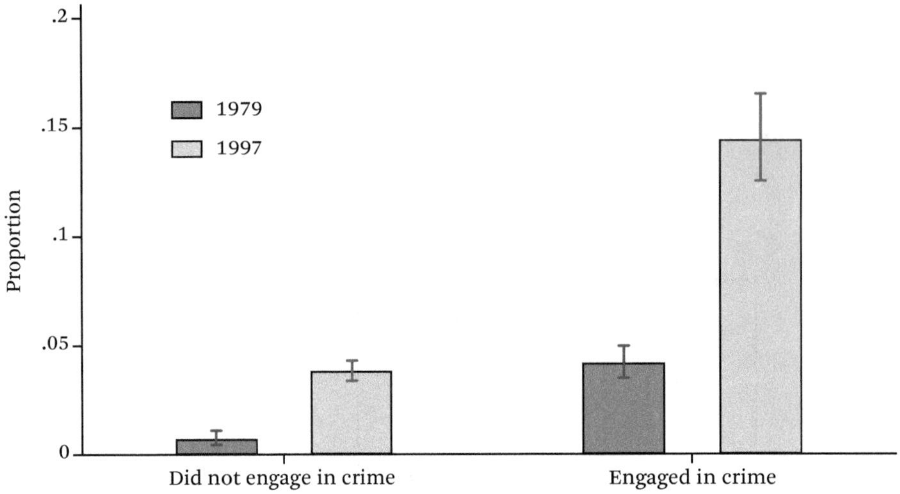

Source: Authors' compilation based on the NLSY (Bureau of Labor Statistics 2014, 2015).

shows, the 1997 cohort shifts decidedly; a greater share of young adult Americans are having contact despite not reporting criminal involvement. Indeed, the share of NLSY respondents in the later cohort who reported no offending and had been arrested was larger (0.21) than those who *had* done something unlawful but evaded arrest in the earlier cohort (0.15).

Figure 3 repeats the basic premise of figure 2 but with a more punitive form of criminal justice contact: incarceration. As with arrest, figure 3 shows that the 1997 cohort experiences a greater level of confinement without reporting offending than the 1979 cohort: 0.04 percent of the 1997 cohort versus 0.01 percent of the 1979 cohort reported having been confined without reporting committing an offense. Moreover, the level of contact is so much higher among the later cohort that, among those engaged in crime, their odds of being incarcerated are roughly equivalent to the odds of arrest for the 1979 cohort.

Finally, figure 4 disaggregates the odds of arrest by race and gender to detect any bivariate relationship. Two important patterns emerge from figure 4. First, the decoupling of criminality from arrest appears to have affected all members of both cohorts. That is, the black, Hispanic, and white respondents of the 1997 cohort all reported increased arrest in the absence of reported offending. This suggests that the decoupling of criminality from contact occurred at perhaps a larger scale than anticipated. However, the second pattern seen in figure 4 is that the decoupling of criminality from arrest was largest for black respondents. The increase in the odds of being arrested without having reported criminal involvement between the 1979 and 1997 cohort of black men is roughly 419 percent. Considered another way, black men who do not report engaging in crime in 1997 have larger odds of arrest than their counterparts who do report it in 1979. That outcome is striking and one we return to later.

Multivariate Results

The bivariate results suggest movement toward the decoupling of criminality from criminal justice contact, but multivariate analyses are needed to more fully understand the underlying relationships. The normative argument guiding our analysis is that the relationship between offending behavior and criminal justice exposure should be quite strong such that offending is a primary predictor of arrest, that the relationship should be relatively stable across the two cohorts, and the connection between criminality and exposure to arrest should not diverge substantially by noncrime statuses such as race or education. We might worry, for example, if Americans committing many vio-

Figure 4. Odds of Arrest by Offending, Demographic Group, and Cohort

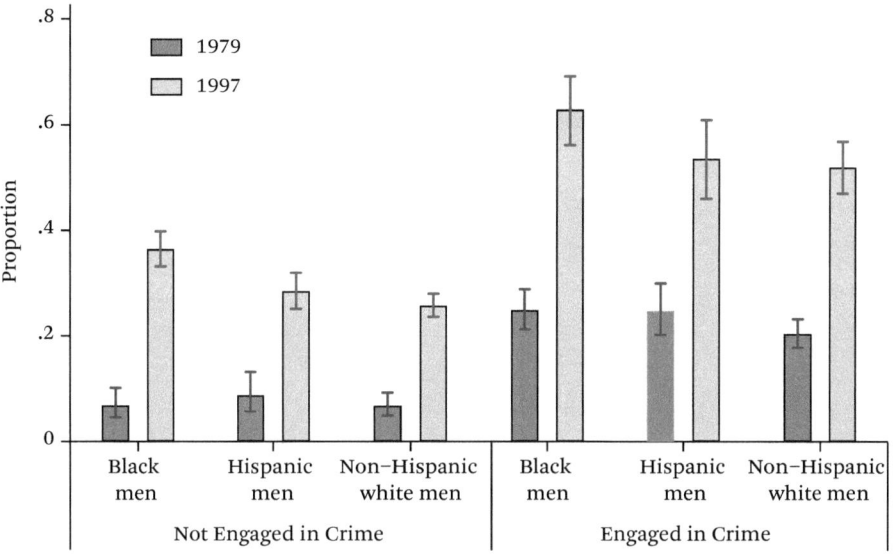

Source: Authors' compilation based on the NLSY (Bureau of Labor Statistics 2014, 2015).

lent acts were never detained or, conversely, if many Americans were being arrested but had not engaged in illegal behavior. It would raise questions about the function of the criminal justice system if arrest patterns had little to do with offending patterns or if the connection between crime and arrest was arbitrary, dwarfed by other factors that have little to do with breaking the law.

We investigate these issues by merging the NLSY cohorts into one data file and conducting our analysis on the combined file with a year variable differentiating the two cohorts. We model arrest outcomes in a logistic regression where the outcome to be explained is reported arrest and our main explanatory variables are the dichotomous (self-reported) property crime and violent crime measures. To account for slight sampling differences across the cohorts, we control for various demographic and socioeconomic measures: age, gender, race, region, urbanicity, education, family income with missing values imputed, and leaving school before completing high school (see table A1).[17] The results of these regressions are presented in figures 5 through 9. Full regression parameters are presented in the appendix (see tables A3 through A6).[18]

As we can see in figure 5, one of the best predictors of being arrested is engaging in property crime or violent crime; both of these parameters are large and statistically significant. Substantively, this indicates a strong relationship between criminal justice exposure (arrest) and self-report of engaging in crime. As we would expect, gender, age, urbanicity, and education level also affect the odds of arrest. Being in the later cohort (that is, the year dummy) has a very large influence on arrest; respondents have a greater probability of being arrested if they were unlucky enough to be moving through young adulthood two decades after the early 1980s cohort.

But the question that our analysis hinges

---

17. We also include sampling weights and run the analyses with and without the weights. Results do not depend on the weights; for convenience, we report the unweighted results.

18. We also produced similar results using a more restrictive measure of arrest—being charged—as well as a noncumulative measure of arrest—arrest in last year only (see table A3). Full results for all models are available from the authors on request.

Figure 5. Results of Logistic Regression Predicting Arrest, 1979 and 1997 NLSY

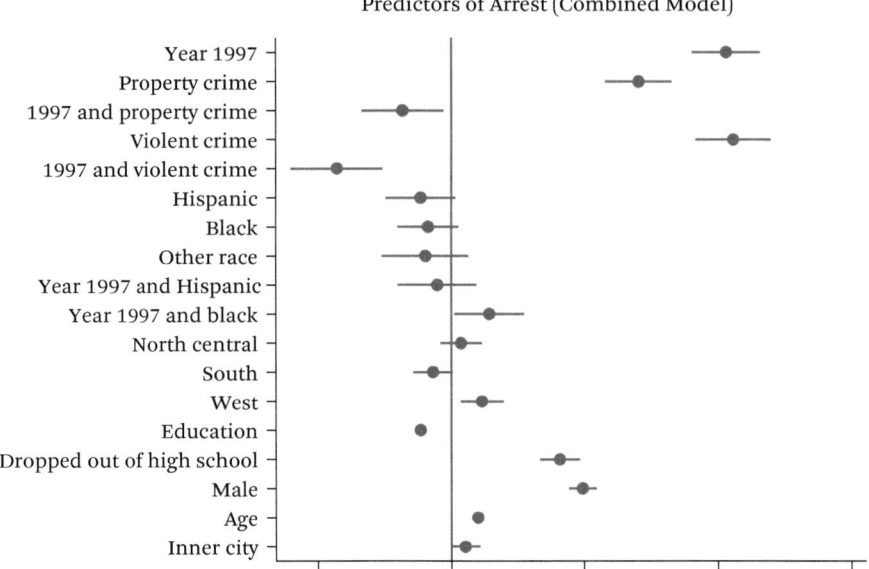

Source: Authors' compilation based on the NLSY (Bureau of Labor Statistics 2014, 2015).

on is whether the influence of criminal offending on arrest likelihood changes across the cohorts. It does, and sharply so. In the logit model predicting arrest, an interaction term that captures the interaction of cohort and self-reported property or violent offending declines in importance for the 1997 cohort relative to respondents in the 1979 cohort. We see this in models with cohort interaction effects as well as if we examine the effects of self-reported offending separately by cohort. For example, for the 1979 cohort, self-reported property and violent offending measures explain 0.08 of the variance in arrest; in 1997, these measures explain 0.05 of the variance in arrest. Committing a property or violent crime (self-report) explains arrest outcomes less well in the 1997 cohort than in the 1979 cohort. That is a concerning dynamic, and one we need to explore further.

Figure 5 also indicates the growing influence of racial membership. A cohort-race interaction term suggests that the influence of being black on arrest grows over time, mattering more for the 1997 cohort than their earlier counterparts.

The analyses thus far provide some support for the idea that self-reported criminal offending and exposure to criminal justice has shifted—decoupled even—over time. The next set of results relies on a different, more elaborate measure of criminal behavior using measures in both iterations of the NLSY. We developed a crime index, a scale of items about the frequency of a respondent's committing one of six crimes—theft under $50, theft over $50, assault, selling drugs, damaging property, and using hard drugs (never, one time, two times, three to five times, six to ten times, eleven to fifty times, and more than fifty times).[19] These six items use relatively similar question wording across the two surveys. The alpha is 0.713, indicating that the items load well as a scale. The results that follow rely on the index of all six delinquency items; analyses were also run using each measure of offending separately to ensure that the results were not being driven by one type of offending. To avoid an abun-

---

19. Marijuana use is excluded in our index because in 1997 the item uses a different scale (last thirty days instead of last year) than in 1979. Results do not change when marijuana use is adapted for the index, however.

Figure 6. Predicted Probability of Arrest by Offending and Cohort

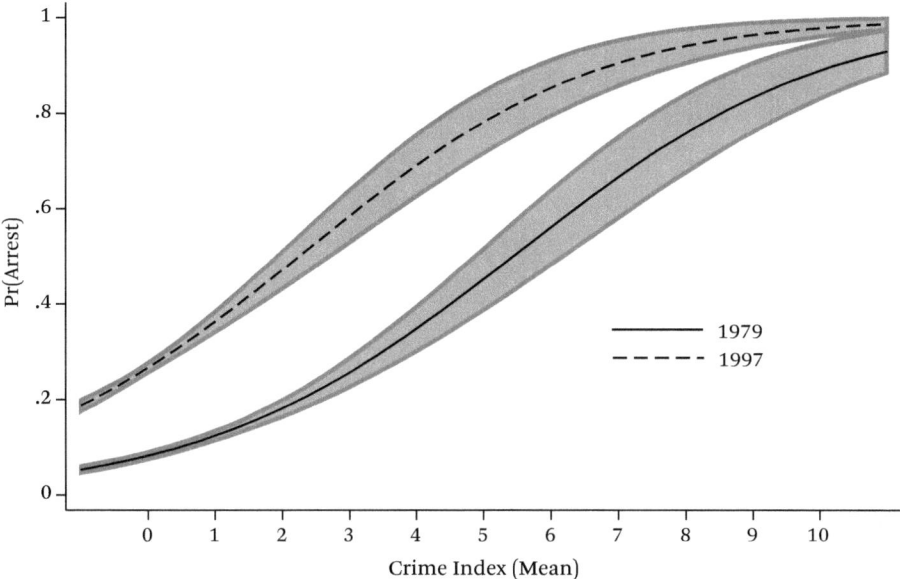

Source: Authors' compilation based on the NLSY (Bureau of Labor Statistics 2014, 2015).
Note: Unweighted. Logistic regressions with controls for age, gender, race, region, urbanicity, education, leaving school before completing high school. Confidence intervals appear in gray.

dance of zeros, we mean-centered the index.[20] The resulting measure has a mean value of 0.16 among the 1979 cohort and -0.19 among the 1997 cohort.

Figure 6 plots the results of a logistic regression where generational cohort is interacted with the continuous measure of self-reported offending, the crime index. Rather than plotting the regression coefficients as before, we plot the marginal probabilities of arrest at each level of crime for each cohort separately. The interaction term allows the relationship between self-reported criminal offending and arrest to have a different slope by cohort. The results are striking. Viewed in this way, one sees clearly that not only is the 1997 cohort more likely to be arrested than the 1979 cohort, the lines do not converge at any point on the crime continuum. The relationship between self-reported crime and arrest is indeed different based on cohort, even if the direction of the relationship (more crime leading to increased probability of arrest) is similar. Moreover, the probability of arrest is higher at every level of self-reported criminality (including no offending) in 1997, and the relationship between self-reported crime and arrest becomes flat sooner. Perhaps the most interesting part of the figure is toward the lower values on the crime index, where the divergence between the probability of being arrested conditional on one's generational cohort is large. For example, committing few to no crimes in 1979 (self-reported) translates into a very low probability of arrest; among those in the later cohort, reporting few to no crimes translates into a much higher risk of arrest, sometimes on the order of 20 percent or more. Thereafter, the odds of arrest among the 1997 cohort grow in a steep line until they level off at around a 7 on the crime index.

20. Because standard models are unable to distinguish between a no-arrest outcome due to no offense and a zero outcome due to other reasons (no enforcement), a zero-inflated Poisson regression was appropriate. Although not presented here, we ran the analysis using a zero-inflated Poisson (ZIP) regression so that we could model separate processes leading to a zero outcome and the diagnostics did not indicate it fitting the model better.

Figure 7. Predicted Probability of Arrest by Self-Reported Offending, 1979

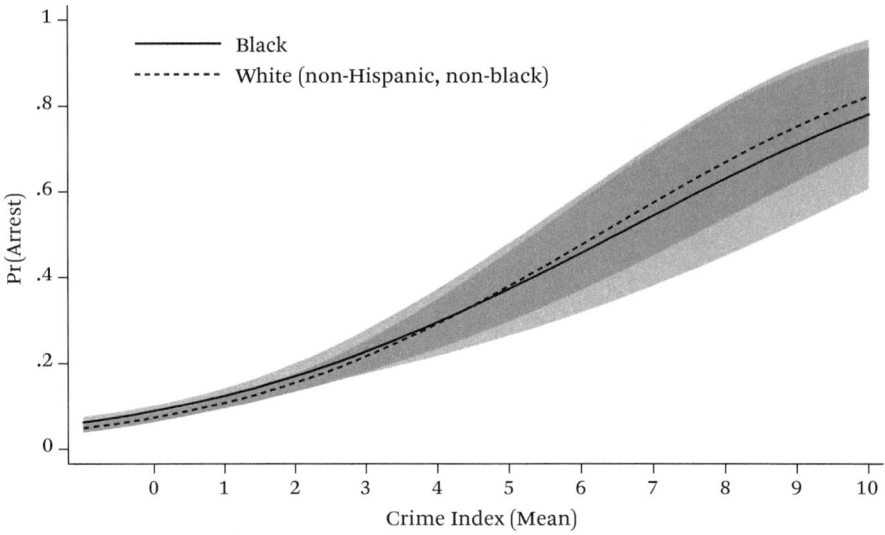

Source: Authors' compilation based on the NLSY (Bureau of Labor Statistics 2014, 2015).
Note: Unweighted. Logistic regressions with controls for age, gender, race, region, urbanicity, education, leaving school before completing high school. Confidence intervals appear in gray.

Among the 1979 cohort, by contrast, arrest probabilities grow more slowly and the steep increase really only sets in after reaching the halfway mark on the index. The cohort lines only begin to converge among those respondents who indicated substantial involvement in crime, but at no point do arrest probabilities mirror each other across the two generations. The 1997 slope takes on a concave downward shape, whereas the 1979 slope is concave upward, at least at the low end of the crime index.[21]

How is this changing relationship between exposure to arrest and reported criminality itself interacting with race? This is where we see some of the most convincing evidence that the crime-arrest connection is increasingly fraught and has become more racially inflected over time. Again, we model the relationship in the same way as before but this time we run separate regressions by year with an interaction term to capture the interacting influence of race and the crime index. Figure 7 plots the margins for the 1979 cohort for blacks and whites separately. Strikingly, the lines for blacks and non-Hispanic whites almost completely overlap, indicating that the relationship be-

---

21. Our finding that one had a much larger likelihood of arrest at low levels of offending or non-offending in the later cohort could be explained by the shift towards probation-related arrests without the commission of a new crime in the later period. Respondents were not asked whether they were specifically arrested for a probation or parole violation until 2008, unfortunately, and they weren't asked this at all in 1979. However, earlier survey waves of the NLSY 1997 cohort do provide a measure of who is currently on probation from prior arrests and convictions. For example, about 332 respondents in the NLSY waves prior to 2002 who were arrested, charged, went to court, and were convicted or pled guilty reported that they were on probation as a result of reported arrests ("Were you put on probation?"). Of these 332, 186 respondents reported no offending since the date of last interview. Of these, only twenty-one respondents reported being arrested in 2002. Thus, the likelihood that our core findings are an artifact of respondents on probation whose new arrests were for probation violations instead of the commission of new crimes is trivial. We repeat the analysis controlling for being on probation in a prior year (that is, those whose new arrest could have been a probation violation) and the results do not change. In addition, the results are nearly identical as before after excluding respondents who reported being on probation in a prior year (1997 to 2001) from the analysis altogether. These results are presented in the appendix.

Figure 8. Predicted Probability of Arrest by Self-Reported Offending, 1997

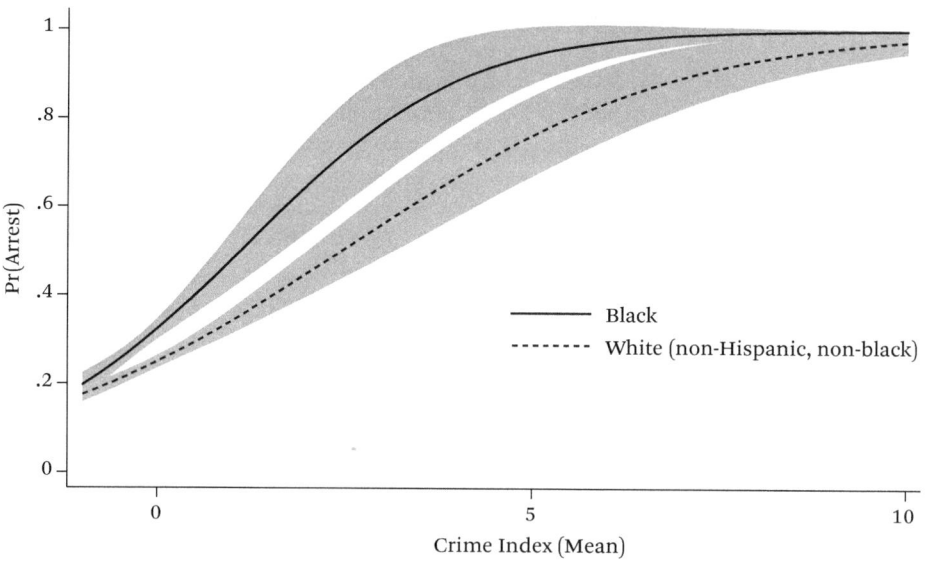

Source: Authors' compilation based on the NLSY (Bureau of Labor Statistics 2014, 2015).
Note: Unweighted. Logistic regressions with controls for age, gender, race, region, urbanicity, education, leaving school before completing high school. Confidence intervals appear in gray.

tween self-reported offending and arrest outcomes is quite similar for blacks and whites in this earlier cohort, and it is similar regardless of where on the crime continuum one focuses. In short, if black young adults are being arrested more than their white peers net of reported criminality, we are hard pressed to find evidence of it in the 1979 NLSY. At least for this generation then, and at least in their early adulthood, arrest outcomes are mostly egalitarian conditional on reported offending. The absence of an obvious racial disparity in arrest among young adults in the 1970s comports with existing bodies of knowledge and is mostly consistent with the chronological development of the carceral state. In his recent book on the turn toward punitive policies, James Forman reminds us that many of the tactics and policies that would drive up arrests, and particularly those of young urban and poor black men, had not yet occurred by the late 1970s and their "catastrophic impact on black communities wasn't yet apparent" (2017, 219). Indeed, in the lead-up to the expansion in prisons and drug arrests, incarceration and arrest rates were low and crime and violence were high and getting worse (Pfaff 2017; Forman 2017).

The situation had changed dramatically by the late 1990s. Figure 8 examines arrest probabilities for blacks and non-Hispanic whites in the cohort that was in early adulthood around 1997 along the same crime index as before. The change from 1979 to 1997 is remarkable. The relationship between reported crime and arrest tilts upward for both blacks and whites, but the increase is much more pronounced among blacks. At the low end of the crime index, both blacks and whites were arrested at a probability of about 0.2. But the odds of arrest for blacks increase and increase more quickly at each point along the crime index. So marked is the increase in arrest conditional on reported crime for blacks that, in contrast to 1979, at no point after the lowest crime value do their odds of arrest intersect with whites. Looking back to figure 7 from the 1979 NLSY, we can see that the racial split that emerges for the 1997 cohort is a break from the relatively recent past, establishing itself in a matter of just one generation. For example, in 1979, both blacks and whites had a probability of about 0.25 of arrest if they were a 3 on the crime index (remember, the index is six crimes with six levels of frequency). In 1997, blacks' probability of arrest jumps to a whopping 0.8 if they were a 3 on the index (relative to 0.6 for whites). Thus, two things are happening—all people experience a significant jump in arrest odds in 1997 relative to earlier and the rise is particularly salient for blacks, who by 1997 experience much higher chances of arrest at every level of reported offending. Put differently, black Americans' exposure to arrest is both higher than their black counterparts of one generation past and markedly different from that of their white counterparts of the same generation. Those two dynamics deserve much more attention than extant scholarship has given them. Many books and essays have been written on the increase in criminal justice exposure over time and their various political causes as well as their racial dimensions, including by us. Many have suggested that crime was only partly a cause. But this is the clearest analysis to date to document that arrest exposure and its relationship to crime changed in one generation, and a racial disparity emerged that was not present before.[22]

Up to this point, we have been concerned with the relationship between reported offending and arrest exposure by generation and racial groups. Let us return to the simple typology that was the springboard for our exploration—the two-by-two of contact and criminality. In the next set of analyses, we divided the NLSY samples into the four quadrants, mirroring our theoretical discussion: arrested, reported a crime; no arrest, reported a crime; arrested, did not report a crime; and no arrest, did not report a crime. Respondents are assigned to the "did not report committing a crime group" if they were a zero on the (non–mean-centered) crime index. Does membership in each quadrant change over time? And if so, is there a distinct pattern for blacks and whites, given that results pointed to an emerging racial disparity among 1997 respondents? Once these quadrants were established, we used a multinomial logit to analyze the relative risk of ending up in one of the quadrants by race and year (with the baseline group being no arrest and no crime). The multinomial approach allows us to model the paired outcomes of arrest and reported offending resulting in four distinct types, rather than using reported offending to predict arrest as we did in the preceding analysis.

Figure 9 plots the predicted probabilities of landing in a quadrant by cohort and race based on the results of the multinomial logit for men only, holding all of the controls at their mean values. Quadrant 1 shows no significant change; the probability of being in this quadrant remains unchanged for blacks and ever so slightly increases for whites. Quadrant 2 shows steep changes in the likelihood of respondents ending up there and in the direction we would expect; for both black and white men, the probability of being in the category of committing crime (self-reported) and not being arrested shifts significantly downward. White men are somewhat more likely than black men to belong to this category in both cohorts, but the change across cohorts is similar for both black and white men. Thus, we might say that the criminal justice system became more adept at making contact with actual offenders, regardless of race.

Quadrant 3 is where much of the action is: it shows a significant and sizable increase in the likelihood of being in the category of experiencing arrest without indicating crime commission and it is especially pronounced for black men. Specifically, for black men, the predicted probability of being in quadrant 3—of being exposed to arrest without having reported breaking a law—rises from about 0.05 in the 1979 cohort to 0.25 in the 1997 cohort. That change occurs net of age, region, urbanicity, and education. White men also experience a surge in the likelihood of belonging to this category from one generation to the next, albeit not as substantial.

This finding exposes a serious and unappreciated distortion in the modern criminal justice system. The established narrative surrounding criminal justice has focused on increasing contacts across the board with occasional nods to racial or other disparities based on neighborhood and various other factors. The key take-

---

22. The effects for men alone are even more pronounced, especially at the lower end of the offending index (results available from the authors).

Figure 9. Multinomial Logit Regression Results

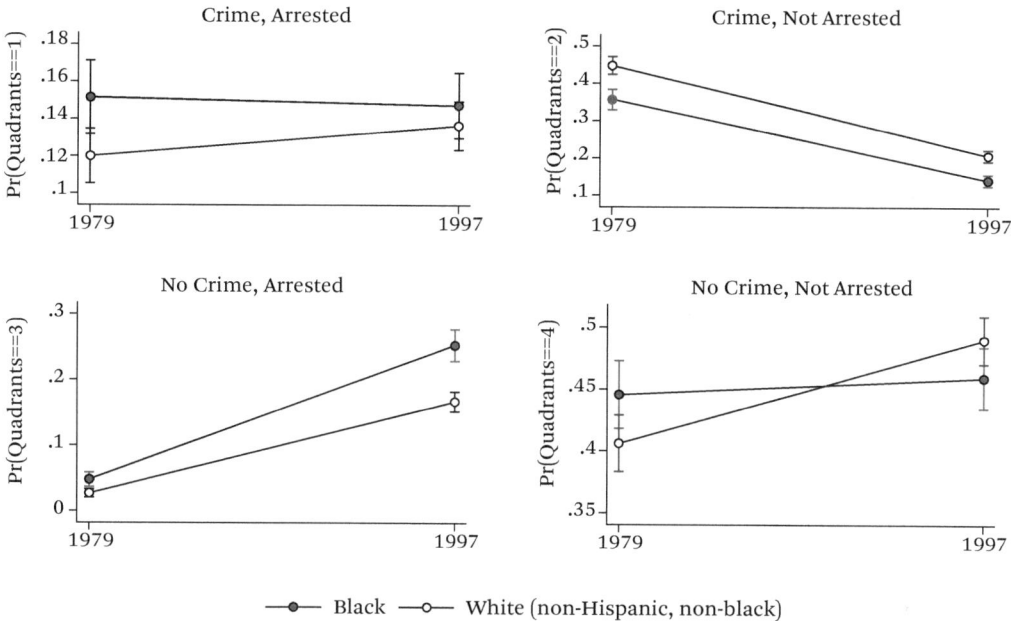

Source: Authors' compilation based on the NLSY (Bureau of Labor Statistics 2014, 2015).

away from our analysis, however, is this: the story of the last four decades is really about quadrant 3. A benefit of our approach is that although some assume that race matters everywhere and all the time in the criminal justice system, and others assume that the relationship between offending and arrest remained unchanged even as arrest increased, we can show that race matters but really comes to matter primarily in one quadrant. By looking at arrest outcomes regardless of offending patterns, scholars conflate quadrants 1 and 3 and thereby underestimate changes happening in the latter. If we focus only on arrest outcomes or only on offending outcomes in isolation from one another, we miss that basic but important pattern. Our criminal justice system, it could be said, got both more and less efficient—more efficient in the sense that offenders (of any race) became more likely to be arrested (quadrant 2), but less efficient and less legitimate in that more law-abiding Americans were exposed to arrest over time, particularly black men (quadrant 3).

Our estimates of the changing relationship across cohorts depend on the assumption that our measures of offending and arrest are reliable and have external validity; it hinges on the claim that under- or overreporting in self-identification of arrests or offending, if it exists, remains constant across cohorts and racial groups. We have good reason to believe that such a strong assumption of equal validity across group-cohort is warranted. Still, even if we relax this assumption and allow that some underreporting of both offending and arrests for blacks, particularly in the later period amid a political discourse around "superpredator" kids and "lock 'em up" policies, and even if we adjusted both estimates up, the basic relationship we find between offending and arrest holds. For such dramatic cross-cohort and race results to be explained entirely by measurement error, it would have to be that underreporting of offending was both worse than prior studies have led us to believe and that underreporting of arrest by blacks declined in the later cohort. In the worst-case scenario, a shift over the cohorts to both overreport arrests and underreport criminality occurred and this shift was greatest for blacks. To the best of our knowledge, no evidence exists in the extant prior literature to support these two possibilities. With all of these considerations in mind, our findings and conclusions are based on one examination of the best dataset we have at present and should be explored in future research with additional datasets.

THE GREAT DECOUPLING

Many explanations have been offered for the expansion in punishment in America before the dawn of the twenty-first century—too much law and too little local democracy, an anxious American public and populist pressures, shifts in modern penology away from the rehabilitative ideal, our dysfunctional political institutions with their weak welfare state and all-powerful prosecutor, neoliberal penality, and the racialized punitive bidding wars of American politics. Such explanations are important. Yet, they all mischaracterize the development as expanding police oversight and punishment in isolation. What transpired in the last half century was not only an expansion of the state's authority and citizens' increased contact with the state's punitive arm, it was a decoupling that transformed the historical relationship between criminality and exposure to arrest among Americans.

According to the NLSY data, perhaps the best data we have to examine a relationship between arrest and offending at the individual level in the early 1980s, self-reported criminality and contact were strongly related. Moreover, blacks were no more likely to be exposed to arrest than whites at a given level of reported offending. Overall and regardless of reported offending patterns, the share of those over eighteen years of age who reported being arrested was 10 percent for both blacks and whites. Among the generation of young adults in the late 1990s, in stark contrast, the ability of criminal behavior to explain variation in arrest outcomes lessened dramatically. And the relationship became especially distorted among blacks, whose odds of arrest surge upward even at low levels of reported offending. Put differently, the offending-contact relationship for the 1979 cohort approximates a system that arrests those who are unlawful and leaves alone those who are law abiding (and does so for blacks and whites equally), though this earlier system likely missed many individuals who engaged in crime (quadrant 2). Over time, it appears that in addition to arresting larger shares of individuals committing crime, the system expanded its purview to those who were not actively offending.

We have modeled this relationship at the individual level among a sample of all Americans. If the shifting upward slope that emerges in 1997, particularly among black Americans, is true to reality, how many arrests does this represent over time? How many Americans were exposed to criminal justice but did not behave unlawfully? Our data do not provide definitive estimates but because black men who had not reported engaging in crime had odds of arrest at 0.36, the number is likely very large. If the decoupling persists or widens over time, we will have institutionalized a system that departs from common normative assumptions that the justice system should target actual offenders and leave alone those who abide by the law.

Such an inquiry may unintentionally reinforce what Naomi Murakawa and Katherine Beckett term "the penology of racial innocence"; they warn scholars, rightly in our view, against the practice of studying criminal justice by "exposing moments of bias" and caution against the widespread practice in our fields of study of controlling for criminality, as though crime itself is innocent of the operation of racial power (Murakawa and Beckett 2010). As others have argued, crime itself exposes key ways the state fails to ameliorate deep social risks: "when persons from the ghetto choose crime, however, they do so under conditions of material deprivation and institutional racism. Thus their criminal activity might express something more, or something other, than a character flaw or a disregard for the authority of morality" (Shelby 2007, 136).

Yet we believe that the quadrant exercise exposes an underlying tendency within our criminal justice system that has been routinely erased in scholarship and has for far too long helped further the "ideology" of black criminality (Muhammad 2011). That is, without knowing how criminality and contact relate, we unwittingly convey a view of our criminal justice system as legitimate and efficient and those who are exposed to it as deserving targets. The implications of shifting quadrants matters not only as an academic exercise, but also as a pressing matter of public policy; reform efforts will likely fail to deliver a more just and fair system if our collective focus remains on lessening the contact in quadrant 1 without attending to the surplus in quadrant 3, those Americans who remain committed to the law but have experienced police sanction. If we do not recognize that decreases in the share of young Americans in quadrant 2 (an outcome to be celebrated, by some more than others perhaps) arguably came at the price of vast and unwarranted expansions in quadrant 3 (which we should all find worrisome), we miss that criminal justice developments can have spillovers born of "improvements" that undermine those very successes. We may also be dismayed when efforts to decarcerate fail to move many people having lower-level contacts into the "no contact" quadrant.

Admittedly, we have only begun to understand the transformation of criminal justice as it related to actual crime. But we hope to have nudged scholars in relevant fields toward greater recognition of the shifting crime-contact link. Our exploration (and findings) were limited to arrest, a key entry point in the criminal justice system to be sure, but only one of the many points where the shifting connection between offending patterns and exposure may be in evidence. Thus, a natural extension to the study would consider other points in the criminal justice system, such as incarceration, and their underlying relationship to offending. Policymakers may naturally consider how to not just decarcerate but how to make criminality less orthogonal to contact. What interventions can repair a system that not only expands the share of the population having contact with surveillant authorities, a system that is both more severe and intrusive, yes, but perhaps just as concerning, more unhinged from actual law breaking?

APPENDIX

Table A1. Sampling Differences and Adjustments in NLSY Cohorts

	NLSY 1979	NLSY 1997	How Our Analysis Deals with Differences Between 1979 and 1997 NLSY Cohorts
Samples	Cross-sectional sample: Nationally representative sample of individuals born 1957 to 1964 and living in United States as of first survey round	Cross-sectional sample: Nationally representative sample of individuals born 1980 to 1984 and living in United States as of first survey round	Because the oversamples of low-SES whites and military servicepeople in the 1979 NLSY are not included in the 1997 NLSY, we omit them from our analysis (as instructed by the NLSY Tutorial on constructing comparable samples, https://www.nlsinfo.org/site/nlsy97/nlsdocs/nlsy97/tutorials/comparing97-79/comparing 97-79_tutorial.html, accessed August 25, 2018)
	Oversamples of black and Hispanic individuals, born 1957 to 1964	Oversamples of black and Hispanic individuals, born 1980 to 1984 (n = 2473)	
	Economically disadvantaged non-black non-Hispanic oversample, born 1957 to 1964		
	Military sample (born 1957 to 1961 and serving in the military as of September 30, 1978)		
Year analyzed	1980 (second round)	2002 (sixth round)	We analyze these rounds because 1980 is the only round for the 1979 NLSY cohort when criminal justice contact and criminal offending variables are asked and 2002 is the round when the age ranges of the 1997 cohort respondents are most similar to the 1980 respondents from the 1979 cohort.

Age range of initial sample	Youth fourteen to twenty-two by December 1978	Youth twelve to sixteen as of December 1978	We examine only youth at least eighteen by 1980 and 2002, the years of our analysis. This omits 3,527 respondents from the NLSY 1979. But the age range of eighteen to twenty-three is now consistent across cohorts.
Sampling design	Stratified multistage area probability sampling	Stratified multistage area probability sampling	
Administration of the survey	PAPI	CAPI	One potential issue in comparing between the two cohorts is that the NLSY switched from using paper and pencil interviews (PAPI) to using computer-assisted personal interviews (CAPI) in 1989 (Interview Methods). This change may have led to differences in reporting delinquent behavior. In 1989, the compatibility of these two methods were tested using CAPI for half of the Ohio interviews and PAPI for the other half (Bradburn et al. 1992, 3). The authors found that of the 139 variables they examined, only four of these "reached conventional levels of significance" (4). Two of these variables were related to alcohol use in CAPI, which leads the authors to consider that CAPI may be a more anonymous form survey and lead to more reporting (8). Therefore, we might potentially expect higher levels of reporting of criminal behavior on the NLSY 97, where only CAPI was used, versus NLSY 79, where PAPI was used for the question regarding criminal behavior.
Question wording on key outcome of interest	"Not counting minor traffic offenses, have you ever been booked or charged for breaking a law, either by the police or by someone connected with the courts?"	"Have you ever been arrested by the police or taken into custody for an illegal or delinquent offense (do not include arrests for minor traffic violations)?" "Since the date of last interview on [], have you, …."	These questions are worded differently and the 1997 version may have been interpreted in a more expansive way to include mere police stops. Therefore, we replicate our analyses using an arrest measure in 1997 that further asks respondents who reported arrest: "did the police charge you with an offense?"

Source: Authors' compilation.

Table A2. Descriptive Statistics

	NLSY 1979 (n = 5,837)	NLSY 1997 (n = 8,683)
Ever arrested (not for minor traffic violations)	10.2	24.9
Ever charged with an offense	10.2	17.4
Arrested in the last year	4.3	6
Mean age of first arrest	17.4	16.3
Criminal offending		
Destroy property	19	3.9
Theft (under $50)	19	5
Theft (over $50)	5	2
Attack with intent to injure or kill	10	6
Marijuana distribution	10	4.5
Hard drugs distribution	2	1.7
Used marijuana	45	21
Used hard drugs	17.5	5
Crime Index (mean)	.306	.127
Men	49	51
Age (mean)	20	20
Less than high school	30	30
Less than high school and not currently enrolled	15	15
High school and not currently enrolled	27.5	23
High school grad and enrolled in college	15	24
Family income (mean)[a]	$18,156	$52,767
Under poverty line[a]	22.7	25.5
Non-Hispanic white	50	51
Hispanic	20	22
Black	30	27
Black men	15	13.5
South	37	39
Northeast	19	17
North central	25	22
West	19	22
Urban	76	76
Central city[b]	23	33

Source: Authors' compilation.
Note: Respondents age eighteen or older only.
[a] Because of high missingness, values were imputed through a multiple imputation procedure.
[b] Of the 1979 cohort, 23 percent are in the central city (though a quarter of the sample is listed as "central city not known").

Table A3. Results of Logistic Regression Predicting Arrest, 1979 and 1997 NLSY Combined

	Ever Arrested	Arrested in Last Year	Ever Charged with Offense	Arrested in Last Year Controlling for Probation
1997 cohort	**2.15*****	**1.06*****	**1.73*****	**1.00*****
	(0.131)	(.210)	(.133)	(.211)
Property offense	**1.39*****	**1.35*****	**1.39*****	**1.35*****
	(0.127)	(.190)	(.127)	(.191)
1997*property offense (interaction)	**−0.348***	.418	−.285	.409
	(0.156)	(.227)	(.159)	(.227)
Violent offense	**2.12*****	**2.03*****	**2.11*****	**2.03*****
	(0.143)	(.205)	(.143)	(.205)
1997*violent offense (interaction)	**−0.857*****	−.211	**−.088*****	−.234
	(0.178)	(.246)	(.180)	(.246)
Hispanic	−0.242	0.189	−.203	0.197
	(0.132)	(.179)	(.133)	(.179)
Black	**−0.191**	−.026	−.179	−.023
	(0.115)	(.162)	(.115)	(.162)
Other race	−0.261	−.107	−.558*	−.100
	(0.192)	(.347)	(.232)	(.349)
1997*Hispanic interaction	−0.142	**−.662****	**−.314***	**−.654****
	(0.150)	(.225)	(.156)	(.225)
1997*black interaction	0.257	−.089	−.030	−.069
	(0.134)	(.202)	(.139)	(.202)
Male	**0.992*****	**1.005*****	**1.028*****	**.983*****
	(0.054)	(.096)	(.059)	(.097)
Education (years)	**−0.215*****	**−.165*****	**−.187*****	**−.162*****
	(0.021)	(.033)	(.022)	(.034)
Dropout	**0.814*****	**.836*****	**.900*****	**.818*****
	(0.079)	(.124)	(.084)	(.124)
Family income	**−2.41e−06****	−7.54e−07	**−2.30e−06****	−7.27e−07
	(7.37e−07)	(1.23e−06)	(8.18e−07)	(1.23e−06)
Age	**0.189*****	.011	.205	.003
	(0.019)	(.030)	(.019)	(.030)
North central	0.072	−0.001	−.086	−0.011
	(0.080)	(0.131)	(0.086)	(0.131)
South	−0.147	−0.088	−0.176	−0.069
	(0.76)	(0.121)	(0.082)	(0.122)
West	**0.213***	**0.077**	**0.172**	0.094
	(0.083)	(0.135)	(0.089)	(0.135)
Urban/rural	.078	.114	**.141***	.101
	(.069)	(.108)	(.072)	(.109)
On probation in prior years				**.641*****
				(.179)
N	12,936	12,939	12,936	12,939

Source: Authors' compilation.
Note: Boldface if significance at the .06 level. Standard errors in parentheses. Sample includes those at least eighteen years old.
*$p < .05$; **$p < .01$; ***$p < .001$

Table A4. Predicted Probability of Arrest by Offending and Cohort

1997 cohort	1.64***	Education	−0.205***
	(0.066)		(0.020)
Mean crime index	0.503***	Dropped out of high school	0.818***
	(0.033)		(0.080)
1997*mean crime index	0.030	Male	1.03***
	(0.052)		(0.054)
Hispanic	−0.411***	Age	0.168***
	(0.079)		(0.019)
White	−0.091	Urban	0.159*
	(0.065)		(0.067)
North central	0.093	Family income	−2.21e−06**
	(0.080)		(7.59e−07)
South	−0.111		
	(0.076)	N	12,766
West	0.189*		
	(0.084)		

Source: Authors' compilation based on the NLSY (Bureau of Labor Statistics 2014, 2015).
*p < .05; **p < .01; ***p < .001

Table A5. Predicted Probability of Arrest by Offending

	1979	1997
White	−0.0045	−0.155
	(0.136)	(0.083)
Mean crime index	0.425***	0.810***
	(0.060)	(0.117)
White*mean crime index (interaction)[a]	0.036	−0.292*
	0.074	(0.128)
Male	1.27***	0.877***
	(0.128)	(0.070)
Urban	0.133	0.235**
	(0.145)	(0.081)
Education (years)	−0.167**	−0.279***
	(0.049)	(0.029)
Dropout	0.979***	0.699***
	(0.175)	(0.109)
Family income	−6.68e−06	−1.41e−06
	3.69e−06	(8.11e−07)
Age	0.153***	0.215***
	(0.039)	(0.026)
North central	0.023	0.051
	(0.166)	(0.166)
South	−0.205	−0.111
	(0.167)	(0.098)
West	0.442*	0.122
	(0.187)	(0.121)
N	4486	5623

Source: Authors' compilation based on the NLSY (Bureau of Labor Statistics 2014, 2015).
[a] Reference category is black.
*p < .05; **p < .01; ***p < .001

Table A6. Multinomial Logit Regression Results, Men Only

Quadrant 1		**Quadrant 2** (*cont.*)	
1997 Cohort	−0.316**	Family income	1.20e−06
	(0.105)		(1.15e−06)
White	0.159	Age	−0.058
	(0.107)		(0.030)
Urban	0.156	North central	−0.114
	(0.110)		(0.109)
Education (years)	−0.265***	South	−0.223*
	(0.041)		(0.108)
Dropout	1.012***	West	−0.050
	(0.146)		(0.133)
Family income	6.63e−07	**Quadrant 3**	
	(1.30e−06)	1997 Cohort	1.71***
Age	0.107**		(0.138)
	(0.034)	White	−0.199*
North central	−0.249		(−0.103)
	(0.137)	Urban	0.324**
South	−0.397**		(0.108)
	(0.132)	Education (years)	−0.315***
West	0.151		(0.039)
	(0.156)	Dropout	0.640***
Quadrant 2			(0.145)
1997 Cohort	−1.75***	Family income	1.60e−08
	(0.094)		(1.15e−06)
White	0.340***	Age	0.245***
	(0.089)		(0.034)
Urban	0.286**	North central	0.232
	(0.093)		(0.138)
Education (years)	−0.032	South	−0.064
	(0.036)		(0.134)
Dropout	0.078	West	−0.040
	(0.141)		(0.173)

Source: Authors' compilation based on the NLSY (Bureau of Labor Statistics 2014, 2015).
Note: Baseline group is 4.
*p < .05; **p < .01; ***p < .001

REFERENCES

Alexander, Michelle. 2012. *The New Jim Crow: Mass Incarceration in the Age of Colorblindness*. New York: The New Press.

Altonji, Joseph G., Prashant Bharadwaj, and Fabian Lange. 2012. "Changes in the Characteristics of American Youth: Implications for Adult Outcomes." *Journal of Labor Economics* 30(4): 783–828.

Andersen, Tia Stevens. 2015. "Race, Ethnicity, and Structural Variations in Youth Risk of Arrest: Evidence from a National Longitudinal Sample." *Criminal Justice and Behavior* 42(9): 900–16.

Apel, Robert, Shawn D. Bushway, Raymond Paternoster, Robert Brame, and Gary Sweeten. 2008. "Using State Child Labor Laws to Identify the Causal Effect of Youth Employment on Deviant Behavior and Academic Achievement." *Journal of Quantitative Criminology* 24(4): 337–62.

Armenta, Amada. 2017. *Protect, Serve, and Deport: The Rise of Policing as Immigration Enforcement*. Oakland: University of California Press.

Bailey, Martha, and Susan Dynarski. 2011. "Gains and Gaps: Changing Inequality in US College Entry and Completion." *NBER* working paper no. w17633. Cambridge, Mass.: National Bureau of Economic Research.

Baumgartner, Frank R., Derek A. Epp, and Kelsey Shoub. 2018. *Suspect Citizens: What 20 Million Traffic Stops Tell Us About Policing and Race*. Cambridge: Cambridge University Press.

Beaver, Kevin M., Matt DeLisi, John Paul Wright, Brian B. Boutwell, J. C. Barnes, and Michael G. Vaughn. 2013. "No Evidence of Racial Discrimination in Criminal Justice Processing: Results from the National Longitudinal Study of Adolescent Health." *Personality and Individual Differences* 55(1): 29–34.

Beckett, Katherine, Kris Nyrop, and Lori Pfingst. 2006. "Race, Drugs, and Policing: Understanding Disparities in Drug Delivery Arrests." *Criminology* 44(1): 105–37.

Beckett, Katherine, Kris Nyrop, Lori Pfingst, and Melissa Bowen. 2005. "Drug Use, Drug Possession Arrests, and the Question of Race: Lessons from Seattle." *Social Problems* 52(3): 419–41.

Belley, Philippe, and Lance Lochner. 2007. "The Changing Role of Family Income and Ability in Determining Educational Achievement." *Journal of Human Capital* 1(1): 37–89.

Bernburg, Jön Gunnar, and Marvin D. Krohn. 2003. "Labeling, Life Chances, and Adult Crime: The Direct and Indirect Effects of Official Intervention in Adolescence on Crime in Early Adulthood." *Criminology* 41(4): 1287–318.

Bersani, Bianca E., and Alex R. Piquero. 2017. "Examining Systematic Crime Reporting Bias Across Three Immigrant Generations: Prevalence, Trends, and Divergence in Self-Reported and Official Reported Arrests." *Journal of Quantitative Criminology* 33(4): 835–57.

Bjerregaard, Beth. 2010. "Gang Membership and Drug Involvement: Untangling the Complex Relationship." *Crime and Delinquency* 56(1): 3–34.

Blumstein, Alfred, and Kiminori Nakamura. 2009. "Redemption in the Presence of Widespread Criminal Background Checks." *Criminology* 47(2): 327–59.

Bobo, Lawrence D., and Victor Thompson. 2010. "Racialized Mass Incarceration: Poverty, Prejudice and Punishment." In *Doing Race: 21 Essays for the 21st Century*, edited by Hazel Rose Markus and Paula M. L. Moya. New York: W. W. Norton.

Bradburn, Norman, Martin Frankel, Reginald Baker and Michael Pergamit. 1992. "A Comparison of CAPI with PAPI in the NLS/Y." In *Information Technology in Survey Research* discussion paper 9. Chicago: NORC.

Brame, Robert W., Shawn D. Bushway, Ray Paternoster, and Michael G. Turner. 2014. "Demographic Patterns of Cumulative Arrest Prevalence by Ages 18 and 23." *Crime and Delinquency* 60(3): 471–86.

Brame, Robert W., Michael G. Turner, Raymond Paternoster, and Shawn D. Bushway. 2012. "Cumulative Prevalence of Arrest from Ages 8 to 23 in a National Sample." *Pediatrics* 129(1): 21–27.

Browning, Sandra Lee, Francis T. Cullen, Liquan Cao, Renee Kopache, and Thomas J. Stevenson. 1994. "Race and Getting Hassled by the Police: A Research Note." *Police Studies* 17(1): 1–11.

Bureau of Labor Statistics, U.S. Department of Labor. 2014. *National Longitudinal Survey of Youth, 1979 cohort, 1979–2012* (rounds 1–25). Columbus, Ohio: Center for Human Resource Research, Ohio State University.

Bureau of Labor Statistics, U.S. Department of Labor. 2015. *National Longitudinal Survey of Youth, 1997 cohort, 1997–2013* (rounds 1–16). Columbus, Ohio: Center for Human Resource Research, Ohio State University.

Bushway, Shawn D. 1998. "The Impact of an Arrest on the Job Stability of Young White American Men." *Journal of Research in Crime and Delinquency* 35(4): 454–79.

Butler, Paul. 2017. *Chokehold: Policing Black Men*. New York: New Press.

Capers, I. Bennett. 2009. "Policing, Race, and Place." *Harvard Civil Rights-Civil Liberties Law Review* 44(1): 43–78.

Castex, Gonzalo, and Evgenia Dechter. 2014. "The Changing Roles of Education and Ability in Wage Determination." *Journal of Labor Economics* 32(4): 685–710.

Del Toro, Juan, Tracey Lloyd, Kim Buchanana, Summer Robins, Lucy Zhang, Meredith Smiedt, Kavita Reddy, and Philip Goff. n.d. "When Policing Causes Crime: The Criminogenic Effects of Police Stops on Adolescent Black and Latino Boys." Working paper, Center for Policing Equity.

Ehrenfreund, Max. 2015. "Black Teens Who Commit a Few Crimes Go to Jail as Often as White Teens Who Commit Dozens." *Washington Post*, January 30. Accessed August 18, 2018. https://www

.washingtonpost.com/news/wonk/wp/2015/01/30/black-teens-who-commit-a-few-crimes-go-to-jail-as-often-as-white-teens-who-commit-dozens.

Elliot, Delbert S. 1995. "Lies, Damn Lies and Arrest Statistics." The Sutherland Award Presentation, The American Society of Criminology Meetings, Boston, MA (November 15–18).

Emmert, Amanda D., Arna L. Carlock, Alan J. Lizotte, and Marvin D. Krohn. 2017. "Predicting Adult Under- and Over-Reporting of Self-Reported Arrests from Discrepancies in Adolescent Self-Reports of Arrests: A Research Note." *Crime & Delinquency* 63(4): 412–28.

Engel, Robin S., Michael R. Smith, and Francis T. Cullen. 2012. "Race, Place, and Drug Enforcement." *Criminology & Public Policy* 11(4): 603–35.

Epp, Charles R., Steven Maynard-Moody, and Donald P. Haider-Markel. 2014. *Pulled Over: How Police Stops Define Race and Citizenship*. Chicago: University of Chicago Press.

Fagan, Jeffrey, and Garth Davies. 2000. "Street Stops and Broken Windows: Terry, Race, and Disorder in New York City." *Fordham Urban Law Journal* 28(2): 457–504.

Fagan, Jeffrey, Amanda Geller, Garth Davies, and Valerie West. 2009. "Street Stops and Broken Windows Revisited." In *Race, Ethnicity, and Policing: New and Essential Readings*, edited by Stephen K. Rice and Michael D. White. New York: New York University Press..

Farrington, David P., Darrick Jolliffe, J. David Hawkins, Richard F. Catalano, Karl G. Hill, and Rick Kosterman. 2010. "Why Are Boys More Likely to Be Referred to Juvenile Court? Gender Differences in Official and Self-Reported Delinquency." *Victims and Offenders* 5(1): 25–44.

Farrington, David P., Rolf Loeber, Magda Stouthamer-Loeber, Welmoet B. Van Kammen, and Laura Schmidt. 1996. "Self-Reported Delinquency and a Combined Delinquency Seriousness Scale Based on Boys, Mothers, and Teachers: Concurrent and Predictive Validity for African-Americans and Caucasians." *Criminology* 34(4): 493–517.

Forman, James, Jr. 2017. *Locking Up Our Own: Crime and Punishment in Black America*. New York: Farrar, Straus and Giroux.

Gase, Lauren Nichol, Beth A. Glenn, Louis M. Gomez, Tony Kuo, Moira Inkelas, and Ninez A. Ponce. 2016. "Understanding Racial and Ethnic Disparities in Arrest: The Role of Individual, Home, School, and Community Characteristics." *Race and Social Problems* 8(4): 296–312.

Gelman, Andrew, Jeffrey Fagan, and Alex Kiss. 2007. "An Analysis of the New York City Police Department's 'Stop-and-Frisk' Policy in the Context of Claims of Racial Bias." *Journal of the American Statistical Association* 102(479): 813–823.

Grogger, Jeffrey. 1995. "The Effect of Arrests on the Employment and Earnings of Young Men." *Quarterly Journal of Economics* 110(1): 51–71.

Grunwald, Ben, and Jeffrey Fagan. Forthcoming. "The End of Intuition-Based High-Crime Areas." *California Law Review* 107.

Hagedorn, John M. 1994. "Neighborhoods, Markets, and Gang Drug Organization." *Journal of Research in Crime and Delinquency* 31(3): 264–94.

Harcourt, Bernard E. 2009. *Illusion of Order: The False Promise of Broken Windows Policing*. Cambridge, Mass.: Harvard University Press.

Hay, Carter, and Walter Forrest. 2008. "Self-Control Theory and the Concept of Opportunity: The Case for a More Systematic Union." *Criminology* 46(4): 1039–1072.

Herrenkohl, Todd I., Eugene Maguin, Karl G. Hill, J. David Hawkins, Robert D. Abbott, and Richard F. Catalano. 2000. "Developmental Risk Factors for Youth Violence." *Journal of Adolescent Health* 26(3): 176–86.

Hindelang, Michael J., Travis Hirschi, and Joseph G. Weis. 1981. *Measuring Delinquency*. Beverly Hills, Calif.: Sage Publications.

Hirschfield, Paul, Tina Maschi, Helene R. White, Leah G. Traub, and Rolf Loeber. 2006. "Mental Health and Juvenile Arrests: Criminality, Criminalization, or Compassion?" *Criminology* 44(3): 593–627.

Huizinga, David, Terrence Thornberry, Kelly Knight, Peter Lovegrove, Rolf Loeber, Karl Hill, and David P. Farrington. 2007. *Disproportionate Minority Contact in the Juvenile Justice System: A Study of Differential Minority Arrest/Referral to Court in Three Cities*. Washington: U.S. Department of Justice.

Jacques, Scott, and Richard Wright. 2015. *Code of the Suburb: Inside the World of Young Middle-Class Drug Dealers*. Chicago: University of Chicago Press.

Jolliffe, Darrick, David P. Farrington, J. David Hawkins, Richard F. Catalano, Karl G. Hill, and Rick Kosterman. 2003. "Predictive, Concurrent,

Prospective and Retrospective Validity of Self-Reported Delinquency." *Criminal Behaviour and Mental Health* 13(3): 179–97.

Jordan, Jeffrey L., Genti Kostandini, and Elton Mykerezi. 2012. "Rural and Urban High School Dropout Rates: Are They Different?" *Journal of Research in Rural Education* 27(12): 1–21.

Keyes, Katherine M., Dahsan S. Gary, Jordan Beardslee, Seth J. Prins, Patrick M. O'Malley, Caroline Rutherford, and John Schulenberg. 2017. "Joint Effects of Age, Period, and Cohort on Conduct Problems Among American Adolescents from 1991 Through 2015." *American Journal of Epidemiology* 187(3): 548–57.

Kirk, David S. 2006. "Examining the Divergence Across Self-Report and Official Data Sources on Inferences About the Adolescent Life-Course of Crime." *Journal of Quantitative Criminology* 22(2): 107–29.

———. 2008. "The Neighborhood Context of Racial and Ethnic Disparities in Arrest." *Demography* 45(1): 55–77.

Kohler-Hausmann, Issa. 2013. "Misdemeanor Justice: Control Without Conviction." *American Journal of Sociology* 119(2): 351–93.

Krohn, Marvin D., Alan J. Lizotte, Matthew D. Phillips, Terence P. Thornberry, and Kristin A. Bell. 2013. "Explaining Systematic Bias in Self-Reported Measures: Factors that Affect the Under- and Over-Reporting of Self-Reported Arrests." *Justice Quarterly* 30(3): 501–28.

Lamberth, John. 1996. "A Report to the ACLU." New York: American Civil Liberties Union.

Lerman, Amy E., and Vesla M. Weaver. 2014. *Arresting Citizenship: The Democratic Consequences of American Crime Control*. Chicago: University of Chicago Press.

Maxfield, Michael G., Barbara Luntz Weiler, and Cathy Spatz Widom. 2000. "Comparing Self-Reports and Official Records of Arrests." *Journal of Quantitative Criminology* 16(1): 87–110.

Meehan, Albert J., and Michael C. Ponder. 2002. "Race and Place: The Ecology of Racial Profiling African American Motorists." *Justice Quarterly* 19(3): 399–431.

Mitchell, Ojmarrh, and Michael S. Caudy. 2017. "Race Differences in Drug Offending and Drug Distribution Arrests." *Crime & Delinquency* 63(2): 91–112.

Mohamed, A. Rafik, and Erik D. Fritsvold. 2010. *Dorm Room Dealers: Drugs and the Privileges of Race and Class*. Boulder, Colo.: Lynne Rienner Publishers.

Morris, Nancy A., and Lee Ann Slocum. 2010. "The Validity of Self-Reported Prevalence, Frequency, and Timing of Arrest: An Evaluation of Data Collected Using a Life Event Calendar." *Journal of Research in Crime and Delinquency* 47(2): 210–40.

Muhammad, Khalil Gibran. 2011. *The Condemnation of Blackness*. Cambridge, Mass.: Harvard University Press.

Murakawa, Naomi, and Katherine Beckett. 2010. "The Penology of Racial Innocence: The Erasure of Racism in the Study and Practice of Punishment." *Law & Society Review* 44(3–4): 695–730.

Natapoff, Alexandra. 2012. "Misdemeanors." *Southern California Law Review* 85(5): 1313–75.

National Longitudinal Survey of Youth. 2014. "Interview Methods." Washington: U.S. Bureau of Labor Statistics. Accessed August 18, 2018. https://www.nlsinfo.org/content/cohorts/nlsy79/intro-to-the-sample/interview-methods.

National Research Council. 2014. *The Growth of Incarceration in the United States: Exploring Causes and Consequences*. Washington, D.C.: The National Academies Press.

Pfaff, John. 2017. *Locked In: The True Causes of Mass Incarceration—and How to Achieve Real Reform*. New York: Basic Books.

Piquero, Alex R., and Robert W. Brame. 2008. "Assessing the Race-Crime and Ethnicity-Crime Relationship in a Sample of Serious Adolescent Delinquents." *Crime & Delinquency* 54(3): 390–422.

Piquero, Alex R., Carol A. Schubert, and Robert W. Brame. 2014. "Comparing Official and Self-Report Records of Offending Across Gender and Race/Ethnicity in a Longitudinal Study of Serious Youthful Offenders." *Journal of Research in Crime and Delinquency* 51(4): 526–56.

Pollock, Wendi, Scott Menard, Delbert S. Elliott, and David H. Huizinga. 2015. "It's Official: Predictors of Self-Reported vs. Officially Recorded Arrests." *Journal of Criminal Justice* 43(1): 69–79.

Ramchand, Rajeev, Rosalie Liccardo Pacula, and Martin Y. Iguchi. 2006. "Racial Differences in Marijuana-Users' Risk of Arrest in the United States." *Drug and Alcohol Dependence* 84(3): 264–72.

Reynolds, John R., and Jennifer Pemberton. 2001. "Rising College Expectations Among Youth in the United States: A Comparison of the 1979 and

1997 NLSY." *Journal of Human Resources* 36(4): 703–26.

Richards, Pamela, Richard A. Berk, and Brenda Forster. 1979. *Crime as Play: Delinquency in a Middle Class Suburb*. Pensacola, Fla.: Ballinger Publishing.

Sampson, Robert J., and John H. Laub. 2003. "Life-Course Desisters? Trajectories of Crime Among Delinquent Boys Followed to Age 70." *Criminology* 41(3): 555–92.

Sampson, Robert J., and Stephen W. Raudenbush. 2004. "Seeing Disorder: Neighborhood Stigma and the Social Construction of 'Broken Windows.'" *Social Psychology Quarterly* 67(4): 319–42.

Shelby, Tommie. 2007. "Justice, Deviance, and the Dark Ghetto." *Philosophy & Public Affairs* 35(2): 126–60.

Singer, Simon I. 2014. *America's Safest City: Delinquency and Modernity in Suburbia*. New York: New York University Press.

Smith, Michael R., and Matthew Petrocelli. 2001. "Racial Profiling: A Multivariate Analysis of Police Traffic Stop Data." *Police Quarterly* 4(1): 4–27.

Stevens, Tia, and Merry Morash. 2014. "Racial/Ethnic Disparities in Boys' Probability of Arrest and Court Actions in 1980 and 2000: The Disproportionate Impact of 'Getting Tough' on Crime." *Youth Violence and Juvenile Justice* 13(1): 77–95.

Stevens, Tia, Merry Morash, and Meda Chesney-Lind. 2011. "Are Girls Getting Tougher, or Are We Tougher on Girls? Probability of Arrest and Juvenile Court Oversight in 1980 and 2000." *Justice Quarterly* 28(5): 719–44.

Tapia, Mike. 2012. *Juvenile Arrest in America: Race, Social Class, and Gang Membership*. El Paso, Tex.: LFB Scholarly Pub.

Thornberry, Terence P., and Marvin D. Krohn. 2000. "The Self-Report Method for Measuring Delinquency and Crime." *Criminal Justice* 4(1): 33–83.

———. 2003. "Comparison of Self-Report and Official Data for Measuring Crime." In *Measurement Problems in Criminal Justice Research: Workshop Summary*, edited by John V. Pepper and Carol V. Petrie. Washington, D.C.: National Academies Press.

Tonry, Michael. 1995. *Malign Neglect: Race, Crime, and Punishment in America*. Oxford: Oxford University Press.

Tonry, Michael, and Matthew Melewski. 2008. "The Malign Effects of Drug and Crime Control Policies on Black Americans." *Crime and Justice* 37(1): 1–44.

Uggen, Christopher. 2000. "Work as a Turning Point in the Life Course of Criminals: A Duration Model of Age, Employment, and Recidivism." *American Sociological Review* 65(4): 529–46.

Unnever, James D., Francis T. Cullen, and J. C. Barnes. 2017. "Racial Discrimination and Pathways to Delinquency: Testing a Theory of African American Offending." *Race and Justice* 7(4): 350–73.

Warren, John Robert, and Emily Forrest Cataldi. 2006. "A Historical Perspective on High School Students' Paid Employment and its Association with High School Dropout." *Sociological Forum* 21(1): 113–43.

Wooden, Wayne S., and Randy Blazak. 1995. *Renegade Kids, Suburban Outlaws: From Youth Culture to Delinquency*. Boston, Mass.: Wadsworth.

PART II
Unexplored Forms of Punishment

Bail and Pretrial Detention: Contours and Causes of Temporal and County Variation

KATHERINE HOOD AND DANIEL SCHNEIDER

Despite growing interest in bail and pretrial detention among both academic researchers and policymakers, systematic research on pretrial release remains limited. In this article, we examine bail and pretrial release practices across seventy-five large U.S. counties from 1990 to 2009 and look at the contextual correlates of bail regime severity. We find tremendous intra-county variation in bail practices, as well as a nationwide decline in the use of nonfinancial release and doubling of bail amounts during this period. This variation is not accounted for by differences in case composition across jurisdictions or over time. Patterns of bail practices are associated with political, socioeconomic, and demographic factors, however. Implications of these findings for future research on bail and pretrial detention are discussed.

Keywords: bail, pretrial detention, inequality

Pretrial detention and release are an important but often overlooked source of inequality in the criminal justice system. Two of every three jail inmates in the United States—20 percent of the total incarcerated population—are being held in pretrial detention (Minton and Zeng 2015). These approximately half a million people have been arrested but not yet convicted of a crime. The burden of detention does not fall evenly on the unconvicted population, however. Black men are significantly more likely than white men to be arrested without engaging in illegal activity (Weaver, Papachristos, and Zanger-Tishler 2019). And once in custody, the overwhelming majority of pretrial detainees remain behind bars because they are unable to pay for the bail needed to secure their release (Phillips 2008). Yet research also shows that detention has considerable collateral consequences. Studies find that pretrial detention fuels further inequality in criminal justice outcomes (Stevenson 2016; Sacks and Ackerman 2014;

Katherine Hood is a graduate student in sociology at the University of California, Berkeley. **Daniel Schneider** is assistant professor of sociology at the University of California, Berkeley.

© 2019 Russell Sage Foundation. Hood, Katherine, and Daniel Schneider. 2019. "Bail and Pretrial Detention: Contours and Causes of Temporal and County Variation." *RSF: The Russell Sage Foundation Journal of the Social Sciences* 5(1): 126–49. DOI: 10.7758/RSF.2019.5.1.06. The authors gratefully acknowledge financial support from the UC Berkeley Department of Sociology and the Institute for Research on Labor and Employment. We received helpful comments and advice from David Harding, Chris Muller, Kristin Turney, Sara Wakefield, and participants in the Russell Sage Foundation conference "Criminal Justice Contact and Inequality." Direct correspondence to: Katherine Hood at khood@berkeley.edu, 410 Barrows Hall, Department of Sociology, University of California Berkeley, Berkeley, CA 94703; and Daniel Schneider at djschneider@berkeley.edu, 480 Barrows Hall, Department of Sociology, University of California Berkeley, Berkeley, CA 94703.

Open Access Policy: *RSF: The Russell Sage Foundation Journal of the Social Sciences* is an open access journal. This article is published under a Creative Commons Attribution-NonCommercial-NoDerivs 3.0 Unported License.

Lowenkamp et al. 2013a; Phillips 2008; Williams 2003), increases recidivism (Gupta, Hansman, and Frenchman 2016; Heaton, Mayson, and Stevenson 2016; Lowenkamp et al. 2013b), and undermines the socioeconomic stability of detainees and their families (Dobbie, Goldin, and Yang 2016; Comfort 2016). Although reformers from across the political spectrum have drawn attention to the inequity of this approach (Harris and Paul 2017), research on the subject remains limited. Despite the size and impact of this system, we know surprisingly little about the bail practices that govern pretrial detention and release.

Existing work on bail and pretrial detention focuses almost exclusively on features of individual cases, looking either in-depth at single jurisdictions or with a broad national sweep to determine how case characteristics shape relevant outcomes. In this article, we shift the focus to consider instead how the varied social, political, and organizational contexts in which cases are processed are associated with patterns of bail and pretrial release. To do this, we look at systematic variation in pretrial practices across time and place. Drawing on the National Archive of Criminal Justice Data State Court Processing Statistics (SCPS) series, we examine variation in bail regimes across the seventy-five largest counties in the United States between 1990 and 2009. We then look at the contextual correlates of bail regime severity, considering how case composition, organizational features, politics, economic conditions, and demographic factors relate to bail-setting practices.

Our analysis reveals considerable variation in pretrial release practices both across the country and over the nearly twenty-year period captured in our data. During this period, counties came to rely increasingly on money bail to determine pretrial release for defendants, while the average (inflation adjusted) cost of bail nearly doubled. This shift toward increasing use of money bail aligns closely with the broader shift toward increasing imprisonment over the same period (Western 2006). Further, given that the burden of arrest falls unevenly across racial categories, that the ability to meet money bail is sharply graded by class, and that pretrial detention is likely to have negative consequences for individual and family well-being, this shift in practices is also likely to have increased inequality in multiple domains.

Specific counties, meanwhile, vary considerably, both in the rates at which they use money bail to determine release and in the amounts at which that bail is set. With few exceptions, however, individual case characteristics do little to explain variation in either time or place. Indeed, our analysis suggests that we would expect more between-county variation in pretrial practices than we see given between-county variation in case characteristics. We do find, however, that patterns of bail outcomes are associated with county- and state-level factors. Higher proportions of African American residents, non-Democrats in the district attorney's office, higher state-level income inequality, and Republican governors were all associated with lower levels of nonfinancial release. Higher unemployment rates, non-Democrats in the district attorney's office, Republican governors, and elected judges were all associated with higher bail amounts.

Together, these findings reveal important sources of inequality in criminal justice contact. They document real differences in bail and release practices over time and across jurisdictions, and they show how local regimes of pretrial practices vary along with the social, political, and economic contexts in which they operate. By highlighting the regimes that produce this inequality, these findings also point to explanations that extend beyond differences in individual detainees to consider instead what drives the choices local jurisdictions make about how to manage the pretrial process.

BACKGROUND

As with many aspects of its carceral system, the United States is a global outlier in how it manages pretrial detention. Officially, the U.S. Constitution outlines a system of bail in which persons awaiting trial may deposit money or property as collateral to ensure they appear in court. As long as defendants do not fail to appear, their bail should be returned. In practice, however, most people turn to commercial bail bonds to secure pretrial release, paying a registered bail agent a nonrefundable fee (usually 10 percent of the bail amount) to purchase a surety bond. The United States and the Philippines are the only two countries in the world that allow this practice (Devine 1991).

Actual bail amounts are determined by a number of factors. Judges and magistrates may consider a defendant's criminal history, ties to the community, or the circumstances of the alleged crime (Spohn 2009). Many jurisdictions, however, rely on bail schedules that base amounts largely on criminal charges. These schedules vary a great deal across state and county lines, and judges and bail magistrates sometimes maintain considerable discretion even when such schedules are used. Yet court officials need not set financial bail on a case at all. Bail may be denied if a person is considered excessively dangerous or likely to flee, and a person considered less risky may be released under supervision conditions or with a promise to appear for subsequent court dates.

Both the decision to set money bail and the amount at which bail is set are important determinants of pretrial detention and release. Research suggests that bail amount is among the most important predictors of the length of pretrial detention (Phillips 2007, 2008; Cohen and Reaves 2007). Even small amounts of bail may keep many people behind bars. One study finds that only one in eight defendants nationwide (12.5 percent) can secure pretrial release when bail is assessed at $50,000 or more, and that number only grows to nearly five in eight (60 percent) when bail is assessed at $5,000 or less (Beck, Bonczar, and Gilliard 1993). While higher bail amounts are thus an important determinant of pretrial detention, many indigent defendants are only able to access pretrial freedom if they are granted release on nonfinancial terms.

The implications of bail decisions can be serious for defendants. In addition to the immediate consequence of incarceration, a small but growing body of research finds that pretrial detention has a number of collateral consequences for detainees. Studies find that pretrial detainees are more likely to be convicted (Stevenson 2016), receive harsher sentences (Sacks and Ackerman 2014; Lowenkamp et al. 2013a; Phillips 2008; Williams 2003), and have higher rates of recidivism (Gupta, Hansman, and Frenchman 2016; Heaton, Mayson, and Stevenson 2016; Lowenkamp et al. 2013b) than similar defendants who are granted pretrial release. Evidence also suggests that pretrial detention is associated with decreased employment and loss of government benefits (Dobbie, Goldin, and Yang 2016). Indeed, even short periods of detention can create considerable instability, because people can quickly lose jobs, housing, and custody of their children while detained. Short-term incarceration can also put great strain on families, extending the consequences of this disruption well beyond individual detainees (Comfort 2016). Indeed, the financial and logistical burdens of securing bail often fall disproportionately on partners and other female caregivers (Page, Piehowski, and Soss 2019).

Yet though bail and pretrial detention have important consequences for inequality within the criminal justice system and for subsequent socioeconomic stability, we know little about patterns of inequality in bail and pretrial release practices. One important exception is a report from the Bureau of Justice Statistics that examines change over time in bail and pretrial detention in large U.S. counties. The report documents a nationwide shift from nonfinancial release to the use of surety bonds in the late 1990s (Cohen and Reaves 2007). This empirical analysis highlights the growing use of financial practices that disadvantage low-income defendants and put additional strain on their families, but it provides no explanation for the trend. And because it pools data from across the country, it provides no information about geographic differences in bail and pretrial patterns. Indeed, because research on bail and pretrial detention tends to look either in-depth at single jurisdictions or broadly at national trends, we know very little about the breadth or variety of bail and pretrial release systems at work across the United States at any given time.

Research on other criminal justice outcomes suggests that criminal case processing can vary widely by time and place, however. The substantial over-time variation in incarceration is very well documented (Garland 2001; Western 2006; Wakefield and Uggen 2010). But, there is also evidence of geographic variation. Bruce Western, for example, shows that although incarceration rates are historically unprecedented in the United States as a whole, states actually vary considerably in the rates at which they imprison people (2006). Whereas in 2003 Louisiana had an incarceration rate of 801 per hundred thousand residents, Maine's rate was only 149 per hundred thousand. A number of studies similarly find systematic differences in sentencing across county lines (Johnson 2006, 2005; Fearn 2005). Studies of geographic differences in pretrial detention, however, have been limited to juvenile offenders. Barry Feld shows that juveniles in Minnesota are detained at higher rates in urban counties than suburban and rural ones, a difference he suggests results from local preferences for the use of formal versus informal social control (1991). Although pretrial detention of juveniles is quite rare and does not rely on the system of money bail so central in adult corrections, this work does suggest that systematic variation in pretrial practices may exist across counties.

This study explores patterns of bail and pretrial practices across time and place and considers the individual and contextual factors associated with variation in each. The overwhelming majority of research looking specifically at bail and pretrial detention focuses on the impact of individual case characteristics on pretrial outcomes, but research on other aspects of criminal case processing suggests a variety of contextual factors that may affect these practices as well. The following section reviews this research and outlines possible determinants of bail and pretrial practices.

DETERMINANTS OF BAIL AND PRETRIAL PRACTICES

We next review existing research on the determinants of bail and pretrial practices. We begin with a look at the literature on individual determinants of pretrial outcomes, then turn to research on other aspects of criminal case processing for insights into contextual factors that may shape the pretrial process.

Individual Case Characteristics

Most systematic research on determinants of bail and pretrial detention focuses on the salience of individual case characteristics for pretrial outcomes. This work is interested primarily in the extent to which outcomes are influenced either by official legal criteria or by extralegal characteristics that might reflect discriminatory decision-making. Studies consistently show that legally relevant factors are important determinants of pretrial outcomes. Severity of charges and criminal history are particularly strong predictors of bail amount, pretrial release, and pretrial detention (Goldkamp and Gottfredson 1985; Cohen and Reaves 2007). Other characteristics that judges are legally allowed to consider, such as community ties, help predict pretrial outcomes as well (Petee 1994; Spohn 2009).

Yet considerable work also finds that extralegal factors play an important role in bail and pretrial release. Most of this research focuses on race and sex and finds that pretrial detention is more common for defendants who are black or Hispanic (Spohn 2009; Cohen and Reaves 2007; Leiber and Fox 2005; Katz and Spohn 1995) and for those who are men (Spohn 2009; Katz and Spohn 1995). Other studies consider the specific components of pretrial detention in more detail. Stephen Demuth and Traci Schlesinger each find that black and Hispanic defendants are less likely to be granted nonfinancial release and more likely to receive higher bail amounts, controlling for other relevant predictors (Demuth 2003; Schlesinger 2005). Studies similarly find that bail amounts are higher for male defendants (Demuth and Steffensmeier 2004; Katz and Spohn 1995).

Given the abundance of research finding that individual-level case characteristics play an important role in pretrial outcomes, it is possible that variation in the composition of cases could drive variation in bail and pretrial release decisions. If the legal characteristics of individual cases and demographic characteristics of individual defendants are important determinants of pretrial decisions, then patterns of bail and pretrial release may simply reflect the cases processed at a given time and place. Variation over time or across jurisdiction would then result from changing case composition from year to year or across county lines.

Organizational Context

Organizational features may also play an important role in bail and pretrial release practices. A sizable literature argues that daily concerns about organizational efficiency and practical constraints drive many of the decisions made by courtroom officials (Eisenstein, Flemming, and Nardulli 1988; Dixon 1995). Studies find evidence that such constraints shape criminal case outcomes. Jeffrey Ulmer and Brian Johnson find that caseload pressures help predict differences in sentencing across Pennsylvania counties, for example, and Johnson finds separately that caseload pressures similarly affect rates of downward departures (Ulmer and Johnson 2004; Johnson 2005). These findings suggest that the relative pressure on courts to efficiently process heavy caseloads shapes the decisions prosecutors and judges make about criminal case processing.

A pair of older studies suggest that similar practical considerations might shape pretrial decisions as well. Comparing pretrial practices in Detroit and Baltimore, Roy Flemming finds that the availability of resources, and particularly the availability of space in local jails, is a critical factor in bail policy (1982). Crowded jails increased the likelihood of pretrial release, while excess jail space resulted in more punitive pretrial detention practices. Jeffrey Roth and Paul Wice similarly find that the occupancy rate of local jails influenced the conditions set for pretrial release in Washington, D.C. (1980). This work suggests that judges consider jail crowding when making decisions about bail, pretrial detention, and release. When jail space is limited, that space may be reserved for the most serious offenders. Jail capacity and occupancy rates may create practical constraints on bail and release decisions, and differences in the availability of jail beds may thus affect differences in patterns of bail setting and pretrial release practices.

Political Context
Research suggests that the political context in which cases are processed may affect outcomes as well. Concerns about law and order have frequently been at the center of American electoral politics in recent decades, and politicians have repeatedly appealed to voters by promising to be tough on crime (Helms and Jacobs 2002). While Democrats and Republicans have both made these appeals, and both parties have been complicit in the expansion of the U.S. carceral system (Gottschalk 2014), there do appear to be meaningful partisan differences in criminal justice policies and outcomes. Republican political leaders have spent more than Democrats on police, courts, and corrections (Caldeira 1983; Davey 1998; Jacobs and Helms 1999). Republican strength at the state and national levels is also associated with higher rates of incarceration (Jacobs and Helms 1996, 1997; Western 2006). Local partisan preferences may also shape sentencing outcomes. Ronald Helms and David Jacobs find that courts embedded in conservative communities produced more sentencing disparities, with longer sentences issued for African Americans and for men (2002).

Political context is likely to affect bail and pretrial detention practices in one of two ways. First, it may shape the discretionary decisions of local officials. District attorneys and judges are often elected and accountable to local voters. A conservative electorate may therefore select candidates with more punitive orientations, and officials may consider local preferences when making discretionary decisions about setting bail or allowing pretrial release.

But partisan politics may also shape policies that affect pretrial outcomes. Elected officials may pass laws that set bail schedules, regulate the commercial sale of bail bonds, or affect the funding of pretrial services agencies that facilitate the use of nonfinancial release. Such policies may be shaped by pro-business partisan politics as much as partisan preferences for tough on crime approaches. Indeed, the conservative American Legislative Exchange Council has worked with Republican state lawmakers to pass laws strengthening commercial bail bonds by undermining pretrial service agencies, organizations that facilitate pretrial release largely at the expense of bail industry profits (NAPSA 2009). All of these policies could affect the amounts at which bail is set and the extent to which detainees are released or detained pretrial.

Socioeconomic Context
Socioeconomic context may also play a role in bail and pretrial detention. Social control scholars argue that criminal justice policies are not used merely to control crime, but also more broadly to manage unruly populations that

might pose a threat to broader social order. Because of this, criminal punishment is directly related to economic conditions.

One line of research in this area considers the relationship between unemployment and criminal punishment. In 1939, Georg Rusche and Otto Kirchheimer laid out an early and influential argument, proposing that punishment historically grows harsher amid labor surpluses and milder when that surplus shrinks (2003). Later scholars have suggested that in a modern capitalist system the state uses incarceration to neutralize the threat posed by unemployed workers, who have a particular propensity to become unruly and disrupt the status quo (Spitzer 1975; Box and Hale 1992). This argument has some empirical support. Studies have found that unemployment rates are related to rates of incarceration independent of the effects of crime (Chiricos and Delone 1992; Yeager 1979; Lessan 1991). Stewart D'Alessio and Lisa Stolzenberg also find evidence that this argument may apply to pretrial outcomes (2002). They find that unemployed defendants have a substantially higher probability of pretrial detention in cities with high unemployment rates and argue that the unemployed population only poses a threat that warrants detention in the context of broader economic decline. This finding suggests that unemployment rates may prompt bail-setting patterns that make it harder to secure pretrial release.

But punishment may also be related to economic inequality itself. Scholars have argued that the wider social distance between marginal populations and criminal justice decision-makers may lead to more punitive outcomes for members of marginal groups (Bridges and Crutchfield 1988). Income inequality may reflect social disadvantage better than unemployment alone. Indeed, Western and his colleagues show that though recent incarceration trends in the United States bear little association with actual crime, they do track closely with income inequality. Income inequality may drive more punitive pretrial decisions as well (2004).

Demographic Context
Last, considerable research finds that criminal justice outcomes may be affected by a jurisdiction's racial composition. Most studies explain this relationship in terms of racial threat. Minority or racial threat occurs when a majority white population perceives a threat from the size of a racial or ethnic minority group. Some scholars suggest that this threat stems from concerns that minority groups will challenge the dominant group's economic and political dominance (Blalock 1967). More recent work, however, suggests that it arises from the white majority's association of large minority populations with crime (Bontrager, Bales, and Chiricos 2005). In either case, empirical evidence supports the racial threat theory. Studies have found that black population size in particular is linked to several criminal justice outcomes, one of which is higher rates of imprisonment (Myers and Talarico 1987; Britt 2000; Weidner, Frase, and Schultz 2005) and with longer sentences (Wang and Mears 2015). Less work considers other minority groups, although Xia Wang and Daniel Mears find that larger Hispanic populations increase the decision to incarcerate (2015).

One study does look at whether racial threat accounts for decisions about bail and pretrial release. Marvin Free compares racial disparities in pretrial outcomes across jurisdictions with different size minority populations, and finds a curvilinear relationship between population size and disparate outcomes (2004). The data underlying this finding comes largely from the 1970s—a very different era in criminal case processing—but the analysis nevertheless suggests that racial threat may continue to shape bail and pretrial release decisions. In jurisdictions where white majority populations feel threatened by the size of nonwhite groups, officials may be more likely to embrace bail and pretrial release policies that increase pretrial detention.

CONTRIBUTIONS
Despite growing interest in bail and pretrial detention among both academic researchers and policymakers, systematic research on pretrial release practices remains limited. This study contributes to knowledge of this important but relatively understudied topic in two ways.

First, we address the surprising lack of systematic information about the bail practices that govern pretrial detention and release by providing an empirical description of bail setting patterns both over time and across major U.S. counties. Because most research on bail and pretrial detention focuses on single locations or collapses geographic differences in national data, we know little about whether and how pretrial practices vary in the United States. Mapping the contours of this variation is thus an important empirical contribution in itself.

Second, we provide insight into the contextual correlates of bail regime severity. Much of what we know about variation in pretrial practices comes from studies that focus exclusively on the influence of individual case characteristics. We assess the relative importance of these characteristics for explaining variation in bail and pretrial release over time and across places. But we also draw on a wide range of literature to consider how the larger organizational, political, economic, and social context in which cases are processed may shape bail and pretrial release decisions. In this way, we shift the focus from individual-level determinants of pretrial outcomes to look instead at how policy choices, and the factors that influence them, shape patterns of pretrial detention and release across the country.

DATA AND METHODS

In the following section, we describe the primary individual-level data that we use in our analysis, the State Court Processing Statistics (SCPS), and then detail our construction of state- and county-level variables that we merge to the SCPS. We then describe our analysis plan.

State Court Processing Statistics

We primarily draw on individual-level data from the SCPS. The SCPS were compiled biannually by the Bureau of Justice Statistics from administrative criminal justice records in a sample of the seventy-five largest counties by population. These counties include more than one-third of the United States population and half of all reported crimes (ICPSR 2016). In a given year, forty of the seventy-five counties are sampled based on a four-strata and two-stage design. First, the counties are allocated to four strata based on the number of filings. The ten counties in the first strata are selected with certainty; those in the second, third, and fourth strata are selected at random with decreasing probability of selection by strata. Second, defendants within counties are sampled by selecting from all felony cases filed in May of the survey year and, depending on the number of filings, either taking a week's worth of cases (strata 1), two weeks (strata 2 and 3), or the full month (strata 4). The resulting individual-level data include detailed information on arrest charges, demographic characteristics, criminal history, pretrial release and detention, adjudication, and sentencing. We pool the available waves of the micro-data, covering the years 1990, 1992, 1994, 1996, 1998, 2000, 2002, 2004, 2006, and 2009. Unfortunately, no data in this series is available after 2009.

We merge this data with county-year-level information on several measures designed to capture the contextual processes that may shape pretrial release. These measures and their sources are described in the following section.

Key Variables

We first describe our three key dependent variables that capture the severity of pretrial detention practices and then detail the individual-level measures of demographics, case charges, and prior criminal justice history that we draw on from the SCPS. Finally, we detail the county-level measures that we have assembled from a variety of data sources.

Pretrial Detention

We construct three dependent variables that capture the severity of pretrial detention practices. First, we code whether a defendant is granted nonfinancial release. Defendants who receive nonfinancial release are coded as 1, and respondents who receive financial release or who are held on bail are coded as 0. Respondents who are granted emergency release, who are denied bail, whose release conditions are unknown, who are detained for unknown reasons, or whose cases are closed (7 percent of cases) are coded as missing.

Second, we measure the amount of bail for respondents who have bail set (and are either held on bail or released having made bail). We inflation adjust the amount of bail to 2012 dollars using the CPI-U series and set bail values above the 99th percentile (approximately $800,000) to missing. Respondents in other release categories are set to missing values.

Third, we recode our measure of the amount of bail, by imputing $0 values for respondents who are granted nonfinancial release rather than setting these respondents to missing. Here too, we set bail values above the 99th percentile (approximately $600,000) to missing. Respondents in the residual release categories are set to missing.

Case-Level Predictors
We code three sets of case-level characteristics from the SCPS data: demographics, charges, and prior criminal justice contact.

Demographics We code a dichotomous variable for gender equal to 1 if defendants are male. We include a continuous measure of age in years, setting ages greater than ninety to missing. We categorize defendants in terms of race-ethnicity as being white, non-Hispanic; black, non-Hispanic; Hispanic of any race; and other race, non-Hispanic.

Charges We construct a fifteen-category variable that captures the most series-specific category of arrest charge, distinguishing murder, rape, robbery, assault, other violent crime, burglary, larceny-theft, motor vehicle theft, forgery, fraud, other property offense, drug sales, other drug offense, weapons offense driving related, or other public order. Although the dataset includes only those with felony charges, we also adjust for an indicator of whether the adjudication charge was ultimately a felony or a misdemeanor.

Prior Criminal Justice Contact We construct a number of measures that capture defendants' prior involvement with the criminal justice system. First, we code if the defendant had an active criminal justice status at arrest, a measure of whether the defendant had any prior arrests, and a measure of whether the defendant had any prior failures to appear. All are coded as dichotomous variables. We also construct a measure of the severity of any prior convictions coded 0 for those with none, 1 for those with misdemeanors, and 2 for those with a felony. Finally, we include a measure of the number of prior convictions that ranges from 0 to 10 (where 10 is inclusive of those with more than 10).

Contextual Predictors

Organizational Context We construct a measure of the county jail occupancy rate using data from the Bureau of Justice Statistics' Annual Survey of Jails. We divide the average daily population of jail facilities located in the county each year by the capacity of those jail facilities to derive the jail occupancy rate for each of the county-year observations represented in the SCPS data.

Political Context We drew on information from government websites to construct a county-year time series of judicial selection processes, coding the initial selection as involving nonpartisan elections, partisan elections, or appointment, and then retention as involving nonpartisan elections, partisan elections, retention election, or reappointment. We coded counties dichotomously by whether judges faced election to maintain their positions. Judges facing popular elections (either contested or retention) were coded 1 and judges who maintained their position by appointment or political confirmation were coded 0. We also constructed a county-year time series of the partisan affiliation of county district attorneys (DAs) based on data from multiple sources in the public record, including county websites, election records, and newspaper coverage. All but three counties used in our analysis have a publicly elected district attorney. We construct a measure of DA partisanship that is equal to 0 if the DA is a Democrat and 1 otherwise. Finally, we code whether the governor is a Republican 1 or not 0 based on the University of Kentucky's Center for Poverty Research's National Welfare Data base (1980–2015).

Economic Context We construct two measures of the economic context. First, we measure the county-level unemployment rate based on annual county-level data published by the Bureau of Labor Statistics through the Local Area Unemployment Statistics program. Second, we use the series of state-level Gini coefficients assembled by Mark Frank from the Internal Revenue Service Statistics of Income (2014).

Demographic Context We capture the demographic context of the county with a measure of the percentage of the county population that is black, dividing the number of black county residents by the total county population in each given county-year using data from the Census Bureau's intercensal estimates.

Analysis

Our analysis proceeds in three parts. First, we take advantage of the merged 1990–2009 SCPS micro-data to document the variation in pretrial detention practices across U.S. counties and over this nearly twenty-year period. We generate the county comparisons by selecting defendants in the forty counties covered by the data in either 2006 or 2009 and estimating ordinary least squares (OLS) regressions of our outcomes as a function of a set of county indicators and year fixed effects. We generate the time trends by selecting the full available analysis sample across all years and counties and estimating OLS regressions of our outcomes as a function of a set of year indicators and county fixed effects.[1] We then present plots of the share of defendants in a given county or in a given year who are released on nonfinancial terms; the mean bail amounts adjusted to 2012 dollars in a given county or a given year, for those who are granted financial release or held on bail; and the mean bail amount set adjusted to 2012 dollars in a given county or in a given year, and those released on nonfinancial terms set to a bail of $0.

Second, we examine whether the between-county and over-time variation in pretrial detention practices can be explained by the composition of cases. We examine the extent to which these two sources of variation are accounted for by the demographic characteristics of those charged, the charges brought, and the prior criminal justice history of those charged.

For the between-county analysis, we again select defendants in the forty counties covered by the data in either 2006 or 2009. As before, we have three key dependent variables: defendants released on nonfinancial terms, bail conditional on financial release or being held on bail, and the amount of bail set unconditional on release type. In the first step, we regress each of the dependent variables on a vector of county indicators and a dummy for year. In the second step, we add a set of measures of defendant demographic characteristics—gender, age, and race-ethnicity. In the third step, we add measures of charges—a set of fifteen dummies for the charge and a dichotomous indicator of the level of the most serious adjudication charge. Finally, in the fourth step, we add measures of defendants' prior criminal justice contact—status at arrest, number of prior arrests, prior failures to appear, number of prior convictions, and most serious prior conviction. After each step, we estimate predicted values (percentage receiving nonfinancial release or mean bail amount) for each county. We assess whether the coefficient of variation for the estimated county-specific fixed effects is reduced by controlling for each additive set of case characteristics.

For the over-time analysis, we pool all of the available data from 1990 through 2009 and follow a set of analytical steps similar to those described for counties. We estimate a first-step model by regressing each of the dependent variables on a vector of county indicators and a vector of year indicators. Then, as before, we sequentially and cumulatively add sets of indicators for defendant demographics, charges, and prior criminal justice history. We estimate predicted values for each dependent variable from each of the models. We assess whether the coefficient of variation for the estimated year-specific fixed effects is reduced by controlling for case characteristics.

Third, we turn from this individual-level analysis to a county-year level analysis in which we examine how county contexts are associated with the severity of pretrial detention policies. To do so, we collapse the SCPS micro-data to the county-year level and estimate OLS

---

1. We use linear probability models for the dichotomous financial release—held on bail versus nonfinancial release outcome (Angrist and Pischke 2008).

models that take either the share of defendants in a given county-year released on nonfinancial terms, the mean bail amount, conditional on financial release or being held on bail, or the mean bail amount for all defendants (with those granted nonfinancial release assigned a bail of $0) in the county-year as the dependent variables. We estimate a first model that includes our county-level predictors as well as year and region fixed effects and then a second model that also adds attributes of the SCPS defendants, but aggregated to the county-year (with weights).[2] We conduct this exercise in two steps because the same county-level factors that bear on pretrial detention may also shape who is arrested, what they are charged with, and what their prior criminal justice contact has been. By controlling for these factors, we may underestimate any total effects of county-level characteristics on pretrial detention.

Although no data are missing at the county-year level (because the file is built by aggregating up from all available individual values), we are required to censor county-year cell values based on small numbers of individual observations in the SCPS. In total, of 395 possible county-year observations, we are missing information on one or more variables suppressed in this way for forty-five observations. We impute forty-three of these forty-five using the county-specific mean for available years. However, in two instances, all of the county-year observations on a variable are missing, so we have no basis for the mean imputation. We delete these two rows. We are also missing data on at least one of the county-level predictors constructed from outside sources for eleven county-year observations.[3] We also remove these by list-wise deletion. Finally, we also remove three county-year observations for which we suppressed data on the outcome variables due to small samples in the SCPS. Our final analysis sample, then, is 379 county-year observations, which is 95 percent of those available.

RESULTS

We organize our presentation of results into three parts, first describing the observed variation in nonfinancial release and bail amount across counties and over time, then examining whether this variation can be accounted for by case characteristics, and then examining the county-level correlates of pretrial detention severity.

Variation in Nonfinancial Release and Bail Amount Across Counties and Over Time

We first examine the degree of variation between counties and over time in our key measures of pretrial detention.

County Variation in Pretrial Detention

We begin by plotting the share of defendants, by county, who are granted nonfinancial release prior to adjudication against the mean amount of bail set (conditional on nonfinancial release not being granted). We graph this data for the forty counties represented in either the 2006 or 2009 waves of the SCPS. The result is shown in figure 1.

Examining the values for each county on the y-axis (share granted nonfinancial release), we see that there is significant variation across counties in the share of defendants who are granted a nonfinancial release (as opposed to either being released after making bail or being held after failing to make bail). Being released without making some financial bail is vanishingly uncommon in Harris County, Texas (home to Houston); Tarrant County, Texas (home to Fort Worth); and Orange County, Florida (home to Orlando), where fewer than 5 percent of those charged were granted nonfinancial release in those counties. Other large counties in Texas, Florida, and California re-

---

2. Here, we use a slightly different set of case characteristics because of high multicolinearity in the models. We adjust for the share of defendants who are male, mean age, share white, non-Hispanic, share charged with violent offense, share with a property offense, share with a drug offense, share with a felony charge at adjudication, criminal justice status at arrest, mean number of prior arrests, share with any prior failure to appears, share with a prior misdemeanor conviction, share with a prior felony conviction, and mean number of prior convictions.

3. These eleven county-year cases are dropped due to missing data on jail capacity for Honolulu, New Haven, and Hartford.

Figure 1. Between-County Variation in Terms of Pre-Trial Detention, 2006/2009 (SCPS)

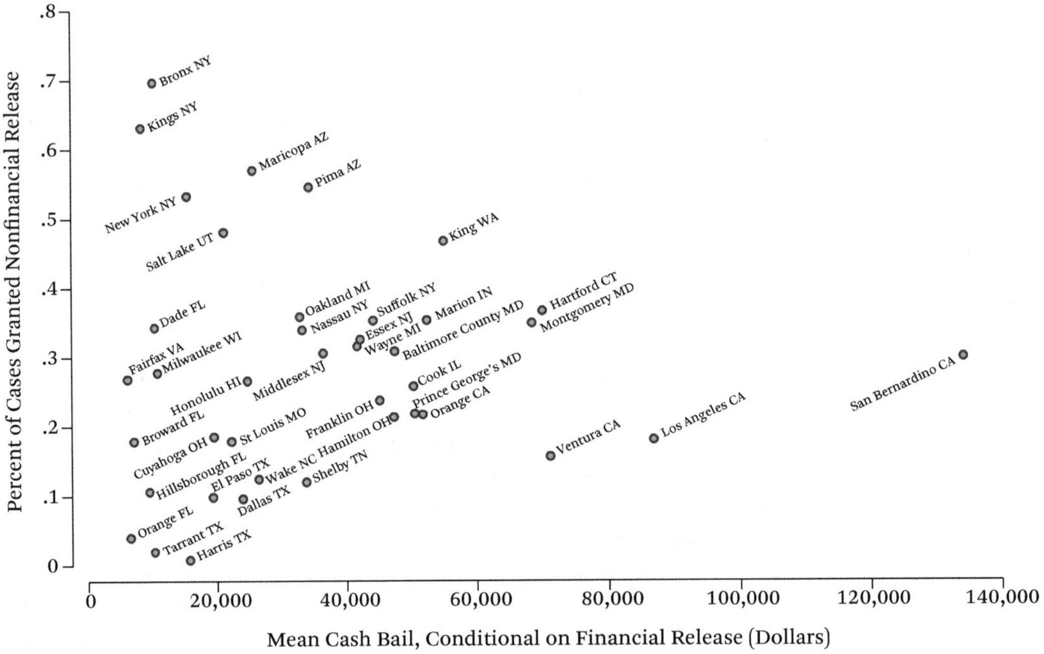

Source: Authors' calculations from the 1990–2009 SCPS (ICPSR 2016).
Note: Plotted values county-specific estimates, adjusting for year of survey and weighted using the survey weights.

leased a somewhat larger share—between 10 percent and 20 percent—on nonfinancial release, but still a relatively small one. At the other end of the distribution, the three New York City counties represented in the data (New York, Bronx, and Kings) each granted nonfinancial release to more than half of defendants; two-thirds of those in the Bronx granted nonfinancial release. The only other counties that came close to granting nonfinancial release to this share of defendants were King County, Washington; Salt Lake, Utah; Pima, Arizona; and Maricopa, Arizona.

The amount of cash bail, conditional on financial release, for each of these counties is plotted along the x-axis. Although the New York City counties are still among the least severe in terms of bail amount, they are now in the company of Orange, Florida; Harris, Texas; and Tarrant, Texas, counties that were very unlikely to grant nonfinancial release. At the other end of the scale, the large California counties have the highest mean bail amounts (conditional on granting financial release or holding on bail), joined by King County, Washington, and Cook County, Illinois, as well as several non–New York City eastern urban counties.

Taken together, we see some evidence of clustering. The counties with high rates of nonfinancial release and low mean bail conditional on financial terms, are in the top left of the plot—primarily the New York City counties. In contrast, counties with low rates of release and high levels of bail are at the far right—primarily California counties. In the bottom left corner, we see a set of Florida and Texas counties in which nonfinancial release is very uncommon, but bail amounts are relatively low.

Over-Time Variation in Pretrial Detention
These analyses focus only on the period between 2006 and 2009, pooling across those years to assess between-county variation in pretrial detention practices, holding temporal change more or less constant. However, just as post-adjudication imprisonment has increased dramatically over the past several decades, so too may have the severity of pretrial practices.

Figure 2. Time Trends in Terms of Pre-Trial Detention, 1990–2009 (SCPS)

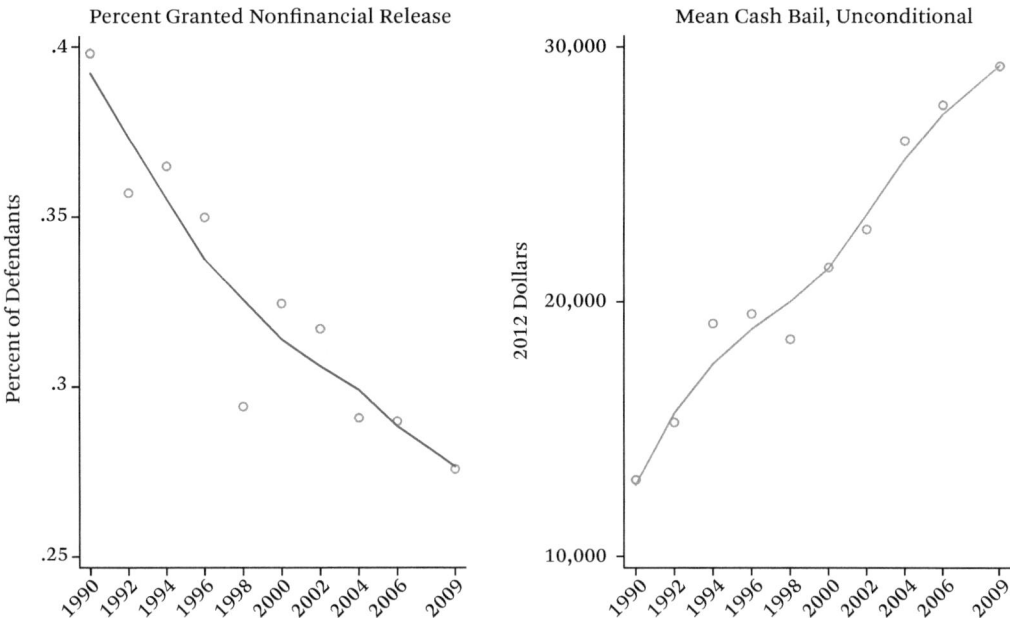

Source: Authors' calculations from the 1990–2009 SCPS (ICPSR 2016).
Note: Hollow circles represent estimates of year-specific predicted values from model with county fixed effects with survey weights. Solid lines apply loess smoother (bandwidth = 0.8).

Figure 2 plots the time trend in two of our key measures of pretrial detention. In each panel, the hollow circles represent predicted values of the dependent variable estimated from a model that also adjusts for a county fixed effect and is weighted using the survey weights. The lines show this series smoothed with a loess regression.

The left panel of figure 2 shows the dramatic decline between 1990 and 2009 in the share of defendants granted nonfinancial release. This share declines from about 40 percent in 1990 to just 27 percent in 2009. The most dramatic decline seems to be between the early 1990s and the late 1990s to early 2000s. The right panel of figure 2 plots the series for the mean level of bail (in 2012 dollars) over the same period. This measure is not conditional on having bail set; instead, it includes defendants released on nonfinancial bail and assigns them a $0 value. Here, mirroring the decline in nonfinancial release, we see a steady rise in the level of bail that is set, from about $12,000 in 1990 to almost $30,000 in 2009. Some of this increase is due to the decline in nonfinancial release, but that is by no means the whole story. If we separately examine the trend in bail, conditional on bail being set, we see that the mean level increased from $20,000 in 1990 to $40,000 by 2009 (not shown in figure 2).

Accounting for Variation as a Function of Case Characteristics
Variation is substantial both across counties and over time in the severity of pretrial detention as measured by the share of defendants granted nonfinancial release and by the level of bail set for those who are not. One possibility is that the variation is the product of compositional differences in the cases brought in different counties and in different periods. Research has carefully documented the role that case characteristics play in shaping pretrial detention (Goldkamp and Gottfredson 1985; Katz and Spohn 1995; Demuth 2003; Schlesinger 2005; Leiber and Fox 2005; Cohen and Reaves 2007; Spohn 2009). If some counties have different kinds of cases than others or if the com-

Table 1. Coefficient of Variation on Adjusted County FE Estimates

Model	Nonfinancial Release	Bail Amount, Conditional	Bail Amount, Unconditional
Baseline	58.7	69.3	65.0
+ Defendant demographics	59.4	69.2	65.5
+ Charges	60.8	71.1	67.4
+ Criminal justice history	61.5	72.3	70.9

Source: Authors' calculations from the 2006–2009 SCPS (ICPSR 2016).

position of cases changed over time, then that could explain county or temporal variation in pretrial detention practices.

Accounting for Between-County Variation
We begin with county-level variation, first augmenting the model that underlies figure 1 with adjustments for defendant gender, age, and race-ethnicity. Second, we add measures of the current charges brought in the case. Third, we add measures of the defendant's history of criminal justice contact. Adjusting for these factors does essentially nothing to account for the between-county variation in the share of defendants granted nonfinancial release. Column 1 of table 1 presents the coefficient of variation calculated from the forty county-specific estimates of the share of defendants granted nonfinancial release, for the baseline model (with just year fixed effects) and then for each of the three models that add in other case characteristics. The coefficient of variation (scaled from 0 to 100) increases as we account for case characteristics. Rather than explain why some counties have less nonfinancial release than others, this analysis suggests that we would expect more between-county variation than we see given the between-county variation in case characteristics.

The same holds true when we examine the extent to which these case characteristics might account for between-county variation in the level of bail conditional on bail being set (column 2), and when we examine the inclusive measure of the level of bail unconditional on whether bail was set and assign those granted nonfinancial release a bail of $0 (column 3). Much of the between-county variation is simply not a function of differences in measurable case characteristics. In short, case composition is not the reason for the substantial variation between counties in pretrial detention practices.

Accounting for Over-Time Variation
We conduct a similar exercise to assess whether these case characteristics might account for the sharp decline between 1990 and 2009 in the share of defendants granted nonfinancial release and the sharp increase in the level of bail set. As before, we estimate a series of models that progressively add groups of case characteristics. For each model and for each outcome, we estimate the predicted values for each of the years in the data. We then calculate the coefficient of variation across the year estimates for each outcome and for each model, assessing the extent to which accounting for these characteristics reduces over-time variation (which we saw previously is essentially monotonic) in pretrial detention practices.

The only hint that these case characteristics matter is found in column 1 of table 2. We see that though accounting for defendant demographics and charges does not reduce the over-time variation, accounting for prior criminal justice contact does play a small role, reducing the coefficient of variation from 12.3 in the baseline model to 9.4. An implication of this result is that accrued criminal justice contact could serve to justify less nonfinancial release, potentially perpetuating entanglement in the criminal justice system. However, this logic does not hold for our other two measures of pretrial detention practices, as adjusting for case characteristics somewhat increases the coefficient of variation on the measures of bail amount.

Table 2. Coefficient of Variation on Adjusted Year FE Estimates

Model	Nonfinancial Release	Bail Amount, Conditional	Bail Amount, Unconditional
Baseline	12.3	20.6	24.9
+ Defendant demographics	13.4	24.4	26.5
+ Charges	12.8	28.2	28.8
+ Criminal justice history	9.4	32.6	31.3

Source: Authors' calculations from the 1990–2009 SCPS (ICPSR 2016).

Table A1 reports the coefficients on the case characteristics from the full model (including defendant demographics, charges, and history of criminal justice contact). We see that even after adjusting for charges and history of criminal justice contact, men are less likely to be granted nonfinancial release and to have higher bail amounts than women, and that older defendants are more likely to be granted nonfinancial release. Hispanic defendants are less likely to be granted nonfinancial release and have higher bail amounts than white, non-Hispanic defendants. Interestingly, we do not see significant black-white gaps in nonfinancial release or in bail amount after adjusting for charges and prior criminal justice contact. However, we note a significant gap between blacks and whites in nonfinancial release without these adjustments and with the adjustments for charges but not criminal justice contact. The gap in bail amount is also significant when only adjusting for demographics. In short, charge severity and prior interactions with the criminal justice system contribute to black-white inequality in pretrial detention practices at the case-level. Turning to charges, we see the expected relationships between severity of charge and nonfinancial release and bail amount. Those charged with felonies are much less likely to be granted nonfinancial release and have much higher bail amounts. Finally, history of criminal justice contact also shapes pretrial detention. Those with prior failure to appears, prior arrests, and prior felony and violent felony convictions are significantly less likely to be granted nonfinancial release, and those with prior felony and violent felony convictions also receive higher bail amounts.

The Role of County Contexts in Shaping Pretrial Detention

These case-level characteristics play an important role in shaping pretrial detention outcomes for individual cases. But, we would also expect that contextual features of counties would affect pretrial detention practices. In table 3, we report estimates from a set of regression models that examine the association between time-varying county-level characteristics and county-level pretrial detention practices, aggregated up to the county-year level from the individual-level SCPS.

Models 1a and 1b examine the association between these county characteristics and the share of defendants in the county-year who are granted nonfinancial release. Models 2a and 2b examine bail for defendants who have financial terms set, and then models 3a and 3b examine the level of bail for all defendants, where those granted nonfinancial release are imputed a $0 bail.

Models 1a, 2a, and 3a include year and region fixed effects and models 1b, 2b, and 3b include both year and region fixed effects as well as time-varying county-year level measures of the defendant characteristics calculated from the individual-level SCPS data. We are somewhat agnostic about the two models. The risk with models 1a, 2a, and 3a is that we undercontrol for case characteristics that could confound the relationship between county characteristics and pretrial detention practices. The risk with models 1b, 2b, and 3b is that we overcontrol, and block one or more of the pathways by which county-level characteristics shape pretrial practices (for instance, if the proportion of blacks in a county shapes the characteristics of those arrested or if the partisan

Table 3. Relationship Between County-Level Characteristics and Pre-Trial Detention Practices

	Nonfinancial Release		Bail, Conditional		Bail, Unconditional	
	M1a	M1b	M2a	M2b	M3a	M3b
Jail occupancy rate (county)	0.0363	0.0614	1,607.9	-2,625.3	1,466.2	-1,720.5
	(0.92)	(1.52)	(0.33)	(-0.55)	(0.45)	(-0.55)
Judges are elected (county)	0.0284	0.0268	3,751.0	5,496.5+	2,796.4	4,103.7*
	(1.33)	(1.02)	(1.42)	(1.75)	(1.59)	(2.00)
DA is not a Democrat (county)	-0.103***	-0.0726***	8,026.4***	9,896.0***	6,715.0***	7,314.6***
	(-6.27)	(-3.80)	(3.96)	(4.38)	(4.97)	(4.92)
Governor is a Republican (state)	-0.0326*	-0.0344*	-4,916.2*	-4,300.2*	-1,274.5	-960.6
	(-1.97)	(-2.13)	(-2.40)	(-2.25)	(-0.93)	(-0.77)
Unemployment rate (county)	-0.00631	-0.00520	1,704.1*	1,594.4*	1,044.6*	924.1+
	(-1.06)	(-0.85)	(2.31)	(2.20)	(2.12)	(1.93)
Gini index (state)	-1.599***	-2.015***	-42,558.7	-37,678.7	-2,366.7	23,69.9
	(-4.79)	(-5.13)	(-1.03)	(-0.81)	(-0.09)	(0.08)
Percent black (county)	-0.0853	-0.335**	440.1	-35,942.5**	5,942.7	-13,691.5
	(-1.12)	(-3.04)	(0.05)	(-2.76)	(0.95)	(-1.60)
Year fixed effects	Y	Y	Y	Y	Y	Y
Region fixed effects	Y	Y	Y	Y	Y	Y
Case controls	N	Y	N	Y	N	Y
N	379	379	379	379	379	379

Source Authors' calculations from the 1990–2009 SCPS (ICPSR 2016).
*p < .05; **p < .01; ***p < .001

affiliation of the district attorney shapes prior criminal justice contact).

We begin by examining how organizational context, operationalizing with the jail occupancy rate, shapes pretrial practices. In models 1a and 1b, we see that the coefficient on jail occupancy is positive, indicating that when occupancy rates are higher, defendants are more likely to be granted nonfinancial release. However, the coefficient is not statistically significant and the estimates of the relationship between jail occupancy rates and bail amounts in models 2a through 3b are inconsistent in direction and not significant.

We next examine how the political context is associated with pretrial detention practices. We measure three political dimensions of local criminal justice systems—the method by which judges are selected, the partisan affiliation of county district attorneys, and the partisan affiliation of the state governor. Here, we see no relationship between judges being elected rather than appointed and the share of defendants granted nonfinancial release. However, the relationship between judges being selected by election and the amount of bail set is positive. Those subject to election tend to set higher bail amounts as seen in the positive coefficients for models 2a and 3a and the positive and significant coefficients in models 3a and 3b.

The partisan affiliation of district attorneys is also strongly related to pretrial detention practices. In counties with non-Democratic district attorneys, defendants are granted nonfinancial release at significantly lower rates and set bail at significantly higher amounts. Figure 3 contrasts the mean bail amounts predicted from model 3b for DAs by partisan affiliation. Mean bail under Democratic DAs is $15,000 versus $22,000 under non-Democrats—a nearly 50 percent difference.

Defendants who go through the pretrial detention process when Republican governors are in office are significantly less likely to be granted nonfinancial release (models 1a and 1b), though the effect is only between one-third

Figure 3. Mean Financial Bail by Political Party of District Attorney

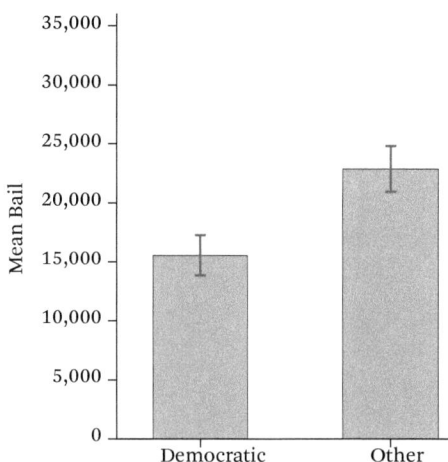

Source: Authors' calculations from the 1990–2009 SCPS (ICPSR 2016) and originally collected data.
Note: Predicted values from model 3b.

and one-half as large as the effect on having a non-Democratic district attorney in the county. However, there is a significant *negative* association between Republican governors and bail amount in models 2a and 2b and no association in models 3a and 3b. One implication is that Republican governors preside over bail regimes that are less likely to grant nonfinancial release and then set lower bail on average given the pool of cases subject to a bail determination.

County-level economic context may also shape pretrial detention practices. There is a negative, but not statistically significant, association between county-level unemployment rate and the share of defendants granted non-financial release. However, a higher unemployment rate is positively and significantly related to the amount of bail in models 2a and 2b and in models 3a and 3b. Figure 4 plots the predicted amount of bail for those with financial terms set from model 2b against the county-level unemployment rate (over the range of values from the 5th through 95th percentile). We see that the predicted bail amount is about $25,500 when unemployment is very low, but

Figure 4. Amount of Money Bail by County Unemployment Rate

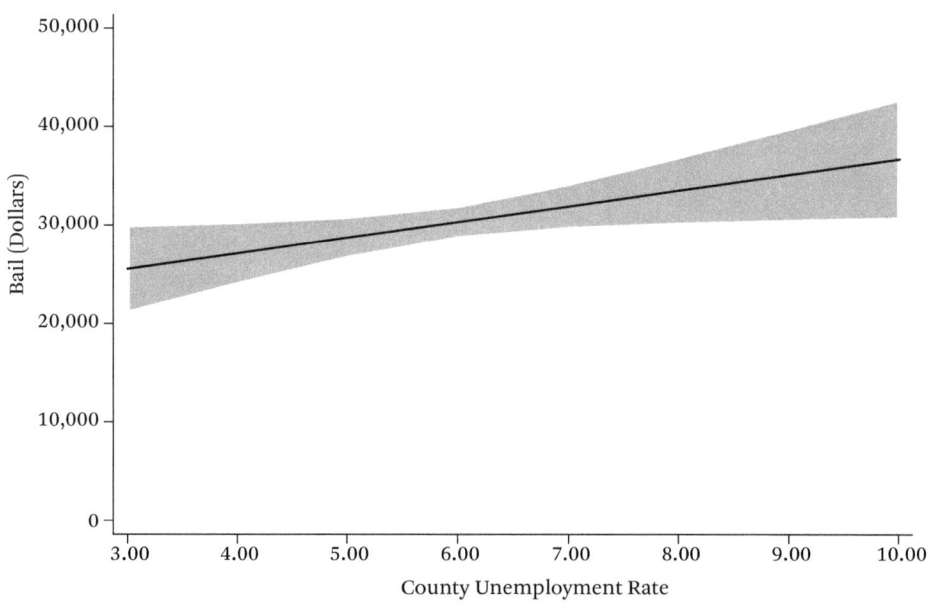

Source: Authors' calculations from the 1990–2009 SCPS (ICPSR 2016) and the Bureau of Labor Statistics Local Area Unemployment Statistics program.
Note: Predicted values from model 2b.

Figure 5. Share of Defendants Granted Nonfinancial Release by Percentage of County Population African American

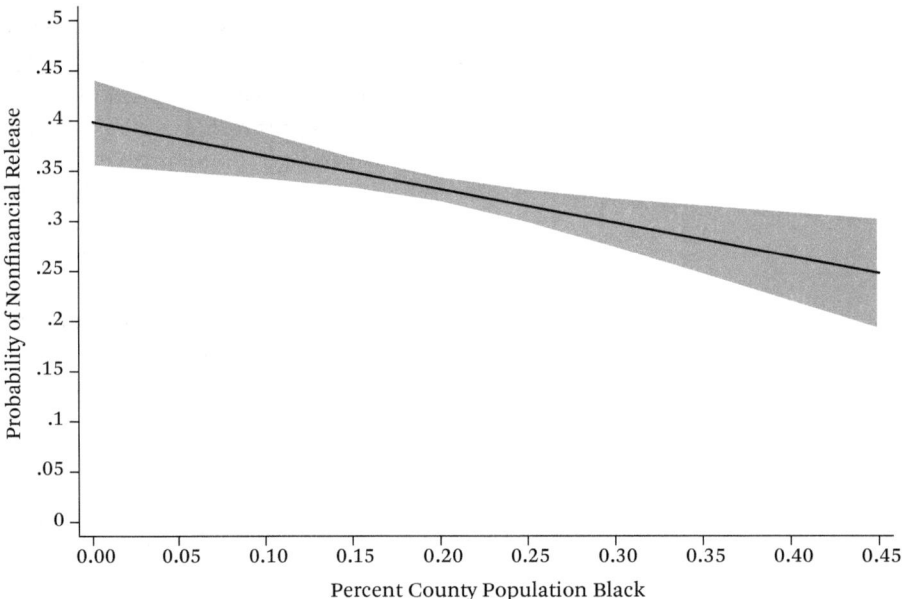

Source: Authors' calculations from the 1990–2009 SCPS (ICPSR 2016) and Census Bureau intercensal estimates.
Note: Predicted values from model 1b.

rises to almost $37,000 in the highest unemployment contexts.

Our second measure of economic context is also associated with pretrial detention practices. The state-level Gini coefficient is strongly and significantly negatively related to the rate of nonfinancial release in models 1a and 1b. Defendants in more unequal places are less likely to be granted nonfinancial release. But, there is no such relationship for the amount of bail.

Finally, the demographic context, in particular the racial composition of the county, may also shape pretrial detention practices. In model 1a, we see that a larger percentage of blacks in the county is negatively associated with lower rate of nonfinancial release. Further, in model 1b, after controlling for case characteristics (including the share of defendants who are black), we find a large and statistically significant negative association between county percent black and the probability of nonfinancial release. Figure 5 plots the predicted share of defendants granted nonfinancial release by the percentage of the county that is black over the effective range of 0 percent (~p5) to 45 percent (~p95). We see that, controlling for the racial composition of defendants, 40 percent of defendants in counties with essentially no black population are granted nonfinancial release against just 25 percent of those in the counties with the largest share of black residents. Although county racial composition matters for nonfinancial release, we find no consistent evidence of a relationship with the amount of bail, but a negative and significant association in model 2b.

DISCUSSION

Bail and pretrial detention have long been an important but overlooked part of the criminal justice system. Yet in spite of growing interest from researchers and policymakers, systematic research on the topic remains limited. Most of what we do know comes from studies that focus narrowly on the relationship between individual case characteristics and pretrial outcomes, ignoring or eliding the considerable geographic and temporal variation that exists in bail and pretrial practices. In this article, we focus instead on that variation. We document patterns of bail and pretrial release across both place and time, and look at whether and how those patterns relate to the larger organizational, political, socioeconomic, and demographic context in which pretrial decisions are made.

Our analysis reveals considerable variation in pretrial practices both across U.S. counties and over the nearly twenty-year period covered in our data. Whereas some counties released more than 50 percent of defendants awaiting trial with no financial conditions, others released fewer than 5 percent on nonfinancial terms. Average bail amounts ranged from less than $10,000 to more than $100,000. Nationwide, nonfinancial release has declined steadily over time, while bail amounts have doubled from $20,000 to $40,000. Yet, for the most part, this variation does not seem to result from differences in the kinds of cases being processed from one place to another or from one year to the next. Defendant demographics, charges, and prior record did nothing to account for pretrial differences between counties. Criminal history does account for some of the decrease in nonfinancial release over time, but declining use of nonfinancial release is unrelated to changes in demographics or charges, while the doubling of bail amounts during this period is not explained by any of these individual case characteristics. These patterns of bail and pretrial release are related to several contextual factors, however. The politicization of judicial offices, partisan affiliations of district attorneys and governors, income inequality, unemployment rates, and the size of the black population all seem to be related to bail-setting practices. Jail occupancy rates, however, are not.

Although variation in both time and place are associated with political, economic, and demographic factors, some of these relationships are easier to interpret than others. Local politics shape pretrial decisions in predictable ways. Elected judges are associated with higher bail amounts than their appointed counterparts, and Democrats in the district attorney's office are linked to both higher rates of nonfinancial release and cheaper bail. This suggests, on the one hand, that judges concerned about reelection make more conservative pretrial decisions, and on the other that Democrats reflect a partisan preference for less-punitive pretrial regimes. Socioeconomic conditions are also important in predictable ways. Higher income inequality is linked to lower financial release, and higher unemployment rates are linked to more expensive bail amounts. In both cases, poorer socioeconomic conditions are related to more punitive pretrial practices.

Other contextual factors, however, show more complicated relationships to bail and pretrial release. Republican governors are associated with lower rates of nonfinancial release, but they are also associated with cheaper bail. Larger black populations are similarly associated with both lower nonfinancial release but cheaper bail. These patterns may suggest a more complicated relationship between state-level politics and pretrial practices, as well as between those practices and local black populations. Alternatively, these patterns might suggest a more complicated relationship between nonfinancial release and bail amounts. Although both nonfinancial release and bail amount are important mechanisms for regulating pretrial detention, they may be governed by different dynamics not well captured in our analysis.

Our findings are descriptive in that they primarily are intended to characterize variation in pretrial detention practices over time and across counties and to show that case-level explanations appear largely insufficient for explaining this variation. However, we also present evidence of associations between contextual-level factors and pretrial detention practices. The Bureau of Justice Statistics has itself stressed that the SCPS are insufficient on their own for making causal inferences (Cohen and Kyckelhahn 2010), and we stress here that we have not attempted to identify the causal effect of any of these measures or underlying constructs on pretrial detention practices. Future work that focuses on a particular explanatory factor could very usefully advance knowledge by attempting such identification. Further, we again emphasize that our descriptive work here is limited in representing only those particular large urban counties that are sampled as part of the complex SCPS design. We are not able to generalize to pretrial detention practices more generally—whether for other urban counties or nationally (National Research Council 2009).

Still, these results suggest tremendous variation in the choices local jurisdictions make about how to manage the pretrial process, choices that do not simply reflect differences in the cases they handle. With distinct bail regimes operating in different counties, the costs of criminal justice contact can differ radically across county lines. Heavy reliance on money bail and high bail amounts increase the price of pretrial freedom for detainees and their families, putting greater financial burden on defendants who do bail out and leaving defendants unable to pay this price facing the long-term costs of detention. Studies show that detainees are more likely than released defendants to be convicted (Stevenson 2016) and receive harsher sentences when they are (Sacks and Ackerman 2014; Lowenkamp et al. 2013a; Phillips 2008; Williams 2003), while even short stays behind bars put people at risk of losing jobs, housing, property, access to government benefits, or custody of their children (Dobbie, Goldin, and Yang 2016; Comfort 2016). Different bail regimes thus have important consequences for inequality both in the criminal justice system and in society more broadly. Yet amid local variation, the trend nevertheless has been toward more punitive pretrial practices over time. Both the steady decline of nonfinancial release and the massive increase in bail amounts during these twenty years make pretrial freedom substantially more expensive and increase the likelihood of pretrial detention across the country.

Going forward, future research on bail and pretrial detention should consider the sizable inequality in pretrial practices and the importance of the contextual factors we have identified here. Indeed, these findings suggest a number of possible avenues for further study. One valuable avenue for future research would be to decompose the within-county and between-county (and within-year and between-year) variation in pretrial detention practices and assess the contribution of case-level factors and county-level characteristics to this variance. Additionally, more research is needed to tease apart the role of political, socioeconomic, and demographic factors in pretrial practices, particularly the seemingly inconsistent relationships of both governor partisanship and race to bail decisions. In light of growing calls for bail reform, future studies should also investigate new types of pretrial management systems, and particularly the use of risk assessment tools. Studies suggest these tools hold considerable promise for reducing the total number of people held in pretrial detention, as well as reducing racial and ethnic disparities in detention practices (Kleinberg et al. 2017). We know little, however, about whether and how their efficacy might be shaped by the patterns we document here. Last, more historical and ethnographic accounts of bail and pretrial release practices could greatly enhance our understanding of the mechanisms driving the patterns we document, and perhaps provide a more complete understanding of how these different contextual factors interact and shape different pretrial regimes.

Table A1. Associations Between Case-Level Characteristics and Pre-Trial Detention and Bail Amount

	Nonfinancial Release	Bail Amount
Gender		
Female	(ref)	(ref)
Male	−0.0745***	7,359.4***
	(−17.06)	(10.73)
Age	0.000581***	51.95
	(3.53)	(1.62)
Race-ethnicity		
White, non-Hispanic	(ref)	(ref)
Black, non-Hispanic	−0.00288	−384.0
	(−0.71)	(−0.52)
Hispanic	−0.0395***	4,168.5***
	(−8.51)	(3.87)
Other, non-Hispanic	−0.00306	3,770.1
	(−0.25)	(1.19)
Charges		
Other drug	(ref)	(ref)
Murder	−0.330***	179,857.9***
	(−18.18)	(11.55)
Rape	−0.240***	76,308.0***
	(−18.53)	(16.33)
Robbery	−0.245***	48,162.8***
	(−37.05)	(29.01)
Assault	−0.186***	33,373.6***
	(−33.41)	(27.23)
Other violent	−0.177***	40,603.3***
	(−21.81)	(19.99)
Larceny-theft	−0.0472***	6,117.9***
	(−7.52)	(7.47)
Motor vehicle theft	−0.101***	2,911.0*
	(−11.78)	(2.36)
Forgery	−0.0449***	5784.7***
	(−4.31)	(4.47)
Fraud	0.0330**	7,978.2***
	(3.16)	(5.87)
Other property	−0.0460***	5,741.4***
	(−5.22)	(4.70)
Drug sales	−0.144***	21,861.5***
	(−26.82)	(20.56)
Weapons	−0.166***	8,794.8***
	(−18.27)	(6.35)
Driving related	−0.0901***	7,392.2***
	(−10.17)	(6.68)
Other, public order	−0.0702***	11,298.2***
	(−8.07)	(8.00)
Most serious adjudication charge		
Midemeanor	(ref)	(ref)
Felony	−0.0440***	14347.1***
	(−8.36)	(21.83)

Table A1. (*continued*)

	Nonfinancial Release	Bail Amount
Status at arrest		
None	(ref)	(ref)
Active	−0.0732***	2,681.9***
	(−19.00)	(3.33)
Number of prior arrests	−0.00614***	−51.20
	(−8.33)	(−0.36)
Failure to appear		
None	(ref)	(ref)
Prior	−0.0240***	375.6
	(−5.70)	(0.43)
Prior convictions		
No prior convictions	(ref)	(ref)
Misdemeanor	0.0135*	−3918.7***
	(2.51)	(−3.67)
Felony	−0.0625***	4,488.3***
	(−10.84)	(3.89)
Violent felony	−0.00301***	479.5**
	(−3.66)	(2.91)
_cons	0.546***	−54,299.2***
	(19.52)	(−17.48)
N	70,321	47,449

Source: Authors' calculations from the 1990–2009 SCPS (ICPSR 2016).
*$p < .05$; **$p < .01$; ***$p < .001$

REFERENCES

Angrist, Joshua D., and Jörn-Steffen Pischke. 2008. *Mostly Harmless Econometrics: An Empiricist's Companion*. Princeton, N.J.: Princeton University Press.

Beck, Allen J., Thomas P. Bonczar, and Darrell K. Gilliard. 1993. *Jail Inmates, 1992*. Washington: U.S. Department of Justice, Bureau of Justice Statistics.

Blalock, Hubert M. 1967. *Toward a Theory of Minority Group Relations*. New York: John Wiley & Sons.

Bontrager, Stephanie, William Bales, and Ted Chiricos. 2005. "Race, Ethnicity, Threat, and the Labeling of Convicted Felons." *Criminology* 43(3): 589–622.

Box, Steven, and Chris Hale. 1992. "Economic Crisis and the Rising Prisoner Population." *Crime and Social Justice* 17(1): 20–35.

Bridges, George S., and Robert D. Crutchfield. 1988. "Law, Social Standing, and Racial Disparities in Imprisonment." *Social Forces* 66(3): 699–724.

Britt, Chester L. 2000. "Social Context and Racial Disparities in Punishment Decisions." *Justice Quarterly* 17(4): 707–32.

Caldeira, Greg A. 1983. "Elections and the Politics of Crime: Budgetary Choices and Priorities in America." In *The Political Science of Criminal Justice*, edited by Stuart Nagel, Erika Fairchild, and Anthony Champaign. Springfield, Ill.: Charles C. Thomas.

Caldeira, Greg A., and Andrew T. Cowart. 1980. "Budgets, Institutions, and Change: Criminal Justice Policy in America." *American Journal of Political Science* 24(3): 413–38.

Chiricos, Theodore G., and Miram A. Delone. 1992. "Labor Surplus and Punishment: A Review and Assessment of Theory and Evidence." *Social Problems* 39(4): 421–46.

Cohen, Thomas H., and Tracey Kyckelhahn. 2010. *Data Advisory: State Court Processing Statistics Data Limitation*. Washington: U.S. Department of Justice, Bureau of Justice Statistics.

Cohen, Thomas H., and Brian A. Reaves. 2007. *Pretrial Release of Felony Defendants in State Court:*

State Court Processing Statistics, 1990–2004. Washington: U.S. Department of Justice, Bureau of Justice Statistics.

Comfort, Megan. 2016. "A Twenty-Hour-A-Day Job: The Impact of Frequent Low-Level Criminal Justice Involvement on Family Life." *Annals of the American Academy of Political and Social Science* 665(1): 63–79.

D'Alessio, Stewart J., and Lisa A. Stolzenberg. 2002. "A Multilevel Analysis of the Relationship Between Labor Surplus and Pretrial Incarceration." *Social Problems* 49(2): 178–93.

Davey, Joseph D. 1998. *The Politics of Prison Expansion: Winning Elections by Waging War on Crime.* Westport, Conn.: Praeger.

Demuth, Stephen. 2003. "Racial and Ethnic Differences in Pretrial Release Decisions and Outcomes: A Comparison of Hispanic, Black, and White Felony Arrestees." *Criminology* 41(3): 873–908.

Demuth, Stephen, and Darrell Steffensmeier. 2004. "The Impact of Gender and Race-Ethnicity in the Pretrial Release Process." *Social Problems* 51(2): 222–42.

Devine, F. E. 1991. *Commercial Bail Bonding: A Comparison of Common Law Alternatives.* New York: Praeger.

Dixon, Jo. 1995. "The Organizational Context of Criminal Sentencing." *American Journal of Sociology* 100(5): 1157–98.

Dobbie, Will, Jacob Goldin, and Crystal Yang. 2016. "The Effects of Pre-Trial Detention on Conviction, Future Crime, and Employment: Evidence from Randomly Assigned Judges." *NBER* working paper no. 22511. Cambridge, Mass.: National Bureau of Economic Research.

Eisenstein, James, Roy Flemming, and Peter Nardulli. 1988. *The Contours of Justice: Communities and Their Courts.* Boston, Mass.: Little, Brown.

Fearn, Noelle E. 2005. "A Multilevel Analysis of Community Effects on Criminal Sentencing." *Justice Quarterly* 22(4): 452–87.

Feld, Barry C. 1991. "Justice by Geography: Urban, Suburban, and Rural Variations in Juvenile Justice Administration." *Journal of Criminal Law and Criminology* 82(1): 156–210.

Flemming, Roy. 1982. *Punishment Before Trial: An Organizational Perspective on Felony Bail Process.* New York: Longman.

Frank, Mark. 2009. "Inequality and Growth in the United States: Evidence from a New State-Level Panel of Income Inequality Measure." *Economic Inquiry* 47(1): 55–68.

Free, Marvin. 2004. "Bail and Pretrial Release Decisions." *Journal of Ethnicity in Criminal Justice* 2(4): 23–44.

Garland, David. 2001. *The Culture of Control: Crime and Social Order in a Contemporary Society.* Chicago: University of Chicago Press.

Goldkamp, John, and Michael Gottfredson. 1985. *Judicial Guidelines for Bail: The Philadelphia Experiment.* Philadelphia, Pa.: Temple University Press.

Gottschalk, Marie. 2014. *Caught: The Prison State and the Lockdown of American Politics.* Princeton, N.J.: Princeton University Press.

Gupta, Arpit, Christopher Hansman, and Ethan Frenchman. 2016. "The Heavy Costs of High Bail: Evidence from Judge Randomization." *Columbia Law and Economics* working paper no. 531. New York: Columbia Law School.

Harris, Kamala D., and Rand Paul. 2017. "To Shrink Jails, Let's Reform Bail." *New York Times*, July 20, A27.

Heaton, Paul, Sandra Mayson, and Megan Stevenson. 2017. "The Downstream Criminal Justice Consequences of Pretrial Detention." *Stanford Law Review* 69(3): 711–94.

Helms, Ronald, and David Jacobs. 2002. "The Political Context of Sentencing: An Analysis of Immunity and Individual Determinants." *Social Forces* 81(2): 577–604.

ICPSR. 2016. "State Court Processing Statistics, 1990–2009: Felony Defendants in Large Urban Counties (ICPSR 2038)." Machine Readable Database and Documentation.

Jacobs, David, and Ronald E. Helms. 1996. "Toward a Political Model of Incarceration: A Time-Series Examination of Multiple Explanations for Prison Admission Rates." *American Journal of Sociology* 102(2): 323–57.

———. 1997. "Testing Coercive Explanations for Order: The Determinants of Law Enforcement Strength over Time." *Social Forces* 75(4): 1361–92.

———. 1999. "Collective Outbursts, Politics, and Punitive Resources: Toward a Political Sociology of Spending on Social Control." *Social Forces* 77(4): 1497–524.

Johnson, Brian. 2005. "Contextual Disparities in Guidelines Departures: Courtroom Social Contexts, Guidelines Compliance, and Extralegal Disparities in Criminal Sentencing." *Criminology* 43(3): 761–96.

———. 2006. "The Multilevel Context of Criminal Sentencing: Integrating Judge- and County-Level Influences." *Criminology* 44(2): 259–98.

Katz, Charles M., and Cassia C. Spohn. 1995. "The Effect of Race and Gender on Bail Outcomes: A Test of an Interactive Model." *American Journal of Criminal Justice* 19:161–84.

Kleinberg, Jon, Himabindu Lakkaraju, Jure Leskovec, Jens Ludwig, and Sendhil Mullainathan. 2017. "Human Decisions and Machine Predictions." Technical report. Cambridge, Mass.: National Bureau of Economic Research.

Leiber, Michael J., and Kristan C. Fox. 2005. "Race and the Impact of Detention on Juvenile Justice Decision-Making." *Crime & Delinquency* 51(4): 470–97.

Lessan, Gloria T. 1991. "Macroeconomic Determinants of Penal Policy: Estimating the Unemployment and Inflation Influences on Imprisonment Rate Changes in the United States, 1948–1985." *Crime, Law and Social Change* 16(2): 177–98.

Lowenkamp, Christopher T., Marie VanNostrand, and Alexander Holsinger. 2013a. "Investigating the Impact of Pretrial Detention on Sentencing Outcomes." Houston, Tex.: Laura and John Arnold Foundation.

———. 2013b. "The Hidden Costs of Pretrial Detention" Houston, Tex.: Laura and John Arnold Foundation.

Minton, Todd D., and Zhen Zeng. 2015. "Jail Inmates at Midyear 2014." Technical Report. Washington: U.S. Department of Justice, Bureau of Justice Statistics.

Myers, Martha A., and Susette M. Talarico. 1987. *The Social Contexts of Criminal Sentencing*. New York: Springer-Verlag.

National Association of Pretrial Services Agencies (NAPSA). 2009. "The Truth About Commercial Bail Bonding in America." *Advocacy Brief* 1(1).

National Research Council. 2009. *Ensuring the Quality, Credibility, and Relevance of U.S. Justice Statistics*, edited by Robert M. Groves and Daniel L. Cook. Washington, D.C.: National Academies Press.

Page, Joshua, Victoria Piehowski, and Joe Soss. 2019. "A Debt of Care: Commercial Bail and the Gendered Logic of Criminal Justice Predation." *RSF: The Russell Sage Foundation Journal of the Social Sciences* 5(1): 150–72. DOI: 10.7758/RSF.2019.5.1.07.

Petee, Thomas A. 1994. "Recommended for Release on Recognizance: Factors Affecting Pretrial Release Recommendations." *Journal of Social Psychology* 134(3): 375–82.

Phillips, Mary T. 2007. "Bail, Detention, and Nonfelony Case Outcomes." New York: City Criminal Justice Agency.

———. 2008. "Bail, Detention, and Felony Case Outcomes." *Research Brief Series* no. 18. New York: Criminal Justice Agency.

Roth, Jeffrey, and Paul Wice. 1980. *Pretrial Release and Misconduct in the District of Columbia*. Washington, D.C.: Institute for Law and Social Research.

Rusche, Georg, and Otto Kirchheimer. 2003 [1939]. *Punishment and Social Structure.* New Brunswick, N.J.: Transaction Books.

Sacks, Meghan, and Alissa R. Ackerman. 2014. "Bail and Sentencing: Does Pretrial Detention Lead to Harsher Punishment?" *Criminal Justice Policy Review* 25(1): 59–77.

Schlesinger, Traci. 2005. "Racial and Ethnic Disparity in Pretrial Criminal Processing." *Justice Quarterly* 22(2): 170–92.

Spitzer, Steven. 1975. "Toward a Marxian Theory of Deviance." *Social Problems* 22(5): 638–51.

Spohn, Cassia C. 2009. "Race, Sex, and Pretrial Detention in Federal Court: Indirect Effects and Cumulative Disadvantage." *Kansas Law Review* 57:879–901.

Stevenson, Megan. 2016. "Distortion of Justice: How the Inability to Pay Bail Affects Case Outcomes." Unpublished working paper, University of Pennsylvania Law School.

Ulmer, Jeffery T., and Brian Johnson. 2004. "Sentencing in Context: A Multilevel Analysis." *Criminology* 42(1): 137–77.

Wakefield, Sara, and Christopher Uggen. 2010. "Incarceration and Stratification." *Annual Review of Sociology* 36: 387–406.

Wang, Xia, and Daniel Mears. 2015. "Sentencing and State-Level Racial and Ethnic Contexts." *Law and Society Review* 49(4): 883–915.

Weaver, Vesla M., Andrew Papachristos, and Michael Zanger-Tishler. 2019. "The Great Decoupling: The Disconnection Between Criminal Offending and Experience of Arrest Across Two Cohorts." *RSF: The Russell Sage Foundation Journal of the Social*

Sciences 5(1): 89-123. DOI: 10.7758/RSF.2019.5.1.05.

Weidner, Robert R., Richard S. Frase, and Jennifer S. Schultz. 2005. "The Impact of Contextual Factors on the Decision to Imprison in Large Urban Jurisdictions: A Multilevel Analysis." *Crime and Delinquency* 51(3): 400-24.

Western, Bruce. 2006. *Punishment and Inequality in America.* New York: Russell Sage Foundation.

Western, Bruce, Meredith Kleykamp, and Jake Rosenfeld. 2004. "Crime, Punishment, and American Inequality." In *Social Inequality*, edited by Katherine Neckerman. New York: Russell Sage Foundation.

Williams, Marion R. 2003. "The Effects of Pretrial Detention on Imprisonment Decisions." *Criminal Justice Review* 28(2): 299-316.

Yeager, Milton G. 1979. "Unemployment and Imprisonment." *Journal of Criminal Law and Criminology* 70(4): 586-88.

A Debt of Care: Commercial Bail and the Gendered Logic of Criminal Justice Predation

JOSHUA PAGE, VICTORIA PIEHOWSKI, AND JOE SOSS

Among the institutions that link criminal justice and inequality in the United States, commercial bail remains one of the most important yet least understood. Each year, the bail industry extracts millions of dollars from lower-income Americans, disproportionately draining resources from poor communities of color. We draw on ethnographic research to explore how the bail system operates as a predatory social process, arguing that gender interacts with class and race to structure resource extraction in this field. Poor women of color are especially subject to bail predation because they are seen within the larger social organization of care as bearing primary responsibility for defendants. Gendered care work and emotional labor are thus central to the field's logic of practice and to bail industry profits.

Keywords: bail, care, gender, ethnography, predatory industries

Among the institutions that link criminal justice systems to social inequalities in the United States, bail remains one of the most important yet least understood. In recent decades, scholars have shown how social subjugation and economic inequality weave their way throughout the origins, operations, and consequences of mass incarceration (for example, Western 2006; Patillo, Weiman, and Western 2004). Policing and judicial action have been subject to extensive scrutiny in this regard (Epp, Maynard-Moody, and Haider-Markel 2014; Lerman and Weaver 2014; Kohler-Hausmann 2014). The collateral consequences and spillover effects that ripple through the social networks of people who become entangled with the system have as well (Clear 2007; Wakefield and Wildeman 2014).

Scholars have begun to clarify how monetary sanctions such as fines and fees compound inequalities as they turn poor people's assets into government revenues (Harris 2016; Harris, Evans, and Becket 2011). Still, knowledge about commercial bail has changed little since legal

Joshua Page is associate professor of sociology and law at the University of Minnesota. **Victoria Piehowski** is a graduate student in the Department of Sociology at the University of Minnesota. **Joe Soss** is Cowles Chair for the Study of Public Service at the University of Minnesota, where he holds faculty positions in the Humphrey School of Public Affairs, Political Science, and Sociology.

© 2019 Russell Sage Foundation. Page, Joshua, Victoria Piehowski, and Joe Soss. 2019. "A Debt of Care: Commercial Bail and the Gendered Logic of Criminal Justice Predation." *RSF: The Russell Sage Foundation Journal of the Social Sciences* 5(1): 150–72. DOI: 10.7758/RSF.2019.5.1.07. We are grateful to AshLee Smith Garret, Ryan Steel, and Chase Hobbs-Morgan for research assistance. Joshua Page received financial support for his research on the bail industry from the Talle Research Fund at the University of Minnesota. Direct correspondence to: Joshua Page at page@umn.edu, 909 Social Sciences Building, 267 19th Ave. South, Minneapolis, MN 55455.

Open Access Policy: *RSF: The Russell Sage Foundation Journal of the Social Sciences* is an open access journal. This article is published under a Creative Commons Attribution-NonCommercial-NoDerivs 3.0 Unported License.

scholar Malcolm Feeley observed in 1979 that "there has been virtually no scholarly interest in the bail bondsman. . . . this neglect and perfunctory dismissal cannot be attributed to the bondsman's lack of importance" (96–97). This blind spot is especially troubling because commercial bail stands at the center of resource extraction in the pretrial process and is one of the most distinctive aspects of the U.S. criminal justice system. The United States and the Philippines are the only countries that permit a for-profit bail bond industry. And in a criminal justice system shot through with efforts to generate revenues for public institutions (such as fines and fees) and private firms (such as prison profiteering), commercial bail is one of the oldest and most enduring sites of extractive public-private partnership. Since the 1910s, it has offered a template for how the machinery of criminal justice can be used to siphon assets from poor communities.

Each year, the bail industry extracts millions of dollars from lower-income communities, disproportionately from poor communities of color and often in cases where defendants are found not guilty (see, for example, Gupta, Frenchman, and Swanson 2016). These revenues flow to state and market institutions alike, but the biggest moneymakers are the large insurance corporations that back the bonds sold in smaller bail businesses. In a field dominated by about thirty-five major players, funds reliably flow to the big sureties. In 2011, they secured about $13.5 billion in bonds; and while auto and property insurers typically pay out 40 to 60 percent of their revenue in losses each year, records suggest that bail surety companies pay less than 1 percent in losses (Bauer 2014).

Against this backdrop, this article builds on prior scholarship in several ways. First, we adopt the bail industry as a focal point for analyzing the interplay of social inequalities and the criminal justice system. In addition to illuminating a rarely studied site of this relationship, the analysis of bail offers a distinctive perspective on the broader practice of resource extraction in the criminal justice field. Research on inequality and bail has laid important foundations for this work, showing, for example, how racial factors affect judges' bail decisions and how pretrial detention can negatively affect legal outcomes, employment, earnings, and access to welfare benefits (on racial factors, Demuth 2003; Schlesinger 2005; on detention, Dobbie, Goldin, and Yang 2016; Gupta, Hansman, and Frenchman 2016). Other studies have made progress in measuring the extent and distribution of bail revenues, focusing on how wealth is disproportionately drawn from poor communities of color (Gupta, Frenchman, and Swanson 2016; Color of Change and ACLU 2017). Pursuing a more process-centered analysis, we examine how the unequal terms of societal relations structure bail practices, including how bail agents pursue extractive relations with clients and how bail practices function as mechanisms for the reproduction of inequality and social control.

Second, this article offers a complement to the *punishment* perspective that typically frames studies of resource extraction in the criminal justice field. Most scholarship on this topic has emerged from the punishment and society subfield and reflected its guiding concerns. Thus, leading scholars conceptualize financial takings in the criminal justice field as "monetary sanctions, sometimes called Legal Financial Obligations (LFOs), [which] include fees, fines, restitution orders, and other financial obligations that courts and other criminal justice agencies may impose on persons accused of crimes" (Harris, Evans, and Beckett 2011, 235–36). Similarly, leading explanations for these practices tend to focus on developments within the criminal justice field, emphasizing how a "culture of punishment" created new needs for revenue streams to fund the penal state, fueling and justifying the push for tougher monetary sanctions (see, for example, Harris 2016).

The punishment frame has fostered a growing scholarly community and important empirical and theoretical advances. By isolating state-centered financial takings in the penal field, however, this frame can obscure analytic and historical questions about how state-implemented takings (such as fines and fees) relate to other modes of targeted financial extraction. Indeed, reliance on the punishment frame helps explain why studies of monetary sanctions have devoted so little attention to closely related practices that have grown in the same decades—such as the systematic resource extractions associated with monetary bail, asset forfeiture, and prison profiteering.

To complement studies that adopt a punishment frame, we draw on the concept of predation as it has been developed in the broader study of political economy and social domination.[1] A predation frame encourages scholars to locate the varied revenue projects woven into the criminal justice system today in the longer historical trajectory of dispossession in the United States—institutionalized takings, past and present, in which state and market actors routinely target subjugated groups for resource extraction. The roots of this approach can be traced to several intellectual traditions: theories of the predatory state (North 1981; Tilly 1992); Marxian analyses of primitive accumulation and dispossession as ongoing features of capitalism (Glassman 2006; Nichols 2017); studies of "racial capitalism" in the black radical tradition (Robinson 1983; Du Bois 1935); and theories of the symbiotic relationship between social contract and social domination (Pateman and Mills 1997).

Challenging liberal-democratic theories of state and society, these varied traditions suggest how a social contract among dominant actors may be premised on and institutionalize various forms of subjugation (Pateman and Mills 1997). Images of free exchange among equal partners to contract, in this view, enable and legitimate exploitation (such as wage-based employment relations) and expropriation (such as of land, labor, or money). Expropriation and exploitation operate as foundational features of a liberal order that, though it appears to be rooted in voluntary agreements among equals, is actually organized around hierarchical power relations rooted in class, race, gender, and other axes of social dominance (Dawson 2016; Fraser 2016). Predatory modes of dispossession, such theorists argue, have long played a central role in enriching dominant groups and building and funding liberal state and market institutions, underwriting civic hierarchies, and sustaining the social order.

From this perspective, fines and fees can be seen not just as burdens imposed as sanctions but as elements of a variegated palette of extractive relations and practices associated with the criminal justice system. In turn, these elements can be drawn into a common frame of analysis with payday lending, subprime auto and home lending, and other predatory projects that exploit marginalized communities as captive markets, creatively converting their disadvantaged social positions into revenue streams. Criminal justice predation can also be located in relation to the longer history of dispossession in the United States, from the antebellum appropriation of labor and land through chattel slavery and settler colonialism through the postbellum systems of debt peonage, sharecropping, and convict leasing. In this article, we analyze the bail field as a complex of socially and politically produced *predation opportunity structures*: frameworks that convert the needs, vulnerabilities, and aspirations of subjugated populations into revenue opportunities for state and market actors. We ask how social inequalities guide these operations and how predatory bail practices, in turn, reinforce social inequalities.

Along a third axis, we extend prior work by responding to calls for greater attention to gender in the study of inequalities and criminal justice practices (see, for example, Haney 2004; Crenshaw 2012). Like other predatory practices in and around the criminal justice system, resource extraction in the bail industry is organized by race and class and guided by their social and spatial coordinates. As we show, however, gender is no less central to the intersectional matrix that organizes action in the field. Just as men of color are disproportionately targeted for arrest and incarceration, women of color disproportionately shoulder the burdens of the criminal justice field's financial takings. The gender basis of bail predation, however, is not simply a matter of sex differences in the distribution of burdens. Instead, to grasp the underlying logic of practice in the field (that is, the largely taken-for-granted dispositions that generate patterns of action), we need to understand how race- and class-focused resource extractions are ad-

---

1. This analytic shift is pursued in greater detail in a book-length project. Joshua Page and Joe Soss, *Preying on the Poor: Criminal Justice as Revenue Racket* (under contract, University of Chicago Press).

vanced through gendered ethics of care and ordered by the gendered organization of care relations.

Much of the work on collateral criminal justice effects focuses on dynamics of exclusion and marginalization. Here, we focus on how gendered bail practices work to draw women cosigners into the criminal justice system's predatory operations. In this regard, our analysis builds on Megan Comfort's ethnographic study of women who visit incarcerated men and the dynamic process of "secondary prisonization," a "less absolute but still powerful form" of socialization and social control associated with prison exposure (2008, 15). We extend this insight to a gender analysis of bail-centered predation. Through the bail contract, cosigners are repositioned as economic actors assuming new debts, as citizens taking on new relations to state powers, and as social actors experiencing new or revised ties to defendants and their relations. Bail processes insert new financial terms into existing relations of care, often reconstructing them in the idiom of debt (LeBaron and Roberts 2010). In this regard, bail-centered predation can be seen as productive— not only in its incorporation of cosigners into criminal justice processes and its reconstruction of women's civic and economic positions, but also in its reordering of gendered social relations and associated ethics of care.

We depart from Comfort's account of secondary prisonization in one important respect. Comfort argues that the women who support prisoners become secondary targets of social control, socialization, and financial extraction. In the bail field, we argue, women cosigners are better conceptualized as primary targets of predation. Few defendants have the resources needed to enter bail contracts on their own. From the start, the defendant functions as an entry point (even a lure) for a predatory process that focuses on locating and securing cosigners. Women, and most of all mothers, are prized among potential bail clients because they are seen as likely to have both the financial means and the obligations to care (that is, the motive) to transfer resources to the bail industry. Thus, social interactions between cosigners and bail agents are suffused with ethics of care and structured by the gendered basis of caring relations in the broader society.

Our analysis is based on an immersive ethnographic study of the bail industry in 2015 and 2016. For about eighteen months, Joshua Page worked as a bail bond agent, participating and observing as an employee on the frontlines of the industry. Drawing on this fieldwork, we ask how gender operates (in conjunction with race and class) as a structure of interpretation and action, guiding practice on "both sides of the desk" in the bail industry. How do participants on each side of the social transaction understand and make use of the gendered rules of the game? How do gender and the gendered basis of care relations position women (especially women of color) as primary targets of predation? And how should scholars of inequality and criminal justice think about the consequences of the bail industry's gendered process of resource extraction?

CARE, INEQUALITY, AND THE CRIMINAL JUSTICE SYSTEM

Throughout the fieldwork, bond agents and cosigners routinely framed efforts to secure bail in terms of obligations to take care of the defendant. The predominance of lower-income women of color among cosigners reflects not only the social targeting of criminal justice practices but also, and equally, the social forces that allocate and regulate caring responsibilities. That is, to understand who cosigns for bail bonds and how bail practices operate, the bail industry needs to be located within the social structure of care relations in the broader society. Because cosigners and defendants engage each other on terms defined by ethics and expectations of care, these concerns define the terrain that bail agents navigate as they recruit and manage cosigners. As a result, the bondsperson's job entails various forms of "emotional labor" calibrated to convey care for the caregiving cosigner and a shared desire to take care of the defendant (Hochschild 2012). We situate our study within the broader interplay of care, social inequalities, and the criminal justice system.

Criminal justice institutions generate needs—physical, financial, emotional, spiritual, and social—which raise fundamental questions of social responsibility, morality, and justice. Who is obligated to address these needs? Why, from a moral standpoint, should someone extend or deny care to an individual caught up in the criminal justice system? And to what extent should the distribution of caring burdens, in the matter at hand and in the longer history of a social relationship, be considered just or unjust? These questions fit neatly into a long tradition of inquiry exploring the operations of care as an ethical standpoint and the construction of care as a gendered site of social obligation and labor. This tradition examines how socially situated actors contemplate their moral obligations in light of their specific attachments, statuses, and roles (Gilligan 1982; Noddings 1984). Yet as political scientist Joan Tronto and others have emphasized, this "ethic of care" does not stand apart from considerations of justice and democracy (Tronto 1993). Indeed, because care is not just an ethical matter but also a practice necessary for societies to function, questions about how care should be organized and how its burdens should be distributed are inseparable from questions of power, justice, and politics (Tronto 1993, 2013; Fineman 2004).

Informed by an interdisciplinary literature in which feminist scholars have often taken the lead, one can see how the forms of caring labor that surround criminal justice institutions reflect the broader ideological and practical construction of gender-, race-, and class-specific labor roles (Federici 2004; Glenn 2010). Historically rooted in a contrast of public and private spheres, gendered divisions of labor have made women primarily responsible for care work in domestic spaces and called on men to serve as the "breadwinning" earners of a family-sustaining wage (Gordon 1994; Fineman 2004). "Men's work," framed as freely exchanged labor, has thus been viewed as deserving of financial compensation; women's unwaged caring labor has been cast as a vocation of devotion supplying its own intrinsic, feminine rewards (Fortunati 1995). In this contrast, women's care work appears to exist in a world apart from market forces—a fulfillment of women's essential nature that expresses loving social bonds and holds the deepest social and even spiritual value. Such myths have endured despite the fact that care work has long taken waged as well as unwaged forms, lower-class women being especially likely to support their families through care-work earnings (Glenn 2010). Further, the disposition to care is often regarded as a trait natural to particular individuals. Tronto reminds us, however, that such inclinations are cultivated through social trainings rooted in institutions (2013). Marriage and family laws in the United States have historically constructed care as a private duty of wives and mothers, reflecting and reinforcing family socialization processes that tend to assign caring roles to girls and women (Glenn 2010).

Yet to speak simply of women and care work is to obscure how gender has always organized care relations in varied ways, depending on its intersections with other dimensions of social subordination. Historically, for example, black women in the United States have occupied a distinctive position. With formative roots in chattel slavery, their care work has never been limited to a "private" sphere defined by family or household membership (Jones 2010; Haley 2016).[2] For centuries, it was expropriated through systems of slavery and then, after the Civil War, exploited through low-wage, domestic-servant arrangements. Because black women have been pressed into care work as social supports for more privileged groups, their commodified caring labor has contrasted with—and helped enable—the halo of private, devotional care attached to white, middle-class women. Indeed, black women charged with taking care of white families have often been deemed "unfit" to care for their own families—deprived of the sanctified images of Republican Motherhood that surrounded white women's care work and often punished for alleged maternal failures in their own homes (Gordon 1994; Roberts 1997). Contemporary child wel-

---

2. We focus on black women's experiences here to clarify a point that can also be elaborated, differently but no less importantly, through consideration of the exploitative care-labor relations experienced by, for example, poor Latina, Asian American, Native American and, in many instances, European-immigrant women (Amott and Matthaei 1996; Glenn 2010).

fare systems, which disproportionately remove children from black and Native American homes, enact this ongoing distrust in socially and materially destructive ways (Roberts 2001).

Like other structures of inequality, intersectionally organized caring relations tend to become entrenched through social repetition (Tronto 2013). Over time, assumptions and social pressures that designate primary caregivers can develop into natural, taken-for-granted features of social reality. Aligning behavior with such gender expectations can become an important part of what it means to be a "normal" man or woman in a society. Consider that, even as women's opportunities in labor markets and other arenas have expanded since the 1960s, gendered care practices have remained a durable feature of American society. Women's share of housework has declined, for example, as their employment rates have risen; yet studies show that working women still perform more than twice as much housework as their male partners (Fuwa and Cohen 2007; Bianchi et al. 2000). Today as in the past, women—and especially poor women of color—"subsidize" the mythical autonomy of the American worker in their disproportionate contributions of unpaid care work in the home, domestic service jobs in other people's homes, and low-paid employment in care centers for children, the elderly, people with disabilities, and people with illnesses (Fineman 2004; Glenn 2010; Duffy 2007). In the United States today, for example, more than 90 percent of home-care workers are women, 50 percent are people of color, 25 percent are immigrants, and 33 percent do not have a high school education (Glenn 2010, 79).

The social organization of caring relations also shapes how care is given, received, and solicited across the criminal justice field. Since the 1970s, policing, adjudication, and incarceration have become increasingly normal life experiences in low-income communities of color (Western 2006; Lerman and Weaver 2014). The rising wave of socially and spatially concentrated criminal justice entanglements has driven a dramatic expansion of similarly concentrated needs for caregiving related to criminal justice. As the collateral consequences literature makes clear, these new needs are hardly limited to the direct adult targets of the legal system (see, for example, Wakefield and Wildeman 2014). Meeting these needs may significantly disrupt and alter the life conditions of the family and friends of legally entangled individuals—especially among women of color who have long endured distinctively intense regimes of state-imposed punishments, deprivations, and risks (Collins 1994; Haley 2016; Gurusami 2018).

The rapid growth of criminal justice resource extraction since the 1990s has turned financial payment into a far more pressing and widely experienced need among targeted populations (Harris 2016; Page and Soss 2017). The women in Comfort's 2008 study of prison visitation provide an illuminating example. Given the limited resources of incarcerated individuals, women typically paid exorbitant rates for collect calls, meeting social needs in ways that simultaneously delivered commissions to telecommunications firms and the California Department of Corrections (Comfort 2008, 89). The women routinely deposited funds their loved ones could use at the prison canteen, and some even went into debt sending this money. In these transactions, they saw themselves as taking care of loved ones' daily needs, expressing loyalty, and providing badly needed emotional support (84).

Comfort (2008) frames her analysis as a process of "secondary prisonization" rooted in punishment, but this common dynamic in poor communities of color can equally be viewed through the lens of predatory governance. For the institutions that receive financial flows, gendered ethics of care function as the social fulcrum in a process that turns penal custody into a revenue-generating asset. Actors in the criminal justice field today thus follow a long history of forging profit from the care work provided by poor women of color. Indeed, an Ella Baker Center report estimates that women make up a remarkable 83 percent of all family members covering costs for incarcerated populations (deVuono-powell et al. 2015).

In the following sections, we explore the financialization of care in the commercial bail system, paying particular attention to its grammars of action, its organization, and its legitimation as we clarify how structural forces position lower-income women of color as primary targets of predation. We also show how the gendered basis of care relations in American society underwrites the logic of practice in the bail field, structuring the understandings and actions of defendants, cosigners, and bail agents alike.

BAIL AS A SITE OF INTERDEPENDENCE AND EXTRACTION

In the pretrial process, the court may hold individuals in custody, release them on their own recognizance, or require them to post bail to ensure that they will return for their court dates. When bail is imposed, most defendants find they cannot afford the full amount, so they turn to a bail company for assistance. The private business charges a premium (usually 10 percent of the bail), generally via contract with a defendant's cosigner, who assumes responsibility for ensuring that the defendant makes it to court. Should the accused fail to appear, the court can collect the full amount of the bail from the company—a threat that motivates bail companies to return defendants to custody, sometimes using bounty hunters. Failing that, the company works to recoup the amount of the bail from the bond's cosigners. The lion's share of revenues generated through this process flow, not to individual bondspersons or "mom and pop" bail companies, but instead to the large insurance companies that, by law in most states, must underwrite the bonds.

The federal government, the District of Columbia, and a handful of states—California, Illinois, Kentucky, Massachusetts, New Jersey, Oregon, and Wisconsin—depart from this model, joining the vast majority of the world in rejecting for-profit bail. These states instead rely on a variety of other techniques to secure the defendant's appearance: having arrestees deposit money with the court, which is returned (minus fines and fees) at the end of their case; charging defendants with new crimes if they fail to appear; denying release on bail (that is, pretrial detention); requiring payment of bail for missing court; or mandating conditions of release, such as wearing an electronic monitor, checking in with court staff, or adhering to a curfew. As these jurisdictions demonstrate, commercial bail is a choice within, not a requirement of, the U.S. legal system; it is a profitable industry constructed through law and policy choices, judicial decision-making, and deliberate market strategies.

In recent decades, jail systems and commercial bail have expanded together, and quickly. Between 1980 and 2015, local jail populations in the United States roughly quadrupled (Sentencing Project 2017). Trends in the bail industry followed right alongside, not only because of the swelling ranks of people passing through jails but also because of changes in judicial behavior. From 1990 to 2009, judges in large counties assigned monetary bail to a growing number of felony defendants, rising from 53 percent to 72 percent of all cases; at the same time, mean bail amounts rose 46 percent (to $61,000), driven mostly by growth in the lucrative "upper tail of defendants [who] now face bail payments in the hundreds of thousands of dollars" (Council of Economic Advisors 2015, 6). Not surprisingly, reports suggest that between 1996 and 2012 the number of bail bond agents in the United States grew from roughly eight thousand to fifteen thousand (Burns and Leone 2005, 122; Justice Policy Institute 2012, 8).

It is estimated that today 450,00 people, 65 percent of the total U.S. jail population, are defendants who have not been convicted (Santo 2015). The vast majority of these people—roughly five in six, or 83 percent—are behind bars because they cannot afford bail, bond companies refuse to bail them out, or the court will not allow them to post bail because of probation or parole violations, mandatory in-custody drug assessments, or other legal matters. Meanwhile, commercial bail agents secure the release of more than two million defendants annually (Cohen and Reaves 2007, 4). Bail is now the dominant method for obtaining pretrial release, surpassing release on recognizance in 1998, and bail amounts set by judges have risen steadily (Cohen and Kychelhahn 2006).

The profitability of commercial bail depends on the fact that accused individuals rarely have the financial means to exit jail on their own. Bail in the United States is typically imposed without regard for ability to pay, and roughly 80 percent of criminal defendants today are indigent enough to qualify for publicly provided legal counsel (Rabuy and Kopf 2016). Bureau of Justice Statistics data indicate just how low median incomes are among this group (Rabuy and Kopf 2016, 10). In 2002, women awaiting trial in local jails typically earned $8,052 per year—below the poverty line of $15,020 for a family of three or $8,860 for a single person. Men in this group typically earned $12,732, with white men ($14,852) leading Hispanic men ($13,368), and black men ($10,800). This racial pattern—made significant by the high concentration of people of color among the pretrial population—held for women as well: The low earnings of white women ($9,756) exceeded those of Hispanic women ($8,508) and stood considerably above those of black women ($6,816). In the month prior to being held in local jails, black men and women ages twenty-three to thirty-nine earned a median income of only $900 and $568, respectively (Color of Change and ACLU 2017, 18).

Against this backdrop of limited resources, the profitability of the bail industry also hinges on people in defendants' lives being able and willing to cosign bonds and pay bail premiums. A cosigner is usually a family member, romantic partner, or close friend who formally accepts financial and legal liability for the defendant making court appearances. "It's like cosigning for a loan," agents explain. That said, the responsibilities and conditions taken on by the cosigner are far more extensive than many expect. If a defendant fails to appear in court, the bail company may charge cosigners costs associated with locating the defendant (for example, expenses for bounty hunters). Contracts include provisions along these lines: "I am responsible for paying for investigation, location and apprehension time; this is billed at a rate of $250 per hour per investigator plus expenses or 10 percent of bond whichever is greater" (UCLA 2017, 17). In addition, contracts may hold cosigners responsible for some fines and fees incurred by the bail company (for example, if the company files to have the court extend or dismiss a delinquent bond). Cosigners also agree to a variety of nonfinancial conditions. A 2017 analysis by the UCLA School of Law Criminal Justice Reform Clinic notes that

Some contracts require the indemnitor [cosigner] to keep the bail bond agent apprised of their living and employment situations. Others force indemnitors to grant the bail bond agent access to private information related to every aspect of their lives, including: telephone records, medical records, school records, worker compensation records, and employment records.... But perhaps the most egregious privacy violation for indemnitors is the authorization for the bail bond agent to physically invade their homes and to track their vehicles. (UCLA 2017, 11)

By signing the contract, cosigners become both agents of social control (in relation to the defendant) and objects of social control (in relation to the bail company and court).

Millions of people agree to this onerous responsibility each year. It is not hard to see why. Local jails are notoriously terrible places, even worse than prisons. They are often dangerous, dirty, chaotic, and mind-numbingly boring (Irwin 1985; Walker 2016). In addition to wanting relief from these conditions, many defendants are eager to get out so they can work on their cases. Indeed, research suggests that defendants who remain in jail are much more likely than those who are released to be convicted, receive longer prison sentences, and get worse results in plea-bargaining processes (Phillips 2010; Oleson et al. 2014; Dobbie, Goldin, and Yang 2016; Gupta, Hansman, and Frenchman 2016). Defendants who remain in jail also make their criminal status visible to others, raising the potential for social stigma. Locked up, they cannot fulfill their parenting obligations and may accrue absences at work or school with dire consequences. To limit the harms of pretrial confinement, then, close relations of the accused may feel tremendous pressure to cosign a bail.

But these conditions provide only a partial explanation for why so many people—and why particular groups of people—become enmeshed in the bail system via cosigning. To illuminate social processes involved, we draw on our ethnographic research in "Rocksville," a large urban county.[3] Page gained access to the

---

3. Names used for the county, bail company, and all coworkers and clients are pseudonyms.

research site, known as A-Team, after several conversations with the owner of the bail bond company. He was upfront about his motivation—to understand the world of bail by participating in it. He presented himself as a curious professor—a "sponge"—who wanted to soak up his coworkers' knowledge of the bail industry; because he knew little about the inner workings of the industry, this presentation was not false, even if he occasionally played it up.

Page's position as a professor facilitated his acceptance within the company. Bail agents receive minimal respect in the legal field, and the media tend to portray them as greedy and ignorant. For some coworkers, having a professor on staff who wanted to learn from them was a source of pride; it signaled that their line of work (and *their* company) was worthy of serious scholarly interest. In fact, on several occasions, Page asked his colleagues not to introduce him as a professor because he wanted other actors in the field (such as lawyers) to interact with him like they would any other agent. Also, he wanted to protect the confidentiality of the company and his coworkers. His coworkers understood and, over time, referred to him as "the professor" less and less.

Downplaying his position as a professor, Page worked hard to show he was a serious bail agent and team player. He engaged in the same activities as his coworkers: solicited business at court, worked daytime and nighttime desk shifts, posted bonds at courthouses throughout the state, developed relationships with attorneys, attended company parties, checked warrants, and followed up with defendants who missed court or did not make payments. (He did not engage in "fugitive recovery"—the company contracted with freelance bounty hunters if needed.) Beyond these everyday tasks, he helped out whenever he could, for example, subbed for coworkers who needed time off, worked undesirable night shifts, and helped write advertisements for hiring new agents. He also engaged in the social life of the company, regularly going for lunch and afternoon coffee with coworkers, attending company parties, and exchanging texts with colleagues about bail, sports, television, movies, and life events (for example, medical procedures).

Page's social position also helped facilitate his acceptance in the research site. Like the vast majority of his coworkers, he is white and upper middle class (and though he has lived in cities for many years, he grew up in the suburbs of Southern California, so he could relate with his colleagues' suburban identities and routines). Moreover, his physical appearance and interests (especially in sports) read as traditionally masculine; he has an athletic build, he practices martial arts, and his arms are covered with tattoos. A-Team is a masculine space—with a couple of exceptions, the agents, both male and female, were aggressive competitors who ribbed each other, specialized in ribald humor, and claimed not to "take shit" from anyone. Likely because of Page's social position, self-presentation, and commitment to learning the trade, his colleagues eventually saw him as part of the team. Therefore, they rarely censored themselves around him, providing a relatively unvarnished view of the bail business in a large urban county.

While working at A-Team, Page was a paid employee. He decided to work for pay to learn what it took to make decent money as an agent. Plus, the owners informed him that he could not legally work for free. Even though he received paychecks (based solely on commissions), he did not use the money for nonresearch purposes. He used it to pay taxes on his bail income (because he was an independent contractor, taxes were not taken out of his paychecks), fund a part-time research assistant, and make donations to an organization that provides legal services to low-income people. Because he did not rely on his pay, he did not feel the same pressures as his coworkers to hustle constantly and engage in profitable but ethically and legally questionable behavior. He was free to take time off and temporarily leave behind the stresses of the job. Even though he did not rely on the income, he still became invested in beating the competition and landing bonds; he developed a strong *will to win*, arguably the defining characteristic of the big city bond agent.

Early on, Page learned that agents work mainly with friends and family rather than with defendants. Because the defendant is in jail, associates on the outside must gather money, secure collateral (if necessary), and recruit cosigners. A-Team requires cosigners to be at least twenty-one years old and to have a "decent-paying" full-time job. The composition of unconvicted jail prisoners in Rocksville (that is, those potentially eligible for bail) aligns with the national picture. According to the 2002 Bureau of Justice Statistics Survey of Inmates in Local Jails, men make up 89.2 percent of the unconvicted jail population (James 2002). Despite being nearly 70 percent of the total U.S. population, white inmates accounted for only 31 percent of the pretrial jail population. Black and Hispanic individuals made up 43 percent and 19.6 percent, respectively. Defendants' education levels matched their incomes, only 12.6 percent having at least some college and 33 percent some high school.

In conversations with coworkers and agents from other companies, Page routinely commented on the gender differences between defendants (typically men) and cosigners (typically women). Without exception, bail workers confirmed the observation, but the preponderance of women cosigners seemed unremarkable to them, Page came to understand, because it fit so easily into their own gendered assumptions about who would take care of defendants. Agents saw the field of play in the pretrial process through a gendered lens that made it seem normal and right that women would secure bail for accused men. One of the bosses at A-Team, for example, regularly instructed agents to begin conversations with defendants by asking, "What's mom's name and number?" A common belief was that mothers would bail out their children and make sure they showed up for court. Grandmothers and long-term romantic partners were good targets as well; short-term girlfriends were avoided because their ties to defendants were considered tenuous.

The selection and pursuit of women as cosigners paralleled agents' tendency to see and describe cosigners as babysitters for defendants—a strongly gendered role employed in the field as an occupational metaphor. In these ways and others, bail agents revealed an intuitive grasp of what Evelyn Nakano Glenn terms "the social organization of care": the "systematic ways in which care for those who need it is allocated and how the responsibility for caring labor is assigned" (2010, 6). Indeed, just as race and class intersect with gender in the social organization of care, these axes of inequality shape evaluations of women as potential cosigners. For agents, race and class categories (operating as racialized assumptions about class and class-inflected conceptions of race) function as rubrics for estimating financial resources and sizing up character, for judging, in ways large and small, whether a person is a good or bad risk. Thus, as the pecking order for desirable clients works through gender roles (for example, mother, wife, daughter), its gradations reflect cultural constructions of groups positioned according to race and class.

White women and middle-class women are typically seen as better bets in these regards, more likely to "be responsible" and have "good jobs." Most agents adopt a view of group culture consistent with "underclass" narratives that portray the poor, racially segregated "ghetto" as a place where "social pathologies" proliferate as products of moral turpitude and dysfunctional norms (rather than social inequality and subjugation). Poor women of color therefore stand at the center of predatory bail targeting (due to the social composition of criminal defendants) but are also subjected to tougher scrutiny via race and class stereotypes. This profiling can have serious consequences. First, it raises the odds that defendants from race- and class-subjugated groups will be unable to bail out of jail—a fate far worse than a bail contract, however predatory its terms may be. Second, it raises the odds that bail will be offered to cosigners from subjugated groups only on riskier or more costly terms—for example, with higher premiums, stronger collateral requirements, and stricter payment conditions.

CARING OBLIGATIONS AND EMOTIONAL LABOR

Agents' gendered expectations regarding cosigners are a social construction built around a real pattern of sex difference in the adoption of bail responsibilities. As the most frequent cosigners, women often express strong feelings of obligation to bail out defendants. In what might appear as straightforward business transactions, cosigners frequently see themselves (and are seen by others) as expressing loyalty and care by arranging premiums, agreeing to onerous contractual obligations, and taking responsibility for getting the defendant to court. Further, like many other forms of care work, the act of bailing someone out of jail is often seen as an effort to create the conditions needed for self-care. Locked behind bars, defendants are unable to meet many of their own physical-emotional needs and social obligations. Cosigning, in this sense, fosters conditions for others' autonomous action.

Still, decisions to cosign are rarely free from ambivalence. Many cosigners feel conflicted about helping the accused and find the bail process a highly emotional experience. Pressures to sign on the dotted line can raise hard questions about what one person owes another, who has done favors for whom in the past, which betrayals can be forgiven, and how much is too much to ask. The act of cosigning may restore long-severed ties to a defendant or rewrite the terms and expectations of an existing social relationship. Many clients become anxious when asked to sign for a bond, especially when former romantic partners worry they will become re-entangled with a defendant's life in unwanted ways.

In this anxious context, the caring dispositions of the cosigner are strategically matched by the bail agent's performance of various forms of "emotional labor" (Hochschild 2012). Seeking to close the deal, agents express kindness and understanding, appreciation for the cosigner's sacrifice. They listen to clients' concerns, offer reassurances, and convey information to allay uncertainties. Before and after the cosigning, the agent offers emotional support and finds ways to indicate that, in their own way, they also care. Although some agents are more adept at and invested in caring labor, all engage in it on occasion. Agents who come off as uncaring, self-interested salespersons risk losing cases to more empathetic competitors. A-Team and its local competitors even strategically hired female agents, believing that as women they would connect emotionally with the mothers, girlfriends, and female friends of defendants. A-Team also retained and rewarded male agents who took pride in helping distraught clients. A few of Page's colleagues seemed to gain a sense of masculine honor, seeing their work as chivalry extended toward women in distress. Engaging in emotional labor helped them make a profit and, perhaps ironically, feel good as men.

To unpack these dynamics, an episode from the fieldwork is instructive. In Rocksville, agents attend first-appearance court for people charged with gross misdemeanors and felony crimes.[4] The goal is to secure a client's business immediately after the judge has ruled on bail. To do so, agents typically engage in a strategic presentation of self, conveying that they are potential allies who "know the ropes" of the legal system and can help worried newcomers understand and navigate the pretrial process (Goffman 1959). After making first contact, agents may work with the defendant's family or friends for several days as they line up money for the premium and a qualified cosigner. It is not unusual for agents to "work a bond" for a week or more (and typically, the bigger the bail, the longer the process). The six days it took for Page to close this deal was par for the course.

At court one day, Page casually introduced himself to two Native American women, the long-term partner of a defendant and his mother. The defendant, Johnny, was charged with statutory rape (sex with a minor); the initial bail was set at $100,000.[5] The women seemed unfamiliar with the court process and appeared to have been crying. Page sat down

---

4. Agents in Rocksville rarely attend misdemeanor court because judges generally release low-level defendants with no or low financial bail.

5. In Rocksville, defendants receive an initial bail amount when the court charges them with a crime. At the first appearance (typically the following weekday), the judge considers the prosecutor's and defense attorney's bail arguments and then typically gives felony defendants a choice between unconditional bail (post a larger bail amount, remain law-abiding, and show up for court appearances) and a conditional bail (post a lower bail amount—or sometimes no money at all—and follow a set of conditions, such as checking in with a probation officer, submitting to drug tests, or avoiding locations).

and explained the proceedings. Striking an optimistic note, he remarked that judges typically lower bail as the process moves forward. Even though the women felt they could not afford the premium for such a high bail, there was still a chance they would be able to get Johnny out of jail.

Over the next hour and a half, they waited for the clerk to call Johnny's case. The session ended without the case being called, but Page had gotten valuable time to establish rapport and expertise. When, for instance, the prosecutor asked if anyone were present for a case that had not been called, Page advised Johnny's partner, Angie, to speak up. The prosecutor explained that Johnny had refused to come to court. Noting that defendants typically get one "pass," he said that if Johnny refused again, staff would probably bring him to court in restraints. As they left together, Angie told Page that Johnny might have refused to come to court because he felt too ashamed to face her. She agreed to meet the following afternoon before court, and Page encouraged her to call him with any questions in the meantime. When Angie replied, "I don't even know what questions to ask," Page assured her that he would try to help with any confusion.

Page's invitation to "call anytime" could easily be read as disingenuous. But by this point in the fieldwork, the offer was more reflexive, based on an intuitive feel for what was socially appropriate. True, the bail agent has financial incentives to provide emotional support; offering the "gift" of kindness and understanding, he or she hopes to receive the reciprocal gift of business.[6] But the expression of care in this context cannot be reduced to a rational actor engaging in conscious dissembling for financial gain. As a bond agent, Page knew that friends and family members are often fearful and worried about defendants' well-being. They feel disoriented by the legal process and, in most cases, do not have a private attorney or public defender available to answer their questions. They do not know where else to turn. The bail agent appears in this unfamiliar and intimidating arena as a knowledgeable person who cares—a person who can and possibly will help someone like Angie care for a loved one in jail.

For the agent, then, the strategic move for securing the client doubles as a humane and sympathetic response to someone in Angie's or Johnny's mother Shawna's position. Care and service are, in fact, highly valued elements of the bail agent's professional identity. To be sure, these values rest uneasily alongside other aspects of the agent's work life, such as the drive to beat out the competition and the agent's pride in being a "good closer." But as agents are socialized to win in the bail game, they are simultaneously immersed in a discourse of service and educated in the arts of care. Becoming attuned and responsive to the needs of potential cosigners is central to the development of the bail agent's occupational habitus—so much so that agents often describe themselves as part counselor.

The next day, Angie was alone when she met Page at court. She had visited Johnny the night before, and he told her he had refused to go to court because he was having a breakdown and was suicidal. She said he felt better after she met with him. Johnny had been having sex with a fifteen-year-old friend of their daughter, she explained, as a preface to insisting that she was not at court because of her feelings for Johnny. She was there "for the kids" she and Johnny coparented. In Page's experience, it was not unusual for cosigners to feel they needed to justify bailing out a defendant. This need to offer *good reasons* for taking care of an accused person was especially common in cases such as Angie's, when the defendant is charged with a strongly stigmatized crime and in cases where the cosigner is the alleged victim (or victim's relative). Caring obligations thus supply what C. Wright Mills called a "vocabulary of motives"—a range of situationally acceptable bases for accounting for one's conduct (1940). Posting bail "for the kids" construes the situation in a way that remains squarely within the idiom of care but shifts the referent of care to "more deserving" actors. Angie wanted Page to know that her actions were a fulfillment of her duties as a mother, not an act of caring for a man who had had sex with a minor outside their relationship.

---

6. On the concept of gift exchange, see Mauss 1954.

When Angie and Page walked into court, they found the public defender talking with the prosecutor. Johnny would not be coming to court, the lawyers said, due to what sounded like a panic attack. (Because of his mental state, jail staff did not exercise their option to bring Johnny to court in restraints.) Angie and Page walked back to A-Team's office, where Angie described the difficulty of caring for her children while dealing with Johnny's situation. She was caught in a bind of competing care obligations. Slumping low in a chair, she became teary as she explained that Johnny had committed the crime on their anniversary and left her in a near-impossible situation. Page tried to comfort Angie. They agreed to meet at court again the following day.

On the third day, with Johnny's mother, Shawna, in attendance, Johnny showed up for court and his case was called soon after the session began. When the judge lowered Johnny's bail from $100,000 without conditions to $15,000 with conditions, Angie breathed a sigh of relief. Afterward, Page walked the women to their car, telling them that, in the short term, they would need "only" $750 to post bail. They could pay off the remaining $750 of the premium over the next couple months. Angie and Shawna hoped to get the money together quickly, Angie explained, because they feared Johnny's mental state would worsen the longer he stayed in jail. With a slightly guilty tone, Shawna said that even though her "baby" did the crime, she still loved him. The women thanked Page for his help and said they would be in touch soon.

Friday and Saturday passed without Angie calling or responding to Page's efforts to reach out. Late Sunday morning, when Angie finally took his call, she told him that she had been contacted by other bail companies. A competitor had offered to do the bail for $750 (a 5 percent premium) with no payments. Bail companies in Rocksville are required to charge 10 percent, but as Page knew at this point in his fieldwork, agents routinely ignored the rule to beat out a competitor. Page got permission from his boss to match the lowest offer and did so immediately. Angie seemed relieved. With the price difference eliminated, she could take the best deal and give Page the "gift" of her business in return for his help and support.

Angie's case reveals a number of dynamics common in the bail process. Significant others (most often, mothers and current or former partners) often feel obligated to take responsibility for defendants. Although Johnny's illegal actions harmed her, Angie felt she had to bail him out for the children. She felt duty-bound to visit Johnny, and Johnny's reported mental health breakdown seemed to intensify her sense that she needed to take care of his bail. Shawna, Johnny's mother, experienced less ambivalence than Angie. As a mother, she had to help her baby—full stop. Page worked to provide emotional and informational support so the women would eventually feel obligated to him rather than the competition. When Angie ultimately accepted Page's offer, she and Shawna lost $750 and became subjects of the bail company. If Johnny missed court or accrued additional costs (if, for instance, A-Team had to send a bounty hunter after him), they would be financially responsible, and the company could access their personal information and subject their properties to search. In the words of Page's bosses, Angie and Shawna were babysitting Johnny as watchful coagents for the bail company, under surveillance themselves as they tended to the company's investment.

SELLING CARE

Friends and family are often less willing than Angie and Shawna to bail out defendants. Bail agents use a variety of strategies to override this reluctance. By describing jail conditions as horrible, dangerous, and unhealthy, for example, agents may ramp up fears and guilt pangs rooted in a perceived duty to care. Sheila, one of Page's coworkers, warned mothers that their daughters were locked up with "prostitutes, murderers, and thieves." Another agent, Sean, routinely told potential clients, "Listen, there's no jail worse than Rocksville County in the state. And I've been to all of them." It was a lie; he had never been inside Rocksville's lock up, let alone the rest of the state's. It was a scare tactic to induce a desire to care for the accused.

Agents also emphasized negative legal outcomes tied to a defendant remaining in jail.

Such defendants, for example, are more likely to take a plea bargain even if they are not guilty (a claim that academic research supports) and might look "more guilty" appearing in court in an orange jumpsuit rather than their own clothes. Freed from lockup, defendants can strategize with attorneys, contact witnesses, and aid their case in other ways. The bottom line, agents conveyed, was that if you really care about the defendant's legal and personal fate—if you really want to take care of them in this awful situation—you will pay the premium and cosign the bond.

Like bail agents, some defendants instrumentalize duties-to-care to get reluctant family or friends to bail them out. Jail inmates routinely call bail companies asking agents to contact possible cosigners. The high cost of the jail's call system makes it unaffordable for many defendants to make these contacts on their own, but bail companies typically allow detainees to call them for free. In such cases, defendants may explicitly ask agents to stress the negative consequences of remaining in jail—losing a job, not receiving medications, or getting victimized by prisoners or guards. Defendants hope agents convey their desperation and how their safety and hopes depend on the person receiving the call. The following description is taken from Page's field notes:

> I got to the office a little before 9 am and received a call from the local jail. The young woman, Annika, was charged with drug possession and her bail was $5,000. She wanted to bail out and go to detox. Her voice shook and her breath was ragged. At her request, I called her mother, who was divorced from her father. When the mother didn't pick up, I left a message. Annika called back around 11:15. Sounding slightly hopeful, she asked if I had reached her mother. When I said I hadn't, she exhaled deeply and went silent. "Who else might be able to help?" I asked. She gave me her dad's number, but her tone suggested that he was unlikely to bail her out. Then she had an idea: I should tell her dad that she needs to go to detox because she is pregnant. Confused and concerned, I responded, "He doesn't know?" He didn't, she replied. "Do you really want me to be the one to tell him?" She said she had just found out and feared that her withdrawals would kill the baby. I agreed to call her dad, but didn't commit to unveiling the news about the man's future grandchild. A powerful combination of caffeine and anxiety sent my heart racing. Before dialing, I took several deep breaths and got a glass of water. When I reached the father, the man seemed to have expected the call and stated matter-of-factly, "I'm not bailing her out." He'd done so several times in the past and his daughter had gone right back to using. I didn't tell him about the pregnancy; in fact, I didn't push at all. I simply thanked the man for his time.

This particular case led Page to reflect on his assumptions about gender and care as a participant in the field. He realized the extent to which he assumed that women (especially mothers, grandmothers, sisters, wives, and long-term partners) would be more open to bailing out defendants. Pushing the men with strategies agents used with women seemed unlikely to be productive, especially if men came across as masculine by acting aloof and disinterested or, like the father in the example, by plainly refusing to help. In the field, Page was rarely surprised when men (even fathers) felt no obligation to cosign a bail agreement. In fact, when men took up the burdens of cosigning, they were far more likely than women to act as if bailing out a friend or family member, especially a woman, was extraordinary. Such cases resonated with bail agents' descriptions of cosigners as babysitters. Like fathers who earn praise for babysitting (rather than simply parenting) their own children, these men saw cosigning as going beyond the basic terms of their relationship to the defendant. That Page and his coworkers saw nothing surprising in this fact underscores how the men's reluctance to cosign reflected shared understandings of the social organization of care. In this sense, many of the apparently deviating cases of men being recruited into the typically feminized role of cosigner are actually consistent with our broader claim: the social terrain on which bail agents operate is defined, in significant ways, by the gendered structure of care relations in the broader society.

Another deviating case offers insight on this front. In a minority of cases, jailed defendants refrain from contacting a bond company because they do not want their loved ones to feel compelled to take care of their bail. Page learned this lesson while prospecting—an aggressive form of solicitation, common in Rocksville and strongly encouraged at A-Team, in which agents cold-call potential cosigners without defendants' knowledge or permission.[7] Prospecting during an evening shift, Page reached a woman whose son, Paul, an African American in his mid-thirties, was accused of drunk driving. The mother worked full-time as a nurse's aide and agreed to pay the premium ($600 down, $600 in payments) and cosign Paul's $12,000 bond.

About an hour later, Paul came to the office to fill out his paperwork. Page cheerfully greeted him at the door and offered bottled water and coffee. But, unlike most released defendants, Paul appeared dejected about getting bailed out. As he scanned the bail contract, he asked, "My mom came down, didn't she?" Perplexed by his unexpected release, Paul wondered aloud who in his circle had informed his mother about his situation. He had intentionally tried to keep her in the dark, though he knew she would help him. He was hoping the state would drop the charges; if not, he was confident he could handle the jail stay. He could do time, as he put it, "standing on his head." The last thing he wanted was for his mother to lose hundreds of dollars just because of his "bullshit case." When Paul found out that she had paid $600 and still owed $600, his frustration turned to sadness: "You have to be kidding me. This is what I feared." Because the deal was done, he reasoned, all he could do now was try to pay her back and "say thank you."

Although exceptional (defendants generally do not get upset when people bail them out), Paul's case is instructive. Paul clearly knows that his mother would feel a duty to take care of him by posting bail, even if it places her (and perhaps others she cares for) at risk. But his reciprocal sense of the caring relationship—he needs to look out for her well-being, too—leads him to strategically withhold information and try to bear his legal entanglement alone. Both sides of this story suggest a working knowledge of the gendered care structure of the social situation. Paul's actions also fit comfortably into a broader societal pattern in which the unwillingness to accept maternal care sometimes functions as a way of declaring one's full status as an independent, respectable adult—or, in more gendered terms, as a means for declaring, "I am a man, capable of taking care of myself without calling my mother to the scene."

ENGENDERING PREDATION
Drawing on this immersive ethnography, we have sought to clarify how relations and practices in the bail field are structured by the broader social organization of care in American society. Bail agents, cosigners, and defendants intuitively grasp this aspect of the social landscape, which underlies their dispositions to act as they do. Women are positioned as primary caregivers in the broader society so, accordingly, players in the bail game look to women first. To be sure, few women pay bail premiums and cosign bond contracts routinely in their daily caregiving. But beneath the distinctive circumstances, gendered caring relations—in this case, women stepping forward to bear the burdens of men's bail needs—operate in a manner that seems ordinary to all involved. Signing forms and making payments at the bail office, women's actions slot into the social organiza-

---

7. Prospecting works like this: When individuals are arrested, the county publishes their name, birthday, and reason for arrest online. When a defendant is charged and initial bail is set, this information is also made public on some (though not all) counties' websites. Bail agents monitor the county's electronic jail roster for prospective clients. When they find good leads, they enter the defendant's name and birthday into a proprietary software program that retrieves contact information for the defendant and his or her family members. Bail companies pay the for-profit software provider a small fee for each search. Agents then call the contacts and "offer" to bail out their friend or family member.

tion of care as well as their personal experience of caregiving duties.[8]

Bail agents strategically target women, expecting that they will feel obligated to care for defendants, and present themselves as caring allies in that effort. By performing various forms of emotional labor—whether offering understanding, patience, and reassurance or providing information and help within a system that often feels dehumanizing and painfully opaque—bond agents try to forge a connection with potential clients, cultivating a sense of reciprocal obligations. When potential clients are reluctant to sign on the dotted line, agents work to leverage whatever care obligations they may feel. Defendants, desperate to get out of jail, may collaborate with bond agents in these instrumental efforts. Woven throughout the fabric of the bail game, gendered ethics of care go a long way toward explaining sex differences in the distribution of cosigning burdens as well as the social processes that advance resource extraction in the bail industry.

We have sought to clarify how gender plays a central role in organizing and facilitating predatory criminal justice practices that are typically (and correctly) understood as being guided by race and class. As we have noted from the outset, however, these complementary axes of social differentiation and power should not be treated as alternative explanations. The gender basis of the bail field cannot be understood outside its intersections with race and class—social structures so central to the criminal justice field in the United States (Western 2006; Soss and Weaver 2017), including its predatory practices of financial extraction (Page and Soss 2017). Low-income people of color are dramatically overrepresented among defendants and, thus, are disproportionately compelled to use the services of bail bond companies. As women are pulled into the bail process, race and class matter greatly in agents' evaluations of which cases to pursue and what terms to offer. Predatory financial extraction in the bail industry today is intersectional, in part, because care duties in American society are intersectionally organized.

At a methodological level, we hope to have underscored the value of ethnography as part of a broader, pluralistic mix of approaches to studying inequality and the criminal justice system. To analyze how the bail industry works and how its practices reflect and reinforce inequalities, a researcher must go inside it. By inserting oneself into the situation, one can thus see how social inequalities structure understandings, relations, decisions, and actions and how institutional incentives and role-based obligations interact in ways that connect social disadvantage to predation. As a participant observer at A-Team, Page was able to see how elements of race, gender, class, national origin, and place of residence infused organizational culture and shaped agents' dispositions in ways that influenced perceptions of risk and worthiness, and, ultimately, financial, social, and legal outcomes. In short, this study reinforces what other scholars of punishment and society have repeatedly shown: ethnography is a critical tool for analyzing inequalities in the criminal justice system, including those related to "spillover effects" and "collateral consequences" (see also Comfort 2008; Lopez-Aguado 2016).

Drawing on the ethnography, we have also sought to clarify how the bail industry operates as a predation opportunity structure in motion. By tracing its logic of practice, we have arrived at a view of targeting that departs somewhat from the norm in scholarly literature. In most studies, the focus of analysis follows the path defined by criminal charges and punishments: the primary targets of criminal justice practices are arrestees, defendants, prisoners, and so on; the people who surround those actors are seen as secondary targets experiencing collateral consequences and spillover effects. By shifting the analytic frame from punishment to predation and analyzing bail as a social process, we

---

8. In addition to caring for family, many potential cosigners also worked as personal care assistants (PCAs). Because of home-care workers' low socioeconomic status and the precariousness of their work, A-Team had an informal policy of not approving PCAs as sole cosigners. The existence of this policy is a clear indication that professional caregivers regularly volunteered to serve as cosigners.

have arrived at an analysis that decenters the defendant. The primary target in this field is not the defendant per se but those individuals (usually women) who possess the requisite resources and feelings of obligation to take care of the defendant.

In other words, although defendants provide the entry point for bail industry revenues, the primary targets of extraction are defined by the social organization of care relations in which the defendant is enmeshed. In some cases, such as Johnny's and Paul's, bail agents may not even speak with a defendant before bailing him or her out. In other cases, such as Annika's, the defendant (motivated by a desire to be freed from jail) may collaborate in the bail agent's efforts to secure a cosigner and their resources. Even when defendants contact bail companies directly, their main function in the process of bail is providing contact information for the industry's real customers: possible cosigners, preferably mothers or long-term partners.

The ethnographic approach taken here also yields important insights into the critical question of how criminal justice actors (in this case, bail agents) construct financial predation as a justifiable if not morally desirable practice (Harris 2016). Although interviews are useful for identifying legitimating discourses, participatory ethnography helps us understand actors' bodily investments in the game (Wacquant 2004). Fierce competition inside and outside of bail companies promotes a strong desire among bail agents to "win." This pushes agents to sidestep questions about morality to aggressively solicit business. But Page's experience as a bail agent also made clear that actors in the bail industry routinely consider questions about the legitimacy and value of their work. They do not unquestioningly embrace a mythos offering a sanitized and idealized vision divorced from their real work. On the contrary, their legitimation is more often rooted in the concrete realities of practice, in which bail agents care for the needs of confused and fearful clients and provide services that clients often receive with gratitude.

As they perform emotional labor, agents come to feel that they are, in fact, valuable service providers helping clients through difficult times—even as they simultaneously work to devise the best strategies to extract revenues from them (Page 2017a). Care and competition are inseparable. In this area as elsewhere in the bail field, gender can play an important role: Page's male coworkers sometimes portrayed themselves as honorable, even chivalrous, as they shepherded distressed women—sometimes women distressed by the discourse those agents offered—through the cosigning process.

Finally, building on Comfort's work, our analysis has highlighted how predation shapes people's social positions, self-conceptions, behaviors, and relationships (Comfort 2008). As reports from advocacy groups such as Color of Change and the ACLU show (2017), commercial bail strips wealth from individuals and communities, especially low-income communities of color. In addition to these systematic "takings," for-profit bail moves defendants and cosigners into positions of debt with regard to bail companies and, potentially, collection agencies. As Alexes Harris shows, criminal justice debt generates stress and may alter behaviors, such as avoidance of legal and social service professionals and institutions (2016). In addition, because bail processes produce new relationships between cosigners and legal and quasi-legal institutions, they can recast the terms of existing relationships, especially between defendants and those who bail them out, reconnecting cosigners to defendants in ways they would not otherwise choose and generating new social obligations and expectations. By making cosigners responsible for monitoring and delivering defendants, the bail process also infuses social relationships with new dynamics of surveillance and social control.

In contemplating these sorts of social dynamics on the ground, it is essential not to lose sight of the ultimate beneficiaries and drivers of commercial bail. Bail companies and their agents are on the frontlines of an industry that delivers vast, reliable profits to sureties every year. To be sure, governments that enable this predatory business model benefit from the bail system, and the owners of some local bail businesses do quite well. But the basic structure of the industry serves to transfer wealth from the lower to the higher levels of social class. The bail industry extracts millions of dollars in resources from lower-income communities of color each year and enhances corporate wealth. What has rarely been noted, even by the strongest critics of commercial bail, is the extent to which this industry operates through and is made possible by the social organization of care and its gendered production of caring obligations, expectations, and dispositions.

A NOTE ON METHODOLOGY

Our analysis of bail takes the form of an extended case study. The core of the study is an institutional ethnography based on Page's participant observation as a bail bond agent. Unlike other methods of data gathering, participant observation allows the researcher to "participate in the action being studied . . . [to produce] the most direct evidence on action as the action unfolds in everyday life" (Lichterman 2002, 120–21). As a longitudinal method pursued across varied contexts, ethnography allows the researcher to compare words and deeds and to empirically investigate why statements, attitudes, and practices vary from one setting or group of actors to another (Wedeen 2009; Jerolmack and Khan 2014). Participatory ethnography allows scholars to "observe how people make sense of their worlds, to chart how they ground their ideas in everyday practices and administrative routines" (Wedeen 2009, 85). Through immersion in the field, the researcher learns (and in various ways, embodies) the cognitive, emotional, and discursive conditions of participation in the activity under investigation (Goffman 1989; Wacquant 2004).

As a participant, Page directly experienced the rules and norms, identities and ideals, and workplace pressures that define and organize bail agents' practices. As an observer, he benefited from long-term investments in watching, listening, and asking while positioned as a co-participant in work activities as they transpired. On occasion, of course, the people he interacted with may have worried about the impression they were making; they may have had incentives to dissemble or make self-serving statements. Over the long haul, however, it is difficult for a loose collection of workers to sustain a misleading self-presentation at all times and places, coordinating a sham around the researcher for more than a year while pursuing the work needed to get their jobs done. At the same time, the slow building of trust and rapport made possible by this method are especially valuable for studies of stigmatized fields, such as commercial bail, in which actors may fear reinforcing negative images of their profession (Goldfarb 1965; Dill 1975; Davis 1984; Page 2017a). As Page became a familiar coworker at A-Team, the noteworthy introduction of a distinctive outsider gave way to the unremarkable routines, conversations, and friendships of the everyday workplace.

Sustained immersion also allows the researcher to experience and analyze the field from varied perspectives over the course of the study. As a standpoint for understanding commercial bail, the courtroom offered opportunities the office did not. Moreover, night shifts differed from day shifts, conversations with lawyers and fellow bail agents painted varied portraits, and so on. And because A-Team typically processed more than one hundred bails each month, Page had repeated opportunities to separate case-specific details and agent-specific styles from organizational routines, standard operating procedures, and the underlying logic of practice—that is, largely taken-for-granted dispositions that generate patterns of action (Bourdieu and Wacquant 1992; Wedeen 2009). Page's growing familiarity with bail work also meant that his standpoint on social action changed in productive ways over time.[9]

Although Page conducted his research at a single local bail company, we analyze it here as a case of a broader class of phenomena. Our "casing" of the study works at two levels. At one, we analyze A-Team's work in Rocksville as a concrete, particular instance of commercial bail practices in the United States. At a second level, we analyze commercial bail as a case of the more general practice of criminal justice predation. Money bail is a mode of resource extraction that differs from others (such as prison profiteering, asset forfeiture, or fines and fees) in many ways but nonetheless can be seen as integral to the broader whole, enmeshed with its other operations, and struc-

---

9. On the complementary advantages of strangeness and familiarity in field research, see Soss 2013, 137.

tured by its general logics of targeting and operation.

A-Team is a professional, well-managed, successful company, selected as a research site, in part, because it is not a deviating "bad actor" or unusually predatory operation. Informal conversations and formal interviews in the field; industry, media, and governmental reports; and direct observations all corroborated that A-Team is not fundamentally different from other bail companies in large urban counties. A-Team and Rocksville, however, should not be mistaken for a representative case of commercial bail in the sense that a statistical sample may be representative of a broader population. In an extended case study, the relationship between the general and the particular works in a different way. Rather than standing in for other local bail operations, A-Team's business operations provide a vantage point for analyzing the more general structures and forces that shape local bail businesses across the United States as a whole. Our analysis illuminates a concrete case of organized actors navigating and grappling with the general conditions of the industry—a goal quite different from providing sample-based estimates of population characteristics.

Thus, as Michael Burawoy explains, "The importance of the single case lies in what it tells us about [a theoretically and practically significant aspect of] society as a whole rather than about the population of similar cases" (2009, 281). In an extended case study, "researchers analyze a particular social situation in relation to the broader social forces shaping it" (Small 2009, 19). Seeking analytic rather than statistical generalization, "the researcher 'extends' his [or her] view of a case by theorizing it as a very specific instance of social and cultural structures or institutional forces at work. . . . In the extended case method, we want to learn, ultimately, 'how' institutional forces, social and cultural structures, shape action in our particular field sites" (Lichterman 2002, 123). Our goal, then, is to use A-Team's operations in Rocksville to advance theoretical understandings of how predatory relations and practices work in and around criminal justice institutions and how they reflect and perpetuate social inequalities.

ON THE ETHICS OF ETHNOGRAPHIC BAIL RESEARCH

A study based on direct participation in the bail industry unavoidably raises questions of research ethics. After all, we argue that commercial bail operations prey on subjugated communities, leveraging the needs and vulnerabilities created by pretrial processes to turn poor people's resources into corporate and governmental revenues. Was it ethical for Page to pursue research by participating as a bail agent at A-Team? A full discussion of the relevant considerations would require far more space than we have here. We have given extensive thought to these questions, however, and take this opportunity to offer some brief comments on the ethics of ethnographic bail research.

Ethnography, by definition, is a form of participation in social life. As such, it shares the ethical complexity of all social action. It is understandable that researchers and their home institutions are often eager to draw a bright line between ethical and unethical research, positioning themselves on the legally and morally pure side of the divide. Ethically speaking, however, participation in social life is rarely such a black-and-white affair. Any given social role or action—as a consumer, worker, citizen, parent, friend, and so on—will raise moral and ethical questions along multiple dimensions, each of which may be judged differently from the vantage point of different moral philosophies.[10] Moreover, as a large literature on "bystanders to injustice" makes clear, a decision to stay on the sidelines, declining to get involved, is not in any universal sense a more ethical or moral position than direct participation. Like passive beneficiaries of collective injustices and citizens who do not vote in the face of government atrocities, scholars do not necessarily occupy higher moral ground simply by declining to get involved.

In this sense, we reject the presumption that by not doing this kind of research, we

---

10. For a classic discussion of the diverse and historically shifting moral standpoints used to assess the ethics of social action, see MacIntyre 2003.

scholars can keep our hands clean. As we argue here and in a larger book-length project,[11] predatory resource extraction from subjugated communities subsidizes both the liberal contract society and the quality of life that more advantaged Americans enjoy. People who benefit from these practices cannot shed responsibility for them simply by declining to go out and do the bond work (or prison work or policing work) themselves. Those of us who neither work in nor are targeted by the industry are not nonparticipants; we simply participate on terms that allow us to benefit while maintaining cognitive distance from our moral responsibility.[12]

Page made his participation in (and responsibility for) criminal justice predation more explicit and direct in order to bring the industry's practices to public light and show how this form of predation is made possible, sustained, organized, legitimated, and carried out on the frontlines. The research intervention reflects ethical and political commitments to *doing something* about the predatory bail industry's ongoing invisibility in scholarship and the broader society. Page took on the ethical burdens of overt participation because this was the only way to really understand the work itself—and thus, to develop an analysis of how it is organized, carried out, and can be effectively reformed or abolished. Fully understanding the industry meant engaging in its core practices, which are by definition predatory, and work in the field provided a foundation for critical scholarly and public interventions.[13]

If Page had stayed on the sidelines and we had forgone this research, the bail industry would have been no less predatory; the distribution of its harms would have been altered in no meaningful way; and our responsibility for industry's harms, though certainly less visible and direct, would have remained. Sometimes ethically complex research—inserting ourselves in troubling modes of action in a more overt way—should be pursued precisely because it offers a way to take responsibility for societal injustices that are already being carried out in our name and already delivering benefits to us as more advantaged members of a community.[14]

No mechanical cost-benefit formula can generate a summary yes-or-no ethical verdict on this research. The procedure-centered judgments of the University of Minnesota's Institutional Review Board, which approved this "human subjects" research as ethical, also should not be seen as the final word on the multiple, complex moral questions involved. In a bail ethnography as in much of social life, participation is a subject that must be wrestled with in light of the real (not ideal) conditions we confront, the many morally relevant aspects of a single social action, and the diversity of ethical perspectives that may be brought to bear. To do so effectively, we must openly acknowledge that the predatory bail industry presents us with no easy answers as we try, both as scholars and community members, to understand how it works, explain what it does, and pursue effective actions in response.

REFERENCES

Amott, Teresa, and Julie Matthaei. 1996. *Race, Gender, and Work: A Multi-cultural Economic History of Women in the United States*. Boston: South End Press.

Bauer, Shane. 2014. "Inside the Wild, Shadowy, and Highly Lucrative Bail Industry." *Mother Jones*, May/June. Accessed October 30, 2017. http://www.motherjones.com/politics/2014/06/bail-bond-prison-industry.

Bianchi, Suzanne, Melissa Milkie, Liana Sayer, and John Robinson. 2000. "Is Anyone Doing the Housework? Trends in the Gender Division of Household Labor." *Social Forces* 79(1): 191–228.

Bourdieu, Pierre, and Loïc Wacquant. 1992. *An Invi-*

---

11. Joshua Page and Joe Soss, *Preying on the Poor: Criminal Justice as Revenue Racket* (under contract, University of Chicago Press).

12. For insight on collective responsibility and cognitive distancing (or "ignorance"), see Hayward 2017.

13. This article offers a scholarly intervention. For a more public intervention, see Page 2017b.

14. For closely related arguments regarding the ethics of ethnographic research that required participation in the violence of slaughterhouse work, see Pachirat 2013, especially chapter 6.

tation to Reflexive Sociology. Chicago: University of Chicago Press.

Burawoy, Michael. 2009. The Extended Case Method: Four Countries, Four Decades, Four Great Transformations, and One Theoretical Tradition. Berkeley: University of California Press.

Burns, Ronald, and Patrick Leone. 2005. "Bounty Hunters: A Look Behind the Hype." Policing: An International Journal of Police Strategies & Management 28(1): 118–38.

Clear, Todd. 2007. Imprisoning Communities: How Mass Incarceration Makes Disadvantaged Neighborhoods Worse. New York: Oxford University Press.

Cohen, Thomas, and Tracey Kychelhahn. 2006. Felony Defendants in Large Urban Counties, 2006. NCJ 228944. Washington: U.S. Department of Justice, Bureau of Justice Statistics.

Cohen, Thomas, and Brian Reeves. 2007. Pretrial Release of Felony Defendants in State Courts. Washington: U.S. Department of Justice, Bureau of Justice Statistics.

Collins, Patricia H. 1994. "Shifting the Center: Race, Class, and Feminist Theorizing About Motherhood." In Mothering: Ideology, Experience, and Agency, edited by Evelyn N. Glenn, Grace Chang, and Linda R. Forcey. New York: Routledge.

Color of Change and ACLU. 2017. Selling Off Our Freedom: How Insurance Corporations Have Taken Over Our Bail System. New York: ACLU.

Comfort, Megan. 2008. Doing Time Together: Love and Family in the Shadow of the Prison. Chicago: University of Chicago Press.

Council of Economic Advisors. 2015. "Fines, Fees, and Bail." Issue Brief, December. Accessed September 15, 2017. https://obamawhitehouse.archives.gov/sites/default/files/page/files/1215_cea_fine_fee_bail_issue_brief.pdf.

Crenshaw, Kimberle. 2012. "From Private Violence to Mass Incarceration: Thinking Intersectionally About Women, Race, and Social Control." UCLA Law Review 59(6): 1418–72.

Davis, David S. 1984. "Good People Doing Dirty Work: A Study of Social Isolation." Symbolic Interaction 7(2): 233–47.

Dawson, Michael C. 2016. "Hidden in Plain Sight: A Note on Legitimation Crises and the Racial Order." Critical Historical Studies 3(1): 143–61.

Demuth, Stephen. 2003. "Racial and Ethnic Differences in Pretrial Release Decisions and Outcomes: A Comparison of Hispanic, Black, and White Felony Arrestees." Criminology 41(3): 873–908.

deVuono-powell, Saneta, Chris Schweidler, Alicia Walters, and Azadeh Zohrabi. 2015. Who Pays? The True Cost of Incarceration on Families. September. Oakland, Calif.: Ella Baker Center, Forward Together, Research Action Design. Accessed August 15, 2018. http://whopaysreport.org/who-pays-full-report.

Dill, Forrest. 1975. "Discretion, Exchange and Social Control: Bail Bondsmen in Criminal Courts." Law & Society Review 9(4): 639–74.

Dobbie, Will, Jacob Goldin, and Crystal Yang. 2016. "The Effects of Pre-Trial Detention on Conviction, Future Crime, and Employment: Evidence from Randomly Assigned Judges." NBER working paper no. 22511. Cambridge, Mass.: National Bureau of Economic Research.

Du Bois, W. E. B. 1935. Black Reconstruction in America: An Essay Toward a History of the Part Which Black Folk Played in the Attempt to Reconstruct Democracy in America, 1860–1880, vol. 6. New York: Oxford University Press.

Duffy, Mignon. 2007. "Doing the Dirty Work: Gender, Race, and Reproductive Labor in Historical Perspective." Gender and Society 21(3): 313–36.

Epp, Charles, Steven Maynard-Moody, and Donald Haider-Markel. 2014. Pulled Over: How Police Stops Define Race and Citizenship. Chicago: University of Chicago Press.

Federici, Sylvia. 2004. Caliban and the Witch: Women, the Body, and Primitive Accumulation. New York: Autonomedia.

Feeley, Malcolm. 1979. The Process is the Punishment: Handling Cases in a Lower Criminal Court. New York: Russell Sage Foundation.

Fineman, Martha. 2004. The Autonomy Myth: A Theory of Dependency. New York: The New Press.

Fortunati, Leopoldina. 1995. The Arcane of Reproduction: Housework, Prostitution, Labor, and Capital. Milan: Autonomedia.

Fraser, Nancy. 2016. "Expropriation and Exploitation in Racialized Capitalism: A Reply to Michael Dawson." Critical Historical Studies 3(1): 163–78.

Fuwa, Makiko, and Phillip Cohen. 2007. "Housework and Social Policy." Social Science Research 36(2): 512–30.

Glassman, Jim. 2006. "Primitive Accumulation, Accumulation by Dispossession, Accumulation by 'Extra-Economic' Means." Progress in Human Geography 30(5): 608–35.

Glenn, Evelyn N. 2010. *Forced to Care: Coercion and Caregiving in America*. Cambridge, Mass.: Harvard University Press.

Goffman, Erving. 1959. *The Presentation of Self in Everyday Life*. New York: Anchor.

———. 1989. "On Fieldwork." *Journal of Contemporary Ethnography* 18(2): 123–32.

Goldfarb, Ronald. 1965. *Ransom: A Critique of the American Bail System*. New York: Harper & Row.

Gordon, Linda. 1994. *Pitied But Not Entitled: Single Mothers and the History of Welfare, 1890–1935*. New York: Free Press.

Gupta, Arpit, Ethan Frenchman, and Douglas Swanson. 2016. "The High Cost of Bail: How Maryland's Reliance on Money Bail Jails the Poor and Costs the Community Millions." Annapolis: Maryland Office of the Public Defender. Accessed August 15, 2018. https://www.nmcourts.gov/uploads/FileLinks/251c46be89664ada8ab0d99c3c426956/High_Cost_of_Bail__Maryland.pdf.

Gupta, Arpit, Christopher Hansman, and Ethan Frenchman. 2016. "The Heavy Costs of High Bail: Evidence from Judge Randomization." Columbia Law and Economics working paper no. 531. New York: Columbia Law School.

Gurusami, Susila. 2018. "Motherwork Under the State: The Maternal Labor of Formerly Incarcerated Black Women." *Social Problems*. Published online February 13. DOI: 10.1093/socpro/spx045.

Haley, Sarah. 2016. *No Mercy Here: Gender, Punishment, and the Making of Jim Crow Modernity*. Chapel Hill: University of North Carolina Press.

Haney, Lynne. 2004. "Introduction: Gender, Welfare, and the States of Punishment." *Social Politics: International Studies in Gender, State & Society* 11(3): 333–62.

Harris, Alexes. 2016. *A Pound of Flesh: Monetary Sanctions as Punishment for the Poor*. New York: Russell Sage Foundation.

Harris, Alexes, Heather Evans, and Katherine Beckett. 2011. "Courtesy Stigma and Monetary Sanctions: Toward a Socio-Cultural Theory of Punishment." *American Sociological Review* 76(2): 234–64.

Hayward, Clarissa Rile. 2017. "Responsibility and Ignorance: On Dismantling Structural Injustice." *Journal of Politics* 79(2): 396–408.

Hochschild, Arlie. 2012. *The Managed Heart: Commercialization of Human Feeling*, 2nd ed. Berkeley: University of California Press.

Irwin, John. 1985. *The Jail: Managing the Underclass in American Society*. Berkeley: University of California Press.

James, Doris J. 2002. "Profile of Jail Inmates." Bureau of Justice Statistics special report NCJ 201932. Washington: U.S. Department of Justice.

Jerolmack, Colin, and Shamus Khan. 2014. "Talk Is Cheap: Ethnography and the Attitudinal Fallacy." *Sociological Methods & Research* 43(2): 178–209.

Jones, Jacqueline. 2010. *Labor of Love, Labor of Sorrow: Black Women, Work, and the Family, from Slavery to the Present*. New York: Basic Books.

Justice Policy Institute. 2012. *For Better or For Profit: How the Bail Bonding Industry Stands in the Way of Fair and Effective Pretrial Release*. Washington, D.C.: Justice Policy Institute.

Kohler-Hausmann, Issa. 2013. "Misdemeanor Justice: Control Without Conviction," *American Journal of Sociology* 119(2): 351–93.

LeBaron, Genevieve, and Adrienne Roberts. 2010. "Toward a Feminist Political Economy of Capitalism and Carcerality." *Signs: Journal of Women in Culture and Society* 26(1): 19–44.

Lerman, Amy, and Vesla Weaver. 2014. *Arresting Citizenship: The Democratic Consequences of American Crime Control*. Chicago: University of Chicago Press.

Lichterman, Paul. 2002. "Seeing Structure Happen: Theory-Driven Participant Observation." In *Methods of Social Movement Research*, edited by Bert Klandermans and Suzanne Staggenborg. Minneapolis: University of Minnesota Press.

Lopez-Aguado, Patrick. 2016. "The Collateral Consequences of Prisonization: Racial Sorting, Carceral Identity, and Community Criminalization." *Sociology Compass* 10(1): 12–23.

MacIntyre, Alasdair. 2003. *A Short History of Ethics: A History of Moral Philosophy from the Homeric Age to the 20th Century*. New York: Routledge.

Mauss, Marcel. 2000 [1954]. *The Gift: The Form and Reason of Exchange in Archaic Societies*. New York: W. W. Norton & Co.

Mills, C. Wright. 1940. "Situated Actions and Vocabularies of Motive." *American Sociological Review* 5(6): 904–13.

Nichols, Robert. 2018. "Theft Is Property! The Recursive Logic of Dispossession." *Political Theory*. 46(1): 3–28.

Noddings, Nel. 1984. *Caring: A Feminine Approach to Ethics and Moral Education*. Berkeley: University of California Press.

North, Douglas. 1981. *Structure and Change in Economic History.* New York: W. W. Norton.

Pachirat, Timothy. 2013. *Every Twelve Seconds: Industrialized Slaughter and the Politics of Sight.* New Haven, Conn.: Yale University Press.

Page, Joshua. 2017a. "Desperation and Service in the Bail Industry." *Contexts* 16(2): 30–37.

———. 2017b. "False Claims Stoke Fears About Reforming California's Bail System." *Sacramento Bee*, May 18. Accessed August 15, 2018. https://www.sacbee.com/opinion/op-ed/soapbox/article151392712.html.

Page, Joshua, and Joe Soss. 2017. "Criminal Justice Predation and Neoliberal Governance." In *Rethinking Neoliberalism: Resisting the Disciplinary Regime*, edited by Sanford Schram and Marianna Pavlovskaya. New York: Routledge.

Pateman, Carole, and Charles W. Mills. 2007. *Contract and Domination.* Malden, Mass.: Polity.

Patillo, Mary, David Weiman, and Bruce Western, eds. 2004. *Imprisoning America: The Social Effects of Mass Incarceration.* New York: Russell Sage Foundation.

Phillips, Mary T. 2010. *Making Bail in New York City: Commercial Bonds and Cash Bail.* New York: New York City Criminal Justice Agency.

Rabuy, Bernadette, and Daniel Kopf. 2016. *Detaining the Poor.* Northhampton, Mass.: Prison Policy Initiative.

Roberts, Dorothy E. 1997. "Spiritual And Menial Housework." *Yale Journal of Law and Feminism* 9(1): 6.

———. 2002. *Shattered Bonds: The Color of Child Welfare.* New York: Basic Books.

Robinson, Cedric. 1983. *Black Marxism: The Making of the Black Radical Tradition.* London: Zed.

Santo, Alysia. 2015. "When Freedom Isn't Free." *The Marshall Project*, February 23. Accessed September 15, 2017. https://www.themarshallproject.org/2015/02/23/buying-time.

Schlesinger, Traci. 2005. "Racial and Ethnic Disparity in Pretrial Criminal Processing." *Justice Quarterly* 22(2): 170–92.

The Sentencing Project. 2017. "Trends in U.S. Corrections: U.S. State and Federal Prison Population, 1925–2016." Fact Sheet, June 2017. Accessed September 12, 2017. http://sentencingproject.org/wp-content/uploads/2016/01/Trends-in-US-Corrections.pdf.

Small, Mario Luis. 2009. "'How Many Cases Do I Need?': On Science and the Logic of Case Selection in Field-Based Research." *Ethnography* 10(1): 5–38.

Soss, Joe. 2013. "Talking Our Way to Meaningful Explanations: A Practice-Centered Approach to In-Depth Interviews for Interpretative Research." In *Interpretation and Method*, edited by Dvora Yanow and Peregrine Schwartz-Shea. New York: M. E. Sharpe.

Soss, Joe, and Vesla Weaver. 2017. "Police Are Our Government: Politics, Political Science, and the Policing of Race-Class Subjugated Communities." *Annual Review of Political Science* 20: 565–91.

Tilly, Charles. 1992. *Coercion, Capital and European States, A.D. 990–1992.* New York: Wiley Blackwell.

Tronto, Joan. 1993. *Moral Boundaries: A Political Argument for an Ethic of Care.* New York: Routledge.

———. 2013. *Caring Democracy: Markets, Equality, and Justice.* New York: New York University Press.

UCLA School of Law Criminal Justice Reform Clinic (UCLA). 2017. *The Devil in the Details: Bail Bond Contracts in California.* Los Angeles: University of California.

Wacquant, Loïc. 2004. *Body & Soul: Notebooks of an Apprentice Boxer.* New York: Oxford University Press.

Wakefield, Sara, and Christopher Wildeman. 2014. *Children of the Prison Boom: Mass Incarceration and the Future of American Inequality.* New York: Oxford University Press.

Walker, Michael. 2016. "Race Making in a Penal Institution." *American Journal of Sociology* 121(4): 1051–78.

Wedeen, Lisa. 2014. "Ethnography as Interpretive Enterprise." In *Political Ethnography: What Immersion Contributes to the Study of Power*, edited by Edward Schatz. Chicago: University of Chicago Press.

Western, Bruce. 2006. *Punishment and Inequality in America.* New York: Russell Sage Foundation.

Statutory Inequality: The Logics of Monetary Sanctions in State Law

BRITTANY FRIEDMAN AND MARY PATTILLO

Monetary sanctions mandated in state statutes include fines, fees, restitution, and other legal costs imposed on persons convicted of crimes and other legal violations. Drawing on content analysis of current legislative statutes in Illinois pertaining to monetary sanctions, we ask three questions: What are defendants expected to pay for and why? What accommodations exist for defendants' poverty? What are the consequences for nonpayment? We find that neoliberal logics of personal responsibility and carceral expansion suffuse these laws, establishing a basis for transferring public costs onto criminal defendants, offering little relief for poverty, and supporting severe additional penalties for unpaid debt. Statutory inequality legally authorizes further impoverishment of the poor, thereby increasing inequality. Major related organizing and advocacy work, however, has created an opening for significant changes toward greater fairness.

Keywords: monetary sanctions, legal financial obligations, poverty, criminal statutes

Section 3-7-6 of the Illinois Unified Code of Corrections reads, in part, "Committed persons shall be responsible to reimburse the Department for the expenses incurred by their incarceration at a rate to be determined by the Department in accordance with this Section" (730 ILCS 5/3-7-6).[1] Backing up this obligation is the state's ability to sue current and former inmates to recover the costs of their incarceration. Between 2000 and 2016, the Illinois attorney general brought 157 lawsuits against inmates under this statute (Madigan 2017). Between 2010 and 2015, these lawsuits recovered roughly $500,000, most of which came from just two prisoners (Mills and Lighty 2016).

In February 2016, Illinois Democratic state senator Daniel Biss introduced Senate Bill (SB) 2465 to repeal this section of the law, eliminating the ability of the attorney general to sue inmates on behalf of the Illinois Department

Brittany Friedman is assistant professor of sociology and faculty affiliate of the Program in Criminal Justice at Rutgers University. **Mary Pattillo** is Harold Washington Professor of Sociology and African American Studies at Northwestern University.

© 2019 Russell Sage Foundation. Friedman, Brittany, and Mary Pattillo. 2019. "Statutory Inequality: The Logics of Monetary Sanctions in State Law." *RSF: The Russell Sage Foundation Journal of the Social Sciences* 5(1): 173–96. DOI: 10.7758/RSF.2019.5.1.08. This research was funded by a grant to the University of Washington from the Laura and John Arnold Foundation (Alexes Harris, PI). We thank the faculty and graduate student collaborators of the Multi-State Study of Monetary Sanctions for their intellectual contributions to the project. We thank the editors of and contributors to this *RSF* volume for their feedback. Direct correspondence to: Mary Pattillo at m-pattillo@northwestern.edu, Northwestern University, 1810 Chicago Ave., Evanston, IL 60208.

Open Access Policy: *RSF: The Russell Sage Foundation Journal of the Social Sciences* is an open access journal. This article is published under a Creative Commons Attribution-NonCommercial-NoDerivs 3.0 Unported License.

1. All statute citations are from Illinois Compiled Statutes (http://www.ilga.gov/legislation/ilcs/ilcs.asp).

of Corrections to recoup their costs. The bill passed the Senate (32 to 19), and more narrowly the House (60 to 54). Illinois Republican Governor Bruce Rauner vetoed it. His proposed amendments echoed the concerns raised in the Senate debates, namely, that eliminating the authority to sue meant that the state would forgo any possibility of recovering costs from wealthy defendants.

The debate over SB 2465 and its ultimate demise raises the central questions of this article about who pays for the institutions of the criminal justice system—police, jails, courts, prisons, and all of the actors in their employ—and how far the law reaches to make people "pay" for their crimes. These questions have taken on greater importance with the growth of all components of the criminal justice apparatus, from the hiring of more police officers (Beckett 1999), to more intensive prosecution of crimes (Pfaff 2017), to the roughly sevenfold increase in the prison population since 1970 (Western 2006). To pay for this growing system—and for other state costs—legislators have turned to additional sources of revenue: higher fines, fees, and other costs charged to the "users" of the criminal justice system. Convicted persons—whether sentenced to prison time or not—are often sentenced to these *monetary sanctions* that go to pay for the police cars that transport them, the computer systems that process them, the attorneys who prosecute them, the parole and probation officers who supervise them, and the collection and storage of their DNA, among dozens of other uses, many of which are far removed from the crime they committed, or any state dollars spent directly on their case.[2] Beyond the official sentenced fines and fees are other financial obligations such as paying for required drug treatment or domestic violence counseling or reimbursing the relevant jurisdiction for the costs of incarceration.

Monetary sanctions, also referred to as legal financial obligations (LFOs), include fines, fees, restitution, surcharges, interest, assessments, and other court costs imposed on people convicted of crimes ranging from traffic violations to violent felonies. These sanctions are mandated in state statutes that define the amounts and ranges to be charged as well as the funds into which the collected monies are to be deposited. We argue that these laws not only set out the specifics of the monetary sanctions system but also convey ideologies about crime, punishment, and offenders that build on two central scripts: the neoliberal trope of personal responsibility and the carceral logic of extended (in terms of reach) and prolonged (in terms of time) surveillance and monitoring. That these policies are disproportionately exacted on poor and working-class people who make up the majority of defendants in the courts, jails, and prisons constitutes what we call statutory inequality. The inability to pay monetary sanctions triggers increased financial and legal penalties such that poverty becomes a guilty sentence of its own, legitimizing people's continued subjection to criminal justice supervision and causing harm to their socioeconomic and general well-being.

Illinois Governor Rauner posited a millionaire inmate who would reimburse the state for its costs. The reality of those involved in the criminal justice system, however, is quite the opposite. More than 80 percent of criminal defendants in the United States are found to be indigent and thus qualified to use the services of a public defender (Harlow 2000). In Cook County, which includes the city of Chicago, that figure is 89 percent (Bellware 2017). Roughly 40 percent of prison inmates nationally do not have a high school diploma (Ewert and Wildhagen 2011). In Illinois, 30 percent of people on probation were unemployed, and just under half earned less than $20,000 annually (Adams, Bostwick, and Campbell 2011). It is difficult to discern what information lawmakers have at their disposal, but these facts should be no secret. Beyond the abundance of research that documents the lower socioeconomic status of

---

2. We use a range of words to refer to those sentenced to monetary sanctions, depending on the context. We prefer *people with court debt* and *defendants*; the former highlights the status that is most relevant for our research and the latter maintains possible innocence. The term *convicted persons* emphasizes that LFOs are mostly levied upon conviction, although there are also pretrial costs that can be passed on to defendants (Logan and Wright 2014).

those processed through the criminal justice system, the journalistic and popular portrayal of the accused and the convicted reinforces, if not overemphasizes, this reality. Thus, it is reasonable to assume that lawmakers recognize to whom they are shifting the burden when they look to defendants as sources of revenue.

In this article, we conduct a content analysis of legislative statutes regarding monetary sanctions in the State of Illinois and ask three questions: What are defendants expected to pay for and why? What accommodations are made (or not) for their ability to pay? What are the consequences for not paying? This analysis uncovers neoliberal ideas of personal responsibility and carceral logics that effectively create indebtedness to the state, especially for poor defendants, which furthers state supervision and punishment, and perpetuates and deepens the socioeconomic insecurity of already fragile populations, thereby exacerbating overall inequalities. We are careful to note, however, that this is a study of law on the books. This project is part of a larger study that includes courtroom observations and interviews with court actors and people with court debt (discussed in the methods section); this article, however, focuses on how what the law *allows* offers a window into the social, cultural, and political moods about criminals and punishment, which necessarily precedes the unequal outcomes.[3] In important new developments, major organizing and advocacy work around this issue has set the foundation for significant changes toward greater fairness.

THE NEOLIBERAL LOGICS OF PERSONAL RESPONSIBILITY AND CARCERAL EXPANSION

We embed our research within theories about the growing effects of neoliberal economic ideologies on a range of societal institutions. Germinating as early as the late 1940s, but flowering by the 1970s, the core of neoliberal ideology is about reducing governmental regulation of the economy and reducing the welfare state to increase the efficiency of markets, even though markets and economies are never unfettered from rule-making and thus are always the productions of societies and their governments (Ong 2006; Prasad 2006). As neoliberal policies began to take firm hold in the 1980s, holes left by the retreat of government- and employer-supported social safety nets were filled with language about personal responsibility and choice. As the theorist David Harvey describes it, "each individual is held responsible and accountable for his or her own actions and well-being. This principle extends into the realms of welfare, education, health care, and even pensions" (2007, 65–66). Of course, the concept of personal responsibility is not new in the criminal justice realm, where the law has always assumed an individual actor who is individually culpable. Hence, in criminal justice, the idea of personal responsibility is simply more heightened—rather than wholly created—by the proliferation of neoliberal ideas. In the criminal justice context, the intensified personal responsibility rhetoric allows for greater certainty of culpability and punitive severity.

As an institution that primarily and increasingly processes and manages poor and working-class people, criminal justice is a domain in which personal responsibility is particularly potent. Loïc Wacquant captures this confluence:

> Comparative analysis of the evolution of penality in the advanced countries over the past decade reveals a close link between the ascendancy of neoliberalism, as ideological project and governmental practice mandating submission to the "free market" and the celebration of "individual responsibility" in all realms, on the one hand, and the deployment of punitive and proactive law-enforcement policies targeting street delinquency and the categories trapped in the margins and cracks

---

3. Alexes Harris, Heather Evans, and Katherine Beckett (2010) focus on how the application of monetary sanctions in practice exacerbates inequality through a threefold mechanism of reducing disposable household income (because monies are going to pay off monetary sanctions); reducing access to housing, employment, and education, which could improve socioeconomic well-being; and increasing the likelihood of rearrest and incarceration.

of the new economic and moral order coming into being under the conjoint empire of financialized capital and flexible wage labor, on the other. (2009, 1)

Like the emphasis on personal responsibility, carceral logics also grow out of neoliberal policymaking and practices. The criminal justice system is part of the answer to the question of how to manage the increased economic and social insecurity that neoliberalism generates for people at the lower end of the socioeconomic spectrum. Wage stagnation, welfare reform, lowered protections for labor unions, and the rise of part-time and contract work dislocate and detach low-skilled workers from the labor market. As work disappears (Wilson 1996), the prison and myriad other forms of social control have grown in importance. Carceral logics "naturalize carceral expansion as part of the 'common sense' of deindustrialized communities reeling from the departures of capital and industry" (Schept 2015, 8). That expansion reaches into neighborhoods (Rios 2011), families (Roberts 2002), schools (Monahan and Torres 2009; Shedd 2015), welfare offices (Soss, Fording, and Schram 2011) and hospitals (Lara-Millán 2014), among many other places.

In this article, we focus on the extension of carceral logics to people's financial lives, which has reverberations far beyond their finances. Individuals sentenced to legal financial obligations are not released from criminal supervision until their debts are paid in full. Monetary sanctions encumber the future income and benefits not only of those sentenced to them, but also of their family members whose contributions to household expenses make up for the money that people with court debt are paying on their fines and fees, not to mention when family members pay directly through bail forfeiture or seizure of monies deposited into inmates' accounts (Katzenstein and Waller 2015). Financial debt in general is a mechanism of social control, but in the case of monetary sanctions the institution that holds the debt is the same one that holds the ultimate authority to deprive people of their liberties through imprisonment.

RESEARCH ON MONETARY SANCTIONS

Given the facts reviewed in the introduction to this issue, criminal justice scholars have rightly paid considerable attention to incarceration. Yet a significant component of sentencing law is financial. That is, rather than incapacitation through jail or prison, people are sentenced to pay for their crimes. Monetary sanctions make literal the figurative description of the criminal justice system as the way to make offenders "pay their debt to society."

Like all states, Illinois imposes offense-specific fines, fees, assessments, interest, surcharges, and restitution on people convicted at the felony, misdemeanor, and traffic levels. Fines are the punitive component of monetary sanctions. Although this makes them directly relevant to the criminal act in question, determining the dollar amount or ranges of a fine is completely a matter of policy and politics; there is no objective financial penalty for aggravated assault, or drug possession, or driving while intoxicated. Fees compensate the state for its labor and services, as well as fund special interests that have varying levels of direct connection to the crime for which a person is sentenced. In Illinois, assessments are mainly tied to drug-related offenses and encourage participation in drug treatment or community service programs. Interest and penalties are levied against those who do not pay their fines or fees within the specified period. Restitution compensates the victim for their loss.[4] The nomenclature of monetary sanctions varies from state to state, and may also include words such as *costs* or *surcharges* (see Harris et al. 2017).

---

4. Although this description suggests a vocabulary with clear definitions, this is far from the case. In several cases in Illinois, defendants have challenged the fines and fees they were ordered to pay and the appellate court found that what was labeled a "fee" in both the statute and the court clerk's accounting was actually a "fine." For example, in *People of the State of Illinois v. Graves*, the court found "that a charge labeled a fee by the legislature may be a fine, notwithstanding the words actually used by the legislature" and concluded in that case that "the charges imposed herein do not seek to compensate the state for any costs incurred as the result of prosecuting the defendant" as a "fee" is supposed to do. *People v. Graves*, 919 N.E.2d 906 (Ill. 2009), 910.

Legal, policy, and scholarly interest in monetary sanctions is increasing across the country. The Justice Department issued a report following its investigation of the Ferguson Police Department, which came under scrutiny for the killing of an unarmed African American man. Among other things, the report found that "Ferguson law enforcement efforts are focused on generating revenue" and "high fines, coupled with legally inadequate ability-to-pay determinations and insufficient alternatives to immediate payment, impose a significant burden on people living in or near poverty" (2015, 9, 52). Several public interest law and advocacy organizations have also issued reports studying monetary sanctions (see, for example, Bannon, Nagrecha, and Diller 2010; Chicago Appleseed Fund for Justice 2016; deVuono-powell et al. 2015; Tran-Leung 2009, 2010). Finally, scholars across the social science fields of sociology, political science, criminology, and law have also begun to empirically document this previously understudied part of the criminal justice system (see, for example, Beckett and Harris 2011; Greenberg, Meredith, and Morse 2016; Harris, Evans, and Beckett 2011; Katzenstein and Waller 2015; Logan and Wright 2014; Piquero and Jennings 2017; Sances and You 2017).

This body of research illustrates that Illinois is by no means unique or an outlier in its legislation of monetary sanctions, nor in the fact that in Illinois "court fines and fees are constantly increasing and outpacing inflation" (Statutory Court Fee Task Force 2016, 20). Alexes Harris documents that statutes authorizing monetary sanctions exist in all fifty states and the District of Columbia (2016, table 2.4). The U.S. Commission on Civil Rights reports that "since 2010, forty-seven states have increased civil and criminal fees" (2017, 7). National Public Radio finds that the vast majority of states authorize charges to defendants for use of a public defender, for their probation and supervision costs, and for their room and board while incarcerated (2014). In their detailed study of fifteen states that cover 60 percent of all state criminal filings in the United States, Alicia Bannon, Mitali Nagrecha, and Rebekah Diller find that all of the states were "introducing new user fees, raising the dollar amounts of existing fees, and intensifying the collection of fees and other forms of criminal justice debt such as fines and restitution" (2010, 1). Fourteen of the studied states charged additional penalties for nonpayment, and Illinois was included among nine states that charged "exorbitant" fees for delinquent accounts (17). None of the states had "adequate mechanisms to reduce criminal justice debt based on a defendant's ability to pay" (13) and all of the states had "jurisdictions that arrest[ed] people for failing to pay debt or appear at debt-related hearings" (2). Alexes Harris, Heather Evans, and Katherine Beckett show that inmates in nearly all states, in the District of Columbia, and at the federal level had been assessed monetary sanctions in 2004 (2010). Prevalence rates were even higher for those sentenced to probation, rather than incarceration; nationally, more than 80 percent of felons and misdemeanants on probation had fines and fees to pay.

Neither is Illinois an outlier in terms of the dollar amounts of monetary sanctions. Harris reports that the maximum defined fines for a felony offense range from a low of $400 in Massachusetts to a high of $500,000 in Alaska and Kansas (2016). The maximum in Illinois is $25,000. In their study of fines and fees in nine states, Harris and her colleagues compare the possible range of court-ordered costs for driving with a suspended license (2017). Illinois has the highest possible total charge of $3,832.50, but its lowest possible charge of $395 (based on Cook County charges) is less than the lowest possible charge in four other states. In general, Illinois fell toward the upper-middle end of the distribution for this offense. Yet, one of the primary findings of the study was the incredible variability of legislated fines and fees across and even within states. The extreme localism of monetary sanctions at the state and municipal levels makes nationwide comparisons difficult, and several state-level comparisons suggest that there is no such thing as a representative state or jurisdiction in the case of monetary sanctions.[5]

---

5. Although states provide overall authorization for monetary sanctions, many states have a decentralized court system with municipal courts handling the majority of traffic and misdemeanor violations. This further

Finally, Illinois is not unique in that the increasing number and amounts of criminal justice monetary sanctions are connected to poor state fiscal health. The anti-tax political climate ascendant since the 1970s has required legislators to look elsewhere for additional revenues. The U.S. Commission on Civil Rights gives the example of Missouri:

> State laws or state constitutions may also preclude (or make it difficult for) cities, towns, and counties to increase taxes. For example, the Missouri state legislature passed an amendment (known as the "Hancock Amendment") in 1980 that required municipalities to conduct a citywide referendum before raising taxes. Fines and "user" fees, on the other hand, can be raised without these formalities by a city in Missouri. As a consequence of these limitations on raising taxes, fines and fees have become one of the easier and faster ways through which local governments can increase revenue. (2017, 9)

In other words, rather than funding the court system—which is a general government purpose and has broad benefits for the general population—with increasingly unpopular tax increases, the system of monetary sanctions directly charges those who are being criminally prosecuted, and who are thus in the weakest social and often financial position to protest.

SETTING, DATA, AND METHODS

In part because of concerted research, advocacy, and litigation, the legislative landscape regarding monetary sanctions is at a moment of significant transformation in Illinois and across the country. Many states are in the process of reforming the imposition of fines, fees, and other costs associated with criminal justice contact (U.S. Commission on Civil Rights 2017, chapter 4 and tables 1–4). In Illinois, the Criminal and Traffic Assessment Act passed both houses of the Illinois legislature in May and was signed into law by the governor in August of 2018 (see State of Illinois 2018). It will take effect in July of 2019 and includes an automatic repeal provision at the end of 2020, if key state agencies determine that it has been detrimental to their finances.

The new law includes two major revisions. First, it establishes a uniform schedule of assessments by offense type (and establishes *assessments* as the general language to refer to fees and costs), eliminating uncertainty and variation at the county level. Second, it allows defendants to apply for fee waivers on a sliding scale: full waivers for persons found to be indigent, and partial waivers for persons earning up to 400 percent of the poverty level. We discuss our theoretical framework in light of the new law, as well as what the new law includes and does not include, in the conclusion. It is a critical time to study the legislative infrastructure of monetary sanctions because lawmakers are poised to review it, not just in Illinois but also across the country.

We conducted the analysis for this article prior to the legislative changes. First, using the publicly accessible, fully searchable online record of the Illinois Compiled Statutes, we created a comprehensive dataset of all state statutes in Illinois that pertained to costs to defendants in criminal cases.[6] We searched the entire legal code for any mention of fines, fees, restitution, reimbursement, assessments, costs, surcharges, forfeitures, interest, payments, penalties, and other words likely to signal a monetary sanction. We identified the following chapters of Illinois law as including information about monetary sanctions for petty, business, traffic, misdemeanor, and felony crimes: chapter 625, vehicles; chapter 705,

---

complicates comparisons across states. Comparing revenues from fines, fees, and forfeitures as a proportion of municipal revenues, Daniel Kopf reports that "Of the top 100 municipalities in terms of revenues from fines, more than two thirds are in just six states: Texas (19), Georgia (17), Missouri (12), Illinois (9), Maryland (6) and New York (6)." For other comparisons of municipalities, see Henricks and Harvey (2017); Sances and You (2017).

6. See "Illinois Compiled Statutes," http://www.ilga.gov/legislation/ilcs/ilcs.asp. We also compiled a dataset for court costs in civil cases, but those data are not relevant for the current analysis.

courts; chapter 720, criminal offenses; chapter 725, criminal procedure; and chapter 730, corrections. State law also authorizes and delimits the collection of fines and fees for counties (chapter 55) and municipalities (chapter 65), which were also included in the database.[7] All statutes that levied any kind of cost on a defendant or convicted person were included in our dataset. Dataset particulars include the statute number, type of offense (if directly related to an offense), last year amended, summary and full text of the statute, whether the monetary sanction is mandatory or discretionary, whether the sanction can be reduced for time served in jail, the sanction amount, whether the court is required to consider ability to pay, punishment for default, whether payment plans are allowed, and the state fund receiving the LFO. We use the full sample to answer the first research question "What are defendants expected to pay for and why?"

To answer the second two questions, we searched the full database for roughly forty keywords and phrases relevant to how the law regards people's socioeconomic status (indigent, ability to pay, unpaid, poor-poverty, nonpayment, default, delinquent, debt, collections, and so on). We used the qualitative data analysis software Atlas.ti to code relevant text with those keywords. Notably, the words *poor* and *poverty* are not used in any statutes regarding monetary sanctions; indigent appears only rarely. More common are discussions of *ability to pay* and the consequences for *default*. The coding for these words yielded ninety-six unique statutory entries pertaining to monetary sanctions and the socioeconomic circumstances of the defendant.[8] We then read the content of each analytic code and wrote memos on preliminary findings. It was often necessary to go back to the full statute to understand the context of the provision.

We also traced some statutes backward and forward. That is, we researched the legislative history of several statutes and reviewed the transcripts of the House or Senate debates when they were considered; we also searched Illinois case law for instances when specific statutes were questioned or appealed, such as lawsuits that challenged the precise amounts defendants were charged, or challenges to demands to reimburse the state for incarceration, or appeals regarding probation revocation decisions based on unpaid LFOs. Overall, this is a qualitative study in which the primary data are the text of specific laws, the words of legislators who debated them, and the decisions of judges who adjudicated them.

This study is part of a larger five-year, eight-state study of monetary sanctions. The full project includes comparable data collection in each state, including: legislative scans (see Harris et al. 2017); surveys and qualitative interviews with judges, prosecutors, defense attorneys, clerks, probation officers, and people with court debt; courtroom ethnographies; and comprehensive quantitative sentencing data by defendant characteristics, crime type, and other relevant variables. The larger project aims to move progressively from law on the books to law in practice to an understanding of the cumulative impact of monetary sanctions

---

7. Matters of criminal justice in Illinois are handled at the Circuit Court level, which is "the court of original jurisdiction" (Illinois Courts 2017). Illinois has twenty-four judicial circuits, no municipal judicial courts, and a system of administrative adjudications. Administrative hearings officers in home rule units have the authority to levy fines of up to $50,000. Municipalities or counties that are not home rule units have the authority to levy fines of up to $750. These administrative hearings at the county and municipal levels are an added layer of financial sentencing outside the scope of this article.

8. A statutory entry is some piece of text (such as a sentence, a paragraph) that does not constitute a full statute but has information relevant to the current study. It may be a full section of the law, but often it is a sub-number or subletter of a section. For example, the paragraph "State's attorneys shall have a lien for their fees on all judgments for fines or forfeitures procured by them and on moneys except revenue received by them until such fees and earnings are fully paid" is coded in our dataset under "lien," and it is just one paragraph among twenty-three in letter (a) of Section 4-2002 of the Illinois Counties Code, which lays out all of the fees to which state's attorneys are entitled in counties with populations of less than three million in Illinois (55 ILCS 5/4-2002(a)).

across the full load of cases in the states in our study.[9]

WHAT ARE DEFENDANTS EXPECTED TO PAY FOR AND WHY?

Table 1 presents a non-exhaustive list of agencies, entities, and special funds that appear as receivers in the statutes authorizing monetary sanctions in criminal cases in Illinois. It covers a broad array of interests. At the highest level are the general revenue funds for the municipalities, counties, and state, and the large state agencies, such as the Secretary of State, which handles most traffic violations. Law enforcement agencies at the municipal, county, and state levels receive payments, which go to both their general operating funds as well as to specialized funds, such as the State Police Merit Board Public Safety Fund. County jails, the Department of Corrections, county sheriffs, and the Circuit Court clerk all receive funding from monetary sanctions. The fees charged to defendants also go to fund both the prosecution and the defense of their cases. Low-income defendants are guaranteed the right to legal representation in a criminal proceeding, but this does not mean states cannot attempt to recoup the costs of court-appointed counsel (Wright and Logan 2006). Illinois county courts may charge up to $500 for defense counsel for misdemeanors, up to $5,000 for felonies, and up to $2,500 for appealing a conviction (725 ILCS 5/113–3.1). Defendants can be charged even if they are ultimately judged not guilty.[10] Monetary sanctions may also be earmarked for a range of specific activities carried out by the institutions within the criminal justice system, such as electronic filing, automation, cameras, document storage, and laboratories. Individual counties may charge additional fees and set up county-level funds not listed in table 1 to support drug courts, teen courts, child advocacy centers, and other such special purposes (55 ILCS 5/5–1101).

Additionally, a number of specialty funds move further away from the actual operations of the criminal justice system. For example, the Prescription Pill and Drug Disposal Fund and the Criminal Justice Information Projects Fund are authorized such that a "$40 assessment shall be assessed by the court, the proceeds of which shall be collected by the Circuit Clerk. Of the collected proceeds, (i) 90% shall be remitted to the State Treasurer for deposit into the Prescription Pill and Drug Disposal Fund; (ii) 5% shall be remitted for deposit into the Criminal Justice Information Projects Fund, for use by the Illinois Criminal Justice Information Authority for the costs associated with making grants from the Prescription Pill and Drug Disposal Fund" (730 ILCS 5/5–9-1.1(f)). The 2012 bill that created this law was "a result of the environmental classes of Antioch Community High School and Pontiac Township High School working together across the state to make a difference in our lives" (State of Illinois 2011, 132). Its intent was to "prevent future contamination of our drinking water, protect our wildlife, [sic] keep drugs out of the hands of teens" (133). The assessment may be charged

---

9. Legislation regarding criminal penalties has both a symbolic and a punitive function. If the Illinois laws are mostly symbolic and not widely implemented, then the present analysis would be important in the abstract for the kinds of ideologies it conveys, but have few consequences for inequality. This is decidedly not the case in Illinois, nor in the other states in the larger study. In our courtroom observations, we have routinely seen people's court debts sent to collection agencies, and we have interviewed people who report frequent contact by those agencies. We have observed people being re-sentenced to prison because of unpaid court fines and fees during their probationary periods. And the appellate cases discussed in this article show that people have been incarcerated for willful nonpayment. Evidence from journalists and advocacy organizations about the certain and severe implementation and enforcement of monetary sanctions is also considerable (Chicago Jobs Council 2018; Sanchez and Kambhampati 2018; Tran-Leung 2009, 36).

10. In *People v. Kelleher*, the court found that "A nonindigent, although acquitted, is ordinarily required, without reimbursement by the State, to pay for counsel. To require an indigent, although acquitted, to reimburse the county, to the extent he is able, for the expense of furnished counsel, tends to put indigents and nonindigents who are acquitted, on the same basis and is consistent with due process" (*People v. Kelleher* 116 Ill. App.3d 186 [1983], 189).

Table 1. Receiving Agencies and Funds of Monetary Sanctions in Illinois

Circuit Court Clerk Operation and Administrative Fund	Law Enforcement Alarm Systems Fund
	Law Enforcement Camera Grant Fund
Conservation Police Operations Assistance Fund	Local Government Treasurer
Cook County Health Fund	Methamphetamine Law Enforcement Fund
County Clerk	Performance-enhancing Substance Testing Fund
County Jail Medical Costs Fund	Prescription Pill and Drug Disposal Fund
County Sheriff	Prisoner Review Board Vehicle and Equipment Fund
County Treasurer	
County Working Cash Fund	Probation and Court Services Fund
Court Automation Fund	Public Defender Records Automation Fund
Crime Laboratory Fund, state	Road Fund
Crime laboratory, local	Roadside Memorial Fund
Criminal Conviction Surcharge Fund	Secretary of State
Criminal Justice Information Projects Fund	Secretary of State DUI Administration Fund
Department of Corrections	Sex Offender Investigation Fund
Department of Corrections Parole Division Offender Supervision Fund	Sexual Assault Services Fund
	Specialized Services for Survivors of Human Trafficking Fund
Department of Corrections Reimbursement and Education Fund	
	Spinal Cord Injury Paralysis Cure Research Trust Fund
Department of Natural Resources Fund	
Document Storage Fund	State Offender DNA Identification System Fund
Domestic Violence Abuser Services Fund	State Police DUI Fund
Domestic Violence Shelter and Service Fund	State Police Merit Board Public Safety Fund
Drivers Education Fund	State Police Operations Assistance Fund
Drug Treatment Fund	State Police Services Fund
Electronic Citation Fund	State Police Streetgang-Related Crime Fund
Fire Prevention Fund	State Toll Highway Authority Fund
Fire Truck Revolving Loan Fund	State Treasurer
General Revenue Funds (municipalities, counties, and state)	State's Attorney Records Automation Fund
	State's Attorney's Office
George Bailey Memorial Fund	Supreme Court Special Purposes Fund
Law enforcement agencies (local, county, state, federal)	Traffic and Criminal Surcharge Fund
	Transportation Safety Highway Hire-back Fund
Law Enforcement Agency Data System (LEADS) Maintenance Fund	Trauma Center Fund
	Violent Crimes Victims Assistance Fund

Source: Authors' analysis of Illinois statutes.
Note: Alphabetical order.

to people who have been "adjudged guilty of a drug related offense involving possession or delivery of cannabis or possession or delivery of a controlled substance, other than methamphetamine" (730 ILCS 5/5-9-1.1).[11] This fund represents an initiative that is—however worthy—only tangentially, if at all, connected to the crime committed by those sentenced to pay.

Other examples of funds that move further away from core criminal justice processes include the George Bailey Memorial Fund, which compensates disabled burn victims using fees charged to arsonists, even if the arson was to property only (705 ILCS 105/27.6(p)), as well as to those convicted of serious traffic violations (625 ILCS 5/16-104d); and the State Police Merit

---

11. Although this charge is authorized in the law, we have not seen it show up on any listing of sentenced fines and fees, nor have we heard it mentioned in the courtroom.

Figure 1. Listing of Fees Owed by Defendant in an Illinois County

```
Case#  ████████████      Criminal Felony
Def:   ████████████                          Owed..........      $3,525.00
                                             Paid..........        $450.00
                                             Balance Due...      $3,075.00

                                             Agency: ██ ████████████
                                             Class: 4   Fine: 1  Fine & Cost

                                             Fine Amount...           $.00

No.  Description                        Owed         Paid       Balance Due
 1   CLERK FEE                         $80.00       $80.00           $.00
 2   STATES ATTORNEY FEE               $30.00       $30.00           $.00
 3   STATES ATTRNY RECORDS AUTO FEE     $2.00        $.00           $2.00
 4   CR. SURCHARGE STATE              $750.00      $210.00         $540.00
 5   CRIME LAB                        $100.00        $.00         $100.00
 6   COURT AUTOMATION FEE              $25.00       $25.00           $.00
 7   COURT SECURITY FEE                $25.00       $25.00           $.00
 8   VICTIM FUND                      $200.00        $.00         $200.00
 9   COURT SYSTEM FEE                  $50.00       $50.00           $.00
10   DOCUMENT STORAGE FEE              $15.00       $15.00           $.00
11   *DRUG FUND-AGENCY*               $525.00        $.00         $525.00
12   DRUG FUND-JUVENILE               $131.25        $.00         $131.25
13   DRUG FUND-COUNTY                 $393.75        $.00         $393.75
14   PROBATION FEES                   $288.00        $.00         $288.00
15   ISP OPERATIONS ASSIST FUND        $15.00       $15.00           $.00
16   STATE POLICE SERVICES FUND        $25.00        $.00          $25.00
17   SPINAL CORD INJURY PARALYSIS F     $5.00        $.00           $5.00
18   DRUG FUND-ASSESSMENT             $500.00        $.00         $500.00
19   TRAUMA FUND                      $100.00        $.00         $100.00
20   DNA ST OFFEND. ID SYSTEM         $250.00        $.00         $250.00
21   STATE POLICE MERIT BOARD          $15.00        $.00          $15.00

                         ** END OF REPORT **
```

Source: Public online court records from Illinois county (unnamed for privacy reasons).

Board Public Safety Fund, which receives the $15 charged to anyone convicted of violating the Criminal Code or the Vehicle Code (705 ILCS 105/27.6(n)). These monies go to support a cadet program and the general operations of the State Police Merit Board, whose mission is "to remove political influence and provide a fair and equitable merit process for the selection of Illinois State Trooper candidates and the promotion and discipline of Illinois State Police officers" (Illinois State Police Merit Board 2017).

Figure 1 presents an example of how these fees appear for someone sentenced to pay court debt.[12] In this case, the person was convicted of a class 4 drug felony, which is the lowest category of drug felony in Illinois. The person was sentenced to a month in county jail, one hundred hours of community service, twenty-four months of probation, and monetary sanctions totaling $3,525. The $450 payment reflected in the ledger was not in fact a payment, but rather the statutorily allowed application of the defendant's bail funds to the monetary sanctions. There is no mandatory fine for a class 4 felony, but the $500 listed as the drug fund assessment is mandatory. Similar to the full list of possible receivers, the fees this defendant must pay go to fund state agencies (such as the state's attorney's office, court clerk), specific activities (court security and automation), and more distant purposes (such as the Spinal Cord Injury Paralysis Cure Research Trust Fund, which is charged to those convicted of DUI (730 ILCS 5/5-9-1(c-7) or drug-related offenses (730 ILCS 5/5-9-1.1(c)).

The answer to what defendants are expected to pay for is thus a broad sweep of state functions that center on the arrest, prosecution, and punishment of those adjudged guilty, but that also stray far from those core uses. The answer to why defendants are held responsible

---

12. Some counties in Illinois offer online systems that allow defendants to check the status of their case and see their monetary sanctions balance. These systems are public. For this example, we typed in a random name into one county's system, which yielded this illustrative record.

for these functions is that state budget shortfalls combine with criminal stigmatization and an emphasis on personal responsibility to create the political support for increased monetary sanctions. The 2002 debate in the Illinois House of Representatives regarding Senate Bill 2074 illustrates a common pattern in the discussions of bills to increase fines and fees or levy new monetary sanctions. The bill, which was eventually passed (725 ILCS 5/124A-10), allows the Circuit Court clerk to add fees of up to 15 percent for delinquent accounts, as well as to report nonpayers to credit reporting agencies. The monies collected by these penalties "shall be used to defray additional administrative costs incurred by the clerk of the court in collecting unpaid fines, costs, fees, and penalties" (725 ILCS 5/124A-10).

The lengthy discussion on the House floor—edited for repetition and procedural dialogue—proceeded as follows (State of Illinois 2002, 12–18):

CLERK ROSSI: Senate Bill 2074, a Bill for an Act in relation to criminal law. Third Reading of this Senate Bill.

SPEAKER HARTKE: Representative Currie.

CURRIE: Thank you, Speaker and Members of the House. This is an initiative of the Illinois Association of Clerks of the Circuit Court. It merely provides that if there are unpaid balances, there's a schedule of interest applied and as with your Visa Bill, after 90 days the Clerk will notify the credit rating agencies that you're a deadbeat. I know of no opposition. This is a Bill that came out of the Senate unanimously, and I'd appreciate your support.

SPEAKER HARTKE: Is there any discussion? The Chair recognizes the Gentleman from . . . McHenry [County], Mr. Franks. . .

FRANKS: I understand the speakers. . . . I'm sorry, the Sponsor's intent with this Bill. But what this Bill does is increases the cost of fines by 5% for costs that remain unpaid after 30 days. And then it increases to 10% and then it increases to 15%. So, what this Bill does is it really penalizes poor people. For those people that can't pay their fines right away, they're getting an extra penalty for not being able to afford it. It's a penalty for being poor. And what this also does, frankly, is it changes the priority in which debtors may pay their Bills. So, if you're a secured creditor and you have a judgement against someone you get statutory interest at 9%. However, what this Bill plans to do is to force people to have to pay fines criminally, before they would pay a secured creditor. So, if you have a judgement, or if you have a mortgage, or anything else, those are going to be put behind anyone who's trying to pay a criminal fine. I believe this is a really bad bill. It really hurts poor people, and it takes away the priorities of what we have set up. And I'd urge you to vote 'no.'

SPEAKER HARTKE: Further discussion? The Chair recognizes the Gentleman from Vermilion [County], Representative Black.

BLACK: Thank you very much, Mr. Speaker and Ladies and Gentlemen of the House. I rise in strong support of the Majority Leader's Bill. If you go into any court facility in the State of Illinois, and by the way we . . . we do not fully fund the court system and we're suppose to [sic] do that, but we don't, we're not able to. Some day [sic] perhaps we can reexamine that. But I . . . I just find it disingenuous that somebody could say if you're found guilty of a criminal offense, and you blow off that fine, as many of them do, talk to many of your court clerks, there are, in some cases, hundreds of thousands of dollars of unpaid fines on the books. Now, if you're just going thumb [sic] your nose at a court ruling, and not pay the fine, then by golly, it only stands to reason, fine, we'll charge you with a little interest. And if that doesn't work, I'll join with the Majority Leader next Session and if they continue to thumb their nose at the court and show total disregard for what they have been convicted of, and refuse to pay their fine then fine, let's just lock 'em up. And they can work it off at so many cents a day. It only makes good sense. This state can't afford deadbeats. We've got a billion dollars in unpaid child support and probably millions of dollars in unpaid fines. And I daresay, I'm generalizing because I don't know, but I daresay many of those unpaid fines are the result of somebody just saying, I'm not going to pay it, come and get me. We'll come and get you, that's fine. . . .

CURRIE: Just to clarify, poor people are not at stake in this measure. Because the court already has and would continue to have the ability to waive fines if people in fact are unable to meet this requirement.

MULLIGAN: So, it's currently the law in Cook County that if they are poor that the fine would be waived?

CURRIE: The court has that opportunity today and nothing would change in that opportunity under this measure. . . .

MULLIGAN: Can they get an automatic judgement against people who are delinquent if they have assets? I mean rather than just heap on the fines, can't they try to collect them by putting a lien on their property or doing something like that?

CURRIE: Sure they can, sure they can. The court can bring them back into court, hold them in contempt. This, we believe, will give people an incentive to pay up before using additional court resources, in order to make sure that they are current with their obligations, just as with your Visa Bill.

MULLIGAN: All right.

CURRIE: You know, ultimately they can send the sheriff after you if you don't pay that either.

MULLIGAN: Right.

CURRIE: But in the meantime, they charge you interest, and they hope that will encourage you to pay up, pay promptly. That's all this measure is about . . . After 30 days unpaid balance, then 5%, and after three months if you continue to thumb your nose at the court then they would be . . . be allowed to notify the credit agencies that you are a deadbeat. . . .

I'd appreciate your 'aye' votes. We've got enough deadbeats. This is a way to encourage people to meet their responsibilities imposed by the courts, just as Visa has a chance to make sure they meet their responsibilities through their decisions to buy. Please vote 'yes.'

SPEAKER HARTKE: The question is, 'Shall the House pass Senate Bill 2074?' All those in favor will signify by voting 'yes'; those opposed vote 'no.' The voting is open. . . . Mr. Clerk, take the record. On this question, there are 97 Members voting 'yes,' 12 Members voting 'no,' 6 Members voting 'present.' And this Bill, have [sic] received a Constitutional Majority, is hereby declared passed. Mr. Clerk for an announcement.

Representative Currie introduces and closes the debate with the term *deadbeats*, illustrating the personalization and stigmatization of the fact of nonpayment. Representative Black chastises people who "thumb [their] nose at a court ruling" and "show total disregard for what they have been convicted of." He ratchets up the punitive tone by suggesting jail time and what amounts to debt bondage when he says that they can "work it off at so many cents a day." Representative Mulligan suggests property liens, for which authorization already existed in the law. Finally, Currie makes explicit the role of personal responsibility: "This is a way to encourage people to meet their responsibilities imposed by the courts." It is notable that the responsibilities here are *imposed* rather than taken on, and they are imposed without consideration of the defendant's ability to take them on or to comply with them.

Representative Franks makes it clear who would bear the brunt of these penalties. "It really penalizes poor people," he says flatly. This argument is dismissed with a reference to judges' discretion in levying fines and fees. Yet contrary to Currie's statements—and betrayed by her imprecise language (such as "the court *has that opportunity*" [emphasis added])—the statute in question does not allow judges to waive fees, only to set up payment plans. Statutory guidance to judges about fine and fee waivers is minimal.[13] We cannot deduce from

---

13. A similar statute about penalties for nonpayment begins "Unless a court ordered payment schedule is implemented or fee requirements are waived pursuant to a court order" (705 ILCS 105/27.5), but there is no guidance about the acceptable (or desirable) reasons for such waivers. In our analysis of the code for "waive[rs]" only one usage explicitly directed the waiver to be about the defendant's socioeconomic situation: "The Court may only waive probation fees based on an offender's ability to pay" (730 ILCS 5/5-6-3(i)).

this debate that the intent of the law was specifically to punish poor defendants, but it is clear that the information about the characteristics of those who would pay the penalties did not sway the legislative body.

The issue of state budget pressures is also apparent in this exchange. Representative Black recognizes that "we do not fully fund the court system and we're suppose to [sic] do that, but we don't, we're not able to." The accounts receivables for criminal justice fines and fees have frequently been used for the state's general purpose budget. Every year and often multiple times a year, the legislature passes laws "concerning finance" that transfer monies from these funds to the general revenue fund. For example, Public Act 100–0023 of 2017, was passed "to maintain the integrity of special funds and improve stability in the General Revenue Fund, the Budget Stabilization Fund, the Healthcare Provider Relief Fund, and the Health Insurance Reserve Fund" (State of Illinois 2017). The law authorized the transfer to those purposes of up to $1.5 million from the Law Enforcement Camera Grant Fund, up to $3.5 million from the State Police Services Fund, up to $3 million from the Trauma Center Fund, and several other authorized transfers from many of the funds listed in table 1. The value of monetary sanctions to states lies not just in funding the criminal justice system, which legislators recognize is underfunded, but also to run the state's general operations.

Understanding the relevance of the reasoning behind what to *charge* defendants *for* (not *with*) requires going back to the statistics recited at the beginning of this article. The overwhelming majority of defendants in Illinois and in the country are poor and near poor. Those who have the means to pay fines and fees outright are unlikely to incur delinquency charges, if they are sentenced to monetary sanctions at all given their better outcomes through the court system (Reiman and Leighton 2015). The remittances of those who are financially able also go to fund the institutions and services listed in table 1, and their payments for speeding tickets and drug possession and domestic violence violations likely comprise a large proportion of the funds collected. But they are not representative of the criminal justice population, and the other payers are poor people for whom these fines and fees represent a much larger proportion of their incomes. Those convicted of crimes are easy targets for funding state functions just because they have wronged society, are the least able to avoid and defend themselves against the purview of criminal justice actors, and are the least powerful to lobby against the ever growing regime of monetary sanctions. Then, when they cannot pay, they are further stigmatized and criminalized for having skirted their responsibility.

WHAT ACCOMMODATIONS ARE MADE FOR DEFENDANTS' ABILITY TO PAY?

Nationally, guidance to criminal courts about how to assess defendants' financial means is scant (U.S. Commission on Civil Rights 2017, 72). In the laws prior to the one passed in 2018, neither the word *poor* nor *poverty* appeared in the Illinois statutes on criminal monetary sanctions; the word *indigent* appeared rarely and only once was it defined, in that case for incarcerated persons having "$20 or less in his or her Inmate Trust Fund" in order to evaluate their ability to pay a medical co-payment (see table 2). The word *low-income* appeared in the municipal codes and is defined as someone who is eligible for the federal earned income tax credit (65 ILCS 5/1–2–1).[14]

The law regarding court-appointed counsel (public defender) requires defendants to file an affidavit with the court to determine eligibility. "Such affidavit shall be in the form established by the Supreme Court containing sufficient information to ascertain the assets and liabilities of that defendant" (725 ILCS 5/113–3). The term *sufficient information*, however, is not further explained. The Illinois Supreme Court rules do not include a standard form, so each county has created its own affidavit, which includes varying questions about assets (such as homes,

---

14. The new law defines indigence as someone who is receiving one or more of several forms of public assistance; whose income is less than 200 percent of the poverty level; or someone who would face "substantial hardship," in the eyes of the court, in paying the assessments (State of Illinois 2018, 166).

cars, bank accounts), and liabilities (number of dependents, monthly expenses, and so on), as well as marital status, employment, and household income from various sources. Yet no formula or standard is in place for evaluating the information on the form. It is entirely up to the judge's discretion to deem someone indigent and thus eligible for court-appointed counsel, or not. Given the absence of any guidance, that same discretion extends to all of the allowances in the law for taking into consideration a defendant's financial wherewithal to pay sentenced fines and fees.

Table 2 lists all of the statutes pertaining to monetary sanctions that consider a person's financial status or ability to pay. More state receivers of monetary sanctions are mentioned in the Illinois law (table 1) than dispensations for poor defendants regarding payment. The language is vague, referring generally to a defendant's *ability to pay* or *financial resources*, but not defining either term. The lengthiest elaboration is for the form that determines prisoners' ability to reimburse the Department of Corrections. Such forms

> shall provide for obtaining the age and marital status of a committed person, the number and ages of children of the person, the number and ages of other dependents, the type and value of real estate, the type and value of personal property, cash and bank accounts, the location of any lock boxes, the type and value of investments, pensions and annuities and any other personalty of significant cash value, including but not limited to jewelry, art work and collectables, and all medical or dental insurance policies covering the committed person. The form may also provide for other information deemed pertinent by the Department in the investigation of a committed person's assets. (730 ILCS 5/3-7-6(a))

Notably, this form collects information only on assets, not on debts or liabilities. Although this statute is for collecting monies from the defendant rather than providing them with relief, we include it because a finding of no or few assets would likely exempt the defendant from prosecution for reimbursement.[15]

The lack of clear guidance on how to evaluate indigence and of explicit admonitions to consider a person's finances creates a silence that can be readily filled with stereotypes, stigma, and the kinds of logics about personal responsibility that suffused the lawmaking process discussed earlier (Van Cleve 2016). The flow of cases through the courtroom is swift, leaving no time for much deliberation and little direct interaction between the judge and defendant. Nonetheless, decisions about sentencing have long-term impacts. In addition to the research on the collateral consequences of incarceration for health, political participation, employment, and other outcomes (Pattillo et al. 2004), monetary sanctions have direct repercussions for people's finances, and more. In the following section, we explore the consequences for nonpayment authorized in Illinois state law to illustrate how the disregard for ability to pay at sentencing sets the stage for the expansion of carceral logics to deal with court debt.

WHAT ARE THE CONSEQUENCES FOR NOT PAYING?

The statutes about consequences for nonpayment are more wordy, detailed, and explicit than the directions regarding indigence. Consider the following excerpts from four laws allowing actions to be taken against people with outstanding court debt:[16]

---

15. Other statutes similarly provide possible relief for poor defendants but do not evaluate financial status. Presentencing monetary credit is granted for bailable offenses when the defendant cannot supply bail. A defendant receives a $5 credit for each day he or she was jailed prior to sentencing (725 ILCS 5/110-14). Because low-income defendants are more likely to lack the funds necessary to make bail and consequently remain incarcerated throughout their trial, this de facto serves as an accommodation for poverty.

16. We present this abundance of text because it illustrates the wordiness regarding collecting fines and fees in comparison to the minimalist or nonexistent language regarding indigence and relief for poor defendants. Consider this text as one might consider the abundance of quantitative information in a regression table that is not discussed but is available for readers to review and interpret for themselves.

The property, real and personal, of a person who is convicted of an offense shall be bound, and a lien is created on the property, both real and personal, of every offender, not exempt from the enforcement of a judgment or attachment, from the time of finding the indictment at least so far as will be sufficient to pay the fine and costs of prosecution. The clerk of the court in which the conviction is had shall upon the expiration of 30 days after judgment is entered issue a certified copy of the judgment for any fine that remains unpaid, and all costs of conviction remaining unpaid. Unless a court ordered payment schedule is implemented, the clerk of the court may add to any judgment a delinquency amount equal to 5% of the unpaid fines, costs, fees, and penalties that remain unpaid after 30 days, 10% of the unpaid fines, costs, fees, and penalties that remain unpaid after 60 days, and 15% of the unpaid fines, costs, fees, and penalties that remain unpaid after 90 days. Notice to those parties affected may be made by signage posting or publication. The clerk of the court may also after a period of 90 days release to credit reporting agencies, information regarding unpaid amounts (725 ILCS 5/124A-10).

As a condition of the assessment, the court may require that payment be made in specified installments or within a specified period of time. If the assessment is not paid within the period of probation, conditional discharge or supervision to which the defendant was originally sentenced, the court may extend the period of probation, conditional discharge or supervision (720 ILCS 550/10.3(c)).

The Clerk of the Circuit Court may enter into an agreement with the Illinois Department of Revenue to establish a pilot program for the purpose of collecting certain fees. The purpose shall be to intercept, in whole or in part, State income tax refunds due the persons who owe past due fees to the Clerk of the Circuit Court in order to satisfy unpaid fees pursuant to the fee requirements of Sections 27.1a, 27.2, and 27.2a of this Act. The agreement shall include, but may not be limited to, a certification by the Clerk of the Circuit Court that the debt claims forwarded to the Department of Revenue are valid and that reasonable efforts have been made to notify persons of the delinquency of the debt. The agreement shall include provisions for payment of the intercept by the Department of Revenue to the Clerk of the Circuit Court and procedures for an appeal/protest when an intercept occurs. The agreement may also include provisions to allow the Department of Revenue to recover its cost for administering the program (705 ILCS 105/27.2b).

(a) An offender who defaults in the payment of a fine or any installment of that fine may be held in contempt and imprisoned for nonpayment. The court may issue a summons for his appearance or a warrant of arrest. (b) Unless the offender shows that his default was not due to his intentional refusal to pay, or not due to a failure on his part to make a good faith effort to pay, the court may order the offender imprisoned for a term not to exceed 6 months if the fine was for a felony, or 30 days if the fine was for a misdemeanor, a petty offense or a business offense. Payment of the fine at any time will entitle the offender to be released, but imprisonment under this Section shall not satisfy the payment of the fine (730 ILCS 5/5-9-3).

These four statutes alone represent consequences ranging from property liens to credit agency reporting to graduated financial penalties to extended probation or supervision to intercepted income tax refunds to incarceration. Other possible outcomes include wage garnishment, referral to private debt collectors, driver's license suspension or revocation, deductions from inmate's accounts, lawsuits, and generally "any and all means authorized for the collection of money judgments" (730 ILCS 5/5-9-3) (also see Tran-Leung 2009).

These methods encumber the financial lives of those sentenced to monetary sanctions, but the final example—730 ILCS 5/5-9-3—is the most extreme: incarceration. The law was passed in 1972, the tail end of decades of civil rights protests and general social unrest, and the moment of a punitive turn in criminal justice policy (Calavita and Jenness 2015; Fortner

Table 2. Considerations of Financial Resources or Ability to Pay in Illinois Law

Statute	Basis for Accommodation	Accommodation
55 ILCS 5/3-15016	"Ability to pay," no definition	May determine amount to be reimbursed to county jails for the cost of incarceration
65 ILCS 5/1-2-1	"Low-income individual" defined as eligible to receive federal EITC	Waiver of fee to pay for required education programs in municipal ordinance violations
105 ILCS 105/27.1(w-3)	"Indigent," no definition	May excuse the payment of the jury services fee in fine-only ordinance violations
720 ILCS 5/26-1(e)	"Indigent," no definition	Possible exemption from reimbursing a public agency for emergency response costs in response to disorderly conduct violation
725 ILCS 5/113-3.1	Affidavit of Assets and Liabilities; "any other information pertaining to the defendant's financial circumstances"; and "as the interest of fairness may require"	May determine amount, payment duration, or suspension of reimbursement to state for court-appointed counsel
730 ILCS 5/3-6-2(f)	"Indigent," defined as a committed person who has $20 or less in his or her Inmate Trust Fund	Exemption from $5 medical services copayment while imprisoned
730 ILCS 5/3-7-6(a)	A detailed form "regarding assets"	May determine reimbursement to state for incarceration costs
730 ILCS 5/5-4-3(j)	"Inability to pay," no definition	May mitigate potential incarceration for nonpayment of mandatory DNA analysis fee
730 ILCS 5/5-5-10	"Ability to pay," no definition	May determine amount of monthly community service fee when supervised by probation or court services department
730 ILCS 5/5-5-3(j-5)	"Inability of the defendant after making a good faith effort to obtain financial aid or pay"	Mitigates failure to pay costs of required coursework toward a high school degree while under mandatory supervised release from prison
730 ILCS 5/5-5-6(f)	"Ability of the defendant to pay, including any real or personal property or any other assets of the defendant"	May determine payment terms in order of restitution

730 ILCS 5/5-6-3	"Inability of the offender to pay the fee," no definition	May determine amount or waiver of monthly probation fees; may determine amount or waiver of additional fees and costs for sex-offenders sentenced to probation; may determine payment of costs or waiver for mandatory drug or alcohol testing and electronic home monitoring while sentenced to probation
730 ILCS 5/5-6-3.1	"Inability of the person . . . to pay the fee," no definition	Same as above, while sentenced to supervision
730 ILCS 5/5-7-1(g)	"Ability to pay," no definition	May determine costs for mandatory drug or alcohol testing and electronic home monitoring while sentenced to periodic imprisonment
730 ILCS 5/5-9-1(d)	"The financial resources and future ability of the offender to pay the fine"	May determine the amount and method of payment of additional fines authorized in this section
730 ILCS 5/5-9-1.4(b)	"Ability to pay" based on a "verified petition," no definition	May suspend all or part of the crime lab fee in drug-related cases.
730 ILCS 5/5-9-1.9(b)	"Ability to pay" based on a "verified petition," no definition	May suspend all or part of the DUI analysis fee
730 ILCS 5/5-9-2	"Upon good cause shown," no definition	Court may revoke or modify method of payment of authorized fines
730 ILCS 125/17	"Reasonably able to pay…including reimbursement from any insurance program or from other medical benefit programs"	May determine amount to be reimbursed to jail wardens for bedding, clothing, fuel, and medical aid
730 ILCS 125/20(a)	"Ability to pay"	May determine amount to be reimbursed to county jails for the cost of incarceration
730 ILCS 148/10(c-5)	"Indigent," no definition	May grant fee waiver for arsonists to register with local and county police

Source: Authors' analysis of Illinois statutes.

2015; Weaver 2007; Western 2006). It began as House Bill 811, which aimed to restructure the corrections system in Illinois, reviewing, consolidating, revising, and writing nearly five hundred bills into what became the Unified Code of Corrections, much of which remains law today. The specific issue of jailing people for failing to pay their fines was not debated on the Senate floor (State of Illinois 1972a). It was a short paragraph in an eighty-page piece of legislation. The text of parts (a) and (b) of Section 5-9-3 has hardly changed since 1972. All of the new language is in part (e). In 1972, it began with the simple sentence "A default in the payment of a fine or any installment may be collected by any means authorized for the collection of money judgments rendered in favor of the State" (State of Illinois 1972b, 834). Now, however, it elaborates on the means of collection; adds fees, costs, and other judgments to what can be collected; adds 9 percent annual interest; and adds a 30 percent fee onto the original amount due and onto any other costs incurred by the state's attorney's office in the process of collections.[17] Hence, 730 ILCS 5/5-9-3 has progressively extended the hand of the correctional state into the pocketbooks of those sentenced to monetary sanctions, and allows for the further deprivation of liberty through incarceration.

This law also stipulates the basis upon which courts are instructed to decide on incarceration as a penalty for nonpayment, namely if that nonpayment was intentional, or what in other statutes is called a "willful refusal to pay" (730 ILCS 5/5-6-4(d)). Illinois is one of forty-four states that allow the incarceration of people with outstanding court debt due to willful nonpayment (Harris 2016, 50), which is in line with the terminology set forth in the U.S. Supreme Court decision in *Bearden v. Georgia* (1983) (Pepin 2016).[18] Willfulness is also the standard for courts when deciding on the revocation of probation. Several defendants have appealed their probation revocation on these grounds, but the bar for disproving willful nonpayment seems high. In *People v. Wright*, a fifty-eight-year-old woman who worked part time at Kentucky Fried Chicken and other temporary jobs was found to have willfully not paid her $2,323 balance in court costs, fees, and restitution. The Illinois Appellate Court held that "Although defendant was employed on multiple occasions and had discretionary cash to purchase cigarettes, she demonstrated she did not consider the financial obligations of her probation conditions to be a priority." She was re-sentenced to a three-year prison term on the original offenses of theft and robbery. In *People v. Colton*, a defendant was re-sentenced to four years in prison when his probation was revoked for, in part, not paying his $685 in fines and fees. Despite also finding that $605 of the $685 in monetary sanctions were improperly charged, the court concluded, "Here, there is no indication that defendant paid any of the fines, fees or costs assessed as part of his probation or attempted to explain his failure to do so. Although defendant argues on appeal that he was a minor without financial resources, he cites no authority for the proposition that underage students are excused from such financial responsibilities."[19] Echoing the language in the legislative discussions of deadbeats thumbing their noses at the system, the transcripts of the probation revocation appeals include words about defendants' responsibility to pay their court costs and their failure to prioritize this debt.

In both the legislation and the case law, we see the application of neoliberal logics about personal responsibility and the appropriate-

---

17. These consequences, from interest to collections referrals, are not just hypothetical, but are enforced throughout the state (see, for example, Martin 2014; Parker 2015).

18. *Bearden v. Georgia*, 461 U.S. 660 (1983).

19. *People v. Wright*, IL App (4th) 110533-U (2012), 5. *People v. Colton*, IL App (1st) 112218-U (2013). Several other examples follow these cases, but we found two cases where the appeals court reversed the Circuit Court decision to revoke probation based on willful nonpayment. In one case, the defendant was legally blind, was unemployed, and had stated assets of $22 (*People v. Bouyer*, IL App (2nd) No. 2-00-1158 (2002)). In the other, the defendant was a single mother of three children who had recently been evicted from her apartment (*People v. Davis*, 576 N.E.2d 510 (Ill. App. Ct. 1991)).

ness of criminal justice punishments for a situation caused by a criminal justice penalty that is disproportionately burdensome for poor defendants. In other words, the crime of not paying a monetary sanction is in many cases the mere state of being poor, yet nonpayment occasions a series of consequences that further ensnare defendants in criminal justice proceedings. One final example illustrates this point. In *People v. Butler-Hobbs*, a fifty-three-year-old woman appealed the revocation of her probation, which stemmed from a 2001 forgery conviction.[20] After several years of criminal justice supervision, including jail time, mandated drug treatment, and frequent court status hearings, she still owed roughly $1,700 in probation fees and court fines and costs. At one status hearing, the judge asked the woman's probation officer, "It's only financial at this point?" The probation officer affirmed. In a later status hearing that the woman failed to attend, the probation officer reported things were "pretty stressful for her right now," regarding her financial status. He added, "She's been off for some time. The treatment and everything is done. It's just an issue of the financial piece right now." Still, the case wore on for another three years with frequent status hearings and requirements for payment, which the woman often did not attend and did not meet. Ultimately, the trial court revoked her probation and the appeals court affirmed that decision. In this instance, the role of monetary sanctions in furthering criminal justice contact is clear. Except for the literal payments, the defendant had paid every other part of her debt to society. Yet not paying the monetary sanctions meant that she did not responsibly complete her sentence, and the corresponding remedy was thirty months of prison time, one year of mandatory supervised released, and additional court costs and fees.

CONCLUSION

Punishment for lawbreaking is a core function of government. We have focused on the legislative domain in one state as a space that authorizes such punishment. The text of statutes, the debates that crafted them, and the case law that adjudicates them together make up a record and reflection of the kinds of ideologies that guide society's position on crime and those who commit them. Monetary sanctions are a particularly underexplored area of law, and the analysis of such laws uncovers the force of ideologies that emphasize personal responsibility and a carceral approach to managing poverty.

In answering the questions of what defendants are expected to pay for, what accommodations are allowed, and what the consequences of nonpayment are, we find the repeated rhetoric that the debts defendants owe are of their own making due to their failing to prioritize and their shirking of responsibilities. We find a willingness to attach additional penalties, reinitiate prosecution, extend supervision, and appease new stakeholders, but very little statutory guidance on a primary fact of the criminal justice system: the majority of people involved are poor or near poor. Poor state finances make poor defendants a clear and easy population upon which to foist the burden of monetary sanctions.

The core term *willful* (as well as *intentional*) is especially instructive because it both assumes an autonomous individual who is in full control of their circumstances and fixes the blame on the individual who acts with clear purpose. The literature on monetary sanctions to date paints quite another picture, however: namely, that of defendants who are barely making ends meet and who often prioritize rent, food, childcare, and health over paying the court that prosecuted them or the jail that imprisoned them (Harris et al. 2010; Harris 2016). Yet the law is clear that these debts are now their responsibility.

We argue that these contradictions constitute statutory inequality. Lawmakers rhetorically conjure a financially capable defendant in order to enact legislation that aims to recoup costs from them. A public defender in one Illinois county opined, "I do, generally, believe that very few of our judges have ever experienced the kind of poverty a majority of my clients live with, so they are often unrealistic about what is possible" (Bannon et al. 2010, 22). That sentiment seems equally applicable to leg-

---

20. *People v. Butler-Hobbs*, IL App (2nd) 100260-U (2011).

islators. Laws that exact financial penalties without attention to the financial circumstances of the majority of defendants—and without primary attention to the ability to pay of individual defendants—in essence legislate inequality of impact. For someone earning $1,000 a month, $1,000 in court costs is an impossible debt to pay; whereas for someone earning $6,000 a month, the same costs are challenging but not impossible. Even more important, cascading penalties—from delinquent charges to extended or revoked probation to incarceration—further separate the person who can pay from the person who cannot, making the latter even less able to go to work or school or pay for daily necessities. Scholars have characterized such laws and practices as constituting "predation" (Page and Soss 2018), "stategraft" (Atuahene and Hodge 2018), and outright "seizure" (Katzenstein and Waller 2015) of the assets of poor people. All of these terms highlight the additional impoverishment of already poor people, in this case through the workings of the law, the effect being larger gaps between poor and nonpoor defendants, which reverberate to poor and nonpoor families and communities.

The new Illinois law will correct some of the issues highlighted in this article. The provision for waivers of monetary sanctions for poor people is extraordinarily significant, and the definition of indigence offers clear guidance for judges and attorneys about who should be eligible for such waivers. However, the law goes only so far. The waivers are applicable only to assessments, not to fines or restitution. The mandatory fine for a first-time driving under the influence of alcohol or drugs offense, for example, is $500, a payable sum for the affluent but not for the poor. Restitution in theft or damage to property cases can run in the thousands. Moreover, the defendant must apply for the waiver within thirty days of conviction; successful implementation of the law will rely heavily on public awareness, compliance with posting requirements, and the proactive counsel of public defenders. Also, the new law is not retroactive and thus offers no relief for people already sentenced to pay monetary sanctions. Neither does it offer relief for services that defendants must pay for as part of their sentence, such as probation fees or the costs of anger management classes or substance abuse treatment. Finally, the consequences for nonpayment are unchanged. Hence, if a person does not apply for the waiver in a timely fashion, the cascade of penalties from interest to collections to imprisonment is still available to the state.

Nonetheless, the new law raises the question of whether the neoliberal logics of responsibility and carceral expansion are crumbling. We argue that some evidence suggests that they are. Successful efforts in Washington, D.C., New Jersey, California, and large jurisdictions, including Cook County, to eliminate bail for many offenders, as well as general movements toward *decarceration*, reflect public opinion moving away from the harshly punitive policies of the 1980s and 1990s, even if only for fiscal reasons (on bail, Wiltz 2017; on decarceration, Pettus-Davis and Epperson 2015). Indeed and curiously, the waivers for LFOs in Illinois got very little attention in the House and Senate floor discussions. Much of the logic for the reformation was on efficiency grounds. As a task force report that preceded the statutory change noted, "A relatively small percentage of assessments imposed in criminal cases is ever collected. Compared to any revenue that they generate, the administrative burden that such assessments impose on court clerks is substantial because criminal cases are not closed if assessments have not been paid" (Statutory Court Fee Task Force 2016, 31). This may be a case of the technocratic logics of neoliberalism triumphing over the personal responsibility logics (see, for example, Fourcade-Gourinchas and Babb 2002).

Yet, in addition to the limitations of the new law discussed, there are also reasons not to be too sanguine. Carceral logics effectively extend into community contexts outside prisons and courthouses (Kohler-Hausmann 2013; Shedd 2015; Soss, Fording, and Schram 2011). This extension suggests that a less concrete infrastructure of surveillance and control is already ensconced to take the place of prisons and jails; that various decriminalization efforts (marijuana being the biggest example) rest on making such offenses "fine-only," which leads back to the statutory inequality described (Natapoff 2015); and that the rhetoric of personal responsibility, especially when applied to the poor, and related policy efforts to increase work and other requirements to access social safety net programs show no signs of abating (Davis 2017). These realities play out just as strongly in Illinois, where the new law to revamp the system of monetary sanctions moves in the direction of reducing statutory inequality, but has much more room to go.

REFERENCES

Adams, Sharyn, Lindsay Bostwick, and Rebecca Campbell. 2011. *Examining Illinois Probationer Characteristics and Outcomes*. Chicago: Illinois Criminal Justice Information Authority. Accessed August 15, 2017. http://www.icjia.state.il.us/assets/pdf/ResearchReports/Examining_IL_probationer_characteristics_and_outcomes_092011.pdf.

Atuahene, Bernadette, and Timothy Hodge. 2018. "Stategraft." *Southern California Law Review* 91(2): 263–302.

Bannon, Alicia, Mitali Nagrecha, and Rebekah Diller. 2010. *Criminal Justice Debt: A Barrier to Re-entry*. New York: Brennan Center for Justice. Accessed August 15, 2017. www.brennancenter.org/page/-/Fees%20and%20Fines%20FINAL.pdf.

Beckett, Katherine. 1999. *Making Crime Pay: Law and Order in Contemporary American Politics*. New York: Oxford University Press.

Beckett, Katherine, and Alexes Harris. 2011. "On Cash and Conviction." *Criminology & Public Policy* 10(3): 509–37.

Bellware, Kim. 2017. "Chicago Judge Orders Access to Free Lawyers at Police Stations." *HuffPost*, March 15. Accessed August 15, 2017. http://www.huffingtonpost.com/entry/chicago-free-legal-aid-police-custody_us_58c87c81e4b09e52f5545e4b.

Calavita, Kitty, and Valerie Jenness. 2014. *Appealing to Justice: Prisoner Grievances, Rights, and Carceral Logic*. Berkeley: University of California Press.

Chicago Appleseed Fund for Justice. 2016. *Statement on "Excessive Court Fines, Fees, and Costs."* Chicago: Collaboration for Justice. Accessed August 15, 2017. http://www.chicagoappleseed.org/wp-content/uploads/2016/05/Collaboration-for-Justice-Policy-Brief-Fines-Fees-and-Costs-May-2016.pdf.

Chicago Jobs Council. 2018. "Living in Suspension: Consequences of Driver's License Suspension Policies." February. Accessed June 29, 2018. https://cjc.net/wp-content/uploads/2018/04/Living-in-Suspension_Report-by-CJC.pdf.

Davis, Julie Hirschfeld. 2017. "Trump's Budget Cuts Deeply into Medicaid and Anti-Poverty Efforts." *New York Times*, May 22. Accessed August 15, 2017. https://www.nytimes.com/2017/05/22/us/politics/trump-budget-cuts.html.

deVuono-powell, Saneta, Chris Schweidler, Alicia Walters, and Azadeh Zohrabi. 2015. *Who Pays? The True Cost of Incarceration on Families*. Oakland, Calif.: Ella Baker Center, Forward Together, Research Action Design. Accessed August 15, 2017. http://www.ellabakercenter.org/sites/default/files/downloads/who-pays.pdf.

Ewert, Stephanie, and Tara Wildhagen. 2011. "Educational Characteristics of Prisoners: Data from the ACS." *Social, Economic and Housing Statistics Division* working paper no. 2011-08. Washington: U.S. Census Bureau. Accessed August 15, 2017. https://www.census.gov/library/working-papers/2011/demo/SEHSD-WP2011-08.html.

Fortner, Michael Javen. 2015. *Black Silent Majority: The Rockefeller Drug Laws and the Politics of Punishment*. Cambridge, Mass.: Harvard University Press.

Fourcade-Gourinchas, Marion, and Sarah L. Babb. 2002. "The Rebirth of the Liberal Creed: Paths to Neoliberalism in Four Countries." *American Journal of Sociology* 108(3): 533–79.

Greenberg, Claire, Marc Meredith, and Michael Morse. 2016. "The Growing and Broad Nature of Legal Financial Obligations: Evidence from Court Records in Alabama." *Connecticut Law Review* 48(4): 1079–122.

Harlow, Caroline Wolf. 2000. "Defense Counsel in Criminal Cases." Bureau of Justice Statistics Special Report. Washington: U.S. Department of Justice. Accessed August 15, 2017. https://www.bjs.gov/content/pub/pdf/dccc.pdf.

Harris, Alexes. 2016. *A Pound of Flesh: Monetary Sanctions as Punishment for the Poor*. New York: Russell Sage Foundation.

Harris, Alexes, Heather Evans, and Katherine Beckett. 2010. "Drawing Blood from Stones: Legal Debt and Social Inequality in the Contemporary United States." *American Journal of Sociology* 115(6): 1753–99.

———. 2011. "Courtesy Stigma and Monetary Sanctions: Toward a Socio-Cultural Theory of Punishment." *American Sociological Review* 76(2): 234–64.

Harris, Alexes, Beth Huebner, Karin Martin, Mary Pattillo, Becky Pettit, Sarah Shannon, Bryan Sykes, Chris Uggen, and April Fernandes. 2017. *Monetary Sanctions in the Criminal Justice System*. Houston, Tex.: Laura and John Arnold Foundation. Accessed August 15, 2017. http://www.monetarysanctions.org/wp-content/uploads/2017/04/Monetary-Sanctions-Legal-Review-Final.pdf.

Harvey, David. 2007. *A Brief History of Neoliberalism*. Oxford: Oxford University Press.

Henricks, Kasey, and Daina Cheyenne Harvey. 2017. "Not One but Many: Monetary Punishment and the Fergusons of America." *Sociological Forum* 32(S1): 930–51.

Illinois Courts. 2017. "Illinois Circuit Court General Information." Springfield: Illinois General Assembly. Accessed August 15, 2017. http://www.illinoiscourts.gov/CircuitCourt/CCInfoDefault.asp.

Illinois State Police Merit Board. 2017. "Welcome to the Illinois State Police Merit Board." Accessed August 15, 2017. https://www.illinoistrooper.com.

Katzenstein, Mary Fainsod, and Maureen R. Waller. 2015. "Taxing the Poor: Incarceration, Poverty Governance, and the Seizure of Family Resources." *Perspectives on Politics* 13(3): 638–56.

Kohler-Hausmann, Issa. 2013. "Misdemeanor Justice: Control Without Conviction." *American Journal of Sociology* 119(2): 351–93.

Kopf, Daniel. 2016. "The Fining of Black America." *Priceonomics*. Accessed December 23, 2017. https://priceonomics.com/the-fining-of-black-america.

Lara-Millán, Armando. 2014. "Public Emergency Room Overcrowding in the Era of Mass Imprisonment." *American Sociological Review* 79(5): 866–87.

Logan, Wayne A., and Ronald F. Wright. 2014. "Mercenary Criminal Justice." *University of Illinois Law Review* 4: 1175–226.

Madigan, Lisa. 2017. "Letter in Response to Freedom of Information Act Request 2017 FOIA 046070." February 1. Sent to the authors.

Martin, Antwon R. 2014. "Court Fines Go to Collection." *Register-Mail*, November 8. Accessed June 29, 2018. http://www.galesburg.com/article/20141108/NEWS/141109787.

Mills, Steve, and Todd Lighty. 2016. "Rauner Vetoes Legislation to Abolish Room-and-Board Lawsuits against Prisoners." *Chicago Tribune*, August 19. Accessed August 15, 2017. http://www.chicagotribune.com/news/local/politics/ct-rauner-prisoner-lawsuits-20160819-story.html.

Monahan, Torin, and Rodolfo D Torres. 2009. *Schools Under Surveillance: Cultures of Control in Public Education*. New Brunswick, N.J.: Rutgers University Press.

Natapoff, Alexandra. "Misdemeanor Decriminalization." *Vanderbilt Law Review* 68(4): 1055–116.

National Public Radio. 2014. "As Court Fees Rise, The Poor Are Paying the Price." *All Things Considered*, May 19. Accessed December 23, 2017. https://www.npr.org/2014/05/19/312158516/increasing-court-fees-punish-the-poor.

Ong, Aihwa. 2006. *Neoliberalism as Exception: Mutations in Citizenship and Sovereignty*. Durham, N.C.: Duke University Press.

Page, Joshua, and Joe Soss. 2018. "Criminal Justice Predation and Neoliberal Governance." Chapter 8 in *Rethinking Neoliberalism: Resisting the Disciplinary Regime*, edited by Sanford F. Schram and Marianna Pavlovskaya. New York: Routledge.

Parker, Molly. 2015. "Cash-Strapped Counties Stepping Up Efforts to Collect Unpaid Court Fines — Some Decades Old." *The Southern*, November 15. Accessed June 29, 2018. https://thesouthern.com/news/local/cash-strapped-counties-stepping-up-efforts-to-collect-unpaid-court/article_cbcedbf9-448a-5e88-b16b-ccc7230c0e35.html.

Pattillo, Mary, Bruce Western, and David Weiman, eds. 2004. *Imprisoning America: The Social Effects of Mass Incarceration*. New York: Russell Sage Foundation.

Pepin, Arthur W. 2016. "The End of Debtors' Prisons: Effective Court Policies for Successful Compliance with Legal Financial Obligations." Policy Paper. Williamsburg, Va.: National Center for State Courts, Conference of State Administrators. Accessed December 23, 2017. http://cosca.ncsc.org/~/media/Microsites/Files/COSCA/Policy%20Papers/End-of-Debtors-Prisons-2016.ashx.

Pettus-Davis, Carrie, and Matthew W. Epperson. 2015. "From Mass Incarceration to Smart Decarceration." *American Academy of Social Work and Social Welfare* working paper no. 4. Columbia,

S.C.: AASWSW. Accessed August 15, 2017. http://aaswsw.org/wp-content/uploads/2015/03/From-Mass-Incarceration-to-Decarceration-3.24.15.pdf.

Pfaff, John. 2017. *Locked In: The True Causes of Mass Incarceration—and How to Achieve Real Reform.* New York: Basic Books.

Piquero, Alex R., and Wesley G. Jennings. 2017. "Justice System–Imposed Financial Penalties Increase the Likelihood of Recidivism in a Sample of Adolescent Offenders." *Youth Violence and Juvenile Justice* 15(3): 325–40.

Prasad, Monica. 2006. *The Politics of Free Markets: The Rise of Neoliberal Economic Policies in Britain, France, Germany, and the United States.* Chicago: University of Chicago Press.

Reiman, Jeffrey, and Paul Leighton. 2015. *The Rich Get Richer and the Poor Get Prison: Ideology, Class, and Criminal Justice.* New York: Routledge.

Rios, Victor M. 2011. *Punished: Policing the Lives of Black and Latino Boys.* New York: New York University Press.

Roberts, Dorothy. 2002. *Shattered Bonds: The Color of Child Welfare.* New York: Basic Books.

Sanchez, Melissa, and Sandhya Kambhampati. 2018. "Driven into Debt: How Chicago Ticket Debt Sends Black Motorists into Bankruptcy." *ProPublica Illinois*, February 27. Accessed June 29, 2018. https://features.propublica.org/driven-into-debt/chicago-ticket-debt-bankruptcy.

Sances, Michael W., and Hye Young You. 2017. "Who Pays for Government? Descriptive Representation and Exploitative Revenue Sources." *Journal of Politics* 79(3): 1090–94.

Schept, Judah. 2015. *Progressive Punishment: Job Loss, Jail Growth, and the Neoliberal Logic of Carceral Expansion.* New York: New York University Press.

Shedd, Carla. 2015. *Unequal City: Race, Schools, and Perceptions of Injustice.* New York: Russell Sage Foundation.

Soss, Joe, Richard C. Fording, and Sanford Schram. 2011. *Disciplining the Poor: Neoliberal Paternalism and the Persistent Power of Race.* Chicago: University of Chicago Press.

State of Illinois. 1972a. *77th General Assembly. Senate Floor Debate.* Springfield: Illinois General Assembly. Accessed August 15, 2017. http://www.ilga.gov/Senate/transcripts/Strans77/ST050972.pdf.

———. 1972b. *Public Act 77-2097. Laws of the State of Illinois Passed by the Seventy-Seventh General Assembly and Approved During the Calendar Year*, Volume 1. Springfield: Illinois General Assembly. Session Laws Library, HeinOnline.

———. 2002. "92nd General Assembly. House of Representatives. Transcription Debate." Springfield: Illinois General Assembly. Accessed August 15, 2017. http://www.ilga.gov/House/transcripts/Htrans92/T042502.pdf.

———. 2011. "97th General Assembly. House of Representatives. Transcription Debate." Springfield: Illinois General Assembly. Accessed August 15, 2017. http://www.ilga.gov/House/transcripts/Htrans97/09700038.pdf.

———. 2017. *Public Act 100-0023: FY2018 Budget Implementation Act.* Springfield: Illinois General Assembly. Accessed August 15, 2017. http://www.ilga.gov/legislation/publicacts/100/100-0023.htm.

———. 2018. *Public Act 100-0987: Criminal and Traffic Assessment Act.* Springfield.: Illinois General Assembly. Accessed September 6, 2018. http://www.ilga.gov/legislation/publicacts/100/100-0987.htm.

Statutory Court Fee Task Force. 2016. *Illinois Court Assessments: Findings and Recommendations for Addressing Barriers to Access to Justice and Additional Issues Associated with Fees and Other Court Costs in Civil, Criminal, and Traffic Proceedings.* Springfield: Illinois General Assembly. Accessed August 15, 2017. www.illinoiscourts.gov/2016_Statutory_Court_Fee_Task_Force_Report.pdf.

Tran-Leung, Marie Claire. 2009. "Debt Arising From Illinois' Criminal Justice System: Making Sense of the Ad Hoc Accumulation of Financial Obligations." Chicago: Sargent Shriver National Center on Poverty Law. Accessed August 15, 2017. http://povertylaw.org/files/docs/debt-report.pdf.

———. 2010. "Assessing the Ad Hoc Nature of Financial Obligations Arising in the Illinois Criminal Justice System." *Journal of Poverty Law and Policy* 43(9–10): 440–47.

U.S. Commission on Civil Rights. 2017. *Targeted Fines and Fees against Communities of Color: Civil Rights & Constitutional Implications.* Washington: U.S. Commission on Civil Rights. Accessed December 23, 2017. www.usccr.gov/pubs/Statutory_Enforcement_Report2017.pdf.

U.S. Department of Justice. 2015. *Investigation of the Ferguson Police Department*. Washington: Government Printing Office. Accessed August 7, 2018. https://www.justice.gov/sites/default/files/opa/press-releases/attachments/2015/03/04/ferguson_police_department_report.pdf.

Van Cleve, Nicole Gonzalez. 2016. *Crook County: Racism and Injustice in America's Largest Criminal Court*. Palo Alto, Calif.: Stanford University Press.

Wacquant, Loic. 2009. *Punishing the Poor: The Neoliberal Government of Social Insecurity*. Durham, N.C.: Duke University Press.

Weaver, Vesla M. 2007. "Frontlash: Race and the Development of Punitive Crime Policy." *Studies in American Political Development* 21(2): 230–65.

Western, Bruce. 2006. *Punishment and Inequality in America*. New York: Russell Sage Foundation.

Wilson, William Julius. 1996. *When Work Disappears: The World of the New Urban Poor*. New York: Alfred A. Knopf.

Wiltz, Teresa. 2017. "Locked Up: Is Cash Bail on the Way Out?" *Stateline* (blog), March 1. Accessed August 15, 2017. http://www.pewtrusts.org/en/research-and-analysis/blogs/stateline/2017/03/01/locked-up-is-cash-bail-on-the-way-out.

Wright, Ronald F., and Wayne A. Logan. 2006. "The Political Economy of Application Fees for Indigent Criminal Defense." *William and Mary Law Review* 47(6): 2045–88.

PART III

Consequences of Criminal Justice Contact

Level of Criminal Justice Contact and Early Adult Wage Inequality

ROBERT APEL AND KATHLEEN POWELL

This study explores heterogeneity in the relationship between criminal justice contact and early adult wages using unconditional quantile regression models with sibling fixed effects, estimated separately by race-ethnicity. The findings support the contention that the relationship between criminal justice contact and wages is heterogeneous in three respects: level of contact, race, and location in the wage distribution. First, entry-level contacts in the form of arrest are largely uncorrelated with wages, whereas wage gaps are evident following late-stage contacts in the form of jail or prison incarceration. Second, the wage gap from incarceration is observable among black respondents, but not whites or Latinos. Third, the size of the wage gap from incarceration is approximately U-shaped with respect to the black wage distribution.

Keywords: arrest, incarceration, wage inequality

In the span of a generation, the criminal justice system metamorphosed into an unprecedented form of state intervention in American life, reaching a scale unmatched by any other society or any other time (Garland 2001a). Imprisonment growth is the most frequently noted and studied symptom of this phenomenon (Garland 2001b; Kirk and Wakefield 2018; Wakefield and Wildeman 2014). The trend is also obvious in noncarceral forms of criminal justice contact, such as those that entail supervision without secure custodial confinement (Phelps 2017).

The contemporary criminal justice system is also notable for its concentration of young men of color (Patterson and Wildeman 2015; Pettit 2012; Pettit and Western 2004; Shannon et al. 2017). This persistent disparity, apparent across all levels of the system, is only partly explained by differences in the frequency or level of criminal offending across racial-ethnic groups (see, for example, Gelman, Fagan, and Kiss 2007; Sampson and Lauritsen 1997). Paired with the system's unparalleled scale, this racial disparity seems to leave little doubt that it is today more of a major vehicle of contemporary social stratification than it historically has been (Wakefield and Uggen 2010).

In this study, we examine the relationship of criminal justice contact with the early adult wages of a large representative sample using a method new to the study of punishment and

Robert Apel is professor at the School of Criminal Justice at Rutgers University–Newark. **Kathleen Powell** is a PhD candidate at the School of Criminal Justice at Rutgers University–Newark.

© 2019 Russell Sage Foundation. Apel, Robert, and Kathleen Powell. 2019. "Level of Criminal Justice Contact and Early Adult Wage Inequality." *RSF: The Russell Sage Foundation Journal of the Social Sciences* 5(1): 198–222. DOI: 10.7758/RSF.2019.5.1.09. Direct correspondence to: Robert Apel at ra437@scj.rutgers.edu, School of Criminal Justice, Rutgers University, 123 Washington St., Newark, NJ 07102.

Open Access Policy: *RSF: The Russell Sage Foundation Journal of the Social Sciences* is an open access journal. This article is published under a Creative Commons Attribution-NonCommercial-NoDerivs 3.0 Unported License.

inequality. We measure different stages of criminal justice contact to determine the degree to which the level of contact is correlated with wages.[1] We also estimate race- and ethnicity-specific models to study whether criminal justice contacts have uniform or distinct effects across sociodemographic groups, which is particularly important in light of the social patterning of criminal justice contact. Finally, we estimate (unconditional) quantile regression models to document heterogeneity in the relationship between criminal justice contact and wages. Taken together, our results point to level-specific effects and distinct racial patterning of early adult wage inequality following criminal justice contact.

RESEARCH ON CRIMINAL JUSTICE CONTACT AND WAGE INEQUALITY

Spanning several decades and countries, an extensive literature documents the impact of criminal justice contact on the labor market. This rich research tradition is mixed with respect to legal jurisdictions, types of contact, age and representativeness of the samples, measurement sources, research designs, and methodological rigor. We refer readers to more comprehensive summaries of employment-related consequences available elsewhere, and focus attention here on the outcomes most germane to our study—wages and earnings (see Apel and Ramakers, forthcoming; Kirk and Wakefield 2018; Travis, Western, and Redburn 2014; Raphael 2014; Wakefield and Uggen 2010).

Research on the relationship between criminal justice contact and wages is not as uniform as one might first suspect. For example, Ross Matsueda and his colleagues do not find any difference in earnings between individuals in the Supported Work evaluation who were formerly incarcerated versus formerly addicted to drugs (1992). They find instead that formerly incarcerated individuals are more likely to earn income illegally. The authors also estimate an inverse relationship between the number of prior arrests and earnings, but an unexpectedly positive relationship for the number of prior weeks in jail. Karen Needels also does not find any relationship between incarceration and earnings among men in the Transitional Aid Research Project evaluation, although she does find that the number of arrests is inversely correlated with long-term earnings (1996).

In Jeffrey Grogger's panel study of individuals arrested in California, arrest is correlated with a modest 4 percent earnings penalty that declines and then disappears after the fourth quarter, whereas conviction is uncorrelated with earnings, and the coefficients are even positive (1995). By comparison, jail incarceration corresponds with a 16 percent earnings decline and prison incarceration a 22 percent decline, both of which persist for at least six quarters. Joel Waldfogel's sample of men convicted for the first time in the federal criminal justice system experience earnings erosion when they are convicted, as well as when they are incarcerated (1994a, 1994b). The effects are particularly large for higher-status workers who are better educated and whose occupations require more trust, indicating that the effects of criminal justice contact is status dependent, to some degree. Daniel Nagin and Waldfogel find that conviction is actually correlated with 10 percent higher earnings among London-area men, controlling for self-report delinquency and crime, and explain this unexpected finding by arguing that criminal conviction relegates individuals to spot market jobs which are high-paying but unstable in the long run (1995, 1998).

Research using state administrative data sources reveals an unexpectedly positive correlation between time served in prison and postrelease earnings. For example, Jeffrey Kling observes that formerly incarcerated men in Florida who serve longer prison terms have initially higher earnings than their counterparts who serve shorter terms (2006). However, two years after incarceration, the differences disappear. Similar findings are reported in Illinois (Jung 2011). Additional evidence from Washington indicates that the earnings of formerly

---

1. To speak of stages of the criminal justice process can be misleading, because it implies a degree of coordination between justice personnel and justice institutions that simply does not exist. While it possesses a distinctly progressive structure, whereby downstream decision-making is influenced by upstream decision-making, the criminal justice process more closely resembles a series of administrative filters than stages.

incarcerated black men grow 21 percent more slowly following release than their white counterparts, contributing to "compound disadvantage" (Lyons and Pettit 2011).

Until recently, the National Longitudinal Survey of Youth 1979 (NLSY79) has been the only large-scale, self-report survey permitting study of the long-term relationship between criminal justice contact and wages in a representative sample.[2] Jeffrey Fagan and Richard Freeman show a consistent inverse correlation between incarceration and earnings (1999; on null effects for earlier interviews, see Bound and Freeman 1992). In a panel study, Bruce Western reports that prior incarceration corresponds with a reduction in wages of about 16 percent relative to non-incarcerated individuals (2002). He also finds that incarceration deflects individuals onto a flatter wage profile, slowing wage growth by 31 percent relative to high-risk men who are never incarcerated. Models estimated separately for white, black, and Hispanic respondents indicate more or less uniform deceleration in wage growth following incarceration. Steven Raphael reports a wage gap of about 15 percent following incarceration, although in his most stringent test (restriction of the sample only to individuals who have been or will be incarcerated), the incarceration-wage correlation disappears (2007). Haeil Jung finds that both youth and adult incarceration are correlated with reductions in adult wages (2015).

Amanda Geller and her colleagues report from the Fragile Families and Child Wellbeing study that men who have ever been incarcerated possess a wage rate 9 to 22 percent lower than their non-incarcerated peers, depending on the model specification (2006). However, sensitivity analysis also indicates the results are not robust to unobserved confounding. Robert Apel and Gary Sweeten, using the 1997 cohort of the National Longitudinal Survey of Youth, report a nonsignificant wage gap of about 9 percent among those who are incarcerated following their first criminal conviction, compared to their similarly first-time convicted peers who are not incarcerated (2010).

To summarize, the nature of the relationship between criminal justice contact and wages remains in doubt. Evidence exists that arrest is inversely correlated with wages, but for either a short period of time or a long period of time. Evidence also exists that conviction has no relationship with wages, that it is inversely correlated with wages, and that it is positively correlated with wages. Additional evidence indicates that incarceration has no relationship with wages, that it is inversely correlated with wages, and that incarceration (length) is positively correlated with wages. It would be seriously mistaken to conclude from this body of research that the correlation between criminal justice contact and wages has been firmly established.

MECHANISMS UNDERLYING CRIMINAL JUSTICE CONTACT AND WAGE INEQUALITY

Three prominent mechanisms are usually invoked to explain why criminal justice contact might be correlated with wages (see also Western, Kling, and Weiman 2001). We consider differential selection, labor demand, and labor supply in turn. However, these mechanisms are more relevant to understanding the correlation between conviction or incarceration and wages, involving decision-making in the court system, but less obviously applicable to understanding entry-level contacts such as arrests.

Differential Selection

Selection mechanisms are implicated if individuals who experience criminal justice contact would have had lower wages or experienced slowed wage growth even in the absence of contact. Criminal justice contact is more heavily concentrated among individuals occupying the lowest rungs of the social ladder. Incarceration, in particular, resembles a sorting mechanism that absorbs socially marginal populations (Wakefield and Uggen 2010).[3] For example, just

---

2. This advantage is offset by the fact that, aside from a self-report crime and criminal justice module administered in the 1980 interview, the only form of criminal justice contact that is possible to measure is whether the interview was conducted in a correctional institution.

3. "Prisons . . . house the jobless, the poor, the racial minority, and the uneducated, not the merely criminal" (393).

32 percent of state prison inmates and 39 percent of local jail inmates have a high school diploma, compared with about 82 percent of the general population and even 58 percent of probationers (Harlow 2003, table 1). Furthermore, in the month prior to their arrest, 53 percent of state prison inmates take home less than $1,000 ($1,525 in 2017 dollars, an annualized equivalent of $18,300), and 25 percent live with someone who receives welfare (Harlow 2003, table 14).

An additional source of selection into the criminal justice system is undoubtedly criminal offending. Simply put, individuals who are more criminally active are more exposed to criminal justice contact, other things equal. Furthermore, a higher volume of police contacts and arrests is correlated with subsequent criminal justice processing. Additionally, a defendant's current offense and criminal history account for the lion's share of variation in judicial sentencing. That said, criminologists have long been aware that, although legal variables tend to be the most salient determinants of criminal justice processing, extralegal variables frequently impinge on criminal justice decision-making, especially at times when officials are entitled to more discretion. For example, Robert Sampson finds that black youth and youth from low-status neighborhoods accumulate significantly more police contacts, net of several forms of delinquent behavior, and a higher volume of police contacts is then highly correlated with court referral (1986; see also Sampson and Laub 1993). The influence of neighborhoods is partly "ecological contamination," as police departments adopt more legalistic practices in low-status and minority neighborhoods (Smith 1986). Yet even in the court system, young black males and individuals from low-status families tend to be subjected to more punishment than can be explained by legally relevant variables alone (Sampson 1986; Steffensmeier, Ulmer, and Kramer 1998).

Labor Demand

Demand-side mechanisms focus on the willingness of employers to knowingly hire individuals with a history of criminal justice contact. The analytical focus is on employers as decision-makers and gatekeepers: criminal justice contact is a stigma that, in the eyes of employers, makes job applicants unemployable or at least undesirable. This mechanism is corroborated by experimental audits and correspondence tests.[4] Devah Pager's studies of entry-level job openings document a callback rate of formerly incarcerated individuals that is just one-half the size, from a 25 to 28 percent baseline, of the rate among their peers with no incarceration (Pager 2003, 2005, 2007; Pager, Western, and Bonikowski 2009; Pager, Western, and Sugie 2009; see also Decker et al. 2015).[5] Formerly incarcerated black applicants experience even larger disparities. Specifically, black applicants without a prison record have a similar callback rate to white applicants with a prison record—being black and formerly incarcerated thus constitutes "double jeopardy" in low-wage labor markets (Pager 2005, 2007). Aside from their categorical exclusion at the point of the decision to hire, further evidence indicates post-hiring, race-coded job channeling whereby blacks are placed into lower-prestige occupations (Pager, Western, and Bonikowski 2009).

Employers also appear to make hiring decisions on the basis of noncarceral contacts

---

4. In a typical study, a pair of applicants, known as auditors or testers, applies for the same job. Relevant background characteristics of the pair (such as gender, race, education, and work history) are matched as best as possible while the key characteristic under study—possession of some kind of criminal history—is randomly varied between the testers. In an audit study, the auditors apply in person for posted job openings, whereas in a correspondence study, résumés or applications with fictitious credentials are submitted. The outcome in either kind of study is the callback, or any form of favorable follow-up from an employer (such as offer of hire, invitation for an interview, or solicitation of more information).

5. Sarah Galgano reports on a correspondence study using female testers in Chicago (2009). She does not observe any difference in callback rates, suggesting that "a criminal history is not as universally stigmatizing for women" (33). Scott Decker and his colleagues also do not find any difference in callback rates in the correspondence portion of their study but do find differences in the audit portion (2015).

when that information is available. Richard Schwartz and Jerome Skolnick report a lower callback rate for conviction, relative to employment files with no criminal record (1962). Even employment files with a trial and acquittal—an applicant who is criminally accused but proclaimed to be without guilt—show lower callback. Christopher Uggen and his colleagues further report that employers incorporate arrests into their hiring decisions, in that applications indicating an arrest receive a callback 29 percent of the time relative to a baseline of 33 percent (2014; see also Vuolo, Lageson, and Uggen 2017). Thus, even individuals who have a minor brush with the law can be stigmatized if potential employers find out about it.[6]

Labor Supply
Supply-side mechanisms emphasize the training and credentials possessed by job seekers that make them more or less attractive hires to potential employers. Education and work experience are crucial components of supply-side explanations. A number of studies indicate that youthful criminal justice contact is correlated with schooling deficits (Bernburg and Krohn 2003; Hirschfield 2009; Hjalmarsson 2008; Kirk and Sampson 2013; Sweeten 2006; Widdowson, Siennick, and Hay 2016). These studies are mixed as to whether the correlation between arrest and schooling withstands rigorous selection controls, but intermediate and especially later stages of criminal justice contact—namely, court involvement and incarceration—are strongly correlated with high school noncompletion.

Criminal justice contact is also correlated with nonwage facets of an individual's work experience that can translate into later wage gaps. Apel and Sweeten report that, among individuals convicted for the first time, those who are incarcerated are subsequently less likely to be employed and work fewer weeks when they are employed (2010). This work experience gap is accounted for largely by labor force nonparticipation, which is a form of work detachment that can worsen long-term employment prospects.[7] A similar phenomenon has recently been reported among formerly incarcerated individuals in Boston, who experience idleness in the weeks following their return to the community—they are neither working nor looking for work (Western et al. 2015). Criminal justice contact can therefore contribute to a spotty work record because of detachment from work, beyond any time out of the labor market due to confinement (Holzer, Raphael, and Stoll 2006).[8]

CRIMINAL JUSTICE CONTACT AND DISTRIBUTIONAL HETEROGENEITY
Research on the consequences of criminal justice contact has focused largely on estimation of differences in (regression-adjusted) mean outcomes, but recognition is growing of the need to unpack average effects to better understand the consequences of criminal justice contact for social inequality (Kirk and Wakefield 2018; Sampson 2011; Wakefield and Wildeman 2014). Only a handful of studies address heterogeneity in outcomes among justice-involved individuals, finding that some precontact characteristics moderate postcontact outcomes in

---

6. On employer use of criminal background checks, see Holzer 1996; Holzer et al. 1996; Stoll and Bushway 2008; Stoll 2009. On policies that prevent employers from inquiring about criminal histories on job applications (such as Ban the Box), see Agan and Starr 2018.

7. Labor force nonparticipants include stay-at-home parents, school-going youth, retirees, and disabled persons. They also include discouraged workers, or those individuals who have given up looking for work. Labor force nonparticipation is different from unemployment, which presumes that an individual is actively seeking work but has not yet been hired (such as having recently filled out a job application or gone on a job interview).

8. Harry Holzer and his colleagues report that 96 percent of employers will hire applicants with only a GED, applicants who are former welfare recipients (92 percent), applicants who have been unemployed for a year or more (83 percent), applicants with a "spotty work record" (59 percent), and applicants with a criminal record (38 percent) (2006). Even if employers lack access to criminal history information, therefore, formerly incarcerated job applicants are quite likely to experience hiring difficulty simply because of the spotty record caused by incarceration-induced work history gaps.

interesting ways. For example, a pair of recent child well-being studies demonstrate that parental incarceration is most harmful to well-being among children from comparatively advantaged family environments—those for whom the confinement of a parent is likely to result in a more substantial, and unexpected, change to the family milieu (Turney 2017; Turney and Wildeman 2015). Sara Wakefield and Kathleen Powell report that children of incarcerated fathers with severe substance abuse problems prior to their confinement exhibit less aggression compared to children of substance-abusing fathers who are not incarcerated (2016). Christopher Dennison and Stephen Demuth find that individuals from high-status backgrounds experience downward mobility following deeper criminal justice contact relative to their low-status counterparts (2018).

Although researchers typically focus on differences in means, differences in other distributional quantities (such as percentiles) are frequently insinuated in inequality scholarship. Inattention to this distributional heterogeneity is especially problematic for the study of an institution—and the criminal justice system is one prominent institution—that more or less routinely interfaces with highly disadvantaged populations. However, predictions diverge about the nature of the relationship between criminal justice contact and wage inequality. For comparatively low-wage workers, criminal justice contact might not have any effect discernible from other facets of their lives that already situate them in a highly disadvantaged milieu. Wages might be similarly inelastic with respect to criminal justice contact among comparatively high-wage workers, who benefit from more privileged social contexts (but see Waldfogel 1994a, 1994b). Alternatively, criminal justice contact (carceral contact, in particular) might further entrench wage inequality among low-wage workers, and at the higher end of the continuum, create wage inequality where it might not have otherwise existed.

We believe a study of distributional heterogeneity more closely aligns with scholarly interest in criminal justice contact as a possible mainspring of wage inequality. We thus propose the unconditional quantile regression model to probe the relationship between criminal justice contact and hourly wage. We explore heterogeneity through estimation of the model at all wage percentiles between the 5th and the 95th. Because of the salience of race-ethnicity in the criminal justice system as well as in the population wage distribution, we estimate the models separately for white, Latino, and black respondents. We also explore different levels of criminal justice contact, and though we focus our attention on only arrest and incarceration for collinearity reasons, we comment on intermediate forms of contact at relevant points.

DATA

The data used for this study come from the National Longitudinal Survey of Youth 1997 (NLSY97), a nationally representative sample of about nine thousand American youth born between 1980 and 1984 (Bureau of Labor Statistics 2015). Funded by the Bureau of Labor Statistics and fielded by the National Opinion Research Center, the first round of the NLSY97 was administered in 1997 and 1998, when respondents were between ages twelve and eighteen. To date, seventeen rounds of data are available, which effectively span ages twelve to thirty-six inclusive. The first fifteen rounds were conducted annually; as of the sixteenth, the survey is biennial. One distinct advantage of the NLSY97 is its goal to document the transition from school to work in a contemporary sample of young people, which means that it provides a broad array of measures related to employment and attainment outcomes. A second distinct advantage, essential for this study, is that the survey regularly inquires about forms of criminal justice contact that transpire between interviews.

The objective of this study is to compare the early adult wage distribution of individuals with a history of criminal justice contact to their counterparts—specifically, their sibling or siblings—with no reported contacts. For each respondent, the last available round is selected for analysis. In most cases, this is the seventeenth round, but for 30 percent of respondents, the last available interview is from an earlier round on account of attrition. The median respondent is 32 years of age at the last available interview.

Hourly Wage

Descriptive statistics for all measures are provided in table A1. The dependent variable is the hourly wage reported in a formal job at the last available interview. In the NLSY97, a formal job is an "employee-type job" defined as "a situation in which the respondent has an ongoing relationship with a specific employer" (Center for Human Resource Research 2002, 96). The hourly wage in 2016 dollars is calculated by pooling wage information across all jobs worked within the reference window, thus assigning heavier weight to longer-duration jobs.[9] At the last available interview, 87.7 percent of all respondents are employed, and the mean wage is higher than $19 per hour (median = $15.68). Respondents who are not employed are excluded from the regression models.

Criminal Justice Contact

The independent variables of interest are forms of criminal justice contact. In each round, NLSY97 survey staff ask respondents a series of questions to ascertain whether, since the last interview, they had been arrested, charged (if arrested), court involved (if charged), convicted (if court involved), and sentenced (if convicted). Respondents who report having been sentenced are then asked whether they served a sentence in a juvenile correctional institution, reform or training school, jail, or adult correctional institution (prison). Those who report institutional confinement are further asked to provide the month and year of entry and exit. The type of incarceration of most interest in this study is that which takes place in either jail or prison, although for the handful of respondents for whom it applies, incarceration in a juvenile correctional institution or a reform or training school is treated as a control variable.[10]

These questions are used to create measures of two distinct types of criminal justice contact: arrests and incarceration spells, the latter being jail or prison.[11] Each is measured using a dummy variable to indicate whether, as of the last available interview, respondents had ever reported that type of contact. These represent accumulative indicators of noncarceral and carceral contacts and are the key measures in the empirical models. More than one-third (35 per-

---

9. To account for the fact that respondents may report more than one job within a reference window, we incorporate job weights. The weight is constructed as the number of weeks worked in job *j*, divided by the sum of the total number of weeks worked across all *K* jobs:

$$Weight_j = \frac{Weeks_j}{\sum_{j=1}^{K} Weeks_j}.$$

The denominator is not the total number of calendar weeks worked, but the sum of the number of calendar weeks worked in all jobs, that is, the sum of *K* job durations. By construction, the job weights sum to unity at each interview. Each reported wage is multiplied by its corresponding job weight; these are then summed across all jobs reported within a reference window.

10. Supplementary information on incarceration can be obtained from at least three additional sources: the location where the respondent's interview was conducted (dormitory, prison, or hospital), the type of dwelling in which the respondent resides as of the interview (jail, prison, detention, or work release), or the type of interview conducted or else the reason that a respondent was not interviewed (interview completed in person or by phone when respondent was incarcerated; not interviewed because of inaccessibility due to imprisonment). However, none of these supplementary sources of information accommodates a clear distinction between jail and prison, so this information is not used.

11. Because the intermediate measures of criminal justice contact (such as charges, convictions) are highly correlated with arrest, they cannot be included simultaneously in a cross-sectional analysis. However, we comment at relevant points on sensitivity analyses which include these measures in place of arrest. Jail and prison spells refer to postconviction sentences (that is, sanctions), rather than post-arrest or pretrial detentions. In other words, in this study, carceral contact should be taken to mean that an individual was punished for a criminal offense with a sentence to a correctional facility.

cent) of the sample has ever been arrested, a figure that aligns with what has been reported elsewhere from the NLSY97 (Brame et al. 2012, 2014). At the "deep end" of the criminal justice system, almost one in ten (9.8 percent) has been sentenced to jail or prison. Among those who have been incarcerated in prison, exactly half have also been incarcerated in jail on a different (usually prior) occasion.

In addition to dummy indicators for criminal justice contact prevalence, two additional measures are created. First, the accumulated frequency of arrests and incarceration spells, as well as the accumulated duration of jail and prison incarceration are obtained by summing the relevant information across all interviews from the first to the last available. These serve as alternative measures of criminal justice contact, used to ascertain whether discrete *stage effects* stem from single contacts or instead *accumulation effects* flow from repeated contacts. Second, the number of years elapsed since the first reported contact is measured based on the respondent's age as of the interviews in which the first arrest and incarceration spell are reported. These are included to determine whether the effects of criminal justice contact fade or grow over time.

Control Variables

The regression models control for a number of other variables, including gender, age at interview (dummy coded), marital status (never married, currently married, currently divorced or separated), cohabitation, dwelling type (house, apartment, other dwelling type), urbanicity (central city, suburb, outside MSA), census region, and number of years in the interview reference window. As mentioned, having ever been incarcerated in a juvenile correctional institution, reform school, or training school is also included as a control variable. We do not include employment- and education-related controls to avoid so-called collider variables that are likely to mediate the relationship between criminal justice contact and early adult wages (Elwert and Winship 2014).

METHODS

We focus here on the intuition underlying the approach (for technical methodological details, see the appendix). In light of our interest in the study of inequality as a distributional phenomenon, the method of choice is the unconditional quantile regression model (Firpo 2007; Firpo, Fortin, and Lemieux 2009). Because the criminal justice contact measures are binary, the model lends itself to estimation of the impact of increasing the proportion of arrested or incarcerated individuals on the marginal or unconditional wage distribution. Rather than yielding a single overall (and possibly unrepresentative) estimate of the impact of criminal justice contact, this approach considers whether criminal justice contact has heterogeneous effects, that is, different effects at different points in the wage distribution. We estimate all models from the 5th to the 95th percentiles of the wage distribution.

To incorporate a quasi-experimental design element that deals with certain forms of selection bias, we estimate the unconditional quantile regression models with fixed effects for siblings. The design of the NLSY97 involved interviewing all age-eligible residents in each sampled household, where age eligibility was defined by birth year (1980–1984).[12] The analytic sample is thus limited to the roughly four thousand respondents (about 45 percent of the sample) that have one or more coresident siblings. Identification of the model derives from a comparison of respondents who have ever experienced criminal justice contact to one or more similar-age siblings who have never experienced contact, which provides a strong control for early neighborhood and family environment as well as social class background, all of which are important correlates of criminal justice contact and early adult wages.

Because wages differ considerably by race and ethnicity, separate models are estimated for white, Latino, and black respondents. Additionally, as a supplement to tests of statistical significance, we use effect-size calculations to judge substantive significance using Cohen's *d* (Cohen 1988). The effect size is routinely judged

---

12. Multiple-respondent households comprise as many as five respondents. Although coresident interviewees are most likely to be siblings, they are not universally so.

Figure 1. Density of Hourly Wage

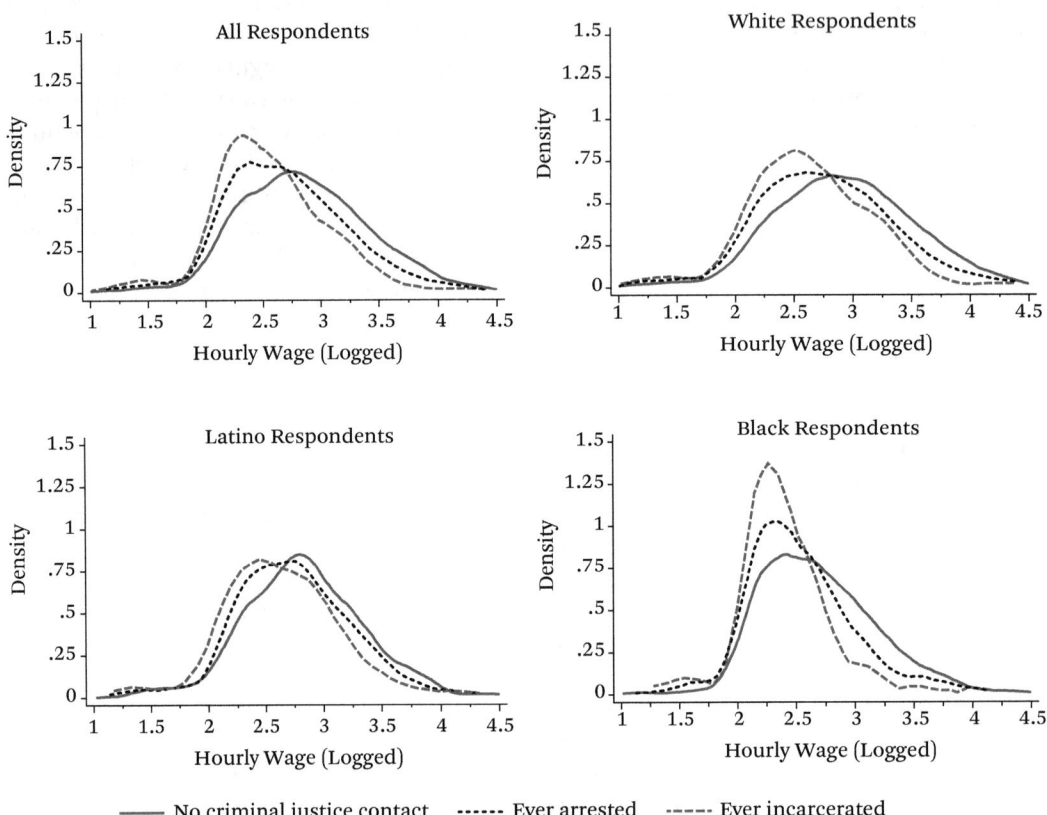

Source: Authors' estimates from respondents' last available round of the National Longitudinal Survey of Youth 1997, rounds 1–17 (Bureau of Labor Statistics 2015).
Note: Estimates are unweighted. The distributions derive from the full sample, not the sibling subsample. The criminal justice contact groups are not mutually exclusive.

against a minimum threshold of 0.20, below which an effect size is generally regarded as uninteresting in terms of practical significance, even if the coefficient is statistically significant.

RESULTS

Figure 1 provides provisional evidence about the nature of the correlation between criminal justice contact and early adult wages, for both the full sample and the race-ethnicity–specific subsamples. The density of log hourly wages is graphed for respondents who have never experienced criminal justice contact, those who have ever been arrested, and those who have ever been incarcerated (for the cumulative distribution of log hourly wages, see figure A1). Individuals with a history of criminal justice contact exhibit wage distributions that are shifted leftward relative to the normative, no-contact distribution. Level of criminal justice contact and wages are also correlated, as indicated by the fact that the wages of individuals who have been incarcerated are consistently lower relative to those who have been arrested.

Figure 1 also documents racial-ethnic differences in the wage distributions as well as in the magnitude of the wage gap for respondents with a history of criminal justice contact. Black respondents with a history of incarceration, in particular, exhibit a visually striking deviation from the no-contact wage distribution relative to their incarcerated white and Latino peers. This is compounded by the fact that the wage distribution of black respondents is noticeably lower than their white and Latino peers to begin with. On its face, this harmonizes with Pager's observations concerning the double jeopardy African Americans with a criminal history experience in low-wage labor markets (2005).

In the empirical analysis, we probe the information conveyed by the wage distributions just shown, to examine whether the noted patterns persist when we account for additional variables. Table 1 provides select estimates of the relationship between criminal justice contact and early adult wages from unconditional quantile regression models with sibling fixed effects. The inclusion of sibling fixed effects means that individuals who have experienced criminal justice contact are compared with their similar-age siblings who have never experienced criminal justice contact. Although it is not necessary that wages are logged for this analysis, doing so means the coefficients are approximate proportional differences in the hourly wage at a given marginal quantile.[13] The reference group for the arrest and incarceration coefficients is respondents who have never experienced criminal justice contact.

The first finding of interest is that, with few exceptions, individuals who have been arrested do not differ in their early adult wages from similar-age siblings who have never been arrested. Some coefficients are even positive in sign, though never close to statistical significance. The only indications of a relationship between arrest and hourly wages are a pair of coefficients which are marginally significant ($p < .10$), one at the 50th percentile among all respondents and another at the 90th percentile among black respondents.

The second finding of interest is that incarceration is correlated with early adult wages among black but not white or Latino respondents. Among black respondents, three of five quantile regression coefficients are significant using a .05 criterion (and one more is significant using a .10 criterion), and it is notable that these three coefficients also differ from their white counterparts ($p < .10$). For example, evaluating at the 25th percentile, blacks who have ever been incarcerated earn a 28 percent lower wage ($e^{-0.33} - 1 = -0.28$) than their similar-age siblings who have never experienced criminal justice contact. Evaluating at the 90th percentile, the wage penalty is 42 percent ($e^{-0.54} - 1 = -0.42$).[14]

Figures 2 and 3 provide the full suite of quantile regression estimates and confidence intervals for arrest (figure 2) and incarceration (figure 3), spanning the wage distribution from the 5th to the 95th percentiles. With respect to arrest, and confirming the impression from the results reported in table 1, no obvious wage disparity is evident between individuals with an arrest record and their counterparts without an arrest record. Above the 85th percentile, the quantile regression estimates exceed minimum effect-size thresholds, but interestingly, the coefficients for whites are positive but negative for Latinos and blacks. However, fewer coefficients are statistically significant than what would be expected merely by chance.

Concerning incarceration, the estimates for whites and Latinos also confirm the prior impression of null findings from table 1. Indeed, not a single estimate is statistically significant at any conventional level, and virtually all are within the bounds of a substantively null effect size. For black respondents, on the other hand, 71 percent of the quantile regression estimates are statistically significant using a .05 criterion (and 87 percent are significant using a .10 criterion). Below the 60th percentile, the effect sizes are small but substantively meaningful (that is, $|d| \geq 0.20$), whereas above the 60th percentile, the effect sizes are well within the medium range (that is, $|d| \geq 0.50$). Although it is not shown, the incarceration coefficients frequently differ at the 10 percent significance level from the arrest coefficients, indicating that carceral contacts have additive effects on

---

13. The interpretation of coefficients as proportional differences is a convenient approximation, but the approximation is overestimated when coefficients are larger than ±0.10. Instead, the transformation $e^b - 1$ yields the technically correct proportional difference in the hourly wage at a given marginal quantile.

14. At the urging of an anonymous reviewer, in a sensitivity analysis we restricted the analytic sample to respondents from households with at least one same-sex sibling. Despite the fact that this reduced the sample from 4,035 to 2,296, all results were replicated, and in fact, the coefficients tended to be larger in magnitude.

Table 1. Select Quantile Regression Estimates of the Difference in Hourly Wage

Percentile	Quantile Wage	Ever Arrested Coeff. (SE)	Ever Incarcerated Coeff. (SE)	Quantile Wage	Ever Arrested Coeff. (SE)	Ever Incarcerated Coeff. (SE)
	(A) All Respondents (N = 3,249)			(B) White Respondents (N = 1,696)		
10th	$8.25	-0.04 (0.05)	-0.15 (0.09)+	$8.41	-0.08 (0.09)	0.01 (0.17)
25th	$10.81	-0.02 (0.05)	-0.10 (0.08)	$11.73	-0.12 (0.09)	0.00 (0.13)
50th	$15.75	-0.08 (0.04)+	-0.20 (0.07)**	$17.98	0.01 (0.07)	-0.08 (0.12)
75th	$23.61	-0.07 (0.05)	-0.19 (0.08)*	$26.74	0.10 (0.08)	-0.02 (0.10)
90th	$35.44	0.05 (0.08)	-0.08 (0.10)	$40.25	0.13 (0.10)	-0.08 (0.12)
Linear (fixed)	—	-0.02 (0.04)	-0.18 (0.08)*	—	0.02 (0.06)	-0.06 (0.09)
	(C) Latino Respondents (N = 768)			(D) Black Respondents (N = 785)		
10th	$9.18	0.11 (0.11)	0.03 (0.17)	$7.74	-0.08 (0.09)	-0.23 (0.15)
25th	$11.60	0.01 (0.10)	-0.02 (0.15)	$9.43	-0.01 (0.09)	-0.33 (0.13)**
50th	$16.00	-0.05 (0.10)	-0.08 (0.13)	$12.50	0.04 (0.08)	-0.22 (0.12)+
75th	$22.64	-0.19 (0.14)	-0.14 (0.18)	$17.66	-0.10 (0.10)	-0.34 (0.15)*
90th	$31.65	-0.35 (0.21)	-0.11 (0.24)	$26.17	-0.24 (0.14)+	-0.54 (0.23)*
Linear (fixed)	—	-0.00 (0.12)	0.00 (0.22)	—	-0.15 (0.08)+	-0.52 (0.13)***

Source: Authors' estimates from respondents' last available round of the National Longitudinal Survey of Youth 1997, rounds 1-17 (Bureau of Labor Statistics 2015).

Note: Estimates are unweighted. The coefficients derive from (unconditional) quantile regression models of log hourly wage with sibling fixed effects. The coefficients for control variables are not shown. Cluster-robust standard errors are reported, and are obtained from the bootstrap with 250 replications. For comparative purposes, coefficients from linear regression models (of the mean) with sibling fixed effects are also shown.

+$p < .10$; *$p < .05$; **$p < .01$; ***$p < .001$ (two-tailed tests)

Figure 2. Full Quantile Regression Estimates of the Relationship Between Arrest and Hourly Wage

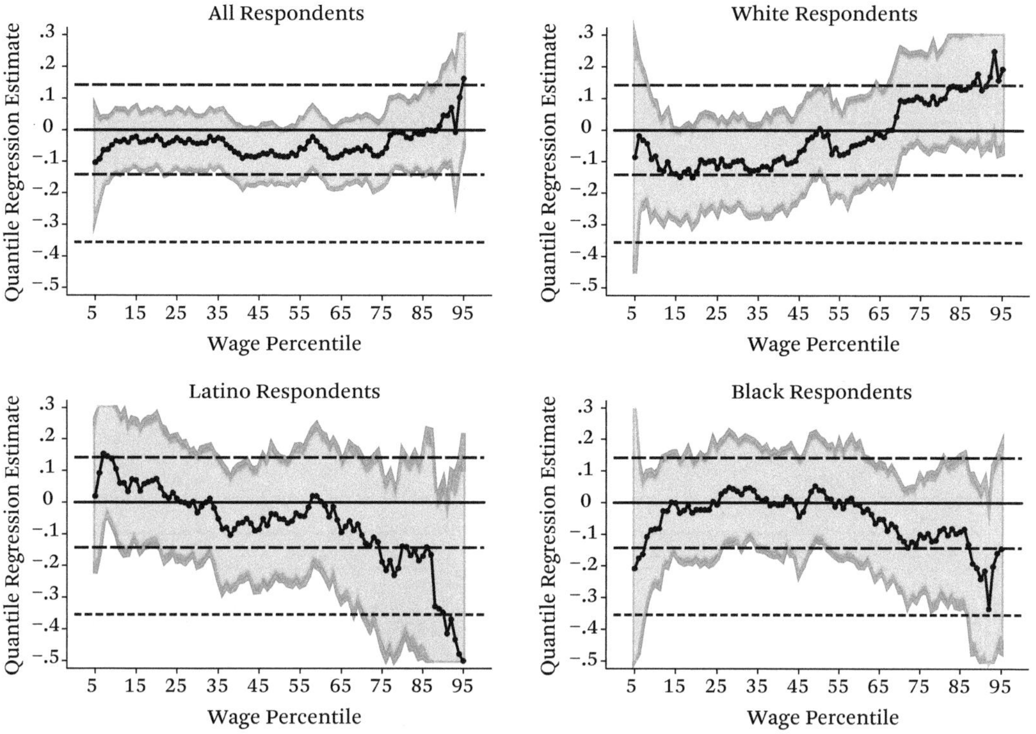

Source: Authors' estimates from respondents' last available round of the National Longitudinal Survey of Youth 1997, rounds 1–17 (Bureau of Labor Statistics 2015).
Note: Estimates are unweighted. The coefficients derive from unconditional quantile regression models of log hourly wage with sibling fixed effects, with cluster-robust standard errors obtained from the bootstrap with 250 replications. The confidence intervals are 90 percent (light gray) and 95 percent (dark gray). For graphing purposes, the coefficients and confidence intervals are censored at +0.3 and −0.5. The solid horizontal line is drawn at zero to judge statistical significance, whereas the dashed horizontal lines are drawn to judge substantive significance. Specifically, the long-dashed lines mark a small effect size (|d| = 0.20), and the short-dashed line marks a medium effect size (|d| = 0.50).

black wages, over and above noncarceral contacts.

Interestingly, the relationship between incarceration and wages is strong and consistent enough among the black respondents that it is observable in the pooled sample. As can be seen in figure 3 (top left panel), above the 40th percentile, many of the quantile regression coefficients are both significant and sizable, as indicated by an abundance of small effect sizes (that is, |d| ≥ 0.20). Indeed, 41 percent of the incarceration coefficients are statistically significant using a .05 criterion (and 58 percent are significant using a .10 criterion). These are apparently driven by the incarceration experiences of the one-quarter of the sample who is black, because when black respondents are removed from the pooled sample, there is just a single significant incarceration coefficient.

Figure 4 graphs the wage gap in dollar metric rather than proportional metric for justice-involved black respondents and their similar-age siblings with no criminal justice contact. At each wage percentile, the estimate averages over the difference in exponentiated marginal predictions derived from the quantile regression models. Given the nonsignificance of arrest, we focus our attention on incarceration. Below the 40th percentile—which is $11.85 per

Figure 3. Full Quantile Regression Estimates of the Relationship Between Incarceration and Hourly Wage

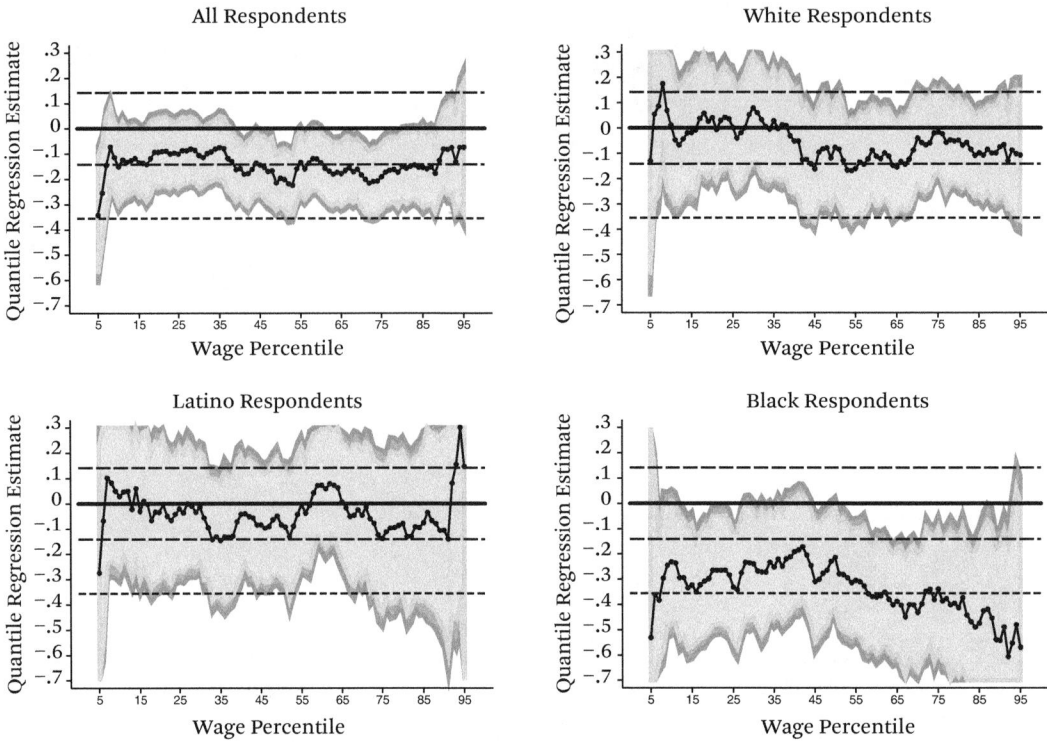

Source: Authors' estimates from respondents' last available round of the National Longitudinal Survey of Youth 1997, rounds 1–17 (Bureau of Labor Statistics 2015).
Note: Estimates are unweighted. The coefficients derive from unconditional quantile regression models of log hourly wage with sibling fixed effects, with cluster-robust standard errors obtained from the bootstrap with 250 replications. The confidence intervals are 90 percent (light gray) and 95 percent (dark gray). For graphing purposes, the coefficients and confidence intervals are censored at +0.3 and −0.7. The solid horizontal line is drawn at zero to judge statistical significance, whereas the dashed horizontal lines are drawn to judge substantive significance. Specifically, the long-dashed lines mark a small effect size ($|d| = 0.20$), and the short-dashed line marks a medium effect size ($|d| = 0.50$).

hour among the baseline, no-contact black respondents—the wage penalty for formerly incarcerated blacks is a roughly constant $2.40. When considered in percentage terms, this implies that the wage gap narrows as the baseline hourly wage grows. Above the 40th percentile, on the other hand, the wage penalty grows in both an absolute and relative sense as the baseline wage grows. In percentage terms, then, the size of the wage penalty is roughly U-shaped when evaluated across the full wage distribution of black respondents.

Supplemental Measures of Criminal Justice Contact

In the appendix, we substitute the binary indicators of criminal justice contact with continuous measures. Table A2 provides quantile regression estimates including arrest frequency and the total time spent incarcerated in jail or prison. (The coefficients and standard errors are multiplied by ten to eliminate zeros.) There is some indication that arrest accumulation culminates in a wage penalty among white respondents at the 50th percentile and lower. For ex-

Figure 4. Implied Relationship Between Criminal Justice Contact and Hourly Wage in 2016 Dollars, Black Respondents

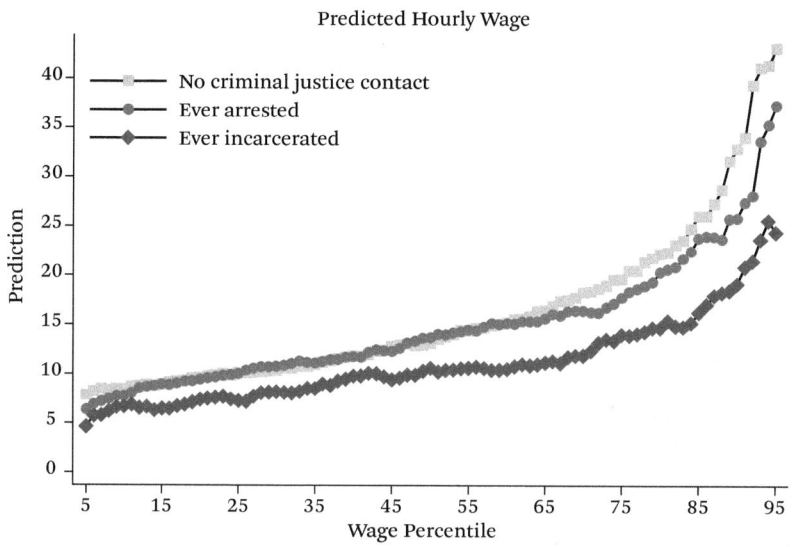

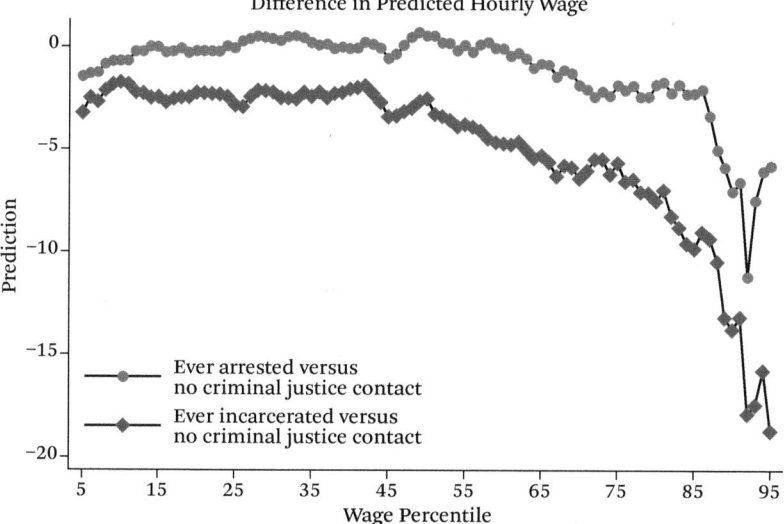

Source: Authors' estimates from respondents' last available round of the National Longitudinal Survey of Youth 1997, rounds 1–17 (Bureau of Labor Statistics 2015).
Note: Estimates are unweighted. The coefficients derive from unconditional quantile regression models of log hourly wage with sibling fixed effects, and average over the difference in exponentiated marginal predictions.

ample, at the 25th percentile, the hourly wage of whites with ten arrests is 21 percent lower ($e^{-0.23} - 1 = -0.21$) than their similar-age siblings with no arrest record. There is also evidence that accumulation of time spent behind bars further corrodes the wages of black respondents beyond the stage effects observed in table 1.

Table A3 provides quantile regression estimates including the number of years elapsed since the first arrest and first incarceration spell. For black respondents, the results indicate that the size of the wage gap grows over time, but the same is not true for other racial/ethnic groups or other forms of criminal justice contact. For example, at the 50th percentile, the hourly wage is estimated to be 12 percent lower ($e^{-0.13} - 1 = -0.12$) if a black respondent was first incarcerated five years earlier, but 24 percent lower ($e^{-0.27} - 1 = -0.24$) if the first incarceration spell was ten years earlier, and 33 percent lower ($e^{-0.40} - 1 = -0.33$) if it was fifteen years earlier.

In a final set of models, we substitute binary indicators for having been charged or convicted with a crime for having been arrested for a crime.[15] In the quantile regression models with charging and incarceration, the only difference from what is reported above concerns white respondents, for whom wages are significantly lower at the 10th percentile ($p < .05$) and 25th percentile ($p < .10$) among those who have been charged compared to their similar-age siblings who have never been charged.[16] The results for Latinos and blacks are otherwise unchanged. In the quantile regression models with conviction and incarceration, the only difference is Latino wages are significantly lower at the 50th percentile ($p < .10$) and 90th percentile ($p < .05$) following conviction. The results for whites and blacks are otherwise unchanged.

DISCUSSION

Whether criminal justice contact is correlated with early adult wages depends to a great extent on a respondent's race-ethnicity and the level of contact. Interestingly, arrest is largely uncorrelated with wages in our analysis. For example, of 91 quantile regression coefficients for arrest, none is statistically significant for whites, and just one is significant for Latinos and blacks (using a 0.05 criterion). There are thus far fewer significant results than what we would expect by chance, even conditional on there being no true relationship between arrest and wages. One possible exception is arrest frequency among white respondents at the 50th percentile and below, for whom there is a weak indication that arrest has incremental effects stemming from the accumulation of repeated contacts. Another exception relates to having been charged (in place of arrest), which is correlated with wage erosion among whites at the 25th percentile and below. In any case, the impact of any single arrest is so small as to be negligible, but repeated arrests and post-arrest criminal justice processing do correspond with a wage gap among low- to middle-wage whites.

Highly consistent evidence of a relationship between criminal justice contact and early adult wages stems from incarceration among black respondents. For whites and Latinos, no empirical evidence supports a wage penalty following carceral contact; the coefficients are both statistically and substantively null. On the contrary, formerly incarcerated blacks earn significantly lower wages than their similar-age siblings with no history of criminal justice contact (and even their similar-age siblings who have an arrest record), and the coefficients are noteworthy in that they are not trivial in magnitude. Across the black wage distribution, the estimates indicate a U-shaped wage penalty, with an inflection point at about the 40th percentile where the wage penalty is smallest in percentage terms. All evaluation points, however, show a corrosive correlation between incarceration and black wages.

The evidence therefore supports the conclusion that the relationship between criminal justice contact and early adult wages is heterogeneous. Namely, the wage gap is more or less limited to incarceration among black respondents, and, with the noted exceptions, there is no wage gap following arrest for blacks, nor a discernible wage gap following any form of criminal justice contact for whites and Latinos. Furthermore, the size of the black wage gap varies along the wage distribution; in percentage terms, it averages roughly 26 percent in the middle half of the wage distribution and 38 per-

---

15. Note that 80 percent of NLSY97 respondents who have ever been arrested reporting having been charged, and 60 percent have been convicted.

16. David Kirk's study of self-report versus official arrest indicates a tendency of some youth (whites in particular) to overreport arrest, suggesting that self-report charges might be more valid as a measure of arrest for this group (2006).

cent in the lower and upper quartiles. The strength and salience of the relationship between incarceration and black wages is further evident from the fact that an incarceration-wage relationship is detectable in a model that pools together whites, Latinos, and blacks—the wage gap in this model is driven by the roughly 3.5 percent of the NLSY97 sample who are formerly incarcerated black respondents.

Our results both harmonize and conflict with prior studies. For example, our conclusions differ from those of Matsueda and his colleagues and Needels, both of whom observe no relationship between incarceration and earnings among mostly black reentry program participants (Matsueda et al. 1992; Needels 1996). They also differ from those of Anke Ramakers and colleagues and Rasmus Landersø, who find no relationship between incarceration (length) and wages or earnings among recently incarcerated individuals in the Netherlands and Denmark (Ramakers et al. 2014; Landersø 2015). On the other hand, our conclusions are in line with the findings of Waldfogel and Grogger, who identify effects of incarceration on administrative earnings (Waldfogel 1994a, 1994b; Grogger 1995); with Grogger's finding that arrest is uncorrelated with long-term (beyond one year) earnings (1995); and with Signe Andersen's finding of long-term income erosion following incarceration (versus community service) among punished individuals in Denmark (2015). The findings align also with those of numerous other studies that estimate self-report wage gaps of varying size in panel data from the NLSY79, Fragile Families, and the NLSY97 (Fagan and Freeman 1999; Western 2002; Geller, Garfinkel, and Western 2006; Raphael 2007; Apel and Sweeten 2010; Jung 2015). However, that incarceration is correlated only with wages for black respondents in our study but not for whites or Latinos conflicts with Western's finding of uniform wage erosion across demographic groups (2002).

Provisional follow-up analyses, which are not shown, indicate that the wage penalty experienced by formerly incarcerated blacks likely stems from a combination of supply-side and demand-side mechanisms. First, we find that formerly incarcerated blacks work fewer weeks than their similar-age siblings with no criminal justice contact, and this is due to their longer duration of labor force nonparticipation rather than to unemployment (see also Apel and Sweeten 2010). Second, we find that formerly incarcerated black workers are employed in less prestigious occupations than their no-contact siblings, consistent with the race-coded job channeling noted by Pager, Western, and Bart Bonikowski (2009a). It thus seems likely that black wage inequality due to incarceration is attributable to a combination of work detachment and low work quality.

By way of limitations, the estimates reported in this study are the long-term effects of criminal justice contact. The typical first arrest occurred almost thirteen years prior to the last available interview, and the typical first incarceration spell was experienced almost nine years prior. Short-term effects that cannot be observed by virtue of our study design are therefore possible. Additionally, because our data are cross-sectional (the last available interview), high collinearity makes it impossible to simultaneously include all available measures of criminal justice contact. It will thus be important to build on this study using panel methods that are capable of exploiting the timing of first contact with different stages of the criminal justice system. Facets of work experience other than hourly wages might also undergo corrosion following criminal justice contact, especially for the whites and Latinos in our study for whom no correlations are consistent. Finally, undoubtedly other sources of confounding than strictly household-based confounding (which can be eliminated using sibling fixed effects) are possible. Criminal offending is an obvious candidate, but it is regrettably measured inconsistently and from poorly defined subsamples over time in the NLSY97. However, when we control for a measure of the total frequency of self-report crime from the first interview (a measure available for the full sample and temporally prior to criminal justice contact), the findings are unchanged.

To bring this study to a close, our findings provide confirmation of "double jeopardy" and "compound disadvantage" of being both black and formerly incarcerated in the labor market (Pager 2005, 2007; Lyons and Pettit 2011). In our data, this is evident from the fact that, at any given percentile, the wages of black respondents are lower than their white counterparts, and black wages carry a penalty from incarceration that white wages do not. There is thus substantial between-race inequality in wages, worsened by within-race inequality that follows incarceration among black respondents but not their non-black counterparts.

Where we believe our results make a new empirical contribution to punishment and inequality scholarship is our finding that black wages following incarceration are lower no matter the point in the wage distribution. Research tends to focus on the marginalization of blacks already in a socially precarious position, for example, those applying for entry-level and low-wage jobs (Pager 2003), those whose school dropout and persistent joblessness are concealed by mass incarceration and thus from national indicators of economic health and racial well-being (Pettit 2012; Western and Beckett 1999), or those who subsist in a racialized caste system reminiscent of the ghetto (Wacquant 2000). Although our findings do not repudiate these concerns, they do suggest that incarceration is a salient barrier to wage mobility for a much larger swath of the black population than is apparent in punishment and inequality discourse.

APPENDIX

In a standard regression model with sibling fixed effects, the basic parameterization would be as follows:

$$Y_{il} = \alpha + \sum_{j=1}^{K} \beta_j X_{ilj} + \delta_1 Arrest_{il} + \delta_2 Incarceration_{il} + u_l + e_{il}, \quad (1)$$

where $i = 1, \ldots, N$ indexes individuals, $l = 1, \ldots, M$ indexes households, and $j = 1, \ldots, K$ indexes control variables. The model assumes that u_l is fixed rather than random, giving rise to the sibling fixed-effects model. The way criminal justice contact is measured, a respondent who has ever been incarcerated has also, by definition, been arrested. The coefficient for incarceration in this regression model thus represents the additive influence of jail or prison confinement on hourly wages, over and above arrest. Summing the arrest and incarceration coefficients yields the relationship between hourly wages and total criminal justice contacts from arrest to incarceration. Specifically, the two quantities of interest are formed as follows:

$$\vec{\delta}_r = \begin{cases} \delta_1 & \text{if Arrested} \\ \delta_1 + \delta_2 & \text{if Incarcerated} \end{cases}. \quad (2)$$

For the resulting coefficients and standard errors, the reference group comprises respondents who have never experienced criminal justice contact.

Quantile regression expands on this approach by probing the distributional effects of criminal justice contact on early adult wages. The unconditional quantile regression model with sibling fixed effects is estimated using the method of Firpo and his colleagues (Firpo, Fortin, and Lemieux 2009; Firpo 2007; for software details, see Borgen 2016). The appeal of this model is the ability to estimate the impact of regressors on the unconditional or marginal quantile of the outcome, as opposed to the conditional quantile as is typical in quantile regression models (Koenker 2005; Koenker and Bassett 1978).[17] This is accomplished via calculation of a recentered influence function (RIF) as a first step:

$$RIF(Y_i; q_\tau, F_Y) = q_\tau + \frac{\tau - 1\{Y_i \leq q_\tau\}}{f_Y(q_\tau)}, \quad (3)$$

---

17. In a standard (conditional) quantile regression model with some form of criminal justice contact as the key regressor, for example, the model estimates would reflect whether respondents with criminal justice contact have a higher or lower wage than what would be expected given their characteristics on the control variables. The control variables influence where in the wage distribution respondents fall, however, so the estimate of criminal justice contact is identified within groups of individuals sharing the same profile on all of the covariates except criminal justice contact. In the unconditional quantile regression model, on the other hand, it is possible to examine how the relationship between criminal justice contact and wages (net of their joint association with the control variables) varies across the outcome distribution. This is because the quantiles are defined with respect to the unconditional distribution rather than the conditional distribution and thus the control variables (for a good description of the distinction, see Killewald and Bearak 2014).

where q_τ is the value of the outcome at quantile τ, $f_Y(q_\tau)$ is the density of the outcome at quantile τ, and $1\{Y_i \leq q_\tau\}$ is a dummy indicator for whether the outcome for individual i is at or below q_τ. Note that the density can be estimated using any suitable kernel weighting function, and in this analysis we choose the Epanechnikov kernel with a bandwidth or half-smoothing window equal to one-quarter of a standard deviation of the outcome trimmed at the 1st and 99th percentiles. For each respondent, at each quantile, the RIF takes on one of two values, resembling a regime switch:

$$RIF(Y_i; q_\tau, F_Y) = \begin{cases} q_\tau - \dfrac{1-\tau}{f_Y(q_\tau)} & \text{if } Y_i \leq q_\tau \\ q_\tau + \dfrac{\tau}{f_Y(q_\tau)} & \text{if } Y_i > q_\tau \end{cases}.$$

At the second step, the estimated RIF is treated as the dependent variable in a cross-sectional, linear regression model that includes sibling fixed effects along with the regressors:

$$\widehat{RIF}(Y_{il}; q_\tau, F_Y) = \alpha + \sum_{j=1}^{K} \beta_j X_{ilj} + \delta_1 Arrest_{il} \quad (4)$$
$$+ \delta_2 Incarceration_{il} + u_l + e_{il},$$

where the terms are all defined as in (1). We also perform the same summing procedure defined in (2) to obtain the two quantities of interest.

As Firpo and his colleagues define it, a coefficient in this model "corresponds to the marginal effect on the unconditional quantile of a small location shift in the distribution of covariates, holding everything else constant" (2009, 954). In the case where the regressor of interest is a dummy variable, as is true for criminal justice contact, the coefficient represents the impact of a change in the probability of experiencing a particular stage of criminal justice contact. Note that we estimate the RIF regression for all percentiles ranging from the 5th to the 95th and obtain cluster-bootstrapped standard errors with 250 replications.

Effect-Size Calculation

As a supplement to standard tests of statistical significance, we devote attention to the substantive significance of results with the use of effect-size calculations. The effect size of choice, Cohen's d, is the standardized difference between means estimated from two independent groups (Cohen 1988). It takes the following elementary form:

$$d = \frac{|\bar{Y}_T - \bar{Y}_C|}{\sqrt{\left[s_{Y_T}^2(N_T - 1) + s_{Y_C}^2(N_C - 1)\right]/(N_T + N_C - 2)}}.$$

Here, T references a treatment or intervention group and C references a comparison or non-intervention group, and the denominator is the pooled variance. This formula is adapted in three ways for the current study. First, the treatment and comparison groups referenced in the formula are defined, respectively, by whether a given stage of criminal justice contact has ever been reached or not. Second, the numerator is replaced by a regression coefficient from the quantile regression model, which yields an adjusted difference in the hourly wage at a given quantile. Third, the denominator is replaced by the pooled variance of the hourly wage at the last interview, from groups defined by the cumulative stage of criminal justice contact.

These modifications give rise to the following effect-size formula:

$$d_r = \frac{|\hat{\delta}_r|}{\sqrt{\left[s_{Y_T}^2(N_T - 1) + s_{Y_C}^2(N_C - 1)\right]/(N_T + N_C - 2)}}, \quad (5)$$

where the numerator is the coefficient for either arrest or incarceration, as defined in (2). Cohen's d is bound by $[0, \infty)$ and is routinely judged against thresholds of 0.20 (small), 0.50 (medium), and 0.80 (large) with respect to substantive significance (Cohen 1988). An effect size smaller than 0.20 is generally regarded as not worth mentioning, even if the coefficient is statistically significant.

Figure A1. Cumulative Distribution of Hourly Wage, by Criminal Justice Contact and Race/Ethnicity

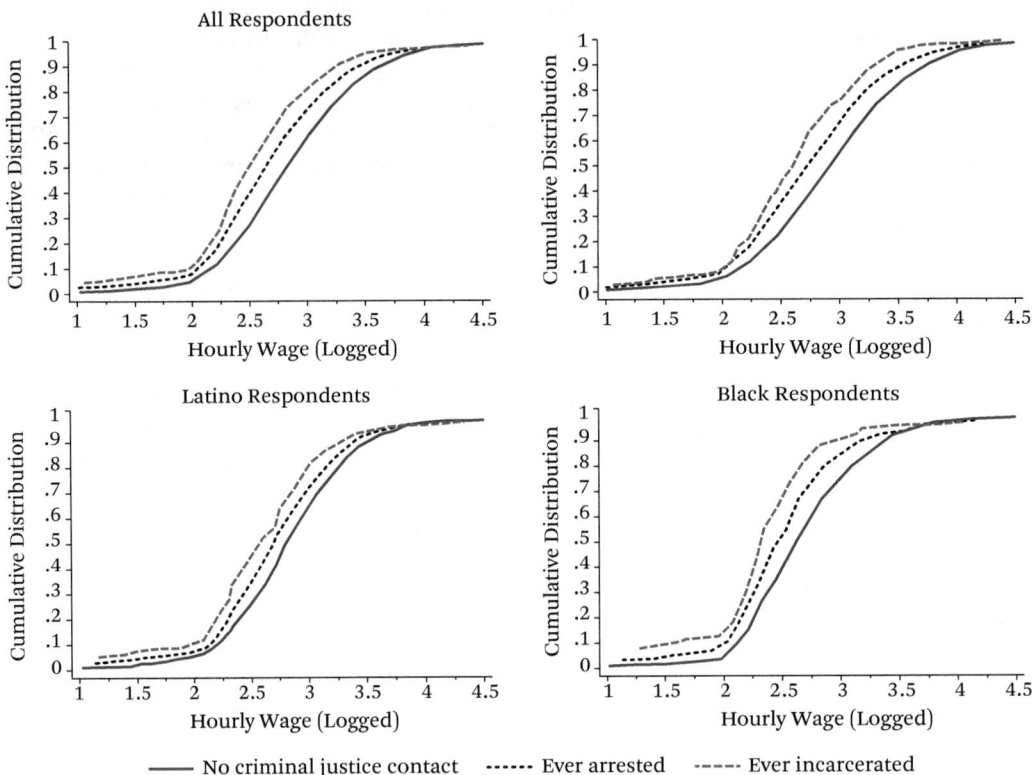

Source: Authors' estimates from respondents' last available round of the National Longitudinal Survey of Youth 1997, rounds 1–17 (Bureau of Labor Statistics 2015).
Note: Estimates are unweighted. The distributions derive from the full sample, not the sibling subsample. The criminal justice contact groups are not mutually exclusive.

Table A1. Descriptive Statistics

Variables	All Respondents Mean (SD)	White Respondents Mean (SD)	Latino Respondents Mean (SD)	Black Respondents Mean (SD)
Nonzero wage	87.7%	89.5%	88.0%	83.8%
Hourly wage[a,b]	19.2 (12.9)	21.1 (14.2)	18.4 (11.1)	15.7 (10.3)
Criminal justice contact				
Ever arrested	35.0%	31.8%	35.3%	41.3%
Ever incarcerated	9.8%	7.9%	10.0%	13.3%
Ever jailed	7.5%	6.6%	8.3%	8.7%
Ever imprisoned	4.6%	3.0%	4.3%	8.0%
Total number of arrests[a]	3.8 (5.2)	3.5 (4.5)	3.9 (5.2)	4.2 (6.1)
Total months incarcerated[a]	12.9 (21.4)	10.2 (18.6)	11.4 (23.4)	17.2 (22.7)
Total months jailed[a]	5.9 (11.5)	5.1 (12.8)	5.2 (7.7)	7.8 (11.6)
Total months imprisoned[a]	17.9 (24.8)	15.7 (20.3)	16.5 (32.3)	20.2 (24.2)
Years since first arrest	12.8 (5.0)	12.9 (5.0)	12.6 (5.2)	12.8 (5.0)
Years since first incarceration	8.8 (4.9)	8.6 (5.0)	8.8 (4.8)	9.0 (4.7)
Control variables				
Male	51.2%	51.7%	51.4%	50.1%
Age	31.9 (4.0)	31.6 (4.3)	32.1 (3.7)	32.4 (3.5)
Marital status				
Never married	51.0%	43.2%	49.7%	68.0%
Currently married	39.7%	47.1%	40.0%	24.3%
Separated or divorced	9.3%	9.7%	10.3%	7.7%
Currently cohabiting	17.4%	17.0%	20.0%	15.9%
Biological children	1.3 (1.4)	1.1 (1.3)	1.5 (1.4)	1.6 (1.6)
Dwelling type				
House or farm	68.8%	74.1%	69.5%	57.6%
Apartment or condo	23.2%	17.9%	25.0%	32.3%
Other dwelling	8.0%	8.0%	5.5%	10.1%
Urbanicity				
MSA central city	40.6%	33.4%	45.2%	51.5%
MSA suburb	53.4%	59.1%	50.3%	44.0%
Outside of MSA	6.1%	7.5%	4.5%	4.5%
Census region				
Northeast	16.2%	18.4%	13.4%	14.0%
Midwest	20.8%	27.6%	9.0%	16.5%
South	40.1%	32.5%	31.6%	62.0%
West	23.0%	21.5%	46.0%	7.5%
Ever incarcerated as juvenile	2.5%	1.7%	3.3%	3.4%
N (full sample)	8,984	4,748	1,901	2,335
N (sibling subsample)	4,035	2,043	947	1,045

Source: Authors' estimates from respondents' last available round of the National Longitudinal Survey of Youth 1997, rounds 1–17 (Bureau of Labor Statistics 2015).
Note: Descriptive statistics are unweighted and are based on the full sample, not the sibling subsample. The means of dummy variables are shown as percentages. Hourly wages are in 2016 dollars and, for descriptive purposes, are trimmed at the 99th percentile.
[a] Descriptive estimate is limited to respondents with nonzero values.
[b] Variable is shown here untransformed, but is logged in the regression models.

Table A2. Sensitivity of Select Quantile Regression Estimates to Alternative Measures of Criminal Justice Contact

	Total Arrest Frequency (÷ 10) Coeff. (SE)	Total Incarceration Months (÷ 10) Coeff. (SE)	Total Arrest Frequency (÷ 10) Coeff. (SE)	Total Incarceration Months (÷ 10) Coeff. (SE)
Percentile	(A) All Respondents		(A) White Respondents	
10th	−0.13 (0.08)	−0.06 (0.04)+	−0.29 (0.15)+	0.01 (0.07)
25th	−0.07 (0.08)	−0.04 (0.04)	−0.23 (0.11)*	0.06 (0.06)
50th	−0.16 (0.08)*	−0.02 (0.04)	−0.20 (0.10)+	0.07 (0.08)
75th	−0.15 (0.08)+	−0.02 (0.02)	−0.02 (0.11)	0.01 (0.04)
90th	0.03 (0.14)	−0.03 (0.03)	−0.05 (0.18)	0.01 (0.06)
Linear (fixed)	−0.06 (0.11)	−0.07 (0.04)+	−0.25 (0.09)**	0.04 (0.02)*
	(C) Latino Respondents		(D) Black Respondents	
10th	0.27 (0.20)	−0.14 (0.09)	−0.01 (0.11)	−0.01 (0.01)
25th	0.00 (0.16)	−0.06 (0.07)	−0.03 (0.13)	−0.10 (0.06)+
50th	−0.03 (0.15)	0.02 (0.06)	0.01 (0.17)	−0.10 (0.06)+
75th	−0.03 (0.21)	0.00 (0.06)	−0.03 (0.14)	−0.10 (0.05)*
90th	0.14 (0.31)	0.02 (0.10)	−0.27 (0.19)	−0.07 (0.08)
Linear (fixed)	0.31 (0.34)	−0.07 (0.05)	−0.08 (0.11)	−0.17 (0.06)**

Source: Authors' estimates from respondents' last available round of the National Longitudinal Survey of Youth 1997, rounds 1–17 (Bureau of Labor Statistics 2015).
Note: Estimates are unweighted. The coefficients derive from (unconditional) quantile regression models of log hourly wage with sibling fixed effects. The coefficients for control variables are not shown. Cluster-robust standard errors are reported, and are obtained from the bootstrap with 250 replications. For comparative purposes, coefficients from linear regression models (of the mean) with sibling fixed effects are also shown.
+$p < .10$; *$p < .05$; **$p < .01$; ***$p < .001$ (two-tailed tests)

REFERENCES

Agan, Amanda, and Sonja Starr. 2018. "Ban the Box, Criminal Records, and Racial Discrimination: A Field Experiment." *Quarterly Journal of Economics* 133(1): 191–235.

Apel, Robert, and Anke Ramakers. Forthcoming. "Impact of Incarceration on Employment Prospects." In *Handbook on Corrections and Sentencing*, Vol. 3. *The Consequences of Sentencing and Punishment Decisions*, edited by Beth Huebner and Natasha Frost. New York: Routledge.

Apel, Robert, and Gary Sweeten. 2010. "The Impact of Incarceration on Employment During the Transition to Adulthood." *Social Problems* 57(3): 448–79.

Andersen, Signe Hald. 2015. "Serving Time or Serving the Community? Exploiting a Policy Reform to Assess the Causal Effects of Community Service on Income, Social Benefit Dependency and Recidivism." *Journal of Quantitative Criminology* 31(4): 537–63.

Bernburg, Jön Gunnar, and Marvin D. Krohn. 2003. "Labeling, Life Chances, and Adult Crime: The Direct and Indirect Effects of Official Intervention in Adolescence on Crime in Early Adulthood." *Criminology* 41(4): 1287–318.

Borgen, Nicolai T. 2016. "Fixed Effects in Unconditional Quantile Regression." *Stata Journal* 16(2): 403–15.

Bound, John, and Richard B. Freeman. 1992. "What Went Wrong? The Erosion of Relative Earnings and Employment Among Young Black Men in the 1980s." *Quarterly Journal of Economics* 107(1): 201–32.

Brame, Robert, Shawn Bushway, Raymond Paternoster, and Michael G. Turner. 2014. "Demographic Patterns of Cumulative Arrest Prevalence by Ages 18 and 23." *Crime and Deliquency* 60(3): 471–86.

Table A3. Sensitivity of Select Quantile Regression Estimates to Alternative Measures of Criminal Justice Contact

Percentile	Years Since First Arrest Coeff. (SE)	Years Since First Incarceration Coeff. (SE)	Years Since First Arrest Coeff. (SE)	Years Since First Incarceration Coeff. (SE)
	(A) All Respondents		(B) White Respondents	
10th	−0.00 (0.00)	−0.01 (0.01)	−0.01 (0.01)	0.01 (0.02)
25th	−0.00 (0.00)	−0.00 (0.01)	−0.01 (0.00)+	0.01 (0.01)
50th	−0.00 (0.00)	−0.01 (0.01)	0.00 (0.01)	−0.00 (0.01)
75th	−0.00 (0.00)	−0.01 (0.01)	0.00 (0.01)	−0.00 (0.01)
90th	−0.00 (0.01)	−0.00 (0.01)	0.00 (0.01)	−0.01 (0.01)
Linear (fixed)	−0.00 (0.00)	−0.01 (0.01)+	−0.00 (0.00)	0.00 (0.01)
	(C) Latino Respondents		(D) Black Respondents	
10th	0.01 (0.01)	−0.01 (0.02)	−0.01 (0.01)	−0.02 (0.01)
25th	−0.00 (0.01)	−0.00 (0.01)	−0.00 (0.01)	−0.03 (0.01)*
50th	0.00 (0.01)	−0.01 (0.01)	0.01 (0.01)	−0.03 (0.01)**
75th	−0.01 (0.01)	0.01 (0.02)	−0.00 (0.01)	−0.02 (0.01)*
90th	−0.01 (0.01)	0.02 (0.02)	−0.01 (0.01)	−0.03 (0.02)
Linear (fixed)	0.01 (0.01)	−0.01 (0.02)	−0.01 (0.01)	−0.04 (0.01)***

Source: Authors' estimates from respondents' last available round of the National Longitudinal Survey of Youth 1997, rounds 1–17 (Bureau of Labor Statistics 2015).
Note: Estimates are unweighted. The coefficients derive from (unconditional) quantile regression models of log hourly wage with sibling fixed effects. The coefficients for control variables are not shown. Cluster-robust standard errors are reported, and are obtained from the bootstrap with 250 replications. For comparative purposes, coefficients from linear regression models (of the mean) with sibling fixed effects are also shown.
+$p < .10$; *$p < .05$; **$p < .01$; ***$p < .001$ (two-tailed tests)

Brame, Robert, Michael G. Turner, Raymond Paternoster, and Shawn D. Bushway. 2012. "Cumulative Prevalence of Arrest from Ages 18 to 23 in a National Sample." *Pediatrics* 129(1): 21–27.

Bureau of Labor Statistics, Department of Labor. 2015. *National Longitudinal Survey of Youth 1997 Cohort, 1997–2015 (Rounds 1–17)*. Columbus, Ohio: Center for Human Resource Research, Ohio State University.

Center for Human Resource Research. 2002. *NLSY97 User's Guide*. Columbus, Ohio: Center for Human Resource Research, Ohio State University.

Cohen, Jacob. 1988. *Statistical Power Analysis for the Behavioral Sciences*, 2nd ed. Hillsdale, N.J.: Lawrence Erlbaum.

Decker, Scott H., Natalie Ortiz, Cassia Spohn, and Eric Hedberg. 2015. "Criminal Stigma, Race, and Ethnicity: The Consequences of Imprisonment for Employment." *Journal of Criminal Justice* 43(2): 108–21.

Dennison, Christopher R., and Stephen Demuth. 2018. "The More You Have, The More You Lose: Criminal Justice Involvement, Ascribed Socioeconomic Status, and Achieved SES." *Social Problems* 65(2): 191–210.

Elwert, Felix, and Christopher Winship. 2014. "Endogenous Selection Bias: The Problem of Conditioning." *Annual Review of Sociology* 40: 31–53.

Fagan, Jeffrey, and Richard B. Freeman. 1999. "Crime and Work." In *Crime and Justice: A Review of Research*, vol. 25, edited by Michael Tonry. Chicago: University of Chicago Press.

Firpo, Sergio. 2007. "Efficient Semiparametric Estimation of Quantile Treatment Effects." *Econometrica* 75(1): 259–76.

Firpo, Sergio, Nicole M. Fortin, and Thomas Lemieux. 2009. "Unconditional Quantile Regressions." *Econometrica* 77(3): 953–73.

Galgano, Sarah W. 2009. "Barriers to Reintegration: An Audit Study of the Impact of Race and Offender Status on Employment Opportunities for Women." *Social Thought and Research* 30(1): 21–37.

Garland, David. 2001a. *The Culture of Control: Crime and Social Order in Contemporary Society*. Chicago: University of Chicago Press.

———, ed. 2001b. *Mass Imprisonment: Social Causes and Consequences*. Thousand Oaks, Calif.: Sage.

Geller, Amanda, Irwin Garfinkel, and Bruce Western. 2006. "The Effects of Incarceration on Employment and Wages: An Analysis of the Fragile Families Survey." Working Paper No. 2006-01-FF. Princeton, N.J.: Princeton University.

Gelman, Andrew, Jeffrey Fagan, and Alex Kiss. 2007. "An Analysis of the New York City Police Department's 'Stop-and-Frisk' Policy in the Context of Claims of Racial Bias." *Journal of the American Statistical Association* 102(479): 813–23.

Grogger, Jeffrey. 1995. "The Effect of Arrests on the Employment and Earnings of Young Men." *Quarterly Journal of Economics* 110(1): 51–71.

Harlow, Caroline Wolf. 2003. "Education and Correctional Populations." NCJ 195670. Washington: Bureau of Justice Statistics.

Hirschfield, Paul. 2009. "Another Way Out: The Impact of Juvenile Arrest on High School Dropout." *Sociology of Education* 82(October): 368–93.

Hjalmarsson, Randi. 2008. "Criminal Justice Involvement and High School Completion." *Journal of Urban Economics* 63(2): 613–30.

Holzer, Harry J. 1996. *What Employers Want: Job Prospects for Less-Educated Workers*. New York: Russell Sage Foundation.

Holzer, Harry J., Steven Raphael, and Michael A. Stoll. 2006. "Perceived Criminality, Criminal Background Checks, and the Racial Hiring Practices of Employers." *Journal of Law and Economics* 49(2): 451–80.

Jung, Haeil. 2011. "Increase in the Length of Incarceration and the Subsequent Labor Market Outcomes: Evidence from Men Released from Illinois State Prisons." *Journal of Policy Analysis and Management* 30(3): 499–533.

———. 2015. "The Long-Term Impact of Incarceration During the Teens and 20s on the Wages and Employment of Men." *Journal of Offender Rehabilitation* 54(5): 317–37.

Killewald, Alexandra, and Jonathan Bearak. 2014. "Is the Motherhood Penalty Larger for Low-Wage Women? A Comment on Quantile Regression." *American Sociological Review* 79(2): 350–57.

Kirk, David S. 2006. "Examining the Divergence Across Self-Report and Official Data Sources on Inferences About the Adolescent Life-Course of Crime." *Journal of Quantitative Criminology* 22(2): 107–29.

Kirk, David S., and Robert J. Sampson. 2013. "Juvenile Arrest and Collateral Educational Damage in the Transition to Adulthood." *Sociology of Education* 86(1): 36–62.

Kirk, David S., and Sara Wakefield. 2018. "Collateral Consequences of Punishment: A Critical Review and Path Forward." *Annual Review of Criminology* 1: 171–94.

Kling, Jeffrey R. 2006. "Incarceration Length, Employment, and Earnings." *American Economic Review* 96(3): 863–76.

Koenker, Roger. 2005. *Quantile Regression*. New York: Cambridge University Press.

Koenker, Roger, and Gilbert Bassett Jr. 1978. "Regression Quantiles." *Econometrica* 46(1): 33–50.

Landersø, Rasmus. 2015. "Does Incarceration Length Affect Labor Market Outcomes?" *Journal of Law and Economics* 58(1): 205–34.

Lyons, Christopher J., and Becky Pettit. 2011. "Compounded Disadvantage: Race, Incarceration, and Wage Growth." *Social Problems* 58(2): 257–80.

Matsueda, Ross L., Rosemary Gartner, Irving Piliavin, and Michael Polakowski. 1992. "The Prestige of Criminal and Conventional Occupations: A Subcultural Model of Criminal Activity." *American Sociological Review* 57(6): 752–70.

Nagin, Daniel, and Joel Waldfogel. 1995. "The Effects of Criminality and Conviction on the Labor Market Status of Young British Offenders." *International Review of Law and Economics* 15(1): 109–26.

———. 1998. "The Effect of Conviction on Income Through the Life Cycle." *International Review of Law and Economics* 18(1): 25–40.

Needels, Karen E. 1996. "Go Directly to Jail and Do Not Collect? A Long-Term Study of Recidivism, Employment, and Earnings Patterns Among Prison Releasees." *Journal of Research in Crime and Delinquency* 33(4): 471–96.

Pager, Devah. 2003. "The Mark of a Criminal Record." *American Journal of Sociology* 108(March): 937–975.

———. 2005. "Double Jeopardy: Race, Crime, and Getting a Job." *Wisconsin Law Review* 2005(2): 617–62.

———. 2007. *Marked: Race, Crime, and Finding Work in an Era of Mass Incarceration.* Chicago: University of Chicago Press.

Pager, Devah, Bruce Western, and Bart Bonikowski. 2009. "Discrimination in a Low-Wage Labor Market: A Field Experiment." *American Sociological Review* 74 (October): 777–99.

Pager, Devah, Bruce Western, and Naomi Sugie. 2009. "Sequencing Disadvantage: Barriers to Employment Facing Young Black Men and White Men with Criminal Records." *Annals of the American Academy of Political and Social Sciences* 623(1): 195–213.

Patterson, Evelyn J., and Christopher Wildeman. 2015. "Mass Imprisonment and the Life Course Revisited: Cumulative Years Spent Imprisoned and Marked for Working-Age Black and White Men." *Social Science Research* 53(September): 325–37.

Pettit, Becky. 2012. *Invisible Men: Mass Incarceration and the Myth of Black Progress*. New York: Russell Sage Foundation.

Pettit, Becky, and Christopher J. Lyons. 2009. "Incarceration and the Legitimate Labor Market: Examining Age-Graded Effects on Employment and Earnings." *Law and Society Review* 43(4): 725–56.

Pettit, Becky, and Bruce Western. 2004. "Mass Imprisonment and the Life Course: Race and Class Inequality in US Incarceration." *American Sociological Review* 69(2): 151–69.

Phelps, Michelle S. 2017. "Mass Probation: Toward a More Robust Theory of State Variation in Punishment." *Punishment and Society* 19(1): 53–73.

Ramakers, Anke, Robert Apel, Paul Nieuwbeerta, Anja Dirkzwager, and Johan van Wilsem. 2014. "Imprisonment Length and Post-Prison Employment Prospects." *Criminology* 52(3): 399–427.

Raphael, Steven. 2014. *The New Scarlet Letter? Negotiating the U.S. Labor Market with a Criminal Record*. Kalamazoo, Mich.: W. E. Upjohn Institute for Employment Research.

Sampson, Robert J. 1986. "Effects of Socioeconomic Context on Official Reactions to Juvenile Delinquency." *American Sociological Review* 51(6): 876–85.

———. 2011. "The Incarceration Ledger." *Criminology and Public Policy* 10(3): 819–28.

Sampson, Robert J., and John H. Laub. 1993. "Structural Variations in Juvenile Court Processing: Inequality, the Underclass, and Social Control." *Law and Society Review* 27(2): 285–312.

Sampson, Robert J., and Janet L. Lauritsen. 1997. "Racial and Ethnic Disparities in Crime and Criminal Justice in the United States." In *Crime and Justice: An Annual Review of Research*. Vol. 21. *Ethnicity, Crime, and Immigration: Comparative and Cross-National Perspectives*, edited by Michael Tonry. Chicago: University of Chicago Press.

Schwartz, Richard D., and Jerome H. Skolnick. 1962. "Two Studies of Legal Stigma." *Social Problems* 10(2): 133–42.

Shannon, Sarah K. S., Christopher Uggen, Jason Schnittker, Melissa Thompson, Sara Wakefield, and Michael Massoglia. 2017. "The Growth, Scope, and Spatial Distribution of People with Felony Records in the United States, 1948–2010." *Demography* 54(5): 1795–818.

Smith, Douglas A. 1986. "The Neighborhood Context of Police Behavior." In *Crime and Justice: A Review of Research. Vol. 8. Communities and Crime*, edited by Albert J. Reiss Jr. and Michael Tonry. Chicago: University of Chicago Press.

Steffensmeier, Darrell, Jeffrey Ulmer, and John Kramer. 1998. "The Interaction of Race, Gender, and Age in Criminal Sentencing: The Punishment Cost of Being Young, Black, and Male." *Criminology* 36(4): 763–97.

Stoll, Michael A. 2009. "Ex-Offenders, Criminal Background Checks, and Racial Consequences in the Labor Market." *University of Chicago Legal Forum* 2009(1): 381–419.

Stoll, Michael A., and Shawn D. Bushway. 2008. "The Effect of Criminal Background Checks on Hiring Ex-Offenders." *Criminology and Public Policy* 7(3): 371–404.

Sweeten, Gary. 2006. "Who Will Graduate? Disruption of High School Education by Arrest and Court Involvement." *Justice Quarterly* 23(4): 462–80.

Travis, Jeremy, Bruce Western, and Steve Redburn, eds. 2014. *The Growth in Incarceration in the United States: Exploring Causes and Consequences*. Washington, D.C.: National Academies Press.

Turney, Kristin. 2017. "The Unequal Consequences of

Mass Incarceration for Children." *Demography* 54(1): 361–89.

Turney, Kristin, and Christopher Wildeman. 2015. "Detrimental for Some? Heterogeneous Effects of Maternal Incarceration on Child Wellbeing." *Criminology and Public Policy* 14(1): 125–56.

Uggen, Christopher, Mike Vuolo, Sarah Lageson, Ebony Ruhland, and Hilary K. Whitham. 2014. "The Edge of Stigma: An Experimental Audit of the Effects of Low-Level Criminal Records on Employment." *Criminology* 52(4): 627–54.

Vuolo, Mike, Sarah Lageson, and Christopher Uggen. 2017. "Criminal Record Questions in the Era of 'Ban the Box'." *Criminology and Public Policy* 16(1): 139–65.

Wacquant, Loïc. 2000. "The New 'Peculiar Institution': On the Prison as Surrogate Ghetto." *Theoretical Criminology* 4(3): 377–89.

Wakefield, Sara, and Kathleen Powell. 2016. "Distinguishing Petty Offenders from Serious Criminals in the Estimation of Family Life Effects." *Annals of the American Academy of Political and Social Science* 665(1): 195–212.

Wakefield, Sara, and Christopher Uggen. 2010. "Incarceration and Stratification." *Annual Review of Sociology* 36: 387–406.

Wakefield, Sara, and Christopher Wildeman. 2014. *Children of the Prison Boom: Mass Incarceration and the Future of American Inequality*. New York: Oxford University Press.

Waldfogel, Joel. 1994a. "Does Conviction Have a Persistent Effect on Income and Employment?" *International Review of Law and Economics* 14(1): 103–19.

———. 1994b. "The Effect of Criminal Conviction on Income and the Trust 'Reposed in the Workmen'." *Journal of Human Resources* 29(1): 62–81.

Western, Bruce. 2002. "The Impact of Incarceration on Wage Mobility and Inequality." *American Sociological Review* 67(4): 526–46.

———. 2006. *Punishment and Inequality in America*. New York: Russell Sage Foundation.

Western, Bruce, and Katherine Beckett. 1999. "How Unregulated Is the U.S. Labor Market? The Penal System as a Labor Market Institution." *American Journal of Sociology* 104(4): 1030–60.

Western, Bruce, Anthony A. Braga, Jaclyn Davis, and Catherine Sirois. 2015. "Stress and Hardship After Prison." *American Journal of Sociology* 120(5): 1512–47.

Western, Bruce, Jeffrey R. Kling, and David F. Weiman. 2001. "The Labor Market Consequences of Incarceration." *Crime and Delinquency* 47(3): 410–27.

Widdowson, Alex O., Sonja E. Siennick, and Carter Hay. 2016. "The Implications of Arrest for College Enrollment: An Analysis of Long-Term Effects and Mediating Mechanisms." *Criminology* 54(4): 621–52.

Racial Inequality in the Transition to Adulthood After Prison

HEATHER M. HARRIS AND DAVID J. HARDING

That formerly incarcerated black men experience poor life-course outcomes relative to other subpopulations is well established, yet our ongoing research indicates substantial racial inequality in outcomes among the formerly incarcerated. Young, black former prisoners lag behind their white counterparts in achieving traditional adulthood markers: education, employment, and residential independence. We examine explanations for these inequalities using longitudinal administrative data on a cohort of male parolees age eighteen to twenty-five. We find that early postprison experiences and social context explain some variation. Considerable racial inequality persists, however, even as we control for pre- and postprison life-course conditions, criminal justice contact, and social context. We discuss this in relation to estimates of discrimination, stigma, and social networks not observable in our data.

Keywords: racial inequality, transition to adulthood, incarceration, group-based multitrajectory models

Heather M. Harris is research fellow at the Public Policy Institute of California. **David J. Harding** is professor of sociology at the University of California, Berkeley.

© 2019 Russell Sage Foundation. Harris, Heather M., and David J. Harding. 2019. "Racial Inequality in the Transition to Adulthood After Prison." *RSF: The Russell Sage Foundation Journal of the Social Sciences* 5(1): 223–54. DOI: 10.7758/RSF.2019.5.1.10. This research was funded by the Russell Sage Foundation, the University of Michigan Center for Local, State, and Urban Policy, the National Poverty Center at the University of Michigan, the National Institute of Justice (2008-IJ-CX-0018), the National Science Foundation (SES-1061018, SES-1060708), and the Eunice Kennedy Shriver National Institute of Child Health and Human Development (1R21HD060160 01A1) and by center grants from the Eunice Kennedy Shriver National Institute of Child Health and Human Development to the Population Studies Centers at the University of Michigan (R24 HD041028) and at UC Berkeley (R24 HD073964). We thank Paulette Hatchett, our collaborator at the Michigan Department of Corrections, for facilitating access to the data and for advice on the research design, and we thank Steve Heeringa and Zeina Mneimneh for advice on the sample design. Charley Chilcote, Brenda Hurless, Bianca Espinoza, Andrea Garber, Jessica Wyse, Jonah Siegal, Jay Borchert, Amy Cooter, Jane Rochmes, Claire Herbert, Jon Tshiamala, Katie Harwood, Elizabeth Sinclair, Carmen Gutierrez, Joanna Wu, Clara Rucker, Michelle Hartzog, Tyrell Connor, Madie Lupei, Elena Kaltsas, Brandon Cory, Keunbok Lee, and Elizabeth Johnston provided excellent research assistance. Direct correspondence to: Heather M. Harris at harris@ppic.org, Public Policy Institute of California, 500 Washington St., Suite 600, San Francisco, CA 94111; and David J. Harding at dharding@berkeley.edu, University of California, Berkeley, Department of Sociology, 462 Barrows Hall, Berkeley, CA 94720.

Open Access Policy: *RSF: The Russell Sage Foundation Journal of the Social Sciences* is an open access journal. This article is published under a Creative Commons Attribution-NonCommercial-NoDerivs 3.0 Unported License.

The number of individuals incarcerated in prisons and jails in the United States has risen dramatically over the last four decades, an increase accompanied by a more general escalation in the number of young Americans who experience formal contact with the criminal justice system. Approximately one-third of young adults can now expect to be arrested by the time they turn twenty-three (Brame et al. 2012). For many of these young people, criminal justice contact continues after arrest: the number of individuals on parole and probation increased dramatically. One in thirty-one American adults is on probation, on parole, or in prison or jail on any given day (Pew Center on the States 2009). Because about 80 percent of prisoners are released under parole supervision, the effects of prison are tightly linked to the experiences and institutions of community supervision (National Research Council 2007).

Increases in contact with the criminal justice system have been linked to increasing racial inequality in access to the opportunities that facilitate successful life-course development. Arrest, incarceration, and community supervision are experienced disproportionately by young, low skill, African American males (Bonczar 2003), whose criminal records further marginalize them socially, educationally, and economically by restricting their access to education, housing, and employment (Visher and Travis 2003). That formerly incarcerated black men experience poor life course outcomes relative to other subpopulations is well established (Western 2006). Yet our ongoing research indicates substantial racial inequality in life-course outcomes even among former male prisoners.

We study young men who are released from prison during the transition to adulthood, a critical developmental period in which key life transitions are typically made and life trajectories often established (Hogan and Astone 1986). Young, male, black former prisoners lag behind their white counterparts in achieving traditional markers of adulthood: completing education, finding employment, and establishing their own households. That they do suggests that we have yet to understand the full complexity of the entanglements between criminal justice contact and racial inequality in access to opportunities and successful life-course development. This article presents evidence of racial inequality in postprison trajectories to adulthood, develops possible explanations for that inequality, and tests whether the explanations account for racial inequality in postprison transitions to adulthood.

The largest racial difference after release from prison is between those who maintain criminal justice contact without meeting traditional markers of adulthood and those who avoid criminal justice contact and meet most traditional adulthood markers. Blacks are more likely to experience the former pathway, whites the latter. The life-course theoretical framework and research on the consequences of criminal justice contact contribute to possible explanations for these racial inequalities.

On entering prison, whites are more advantaged than blacks in terms of their life-course development, in particular, the progress they have made transitioning to adulthood. However, they exhibit more substance abuse and mental health problems, which can impede those transitions and contribute to criminal justice contact. In general, the evidence suggests that young black men are disproportionately subject to criminal justice contact. Racial inequality in criminal justice system contact before prison may have cumulative effects on life-course outcomes that disproportionately affect black former prisoners (Sampson and Laub 1997).

After prison, young black men are far more likely than their white counterparts to return to disadvantaged social contexts—such as neighborhoods and counties—that provide fewer resources for life-course development (Wilson 1987; Krivo and Peterson 1996). In these contexts, the processes that contributed to their pre-prison transitions to adulthood resume and set the stage for later outcomes, a form of postprison path dependence. To the extent that employment and education are inhibited and criminal justice contact and substance use are facilitated, disadvantaged social environments disproportionately set young black former prisoner onto adulthood transitions that negatively affect their long-term life-course trajectories.

We examine whether the explanations we

developed account for racial inequality in postprison transitions in a sample of young men released from prison during the transition to adulthood. We include measures that capture pre- and postprison formal contact with the criminal justice system, pre- and postprison life-course development, within prison experiences, and the postprison neighborhood and county context. Yet these measures fail to completely explain the racial inequality in outcomes. We discuss other potential explanations for the residual inequality we are not able to test with our data but that have been discussed extensively in the literature, including racial discrimination, the stigma of a criminal record, and social network support.

THE LIFE-COURSE FRAMEWORK AND THE TRANSITION TO ADULTHOOD

To develop specific hypotheses, we draw on the life course and transition to adulthood frameworks and research on racial inequality in contact with the criminal justice system. The life-course framework is a developmentally informed theoretical perspective that emphasizes the connections between life-course stages (Sampson and Laub 1992). A central assumption is that life events (such as marriage, employment, and school completion) are linked over time, directing attention to the sequences and patterns of events that unfold (Elder 1988).

Trajectories and transitions are the two primary concepts that link individual experiences over the life course and structure life outcomes (Sampson and Laub 1992, 1993). Trajectories are long-term patterns or sequences of behaviors and social roles. Transitions are discrete changes in roles and behaviors connected to "salient life events" such as marriage, school completion, entry into military service, or, for our study population, various contacts with the criminal justice system (Elder 1988; Pettit and Western 2004). For instance, in a common pathway parents provide material support while children accrue human capital through education, which enables the transition to work and the eventual establishment of an independent household.

The transition to adulthood is a developmental period during which important role transitions are made and long-term life trajectories are established. Dennis Hogan and Nan Astone stress that the transition to adulthood is a process, rather than a discrete event, which involves the assumption of progressively more adult social roles across multiple life-course domains (1986). Current conceptualizations of that process emphasize nonuniformity in the achievement of markers of stability and independence in the domains of education, employment, and housing (Waters et al. 2011; Schoon 2015). For example, as the transition to adulthood period has lengthened, events such as high school completion, college enrollment, stable employment, marriage, and childbearing are no longer assumed to follow each other successively or immediately: multiple trajectories to adulthood that include diverse event orderings have been identified (Furstenburg 2006). Marriage may follow childbearing, or not occur at all, or postsecondary schooling may follow stable labor market involvement and occur later in life. Children may leave and then return to the parental home multiple times.

The life-course framework highlights the importance of life events that occur during the transition to adulthood in creating and maintaining inequality in the kinds of opportunities available to people during transitional processes and their life-course outcomes. Life events may either hasten or interrupt role transitions, which in turn establish life-course trajectories and can lead to what Glen Elder calls the "accumulation of disadvantage" (Furstenberg 2006; Kerckhoff 1993; Elder 1988). As a result, racial and other inequalities in adult outcomes often originate during the transition to adulthood. However, the life-course framework also suggests that transitions and their effects are reversible and trajectories can be shifted (Laub and Sampson 2001). This leads researchers to focus also on resilience or "how some individuals succeed in the face of difficult circumstances" (Osgood et al. 2006). The transition to adulthood has often been characterized as an era of "opportunity" and "possibility" during which emerging adults have the ability to "transform their lives," yet many young adults leave prison only to return again or struggle to transition to adulthood and achieve economic and residential independence (Arnett 2005).

RACIAL INEQUALITY IN THE TRANSITION TO ADULTHOOD AFTER PRISON

In discussing possible explanations for racial inequality in transition to adulthood outcomes that include desistance, employment, living independently, and college enrollment, we begin with explanations based on inequality in pre-prison experiences: criminal justice contact, human capital accumulation, household formation, and family transitions (which we collectively refer to as "adulthood transitions"), and substance abuse and mental health. We then turn to prison and postprison experiences, including racially unequal social contexts and path dependence.

Pre-Prison Criminal Justice System Contact

Racial inequality in the onset and frequency of ongoing criminal justice contact may help account for inequality in postprison outcomes. Considerable evidence suggests that racial inequality in criminal justice system contact originates at arrest and compounds through incarceration. Forty-nine percent of black males but only 38 percent of their white counterparts experience an arrest by age twenty-three (Harris et al. 2009; Brame et al. 2014). The racial inequality at arrest seems to widen through the stages of criminal justice system processing, about 20 percent of black males but only 3 percent of white males being incarcerated in young adulthood (Bonczar 2003; Pettit and Western 2004).

How prior contact with the criminal justice system cumulatively contributes to inequality in postprison life-course outcomes is largely unknown because most studies of racial inequality in the criminal justice system focus on a single point of criminal justice contact, such as sentencing or incarceration (see, for example, Zatz 2000; Raphael 2007). Earlier and more frequent arrests result in longer criminal records, which can lead to harsher sentences, more stringent treatment in prison, and more intense supervision after release (Bushway and Piehl 2007; Frase 2009; Petersilia and Turner 1993). More frequent arrests, convictions, and punishments during adolescence and early adulthood can interrupt schooling and the accumulation of work experience, delaying postprison adult transitions as the justice-involved try to rebuild their lives on weak human capital foundations (Bernberg and Krohn 2003). Substance use that begins with experimentation can morph into abuse as individuals find themselves with few licit opportunities and instead turn to illicit work (Hart 2013). Finally, if the experience of early criminal justice system contact and incarceration separates young people from supportive family members by severing or weakening social ties, they will have fewer social resources on which to draw as they attempt to rebuild their lives after prison (Desmond 2012; Western et al. 2015). Together these findings suggest that ongoing exposure to the criminal justice system before prison may have long-term consequences—cascading effects on early life, prison, and reentry experiences—that exacerbate racial disparity in transitions to adulthood.

Pre-Prison Adulthood Transitions

If whites are advantaged relative to blacks with regard to their pre-prison life-course development, those differences may explain differences in postrelease outcomes. Across multiple life-course domains, young black men are disadvantaged relative to their white counterparts. They consistently lag behind in terms of high school graduation and employment rates. For those whose education may be interrupted by early arrest and juvenile justice system contact, levels of education and employment lag behind those in the general population (Kirk and Sampson 2013; Western and Pettit 2005; Holzer, Offner, and Sorenson 2009). Among male state prison inmates age eighteen to twenty-four in 2004, only 14.3 percent of blacks and 19.6 percent of whites had finished high school (Ewert and Wildhagen 2011). For example, as shown in table 1, only 64.5 percent of young black men in our sample had ever been employed prior to their incarceration, whereas 76.5 percent of young white men were. If employment prospects are further hindered by stigma associated with criminal records, these inequalities are likely to grow even larger (Pager 2003).

Similar racial inequality exists in establish-

Table 1. Descriptive Statistics for Sample

Variable	Overall		Blacks		Whites		
	Mean	SD	Mean	SD	Mean	SD	
Pre-prison criminal justice contact							
First arrest age	15.415	2.496	15.462	2.500	15.372	2.494	
Juvenile commitment	0.440		0.428		0.451		
Number arrests	3.222	2.011	3.085	1.945	3.344	2.062	*
Number prior probation	0.808	0.951	0.789	0.947	0.824	0.956	
Number prior custody	2.298	1.475	2.100	1.334	2.474	1.570	*
Prison enter age	20.818	1.990	20.917	1.980	20.731	1.996	
Pre-prison transition to adulthood markers							
Has dependent	0.405		0.489		0.330		*
Ever married	0.051		0.046		0.055		
High school graduate	0.085		0.093		0.077		
Earned GED	0.304		0.209		0.388		*
Employed	0.706		0.645		0.760		*
Lived independent	0.338		0.325		0.349		
Pre-prison mental health and substance abuse							
Mentally ill	0.195		0.088		0.289		*
Daily alcohol use	0.108		0.078		0.134		*
Daily marijuana use	0.270		0.275		0.266		
Daily stimulant use	0.074		0.062		0.084		
Daily depressant use	0.025		0.015		0.035		*
Prison experiences							
Months in prison	22.388	19.123	24.029	20.277	20.928	17.922	*
Earned GED in prison	0.314		0.265		0.358		*
Had misconduct	0.608		0.663		0.560		*
Days in solitary	11.356	67.661	11.101	56.646	11.583	76.173	

(continued)

Table 1. (continued)

Variable	Overall Mean	SD	Blacks Mean	SD	Whites Mean	SD	
First postprison year social context							
Days in Detroit	53.912	118.216	106.070	150.282	7.515	41.937	*
Tract disadvantage score	0.531	1.187	1.362	1.109	-0.216	0.627	*
Tract affluence score	-0.380	0.563	-0.365	0.500	-0.394	0.614	
County crime rate per 1K	6.116	2.784	7.394	2.707	4.970	2.314	*
First postprison year criminal justice system contact							
Electronic monitoring	0.355		0.296		0.407		*
Number parole violations	1.139	1.351	1.123	1.426	1.154	1.281	
Number arrests	0.538	0.778	0.596	0.790	0.485	0.765	*
Days held in custody	47.587	83.293	47.984	81.326	47.234	85.062	
First postprison year transition to adulthood markers							
Continued education	0.066		0.059		0.073		
Employed	0.535		0.410		0.647		*
Earnings	$1,555.23	$2,427.86	$950.48	$1,849.99	$2,093.18	$2,736.06	*
Days lived independent	87.183	121.370	84.129	122.572	89.900	120.315	
First postprison year substance abuse							
Percent positive drug tests	0.109	0.224	0.138	0.252	0.083	0.193	*
Days in residential treatment	6.448	21.453	4.438	19.335	8.235	23.042	*
N	1300		612		688		

Source: Authors' calculations based on data from MDOC, MSP, MUI, MWDA, NSC, and USC.

Note: Fourteen Asian and Native American parolees were grouped with the white parolees. "Stimulants" are mainly cocaine, but also include methamphetamines and prescription stimulants such as Ritalin and Adderall. "Depressants" are mainly heroin and prescription opioids, but also include sedatives, tranquilizers, barbiturates, and benzodiazepines. Lived independent means living in a non-institutional, private residence apart from parents or older relatives (that is, alone, with a romantic partner, friend, or roommate). Continued education indicates that the young man either earned a GED or enrolled in college in the first year after prison. The tract and county variables are averages over all of the characteristics of the residential addresses where a young man lived during the first postprison year. We lack a non-institutional neighborhood address in the first postprison year for twenty-four parolees. The disadvantage and affluence scores were generated via factor analysis and are orthogonal to each other. The disadvantage score loads on percent black, poverty and unemployment rates, female-headed households, and welfare receipt. The affluence score loads on higher education, professional and managerial occupations, and higher median income. The scores are preferred due to multicollinearity between the indicators.

* indicates a statistically significant (at $p \leq .05$) difference between the black and white means.

ing residential independence. In a study of neighborhood change during transition to adulthood, Patrick Sharkey finds that 20 percent of young white people but only 13 percent of young black people lived independently as eighteen-year-olds (2012). To the extent that early life-course development sets the stage for later life-course development as theorized, these pre-prison racial inequalities should persist, and perhaps even widen after prison (see, for example, South et al. 2016)

Pre-Prison Substance Use and Mental Health
Although white former prisoners have more education and formal work experience than black former prisoners, they also have higher rates of identified mental illness and substance use. In 2005, 55 percent of surveyed male state prison inmates (62.2 percent of whites and 54.7 percent of blacks) reported a mental health problem. Prior to their incarceration, state inmates who reported mental health problems were more likely than those who did not to be unemployed (29.9 percent versus 24.4 percent), experience homelessness (13.2 percent versus 6.3 percent), and report daily or almost daily drug and alcohol use (87.1 percent versus 77.2 percent) (James and Glaze 2006).

Between 2007 and 2009, 40.9 percent of male state prison inmates reported that they were under the influence of drugs or alcohol when they committed their offense. Over that same time period, black state prison inmates were less likely than white state prison inmates to report using cocaine (28.0 percent versus 41.7 percent), heroin (7.6 percent versus 24.7 percent), and methamphetamine (2.1 percent versus 34.0 percent). Only 28.5 percent of drug-dependent state prison inmates received substance use treatment while incarcerated (Bronson et al. 2017).

Prison Experiences
The experience of prison may also exacerbate racial inequality in postprison transitions to adulthood. Blacks are more likely than whites to serve longer sentences, which creates larger gaps in their development during a critical period (Rehavi and Starr 2014). Although research on prison experiences has expanded in recent years, it is limited in scope, focusing mainly on time served and behavior during incarceration (see, for example, Meade et al. 2013; Mears et al. 2016; Tiedt and Sabol 2015).

Misconduct violations can impact later life outcomes because they indicate continuity in proscribed and potentially criminal behavior and because the sanctions that often follow, such as solitary confinement, increased prison time, or the loss of treatment and educational opportunities, can have a negative impact on physical and psychological health (Morris 2016; Steiner and Cain 2017; Haney 2003; Smith 2006). The evidence on racial inequality in being cited for misconduct is mixed. Some researchers found racial disparity, whereas others did not (Gendreu, Goggin, and Law 1997; Steiner, Butler, and Ellison 2014). However, the greater tendency of young black men to engage in violence, which has been documented outside prison, also persists inside prison (LaFree, Baumer, and O'Brien 2010; Goetting and Howsen 1986; Harer and Steffensmeier 1996).

Blacks and whites may also receive different opportunities for human capital development in prison. For example, because they have weaker human capital foundations as they enter prison, young black prisoners may be less likely than their white counterparts to earn a GED during incarceration. To the extent that young black men have more harmful experiences in prison, racial inequality will be perpetuated during incarceration and young black men may experience poorer postprison life-course outcomes.

Racially Segregated and Unequal Social Contexts
Social contexts—both local neighborhoods and broader geographies such as cities, counties, and labor markets—influence the social networks individuals form and the resources to which they have access. Racial, economic, and geographic inequalities in access to supportive social contexts and institutions, such as effective schools and colleges, may account for some of the poor outcomes of young black men relative to their white counterparts.

Many former prisoners return to particularly disadvantaged neighborhoods, characterized by poverty, joblessness, and high rates of crime and disorder (Cadora, Swartz, and Gordon

2003; Lynch and Sabol 2004; Solomon, Thomson, and Keegan 2004). Racial differences in the neighborhood contexts in which white and black former prisoners live, however, are stark (Massoglia, Firebaugh, and Warner 2013). Only whites experience worse neighborhood conditions after prison than before (Massoglia, Firebaugh, and Warner 2013; Warner 2014). Blacks in general return to poorer neighborhoods than whites after prison, mainly given the more general landscape of residential segregation by race rather than the impact of incarceration itself (Massoglia, Firebaugh, and Warner 2013; Lee, Harding, and Morenoff 2016).

Returning to disadvantaged neighborhoods after prison increases the risk of recidivism and reduces employment (Hipp, Petersilia, and Turner 2010; Kubrin and Stewart 2006; Mears et al. 2008; Morenoff and Harding 2011). Research suggests five processes through which social contexts affect formerly incarcerated young adults. First, disadvantaged neighborhoods tend to exert lower levels of informal social control over their residents and have higher rates of crime and disorder (Sampson, Morenoff, and Earls 1999; Sampson, Raudenbush, and Earls 1997). Former prisoners who return to neighborhoods with lower social control will face fewer barriers to returning to crime and substance abuse and therefore may also see employment and education as less appealing. Second, if disadvantaged neighborhoods are located in local labor markets with higher unemployment rates, returning to such neighborhoods will potentially increase unemployment and recidivism (Raphael and Weiman 2007; Sabol 2007). Third, residents of disadvantaged neighborhoods are often socially isolated, particularly from networks that might provide information about employment and education (Smith 2007; Wilson 1987; Young 2004). Fourth, disadvantaged neighborhoods tend to be located far from jobs (Mouw 2000; Wilson 1987). Finally, differential criminal opportunity theory suggests that disadvantaged neighborhoods provide more opportunities to engage in crime and substance abuse, both of which may lower prospects for employment or schooling (Cloward and Ohlin 1960). For example, disadvantaged neighborhoods tend to have a higher concentration of former prisoners and higher rates of alcohol and drug use (Clear 2007; Freisthler et al. 2005; Hill and Angel 2005).

Path Dependence

To the degree that whites are initially exposed to more supportive contexts and institutions in the period after their release from prison, those inequalities have the potential to magnify over time as longer-term trajectories are established. The emphasis on transitions and trajectories in the life-course framework suggests that early experiences after release from prison may be especially important for determining longer-term trajectories. Qualitative research has documented the optimism most formerly incarcerated individuals feel at the moment of release (Comfort 2012; Seim 2016; Harding et al. 2017). This suggests that motivation to work, enroll in school, and avoid further criminal justice contact could be maintained if the individual experiences supportive social institutions and contexts after release.

Initial post-incarceration successes may lead to future opportunities and exposure to supportive institutions and contexts. For example, stable housing may be the foundation on which other aspects of successful reentry rely (Bradley et al. 2001). Finding and maintaining employment, family connections, and health care, and avoiding substance use can be challenging without stable housing (Lutze, Rosky, and Hamilton 2013). Likewise, early success in the labor market or schooling may mitigate some of the stigma of a criminal record in the eyes of employers or landlords. Together, these ideas suggest that we should observe some degree of path dependence. Early post-prison experiences should predict later transitions to adulthood. To the extent that these early experiences are racially patterned, they may explain racial inequalities in longer-term trajectories.

DATA

We collected administrative data for a randomly selected two-thirds sample of eighteen- to twenty-five-year-old males who were released on parole from Michigan prisons in 2003 (n = 1,300) and followed for five to ten years, depending on the outcome. We collected and matched data from multiple sources: the Michigan Department of Corrections (MDOC), the Michigan State Police (MSP), the Michigan unemployment insurance system (MUI), the Michigan Workforce Development Agency (MWDA), which tracks GED certifications, the National Student Clearinghouse (NSC), and the 2000 United States Census (USC).[1] Summary statistics are presented in table 1.

Transition to Adulthood Outcomes
We focus on four transitional marker outcomes: residential independence, formal labor market participation, college enrollment, and desistance from criminal justice system contact. These outcomes reflect the transition to adulthood markers young Americans have traditionally been expected to meet (Arnett 2000; Danziger and Rouse 2007). To be clear, we expect young adults to complete and for many to continue their education, enter the labor market and ideally achieve full-time employment, and exit the homes of their parents and older relatives to live alone, with roommates, or a romantic partner. Although incarceration may constitute a "new stage in the life course" for many young Americans, particularly young black men, the markers of adulthood for individuals reentering society should reflect these characterizations of successful transitions to adulthood (Pettit and Western 2004, 151).

We created six-month indicators for each transitional marker. Continuing education is measured as enrollment in postsecondary educational institutions.[2] Residential independence, recorded by parole agents, is defined as living in a noninstitutional setting and apart from parents or older relatives.[3] Employment in the formal labor market is measured using quarterly unemployment insurance (UI) records from 1997 to 2010, which include all earnings paid to that individual in each quarter. More than 90 percent of workers are covered by Michigan's UI system, but informal employment is not covered, even if it is legal. However, we view formal employment as an important indicator of economic reintegration after prison, both because of the greater social protections that formal employment provides (such as workers compensation insurance, social security eligibility) and because formal employment is a stronger signal of integration into mainstream society. Given that our sample is justice involved, we measure periods during which the young men were neither arrested nor incarcerated to create a desistance indicator. We follow college enrollments for ten postprison years, desistance for seven, and residential independence and employment for five.

Pre-Prison Experiences
Unlike much existing prior work on racial inequality in the criminal justice system, our data allow us to control for most of the criminal justice system contacts experienced by an individual prior to incarceration. Our indicators of juvenile justice system contact include first arrest age and whether the young men had been committed as juveniles. We have complete arrest, conviction, and punishment records that include whether probation or a custodial (jail or prison) sentence resulted from each conviction. Thus we are able to account for and ex-

---

1. Unemployment insurance data were matched on social security numbers, birthdates, and names, including all available aliases. Education data were matched on birthdates and names, including all available aliases.

2. Degree receipt is unfortunately not included in the National Student Clearinghouse data for all institutions during the time period we are studying.

3. We examined the quality of the residential data recorded by parole agents and find high levels of agreement between these data and another source. The principal investigator conducted a separate but related longitudinal qualitative study of twenty-four former prisoners who were interviewed once in prison prior to release and at regular interviews for the two years after release. For eighteen of those subjects, we were able to compare self-reported residential histories from our own interviews for the first few months after release with those recorded in Michigan Department of Corrections administrative data. Fourteen (78 percent) of these residential histories matched exactly; the remaining four had one missing address each. Overall, thirty-three of thirty-seven addresses were correctly recorded by MDOC parole agents. Missing addresses were either brief stays or short periods of living on the streets, and those with missing addresses tended to be more residentially mobile, suggesting that the administrative data will understate mobility slightly for some parolees.

amine which criminal justice system contacts are most determinative of eventual incarceration.

Our transition to adulthood measures characterize the progress each young man had made before prison. They include whether he had finished high school, earned a GED, held a job, or lived independently. We also have pre-prison indicators of parenthood and marriage. Other measures include self-reported mental illness and self-reported daily substance use, each of which signifies a potential impediment to postprison transitions.

Prison Experiences
The MDOC data include indicators of elements of the prison experience that may influence the postprison life course in both positive and negative ways. We created variables that allow us to control for months in prison, misconducts charged during that time, and the number of days spent in solitary confinement. Finally, we also control for a potentially beneficial aspect of the prison experience: earning a GED while incarcerated.

First Postprison Year Experiences
We observe the characteristics of the neighborhoods (census tracts), cities, and counties in which each subject lived during the first postprison year. Because many neighborhood metrics are highly correlated, we created standardized, orthogonal neighborhood disadvantage and advantage scores using factor analysis. The disadvantage score loads on percentage black, median family income, the poverty and unemployment rates, the proportion of residents with less than a high school degree, and the percentage of households that receive public assistance and are headed by females. The advantage score loads on the percentage of people who have jobs in managerial professions and college degrees, the proportion of families whose income exceeds $75,000, and the median income. When an individual lives in more than one neighborhood during the first postprison year, we create weighted (by the number of days) averages of the disadvantage and advantage scores. We similarly control for county crime rates. To ameliorate concerns about the extreme disadvantage of people living in Detroit, we also control for the number of days each parolee lived in Detroit during the first postprison year.

To account for postprison path dependence, we create indicators of criminal justice contact, transition to adulthood marker achievement, and substance abuse for the first year. We observe several kinds of criminal justice contact: whether they were electronically monitored and the number of parole violations, arrests, and days incarcerated they experienced. Likewise, we observe several transitional markers: days lived independently, continuing education (that is, GED completion or college enrollment), employment, and earnings. Two measures indicate substance abuse: days spent in residential substance abuse treatment and the percentage drug tests that were positive. Subjects spend, on average, just under one week in residential treatment, far below the recommended three to nine months (Farabee, Prendergrast, and Anglin 1998). Residential treatment therefore is likely more indicative of a substance abuse problem than effective treatment for it.

METHODS
The transition to adulthood literature has been limited by the inability to consider more than one transitional outcome at a time or to consider the relationships between more than two markers at a time (Shanahan 2000). Without the capacity to consider adult transitions in their entirety, it is impossible to ascertain the interrelationships between the markers. Just as the transition to adulthood literature has been limited by the inability to consider multiple outcomes simultaneously, the criminological literature has been limited by predicting life-course outcomes without considering multiple types of contact with the criminal justice system simultaneously. Our methodological approach overcomes these limitations.

Group-Based Multitrajectory Models
Both the life-course and transition to adulthood frameworks emphasize the importance of examining trajectories or pathways, rather than single points in time, to more completely capture outcomes. Single point-in-time outcome measures may poorly summarize former

prisoners' postrelease experiences, particularly if those experiences evolve in fits and starts as they wrestle with the joint processes of reintegration into society and desistance from criminal justice contact (Sampson and Laub 2003; Paternoster and Bushway 2009). Moreover, point-in-time measures may not fully capture divergent trends across individuals because they are often noisy, meaning they neither entirely capture the construct of interest nor do they *only* capture the construct of interest. Many noisy measurements captured over time and compared between individuals can create a more accurate representation of the underlying construct than a single point-in-time measure (Sweeten 2012).

To adhere to the life-course and transition to adulthood frameworks, we map postprison trajectories with a recent extension to group-based trajectory modeling (GBTM) called group-based multitrajectory modeling (GBMTM). GBTM was developed to study life-course development in justice-involved samples such as ours (Nagin and Land 1993; Nagin 2005). It combines features of latent class analysis and multilevel modeling to characterize variation in longitudinal outcomes and the processes that generate them. The models identify latent groups of individuals who follow similar outcome trajectories, producing three pieces of information: the number of groups that best describe the data, a description of the average trajectory for each group, and an estimate of the probability that each person belongs to each group.

Unlike GBTM, in which a single trajectory is modeled, GBMTM allows multiple measures of the same underlying construct to be modeled simultaneously (Nagin et al. 2016). In contrast to dual trajectory modeling, in which two coevolving processes are modeled, GBMTM models a single process for which multiple indicators exist. Thus GBMTM models each of the indicators separately and in relation to each other producing, in effect, multitrajectory groups comprised of trajectory groups.

We use GBMTM to model the transition to adulthood, a process for which we have four indicators: employment, residential independence, college enrollment, and desistance from criminal justice contact. Via GBMTM, we examine how the achievement of one transitional marker relates to the achievement of others. The software models each of the transition to adulthood marker trajectories separately and in conjunction with each other to produce multitrajectory groups that characterize the postprison life-course outcomes of the young men in our sample, beginning with the second postprison year and following them at six-month intervals through the last observation year for each marker.

To determine the optimal number of latent groups, we follow the conventional advice of considering a combination of measures of fit (the Bayesian Information Criterion and appropriateness of functional form), classification (the average posterior probability of group assignment and the odds of correct classification [OCC]), group size and composition, and extant theory and evidence to determine whether the resultant groups "communicate the distinct features of the data" (Nagin 2005, 77). The last criterion, admittedly subjective, means that if an additional trajectory group has a substantively similar trajectory pattern as another group, then the model with fewer groups should be preferred.

Post-Trajectory Analysis

After mapping the postprison transition to adulthood trajectories, we examine the characteristics of the members of each multitrajectory group to determine whether and how blacks and whites cluster differentially into trajectory groups. The postprison trajectory groups then become our dependent variables in a series of multinomial logit models. The key independent variables are the groups of explanatory variables that capture each of our potential explanations for racial inequality in postprison transition outcomes: pre-prison criminal justice contact, pre-prison adult transitions, pre-prison substance use and mental health problems, in-prison experiences, the first postprison year social context, and the first postprison year path dependence. To address the noncomparability of coefficients from logit models with different explanatory variables, we compare average marginal effects, focusing on the effect of race as we add the explanatory variables in groups (Mood 2010).

RESULTS

To determine the potential sources of racial inequality in the transition to adulthood after prison, we describe the pre-prison and one-year postprison life-course conditions of the parolees; describe postprison transition to adulthood trajectories and how they vary by race and other preprison and one-year postprison characteristics; and determine how well the explanations we have proffered explain racial inequality in postprison transition to adulthood trajectories.

Pre-Prison and Postprison Racial Differences

If we observe racial inequality in pre-prison criminal justice contact and life-course development and one-year postprison social context, criminal justice contact, and health and human capital investments, we can expect those inequalities to account for racial inequality in the postprison transition to adulthood. Here we present evidence of racial inequality in our proposed determinants of postprison transition to adulthood trajectories (see table 1). The implications of those differences vary, depending on the postprison transitional trajectories the young men follow.

Prior Criminal Justice System Contact

At prison entry, whites and blacks do not differ in terms of their age or juvenile histories. They do, however, differ on most measures of adult criminal justice system contact. Before their incarceration, whites experience more prior arrests, convictions, and postconviction custodial sentences.[4] In other words, blacks are incarcerated after fewer criminal justice contacts than whites are. Although the racial differences in prior record length are absolutely small, ranging from 0.2 arrests to 0.4 custodial sentences, they are statistically significant.

Prior Life-Course Development

Table 1 also shows that differences between blacks and whites in terms of their pre-prison life-course development are statistically significant. Blacks are 48.1 percent more likely than whites to have children and to live independently. Although high school graduation rates do not differ by race, whites are 17.8 percent more likely to be employed and 61.1 percent more likely to earn GEDs. However, whites are also more than twice as likely to report mental illness and about twice as likely to use both legal and illegal substances daily.

Postprison Social Context

To document the vastly different social contexts to which blacks and whites return from prison, we present the average characteristics of the postprison census tracts and counties in which the parolees lived during their first postprison year in table 2. Racial differences on each tract and county characteristic are substantial. County crime rates are 48.8 percent higher in the counties to which blacks return than they are in the counties to which whites return. At the neighborhood level, we observe that people in the neighborhoods to which the blacks returned are, on average, twice as poor, almost twice as likely to be unemployed, and 38 percent less likely to have achieved a high school education.

One-Year Postprison Path Dependence

During the first postprison year, young white men are 37.6 percent more likely to be on electronic monitoring than young black men are (see table 1). This may be because, on average, black men serve 129.6 percent of their minimum sentence, and white men only 90.9 percent of their minimum sentence and may be electronically monitored until they reach their minimum. Despite the more stringent postprison surveillance of young white men, young black men are 22.9 percent more likely to be rearrested after release.

In addition, young white men seem able to develop more human capital than young black men during the first postprison year. Whites are 57.7 percent more likely to be employed. When employed, young white men earn more than twice as much as their black counterparts.

In terms of postprison substance use, young white men (21.7 percent) are more likely than black (15.4 percent) to enter residential substance abuse treatment, which may reflect deeper substance abuse problems, as indicated

---

4. Just as arrests do not necessarily result in conviction, convictions do not necessarily result from arrests.

Table 2. Postprison Social Context for Blacks and Whites

	Overall		Blacks		Whites		
	Mean	SD	Mean	SD	Mean	SD	
Poverty rate	0.178	0.116	0.236	0.113	0.125	0.090	*
Unemployment rate	0.087	0.047	0.113	0.049	0.063	0.029	*
Percent did not graduate	0.195	0.088	0.229	0.087	0.165	0.078	*
Percent single mothers	0.257	0.142	0.349	0.125	0.174	0.098	*
Percent black	0.350	0.365	0.631	0.322	0.097	0.157	*
Median income	$44,470.94	$16,359.12	$36,965.89	$13,850.87	$51,216.56	$15,486.83	*
Percent owner occupied	0.665	0.177	0.589	0.157	0.733	0.165	*
Percent same address	0.746	0.083	0.736	0.083	0.756	0.082	*
Percent professional	0.239	0.096	0.218	0.097	0.257	0.091	*
Percent high income	0.219	0.126	0.173	0.103	0.261	0.131	*
Percent on assistance	0.091	0.091	0.117	0.100	0.067	0.075	*
N	1300		612		688		

Source: Authors' calculations based on data from USC.

Note: Each indicator is an average over all of the neighborhoods, defined as census tracts, in which each parolee lived in the first year after prison. Twenty-four parolees do not have a known noninstitutional residential tract during the first postprison year.

* indicates a statistically significant (at $p \leq .05$) difference between the black and white means.

Table 3. Initial Postprison Transition to Adulthood Multitrajectory Model Comparisons

Number of groups	4	4	5	5
Bayesian information criterion	−22,616	−22,851	−22,215	−22,133
Lowest average group membership probability	92.8	91.4	91.5	89.6
Lowest group odds of correct classification	42.4	31.8	28.8	34.8
Lowest number of group members	111	230	102	92
Highest number of group members	536	388	354	300

Source: Authors' calculations based on data from MDOC, MSP, MUI, MWDA, NSC, and USC.
Note: The fit of each of the potential multitrajectory group models to the data appears very good. The lowest group membership probabilities are well above the recommended 70 percent threshold for each model. Likewise, the lowest odds of correct classification far exceed the recommended threshold of five in each model. Combined these statistics indicate clear group distinctions and accurate classification of sample members into trajectory groups. The downward trend in the BIC as more groups are added also conforms to expectation. However, these conventional measures of fit do not isolate the optimal model with precision. Instead we rely on group size and composition to select the five-group model, which includes reasonably sized groups with easily identifiable differentiating characteristics. To clarify, were we to accept the first four-group model, 41.2 percent of the sample would cluster into the largest group that does not distinguish between the parolees who maintain low levels of employment, independence, and desistance, and those who do not. Were we to accept the second four-group model, the parolees whose commitment to education distinguishes them would be subsumed into the other groups. Similarly, if a sixth group is added, it does not differ substantively from the group that maintains low levels of employment, independence, and desistance.

by their higher pre-prison prevalence of cocaine and heroin abuse. Young black men, on the other hand, are 66.5 percent more likely than white men to test positive for drugs when tested, which may be because their drug of choice, marijuana, lingers longer in the bloodstream (Visher 1991).

Postprison Desistance and Transitional Outcome Trajectories

To examine post-incarceration adult transitions holistically, we estimate a group-based multitrajectory model that incorporates four trajectory markers measured at six-month intervals for five to ten years after prison, starting with the second postprison year: college enrollment, employment, living independently (that is, not with parents or older relatives), and desistance (that is, no arrest or incarceration). We implement GBMTM with the *traj* module in STATA. We considered models with four through six groups, as shown in table 3. We discuss how we settled on the five-group model in the notes to table 3. The five-group model we chose is shown in figure 1 and described in table 4.

Postprison Transitions to Adulthood
As shown in figure 1 and table 4, five developmental trajectories characterize the postprison transitions to adulthood of the young men (n = 1,300) in our sample. We named the trajectories to highlight the key differences between them, not to comprehensively summarize the experiences of the young men who follow each trajectory across all four domains.

Relative to the young men who follow other trajectories, those who follow *transitioning* trajectories (n = 321) most consistently meet a majority of the adulthood markers. These transitioners are unlikely to attend college. However, they maintain a high probability of employment (approximately 75 percent or greater) and a moderate probability of living independently (approximately 50 percent or greater), although their ability to maintain their independence declines over time. Additionally, these young men are increasingly likely to avoid arrest and incarceration during follow-up.

Young men on *continuing education* trajectories (n = 102) display a commitment to education that sets them apart from the young

Figure 1. Postprison Transition to Adulthood Multitrajectories Beginning One Year After Release from Prison

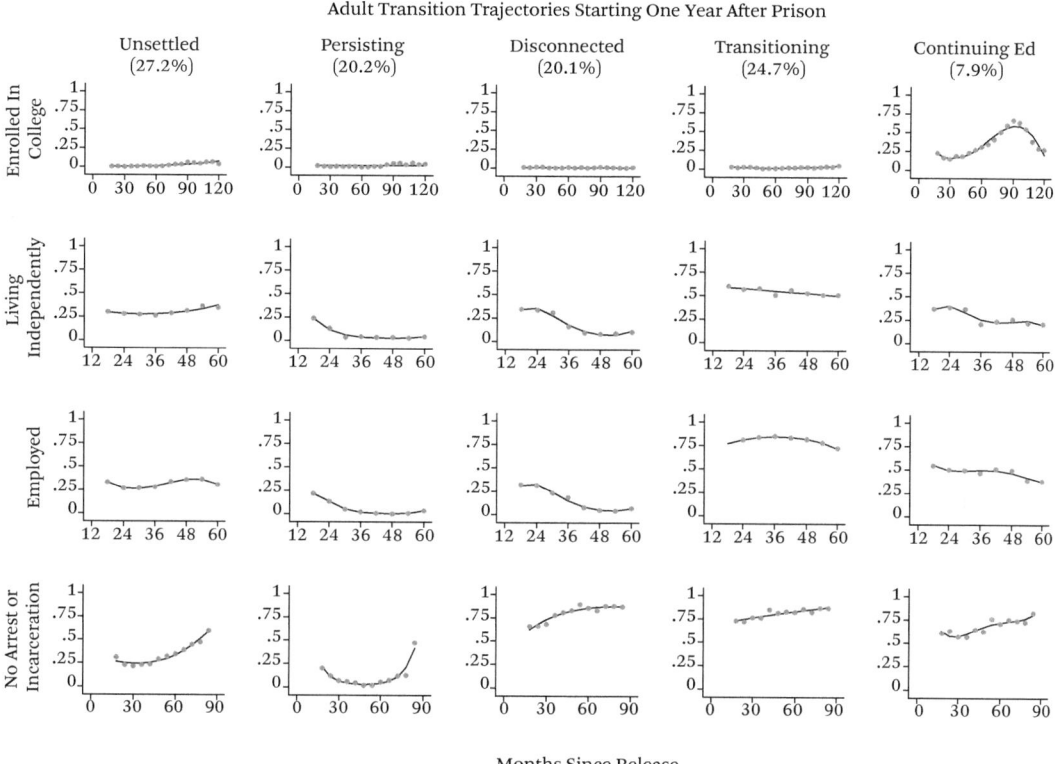

Source: Authors' calculations based on data from MDOC, MSP, MUI, MWDA, NSC, and USC.

Table 4. Postprison Groups, Group Membership Probabilities, and Odds of Correct Classification

Group Number	Group	N	Percentage of Sample	Mean Probability of Group Membership	Odds of Correct Classification
1	Unsettled	354	27.23	91.52	28.83
2	Persisting	262	20.15	94.94	74.31
3	Disconnected	261	20.08	92.43	48.60
4	Transitioning	321	24.69	95.15	59.88
5	Continuing education	102	7.85	94.65	207.95

Source: Authors' calculations based on data from MDOC, MSP, MUI, MWDA, NSC, and USC.

men on each of the other trajectories. Like the transitioners, these young men increasingly avoid contact with the criminal justice system. They struggle to meet the markers of adulthood, however. Their initially moderate probabilities of employment and independence erode over time. Their low probability of employment five years after prison may motivate their continuing education, which peaks several years later. That these young men have the means to enroll in postsecondary education despite meager earnings suggests that they are relying heavily on social support from parents or older relatives who are likely less disadvantaged than those of the young men on other trajectories.

Relative to the other young men, those who follow *persisting* trajectories (n = 262) most consistently do not meet the adulthood markers. Instead, they remain deeply justice-involved, maintaining high probabilities of arrest and incarceration. By the fourth postprison year, the likelihood that they will be incarcerated or arrested is near certain. Accordingly, by the third postprison year and continuing until the end of follow-up, persisters have zero or near zero probability of employment, independent living, or college enrollment.

By contrast, young men on *unsettled* trajectories (n = 354) make some progress on their adult transitions even as they also remain justice involved. They maintain low but nontrivial probability of employment and independent living (approximately 25 percent) while sustaining moderate (25 to 50 percent) probability of arrest or incarceration throughout follow-up. As is true of the other groups, unsettled young men have near zero probability of continuing their education after incarceration.

Those who follow *disconnected* trajectories (n = 261) avoid contact with the criminal justice system, but also do not participate in the labor market or educational institutions. Like persisters, the disconnected have zero or near zero probability of meeting any of the four adulthood markers by four years after prison. However, unlike persisters and more in line with transitioners, disconnected young men increasingly avoid criminal justice contact over time. Based on research on the role of family in providing support for the formerly incarcerated, we suspect that young men who follow disconnected trajectories are relying heavily on social support to meet their basic material needs (see Harding et al. 2014).

Differences Between Trajectories
As shown in table 5, we tested for racial differences between the five postprison trajectory groups using ANOVA. We find statistically significant differences in racial composition. The most distinct is between the persisting and transitioning trajectories: 71.3 percent of transitioners are white, but only 37.0 percent of persisters are. The other trajectories are more racially balanced. Young men on unsettled trajectories are majority white (52.5 percent), whereas those who follow disconnected (49.0 percent white) and continuing education (47.1 percent) are majority black.

Many of the statistically significant differences shown in table 5 distinguish the trajectories from each other.[5] Transitioners have better overall life-course conditions than the young men who follow the other postprison trajectories, even though they are not always the most advantaged (for example, with respect to education). Prior to their incarceration, young men on transitioning trajectories have the highest levels of employment and residential independence and the lowest levels of substance use. After prison, they return to far less disadvantaged neighborhoods, where they have the highest probability of employment and the lowest levels of criminal justice contact during the first postprison year.

Education clearly differentiates the young men following continuing education trajectories from transitioners and those on the other trajectories. Young men who continue their education are the most likely to graduate high school, earn GEDs in prison, and enroll in college during the first postprison year. They also return from prison to the most affluent neighborhoods, which suggests that they have access to the means to enroll in postsecondary education.

By contrast, lack of engagement in human capital development distinguishes the young men who follow disconnected trajectories from those on other trajectories. Although they are oldest at prison entry, disconnected young men are least likely to have completed secondary education or to have held a job. That trend continues during and after prison. Disconnected young men are least likely to earn a GED in prison and are only more likely than the persisters to hold a job in the first postprison year. They appear to benefit from greater social support, however. Despite low employment and

---

5. Table A1 shows the same information as table 5 separately by race.

Table 5. Average Characteristics of Postprison Group Members

Covariate		F-Statistic	Unsettled	Persisting	Disconnected	Transitioning	Continuing Education
Is white	*	19.343	52.542	37.023	49.042	71.340	47.059
First arrest age	*	27.253	14.621	14.805	16.176	16.106	15.608
Juvenile commitment	*	15.075	0.534	0.561	0.333	0.324	0.441
Number arrests	*	7.246	3.415	3.573	2.713	3.146	3.196
Number probation		0.792	0.777	0.809	0.805	0.875	0.706
Number custody	*	4.383	2.497	2.363	2.008	2.283	2.225
Prison enter age	*	2.670	20.766	20.561	21.080	20.922	20.667
Has dependent		0.585	0.395	0.416	0.425	0.408	0.343
Ever married		1.109	0.045	0.034	0.065	0.050	0.078
High school graduate	*	4.892	0.088	0.046	0.073	0.090	0.186
Earned GED	*	2.650	0.308	0.317	0.230	0.352	0.294
Employed	*	8.318	0.715	0.641	0.625	0.816	0.706
Lived independent	*	4.223	0.339	0.260	0.310	0.414	0.363
Mentally ill		0.669	0.203	0.214	0.165	0.187	0.216
Daily alcohol use	*	7.565	0.175	0.122	0.057	0.078	0.059
Daily marijuana use	*	11.364	0.356	0.351	0.188	0.181	0.255
Daily stimulant use	*	6.202	0.113	0.107	0.054	0.028	0.049
Daily depressant use		1.519	0.034	0.038	0.015	0.012	0.029
Months in prison		0.576	21.707	23.815	21.762	22.285	23.016
Earned GED in prison		0.865	0.319	0.317	0.272	0.324	0.363
Had misconduct	*	3.688	0.638	0.679	0.598	0.558	0.510
Days in solitary		2.734	11.503	22.950	7.678	5.838	7.843
Days in Detroit		2.314	48.359	60.622	69.640	46.760	38.206
Tract disadvantage	*	13.394	0.527	0.791	0.769	0.185	0.368
Tract affluence	*	3.055	−0.425	−0.358	−0.391	−0.395	−0.209
County crime rate	*	5.801	6.009	6.722	6.281	5.795	5.514
Electronic monitoring		2.520	0.421	0.313	0.330	0.346	0.324
Number parole violations	*	22.556	1.517	1.450	0.885	0.704	1.049
Number arrests	*	35.923	0.709	0.889	0.322	0.274	0.422
Days held in custody	*	40.366	69.229	85.134	20.287	19.704	33.637
Continued education	*	15.212	0.045	0.050	0.046	0.062	0.245
Employed	*	32.840	0.492	0.351	0.452	0.766	0.647
Wages	*	40.016	$1,086.99	$873.15	$1,093.25	$2,893.29	$1,903.49
Days lived independent	*	15.229	66.161	61.500	93.241	127.424	83.971
Percent positive tests	*	6.840	0.111	0.167	0.096	0.081	0.070
Days treatment		0.362	6.116	5.706	7.245	7.162	5.216

Source: Authors' calculations based on data from MDOC, MSP, MUI, MWDA, NSC, and USC.
Note: Within group means and group differences as determined by ANOVA reported.
* indicates a statistically significant (at $p \leq .05$) difference between the group means.

education levels, many are able to live independently.

Finally, the young men on persisting and unsettled trajectories are most similar to one another before and during incarceration. They are youngest at first arrest and most likely to have juvenile commitments. They are most likely to abuse all types of drugs and alcohol. Interestingly, substance use is more prevalent among the unsettled, suggesting that this may be the primary challenge for these young men as they transition to adulthood. During prison, persisting and unsettled young men are the most likely to be cited for misconduct.

The first postprison year distinguishes persisters from the unsettled. Persisters are arrested more often and held in custody longer than unsettled young men are. Persisters are also 14.1 percentage points less likely to be employed during the first postprison year. When employed, persisters on average earn the least money. Therefore, the first postprison year may be a crucial period for intervention.

Accounting for Racial Inequality

Only 25 percent of the young men in our sample follow the postprison trajectory that suggests they are transitioning to adulthood. Seventy-one percent of them are white. To determine why formerly incarcerated young white men make more progress than their black counterparts, we estimate multinomial logit models that predict the probability that individuals will follow each of the other trajectories, relative to the transitioning trajectory. As shown in table 6, we then calculate the average marginal effect (AME) of race as variables that reflect those explanations are added to the model (full model results provided in table A2; baseline group differences in race provided in appendix table A1). We examine whether the racial differences between the young men who follow transitioning trajectories and those who follow others can be explained by pre-prison criminal justice contact, pre-prison transitional marker achievement, pre-prison substance use and mental health, in-prison experiences, postprison social context, postprison criminal justice contact, postprison substance use, or postprison path dependence.

Persisting Versus Transitioning Trajectories
The largest uncontrolled racial difference in trajectory group membership is between the persisting and transitioning trajectories. Whites are 12.9 percentage points less likely than blacks to be persisters. Controlling for pre-prison criminal justice contact, human capital development, and substance use and mental health exacerbates that inequality. After accounting for those pre-prison differences, young white men are 17.1 percentage points less likely than black to follow the persisting trajec-

tory. Ordinarily, controlling for a variable associated with race and with the outcome would reduce the racial difference. However, these variables are what methodologists call suppressor variables. When uncontrolled, they suppress the racial difference, making it appear smaller than it is (see MacKinnon, Krull, and Lockwood 2000). Substantively, this means that if whites had the same values on these variables as blacks, they would be even more likely than blacks to follow a persisting trajectory.

In contrast, controlling for postprison social context and path dependence has the expected effect. Racial inequality is reduced but not eliminated. After including variables related to social context, criminal justice contact, transitional marker achievement, and substance abuse during the first postprison year, whites are 10.5 percentage points less likely than blacks to follow the persisting trajectory. Most of the reduction is due to racial differences in social contexts, though some is also due to criminal justice contact. The residual racial difference is statistically significant.

Unsettled Versus Transitioning Trajectories
Blacks and whites are equally likely to follow unsettled trajectories relative to transitioning trajectories (the unconditional AME is –0.004). Although conditioning on our explanatory variables causes the race AME to fluctuate somewhat, it is not statistically significant in any model.

Disconnected Versus Transitioning Trajectories
In the unconditional model, young white men are somewhat less likely than their black counterparts (3.1 percentage points) to follow disconnected trajectories, although the difference is not statistically significant. As we add our explanatory variables to this model, the racial difference shrinks to close to zero and then becomes more and more positive. Again, we observe the suppressing influence of some explanatory variables. That is, once we hold constant pre-prison experiences, in-prison experiences, postprison social context and first postprison year adult markers, whites are actually more likely than blacks to follow disconnected relative to transitioning trajectories.

In contrast, controlling for the postprison

Table 6. Average Marginal Effect (AME) of Being White Relative to Being Black as Explanatory Variable Groups Are Added to the Multinomial Logit Model

	Pre-Prison Life Course					Postprison Path Dependence			
	Race	Pre-Prison Criminal Justice Contact	Pre-Prison Adult Markers	Pre-Prison Substance Use and Mental Health	Prison Experiencee	First Postprison Year Social Context	First Postprison Year Criminal Justice Contact	First Postprison Year Adult Markers	First Postprison Year Substance Abuse
Unsettled versus transitioning pathways									
White	-0.004	-0.028	-0.028	-0.036	-0.036	-0.040	-0.024	-0.018	-0.015
SE	0.025	0.026	0.028	0.030	0.031	0.040	0.041	0.042	0.043
t	-0.168	-1.051	-0.988	-1.214	-1.161	-0.994	-0.584	-0.429	-0.355
Persisting versus transitioning pathways									
White	-0.129	-0.148	-0.154	-0.171	-0.172	-0.126	-0.113	-0.110	-0.105
SE	0.022	0.023	0.024	0.026	0.027	0.034	0.034	0.035	0.035
t	-5.763	-6.475	-6.364	-6.708	-6.442	-3.734	-3.369	-3.148	-3.010
Disconnected versus transitioning pathways									
White	-0.031	-0.003	0.021	0.032	0.049	0.067	0.061	0.078	0.073
SE	0.022	0.022	0.023	0.023	0.025	0.034	0.035	0.036	0.036
t	-1.401	-0.134	0.920	1.365	1.994	1.995	1.740	2.169	2.030
Continuing education versus transitioning pathways									
White	-0.018	-0.021	-0.027	-0.028	-0.041	-0.063	-0.070	-0.077	-0.078
SE	0.015	0.017	0.017	0.018	0.017	0.021	0.023	0.022	0.022
t	-1.229	-1.259	-1.608	-1.571	-2.341	-2.965	-3.085	-3.486	-3.499
N	1300	1300	1300	1300	1300	1276	1276	1276	1276

Source: Authors' calculations based on data from MDOC, MSP, MUI, MWDA, NSC, and USC.

Note: In the final multinomial logit model, each set of explanatory variables is jointly statistically significant at $p \leq .05$. See the appendix for the final model.

year criminal justice contact and substance abuse variables reduces the white-black inequality. In other words, greater postprison criminal justice contact and substance abuse among blacks increases the probability of blacks following disconnected trajectories, although not enough to offset the other factors that favor blacks in this comparison. In the fully specified model, young white men are more likely than black (7.3 percentage points) to disconnect rather than transition, a statistically significant residual racial difference.

Continuing Education Versus Transitioning Trajectories
In the uncontrolled model, whites are 1.8 percentage points less likely than blacks to follow continuing education rather than transitioning trajectories, a difference that is not statistically significant. Adding explanatory variables consistently widens, rather than closes, this gap. That is, conditioning on pre-prison adult markers, in-prison experiences, the first year postprison social context, and first postprison year path dependence increases the black-white inequality in these two groups. These too are suppressor variables. If blacks had the same markers, experiences, social contexts, and outcomes as whites, they would be even more likely than whites to continue their education. In the final specification, young black men are 7.8 percentage points more likely than white to follow continuing education trajectories. Once again, the residual racial difference is statistically significant.

DISCUSSION

In our sample of eighteen- to twenty-five-year-old men who were paroled from Michigan state prisons in 2003 and followed for five to ten years, we observe racial inequality in transition to adulthood outcomes that include enrolling in college, finding employment, achieving residential independence, and desisting from criminal justice contact. In estimating postprison trajectories to adulthood, we address what had been a persistent shortcoming in the literature: the inability to consider multiple adulthood markers at the same time. We use group-based multitrajectory modeling to map the former prisoners' transitions to adulthood.

We find that the considerable variation in postprison trajectories does not correspond to a simple relationship between continued criminal justice contact and outcomes in other domains. Rather than simply identifying persisters and desisters, our analysis reveals five trajectories the young men follow after prison that differ in substantively meaningful ways. These trajectories enrich our understanding of desistance and post-incarceration life-course development because they describe how desistance relates to key life-course transitions.

Two of the trajectories we identify coincide with expectations about the relationship between criminal justice contact and life-course development. About 25 percent of our sample belongs to a transitioning group, which avoids criminal justice contact and maintains high employment and residential independence, and about 20 percent to a persisting group, which experiences high rates of continued criminal justice contact and little employment or residential independence.

More than half of the sample belongs to one of three other groups, which complicates our understanding of the transition to adulthood after prison. The largest group, at 27 percent, includes those we term unsettled young men. They maintain low but nonzero levels of criminal justice contact but also experience some formal employment and residential independence. This group seems to capture young men who are waffling between conventional pathways such as employment and residential independence and continued contact with the criminal justice system. Such young men might be most amenable to policy intervention, particularly substance abuse treatment, during the first postprison year. The fourth group, 20 percent of the sample, includes those we call disconnected. They also show little to no employment or residential independence but in addition have no further contact with the criminal justice system. This group has not achieved conventional markers of adulthood but also has managed to avoid further criminal justice contact. To improve their transitional marker outcomes, policymakers might focus on fostering their engagement in the labor market and educational institutions (see, for example, Uggen 2000). The final group, at about 8 percent of the sample, has declining employment and residential independence but instead of engaging in criminal justice contact, these young men eventually enroll in postsecondary schooling. This final group follows an alternative pathway to adulthood other than employment, albeit one that takes longer to realize.

A second and related finding is that many formerly incarcerated young men are struggling to transition to adulthood, at least by conventional measures. On the one hand, more than half of our sample follow trajectories that exhibit approximately 25 to 40 percent initial probabilities of criminal justice contact that decrease over time. On the other hand, the likelihood that these young men will achieve one or more of the traditional markers of adulthood remains low. The average probability of achieving residential independence by the fifth postprison year is below 50 percent across all groups. Only among transitioners is the average probability of employment above 50 percent by the fifth year after release. Those on continuing education trajectories have between a 25 and 50 percent chance of enrolling in college during the ten years after their release from prison, but theirs is the smallest group.

Finally, we find sizable racial inequalities in transition to adulthood outcomes that we are unable to explain. Young black men experience poorer transition to adulthood outcomes than young white men. We identify and test several possible explanations for racial inequality in transition to adulthood outcomes: pre-prison criminal justice contact, pre-prison adult transitions, pre-prison substance use and mental health, postprison social context, and postprison path dependence. We do so by comparing transitioners with the young men on other trajectories using multinomial logit models, to which we sequentially add variables to control for these explanations.

A number of the potential explanations are clearly unable to account for these racial differences, at least with the measures available to us. None of the pre-prison or in-prison variables explained racial inequalities in postprison transition to adulthood trajectories. Indeed, conditioning on these variables sometimes exacerbated racial inequalities. For example, in each of the trajectory group comparisons, pre-prison substance abuse and mental health problems negatively affect each transition to adulthood marker achievement. Young white men are far more likely than their black counterparts to abuse drugs and alcohol and to report mental health problems. As a result, controlling for those factors makes the racial inequality more apparent.

Such *suppression effects* also explain why controlling for pre-prison criminal justice contact increases the apparent racial inequality in the comparisons between persisters and transitioners and between those who belong to the continuing education versus transitioning group. Young men who had more pre-prison criminal justice contact are more likely to persist or continue their education than they are to transition; and young white men have more pre-prison criminal justice contact than their black counterparts.

Substantively, that young white men have more serious prior criminal histories suggests differential treatment by young black men in the criminal justice system. Most of the men in our sample are first-time inmates. Relative to their white counterparts, young black men are incarcerated after fewer arrests and prior convictions involving custodial sentences, in part because they are more likely to be convicted of weapons offenses, violent offenses, and drug offenses, which are punished severely. Put another way, if young black men had the pre-prison criminal justice contact of their white counterparts, they would be 1.9 percentage points more likely to persist and 2.8 percentage points more likely to disconnect than to transition.

What, then, does explain racial inequalities in transition to adulthood outcomes? The starkest difference is between the persisting versus transitioning trajectories. Young white men are more likely to follow transitioning trajectories, and young black men more likely to follow persisting. The difference is 17 percentage points after pre-prison and in-prison experiences are controlled. That racial difference is reduced to just over 10 percentage points by conditioning on postprison experiences. Postprison social contexts and criminal justice contact account for almost all of this reduction.

Racial inequality in the first postprison year social context accounts for 26.5 percent of the racial inequality in transition to adulthood outcomes between the young men who follow these two trajectories. In addition, first postprison year criminal justice contact and substance abuse explain some of the racial difference in membership between the two trajectories.

These findings are generally congruent with research that has found "little evidence" that long-term trajectories of criminal justice contact can be predicted from static early life-course conditions (Sampson and Laub 2005, 31). In fact, as Edward Mulvey and colleagues predict, we find considerable evidence that dynamic early postprison experiences in life-course domains other than criminal justice contact explain some of the longer-term variation we observe in the postprison transition to adulthood (Mulvey et al. 2010). Our work therefore also supports research that implicates early reintegration experiences in determining life-course and criminal justice outcomes among the formerly incarcerated.

Finally, we find that blacks are more likely than whites to follow continuing education trajectories relative to transitioning trajectories. This difference is 4 percentage points after preprison and in-prison experiences are controlled and almost 8 percentage points after postprison experiences are also controlled. This finding indicates that further education is a particularly salient pathway to adulthood for black young men recently released from prison. One interpretation is that young black men with a criminal record have such dismal prospects for upward mobility in the labor market that they turn to higher education to improve their job skills. This would be consistent with Karl Alexander, Doris Entwisle, and Linda Olson's more general argument that working-class white young adults are able to leverage social networks to gain access to good paying jobs in the skilled trades that do not require a college education, but working-class young blacks are not, prompting them to turn to postsecondary education (2014).

Although we control for most formal contact the young men have with the criminal justice system before prison, their pre-prison life-course conditions, in-prison experiences, postprison social context, and early postprison outcomes, we are unable to account for a substantial proportion of the racial inequality we observe in the postprison transition to adulthood. Large and statistically significant residual racial differences remain in three of our four trajectory group comparisons. One possible explanation is that unobserved differences by race in our subjects' early life experiences are important ones. The processes of what we might call selection into prison are quite different by race, as evidenced by large racial differences in rates of imprisonment. Our sample is selected based on imprisonment at an early age, and whites who experience imprisonment at an early age may be very different from blacks who do so. Such differences might account for blacks' greater residual likelihood of continuing education and lower residual likelihood of following disconnected rather than transitioning trajectories.

In addition, we see two possible explanations for blacks' greater likelihood of following persisting rather than transitioning trajectories: stigma, combined with discrimination, and social network support. The impact of the stigma of a criminal record has been extensively studied, particularly for employment outcomes (Petersilia 2003; Pager, Western, and Bonikowski 2009; Pager 2003; Pager 2007; Uggen et al. 2014). In her in-person audit study, Devah Pager finds that criminal record stigma differentially affects black men relative to white men in terms of their employment prospects (2003). Five percent of black men with a criminal record received callbacks, whereas 17 percent of their white counterparts did, a difference of 12 percentage points. In a subsequent in-person audit study focused on isolating the impact of racial discrimination, independent of the stigma of a criminal record, Pager, Bart Bonikowski, and Bruce Western find that black men received a callback or a job offer 15.2 percent of the time, whereas white men were hired or called back 31.0 percent of the time, a difference of 15.8 percentage points (2009). They also find that black men were often channeled into lower prestige and visibility jobs (such as a busboy rather than a server). Thus, even when blacks are hired, racial discrimination is implicated in relegating them to more precarious work with lower wages.

Racial discrimination and the stigma of a criminal record seem to be linked. In subsequent work on specific industries, Pager finds that restaurants, which tend not to do background checks, are most likely to hire whites with criminal records but least likely to hire blacks with criminal records (2007). In a correspondence audit study, Amanda Agan and Sonja Starr find that the white-black differential in callbacks grew by 36 percentage points (from 7 percent to 43 percent) after the passage of ban-the-box legislation (2018). Together, these research findings suggest discrimination in the labor market against blacks in general, which may be in part due to employers associating race with a criminal record when they lack information to the contrary. Similar patterns of racial discrimination and criminal record stigma have been observed in housing markets (see, for example, Page 1995; Pager and Shepherd 2008; Ewens, Tomlin, and Wang 2014). The combination of discrimination and stigma may therefore account for racial inequality in post-prison outcomes among young adults.

Estimates of the impact of racial discrimination and the stigma of a criminal record on employment are large. A 50 percent differential appears to be the floor (Pager 2007; Pager and Shepherd 2008). In fact, the magnitude of previously estimated effects of racial discrimination and the stigma of a criminal record on employment, which range from 12 to 15 percentage points, exceed the remaining unexplained racial inequality in our transition to adulthood outcomes, which range from 7 to 11 percentage points. Thus, it is not unreasonable to attribute the residual to some combination of these two factors. However, further research is needed to provide direct evidence of the degree to which criminal record stigma and racial discrimination account for racial inequality in transition to adulthood outcomes.

A final explanation for residual racial inequality is differences in social network support, particularly in the labor market. Deirdre Royster finds that whites are able to monopolize better paying working-class jobs in industries like construction through the use of social networks for hiring and securing apprenticeships (2003). Sandra Smith finds that blacks are less likely to provide job referrals and references to friends, neighbors, and family members (2007). These arguments are also consistent with the racialized trajectories into the labor market among young adults that Alexander and his colleagues identify (2014). Future research should investigate the role of social network support in integration into the labor market following prison release among young blacks and whites.

Table A1. Average Characteristics of Postprison Group Members by Race

	Unsettled				Persisting			
Covariate	Black Mean	White Mean			Black Mean	White Mean		
First arrest age	14.66	14.59			14.98	14.52		
Juvenile commitment	0.52	0.55			0.54	0.60		
Number arrests	3.34	3.48			3.41	3.85		
Number probation	0.82	0.74			0.76	0.89		
Number custody	2.30	2.68	*		2.13	2.75	*	
Prison enter age	20.77	20.76			20.73	20.28		
Has dependent	0.48	0.32	*		0.50	0.28	*	
Ever married	0.04	0.05			0.03	0.04		
High school graduate	0.09	0.09			0.05	0.03		
Earned GED	0.20	0.40	*		0.27	0.39	*	
Employed	0.66	0.76	*		0.60	0.71		
Lived independent	0.38	0.31			0.25	0.27		
Mentally ill	0.11	0.28	*		0.13	0.36	*	
Daily alcohol use	0.13	0.22	*		0.08	0.20	*	
Daily marijuana use	0.37	0.34			0.30	0.43	*	
Daily stimulant use	0.09	0.13			0.08	0.14		
Daily depressant use	0.03	0.04			0.02	0.07	*	
Months in prison	24.79	18.92	*		22.54	25.97		
Earned GED in prison	0.32	0.32			0.24	0.45	*	
Had misconduct	0.70	0.58	*		0.68	0.68		
Days in solitary	17.96	5.67			10.24	44.58	*	
Days in Detroit	90.95	9.89	*		94.21	3.49	*	
Tract disadvantage	1.30	−0.18	*		1.39	−0.24	*	
Tract affluence	−0.43	−0.42			−0.33	−0.40		
County crime rate	7.18	4.94	*		7.67	5.11	*	
Electronic monitoring	0.36	0.47	*		0.27	0.38		
Number parole violations	1.44	1.59			1.38	1.57		
Number arrests	0.73	0.69			0.88	0.90		
Days held in custody	61.84	75.90			78.61	96.23		
Continued education	0.04	0.05			0.06	0.03		
Employed	0.41	0.56	*		0.27	0.48	*	
Wages	$783	$1,361	*		$619	$1,306	*	
Days lived independent	81.85	51.99	*		62.19	60.33		
Percent positive tests	0.11	0.11			0.22	0.08	*	
Days treatment	3.20	8.75	*		3.65	9.21	*	

Source: Authors' calculations based on data from MDOC, MSP, MUI, MWDA, NSC, and USC.
* indicates a statistically significant (at $p \leq .05$) difference between the black and white means.

	Disconnected			Transitioning			Continuing Education		
	Black Mean	White Mean		Black Mean	White Mean		Black Mean	White Mean	
	16.48	15.86	*	16.17	16.08		15.72	15.48	
	0.27	0.40	*	0.29	0.34		0.43	0.46	
	2.44	2.99	*	2.88	3.25		3.22	3.17	
	0.80	0.81		0.80	0.90		0.74	0.67	
	1.77	2.25	*	2.12	2.35		2.15	2.31	
	21.33	20.82	*	21.22	20.80		20.43	20.94	
	0.50	0.34	*	0.50	0.37	*	0.44	0.23	*
	0.07	0.06		0.05	0.05		0.04	0.13	
	0.10	0.05		0.12	0.08		0.17	0.21	
	0.13	0.34	*	0.22	0.41	*	0.22	0.38	
	0.60	0.65		0.76	0.84		0.65	0.77	
	0.30	0.32		0.36	0.44		0.39	0.33	
	0.02	0.31	*	0.08	0.23	*	0.07	0.38	*
	0.03	0.09		0.08	0.08		0.06	0.06	
	0.20	0.17		0.17	0.18		0.24	0.27	
	0.05	0.06		0.02	0.03		0.02	0.08	
	0.01	0.02		0.00	0.02		0.00	0.06	
	22.62	20.87		26.00	20.79	*	26.32	19.29	
	0.19	0.36	*	0.27	0.34		0.37	0.35	
	0.65	0.54		0.62	0.53		0.59	0.42	
	7.35	8.02		4.45	6.40		12.98	2.06	
	131.11	5.77	*	139.23	9.61	*	71.22	1.06	*
	1.64	-0.17	*	1.27	-0.26	*	0.92	-0.23	*
	-0.41	-0.37		-0.35	-0.41		-0.18	-0.24	
	7.47	5.02	*	7.62	5.05	*	6.64	4.25	*
	0.27	0.39	*	0.25	0.38	*	0.30	0.35	
	0.78	0.99		0.52	0.78	*	1.20	0.88	
	0.38	0.27		0.24	0.29		0.44	0.40	
	20.19	20.39		16.20	21.11		33.91	33.33	
	0.03	0.06		0.07	0.06		0.19	0.31	
	0.34	0.57	*	0.65	0.81	*	0.59	0.71	
	$772	$1,427	*	$1,799	$3,333	*	$1,480	$2,380	
	81.44	105.50		123.50	129.00		97.80	68.42	
	0.11	0.08		0.10	0.07		0.09	0.04	
	7.01	7.49		5.77	7.72		2.09	8.73	*

Table A2. Fully Specified Multinomial Logit Model, Odds Ratios Reported

	Unsettled	Persisting	Disconnected	Continuing Education
White	0.532	0.328	0.814	0.177
	−2.336	−3.908	−0.719	−4.855
First arrest age	0.828	0.898	0.981	0.997
	−4.142	−2.064	−0.400	−0.043
Committed as juvenile	1.274	1.544	0.963	1.551
	1.098	1.868	−0.163	1.477
Number prior arrests	0.952	1.104	0.898	1.031
	−0.773	1.397	−1.637	0.345
Number prior probation convictions	0.917	0.958	1.036	0.864
	−0.795	−0.371	0.304	−0.873
Number prior custody convictions	1.121	0.990	0.942	1.045
	1.317	−0.099	−0.644	0.356
Age entered prison	1.037	0.946	1.179	0.969
	0.554	−0.770	2.518	−0.363
Has one or more dependents	0.803	0.886	0.886	0.759
	−1.104	−0.562	−0.591	−0.989
Ever married	1.337	1.177	1.962	2.672
	0.587	0.296	1.511	1.701
Finished high school	1.860	1.069	0.712	6.457
	1.773	0.146	−0.886	3.840
Earned GED	0.959	1.193	0.538	3.151
	−0.169	0.640	−2.416	2.748
Employed prior	1.021	0.796	0.543	0.595
	0.093	−0.932	−2.728	−1.680
Independence (base = older relative)				
Lived independently	0.874	0.553	0.719	1.082
	−0.685	−2.599	−1.632	0.283
Residential treatment	1.728	2.156	2.052	1.724
	0.580	0.936	1.030	0.594
Jail, prison, or detention center	3.114	2.121	2.020	1.260
	2.233	1.474	1.374	0.308
Homeless or unknown	1.463	0.685	1.423	1.434
	0.693	−0.560	0.620	0.442
Reports mental illness	1.016	1.330	1.085	1.470
	0.067	1.102	0.318	1.190
Daily alcohol use	1.281	0.788	0.594	0.496
	0.758	−0.615	−1.301	−1.295
Daily marijuana use	1.260	1.511	0.864	1.160
	1.033	1.669	−0.582	0.480
Daily stimulant use	3.516	3.311	3.096	2.649
	2.563	2.249	2.064	1.531
Daily depressant use	1.729	2.073	1.017	1.244
	0.799	0.946	0.019	0.266
Months in prison	1.002	1.002	1.000	0.991
	0.321	0.234	0.011	−0.989
Earned GED in prison	1.170	1.267	0.751	4.626
	0.607	0.833	−1.083	3.515

Table A2. (*continued*)

	Unsettled	Persisting	Disconnected	Continuing Education
Misconduct in prison	1.195	1.150	1.144	0.608
	0.838	0.577	0.597	−1.698
Days in solitary confinement	1.004	1.005	1.003	1.002
	1.305	1.577	0.845	0.524
Days in Detroit year 1 post	1.000	0.999	0.999	0.999
	0.180	−0.832	−1.163	−0.810
Tract disadvantage score year 1 post	1.164	1.280	1.240	1.028
	1.222	1.899	1.670	0.160
Tract affluence score year 1 post	1.063	1.418	1.156	1.575
	0.359	1.959	0.823	2.108
County crimes per 1,000 year 1 post	0.991	1.023	0.995	0.883
	−0.221	0.468	−0.111	−1.930
Electronic monitoring year 1 post	1.659	1.137	1.127	0.758
	2.586	0.584	0.587	−0.981
Number parole violations year 1 post	1.381	1.293	1.117	1.207
	3.979	2.827	1.265	1.590
Number arrests year 1 post	1.356	1.619	1.075	1.392
	2.064	3.126	0.432	1.544
Days in custody year 1 post	1.003	1.005	0.996	0.999
	1.919	3.069	−2.037	−0.443
Continued education year 1 post	0.641	1.038	0.672	6.301
	−1.115	0.086	−0.993	5.145
Employed year 1 post	0.695	0.418	0.556	0.824
	−1.530	−3.426	−2.328	−0.604
Earnings year 1 post	1.000	1.000	1.000	1.000
	−3.048	−1.380	−3.301	−1.085
Days independent year 1 post	0.997	0.998	0.998	0.997
	−3.486	−2.544	−2.082	−2.561
Positives per test year 1 post	1.022	2.075	0.548	0.390
	0.050	1.609	−1.212	−1.394
Days in treatment year 1 post	0.991	0.997	0.997	0.995
	−2.029	−0.828	−0.722	−1.149
Observations	1276	1276	1276	1276

Source: Authors' calculations based on data from MDOC, MSP, MUI, MWDA, NSC, and USC.
Note: t-statistics shown below coefficients.

REFERENCES

Agan, Amanda Y., and Sonja B. Starr. 2018. "Ban the Box, Criminal Records, and Statistical Discrimination: A Field Experiment." *Quarterly Journal of Economics* 133(1): 191–235.

Alexander, Karl L., Doris. R. Entwisle, and Linda S. Olson. 2014. *The Long Shadow: Family Background, Disadvantaged Urban Youth and the Transition to Adulthood*. New York: Russell Sage Foundation.

Arnett, Jeffrey Jensen. 2000. "Emerging Adulthood: A Theory of Development from the Late Teens through the Early Twenties." *American Psychologist* 55(5): 469–80.

———. 2005. "The Developmental Context of Substance Use in Emerging Adulthood." *Journal of Drug Issues* 35(2): 235–53.

Bernberg, Jon Gunnar, and Marvin Krohn. 2003. "Labeling, Life Chances, and Adult Crime: The Direct and Indirect Effects of Official Intervention in Adolescence on Crime in Early Adulthood." *Criminology* 41(4): 1287–318.

Bonczar, Thomas P. 2003. *Prevalence of Imprisonment in the US Population, 1974–2001*. Washington: Bureau of Justice Statistics.

Bradley, Katharine H., R. B. Michael Oliver, Noel C. Richardson, and Elspeth M. Slayter. 2001. "No Place Like Home: Housing and the Ex-Prisoner." Policy Brief. Boston, Mass.: Community Resources for Justice.

Brame, Robert, Shawn D. Bushway, Ray Paternoster, and Michael G. Turner. 2014. "Demographic Patterns of Cumulative Arrest Prevalence by Ages 18 and 23." *Crime and Delinquency* 60(3): 471–86.

Brame, Robert, Michael G. Turner, Ray Paternoster, and Shawn D. Bushway. 2012. "Cumulative Prevalence of Arrest from Ages 8 to 23 in a National Sample." *Pediatrics* 129(1): 21–27.

Bronson, Jennifer, Jessica Stroop, Stephanie Zimmer, and Marcus Berzofsky. 2017. *Drug Use, Dependence, and Abuse Among State Prisoners and Jail Inmates, 2007–2009*. NCJ 250546. Washington: Bureau of Justice Statistics.

Bushway, Shawn D., and Anne M. Piehl. 2007. "Social Science Research and the Legal Threat to Presumptive Sentencing Guidelines." *Criminology and Public Policy* 6(3): 461–82.

Cadora, Eric, Mannix Gordon, and Charles Swartz. 2003. "Criminal Justice and Health and Human Services: An Exploration of Overlapping Needs, Resources, and Interests in Brooklyn Neighborhoods." In *Prisoners Once Removed: The Impact of Incarceration and Reentry on Children, Families, and Communities*, edited by Waul Travis. Washington, D.C.: Urban Institute Press.

Clear, Todd. 2007. *Imprisoning Communities*. New York: Oxford University Press.

Cloward, Richard A., and Lloyd E. Ohlin. 1960. *Delinquency and Opportunity: A Theory of Delinquent Gangs*. New York: Free Press.

Comfort, Megan. 2012. "It Was Basically College to Us: Poverty, Prison, and Emerging Adulthood." *Journal of Poverty* 16(3): 308–22.

Danziger, Sheldon, and Cecilia Elena Rouse. 2007. "Introduction: The Price of Independence: The Economics of Early Adulthood." In *The Price of Independence: The Economics of Early Adulthood*, edited by Sheldon Danziger and Cecilia Elena Rouse. New York: Russell Sage Foundation.

Desmond, Matthew. 2012. "Disposable Ties and the Urban Poor." *American Journal of Sociology* 117(5): 1295–335.

Elder, Glen H., Jr. 1988. "The Life Course as Developmental Theory." *Child Development* 69(1): 1–12.

Ewens, Michael, Bryan Tomlin, and Liang Choon Wang. 2014. "Statistical Discrimination or Prejudice? A Large Sample Field Experiment." *Review of Economics and Statistics* 96(1): 119–34.

Ewert, Stephanie, and Tara Wildhagen. 2011. "Educational Characteristics of Prisoners: Data from the ACS." Paper presented to the Annual Meeting of the Population Association of America. Washington (March 31).

Farabee, David, Michael Prendergast, and M. Douglas Anglin. 1998. "The Effectiveness of Coerced Treatment for Drug-Abusing Offenders." *Federal Probation* 62(1): 3–10.

Frase, Robert S. 2009. "What Explains Persistent Racial Disproportionality in Minnesota's Prison and Jail Populations?" *Crime and Justice* 38(1): 201–80.

Freisthler, Bridget, Elizabeth A. Lascala, Paul J. Gruenewald, and Andrew J. Treno. 2005. "An Examination of Drug Activity: Effects of Neighborhood Social Organization on the Development of Drug Distribution Systems." *Substance Use and Misuse* 40(5): 671–86.

Furstenberg, Frank F. 2006. "Diverging Development: The Not-So-Invisible Hand of Social Class in the United States." *MacArthur Network on Transitions to Adulthood* working paper. Philadelphia: University of Pennsylvania.

Gendreu, Paul, Claire E. Goggin, and Moira A. Law 1997. "Predicting Prison Misconducts." *Criminal Justice and Behavior* 24(4): 414–31.

Goetting, Ann, and Roy Michael Howsen. 1986. "Correlates of Prisoner Misconduct." *Journal of Quantitative Criminology* 2(1): 49–67.

Haney, Craig. 2003. "Mental Health Issues in Long-Term Solitary and 'Supermax' Confinement." *Crime and Delinquency* 49(1): 124–56.

Harding, David J., Jessica J.B. Wyse, Cheyney C, Dobson, and Jeffrey D. Morenoff. 2014. "Making Ends Meet After Prison." *Journal of Policy Analysis and Management* 33(2): 440–70.

———. 2017. "Narrative Change, Narrative Stability and Structural Constraint: The Case of Prisoner Reentry Narratives." *American Journal of Cultural Sociology* 5(1): 261–304.

Harer, Miles D., and Darrell J. Steffensmeier. 1996. "Race and Prison Violence." *Criminology* 34(3): 323–55.

Harris, Casey T., Darrell Steffensmeier, Jeffrey T. Ulmer, and Noah Painter-Davis. 2009. "Are Blacks and Hispanics Disproportionately Incarcerated Relative to Their Arrests? Racial and Ethnic Disproportionality Between Arrest and Incarceration." *Race and Social Problems* 1(4): 187–99.

Hart, Carl. 2013. *High Price: A Neuroscientist's Journey of Self-Discovery that Challenges Everything You Know About Drugs and Society*. New York: Harper Collins.

Hill, Terrence D., and Ronald J. Angel. 2005. "Neighborhood Disorder, Psychological Distress, and Heavy Drinking." *Social Science and Medicine* 61(5): 965–75.

Hipp, John R., Joan Petersilia, and Susan Turner. 2010. "Parolee Recidivism in California: The Effect of Neighborhood Context and Social Service Agency Characteristics." *Criminology* 48(4): 947–79.

Hogan, Dennis P., and Nan Marie Astone. 1986. "The Transition to Adulthood." *Annual Review of Sociology* 12: 109–30.

Holzer, Harry J., Paul Offner, and Elaine Sorensen. 2005. "Declining Employment Among Young Black Less-Educated Men: The Role of Incarceration and Child Support." *Journal of Policy Analysis and Management* 24(2): 329–50.

James, Doris J., and Lauren E. Glaze. 2006. "Mental Health Problems of Prison and Jail Inmates." Bureau of Justice Statistics special report no. NCJ 213600. Washington: U.S. Department of Justice, Office of Justice Programs.

Kerckhoff, Alan C. 1993. *Diverging Pathways: Social Structure and Career Deflections*. New York: Cambridge University Press.

Kirk, David S., and Robert J. Sampson. 2013. "Juvenile Arrest and Collateral Educational Damage in the Transition to Adulthood." *Sociology of Education* 86(1): 36–62.

Krivo, Lauren J., and Ruth D. Peterson. 1996. "Extremely Disadvantaged Neighborhoods and Urban Crime." *Social Forces* 75(2): 619–48.

Kubrin, Charis E., and Eric A. Stewart. 2006. "Predicting Who Reoffends: The Neglected Role of Neighborhood Context in Recidivism Studies." *Criminology* 44(1): 165–97.

LaFree, Gary, Eric P. Baumer, and Robert M. O'Brien. 2010. "Still Separate and Unequal? A City-Level Analysis of the Black-White Gap in Homicide Arrests Since 1960." *American Sociological Review* 75(1): 75–100.

Laub, John H., and Robert J. Sampson. 2001. "Understanding Desistance from Crime." In *Crime and Justice: A Review of Research*, vol. 28, edited by Michael Tonry. Chicago: University of Chicago Press.

Lee, Keun Bok, David J. Harding, and Jeffrey D. Morenoff. 2017. "Trajectories of Neighborhood Attainment After Prison." *Social Science Research* 66 (August): 211–33.

Lutze, Faith E., Jeffrey W. Rosky, and Zachary K. Hamilton. 2013. "Homelessness and Reentry: A Multisite Outcome Evaluation of Washington State's Reentry Housing Program for High Risk Offenders." *Criminal Justice and Behavior*. 41(4): 471–91.

Lynch, James P., and William J. Sabol. 2004. "Assessing the Effects of Mass Incarceration on Informal Social Control in Communities." *Criminology and Public Policy* 3(2): 267–94.

MacKinnon, David P., Jennifer L. Krull, and Chondra M. Lockwood. 2000. "Equivalence of the Mediation, Confounding, and Suppression Effect." *Prevention Science* 1(4): 173–86.

Massoglia, Michael, Glenn Firebaugh, and Cody Warner. 2013. "Racial Variation in the Effect of Incarceration on Neighborhood Attainment." *American Sociological Review* 78(1): 142–65.

Meade, Benjamin, Benjamin Steiner, Matthew Makarios, and Lawrence Travis. 20136. "Estimating a Dose-Response Relationship Between Time

Served in Prison and Recidivism." *Journal of Research in Crime and Delinquency* 50(4): 525–50.

Mears, Daniel P., Xia Wang, Carter Hay, and William D. Bales. 2008. "Social Ecology and Recidivism: Implications for Prisoner Reentry." *Criminology* 46(2): 301–40.

Mears, Daniel P., Joshua C. Cochran, William D. Bales, and Avinash Bhati. 2016. "Recidivism and Time Served in Prison." *Journal of Criminal Law and Criminology* 106(1): 81–122.

Mood, Carina. 2010. "Logistic Regression: Why We Cannot Do What We Think We Can Do, and What We Can Do About It." *European Sociological Review* 26(1): 67–82.

Morenoff, Jeffrey D., and David J. Harding. 2001. *Final Technical Report: Neighborhoods, Recidivism, and Employment Among Returning Prisoners*. Washington: U.S. Department of Justice.

Morris, Robert G. 2016. "Exploring the Effect of Exposure to Short-Term Solitary Confinement Among Violent Prison Inmates." *Journal of Quantitative Criminology* 32(1): 1–22.

Mouw, Ted. 2000. "Job Relocation and the Racial Gap in Unemployment in Detroit and Chicago, 1980 to 1990." *American Sociological Review* 65(5): 730–53.

Mulvey, Edward, Laurence Steinberg, Alex R. Piquero, Michelle Besana, Jeffrey Fagan, Carol Schubert, and Elizabeth Cauffman. 2010. "Trajectories of Desistance and Continuity in Antisocial Behavior Following Court Adjudication Among Serious Adolescent Offenders." *Development and Psychopathology* 22(2): 453–75.

Nagin, Daniel S. 2005. *Group-Based Modeling of Development*. Cambridge, Mass.: Harvard University Press.

Nagin, Daniel S., Bobby Jones, Valerie Lima Passos, and Richard E. Tremblay. 2016. "Group-Based Multi-Trajectory Modeling." *Statistical Methods in Medical Research* 27(7): 2015–23.

Nagin, Daniel S., and Kenneth C. Land. 1993. "Age, Criminal Careers, and Population Heterogeneity: Specification and Estimation of a Nonparametric, Mixed Poisson Model." *Criminology* 31(3): 327–62.

National Research Council. 2007. *Parole, Desistance from Crime, and Community Integration*. Washington, D.C.: The National Academies Press.

Osgood, D. Wayne, E. Michael Foster, Constance Flanagan, and Gretchen R. Ruth, eds. 2006. *On Your Own Without a Net: The Transition to Adulthood for Vulnerable Populations*. Chicago: University of Chicago Press.

Page, Marianne. 1995. "Racial and Ethnic Discrimination in Urban Housing Markets: Evidence from a Recent Audit Study." *Journal of Urban Economics* 38(2): 183–206.

Pager, Devah. 2003. "The Mark of a Criminal Record." *American Journal of Sociology* 108(5): 937–75.

———. 2007. *Marked: Race, Crime, and Finding Work in an Era of Mass Incarceration*. Chicago: University of Chicago Press.

Pager, Devah, and Hana Shepherd. 2008. "The Sociology of Discrimination: Racial Discrimination in Employment, Housing, Credit, and Consumer Markets." *Annual Review of Sociology* 34: 181–209.

Pager, Devah, Bruce Western, and Bart Bonikowski. 2009. "Discrimination in a Low-Wage Labor Market A Field Experiment." *American Sociological Review* 74(5): 777–99.

Paternoster, Raymond, and Shawn Bushway. 2009. "Desistance and the Feared Self: Toward an Identity Theory of Criminal Desistance." *Journal of Criminal Law and Criminology* 99(4): 1103–56.

Petersilia, Joan. 2003. *When Prisoners Come Home: Parole and Prisoner Reentry*. Oxford: Oxford University Press.

Petersilia, Joan, and Susan Turner. 1993. "Intensive Probation and Parole." *Crime and Justice* 17:281–335.

Pettit, Becky, and Bruce Western. 2004. "Mass Imprisonment and the Life Course: Race and Class Inequality in US Incarceration." *American Sociological Review* 69(2): 151–69.

Pew Center on the States. 2009. *One in 31: The Long Reach of American Corrections*. Washington, D.C.: Pew Charitable Trusts.

Raphael, Steven. 2007. "Early Incarceration Spells and the Transition to Adulthood." In *The Price of Independence: The Economics of Early Adulthood*, edited by Sheldon Danziger and Cecilia Rouse. New York: Russell Sage Foundation.

Raphael, Stephen, and David F. Weiman. 2007. "The Impact of Local Labor Market Conditions on the Likelihood that Parolees are Returned to Custody." In *Barriers to Reentry? The Labor Market for Released Prisoners in Post-Industrial America*, edited by Shawn D. Bushway, Michael S. Stoll, and David F. Weiman. New York: Russell Sage Foundation.

Rehavi, M. Marit, and Sonja B. Starr. 2014. "Racial Disparity in Federal Criminal Sentences." *Journal of Political Economy* 112(6): 1320–54.

Royster, Deirdre. 2003. *Race and the Invisible Hand: How White Networks Exclude Black Men from Blue Collar Jobs.* Berkeley: University of California Press.

Sabol, William J. 2007. "Local Labor Market Conditions and Post-Prison Employment Experiences of Offenders Released from Ohio State Prisons." In *Barriers to Reentry? The Labor Market for Released Prisoners in Post-Industrial America*, edited by Shawn D. Bushway, Michael S. Stoll, and David F. Weiman. New York: Russell Sage Foundation.

Sampson, Robert J., and John H. Laub. 1992. "Crime and Deviance in the Life Course." *Annual Review of Sociology* 18: 63–84.

———. 1993. *Crime in the Making: Pathways and Turning Points Through Life.* Cambridge, Mass.: Harvard University Press.

———. 1997. "A Life-Course Theory of Cumulative Disadvantage and the Stability of Delinquency." In *Developmental Theories of Crime and Delinquency*, edited by Terence Thornberry. New York: Routledge.

———. 2003. "Life-Course Desisters? Trajectories of Crime Among Delinquent Boys Followed to Age 70." *Criminology* 41(3): 555–92.

———. 2005. "A Life-Course View of the Development of Crime." *Annals of the American Academy of Political and Social Science* 602(1): 12–45.

Sampson, Robert J., Jeffrey D. Morenoff, and Felton Earls. 1999. "Beyond Social Capital: Spatial Dynamics of Collective Efficacy for Children." *American Sociological Review* 64(5): 633–60.

Sampson, Robert J., Stephen W. Raudenbush, and Felton Earls. 1997. "Neighborhoods and Violent Crime: A Multilevel Study of Collective Efficacy." *Science* 277(5328): 918–24.

Schoon, Ingrid. 2015. "Diverse Pathways: Rethinking the Transition to Adulthood." In *Families in an Era of Increasing Inequality*, edited by Paul R. Amato, Alan Booth, Susan M. McHale, and Jennifer Van Hook. New York: Springer.

Seim, Josh. 2016. "Short-Timing: The Carceral Experience of Soon-to-Be-Released Prisoners." *Punishment and Society* 18(4): 442–58.

Shanahan, Michael J. 2000. "Pathways to Adulthood in Changing Societies: Variability and Mechanisms in Life Course Perspective." *Annual Review of Sociology* 26: 667–92.

Smith, Peter Scharff. 2006. "The Effects of Solitary Confinement on Prison Inmates: A Brief History and Review of the Literature." *Crime and Justice* 34(1): 441–528.

Smith, Sandra S. 2007. *Lone Pursuit: Distrust and Defensive Individualism among the Black Poor.* New York: Russell Sage Foundation.

Solomon, Amy L., Gillian L. Thomson, and Sinead Keegan. 2004. *Prisoner Reentry in Michigan.* Washington, D.C.: The Urban Institute.

South, Scott J., Ying Huang, Amy Spring, and Kyle Crowder. 2016. "Neighborhood Attainment over the Adult Life Course." *American Sociological Review* 81(6): 1276–1304.

Steiner, Benjamin, and Callie M. Cain. 2017. "The Effect of Removing Sentencing Credits on Inmate Misbehavior." *Journal of Quantitative Criminology.* DOI: 10.1007/s10940-017-9372-7.

Steiner, Benjamin, H. David Butler, and Jared M. Ellison. 2014. "Causes and Correlates of Prison Inmate Misconduct: A Systematic Review of The Evidence." *Journal of Criminal Justice* 42(6): 462–70.

Sweeten, Gary S. 2012. "Scaling Criminal Offending." *Journal of Quantitative Criminology* 28(3): 533–57.

Tiedt, Andrew D., and William J. Sabol 2015. "Sentence Length and Recidivism Among Prisoners Released Across 30 States in 2005: Accounting for Individual Histories and State Clustering Effects." *Justice Research and Policy* 16(1): 50–64.

Uggen, Christopher. 2000. "Work as a Turning Point in the Life Course of Criminals: A Duration Model of Age, Employment, and Recidivism." *American Sociological Review* 67(4): 529–46.

Uggen, Christopher, Mike Vuolo, Sarah Lageson, Ebony Ruhland, and Hilary Whitham. 2014. "The Edge of Stigma: An Experimental Audit of the Effects of Low-Level Criminal Records on Employment." *Criminology* 52(4): 627–54.

Visher, Christy A. 1991. *A Comparison of Urinalysis Technologies for Drug Testing in Criminal Justice.* NCJ 132397. Washington, D.C.: National Institute of Justice.

Visher, Christy A., and Jeremy Travis. 2003. "Transitions from Prison to Community: Understanding Individual Pathways." *Annual Review of Sociology* 29: 89–113.

Warner, Cody. 2014. "The Effect of Incarceration on Residential Mobility Between Poor and Non-Poor Neighborhoods." Paper presented at the Annual Meetings of the American Sociological Association. San Francisco (August 16–19).

Waters, Mary C., Patrick J. Carr, Maria J. Kefalas, and Jennifer Holdaway, eds. 2011. *Coming of Age in America: The Transition to Adulthood in the Twenty-First Century*. Berkeley: University of California Press.

Western, Bruce. 2006. *Punishment and Inequality in America*. New York: Russell Sage Foundation.

Western, Bruce, and Becky Pettit. 2005. "Black-white wage inequality, employment rates, and incarceration." *American Journal of Sociology* 111(2): 553–78.

Western, Bruce, Anthony A. Braga, Jaclyn Davis, and Catherine Sirois. 2015. "Stress and Hardship After Prison." *American Journal of Sociology* 120(5): 1512–47.

Wilson, William J. 1987. *The Truly Disadvantaged: The Inner City, the Underclass, and Public Policy*. Chicago: University of Chicago Press.

Young, Alford. 2004. *The Minds of Marginalized Black Men: Making Sense of Mobility, Opportunity, and Future Life Chances*. Princeton, N.J.: Princeton University Press.

Zatz, Marjorie S. 2000. "The Convergence of Race, Ethnicity, Gender, and Class on Court Decision-Making: Looking Toward the 21st Century." *Criminal Justice* 3(1): 503–52.

Where the Other 1 Percent Live: An Examination of Changes in the Spatial Concentration of the Formerly Incarcerated

DAVID S. KIRK

Traditionally, prisoner reentry has been regarded as an urban phenomenon, with most returning prisoners concentrating into a select few disadvantaged urban neighborhoods. However, metropolitan-area changes—including the demolition of public housing, the suburbanization of poverty, and desegregation—may have altered the prevailing spatial distribution of returning prisoners, thereby spreading the challenges of prisoner reintegration to new geographic domains. Accordingly, I examine the extent to which the geographic distribution of formerly incarcerated individuals in Chicago and Illinois has changed since the late 1990s, including both the causes and consequences of changes, drawing on sixteen years of prisoner release data from the Illinois Department of Corrections, combined with data from the U.S. Census, the American Community Survey, the Chicago Police Department, and the Chicago Housing Authority.

Keywords: mass imprisonment, neighborhoods, prisoner reentry, inequality, suburbanization, segregation

From 1925 to 1975, the imprisonment rate in the United States hovered around 110 per hundred thousand residents (Maguire 2010). The remarkable stability of the imprisonment rate occurred across both prosperous and recessionary periods as well as in times of war and of relative peace. However, since the mid-1970s, the use of imprisonment in the United States has skyrocketed to previously unfathomable levels (for example, see Blumstein and Cohen 1973), leading David Garland to coin the term *mass imprisonment* to characterize the colossal shift in the scale of the use of imprisonment (2001). The imprisonment rate currently stands at approximately five hundred per hundred thousand residents, which includes only incarcerations in prisons (Maguire 2010). If we include incarcerations in jails, which house individuals convicted of short sentences as well as those awaiting trial, then 1 percent of the adult population in the United States is currently in prison or jail (NRC 2014).

The academic research literature has coalesced around a general agreement that the tough-on-crime era and the rise of mass imprisonment has produced dramatic social costs in terms of unemployment, housing insecurity, debt, ill health, disintegration of families, civic

David S. Kirk is professor of sociology at the University of Oxford and professorial fellow of Nuffield College.

© 2019 Russell Sage Foundation. Kirk, David S. 2019. "Where the Other 1 Percent Live: An Examination of Changes in the Spatial Concentration of the Formerly Incarcerated." *RSF: The Russell Sage Foundation Journal of the Social Sciences* 5(1): 255–74. DOI: 10.7758/RSF.2019.5.1.11. Direct correspondence to: David S. Kirk at david.kirk@sociology.ox.ac.uk, Department of Sociology, University of Oxford, Nuffield College, New Road, Oxford OX1 1NF, United Kingdom.

Open Access Policy: *RSF: The Russell Sage Foundation Journal of the Social Sciences* is an open access journal. This article is published under a Creative Commons Attribution-NonCommercial-NoDerivs 3.0 Unported License.

death, and more (Turney and Wakefield 2019; see Kirk and Wakefield 2018; NRC 2014). Given the reach of the criminal justice system into U.S. society, the scholarly community has come to see mass imprisonment as an "engine of inequality" (Western 2006, 198) that serves as one of the major stratifying mechanisms of modern society (Wakefield and Uggen 2010).

In a recent issue of this journal, George Galster and Patrick Sharkey argue that "space is a particularly severe, and underappreciated, dimension of inequality in the United States" (2017, 21–22). Consistent with their argument, Robert Sampson observes that incarceration is unevenly distributed across geographic space—that is, "a small proportion of communities bear the disproportionate brunt of U.S. crime policy's experiment with mass incarceration" (2012, 102). Traditionally, returning prisoners have been highly concentrated in a relatively small number of urban neighborhoods. For instance, Nancy La Vigne, Cynthia Mamalian, and colleagues find that more than half of individuals released from Illinois prisons in 2001 returned to the city of Chicago; among these, one-third were concentrated in just six of the seventy-seven community areas in the city (2003). In this sense, the conception of mass imprisonment may conjure up misleading images of individuals being scooped up by the law in neighborhoods throughout the country (Sampson and Loeffler 2010). In reality, mass imprisonment occurs in relatively few, extremely affected neighborhoods. But has the geographic location of mass imprisonment changed over time? Do the same neighborhoods year after year continue to bear the brunt of America's exceptionalism in punishment practices?

Sampson convincingly shows that spatial inequality has a durable nature (2012). Multiple forms of social disadvantage—poverty, violence, physical abuse, infant mortality, disease, injury, educational failure—remain stubbornly entrenched, such that the hierarchy of neighborhoods by disadvantage within any given U.S. city reproduces itself year after year. Yet, the early twenty-first century has witnessed substantial changes to urban and suburban environments. To name but a few changes, the Great Recession produced dramatic economic consequences for metropolitan areas, including spikes in unemployment and the collapse of the housing market characterized by a steep rise in mortgage defaults and foreclosures (Grusky, Western, and Wimer 2011). Poverty has fluctuated since 2000 and has suburbanized. On the other hand, even through the Great Recession, the "Great Crime Decline" that began in the early 1990s marched on (Sharkey 2018). Progress in the form of declining racial residential segregation also continued, as it has since the 1970s (Glaeser and Vidgor 2012; Krysan and Crowder 2017). Gentrification and immigration, too, have altered metropolitan environments. Did the typical locations of residence for the formerly imprisoned remain fixed in place over the past two decades, or did they change in sync with the transformations of metropolitan areas?

This article seeks to unite two streams of research that often operate in isolation despite considerable synergies: examinations of the collateral consequences of criminal justice contact (particularly imprisonment) and the study of the spatial inequality of neighborhoods. To do so, I take stock of the geographic distribution of returning prisoners in one U.S. metropolitan area (Chicago) and how it has changed over time.

This longitudinal perspective is unique. Existing studies of the geographic distribution of either prison admissions or exiting prisoners tend to be based on just a snapshot in time (for an exception focused on prison admissions, see Sampson and Loeffler 2010). Neighborhoods and metropolitan areas are dynamic entities, however, and the study of spatial inequality should therefore employ a dynamic analytical approach (for a discussion, see Kirk and Laub 2010). Accordingly, I ask four questions: To what extent are the formerly incarcerated geographically concentrated in space and how persistent is the geographic concentration of returning prisoners over time? To the extent that the residential locations of former prisoners have changed since the turn of the millennium, which urban and suburban locations have seen declines in the rates of former prisoners and which areas have had increases? What factors account for changes to the geography of returning prisoners? And, finally, what have changes in the geographic distribution of returning prisoners meant in terms of the neighborhood conditions that former prisoners face?

THE CONTEXT OF MASS IMPRISONMENT AND MASS REENTRY

An underappreciated fact of the era of mass imprisonment is that 95 percent of prisoners are eventually released from incarceration and returned to society (Langan and Levin 2002). In 1978, roughly 140,000 individuals were released from U.S. prisons. By 2008, yearly releases surpassed 735,000, representing more than a 400 percent increase in three decades (Carson and Mulako-Wangota 2018). The number of yearly releases has declined recently, but the volume still surpasses 625,000 each year. In total, roughly five million formerly imprisoned individuals live in U.S. neighborhoods at this moment (Shannon et al. 2017).

As noted, research by the Urban Institute revealed that more than half of prisoners released from Illinois prisons in 2001 returned to Chicago, and one-third of them were concentrated in only six community areas (La Vigne, Mamalian, et al. 2003). Similarly, in Maryland, nearly 60 percent of prisoners released in 2001 returned to Baltimore, and 30 percent of them were concentrated in just six neighborhoods (La Vigne, Kachnowski, et al. 2003). Of course, metropolitan areas in the United States have changed considerably since the turn of the millennium and the publication of these studies. Still, outside a select few studies, research on the changing geographic patterns of formerly incarcerated individuals is underexplored (see, for example, Harding, Morenoff, and Herbert 2013; Kirk 2016; Simes 2018a). Research exploring geographic patterns outside of urban areas is virtually nonexistent (but see Simes 2018a).

WHY CONCENTRATED?

The reasons ex-prisoners have tended to concentrate in the same neighborhoods is understandably associated with the fact that crime and other social problems are highly concentrated in space and that people admitted to prison generally come from the same relatively few neighborhoods to which they ultimately return (Kirk 2009; Sampson and Loeffler 2010). Many ex-prisoners move back to home neighborhoods, even those who express an interest in avoiding such places, because of a lack of housing opportunities elsewhere and because of the availability of family and social supports in their pre-prison neighborhoods (Western 2018). Indeed, recent estimates from Michigan suggest that the first postprison place of residence for roughly 35 percent of newly released prisoners is within one mile of their pre-prison place of residence, and that a full 60 percent reside within five miles (Harding, Morenoff, and Herbert 2013). As a result, prison admissions and prison releases generally churn in and out of the same neighborhoods (Clear 2007).

Macro Dynamics

The reasons for this concentration of returning prisoners are many and include individual-level factors related to preferences and social networks as well as macroeconomic factors and the dynamics of the housing market. At the macro-level, over the past four decades the relative share of total income held by the top decile of the income distribution in the United States increased from 35 percent to 50 percent (Piketty 2014). Yet inequality has expanded not just between the top 10 and the bottom 90 percent of the distribution; it has also increased *within* the bottom 90 percent.

In conjunction with these macro patterns of income inequality, analyses by Sean Reardon and Kendra Bischoff reveal a growing segregation by income across neighborhoods (2011, 2016). They find that the percentage of metropolitan families in the United States residing in "poor" neighborhoods—defined in their analysis as neighborhoods in which the median family income is less than 0.67 of the metropolitan-area median income—has increased dramatically since 1970. In that year, only 8.4 percent of metropolitan-area families lived in such neighborhoods. By 2012, 18.6 percent of families lived in neighborhoods in which the median income of the neighborhood was less than 0.67 of the metro-area median family income.

This growing income segregation contributes to both the persistence of concentrated poverty and concentrated affluence over time. In a recent study, Robert Sampson analyzes the persistence in levels of median family income by neighborhood from 1990 to the 2008 to 2012 period for all metropolitan-area census tracts in the United States (2016). To do so, he divides all census tracts into quintiles by median family income for three periods: 1990, 2000, and from 2008 to 2012. Despite widespread evidence of gentrification in many urban areas as well as the demolition and redevelopment of public housing, upward mobility of neighborhoods was more the exception than the rule. Similarly, despite the foreclosure crisis and the other ramifications of the Great Recession, he finds little evidence of downward mobility among upper-income neighborhoods. Roughly 80 percent of tracts that were in the bottom or top quintiles by neighborhood median income in 2000 remained in the same quintile between 2008 and 2012 (and the same was true from 1990 to 2000). Hence, income segregation and poverty are quite entrenched, although some neighborhoods transitioned to better socioeconomic positions over time.

Housing Market Dynamics

Along with the lack of income and unstable employment, access to housing for persons with criminal records is hindered by the dearth of affordable housing in the United States. The number of cost-burdened renter households in the United States—defined as households spending more than 30 percent of their income on housing—increased from 17.7 million in 2008 to 21 million in 2017 (Joint Center for Housing Studies 2016, 2018). There are eleven million renter households paying more than 50 percent of income for housing.

Also related to limited housing opportunities for ex-prisoners is the rental vacancy rate. Rental vacancy rates plunged to a thirty-one-year low in 2016, down from double digits to 6.9 percent, before rising slightly to 7.2 percent in 2017 (Joint Center for Housing Studies 2017, 2018).

Given the few possibilities for housing in the private market, the formerly incarcerated may look to the public housing market. However, public housing and voucher programs tend not to be viable options for people with substantial criminal records, or even people without criminal records. Based on analysis of the 2013 American Housing Survey, the Center on Budget and Policy Priorities reports that only 25 percent of families eligible for federal rental assistance actually receive it—that is, all families, not just those with a member with a criminal record (Fischer and Sard 2017; see also Joint Center for Housing Studies 2017).

Of the subsidized housing available for lower-income populations in the United States, much of it is out of reach to people with serious criminal records. Technically, only two circumstances under federal law legally preclude eligibility for public housing assistance: an individual is a lifetime registered sex offender or has been convicted of manufacturing methamphetamine on the premises of federally assisted housing (Federal Interagency Reentry Council 2011). Public housing bans for other crimes, including drug crimes, are *discretionary*. Specifically, the Government Accountability Office explains that "Under federal law and implementing regulations, PHAs have the discretion to evict tenants for drug-related criminal activity but are not required to evict such tenants. Rather, they are required to use leases that provide that any drug-related criminal activity on or off the premises by a public housing tenant shall be cause for termination of the tenancy" (2005, 63). An example of such discretionary practices, which were widely used during the rise of mass imprisonment, was President Clinton's infamous "one strike and you're out" public housing policy, in which families could be denied admission or evicted from public housing for the alleged criminal behavior of an occupant or a guest, even if the criminal behavior had not been prosecuted (Kirk 2018).

During the Obama presidency, the Department of Housing and Urban Development (HUD) took steps toward removing barriers to assisted housing for individuals with criminal records. However, continued disinvestment in federal housing and stringent admission criteria still mean that the formerly incarcerated have little hope of accessing federally assisted housing.

As a result of these dynamics in the private and public housing markets, the formerly incarcerated are left with few possibilities for housing. The options for housing are generally confined to those few neighborhoods from where the formerly incarcerated originated and where a relative who can offer shelter resides (Western 2018).[1]

URBAN TRANSFORMATIONS AND NEIGHBORHOOD CHANGE

Despite abundant reasons to presume that the formerly incarcerated will remain clustered in a relatively small number of neighborhoods in a given metropolitan area, whether that cluster remains entrenched in the exact same neighborhoods or transitions to another set of neighborhoods is an empirical question. Several related urban transformations, including the demolition of public housing, the suburbanization of poverty, and desegregation, may have produced shifts in the residential locations of the formerly incarcerated.

One of the most important changes over the past two decades to impoverished urban neighborhoods has been the demolition of many high density public housing developments, with much of the demolition funded through grants from the federal HOPE VI program. This massive effort sought to redevelop those communities plagued by severely distressed public housing (Kirk and Laub 2010; Tach and Emory 2017). These demolitions embody a shift in federal and local strategies from providing housing assistance through high-rise public housing to low-density scattered-site housing as well as housing vouchers. In 1990, 1.2 million housing vouchers were issued to households in the United States and 1.4 million public housing units were available for residence (Schwartz 2015). In contrast, by 2012, the number of voucher holders had increased to nearly 1.7 million households whereas the number public housing units had declined to 1.15 million (Schwartz 2015).

The impetus for changes in the volume of public housing stock has been the well documented consequences of the concentration of poverty (Wilson 1987). As Laura Tach and Allison Dwyer Emory note, although public housing constituted a relatively small share of the total housing stock in the United States even at its peak, such housing was disproportionately sited in disadvantaged areas, and public housing has been a common fixture of many of the poorest neighborhoods in the country (2017).

One consequence of the demolition of public housing, in conjunction with other metropolitan developments, has been a deconcentration of poverty in urban areas and also a substantial growth in suburban poverty over the past two decades (Chaskin and Joseph 2015; Tach and Emory 2017). Between 2000 and 2014, poverty grew by 65 percent in U.S. suburbs, doubling the growth rate of poverty in major urban areas (Kneebone 2016). In fact, there are more impoverished households in the suburbs in the United States than in urban areas, and that has been true since at least the 2000 Census (Allard 2017; Kneebone and Berube 2013).

Along with the demolition of public housing as well as the suburbanization of poverty has been a decline in racial residential segregation in most metropolitan areas of the United States (Tach and Emory 2017). Edward Glaeser and Jacob Vigdor observe that black-white segregation, as measured by the dissimilarity index, was lower in 2010 than in 1970 in all but one of the 658 housing markets the Census Bureau tracts (2012). When instead assessing the exposure of black residents to other groups, they find that none of the 658 housing markets had a higher level of isolation in 2010 than it did in 1970. Relatedly, Maria Krysan and Kyle Crowder find that the number of all-white metropolitan-area neighborhoods in the United States (that is, with 90 percent or more white residents) decreased from 35,409 in 1980 to 14,214 by 2010, and the number of all-black neighborhoods decreased from 1,889 to 1,787 (2017). Although Glaeser and Vigdor do find evidence that immigration and gentrification spurred some integration of urban neighborhoods, they attribute much of the progress toward declining segregation to population loss in predominantly black neighborhoods, particularly in urban areas in the Midwest and Northeast, which have long been sites of hypersegregation (2012).

In summary, returning prisoners tend to be geographically concentrated into the same

---

1. See, in this volume, Heather Harris and David Harding's analysis of the correlates associated with residential dependence of the formerly incarcerated on parents and family members (2019).

neighborhoods, but twenty-first-century changes to metropolitan areas call into question whether clusters of returning prisoners remain embedded in urban cores or have followed changes such as the demolition of public housing, the suburbanization of poverty, and declining levels of metropolitan-area residential segregation.

Data and Research Design
Much of what is known about the geographic distribution of returning prisoners is from an earlier period of the mass imprisonment era prior to the peak in 2009. I proceed now with an examination of more recent patterns of prisoner reentry and its causes and consequences. My focus is on the Chicago metropolitan area, both the city and suburban Cook County.

Data used in this study come from five sources: the Illinois Department of Corrections (IDOC); the 2000 Census; multiple years—2007–2011, 2008–2012, 2009–2013, 2010–2014, and 2011–2015—of the American Community Survey (ACS); the Chicago Police Department; and the Chicago Housing Authority (2018). IDOC data are available by zip code, and represent the location where individuals first lived after release from prison. Zip code is the unit of analysis I use throughout the study.[2]

The IDOC data were obtained from the Illinois Criminal Justice Information Authority and consist of information on the geographic distribution of prisoners released from prisons in Illinois from fiscal year 1998 to 2013.[3] Releases include those from new court commitments as well as rereleases from prison following a recommitment from a parole violation. I draw on all sixteen years of data for descriptive analyses, and then in later analysis examining the predictors of change in rates of prisoner reentry I focus on the years overlapping the 2000 Census and the ACS data—that is, from 1998 to 2000 and from 2011 to 2013.

In this study, I use two measures of the concentration of returning prisoners—one based on the count of returning prisoners and the other based on the relative share of returning prisoners in a zip code compared to the rest of the population in the zip code.[4] For the latter, I created a yearly measure of the concentration of released prisoners per thousand adult residents in a zip code by dividing the total number of prisoners released to a zip code in a given year over the estimated adult population size (age eighteen to sixty-four) in the zip code, and then multiplying by one thousand. I used interpolation to derive estimates of the adult population count by zip code in the intercensal years.

In regression analyses, I also use a measure of the residual change in the relative share of former prisoners among residents of each neighborhood. This measure is constructed by regressing the 2011 to 2013 average yearly share on the 1998 to 2000 average share. I then output the residual following estimation. These residuals represent the unexpected change in the share of released prisoners after the prior share of former prisoners among neighborhood residents is accounted for. Because a residual change score is the dependent variable, the measure of change in the share of returning prisoners during the first decade of the 2000s is uncorrelated with the initial concentrations of returning prisoners (that is, the share in 1998 to 2000). Residual change scores are useful for

---

2. I recognize that zip codes do not necessarily constitute neighborhoods, particularly outside of Chicago where a zip code may be quite expansive in terms of geographic space. Nevertheless, I do occasionally use the terms *zip code* and *neighborhood* interchangeably for the purposes of making a neighborhood-level argument.

3. The fiscal year in Illinois starts on July 1 and includes the last six months of the prior calendar year through the first six months of the next calendar year (for example, FY1998 ran from July 1, 1997, through June 30, 1998).

4. Housing instability is common among the formerly incarcerated (Kirk 2018). David Harding, Jeffrey Morenoff, and Claire Herbert find that parolees in Michigan move an estimated 2.6 times per year for the median parolee (2013). Again drawing on data from Michigan, Herbert, Morenoff, and Harding find that most periods of residence for parolees last just a few months, with 50 percent of the residential periods lasting eight weeks or less (2015). Accordingly, it is likely that the newly released individuals in Illinois change residences with some frequency, although given the expansiveness of zip codes, it is highly likely that the residential moves occurred within the same zip code in which the individual first resided, or an adjacent zip code.

identifying neighborhoods that changed more or less than expected, where the expected change is a function of citywide changes in shares of returning prisoners.

I use two time points of sociodemographic indicators from the 2000 Census and the 2009–2013 ACS, respectively: the percentages of impoverished residents, of female-headed family households, of individuals age sixteen and older who are unemployed, of households receiving public assistance, of non-Latino black population, of Latino population, and of owner-occupied dwellings in the zip code. For the first four of these indicators, I pooled data from both datasets (that is, each zip code had two observations) and used factor analysis to construct a measure of concentrated poverty. By pooling the data, the factor loadings for each of these indicators do not vary across the two time points, thus ensuring comparability across time. I follow the same procedure to construct residual change scores of the sociodemographic indicators and then use these change scores in regression analysis.

Incident-level crime data were obtained from the Chicago Police Department via the City of Chicago Open Data Portal.[5] Stored on the Data Portal is a file of all criminal incidents by longitude and latitude from 2001 to the present. I subset the data to only include Index crimes, and then created separate files for 2001 Index crimes and 2011 Index crimes. I then spatially joined the point-level longitude/latitude data to Chicago zip codes via tools in ArcGIS.[6] I created measures of the 2001 and 2011 Index crime rates per zip code per 1,000 adult residents by dividing the count of crimes by the adult population size age 18 to 64 and then multiplying by 1,000. I also created a residual change score of the change in the crime rate from 2001 to 2011.

Finally, drawing upon information on the demolition and redevelopment of public housing from the Chicago Housing Authority's website and its Moving to Work annual reports, I constructed a binary measure indicating whether zip codes contained public housing that had been renovated or demolished and redeveloped anytime over the study period from the late-1990s through 2010.[7]

Analytical Framework

Analyses follow five paths. First, I use descriptive analyses based on the count of formerly incarcerated individuals in the various Chicago metropolitan zip codes to examine temporal patterns of the geography of prisoner reentry, including changes over time in the clustering and segregation of the formerly incarcerated in Chicago and Cook County. Second, I map the concentrations of returning prisoners in Cook County in 2013 as well as the change over time in the rate of prisoners returning to Cook County zip codes.

Third, I split the distribution of the rates of returning prisoners by zip code into quintiles for two time points: 1998 and 2013. I then compute a transition matrix (that is, a cross-tab) comparing the two years. The intent is to examine whether any upward or downward mobility is discernible in the concentration of returning prisoners in Chicago. For instance, do most of the zip codes with the highest concentrations of returning prisoners in 1998 still have the highest concentrations in 2013? In many ways, the Chicago metropolitan area over the past several decades has seen considerable change, including a changing geographic distribution of employment, gentrification, public housing demolition, the suburbanization of poverty, and mass foreclosures in the wake of the Great Recession (Allard 2017; Hyra 2008; Kirk and Hyra 2012; Pattillo 2007; Sampson 2012). It is therefore important to examine

---

5. See the Chicago Open Data Portal (https://data.cityofchicago.org/Public-Safety/Crimes-2001-to-present/ijzp-q8t2, accessed September 18, 2018).

6. For a list of index crime classifications used by the Chicago Police Department, see the "Illinois Uniform Crime Reporting (IUCR) Codes" (https://data.cityofchicago.org/Public-Safety/Chicago-Police-Department-Illinois-Uniform-Crime-R/c7ck-438e, accessed September 18, 2018).

7. See Chicago Housing Authority (http://www.thecha.org/about/plans-reports-and-policies, accessed September 18, 2018).

Figure 1. Illinois Prison Releases Returning to Chicago

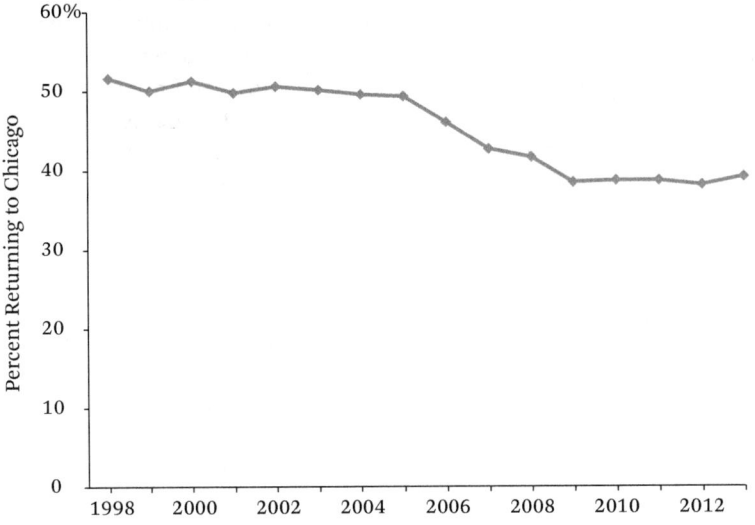

Source: Author's calculations of IDOC data.

whether the pockets of returning prisoners in the city changed measurably over the course of the transformation of the region.

Fourth, I use a linear regression model to examine the predictors of zip code changes in the concentration of returning prisoners over time. For this analysis, it is important to account for the influence of geographic and temporal patterns of crime as a predictor of the geographic distribution of returning prisoners. Point-level crime data are readily available for Chicago zip codes from the City of Chicago Open Data Portal but are not available outside the city limits. Accordingly, I restrict regression models to zip codes within the Chicago city limits. For this analysis, I use the residual change from 1998 through 2000 to 2011 through 2013 in the relative share of former prisoners among residents of each zip code as the dependent variable.

Finally, given evidence of the changing geographic distribution of former prisoners, I examine the consequences in terms of the types of neighborhood conditions to which former prisoners are exposed. Specifically, I examine to the extent to which exposure to neighborhood poverty and racial isolation by former prisoners may have changed over the past two decades.

RESULTS

To start, I examine temporal patterns in the residential location of formerly incarcerated individuals in Chicago. Figure 1 demonstrates that the percentage of IDOC prison releases returning to Chicago in a given year declined from 52 percent in 1998 to 39 percent in 2013. Although not shown in the figure, the decline in the percent of Illinois prisoners returning to Chicago is the product of two shifts: a declining share of IDOC releases to the wider Chicago-Naperville-Elgin core-based statistical area (CBSA) and a suburbanization of releases in the Chicago-Naperville-Elgin CBSA to suburban areas located outside of the Chicago city limits. In the late 1990s, roughly 75 percent of the newly released prisoners to the CBSA lived within Chicago city limits. By 2013, 64 percent did.

The Segregation of the Formerly Incarcerated

Given the suburbanization of former prisoners into zip codes previously inhabited by few formerly incarcerated individuals, it is likely that the spatial concentration of former prisoners would have dissipated in Cook County. This is what we see in the top line in figure 2 (the Cook County line reflects all zip codes in Cook

Figure 2. Prison Releases in the Top 20 Percent of Neighborhoods in Cook County and Chicago by Volume of Returning Prisoners

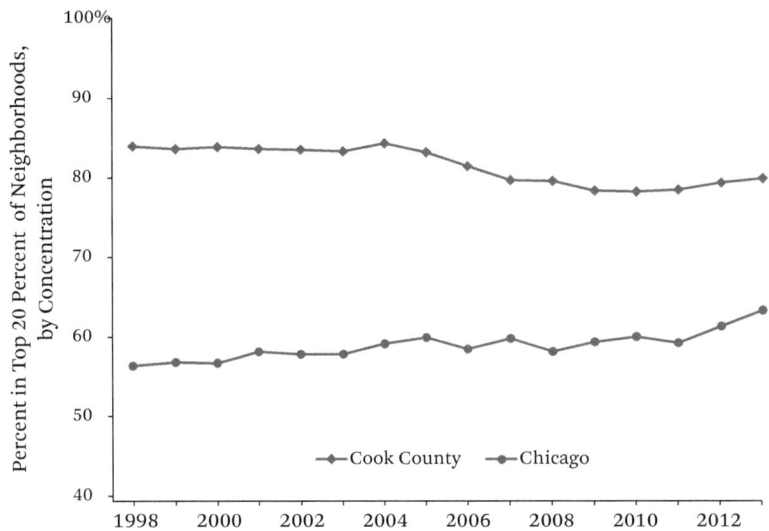

Source: Author's calculations of IDOC data.

County, including Chicago).[8] In the late 1990s, roughly 84 percent of prison releases residing in the Chicago CBSA were concentrated in just 20 percent of the zip codes. This percentage steadily declined until 2011 before increasing slightly more recently. Nevertheless, in Cook County as a whole, the suburbanization of the formerly incarcerated has led to a reduction in at least one measure of neighborhood inequality—that is, the clustering of the formerly incarcerated in a select few zip codes.[9]

Interestingly, the bottom line in figure 2, which focuses on zip codes within the Chicago city limits rather than all of Cook County, reveals that the concentration of the formerly incarcerated has steadily increased over time. In the late 1990s, 57 percent of prison releases in Chicago were concentrated in just 20 percent of the zip codes. By 2013, this figure had increased to 63 percent. Hence, the Chicago zip codes diverge from the rest of the county and wider metropolitan area; the concentration of former prisoners by zip code in Chicago is increasing, but declining in Cook County and the metro region as a whole.

Another way to visualize the geographic patterns in Cook County and Chicago is to examine trends in segregation measures. Presented

---

8. For the analysis presented in figure 2 and the remainder of the article, I excluded five zip codes that contain jails, immigrant detention centers, and adult transition centers (types of halfway houses). These zip codes receive large numbers of returning prisoners, but many of them are immediately reincarcerated in another facility and are never actually released from custody. For instance, zip code 60608 is the location of the Cook County jail, where individuals with an active criminal case and detainer in Cook County may be transferred on release from an IDOC prison. Zip code 60155 is the location of the Broadview immigration detention center, which may process released IDOC prisoners for deportation. I exclude these zip codes because many of the prisoners released to them remain in institutional environments rather than in residential environments, and including them would artificially inflate the counts of former prisoners in certain parts of the metropolitan area.

9. Similar findings emerge when I expand the analysis to include not just Cook County but all of the Illinois counties in the wider Chicago-Naperville-Elgin CBSA (that is, Cook, DeKalb, DuPage, Grundy, Kane, Kendall, Lake, McHenry, and Will counties). In this case, 87 percent of prison releases residing in the CBSA in the late 1990s concentrated in just 20 percent of the zip codes versus 81 percent in 2013.

Figure 3. Index of Dissimilarity of Evenness of Prison Releases in Cook County and Chicago

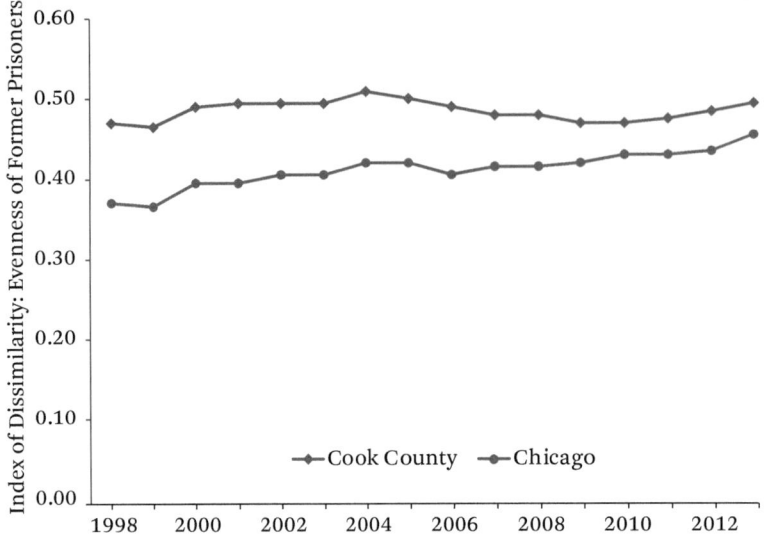

Source: Author's calculations of IDOC data.

in figure 3 are the patterns in the index of dissimilarity, which in this case measures how evenly spread the formerly incarcerated are across Cook County, the top line, and Chicago alone, the bottom line (Massey and Denton 1988). The dissimilarity index measures the percentage of a group's population, typically based on race and ethnicity, that would need to change residence for each zip code to have the same percentage of that group as the total geographic area overall. My focus here is on the segregation of the formerly incarcerated from the nonincarcerated. In Cook County the trend in segregation is mostly flat. In 2013, 49 percent of former prisoners would have needed to change zip codes for the distribution of the formerly incarcerated across the county to be evenly spread.[10] Subset to the Chicago zip codes, we see a pronounced increase in segregation, from a dissimilarity index of 0.37 in 1998 to 0.46 in 2013.

To summarize, by the 80:20 inequality ratio, the suburbanization of released prisoners has produced a more even geographic spread of the formerly incarcerated in Cook County than in prior decades. The dissimilarity index for Cook County mostly reveals a flat trend in the segregation of the formerly incarcerated. For Chicago, however, both the 80:20 ratio and the dissimilarity index reveal increasing patterns of clustering and segregation of former prisoners.

Mapping the Changing Geography of the Formerly Incarcerated

Figures 1, 2, and 3 reveal a complex temporal dynamic among individuals released from prison in Illinois: proportionally fewer of them live in the Chicago city limits, leading to a dispersion in the spatial concentration of former prisoners when looking at the wider Chicago metropolitan area as a whole. However, those former prisoners residing within the city limits are increasingly concentrated and segregated spatially. These findings lead to several important questions: which sections of suburban Cook County may have absorbed the formerly incarcerated who would have resided in Chicago in prior decades, and which parts of Chicago still have a large volume of formerly incarcerated residents?

Figure 4 begins to answer these questions.

10. If I expand the analysis to focus on the wider Chicago-Naperville-Elgin CBSA, I find notably similar patterns and levels of segregation as in the analysis subset to Cook County.

Figure 4. Change in Rate of Returning Prisoners in Cook County by Zip Code, 1998–2000 to 2011–2013

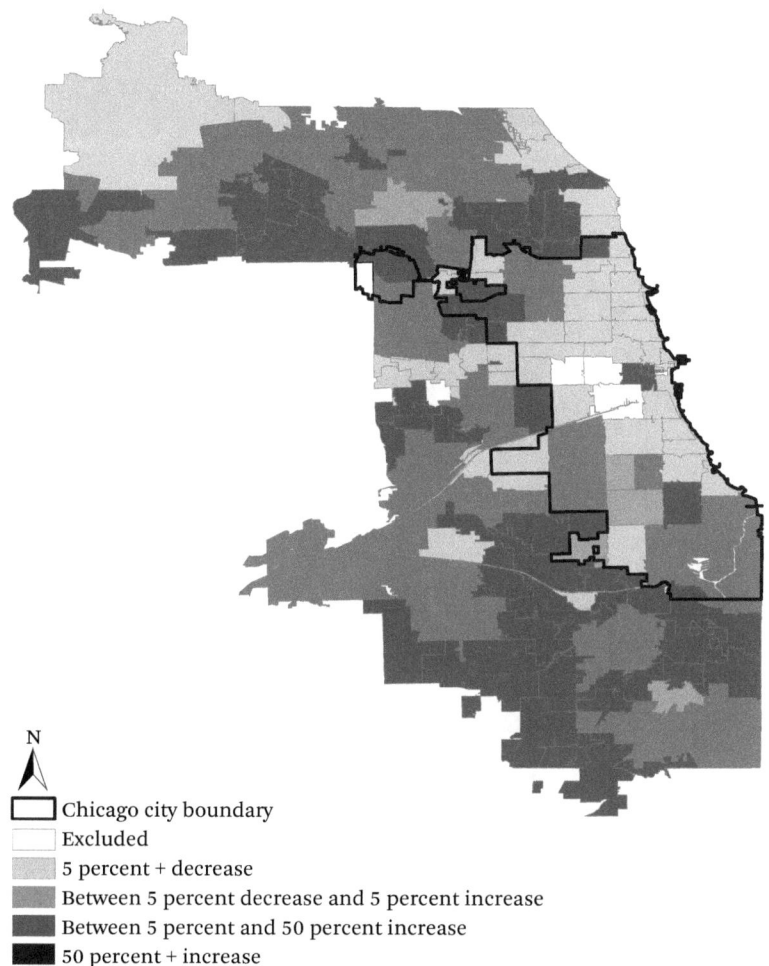

- Chicago city boundary
- Excluded
- 5 percent + decrease
- Between 5 percent decrease and 5 percent increase
- Between 5 percent and 50 percent increase
- 50 percent + increase

Source: Author's calculations of IDOC data.

It displays the changing pattern of the formerly incarcerated in Cook County from 1998 through 2000 to 2011 through 2013. Figure 4 is based upon the rate of recently released individuals in the zip code—that is, the count of released prisoners divided by the size of the adult population, and then multiplied by a thousand. The light gray shading in figure 4 represents declines in the relative share of former prisoners among the adult residents in the zip code. The dark gray shading represents an increasing share.

Figure 4 reveals that for most of the Chicago city limits, zip codes had declining proportions of formerly incarcerated residents. The exceptions are the Near West Side near downtown Chicago as well as the southern border of the city. In contrast, just outside the city limits in the west and especially southwest sections of Cook County, growth in the relative share of formerly incarcerated individuals in the zip codes was substantial. For instance, zip code 60409 in Calumet City, on the border with Indiana in the southern part of the Chicago metropolitan area, was on the receiving end of 164 returning prisoners in 2013 and forty-seven in 1998. Zip code 60419 in Dolton, just across the southern border of the Chicago city limits, had 101 returning prisoners in 2013 and fifty-nine in 1998. Zip code 60402 in Berwyn, just west of

Figure 5. Number of Returning Prisoners in Cook County by Zip Code, 2013

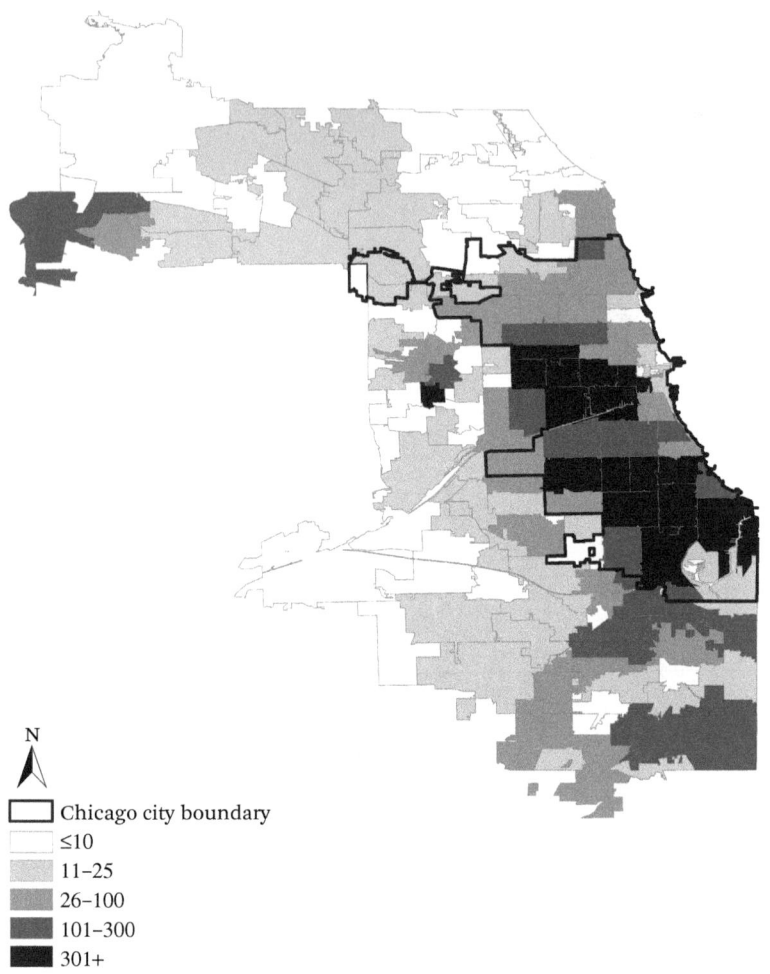

Chicago city boundary
≤10
11–25
26–100
101–300
301+

Source: Author's calculations of IDOC data.

Chicago, had ninety returning prisoners in 2013 versus sixty-two in 1998. Zip code 60120 in Elgin, which lies in the northwest part of Cook County and is its second largest city, also saw an increase in the number of returning prisoners between 1998 and 2013, from sixty-five to 123.

Whereas the growth in the rate of returning prisoners has mainly occurred outside the Chicago city limits, Chicago zip codes still have a disproportionate volume of returning prisoners even if prisoner reentry has been suburbanized. Figure 5 depicts the count of newly released prisoners in each zip code in Cook County. Clearly the largest counts are still within the city, particularly areas west and south of downtown.

Transition Matrices to Assess Zip Code Stability and Change

Another way to visualize stability and change in the concentration of returning prisoners over the course of the last two decades is through transition matrices. Transition matrices are a common method for examining social mobility—for example, to examine upward and downward socioeconomic mobility of children relative to their parents. In this case, I examine

Figure 6. Quintiles of Ex-prisoner Concentration in Cook County, 1998 to 2013

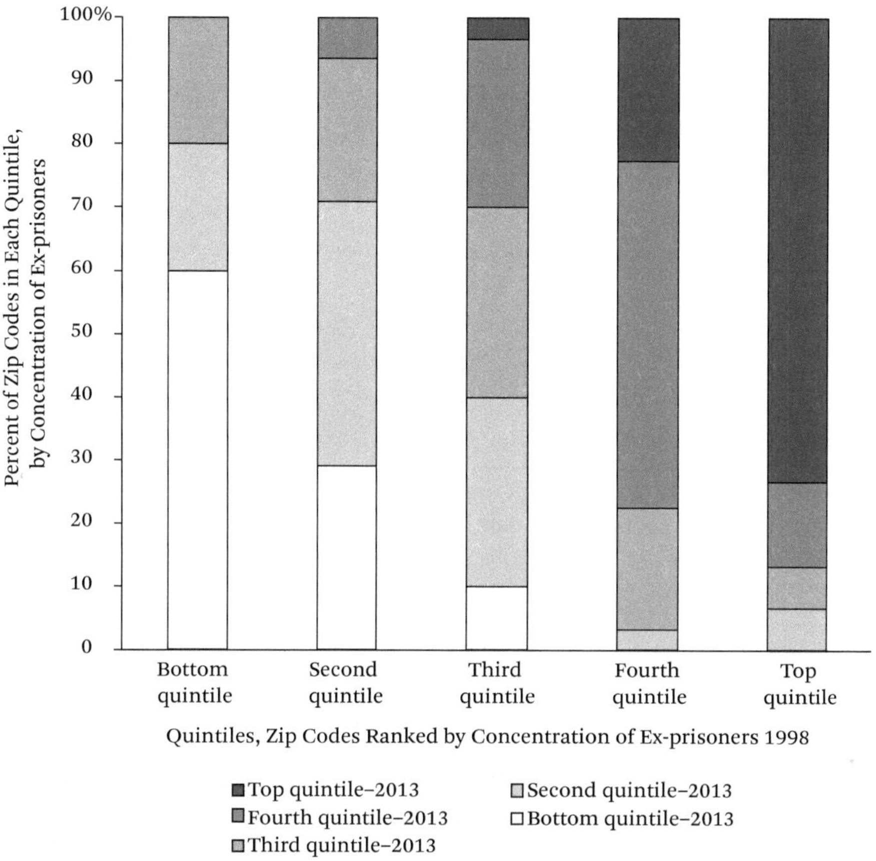

[Stacked bar chart showing percent of zip codes in each quintile by concentration of ex-prisoners, with x-axis showing quintiles ranked by concentration of ex-prisoners in 1998 (Bottom, Second, Third, Fourth, Top), and legend indicating Top quintile–2013, Fourth quintile–2013, Third quintile–2013, Second quintile–2013, Bottom quintile–2013.]

Source: Author's calculations of IDOC data.

the upward and downward mobility of zip codes as measured by their concentration of returning prisoners relative to other zip codes in the metropolitan area.

Figure 6 presents the neighborhood change in rates of ex-prisoner concentration for all zip codes in Cook County from 1998 to 2013, ranked from those with few to no former prisoners (bottom quintile) to those with a high proportion of residents who were formerly incarcerated (top quintile). If transitioning of zip codes in terms of the rank ordering by concentration of returning prisoners was minimal, then a given column would be shaded mostly the same throughout.

This figure reveals both persistence and change in the concentration of returning prisoners. Sixty percent of zip codes in the bottom group in 1998 (the white portion of the bar) were still in the bottom grouping in 2013. These zip codes had few to no returning prisoners in 1998 and remained that way in 2013. However, another 20 percent of the bottom group in 1998 transitioned to the second quintile by 2013 and another 20 percent transitioned to the third quintile. These zip codes started out with essentially zero returning prisoners in 1998, but saw growth in the rate of returning prisoners over the fifteen-plus-year period.

Seventy-three percent of zip codes in the top quintile in 1998 were still in the same quintile in 2013. However, the remaining 27 percent transitioned to a relatively lower ranking by 2013. In summary, figure 6 reveals that although many geographic areas with high concentrations of former prisoners tend to persist over time, there is some transitioning in the rank ordering of zip codes.

Table 1. Residual Change in Geographic Concentration of Former Prisoners, Chicago Zip Codes 1998–2000 to 2011–2013

	b	(Robust SE)	β
Intercept	0.718	(1.735)	
Concentrated poverty, 2000	4.449	(0.738)***	0.910
Change in concentrated poverty	5.167	(1.596)**	0.644
Percent African American, 2000	−2.596	(1.845)	−0.187
Change in percent African American	−3.804	(8.639)	−0.037
Percent Latino, 2000	−5.256	(2.132)*	−0.218
Change in percent Latino	−8.938	(4.082)*	−0.147
Percent owner-occupied housing	3.769	(2.157)	0.158
Change in owner-occupied housing	−10.812	(10.256)	−0.131
Index crime rate, 2001	0.017	(0.005)**	0.355
Change in index crime rate	0.003	(0.016)	0.012
Public housing demolition/renovation	−2.785	(0.755)***	−0.204

Source: Author's calculations using IDOC, 2000 U.S. Census, 2009–2013 ACS, Chicago Police Department, and Chicago Housing Authority (2018) data.
Note: N = 48.
*p < .05; **p < .01; ***p < .001

Correlates of the Changing Geography of Former Prisoners

Given the general stability in the concentration of returning prisoners and many other indicators of social disadvantage, what accounts for some transitioning among neighborhoods in figure 6 in terms of their relative ranking of density of returning prisoners (see Sampson 2012)?

One possibility is that the geographic distribution of returning prisoners is following changes in the volume and geographic distribution of crime. Whereas Chicago has made far too many headlines in recent years for bursts of lethal violence, it is still true that since the early 1990s crime is dramatically down in Chicago, just as it is in many major U.S. cities, particularly in neighborhoods where violence and poverty have historically been most severe (Sharkey 2018). Research reveals that suburbs, too, saw declines in crime from 1990 to the present, although cities had larger declines, on average (Kneebone and Raphael 2011). Of importance, the crime decline has been uneven within suburban areas. Older, inner-ring suburbs generally had large declines in violent and property crime from 1990 to the present, but newer, emerging suburbs as well as exurban areas actually had increases in crime and violence over the same period (Kneebone and Raphael 2011). These trends would suggest that suburban and exurban areas would therefore have a relatively greater share of prison admission and releases than in the past.

Besides the changing distribution of crime as a likely contributor to the changing geography of returning prisoners, it is likely that other socioeconomic shifts—such as the razing of public housing, the suburbanization of poverty, and the decline in residential segregation in Chicago—are also correlated with changes in the location of the formerly incarcerated.

In table 1, I focus on zip codes in the Chicago city limits to examine why, as seen in figure 4, many neighborhoods in Chicago have had declining rates of returning prisoners since the late 1990s. Specifically, table 1 presents regression estimates of the residual change in the zip code share of returning prisoners from 1998 through 2000 to 2011 through 2013, unstandardized coefficients in the second column and standardized coefficients in the fourth.[11] Con-

---

11. As in the other analyses (see footnote 6), I exclude zip codes that contain jails, immigrant detention centers, and adult transition centers. I also exclude the zip code that largely consists of O'Hare airport (60666) as well those with populations of less than five hundred as of the 2000 Census.

sistent with research on neighborhood variation in prison admissions and to improve the precision of my measurement of prisoner return rates, I pool data from three-year periods (see Sampson and Loeffler 2010; Simes 2018a). Analyses presented in figures 2, 3, and 5 reveal that former prisoners are clustered within a relatively small subset of zip codes in the city, evidence of the spatial clustering of returning prisoners. However, in preliminary analysis I examined whether spatial autocorrelation existed in the residual change in returning prisoners net of controls for crime and other zip code characteristics, but did not find evidence of any dependence. Accordingly, I estimate a linear regression model rather than a spatial regression model.

It can be seen in table 1 that there is positive association between the residual change in prisoner reentry and the poverty rate at baseline as well as the growth in poverty (here and elsewhere, *baseline* refers to the first time point of data, typically the year 2000). As expected, zip codes with increasing levels of concentrated poverty are more likely to have gains in the share of former prisoners. Conversely, neighborhoods with declining rates of poverty, as occurred in many Chicago neighborhoods through gentrification and the redevelopment of public housing, are predicted to have declining shares of returning prisoners.

The baseline share of black population is negatively predictive of concentrated prisoner reentry, although baseline concentrated poverty and the baseline percentage of black population are highly correlated with a variance inflation factor for each close to 9. If I remove concentrated poverty from the analysis as I did in a supplementary analysis, I find a positive relationship between the baseline percentage of black population and the concentration of returning prisoners.[12] I do not find evidence of an association between changes in the share of returning prisoners and changes in the share of black population in a zip code, net of other predictors.

Both the baseline share and growth in the Latino population are related to declines in the concentration of returning prisoners, whereas the level and growth in home ownership in a zip code is unrelated to share of former prisoners in the neighborhood.

As expected, I find that the geographic distribution of returning prisoners is correlated with the distribution of crime, at least at baseline. Also as expected, zip codes where public housing has been demolished or renovated had declining rates of prisoner reentry.

Standardized coefficients in the far right column of table 1 reveal the importance of poverty in explaining the geographic distribution of the formerly incarcerated. Whereas I have not in this analysis estimated the reciprocal association between neighborhood poverty and the locations of returning prisoners, in all likelihood they are mutually reinforcing. At the most basic level, mass imprisonment and mass prisoner reentry may exacerbate the concentration of poverty by inundating neighborhoods with undereducated individuals with limited skills and enormous debt who face the daunting task of overcoming the numerous barriers to postprison employment such as denials of occupational licensing and discrimination in hiring (see, in this volume, Apel and Powell 2019; Friedman and Pattillo 2019).

Neighborhood Attainment

Results suggest that the geographic shift in the residential locations of returning prisoners is the product of several forces, including the changing geographies of poverty and crime, but what has this shift meant in terms of the neighborhood conditions to which the formerly incarcerated are exposed? The literature shows a growing emphasis on understanding the neighborhood conditions the formerly incarcerated face after leaving prison (Lee, Morenoff, and Harding 2016; Massoglia, Firebaugh, and Warner 2013; Simes 2018b). The emphasis, however, is typically on racial-ethnic differences in neighborhood attainment rather than changes in neighborhood conditions over time. To complete the analysis, I examine neighborhood attainment in terms of two characteristics: family poverty rate and percentage of black population in zip codes. Figure 7 displays the mean racial composition and mean poverty rate of

---

12. Results available from the author.

Figure 7. Neighborhood Characteristics of Average Residential Locations of Returning Prisoners in Cook County, 1998–2013

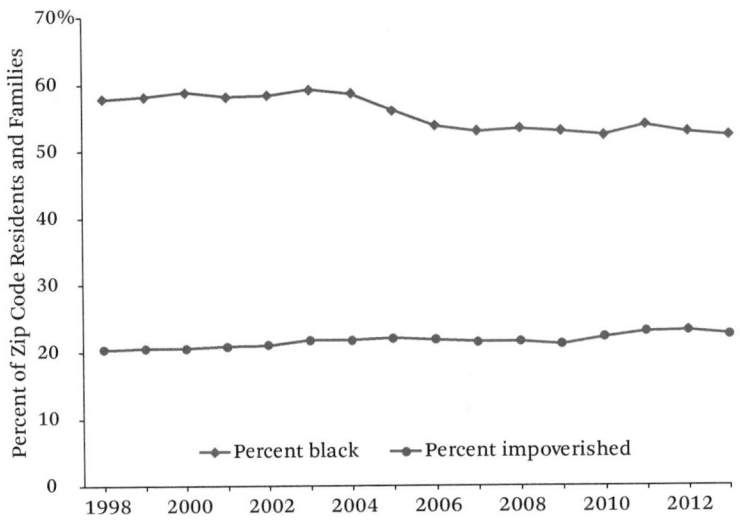

Source: Author's calculations of IDOC, 2000 U.S. Census, and American Community Survey data (2007–2011, 2008–2012, 2009–2013, 2010–2014, 2011–2015).

the zip codes inhabited by newly released prisoners each year from 1998 to 2013.

In terms of racial composition, it is pertinent to note that the size of the non-Hispanic black population in Chicago fell dramatically over the period of investigation, from 1.054 million in 2000 to 863,000 in 2009 through 2013. In comparison, the total population of Chicago fell from 2.9 million to 2.7 million during the same time frame. Similarly, in Cook County, the non-Hispanic black population declined from 1.39 million in 2000 to 1.26 million in 2009 to 2013, whereas the total population size fell from 5.38 million to 5.2 million. In terms of segregation, the dissimilarity index measuring black-white segregation in Chicago declined from 85.2 to 82.5 between the 2000 and 2010 U.S. censuses, and declined from 80.4 to 75.2 for the Chicago metropolitan area as a whole (American Communities Project 2018).

Consistent with trends in desegregation and the declining size of the black population in Chicago and Cook County, the formerly incarcerated in Cook County live in zip codes characterized by an average of 52 percent black residents versus 58 percent back in 1998. In terms of poverty, figure 7 reveals an increasing exposure to poverty even though, as we saw in figures 1 and 4, the location of returning prisoners since the late 1990s has shifted from concentration in core urban neighborhoods to suburban areas. This increasing exposure to poverty is the product of two trends: that the suburbanization of prisoner reentry echoed the suburbanization of poverty such that former prisoners in the suburbs are still largely located in impoverished areas, and that former prisoners in Chicago remain concentrated in areas of severe disadvantage. In sum, the residential experiences of returning prisoners have changed over the past couple of decades: the formerly incarcerated of the current decade are residing in relatively more impoverished areas than their counterparts in the late 1990s, on average, but in areas with a smaller share of black residents.

DISCUSSION

In this study, I sought to examine the extent to which the geographic distribution of formerly incarcerated individuals in Chicago and Illinois has changed, if at all, since the late 1990s as metropolitan areas underwent substantial changes related to the Great Recession, the demolition of public housing, declining levels of racial residential segregation, and the deconcentration of poverty in central cities and the expansion of poverty to the suburbs. Specifically, I asked four questions: To what extent are the formerly incarcerated geographically concentrated in space and how persistent is the geographic concentration of returning prisoners over time? Which urban and suburban locations have seen declines in the rates of former prisoners and which areas have had increases? What factors account for changes to the geography of returning prisoners? What have changes in the geographic distribution of returning prisoners meant in terms of the neighborhood conditions that former prisoners face?

Data brought to bear on these questions reveal several novel findings. Prisoner reentry is not just a city issue, because proportionally fewer (and absolutely fewer) exiting prisoners are returning to the Chicago city limits than in the past, more going to suburban locations as well as other cities in the state. When the formerly incarcerated do reside in Chicago, they tend to be more tightly clustered and segregated from the larger population than in previous periods of the mass imprisonment era. Both stability and change are to be found in the densest clustering of the formerly incarcerated in Chicago, with the West Side long a residential site for returning prisoners and with newer pockets on the far South Side. Transition matrices reveal both stability and change in the rank ordering of zip codes by concentrated prisoner reentry. Changes in the geographic distribution of returning prisoners tend to mirror changes in the distribution of poverty. Last, these various changes mean that former prisoners now reside, on average, in areas with proportionally fewer black residents but more poor residents than in the past.

These findings point to several additional areas of inquiry for future research. For instance, what are the implications of the changing geography of returning prisoners on their ability to reintegrate back into society? Are local and state criminal justice and social service systems even aware of the changing geographic patterns of returning prisoners, and are they equipped to manage the implications of this change? As Scott Allard explores in detail, the social service infrastructure in the suburbs, including government programs as well as nonprofits, is often severely limited and strained (2017). Relative to urban environments, the suburbs have fewer social service organizations and their operations are stretched across a far more expansive service delivery area given the definitional sprawl of suburbs. Because social services for the formerly incarcerated typically concentrate in central cities, the migration of the formerly incarcerated to the suburbs means that it is more challenging for former prisoners to access services such as drug and mental health treatment that are so critical to well-being and desistance from crime. An in-depth exploration of the consequences of the changing geography of returning prisoners on rehabilitation and reintegration is warranted.

An additional line of inquiry is to examine the reciprocal relation between new geographic patterns of prisoner reentry and community conditions, including the concentration of poverty (Kirk 2015). For instance, does an influx of returning prisoners lead to a spike in unemployment in a neighborhood? Are returning prisoners a burden on households to the extent that some households fall below the poverty line? Do neighborhoods on the receiving end of many formerly incarcerated individuals become stigmatized, thereby leading to the outmigration of working and middle-class populations as well as neighborhood institutions and businesses? These questions must be addressed in the future for us to fully comprehend how the geography of mass imprisonment and prisoner reentry has affected spatial inequality in the United States.

REFERENCES

Allard, Scott W. 2017. *Places in Need: The Changing Geography of Poverty.* New York: Russell Sage Foundation.

American Communities Project. "Diversity and Disparities." Accessed July 10, 2018. https://s4.ad.brown.edu/projects/diversity/Data/Data.htm.

Apel, Robert, and Kathleen Powell. 2019. "Level of Criminal Justice Contact and Early Adult Wage Inequality." *RSF: The Russell Sage Foundation Journal of the Social Sciences* 5(1): 198–222. DOI: 10.7758/RSF.2019.5.1.09.

Blumstein, Alfred, and Jacqueline Cohen. 1973. "A Theory of the Stability of Punishment." *Journal of Criminal Law and Criminology* 64(2): 198–207.

Carson, E. Ann, and Joseph Mulako-Wangota. 2018. "Corrections Statistical Analysis Tool (CSAT)—Prisoners." Washington: U.S. Department of Justice, Bureau of Justice Statistics. Accessed September 4, 2018. https://www.bjs.gov/index.cfm?ty=nps.

Chaskin, Robert J., and Mark L. Joseph. 2015. *Integrating the Inner City: The Promise and Perils of Mixed-Income Public Housing Transformation*. Chicago: University of Chicago Press.

Chicago Housing Authority. 2018. "MTW Annual Reports." Accessed September 14, 2018. http://www.thecha.org/about/plans-reports-and-policies.

Clear, Todd R. 2007. *Imprisoning Communities: How Mass Incarceration Makes Disadvantaged Neighborhoods Worse*. New York: Oxford University Press.

Federal Interagency Reentry Council. 2011. "Reentry Mythbuster: On Public Housing." New York: The National Reentry Resource Center. Accessed September 4, 2018. https://csgjusticecenter.org/wp-content/uploads/2012/12/Reentry_Council_Mythbuster_Housing.pdf.

Fischer, Will, and Barbara Sard. 2017. *Chart Book: Federal Housing Spending Is Poorly Matched to Need*. Washington, D.C.: Center on Budget and Policy Priorities.

Friedman, Brittany, and Mary Pattillo. 2019. "Statutory Inequality: The Logics of Monetary Sanctions In State Law." *RSF: The Russell Sage Foundation Journal of the Social Sciences* 5(1): 173-96. DOI: 10.7758/RSF.2019.5.1.08.

Galster, George, and Patrick Sharkey. 2017. "Spatial Foundations of Inequality: A Conceptual Model and Empirical Overview." *RSF: The Russell Sage Foundation Journal of the Social Sciences* 3(2): 1-33. DOI: 10.7758/RSF.2017.3.2.01.

Garland, David. 2001. *Mass Imprisonment: Social Causes and Consequences*. London: Sage Publications.

Glaeser, Edward, and Jacob Vigdor. 2012. *The End of the Segregated Century: Racial Separation in America's Neighborhoods, 1890-2010*. New York: The Manhattan Institute.

Grusky, David, Bruce Western, and Christopher Wimer. 2011. *The Great Recession*. New York: Russell Sage Foundation.

Harding, David J., Jeffrey D. Morenoff, and Claire Herbert. 2013. "Home Is Hard to Find: Neighborhoods, Institutions, and the Residential Trajectories of Returning Prisoners." *The Annals of the American Academy of Political and Social Science* 647(1): 214-36.

Harris, Heather M., and David J. Harding. 2019. "Racial Inequality in the Transition to Adulthood After Prison." *RSF: The Russell Sage Foundation Journal of the Social Sciences* 5(1): 223-54. DOI: 10.7758/RSF.2019.5.1.10.

Herbert, Claire W., Jeffrey D. Morenoff, and David J. Harding. 2015. "Homelessness and Housing Insecurity Among Former Prisoners." *RSF: The Russell Sage Foundation Journal of the Social Sciences* 1(2): 44-79. DOI: 10.7758/RSF.2015.1.2.04.

Hyra, Derek S. 2008. *The New Urban Renewal: The Economic Transformation of Harlem and Bronzeville*. Chicago: University of Chicago Press.

Joint Center for Housing Studies of Harvard University. 2016. *The State of the Nation's Housing: 2016*. Cambridge, Mass.: Harvard University.

———. 2017. *The State of the Nation's Housing: 2017*. Cambridge, Mass.: Harvard University.

———. 2018. *The State of the Nation's Housing: 2018*. Cambridge, Mass.: Harvard University.

Kirk, David S. 2009. "A Natural Experiment on Residential Change and Recidivism: Lessons from Hurricane Katrina." *American Sociological Review* 74(3): 484-505.

———. 2015. "A Natural Experiment of the Consequences of Concentrating Former Prisoners in the Same Neighborhoods." *Proceedings of the National Academy of Sciences* 112(22): 6943-48.

———. 2016. "Prisoner Reentry and the Reproduction of Legal Cynicism." *Social Problems* 63(2): 222-43.

———. 2018. "The Collateral Consequences of Incarceration for Housing." In *Handbook on the Consequences of Sentencing and Punishment Decisions*, edited by Beth M. Huebner and Natasha Frost. New York: Routledge.

Kirk, David S., and Derek S. Hyra. 2012. "Home Foreclosures and Community Crime: Causal or Spurious Association?" *Social Science Quarterly* 93(3): 648-70.

Kirk, David S., and John H. Laub. 2010. "Neighborhood Change and Crime in the Modern Metropolis." *Crime and Justice: A Review of Research* 39(1): 441-502.

Kirk, David S., and Sara Wakefield. 2018. "Collateral Consequences of Punishment: A Critical Review and Path Forward." *Annual Review of Criminology* 1: 171-94.

Kneebone, Elizabeth. 2016. *Suburban Poverty Is Missing from the Conversation about America's Future*. Washington, D.C.: Brookings Institution.

Kneebone, Elizabeth, and Alan Berube. 2013. *Confronting Suburban Poverty in America*. Washington, D.C.: Brookings Institution Press.

Kneebone, Elizabeth, and Steven Raphael. 2011. *City and Suburban Crime Trends in Metropolitan America*. Washington, D.C.: Brookings Institution.

Krysan, Maria, and Kyle Crowder. 2017. *Cycle of Segregation: Social Processes and Residential Stratification*. New York: Russell Sage Foundation.

Langan, Patrick A., and David J. Levin. 2002. *Recidivism of Prisoners Released in 1994*. Washington: U.S. Department of Justice.

La Vigne, Nancy G., Vera Kachnowski, Jeremy Travis, Rebecca Naser, and Christy Visher. 2003. *A Portrait of Prisoner Reentry in Maryland*. Washington, D.C.: Urban Institute.

La Vigne, Nancy G., Cynthia A. Mamalian, Jeremy Travis, and Christy Visher. 2003. *A Portrait of Prisoner Reentry in Illinois*. Washington, D.C.: Urban Institute.

Lee, Keunbok, David J. Harding, and Jeffrey D. Morenoff. 2017. "Trajectories of Neighborhood Attainment after Prison." *Social Science Research* 66(1): 211–33.

Maguire, Kathleen, ed. 2010. *Sourcebook of Criminal Justice Statistics*, Table 6.28.2010. Albany, N.Y.: Hindelang Criminal Justice Research Center. Accessed September 4, 2018. http://www.albany.edu/sourcebook/pdf/t6282010.pdf.

Massey, Douglas S., and Nancy A. Denton. 1988. "The Dimensions of Residential Segregation." *Social Forces* 67(2): 281–315.

Massoglia, Michael, Glenn Firebaugh, and Cody Warner. 2013. "Racial Variation in the Effect of Incarceration on Neighborhood Attainment." *American Sociological Review* 78(1): 142–65.

National Research Council (NRC). 2014. *The Growth of Incarceration in the United States: Exploring Causes and Consequences*, edited by Jeremy Travis, Bruce Western, and Steve Redburn. Washington, D.C.: National Academies Press.

Pattillo, Mary. 2007. *Black on the Block: The Politics of Race and Class in the City*. Chicago: University of Chicago Press.

Piketty, Thomas. 2014. *Capital in the Twenty-First Century*. Cambridge, Mass.: The Belknap Press of Harvard University Press.

Reardon, Sean F., and Kendra Bischoff. 2011. "Income Inequality and Income Segregation." *American Journal of Sociology* 116(4): 1092–153.

———. 2016. "The Continuing Increase in Income Segregation, 2007–2012." Stanford, Calif.: Stanford Center for Education Policy Analysis. Accessed September 4, 2018. http://cepa.stanford.edu/content/continuing-increase-income-segregation-2007-2012.

Sampson, Robert J. 2012. *Great American City: Chicago and the Enduring Neighborhood Effect*. Chicago: University of Chicago Press.

———. 2016. "Individual and Community Economic Mobility in the Great Recession Era: The Spatial Foundations of Persistent Inequality." In *Economic Mobility: Research and Ideas on Strengthening Families, Communities and the Economy*, edited by the Federal Reserve Bank of St. Louis and the Board of Governors of the Federal Reserve System. St. Louis, Mo.: Federal Reserve Bank of St. Louis.

Sampson, Robert J., and Charles Loeffler. 2010. "Punishment's Place: The Local Concentration of Mass Incarceration." *Daedalus* 139(3): 20–31.

Schwartz, Alex F. 2015. *Housing Policy in the United States*, 3rd ed. New York: Routledge.

Shannon, Sarah K. S., Christopher Uggen, Jason Schnittker, Melissa Thompson, Sara Wakefield, and Michael Massoglia. 2017. "The Growth, Scope, and Spatial Distribution of People with Felony Records in the United States, 1948 to 2010." *Demography* 54(5): 1795–818.

Sharkey, Patrick. 2018. *Uneasy Peace: The Great Crime Decline, the Renewal of City Life, and the Next War on Violence*. New York: W. W. Norton.

Simes, Jessica T. 2018a. "Place and Punishment: The Spatial Context of Mass Incarceration." *Journal of Quantitative Criminology* 34(2): 513–33.

Simes, Jessica T. 2018b. "Place After Prison: Neighborhood Attainment and Attachment During Reentry." *Journal of Urban Affairs*. Published online August 2, 2018. DOI: 10.1080/07352166.2018.1495041.

Tach, Laura, and Allison Dwyer Emory. 2017. "Public Housing Redevelopment, Neighborhood Change, and the Restructuring of Urban Inequality." *American Journal of Sociology* 123(3): 686–739.

Turney, Kristin, and Sara Wakefield. 2019. "Criminal Justice Contact and Inequality." *RSF: The Russell Sage Foundation Journal of the Social Sciences* 5(1): 1–23. DOI: 10.7758/RSF.2019.5.1.01.

U.S. Government Accountability Office (GAO). 2005. *Drug Offenders: Various Factors May Limit the Impacts of Federal Laws That Provide for Denial of Selected Benefits*. GAO-05-238. Washington: Government Printing Office.

Wakefield, Sara, and Chris Uggen. 2010. "Incarceration and Stratification." *Annual Review of Sociology* 36: 387–406.

Western, Bruce. 2006. *Punishment and Inequality in America*. New York: Russell Sage Foundation.

———. 2018. *Homeward: Life in the Year After Prison*. New York: Russell Sage Foundation.

Wilson, William J. 1987. *The Truly Disadvantaged: The Inner City, the Underclass, and Public Policy*. Chicago: University of Chicago Press.